Harnessing Java™ 7

A Comprehensive Approach to Learning Java™

Volume - 1

Kishori Sharan

Trademarks

Trademarked names may appear in this book. Trademarks and product names used in this book are the property of their respective trademark holders. The author of this book is not affiliated with any of the entities holding those trademarks that may be used in this book.

Oracle and Java are registered trademarks of Oracle and/or its affiliates. Other names may be trademarks of their respective owners.

Cover Design & Images By: Richard Castillo (http://www.digitizedchaos.com)

Printing History:

August 2011   First Print

ISBN-10: 1-46-376771-4

ISBN-13: 978-1-463-76771-6

Dedicated

To

Three of my college professors who have influenced my academic career the most:

Sri Subir Kumar Roy,

Late Sri Madan Sharma, and

Sri Subhash Sareen

Table of Contents

Preface

My first encounter with the Java programming language was during a one-week Java training session in 1997. I did not then get a chance to use Java in a project until 1999. I read two Java books and took a Java 2 Programmer certification examination. I did very well in the test by scoring ninety five percent. The three questions that I missed on the test made me realize that the books that I had read did not adequately cover details of all the topics necessary about Java. I made up my mind to write a book about the Java programming language. So, in 2001, I formulated a plan to cover most of the topics that a Java developer needs to use the Java programming language effectively in a project, as well as to get a certification. I initially planned to cover all essential topics in Java in seven hundred to eight hundred pages.

As I progressed, I realized that a book covering most of the Java topics in detail could not be written in seven to eight hundred pages. One chapter alone that covered data types, operators, and statements spanned ninety pages. I was then faced with the question, "Should I shorten the content of the book or include all the details that I think a Java developer needs?" I opted for including all the details in the book, rather than shortening its content to keep the number of pages low. It has never been my intent to make lots of money from this book. I was never in a hurry to publish the book, because it could have compromise the quality of its contents. In short, I wrote this book to help the Java community understand and use the Java programming language effectively, without having to read many books on the same subject. I wrote this book keeping in mind that this book would be a comprehensive one-stop reference for everyone who wants to learn and grasp the intricacies of the Java programming language.

One of my high school teachers used to tell us that if one wanted to understand a building, one must first understand the bricks, steel and mortar, because a building is made up of these smaller things. The same logic applies to most of the things that we want to understand in our lives. It also applies to an understanding of the Java programming language. If you want to master the Java programming language, you must start with understanding its basic building blocks. I have used this approach throughout this book endeavoring to build each topic by describing the basics first. In this book, you will rarely find a topic described without first learning its background. Wherever possible, I have tried to correlate the programming practices with activities in our daily-life. Most of the books about the Java programming language available in the market, either do not include any pictures at all, or have only a few. I believe in the adage, "A picture is worth a thousand words." To a reader, a picture makes a topic easier to understand and remember. I have included over two hundred and sixty graphical representations in this book (spanning three volumes) to aid readers in understanding and visualizing its contents. Developers who have little or no programming experience have difficulty in putting things together to make it a complete program. Keeping those developers in mind, I have included over five hundred complete Java programs that are ready to be compiled and run.

As I finished a chapter, I distributed copies to Java students and developers to get their feedback. Their feedback included a common observation that the material in this book is simple yet detailed. That kept me motivated to write the succeeding chapters. One feedback received in the beginning was about the coverage of setting the classpath in this book. I have seen some Java developers with quite a bit programming experience struggle with setting the classpath for a Java application. Most of the developers start programming using a Java editor. Java editors make it easy for the developers to set the classpath. Most of the time, a developer is unaware of the classpath settings when he uses a Java editor. In reality, a Java developer has to debug issues that are related to classpath settings on a machine or an application server. Keeping the principle of describing the basics of a topic, I devoted a chapter on writing a very basic Java program (the chapter name is *Writing Java Programs*) that also describes setting the classpath in detail. I gave this chapter to many Java students and some Java developers with over five years of experience. All of them reported, "Now, I know how to work with the classpath."

I spent countless hours doing research for writing this book. My main source of research was the Java Language Specification, white papers and articles on Java topics, and Java Specification Requests (JSRs). I also spent quite a bit of time reading the Java source code to learn more about some of the Java topics. Sometimes, it took a few months researching a topic, before I could write the first sentence of the topic. Finally, it was always fun to play with Java programs, sometimes for hours, to add them to the book.

I encountered many hurdles and pauses (some long ones) along the way of writing this book. I registered for a master degree program after I finished a few chapters. As I was working on my master program, I could not work on the book for over two years. Sometimes, the extra workload at work prevented me from doing any work on this book for months. It took me ten years (You read it right. Ten years is called a decade.) to finish this book. If I had devoted all my time on writing this book, I could say that it would have taken me about two years to finish it. I also had to keep adding new material to cover the newer versions of Java. I started writing this book using Java 1.2 and finished it using Java 1.7. Finally, it turned out to be almost a two thousand page book, which had to be split in three volumes, because of the restrictions on the number of pages a print-on-demand book can have. At this point, all I can say is, "All's well that ends well."

Kishori Sharan

Structure of the Book

This book contains thirty-four chapters and three appendixes spread across three volumes. The print-on-demand technology puts a restriction on the maximum number of pages in a book. This made me divide the book into three volumes. To get the most out of this book, a reader is suggested to read from the first chapter to the last. Each chapter builds upon the previous chapters. Volumes and chapters inside a volume have been arranged in a way that presents the most basic material about the Java programming language first. Sections in a chapter are arranged in an order of increasing complexity, the least complex section being the first. The following is the list of topics covered in the three volumes.

Volume - 1	Volume - 2	Volume - 3
• Programming Concepts	• Interfaces	• Swing
• Data Types	• Annotations	• Applets
• Operators	• Inner Classes	• Network Programming
• Statements	• Enum	• JDBC API
• Classes & Objects	• Reflection	• Remote Method Invocation
• Object and Objects Classes	• Generics	• Java Native Interface
• AutoBoxing	• Threads	
• Exception Handling	• Input/Output	
• Assertions	• Archive Files	
• Strings & Dates	• Collections	
• Formatting Objects		
• Regular Expressions		
• Arrays		
• Garbage Collection		
• Inheritance		

Audience

This book is designed to be useful for anyone who wants to learn about the Java programming language. If you are a beginner, with little or no programming background, you need to read from the first chapter to the last, in order. The book contains topics of various degrees of complexity. As a beginner, if you find yourself overwhelmed while reading a section in a chapter, you can skip to the next section or the next chapter and revisit them later, when you gain more experience.

If you are a Java developer with intermediate or advanced level of experience, you can jump to a chapter or to a section in a chapter directly. If a section uses an unfamiliar topic, you need to visit that topic before continuing the current one. You may only want to read volumes of this book that cover the topics of your interest.

If you are reading this book to get a certification in the Java programming language, you need to read almost all chapters paying attention to all the detailed descriptions and rules. Most of the certification programs test your fundamental knowledge of the language, not the advanced knowledge. You need to read only those topics that are part of your certification test. Compiling and running over five hundred complete Java programs will help you prepare for your certification.

If you are a student who is attending a class in the Java programming language, you need to read the first six chapters in Volume 1, thoroughly. These chapters cover the basics of the Java programming languages in detail. You cannot do well in a Java class unless you first master the basics. After covering the basics, you need to read only those chapters that are covered in your class syllabus. I am sure, as a Java student, you do not need to read the entire book page-by-page.

How to Use This Book

This book is the beginning, not the end, for you to gain the knowledge of the Java programming language. If you are reading this book, it means you are heading in the right direction to learn the Java programming language that will enable you to excel in your academic and professional career. However, there is always a higher goal for you to achieve and you must constantly work harder to achieve it. The following quotations from some great thinkers may help you understand the importance of working hard and constantly looking for knowledge with both your eyes and mind open.

Be curious always, for knowledge will not acquire you; you must acquire it. - Sudie Back

Knowledge comes by eyes always open and working hard, and there is no knowledge that is not power. - Jeremy Taylor

The learning and knowledge that we have, is, at the most, but little compared with that of which we are ignorant. - Plato

True knowledge exists in knowing that you know nothing. And in knowing that you know nothing, that makes you the smartest of all. - Socrates

Readers are advised to use the API documentation for the Java programming language, as much as possible, while using this book. The Java API documentation is the place where you will find a complete list of documentation for everything available in the Java class library. You can download (or view) the Java API documentation from the official website of Oracle Corporation at *http://www.oracle.com*. While you read this book, you need to practice writing Java programs yourself. You can also practice by tweaking the programs provided in the book. It does not help much in your learning process, if you just read this book and do not practice by writing your own programs. Remember - "Practice makes a person perfect", which is also true in learning how to program in Java.

Java 7 New Features

Java 7 has added many new language level features. This book covers all Java 7 language level new features. A complete chapter in Volume - 2 has been devoted to discuss the NIO 2.0 in detail. The new features in Java 7 have been discussed in the related chapters. The following is the list of the new features of Java 7 covered in three volumes of this book.

Volume - 1	Volume - 2	Volume - 3
• Binary Numeric Literals	• Generic Type Inference	• JLayer Swing Component
• Underscores in Numeric Literals	• Heap Pollution	• Translucent Window
• Strings in a switch Statement	• Improved Compiler Warnings and Errors When Using Non-Reifiable Formal Parameters with Varargs Methods	• Shaped Window
• try-with-resources Statement		• Asynchronous Socket IO
• Catching Multiple Exception Types	• Improved File and Channel Closing Mechanism using a try-with-resources Statement	• Multicast DatagramChannel
• Re-throwing Exceptions with Improved Type Checking	• New Input/Output 2.0 (NIO 2.0)	• RowSetFactory
• The java.util.Objects class	• Fork/Join Framework	
	• Phaser Synchronization Barrier	
	• TransferQueue Collection	

Acknowledgements

This book could not have been written without the encouragements, supports and contributions from many people.

First, I would like to thank the authors of all the books, articles, white papers and Java Specification Requests (JSRs) related to the Java programming language that I read and consulted to gain my own knowledge of the Java programming language.

My heartfelt thanks are due to my father-in-law Mr. Jim Baker for displaying extraordinary patience in proof reading the book. I am very grateful to him for spending so much of his valuable time teaching me quite a bit of English grammar that helped me in producing better material, and hence less work for him during his proof reading sessions. I would also like to thank my mother-in-law Ms. Kim Baker for providing him delicious food (including letting him eat ice cream) and regularly reminding him to finish proof reading this book.

My wife Ellen was always patient when I spent long hours at my computer desk working on this book. She would happily bring me snacks, fruit, and a glass of water every thirty minutes or so to sustain me during that period. I want to thank her for all her support in writing this book. She also deserves my sincere thanks for proofreading many of the chapters and providing valuable feedback.

I would like to thank my sister-in-law Patty Boyd for cooking delicious food for me while I worked on the book. Thanks also go to my brother-in-law Jeff Boyd and my nephew Christopher Estes for helping me in many ways to save my time, so that I can focus on the book.

I would like to thank my friend Kannan Somasekar for his support and hard work to get an appropriate subtitle for this book. I would also like to thank him for time spent in researching the possible publishing options. His research helped me choose the print-on-demand publishing option. I would like to thank Kannan's wife, Divya Somasekar, for taking care of their two lovely sons, Krish and Rishi, while Kannan spent time at his computer desk to help me finish this book.

My special thanks go to my friend and colleague, Richard Castillo, for proof reading this book very thoroughly. He deserves a big thank-you for designing the cover pages and suggesting the title of the book.

I would like to thank my friends and colleagues Christopher Coley, Tanu Mutreja, Rahul Jain, Raju Mudunuri, Willie Baptiste, Tejas Dholakia, Amita Dholakia, Lorenzo Braxter, and Mahbub Chowdhury, for providing valuable feedback. Willie Baptiste, Tejas Dholakia, Amita Dholakia, Lorenzo Braxter, and Mahbub Chowdhury deserve little extra thanks for giving me the opportunity to teach them Java, which gave me more insight on how to explain things in the book to make it easier for the readers to understand.

There is one good thing about members of anybody's family, including mine. Once you tell them that you are working on writing a book, they will remind you periodically about the status of your book, which keeps you always aware that you have one unfinished job at your hand and you must finish it sometime in your life! Finishing this book was not possible without the blessings of my parents, Ram Vinod Singh and Pratibha Devi, and my elder brothers, Janki Sharan and Dr. Sita Sharan. My most sincere and heartfelt thanks go to them for their support and encouragement during the entire period I was working on the book. I would also like to thank my sister Ratna Kumari and brother-in-law Abhay Kumar Singh, my nephew Navin Kumar and daughter-in-law Anjali Singh, my niece Vandana Kumari and son-in-law Prem Prakash, my nephew Neeraj Kumar and daughter-in-law Pallavi, and my nephews Gaurav Sharan and Saurav Kumar, for their interest.

I would like to thank Chitranjan Sharma, my nephew and a student of Bachelor of Computer Applications at Gaya College Gaya, for his diligent efforts to learn Java using this book and providing me valuable feedback.

I would like to thank the following colleagues for their support, encouragement and for being always supportive, while I worked with the Department of Children Service, State of Tennessee: John Jacobs, Reddy Matta, Donna Duncan, Katrina Hills, LaTondra Okeke, Prasanna Despande, Geshan Alvis, Buddy Rice, Jack Parker, Jags.Pinni, Bettye Clark, Charles O' Riley, Basir Kabir, Barbara Gentry, Paula Daugherty, Dinesh Sankala, Elaine Blaylock, Lisa Simmons, Deborah Hurd, Wallace Inman, Pravin Lokhande, Priyanka Sharma, Amitabh Sharma, and Wanda Jackson. I know that some of them did not know that I had been writing a book. But, I feel they deserve mention, because it helped me in the writing of this book at home, when they all were nice and supportive at work. After all, good attitude is contagious!

I would like to thank the following colleagues for their support and helping me learn the intricacies of Java while I worked for Kingsway America in Mobile, Alabama: Larry Brewster, Biju Nair, Jim Jacobs, Ram Atmakuri, Srinivas Kakkera, James Pham, Megan Bodiford, Udhaya Kumar, Matt Flowers, and Greg Langham.

I would like to thank the following colleagues for their support while I worked at ProAssurance in Birmingham, Alabama: LaRonda Lanier, Christy Mueller-Smith, Darren Jackson, Bob Waldrop, Tatiana Telioukova, Russell Thomas, Cameron Ellison, Brandon Russell, Devaraj Rajan, Frank Lay, Andriy Shlykov, Andy Purvis, Rob Ballard, Marty Heim, and Troy Dotson. As I have mentioned earlier, some of my colleagues may not even be aware that I have been writing a book. However, their support in creating a cordial and helping working environment at work helped me carrying the good frame of mind to home in the evening to spend a few hours of my time on this book. So, all of you deserve my sincere thanks.

I would like to thank the following managers for their support while I worked in different projects: Robert Holloway, Connie Spradlin, Ed Bennett, Kieran Cloonan, and Donovan Fitzgerald at Department of Children Services, Nashville, TN; Leslie Zanders, Cheryl Lawrence, and Kelly Dumas at Kingsway America in Mobile, AL; Kirby Sims, Douglas Dyer, Brian Russell, Lael Boyd, and Vivi Gin at ProAssurance in Birmingham, AL; Heath Wade and Amy Gartman at Doozer Inc.

I would like to thank the following friends for their support and encouragement: Rahul Nagpal, Ravi Datla, Anil Kumar Singh, Balram Kumar, Dilip Kumar, Ramta Prasad Singh, Pratap Chandra, Sanjeev Choudhary, Pramod Kumar, Prakash Chandra, Dharmendhra Kumar Mishra, Rajeev Kumar Verma, Randy Lucas, Sanjay Pandey, Suman Kumar Singh, Amarjeet Kumar, Vijay Kumar Tarun, Raju Mishra, Jayshankar Prasad Singh, Mukesh Sinha, Rajesh Kumar, Vishwa Mohan, Ranjeet Ekka, Sanjay Singh, Kamal Singh, Pankaj Kumar, Ranjeet Kumar, Krishna Kumar, and Anuj Sinha.

Source Code and Errata

Source code and errata for this volume may be downloaded from *http://www.jdojo.com*.

Questions and Comments

Please direct all your questions and comments to *ksharan@jdojo.com*

.

Chapter 1. Programming Concepts

What is Programming?

The term "programming" is used in many contexts. We will discuss the meaning of this term in the context of human-to-computer interaction. In the simplest terms, programming is the way of writing a sequence of instructions to tell a computer to perform a specific task. The sequence of instructions for a computer is known as a *program*. A set of well-defined notations is used to write a program. The set of notation used to write a program is called a *programming language*. The person who writes a program is called a *programmer*. A programmer uses a programming language to write a program.

How does a person tell a computer to perform a task? Can a person tell a computer to perform any task or does a computer have a pre-defined set of tasks that it can perform? Before we look at human-to-computer communication, let us look at human-to-human communication. How does a human communicate with another human? You would say that a human-to-human communication is accomplished using a spoken language e.g. English, German, Hindi, etc. Spoken language is not the only means of communication between humans. We also communicate using written languages or using gestures without uttering any words. Some people can communicate sitting miles away from each other without using any words or gestures. They can communicate at thought level. To have a successful communication, it is not enough just to use a medium of communication like a spoken or written language. The main requirement for a successful communication between two parties is the ability of both parties to understand what is communicated from other party. For example, suppose there are two persons. One person knows how to speak English and other one knows how to speak German. Can they communicate with each other? The answer is no, because they cannot understand each other's language. What happens if we add an English-German translator between them? We would agree that they would be able to communicate with the help of a translator even though they do not understand each other directly.

Computers understand instructions only in binary format - sequence of zeros and ones. The sequence of 0s and 1s, which all computers understand, is called *machine language* or *machine code*. A computer has a fixed set of basic instructions that it understands. Each computer has its own set of instructions. For example, 0010 may be an instruction to add two numbers on one computer and 0101 as an instruction to add two numbers on another computer. Therefore, programs written in machine language are machine-dependent. Sometimes, machine code is referred to as *native code* as it is native to the machine for which it is written. Programs written in machine language is very difficult, if not impossible, to write, read, understand and modify. Suppose we want to write a program that adds two numbers – 15 and 12. The program to add two numbers in machine language will look similar to the one shown below. You do not need to understand the sample code written in this section. They are only for the purpose of discussion and illustration.

```
0010010010   10010100000100110
0001000100   01010010001001010
```

The above instructions are to add two numbers. How difficult will it be to write a program in machine language to perform a complex task? Now, you may realize that it is difficult to write, read, and understand a program written in a machine language. Computers are supposed to make our jobs easier and not more difficult. We needed to represent the instructions for computers in some notations that were easier to write, read and understand. Computer scientists came up with another language called *assembly language*. Assembly language provides different notations to write instructions for computers. It is little easier to write, read and understand than its predecessor machine language. Assembly language uses mnemonics to represent instructions as opposed to binary (0s and 1s) used in machine language. A program written in assembly language to add two numbers look similar to those shown below.

```
li $t1, 15
add $t0, $t1, 12
```

If you compare the programs written in machine language and assembly language to perform the same task, you would realize that assembly language is easier to write, read and understand than the machine language. There is one-to-one correspondence between an instruction in machine language and assembly language for a given computer architecture. Recall that a computer understands instructions only in machine language, which consists of 0s and 1s. The instructions that are written in an assembly language must be translated to the machine language before they can be executed by the computer. A program that translates the instructions written in an assembly language to a machine language is called an *assembler*. Figure 1-1 shows the relationship between assembly code, an assembler, and machine code.

Figure 1-1: Relationship between assembly code, assembler and machine code

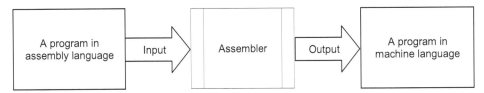

Machine language and assembly language are also known as *low-level languages*. They are called low-level languages, because a programmer must understand low-level details of the computer to write a program those languages. For example, if you were writing programs in machine and assembly languages, you need to know what memory location you are writing to or reading from, which register to use to store a specific value, etc. Soon programmers realized a need for a high-level programming language that will hide the low-level details of computers from them. The need to hide the low-level details of computers from programming gave rise to the development of high-level programming languages like COBOL, Pascal, FORTRAN, C, C++, Java, C#, etc. The high-level programming languages use English-like words, mathematical notations and punctuations to write a program. A program written in a high-level programming language is also called *source code*. They are closer to written languages that humans are familiar with. The instructions to add two numbers can be written in a high-level programming language e.g. Java, which looks similar to the following.

```
int x = 15 + 27;
```

You may notice that the programs written in a high-level language is easier and more intuitive to write, read, understand and modify than the programs written in machine and assembly languages. You might have realized that computers do not understand programs written in high-level languages, as they understand only sequences of 0s and 1s. We need a means to translate a program written in high-level language to machine language. The translation of the program written in a high-level programming language to machine language is accomplished by a compiler, an *interpreter* or combination of both. A compiler is a program that translates a program written in a high-level programming language into machine language. Compiling a program is an overloaded phrase. Typically, it means translating a program written in a high-level language into machine

---

language. Sometimes, it is used to mean translating a program written in a high-level programming language into a lower-level programming language, which is not necessarily the machine language. The code that is generated by a compiler is called *compiled code*. The compiled program is executed by the computer. Another way to execute a program written in high-level programming language is to use an interpreter. An interpreter does not translate the whole program into machine language at once. Rather, it reads one instruction written in a high-level programming language at a time, translates it into machine language, and executes it. You can view an interpreter as a simulator. Sometimes, a combination of a compiler and an interpreter may be used to compile and run a program written in a high-level language. For example, a program written in Java is compiled into an intermediate language called *bytecode*. An interpreter, which is called a Java Virtual Machine (JVM), is used to interpret the bytecode and execute it. An interpreted program runs slower than a compiled program. Most of the JVMs today use just-in-time compilers (JIT), which compile the entire Java program into machine language. Sometimes, another kind of compiler, which is called ahead-of-time compiler (AOT), is used to compile a program in intermediate language (e.g. Java bytecode) to machine language. Figure 1-2 shows the relationship between the source code, a compiler, and the machine code.

Figure 1-2: Relationship between a source code, a compiler, and a machine code

Components of a Programming Language

A programming language is a system of notations that are used to write instructions for computers. A programming language can be described using the following three components.

* Syntax
* Semantics and
* Pragmatics

The syntax part deals with forming valid programming constructs using available notations. The semantics part deals with the meaning of the programming constructs. The pragmatics part deals with the use of the programming language in practice.

Like a written language (e.g. English), a programming language has vocabulary and grammar. The vocabulary of a programming language consists of a set of words, symbols and punctuation marks. The grammar of a programming language defines rules on how to use vocabulary of the language to form valid programming constructs. You can think of a valid programming construct in programming language like a sentence in a written language. A sentence in a written language is formed using vocabulary and grammar of the language. Similarly, a programming construct is formed using vocabulary and the grammar of the programming language. The vocabulary and rules to use vocabulary to form valid programming constructs is known as *syntax* of the programming language.

In a written language, you may form a grammatically correct sentence, which may not have any valid meaning. For example, "The stone is laughing." is a grammatically correct sentence. However, it does not make any sense. In a written language, this kind of ambiguity is allowed. A programming language is meant to communicate instructions to computers, which have no room for any ambiguity. We cannot communicate with computers using ambiguous instructions. There is another component of a programming language, which is called *semantics*. Semantics of a programming language explains the meaning of the syntactically valid programming constructs. The semantics of a programming language answers the question – "What does this program do when it is run on a computer?" Note that a syntactically valid programming construct may not also be semantically valid. A program must be syntactically and semantically correct before it can be executed by a compute.

The pragmatics of a programming language describes its uses and its effects on the users. A program written in a programming language may be syntactically and semantically correct. However, it may not be easily understood by other programmers. This aspect is related to the pragmatics of the programming language. The pragmatics is concerned with the practical aspect of a programming language. It answers questions about a programming language like its ease of implementation, suitability for a particular application, efficiency, portability, support for programming methodologies, etc.

Programming Paradigms

The online Merriam-Webster's Learner's dictionary defines the word paradigm as follows.

> *"A paradigm is a theory or a group of ideas about how something should be done, made, or thought about."*

In the beginning, it is little hard to understand the word "paradigm" in programming context. Programming is about providing a solution to a real-world problem using computational models supported by the programming language. The solution to the real-world problem that we provide in terms of computational models is called a program. Before we provide a solution to a problem in the form of a program, we always have a mental view about the problem and its solution. Before we discuss how we solve a real-world problem using computational model, let us take an example of a real-world social problem, which has nothing to do with computers. Suppose there is a place on the earth that has a food problem. People in that place do not have enough food to eat. The problem is, "shortage of food." Let us ask three people to provide a solution to this problem. The three people are a politician, a philanthropist, and a monk. A politician will have a political view about the problem and its solution. He may think about it as an opportunity to serve his countrymen by enacting some laws to provide food to the hungry people. A philanthropist will offer some money/food to help those hungry people because he feels compassion for all humans and so for those hungry people. A monk will try to solve this problem using his spiritual views. He may preach to them to work and make livings for themselves; he may appeal to rich people to donate food to the hungry; or he may teach them yoga to conquer their hunger! Did you see how three people have different views about the same reality, which is "shortage of food"? The ways they look at the reality are their paradigms. You can think of a paradigm as a mindset with which a reality is viewed in a particular context. It is usual to have multiple paradigms, which let one view the same reality differently. For example, a person who is a philanthropist and politician will have his ability to view the "shortage of food" problem and its solution differently – once with his political mindset and once with his philanthropist mindset. Three people were given the same problem. All of them provided the solution to the problem. However, their perceptions about the problem and its solution were not the same. We can define the term paradigm as a set of concepts and ideas that constitutes a way of viewing a reality.

Why do we need to bother about a paradigm anyway? Does it matter if a person used his political, philanthropist or spiritual paradigm to arrive at the solution? Eventually, we get a solution to our problem. Don't we? It is not enough just to have a solution to a problem. The solution must be practical and effective. Since the solution to a problem is always related to the way the problem and the solution are thought about, the paradigm becomes paramount. You can see that the solution provided by the monk may kill the hungry people before they can get any help. The philanthropist's solution may be a good short-term solution. The politician's solution seems to be a long term and the best solution. It is always important to use the right paradigm to solve a problem to arrive at a practical and the most effective solution. Note that one paradigm cannot be the right paradigm to solve all kinds of problem. For example, if a person is seeking eternal happiness, he needs to consult a monk and not a politician or a philanthropist.

Here is a definition of the term "programming paradigm" by Robert W. Floyd, who is a reputed computer scientist. He gave this definition in his 1979 ACM Turing Award lecture titled "The Paradigms of Programming".

> "A programming paradigm is a way of conceptualizing what it means to perform computation, and how tasks that are to be carried out on a computer should be structured and organized."

You can observe that the word "paradigm" in programming context has a similar meaning to that used in the context of daily life. Programming is used to solve a real-world problem using computational models provided by a computer. The programming paradigm is the way you think and conceptualize about the real-world problem and its solution in the underlying computational models. The programming paradigm comes into the picture well before you start writing a program using a programming language. It is in the analysis phase when you use a particular paradigm to analyze a problem and its solution in a particular way. A programming language provides a means to implement a particular programming paradigm suitably. A programming language may provide features that make it suitable for programming using one programming paradigm and not the other.

A program has two components - data and algorithm. Data is used to represent pieces of information. Algorithm is a set of steps that operates on data to arrive at a solution to a problem. Different programming paradigms involve viewing the solution to a problem by combining data and algorithms in different ways. Many paradigms are used in programming. The following are some commonly used programming paradigms,

- Imperative Paradigm
- Procedural Paradigm
- Declarative Paradigm
- Functional Paradigm
- Logic Paradigm
- Object-Oriented Paradigm

Imperative Paradigm

Imperative paradigm is also known as algorithmic paradigm. In imperative paradigm, a program consists of data and an algorithm (sequence of commands) that manipulates the data. The data at a particular point in time defines the state of the program. The state of the program changes as the commands are executed in a specific sequence. The data are stored in memory. Imperative programming languages provide variables to refer to the memory locations, an assignment operation to change the value of a variable and other constructs to control the flow of a program. In imperative programming, you need to specify the steps to solve a problem. Suppose you have an integer, say 15, and you want to add 10 to it. Your approach would be to add 1 to 15 ten times and you get the result 25. You can write a program using imperative language to add 10 to 15 as follows. You do not need to understand the syntax of the following code. Just try to get the feeling of it.

```
int num = 15;           // num holds 15 at this point
int counter = 0;        // counter holds 0 at this point
```

```
while(counter < 10) {
    num = num + 1;              // Modifying data in num
    counter = counter + 1;  // Modifying data in counter
}
// num holds 25 at this point
```

The first two lines are variable declarations that represent the data part of the program. The code inside the while-loop represents the algorithm part of the program that operates on the data. The code inside the while-loop is executed 10 times. The loop increments the data stored in num variable by 1 in its each iteration. When the loop ends, it has incremented the value of num by 10. Note that data in imperative programming is transient and algorithm is permanent.

Procedural Paradigm

Procedural paradigm is similar to imperative paradigm with one difference that it combines multiple commands in a unit called a *procedure*. A procedure is executed as a unit. Executing the commands contained in a procedure is known as calling or invoking the procedure. A program in procedural language consists of data and a sequence of procedure calls that manipulate the data. The following piece of code is a typical code for a procedure named addTen.

```
void addTen(int num) {
    int counter = 0;
    while(counter < 10) {
        num = num + 1;              // Modifying data in num
        counter = counter + 1;  // Modifying data in counter
    }
    // num has been incremented by 10
}
```

The addTen procedure uses a placeholder (also known as parameter) num, which is supplied at the time of its execution. The code ignores the actual value of num. It simply adds 10 to the current value of num. We will use the following piece of code to add 10 to 15. Note that the code for addTen procedure and the following code are not written using any specific programming language. They are provided here only for the purpose of illustration.

```
int x = 15;    // x holds 15 at this point
addTen(x);     // Call addTen procedure that will increment x by 10
// x holds 25 at this point
```

You may observe that the code in imperative paradigm and procedural paradigm are similar in structure. Using procedures results in modular codes and increases reusability of algorithms. Some people ignore this difference and treat the two paradigms, imperative and procedural, as the same. Note that even if they are different, a procedural paradigm always involves imperative paradigm. In procedural paradigm, the unit of programming is not a sequence of commands. Rather, you abstract a sequence of commands into a procedure and your program consists of a sequence of procedures instead. A procedure has side effect. It modifies the data part of the program as it executes its logic.

Declarative Paradigm

In declarative paradigm, a program consists of the description of a problem and the computer finds the solution. The program does not specify how to arrive at the solution to the problem. It is computer's job to arrive at a solution when a problem is described to it. Contrast the declarative paradigm with imperative paradigm. In imperative paradigm, we are concerned about the "how" part of the problem. In declarative paradigm, we are concerned about the "what" part of the problem. We are concerned about what the problem is, rather than how to solve it. Functional paradigm and logic paradigm, which are described next, are examples of declarative paradigm. Writing a database query using structured query language (SQL) falls under programming based on declarative paradigm where you specify what data you want and the database engine figures out how to retrieve the data for you. Unlike imperative paradigm, the data is permanent and the algorithm is transient in declarative paradigm. In imperative paradigm, the data is modified as the algorithm is executed. In declarative paradigm, data is supplied to the algorithm as input and the input data remains unchanged as the algorithm is executed. Algorithm produces new data rather than modifying the input data. In other words, in declarative paradigm, execution of an algorithm does not produce side effects.

Functional Paradigm

Functional paradigm is based on the concept of mathematical functions. You can think of a function as an algorithm that computes a value from some given input. Unlike a procedure used in procedural programming, a function does not have a side effect. In functional programming, values are immutable. A new value is derived by applying a function to the input value. The input value does not change. Functional programming languages do not use variables and assignment, which are used for modifying data. In imperative programming, a repeated task is performed using a loop construct e.g. a while-loop. In functional programming, a repeated task is performed using *recursion*, which is a way in which a function is defined in terms of itself. A function always produces the same output when it is applied on the same input. A function, say add, that can be applied to an integer, x, to add an integer, n, to it may be defined as follows.

```
int add(x, n) {
    if (n == 0) {
        return x;
    }
    else {
        return 1 + add(x, n-1); // Apply add function recursively
    }
}
```

Note that the add function does not use any variable and does not modify any data. It uses recursion. You can call the add function to add 10 to 15 as follows.

```
add(15, 10); // Results in 25
```

Logic Paradigm

Unlike the imperative paradigm, logic paradigm focuses on the "what" part of the problem rather than how to solve it. All you need to specify is what needs to be solved. The program will figure out the algorithm to solve it. Algorithm is of less importance to the programmer. The primary task of the programmer is to describe the problem as closely as possible. In logic paradigm, a program consists of a set of axioms and a goal statement. The set of axioms is the collection of facts and inference rules, which makes up a theory. The goal statement is a theorem. The program uses deductions to prove the theorem within the theory. Logic programming uses a mathematical concept called *relation* from set theory. A relation in set theory is defined as a subset of the Cartesian product of two or more sets. Suppose there are two sets, `Persons` and `Nationality`, as defined below.

```
Person = {John, Li, Ravi}
Nationality = {American, Chinese, Indian}
```

The Cartesian product of the two sets, denoted as `Person x Nationality`, would be another set as shown below.

```
Person x Nationality = {{John, American}, {John, Chinese},
                        {John, Indian}, {Li, American}, {Li, Chinese},
                        {Li, Indian}, {Ravi, American}, {Ravi, Chinese},
                        {Ravi, Indian}
                        }
```

Every subset of `Person x Nationality` is another set and it defines a mathematical relation. Each element of a relation is called a tuple. Let `PersonNationality` be a relation defined as follows.

```
PersonNationality = {{John, American}, {Li, Chinese}, {Ravi, Indian}}
```

In logic programming, you can use `PersonNationality` relation as the collection of facts that are known to be true. You can state the goal statement (or the problem) like

```
PersonNationality(?, Chinese)
```

which means – "Give me all names of the persons who are Chinese". The program will search through the `PersonNationality` relation and extract the matching tuples, which will be the answer (or the solution) to your problem. In this case, the answer will be `Li`.

Prolog is an example of programming language that supports logic paradigm.

Object-Oriented Paradigm

In object-oriented (OO) paradigm, a program consists of interacting objects. An object encapsulates data and algorithms. Data define the state of an object. Algorithms define the behavior of an object. An object communicates with other objects by sending messages to them. When an object receives a message, it responds by executing one of its algorithms, which may modify its state. Contrast object-oriented paradigm with imperative and functional paradigms. In imperative and functional paradigms, data and algorithms are separated, whereas in object-oriented paradigm, data and algorithms are not separate. Rather, they are combined in one entity, which is called object.

Classes are the basic units of programming in the object-oriented paradigm. Similar objects are grouped into one definition called *class*. A class' definition is used to create an object. An object is also known as an *instance* of the class. A class consists of instance variables and methods. The values of instance variables of an object define the state of the object. Different objects of a class maintain their states separately. That is, each object of a class has its own copy of the instance variables. The state of an object is kept private to that object. That is, the state of an object cannot be accessed or modified directly from outside the object. Methods in a class define the behavior of its objects. A method is like a procedure (or subroutine) in procedural paradigm. Methods can access/modify the state of the object. A message is sent to an object by invoking one of its methods.

Suppose we want to represent real-world persons in our program. We will create a `Person` class and its instances will represent persons in our program. The `Person` class can be defined as listed in Listing 1-1. This example uses syntax of Java programming language. You do not need to understand the syntax used in the programs that we are writing at this point. We will discuss the syntax to define classes and create objects in subsequent chapters.

Listing 1-1: The definition of the Person class whose instances represent real-world persons in a program

```java
public class Person {
    private String name;
    private String gender;

    public Person(String initialName, String initialGender) {
        name = initialName;
        gender = initialGender;
    }

    public String getName() {
        return name;
    }

    public void setName(String newName) {
        name = newName;
    }

    public String getGender() {
        return gender;
    }
}
```

The `Person` class includes three things:

- Two instance variables - `name` and `gender`.
- One constructor - `Person(String initialName, String initialGender)`
- Three methods - `getName()`, `setName(String newName)` and `getGender()`

Instance variables store internal data for an object. The value of each instance variable represents the value of a corresponding property of the object. Each object of the `Person` class will have a copy of `name` and `gender` data. The values of all properties of an object at a point in time (stored in instance variables) collectively define the state of the object at that time. In real-world, a person possesses many properties, e.g., name, gender, height, weight, hair color, addresses, phone numbers, etc. However, when you model the real-world person using a class, you include only those properties of the person, which are relevant to the system being modeled. For our current demonstration purpose, we decided to model only two properties, `name` and `gender`, of a real-world person as two instance variables in the `Person` class.

A class contains the definition (or blueprint) of objects. There needs to be a way to construct (to create or to instantiate) objects of a class. An object also needs to have the initial values for its properties that will determine its initial state at the time of its creation. A *constructor* of a class is used to create an object of that class. A class can have many constructors to facilitate the creation of its objects with different initial states. The `Person` class provides one constructor, which lets you create its object by specifying the initial values for `name` and `gender`. The following snippet of code creates two objects of the `Person` class.

```
Person john = new Person("John Jacobs", "Male");
Person donna = new Person("Donna Duncan", "Female");
```

The first object is called `john` with `John Jacobs` and `Male` as the initial values for its `name` and `gender` properties respectively. The second object is called `donna` with `Donna Duncan` and `Female` as the initial values for its `name` and `gender` properties respectively.

Methods of a class represent behaviors of its objects. For example, in real-world, a person has a name and his ability to respond when he is asked for his name is one of his behaviors. Objects of our `Person` class have abilities to respond to three different messages – `getName`, `setName` and `getGender`. The ability of an object to respond to a message is implemented using methods. You can send a message, say `getName`, to a `Person` object and it will respond by returning its name. It is same as asking a question to a person – "What is your name?" and he responds by telling his name.

```
String johnName = john.getName();   // Send getName message to john
String donnaName = donna.getName(); // Send getName message to donna
```

The `setName` message to the `Person` object asks him to change his current name to a new name. The following snippet of code changes name of `donna` object from `Donna Duncan` to `Donna Jacobs`.

```
donna.setName("Donna Jacobs");
```

If you send the `getName` message to `donna` object at this point, it will return `Donna Jacobs` and not `Donna Duncan`.

You may notice that our `Person` objects do not have the ability to respond to a message such as - `setGender`. The gender of `Person` object is set when the object is created and it cannot be changed afterwards. However, you can query the gender of a `Person` object by sending `getGender` message to it. What messages an object may (or may not) respond to is decided at design-time based on the need of the system being modeled. In the case of the `Person` objects, we decided that they would not have the ability to respond to the `setGender` message by not including a `setGender(String newGender)` method in the `Person` class..

In object-oriented paradigm, the state of an object is kept private to the object. That is, users of the object (or client code) cannot access/modify the state of the object directly. Users of the object use one of the interfaces provided by the object to access or modify the state of the object. The methods defined in the class that are accessible to the client code constitute the interface for objects. Figure 1-3 shows the state and interface of the `Person` object called `john`.

TIP
In object-oriented paradigm, an object consists of state (data) and interface (behavior). The users of the object interact with it using the interface. The state of the object cannot be accessed directly from outside the object. Interfaces are used to access/modify the state of the object.

Figure 1-3: The state and the interface for a Person object

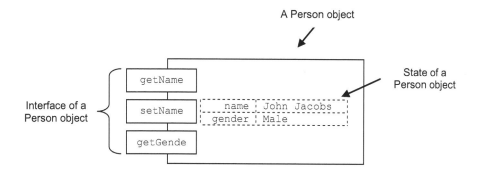

The object-oriented paradigm is a very powerful paradigm to model real-world phenomena in computational model. We are used to working with objects all around us in our daily-life. It is taught that object-oriented paradigm is natural and intuitive as it lets you think in terms of objects. However, it does not give you ability to think in terms of objects correctly. Sometimes, solution to a problem does not fall into the domain of object-oriented paradigm. In such cases, you need to use the paradigm that suits the problem domain the most. Object-oriented paradigm has a learning curve. It is much more than just creating and using objects in your program. Abstraction, encapsulation, polymorphism, and inheritance are some of the important features of object-oriented paradigm. You must understand and be able to use these features to take the full advantage of the object-oriented paradigm. We will discuss these features of Object-oriented paradigm in the sections to follow. In subsequent chapters, we will discuss these features and how to implement them in a program in detail.

To name a few, C++, Java and C# (pronounced as CSharp)) are programming languages that support object-oriented paradigm. Note that a programming language itself is not object-oriented. It is the paradigm that is object-oriented. A programming language may or may not have features to support the object-oriented paradigm.

What is Java?

Java is a general purpose programming language. It has features to support programming based on object-oriented paradigm as well as procedural paradigm. You often read a phrase like – "Java is an object-oriented programming language". What is meant is that Java language has features that support object-oriented paradigm. A programming language is not object-oriented. It is the paradigm that is object-oriented and a programming language may have features that make it easy to implement the object-oriented paradigm. Sometimes, programmers have misconceptions that all programs written in Java are always object-oriented. Java also has features that support procedural paradigm. You can write a program in Java, which is a 100% procedural program without an iota of object-orientedness in it,

Java was released by Sun Microsystems (part of Oracle Corporation since January, 2010) in 1995. Development of Java language was started in 1991. Initially, the language was called Oak and it was meant to be used in the set-top box for televisions.

Soon after its release in 1995, Java became a very popular programming language. One of the most important features for its popularity was its "Write Once, Run Everywhere" (WORE) feature. This feature lets you write a Java program once, which can be run on any platform. For example, you can write and compile a Java program on UNIX and run it on Microsoft Windows, Macintosh or

UNIX without any modifications to the source code. WORE is achieved by compiling a Java program into an intermediate language called *bytecode*. The format of bytecode is platform-independent. A virtual machine, which is called Java Virtual Machine (JVM), is used to run the bytecode on each platform. Note that JVM is a program implemented in software. It is not a physical machine and this is the reason it is called "virtual" machine. The job of JVM is to transform the bytecode into executable code according to the platform it is running on. This feature makes Java programs platform-independent. That is, the same Java program can be run on multiple platforms without any modifications.

Java became a very popular programming language in a very brief period after its first release in 1995. Following are a few characteristics of Java behind its popularity and acceptance in software industry.

- Simplicity
- Wide variety of usage environments
- Robustness

Simplicity may be a subjective word in this context. C++ was the popular and powerful programming language widely used in software industry at the time Java was released. If you were a C++ programmer, Java would provide simplicity for you in its learning and use over C++ experience you had. Java retained most of the syntax of C/C++, which helps a C/C++ programmer learn the new language. It excluded some of the most confusing and hard to use correctly features (though powerful) of C++. For example, Java does not have pointers and multiple inheritance, which were included in C++. If you are learning Java as your first programming language, whether it is still a simple language to learn may not be true for you. This is the reason, we stated in the beginning of this section that simplicity of Java or any programming language is very subjective.

Java can be used to develop programs that can be used in different environments. You can write programs in Java that can be used in a client-server environment. The most popular use of Java programs in its early days was to develop applets. An applet is a Java program that is embedded in a web page, which uses HyperText Markup Language (HTML), and it is displayed in a web browser such as Microsoft Internet Explorer, Google Chrome, etc. An applet's code is stored on a web server, downloaded to the client machine when HTML page is loaded by the browser, and run on the client machine. Java includes features that make it easy to develop distributed applications. A distributed application consists of programs running on different machines connected through a network. Java has features that make it easy to develop concurrent application. A concurrent application has multiple interacting threads of execution running in parallel. We will discuss of these features of Java language in details in subsequent chapters in this book.

Robustness of a program refers to its ability to handle unexpected situations reasonably. The unexpected situation in a program is also known as an *error*. Java provides robustness by providing many features for error checking at different points during a program's lifetime. Following are three different types of errors that may occur in a Java program:

- Compile-time error
- Runtime error
- Logic error

Compile-time errors are also known as syntax errors. They are caused by incorrect use of the Java language syntax. Compile-time errors are detected by the Java compiler. A program with compile-time error does not compile into bytecode until the errors are corrected. Missing a semi-colon at the end of a statement, assigning a decimal value, say 10.23, to a variable of integer type, etc. are the examples of compile-time errors.

Runtime errors occur when a Java program is run. This kind of error is not detected by compiler because a compiler does not have all runtime information available to it. Java is a strongly typed languages and it has a robust type checking at compile-time as well as runtime. Java provides a neat exception handling mechanism to handle runtime errors. When a runtime error occurs in a Java program, JVM throws an exception, which the program may catch and deal with. For example, dividing an integer by zero (e.g. 17/0) generates a runtime error. Java avoids critical runtime errors, such as memory overrun and memory leaks, by providing a built-in mechanism for automatic memory allocation and de-allocation. The feature of automatic memory de-allocation is known as *garbage collection*.

Logic errors are the most critical errors in a program, and they are hard to find. They are introduced by the programmer by implementing the functional requirement incorrectly. This kind of error cannot be detected by Java compiler or Java runtime. They are detected by application testers or users when they compare the actual behavior of a program with its expected behavior. Sometimes, few logic errors sneak into production environment and they go unnoticed even after the application is decommissioned.

An error in a program is known a bug. The process of finding and fixing bugs in a program is known as debugging. All modern Integrated Development Environments (IDE) such as NetBeans, Eclipse, JDeveloper, JBuilder, etc, provide programmers with a tool called debugger, which lets them run the program step-by-step and inspect the program's state at every step to detect the bug. Debugging is a reality of programmer's daily activities. If you want to be a good programmer, you must learn and be good at using debuggers that comes with the development tools that you use to develop your Java programs.

Object-Oriented Paradigm and Java

Abstraction

A program provides solutions to a real-world problem using computational model. A program size may range from a few lines to a few millions of lines. A program may be written as a monolithic structure running from the first line to millionth line in one place. A monolithic program becomes harder to write, understand and maintain if its size is over 25 to 50 lines. For easier maintainability, a big monolithic program must be decomposed into smaller sub-programs. The sub-programs are then assembled together to solve the original problem. Care must be taken when a program is being decomposed into sub-programs. All sub-programs must be simple and small enough to be understood by themselves. When they are assembled together, they must solve the original problem.

Let us consider the following requirement for a device.

Design and develop a device that should let its user type text using all English alphabets, digits and symbols.

One way to design such a device is to provide a keyboard that has keys for all possible combinations of all alphabets, digits and symbols. This solution is not reasonable as the size of the device will be huge. You may realize that we are talking about designing a keyboard. Look at your keyboard and see how it has been designed. It has broken down the problem of typing text into typing an alphabet, a digit or a symbol one at a time, which represents the smaller part of the original problem. If you can type all alphabets, all digits, and all symbols one at a time, you can type text of any length. Another decomposition of the original problem may include two keys – one to type a horizontal line and another to type vertical line. A user can use the two keys combinations to type in E, T, I, F, H, and L because these alphabets consist of only horizontal and vertical lines. With this solution, a user can type six alphabets using the combination of just two keys. However, with your experience using keyboard you may realize that decomposing the keys so that a key can be used to type in only part of an alphabet is not a reasonable solution although it is a valid solution.

Why is providing two keys to type six alphabets not a reasonable solution? Aren't we saving space and number of keys on the keyboard? The use of the phrase "reasonable" is relative in this context. From a purist point of view, it may be a reasonable solution. Our reasoning behind calling it "not reasonable" is that it is not easily understood by users. It exposes more details to its users than needed. A user would have to remember that the horizontal line is placed at the top for T and at bottom for L. When a user gets a separate key for each alphabet, he does not have to deal with these details. It is important that the sub-programs, which provide solutions to parts of the original problem, must be simplified to have the same level of detail to work together seamlessly. At the same time, a sub-program should not expose details that are not necessary for someone to know in order to use it. Finally, all keys are mounted on a keyboard and they can be replaced separately. If a key is broken, it can be replaced without worrying about other keys. Similarly, when a program is decomposed into sub-programs, a modification in a sub-program should not affect other sub-programs. Sub-programs can also be further decomposed by focusing on different level of details and ignoring other details. A good decomposition of a program aims at providing the following characteristics.

- Simplicity
- Isolation
- Maintainability

Each sub-program should be simple enough to be understood by itself. Simplicity is achieved by focusing on the relevant pieces of information and ignoring the irrelevant ones. What pieces of information are relevant and what are irrelevant depends on the context.

Each sub-program should be isolated from other sub-programs so that any changes in a sub-program should have localized effects. A change in one sub-program should not affect any other sub-programs. A sub-program defines an interface to interact with other sub-programs. The inner details about the sub-program are hidden from the outside world. As long as the interface for a sub-program remains unchanged, the changes in its inner details should not affect the other sub-programs that interact with it.

Each sub-program should be small enough to be written, understood and maintained easily.

All of the above characteristics are achieved during decomposition of a problem (or program which solves a problem) using a process called *abstraction*. What is abstraction? Abstraction is a way to perform decomposition of a problem by focusing on relevant details and ignoring the irrelevant details about it in a particular context. Note that no details about a problem are irrelevant. In other words, every detail about a problem is relevant. However, some details may be relevant in one context and some in another. It is important to note that it is the "context" that decides what details are relevant and what are irrelevant. For example, consider the problem of designing and developing a keyboard. For a user's perspective, a keyboard consists of keys that can be pressed and released to type text. Number, type, size and position of keys are the only details that are relevant to the users of a keyboard. However, keys are not the only details about a keyboard. A keyboard has an electronic circuit and it is connected to a computer. A lot of things occur inside the keyboard and the computer when a user presses a key. The internal workings of a keyboard are relevant for keyboard designers and manufactures. However, they are irrelevant to the users of a keyboard. You can say that different users have different views of the same thing in different contexts. What details about the thing are relevant and what are irrelevant depends on the user and the context.

Abstraction is not about removing or hiding details from a problem. It is about considering details that are necessary to view the problem in the way that is appropriate in a particular context and ignoring (hiding or suppressing or forgetting) the details that are unnecessary. Terms like "hiding' and "suppressing" in the context of abstraction may be misleading. These terms may mean hiding of some details of a problem. Abstraction is concerned about what details of a thing that should be considered and what not for a particular purpose. It does imply hiding of the details. How things are hidden is another concept called *information hiding*, which is discussed in the following section.

The term abstraction is used to mean one of the two things – a process or an entity. As a process, it is a technique to extract relevant details about a problem and ignoring the irrelevant details. As an entity, it is a particular view of a problem, which considers some relevant details and ignores the irrelevant details.

Let us discuss application of abstraction in a real-world programming. Suppose we want to write a program that will compute the sum of all integers between two integers. Suppose we want to compute the sum of all integers between 10 and 20. We can write the program as follows. Do not worry if you do not understand the syntax used in programs in this section. Just try to grasp the big picture of how abstraction is used to decompose a program.

```
int sum = 0;
int counter = 10;
while(counter <= 20) {
    sum = sum + counter;
    counter = counter + 1;
}
System.out.println(sum);
```

The above snippet of code will add 10 + 11 + 12 + … + 20 and print 165. Suppose we want to compute sum of all integers between 40 and 60. Here is the program to achieve just that.

```
int sum = 0;
int counter = 40;
while(counter <= 60) {
    sum = sum + counter;
    counter = counter + 1;
}
System.out.println(sum);
```

The above snippet of code will perform the sum of all integers between 40 and 60, and it will print 1050. Note the similarities and differences between the two snippets of code. The logic is same in both. However, the lower limit and the upper limit of the range are different. If we can ignore the differences that exist between the two snippets of code, we will be able to avoid the duplicating of logic at two places. Let us consider the following snippet of code.

```
int sum = 0;
int counter = lowerLimit;
while(counter <= upperLimit) {
    sum = sum + counter;
    counter = counter + 1;
}
System.out.println(sum);
```

This time, we did not use any actual values for lower and upper limits of any range. Rather, we have used lowerLimit and upperLimit placeholders that are not known at the time the code is written. By using lowerLimit and upperLimit placeholders in our code, we are hiding the identity of the lower and upper limits of the range. In other words, we are ignoring their actual values when writing the above piece of code. We have applied the process of abstraction in the above code by ignoring the actual values of the lower and upper limits of the range.

When the above piece of code is executed, the actual values must be substituted for `lowerLimit` and `upperLimit` placeholders. This is achieved in a programming language by packaging the above snippet of code inside a module (subroutine or sub-program) called procedure. The placeholders are defined as formal parameters of that procedure. Listing 1-2 has the code for such a procedure.

Listing 1-2: A procedure named getRangeSum to compute the sum of all integers between two integers

```
int getRangeSum(int lowerLimit, int upperLimit) {
    int sum = 0;
    int counter = lowerLimit;
    while(counter <= upperLimit) {
        sum = sum + counter;
        counter = counter + 1;
    }
    return sum;
}
```

A procedure has a name, which is `getRangeSum` in our case. A procedure has a return type, which is specified just before its name. The return type indicates the type of value that it will return to its caller. The return type is `int` in our case, which indicates that the result of computation will be an integer. A procedure has formal parameters (possibly zero), which are specified within parentheses following its name. A formal parameter consists of data type and a name. In our case, the formal parameters are named as `lowerLimit` and `upperLimit`, and both are of the data type `int`. It has a body, which is placed within braces. The body of the procedure contains the logic.

When we want to execute the code for a procedure, we must pass the actual values for its formal parameters. We can compute and print the sum of all integers between 10 and 20 as follows.

```
int s1 = getRangeSum(10, 20);
System.out.println(s1);
```

The above snippet of code will print 165. To compute the sum all integers between 40 and 60, we can execute the following snippet of code.

```
int s2 = getRangeSum(40, 60);
System.out.println(s2);
```

The above snippet of code will print 1050, which is exactly the same result we had achieved before.

The abstraction method that we used in defining `getRangeSum` procedure is called abstraction by parameterization. The formal parameters in a procedure are used to hide the identity of the actual data on which the procedure's body operates. The two parameters in `getRangeSum` procedure hide the identity of the upper and lower limits of the range of integers. You have seen the first concrete example of abstraction. Abstraction is a vast topic. We will cover some more basics about abstraction in this section.

Suppose a programmer writes the code for `getRangeSum` procedure as shown in Listing 1-2 and another programmer wants to use it. The first programmer is the designer and writer of the procedure and the second one is the user of the procedure. What pieces of information does the user of the `getRangeSum` procedure needs know in order to use it? Before we answer this question, let us consider a real-world example of designing and using a DVD player (**D**igital **V**ersatile **D**isc player). A DVD player is designed and developed by Electronic engineers. How do you use a DVD player? You do not open a DVD player to study all the details about its parts that are based on Electronics engineering theories before you use it. When you buy a DVD player, it comes with a manual on how to use it. A DVD player is wrapped in a box. The box hides the details of the player inside. At the same time, the box exposes some of the details about the player in the form of interface to the outside world. The interface for a DVD player consists of the following items.

- Input and output connection ports to connect to a power outlet, a TV set, etc.
- A panel to insert a DVD
- A set of buttons to perform operations such as eject the DVD disc, play, pause, fast forward, etc.

The manual that comes with the DVD player describes the usage of the player's interface meant for its users. A DVD user need not worry about the details about how a DVD player works internally. The manual also describes some conditions to operate the DVD player. For example, you must plug the power cord to a power outlet and switch on the power before you can use the DVD player.

A program is designed, developed and used in the same way as a DVD player. The user of the program shown in Listing 1-2 need not worry about the internal logic that is used to implement the program. A user of the program needs to know only its usage, which includes – interface to use it, and conditions that must be met before and after using it. In other words, we need to provide a manual for the `getRangeSum` procedure that will describe its usage. The user of the `getRangeSum` procedure will need to read its manual to use it. The "manual" for a program is known as its *specification*. Sometimes, specification for a program is also known as *documentation* or *comments*. The specification for a program provides another method of abstraction, which is called *abstraction by specification*. It describes (or exposes or focuses) the "what" part of the program and hides (or ignores or suppresses) the "how" part of the program from the users of the program.

Listing 1-3: The getRangeSum procedure with its specification for Javadoc tool

```
/**
 * Computes and returns the sum of all integers between two
 * integers specified by lowerLimit and upperLimit parameters.
 *
 * The lowerLimit parameter must be greater than or equal to the
 * upperLimit parameter. If the sum of all integers between the
 * lowerLimit and the upperLimit exceeds the range of the int data
 * type then result
 * is not defined.
 *
 * @param lowerLimit The lower limit of the integer range
 * @param upperLimit The upper limit of the integer range
 * @return The sum of all integers between lowerLimit (inclusive)
 *         and upperLimit (inclusive)
 */
public static int getRangeSum(int lowerLimit, int upperLimit) {
    int sum = 0;
    int counter = lowerLimit;
```

```
    while(counter <= upperLimit) {
        sum = sum + counter;
        counter = counter + 1;
    }
    return sum;
}
```

Listing 1-3 shows the same `getRangeSum` procedure code with its specification. It uses Javadoc standards to write specification for a Java program that can be processed by Javadoc tool to generate HTML pages. In Java, specification for a program element is placed between `/**` and `*/`. The specification is meant for the users of the `getRangeSum` procedure. Javadoc tool (refer to *Appendix - B* for details) will generate the following specification (partially shown) for `getRangeSum` procedure.

---

getRangeSum
`int getRangeSum(int lowerLimit, int upperLimit)`

Computes and returns the sum of all integers between two integers specified by lowerLimit and upperLimit parameters.

The lowerLimit parameter must be less than or equal to the upperLimit parameter. If the sum of all integers between the lowerLimit and the upperLimit exceeds the range of the int data type then result is not defined.

Parameters:
`lowerLimit` - The lower limit of the integer range
`upperLimit` - The upper limit of the integer range

Returns:
The sum of all integers between `lowerLimit` (inclusive) and `upperLimit` (inclusive)

The above specification provides the description (the "what" part) of the `getRangeSum` procedure. It also specifies two conditions, known as pre-conditions that must be true when the procedure is called. The first pre-condition is that the lower limit must be less than or equal to the upper limit. The second pre-condition is that the value for lower and upper limits must be small enough so that the sum of all integers between them fits in the size of the `int` data type. It specifies another condition that is called post-condition, which is specified in "*Returns*" clause. The post-condition holds as long as pre-conditions hold. The pre-conditions and post-conditions are like a contract (or an agreement) between the program and its user. It states that as long as the user of the program makes sure that the pre-condition holds true, the program guarantees that the post-condition will hold true. Note that the specification never tells the user about how the program fulfils (implementation details) the post-condition. It only tells "what" it is going to do rather than "how" it is going to do it. The user of the `getRangeSum` program, who has the specification, need not look at the body of the `getRangeSum` procedure to figure out the logic that it uses. In other words, we have hidden the details of implementation of `getRangeSum` procedure from its users by providing the above specification to them. That is, users of the `getRangeSum` procedure can ignore its implementation details for the purpose of using it. This is another concrete example of abstraction. The method of hiding implementation details of a sub-program (the "how" part) and exposing its usage (the "what" part) by using specification is called *abstraction by specification*.

Abstraction by parameterization and abstraction by specification let the users of a program view the program as a black box, where they are concerned only about the effects that program produces rather than how the program produces those effects. Figure 1-4 depicts the user's view of getRangeSum procedure. Note that a user does not see or need not see the body of the procedure that has the details for computing the sum of integers between two integers. The details for computing the sum of integers between two integers are relevant only for the writer of the program and not its users.

Figure 1-4: User's view of the getRangeSum procedure as a black box using abstraction

What advantages did we achieve by applying the abstraction to define getRangeSum procedure? One of the most important advantages is *isolation*. It is isolated from other programs. If we modify the logic inside its body, other programs, including the ones that are using it, need not be modified at all. To print the sum of integers between 10 and 20, we used the following program.

```
int s1 = getRangeSum(10, 20);
System.out.println(s1);
```

The body of the procedure uses a while-loop, which is executed as many times as the number of integers between lower and upper limits. The while-loop inside getRangeSum procedure executes n times where n is equal to (upperLimit - lowerLimit + 1). The number of instructions that need to be executed depends on the input values. There is a better way to compute the sum of all integers between two integers, lowerLimit and upperLimit, using a formula as follows.

```
n = upperLimit - lowerLimit + 1;
sum = n * (2 * lowerLimit + (n-1))/2;
```

If we use the above formula, the number of instructions that are executed to compute the sum of all integers between two integers is always the same. We can rewrite the body of the getRangeSum procedure as shown in Listing 1-4. The specification of getRangeSum procedure is not shown here.

Listing 1-4: Another version of getRangeSum procedure with logic changed inside its body

```
public int getRangeSum(int lowerLimit, int upperLimit) {
    int n = upperLimit - lowerLimit + 1;
    int sum = n * (2 * lowerLimit + (n-1))/2;
    return sum;
}
```

Note that the body (implementation or the "how" part) of the getRangeSum procedure has changed between Listing 1-3 and Listing 1-4. However, the users of getRangeSum procedure are not affected by this change at all because the details of the implementation of this procedure were kept hidden from its users by using abstraction. If you want to compute the sum of all integers between 10 and 20 using the version of getRangeSum procedure as shown in Listing 1-4, your old code shown below is still valid.

```
int s1 = getRangeSum(10, 20);
System.out.println(s1);
```

You have just seen one of the greatest benefits of abstraction in which the implementation details of a program (in this case a procedure) can be changed without warranting any changes in the code that uses the program. This benefit also gives you a chance to rewrite your program logic to improve performance in future without affecting other parts of the application.

We will consider two types abstraction in this section.

- Procedural abstraction
- Data abstraction

Procedural abstraction lets you define a procedure, for example `getRangeSum`, that you use as an action or a task. So far, in this section, we have been discussing procedural abstraction. Abstraction by parameterization and abstraction by specification are two methods to achieve procedural as well as data abstraction.

Object-oriented programming is based on data abstraction. We need to discuss about data type briefly, before we discuss about data abstraction. A data type (or simply a type) is defined in terms of three components.

- A set of values (or data objects)
- A set of operations that can be applied to all values in the set
- A data representation, which determines how the values are stored

Programming languages provide some pre-defined data types, which are known as built-in data types. They also let programmers define their own data types, which are known as user-defined data types. A data type that consists of an atomic and indivisible value, and that is defined without the help of any other data types, is known as a primitive data type. For example, Java has built-in primitive data types such as `int`, `float`, `boolean`, `char`, etc. Three components that define the `int` primitive data type in Java are as follows.

- An `int` data type consists of a set of all integers between -2147483648 and 2147483647
- Operations such as addition, subtraction, multiplication, division, comparison and many more are defined for `int` data type.
- A value of `int` data type is represented in 32-bit memory in 2's compliment form.

All three components of `int` data type are pre-defined by Java language. You cannot extend or re-define the definition of `int` data type as a programmer. You can give a name to a value of the `int` data type as:

```
int n1;
```

The above statement states that `n1` is a name (technically called an identifier) that can be associated with one value from the set of values that defines values for `int` data type. For example, we can associate integer `26` to the name `n1` using an assignment statement as:

```
n1 = 26;
```

You may ask a question at this stage, "Where in memory the value `26`, which is associated with the name `n1`, is stored?" We know from definition of `int` data type that `n1` will take 32-bit memory. However, we do not know, cannot know, and need not know, where in the memory that 32-bit is allocated for `n1`. Do you see an example of abstraction here? If you see an example of abstraction in this case, you are right. This is an example of abstraction, which is built into the Java language. In this instance, the pieces of information about the data representation of the data value for `int` data type is hidden from the users (programmers) of the data type. In other words, a programmer ignores the memory location of `n1` and focuses on its value and operations that can be performed on it. A programmer does not care if the memory for `n1` is allocated in a register, RAM or the hard disk.

Object-oriented programming languages, e.g., Java, let you create new data types using an abstraction mechanism called *data abstraction*. The new data types are known as **A**bstract **D**ata **T**ypes (ADT). The data objects in ADT may consist of a combination of primitive data types and other ADTs. An ADT defines a set of operations that can be applied to all its data objects. The data representation is always hidden in ADT. For users of an ADT, it consists of operations only. Its data elements may only be accessed and manipulated using its operations. The advantage of using data abstraction is that its data representation can be changed without affecting any code that uses the ADT.

TIP

Data abstraction lets programmers create a new data type called Abstract Data Type, where the storage representation of the data objects is hidden from the users of the data type. In other words, ADT is defined solely in terms of operations that can be applied to the data objects of its type without knowing the internal representation of the data. The reason this kind of data type is called abstract is that users of ADT never see the representation of the data values. Users view the data objects of an ADT in an abstract way by applying operations on them without knowing the details about representation of the data objects. Note that an ADT does not mean absence of data representation. Data representation is always present in an ADT. It only means hiding of the data representation from its users.

Java language has two constructs, class and interface, that let you define new ADTs. When you use a class to define a new ADT in Java, you need to be careful to hide the data representation so that your new data type is really abstract. If the data representation in a Java class is not hidden, that class creates a new data type, but not an ADT. A class in Java gives you features that you can use to expose the data representation or hide it. In Java, the set of values of a class data type are called objects. Operations on the objects are called methods. Instance variables (also known as fields) of objects are the data representation for the class type.

A class in Java also lets you provide implementation of operations that operates on the data representation. An interface in Java lets you create pure ADT. An interface lets you provide only the specification for operations that can be applied to the data objects of its type. No implementation for operations or data representation can be mentioned in an interface. Listing 1-1 shows the definition of the `Person` class using Java language syntax. By defining a class named `Person`, we have created a new ADT. Its internal data representation for name and gender uses `String` data type (`String` is built-in ADT provided by Java class library). Note that the definition of the `Person` class uses the `private` keyword in the `name` and `gender` declarations to hide it from the outside world. Users of the `Person` class cannot access the `name` and `gender` data elements. It provides four operations – a constructor, and three methods - `getName`, `setName`, and `getGender`.

A constructor operation is used to initialize a newly constructed data object of `Person` type. The `getName` and `setName` operations are used to access and modify the name data element respectively. The `getGender` operation is used to access the value of the gender data element.

Users of the `Person` class must use only these four operations to work with data objects of `Person` type. Users of the `Person` type are oblivious to the type of data storage being used to store `name` and `gender` data elements. We are using three terms, `type`, `class` and `interface`, interchangeably because they mean one and the same thing in the context of a data type. It gives the developer of the `Person` type freedom to change the data representation for name and gender data elements without affecting any users of `Person` type. Suppose one of the users of `Person` type has the following snippet of code.

```
Person john = new Person("John Jacobs", "Male");
String intialName = john.getName();
john.setName("Wally Jacobs");
String changedName = john.getName();
```

Note that the above snippet of code has been written only in terms of the operations provided by `Person` type. It has never referred (and could not refer) to the name and gender instance variables directly. Let us see how we can change the data representation of `Person` type without affecting the above snippet of code. Listing 1-5 shows the code for newer version for the `Person` class. Compare the code in Listing 1-1 and Listing 1-5. This time we have replaced the two instance variables (name and gender), which were the data representation for `Person` type in Listing 1-1 by a `String` array of two elements. Since operations (or methods) in a class operate on the data representation, we had to change the implementations for all four operations in `Person` type. The above client code was written in terms of the specifications of the four operations and not their implementation. Since we have not changed the specification of any of the operation, we do not need to change the above snippet of code that uses the `Person` class. It is still valid with the newer definition of `Person` type as shown in Listing 1-5. Some methods in the `Person` class use the abstraction by parameterization and all of them use the abstraction by specification. We have not shown the specification for the methods here, which would be Javadoc comments.

Listing 1-5: Another version of the Person class that uses a String array of two elements to store name and gender values as opposed to two String variables

```java
public class Person {
    private String[] data = new String[2];

    public Person(String initialName, String initialGender) {
        data[0] = initialName;
        data[1] = initialGender;
    }

    public String getName() {
        return data[0];
    }

    public void setName(String newName) {
        data[0] = newName;
    }

    public String getGender() {
        return data[1];
    }
}
```

We have seen two major benefits of data abstraction in this section.

- It lets you extend the programming language by letting you define new data types. What new data types you create depends on the application domain. For example, for a banking system, `Person`, `Currency`, and `Account` may be good choices for new data types, whereas for an auto insurance application, `Person`, `Vehicle`, and `Claim` may be good choices for new data types. What operations are included in a new data type depends on the need of the application.
- The data type created using data abstraction may change the representation of the data without affecting the client code using the data type.

Encapsulation and Information Hiding

The term encapsulation is used to mean two different things – a process or an entity. As a process, it is an act of bundling one or more items into a container. The container could be physical or logical. As an entity, it is a container that holds one or more items.

Programming languages support encapsulations in many ways. A procedure is an encapsulation of steps to perform a task; an array is an encapsulation of several elements of the same type, etc. In object-oriented programming, encapsulation is bundling of data and operations on the data into an entity called a *class*.

Java supports encapsulation in various ways.

- It lets you bundle data and methods that operate on the data in an entity called class.
- It lets you bundle one or more logically related classes in an entity called package. A package in Java is a logical collection of one or more related classes. A package creates a new naming scope in which all classes must have unique names. Two classes may have the same name in Java as long as they are bundled (or encapsulated) in two different packages.
- It lets you bundle one or more related classes in an entity called a *compilation unit*. All classes in a compilation unit can be compiled separately from other compilation units.

While discussing the concepts of object-oriented programming, the two terms, *encapsulation and information hiding,* are often used interchangeably. However, they are different concepts in object-oriented programming, and they should not be used interchangeably as such. Encapsulation is simply bundling of items together into one entity. Information hiding is the process of hiding implementation details that are likely to change. Encapsulation is not concerned with whether the items that are bundled in an entity are hidden from other modules in the application or not. What should be hidden (or ignored) and what should not be hidden is the concern of abstraction. Abstraction is only concerned about which item should be hidden. Abstraction is not concerned about how the item should be hidden. Information hiding is concerned about how an item is hidden. Encapsulation, abstraction and information hiding are three separate concepts. They are very closely related though. One concept facilitates workings of others. It is important to understand the subtle differences in roles they play in object-oriented programming.

It is possible to use encapsulation with or without hiding any information. For example, the `Person` class in Listing 1-1 shows an example of encapsulation and information hiding. The data elements (`name` and `gender`) and methods (`getName()`, `setName()` and `getGender()`) are bundled together in a class called `Person`. This is encapsulation. In other words, we can state that the `Person` class is an encapsulation of data elements - `name` and `gender`, and methods – `getName()`, `setName()` and `getGender()`. The same `Person` class uses information hiding by hiding the data elements – `name` and `gender`, from the outside world. Note that `name` and `gender` data elements use the Java keyword `private`, which essentially hides them from the outside world. Listing 1-6 shows code for the `Person2` class. The code in Listing 1-1 and Listing 1-6 are essentially the same except for two small differences. The `Person2` class uses the keyword `public` to declare the `name` and the `gender` data elements. The `Person2` class uses encapsulation exactly the same way as the `Person` class uses. However, data elements, `name` and `gender`, are not hidden. That is, the `Person2` class does not use data hiding (Data hiding is an example of information hiding). If you look at the constructor and methods of `Person` and `Person2` classes, their bodies use information hiding, because the logic written inside their bodies is hidden from their users.

Listing 1-6: The definition of Person2 class in which data elements are not hidden by declaring them public

```
public class Person2 {
    public String name;    // Not hidden from its users
    public String gender;  // Not hidden from its users

    public Person2(String initialName, String initialGender) {
        name = initialName;
        gender = initialGender;
    }

    public String getName() {
        return name;
    }

    public void setName(String newName) {
        name = newName;
    }

    public String getGender() {
        return gender;
    }
}
```

TIP
Encapsulation and information hiding are two distinct concepts of object-oriented programming. Existence of one does not imply the existence of other.

Inheritance

Inheritance is another important concept in object-oriented programming. It lets you use abstraction in a new way. We have seen how a class represents an abstraction in previous sections. The `Person` class shown in Listing 1-1 represents an abstraction for a real-world person. Inheritance mechanism lets you define a new abstraction by extending an existing abstraction. The existing abstraction is called a *supertype*, a *superclass*, a *parent class,* or a *base class*. The new abstraction is called a *subtype*, a *subclass*, a *child class*, or a *derived class*. It is said that subtype is derived (or inherited) from supertype; supertype is a generalization of subtype; and subtype is a specialization of supertype. The inheritance can be used to define new abstractions at more than one level. A subtype can be used as a supertype to define another subtype and so on. Inheritance gives rise to a family of types arranged in a hierarchical form.

Inheritance allows you to use varying degrees of abstraction at different levels of hierarchy. In Figure 1-5, the `Person` class is at the top (highest level) of the inheritance hierarchy. `Employee` and `Customer` classes are at the second level of inheritance hierarchy. As we move up the inheritance level, we focus on more important pieces information. In other words, at higher level of inheritance, we are concerned about the bigger picture; and at lower levels of inheritance, we are concerned about more and more details. There is another way to look at inheritance hierarchy from abstraction point of view. At `Person` level in Figure 1-5, we focus on the common characteristics of `Employee` and `Customer`, and we ignore the difference between them. At `Employee` level, we focus on common characteristics of `Clerk`, `Programmer` and `Cashier`, and we ignore the differences between them.

In inheritance hierarchy, a supertype and its subtype represent an "is-a" relationship. That is, an `Employee` is a `Person`; a `Programmer` is an `Employee`, etc. Since the lower level of inheritance means more pieces of information, a subtype always includes what its supertype has and maybe some more. This characteristic of inheritance leads to another feature in object-oriented programming, which is known as *principle of substitutivity*. It means that a supertype can always be substituted with its subtype. For example, we have considered only `name` and `gender` information for a person in our `Person` abstraction. If we inherit `Employee` from `Person`, `Employee` includes `name` and `gender` information, which it inherits from `Person`. `Employee` may include some more pieces of information such as employee id, hire date, salary, etc. If a `Person` is expected in a context, it implies that only `name` and `gender` information are relevant in that context. We can always replace a `Person` in this context with an `Employee`, a `Customer`, a `Clerk`, or a `Programmer` because being a subtype (direct or indirect) of the `Person` these abstractions guarantee that they have the ability to deal with at least `name` and `gender` information.

At programming level, inheritance provides a code reuse mechanism. The code written in supertype may be reused by its subtype. A subtype may extend the functionality of its supertype by adding more functionality or by redefining existing functionalities of its supertype.

Inheritance is a vast topic. This book devotes a complete chapter to inheritance. We will discuss how Java allows us to use inheritance mechanisms in *Chapter 9 - Inheritance and Reusability*

Figure 1-5: Inheritance hierarchy for the Person class

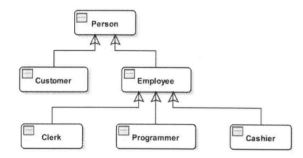

Polymorphism

The word "Polymorphism" has its root in two Greek words – "poly" (means many) and "morphos" (means form). In programming, polymorphism is the ability of an entity (e.g. variable, class, method, object, code, parameter, etc) to take on different meanings in different contexts. The entity that takes on different meanings is known as polymorphic entity. Various types of polymorphism exist. Each type of polymorphism has a name that usually indicates how that type of polymorphism is achieved in practice. The proper use of polymorphism results in generic and reusable codes. The purpose of polymorphism is writing reusable and maintainable code by writing codes in terms of a generic type that works for many types (or ideally all types).

Polymorphism can be categorized in the following two categories.

- Ad hoc Polymorphism
- Universal Polymorphism

If types for which a piece of code works is finite and all those types must be known when code is written, it is known as ad hoc polymorphism. Ad hoc polymorphism is also known as apparent polymorphism because it is not a polymorphism in a true sense. Some computer science purists do not consider ad hoc polymorphism as polymorphism at all. Ad hoc polymorphism is divided into two types – overloading polymorphism and coercion polymorphism.

If a piece of code is written in such a way that it works for infinite number of types (will also work for new types not known at the time the code is written), it is called universal polymorphism. In universal polymorphism, the same code works on many types, whereas in ad hoc polymorphism different implementations of code are provided for different types giving an apparent impression of polymorphism. Universal polymorphism is divided into two types – inclusion polymorphism and parametric polymorphism.

Overloading Polymorphism

Overloading is an ad hoc polymorphism. Overloading results when a method (called method in Java and function in other languages) or an operator has at least two definitions that work on different types. In such cases, the same method or operator name is used for different definitions of the method or the operator. That is, the same name exhibits many behaviors and hence the polymorphism. Such methods and operators are called overloaded methods and overloaded operators. Java lets you define overloaded methods. Java has some overloaded operators. Java does not let you overload an operator in your code. You cannot provide a new definition for an operator in Java.

Listing 1-7: An example of an overloaded method in Java

```java
public class MathUtil {
    public static int max(int n1, int n2) {
        // Code to determine the maximum of two integers goes here
    }

    public static float max(double n1, double n2) {
        // Code to determine the maximum of two floating-point numbers
        // goes here
    }

    public static int max(int[] num) {
        // Code to determine the maximum an array of integers goes here
    }
}
```

Listing 1-7 shows code for a class named MathUtil. The max() method of MathUtil class is overloaded. It has three definitions and each of its definitions performs the same task of computing maximum, but on different types. The first definition computes maximum of two numbers of int data type; second one computes maximum of two floating-point numbers of double data type and third one computes maximum of an array of numbers of int data type. The following snippet of code makes use of all three definitions of the overloaded max() method.

```java
int max1 = MathUtil.max(10, 23);        // Uses max(int, int)
```

```
int max2 = MathUtil.max(10.34, 2.89); // Uses use max(float, float)
int max3 = MathUtil.max(new int[]{1, 89, 8, 3}); // Uses max(int[])
```

Note that method overloading gives you only sharing of the method name. It does not result in the sharing of definitions. In Listing 1-7, the method name `max` is shared by all three methods, but they all have their own definition of computing maximum of different types. In method overloading, the definitions of methods do not have to be related at all. They may perform entirely different things and share the same name.

The following code snippet shows an example of operator overloading in Java. The operator is +. In the following three statements, it performs three different things.

```
int n1 = 10 + 20;          // Adds two integers
double n2 = 10.20 + 2.18;  // Adds two floating-point numbers
String str = "Hi " + "there"; // Concatenates two strings
```

In the first statement, the + operator performs addition on two integers - 10 and 20 and returns 30. In the second statement, it performs addition on two floating-point numbers – 10.20 and 2.18 and returns 12.38. In the third statement, it performs concatenation of two strings and returns "Hi there".

In overloading, the types of actual method's parameters (types of operands in case of operators) are used to determine which definition of the code to use. Method overloading provides only the reuse of the method name. You can remove method overloading by simply supplying a unique name to all versions of an overloaded method. For example, you could rename three versions of `max()` method as `max2Int()`, `max2Double()` and `maxNInt()`. Note that all versions of an overloaded method or operator do not have to perform related or similar tasks. In Java, the only requirement to overload a method name is that all versions of the method must differ in number and/or type of their formal parameters.

Coercion Polymorphism

Coercion is an ad hoc polymorphism. Coercion occurs when a type is implicitly converted (coerced) to another type automatically even if it was not intended explicitly. Consider the following statements in Java.

```
int num = 707;
double d1 = (double)num;  // Explicit conversion of int to double
double d2 = num;  // Implicit conversion of int to double (coercion)
```

The variable `num` has been declared to be of `int` data type, and it has been assigned a value of 707. The second statement uses cast, `(double)`, to convert the `int` value stored in `num` to `double`, and assigns the converted value to `d1`. This is the case of explicit conversion from `int` to `double`. In this case, the programmer makes his intention explicit by using the cast. The third statement has exactly the same effect as the second one. However, it relies on implicit conversion (called widening conversion in Java) provided by Java language that converts an `int` to `double` automatically when needed. The third statement is an example of coercion. A programming language (including Java) provides different coercions in different contexts – assignment (shown above), method parameters, etc.

Let us consider the following snippet of code that shows definition of a `square()` method, which accepts a parameter of `double` data type.

Object-Oriented Paradigm and Java

```
double square(double num) {
    return num * num;
}
```

The `square()` method can be called with actual parameter of `double` data type as:

```
double d1 = 20.23;
double result = square(d1);
```

The same `square()` method may also be called with actual parameter of `int` data type as:

```
int k = 20;
double result = square(k);
```

We have just seen that the `square()` method works on `double` data type as well as `int` data type although we have defined it only once in terms of a formal parameter of `double` data type. This is exactly what polymorphism means. In this case, `square()` method is called polymorphic method with respect to `double` and `int` data type. In this case, `square()` method is exhibiting polymorphic behavior even though the programmer who wrote code did not intend it. The `square()` method is polymorphic because of implicit type conversion (coercion from `int` to `double`) provided by Java language. Here is a more formal definition of a polymorphic method.

Suppose m *is a method that declares a formal parameter of type* T. *If* S *is a type that can be implicitly converted to* T, *the method* m *is said to be polymorphic with respect to* S *and* T.

Inclusion Polymorphism

Inclusion is a universal polymorphism. It is also known as subtype (or subclass) polymorphism because it is achieved using subtyping or subclassing. This is the most common type of polymorphism supported by object-oriented programming languages. Java supports it. Inclusion polymorphism occurs when a piece of code that is written using a type works for all its subtypes. This type of polymorphism is possible based on the subtyping rule that a value that belongs to a subtype also belongs to the supertype. Suppose `T` is a type and `S1, S2, S3...` are subtypes of `T`. A value that belongs to `S1, S2, S3...` also belongs to `T`. This subtyping rule makes us write code as follows.

```
T t;
S1 s1;
S2 s2;
...
t = s1; // A value of type s1 can be assigned to variable of type T
t = s2; // A value of type s2 can be assigned to variable of type T
```

Java supports inclusion polymorphism using inheritance, which is a subclassing mechanism. You can define a method in Java using a formal parameter of a type, e.g., `Person`, and that method can be called on all its subtypes, e.g., `Employee`, `Student`, `Customer`, etc. Suppose we have a method `processDetails()` as follows.

```
void processDetails(Person p) {
    /* Write code using the formal parameter p, which is
       of type Person. The same code will work if an object
       of any of the subclass of Person is passed to this method
    */
```

```
}
```

The `processDetails()` method declares a formal parameter of Person type. You can define any number of classes that are subclasses of the `Person` class. The `processDetails()` method will work for all subclasses of the `Person` class. Assume that `Employee` and `Customer` are subclasses of the `Person` class. We can write code like:

```
Person p1 = create a Person object;
Employee e1 = create an Employee object;
Customer c1 = create a Customer object;
processDetails(p1); // Use Person type
processDetails(e1); // Use Employee type, which is a subclass of Person
processDetails(c1); // Use Customer type, which is a subclass of Person
```

The effect of the subtyping rule is that the supertype includes (hence the name inclusion) all values that belong to its subtypes. A piece of code is called universally polymorphic only if it works on infinite number of types. In the case of inclusion polymorphism, the number of types for which the code works is constrained but infinite. The constraint is that all types must be the subtype of the type in whose term the code is written. If there is no restriction on how many subtypes a type can have, the number of subtypes is infinite (at least in theory). Note that inclusion polymorphism not only lets you write reusable code, it also lets you write extensible and flexible code. The `processDetails()` method works on all subclasses of the `Person` class. It will keep working for all subclasses of the `Person` class, which will be defined in future, without any modifications. Java uses other mechanisms, like method overriding and dynamic dispatch (also called late binding), along with subclassing rules to make the inclusion polymorphism more effective and useful.

Parametric Polymorphism

Parametric is a universal polymorphism. It is also called "true" polymorphism, because it lets you write true generic code that works for any types (related or unrelated). Sometimes, it is also referred to as generics. In parametric polymorphism, a piece of code is written in such a way that it works on any type. Contrast parametric polymorphism with inclusion polymorphism. In inclusion polymorphism, code is written for one type and it works for all of its subtypes. It means all types for which the code works in inclusion polymorphism are related by supertype-subtype relationship. However, in parametric polymorphism, the same code works for all types, which are not necessarily related. Parametric polymorphism is achieved by using a type variable while writing the code rather than using any specific type. The type variable assumes a type for which the code needs to be executed. Java supports parametric polymorphism since Java 5 through generics. Java supports polymorphic entity (e.g. parameterized classes) as well as polymorphic method (parameterized methods) that use parametric polymorphism.

All collection classes in Java 5 have been retrofitted to use generics (parametric polymorphism is achieved in Java using generics). You can write code using generics as shown below. It uses a List object as a list of String type and Integer type. Using generics, you can treat a List object as a list of any type in Java. Note the use of <XXX> (angle brackets) in code to specify the type for which you want to instantiate the List object.

```
// Use List for String type
List<String> sList = new ArrayList<String>();
sList.add("string 1");
sList.add("string 2");
String s2 = sList.get(1);

// Use List for Integer type
```

```
List<Integer> iList = new ArrayList<Integer>();
iList.add(10);
iList.add(20);
int i2 = iList.get(1)
```

Chapter 2. Writing Java Programs

This chapter discusses how to write a program Java program. It describes the steps to write, compile, and run a simple Java program. The program prints a message on the console, e.g., DOS prompt on Windows. This chapter explains only the basics involved in writing a Java program. Detailed explanation of all aspects of a Java program will be explained in subsequent chapters.

A Java program involves three steps:

- Writing the source code
- Compiling the source code
- Running the compiled code

You can write the Java source code using a text editor of your choice, for example, Notepad on Windows, vi editor on UNIX, etc. The source code is compiled into the object code, also known as bytecode, using a Java compiler. The compiled code (object code or bytecode) is then run by a Java virtual machine (JVM).

Writing the Source Code

The source code, also known as compilation unit, for a Java program can be written using any text editor available on the host system, for example, Notepad on Windows; Pico or vi editor on UNIX; SimpleText on Mac, etc. When you finish writing the source code, you must save the file with extension `.java`. We are going to name our source code file as `Welcome.java`. Note that any extension to the file other than `.java` is not acceptable. For example, the names `Welcome.txt` and `Welcome.doc` are not valid source code file names for a Java program. When you write the Java source code, you must follow the grammar of Java language. Whenever you use a language to write something (in our case, Java source code), you need to follow the grammar of that language, and use a specific syntax depending on the thing you are writing. Let us take an example of writing a letter to your friend using English language. A typical letter to your friend will look similar to the one shown below.

2601 Vaughn Lakes Blvd. #1717
Montgomery, AL 36117

January 20, 2001

Dear Anna

Today, I am going to write my first Java program. While writing a Java program one has to follow the grammar specified in Java Language Specification. I just wanted to brush up my memory of the English grammar and the format one should follow while writing a letter to one's friend. I hope I enjoy learning Java programming language.

Your friend,
Joe

The above letter contains five parts each shown in a rectangular box. The five parts are used to specify the following five different things in the letter.

- *The Heading*: It contains your return address and the date on which you write the letter
- *The Greeting*: It contains salutation. For a friend, you use the word "Dear" whereas for your boss, you use the word "Sir" as salutation. Here, you can say the words, "Dear" and "Sir", are keywords for salutation. Other languages may use different words to convey the same meaning. Keywords are words that are used in a specific context to convey special meanings.
- *The Body*: It contains the main message.
- *The Closing*: It contains complimentary closing statement.
- *The Signature*: It tells who wrote the letter.

In this letter, it is not just important to put all five parts together; rather, they should also be placed in a specific order. For example, "The Closing" part needs to follow "The Body" part of the letter. Some parts in a letter may be optional and others mandatory. For example, it is fine to exclude return address in a letter to your friend, whereas it is mandatory in a business letter.

In the beginning, you can think of writing a Java program similar to writing a letter. Let us start writing the Java source code. There are three parts in a Java source code.

- Zero or one package declaration
- Zero, one, or more import declarations
- Zero, one, or more type declarations – a `class`, an `interface`, or an `enum` declaration

All three parts are optional in a Java source code. The three parts, if present, in a Java source code must be specified in the above-mentioned order. The Java source code starts with a package declaration. The import declarations follow the package declaration. The type declarations follow the import declarations.

Package Declaration

The general syntax for a package declaration is:

```
package <<your-package-name>>;
```

A package declaration starts with the keyword `package`. The package name follows the `package` keyword. One or more whitespaces (spaces, tabs, new lines, carriage returns, tabs, and form-feeds) separate the `package` keyword and the package name. A semi-colon (`;`) ends the package declaration. Figure 2-1 shows the parts of a package declaration. For example, the following is the package declaration for a package named `com.jdojo.chapter2`.

```
package com.jdojo.chapter2;
```

Figure 2-1: Parts of a package declaration in a Java program

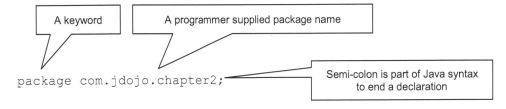

The programmer supplies the package name. A package name may consist of one or more parts separated by a dot (.). Our package name consists of three parts: `com`, `jdojo`, and `chapter2`. There is no limit on the number of parts in a package name. However, if a package declaration appears in a Java source code, it must contain a package name, which must have at least one part. You can have maximum of one package declaration in a Java source code (to be more specific, in a compilation unit). Examples of some valid package declarations are:

```
package chapter2;
package com.jdojo.chapter2.common;
package com.ksharan;
```

Why do we use a package declaration in a Java source code? A package is a logical repository for Java types (`class`, `interface`, and `enum`). In other words, it provides a logical grouping for related Java types. A package can be stored in a host specific file system, in a database or in a network location. In a file system, each part of a package name denotes a directory on the host system. For example, the package name `com.jdojo.chapter2` indicates the existence of a directory named `com`, which contains a sub-directory `jdojo`, which contains a sub-directory `chapter2`. The directory `chapter2` will contain the compiled Java code. If you are working on Windows, you can think of a directory structure `com\jdojo\chapter2\<<Class File Name>>` whereas on UNIX-like operating systems, e.g. Linux, Solaris and Mac OS X, it will look like `com/jdojo/chapter2/<<Class File Name>>`. A dot (.), which is used to separate parts of a package name, is treated as a file-separator character on the host system. A back slash (\) is the file-separator character on Windows, and a forward slash (/) on UNIX-like operating system. A package specifies only the partial directory structure in which the compiled Java program (class files) must exist. It does not specify the full path of the class files. In our example shown above, the package declaration for `com.jdojo.chapter2` does not specify where the `com` folder will be placed. It may be placed under `C:\` directory or `C:\myprograms` directory or under any other directory in the file system.

Knowing just the package name is not enough to locate a class file, because it specifies only a partial path to the class file. The leading part of the class file path on the file system is used from an environment variable called CLASSPATH. We will discuss CLASSPATH in details shortly.

The package declaration is an optional part in a Java source code. What repository does your Java program belong if you omit the package declaration from the Java source code? A Java program (strictly speaking a Java type), which does not have a package declaration, is said to be part of an *unnamed package* (also called *default package*). We will discuss more about unnamed package in sections to follow.

Java source code is case sensitive. The keyword `package` has to be written as is – in all lowercase. The word `Package` or `packAge` cannot replace the keyword `package`. The package name is also case sensitive. On some operating systems, names of files and directories are case sensitive. On those systems, the package names will be case sensitive, as you have seen that the package name is treated as a directory name on the host system. The package names, `com.jdojo.chapter2` and `Com.Jdojo.chapter2`, may not be the same depending on the host system that you are working on. It is recommended to use package names in all lowercase.

The package declaration is a simple and important part of a Java source code. It is recommended that you always use a package declaration in your source code. Typically, a package name starts with a reverse domain name of the company such as `com.yahoo` for Yahoo, `com.google` for Google etc. Using the reverse domain name of the company as the leading part of the package name for all Java code, which is written in a company, guarantees that a package name will not conflict with package names used by other companies.

Import Declaration

The import declaration part in a Java source code is optional. However, unlike the package declaration, which is optional but becomes inevitable when developing a big Java application, the import declarations part is truly optional. You may develop a Java application without using even a single import declaration. Why is an import declaration needed at all? Using import declarations in your code makes your programming life easier. It saves you some typing time while writing code and makes your code cleaner and easier to read. In an import declaration, you tell the Java compiler that you may use one or more classes from a particular package. Whenever a type (a class, an interface, or an enum) is used in Java source code, it must be referred to by its fully qualified name. Using an import declaration for a type lets you refer to it using its simple name. We will discuss about simple and fully qualified name of a type shortly.

Unlike a package declaration, there is no restriction on the number of import declarations in a source code. Two import declarations are shown below.

```
import com.jdojo.chapter2.Account;
import com.jdojo.util.*;
```

We will discuss import declarations in detail in the chapter on *Classes and Objects*. In this section, we will discuss only the meaning of all parts of an import declaration. Like a package declaration, an import declaration starts with the keyword `import`. The second part in an import declaration consists of two parts:

- A package name from which you want to use the classes in the current source code
- A class name or an asterisk (*) to indicate that you may use one or more of the classes stored in the package

Finally, an import declaration ends with a semi-colon (;).

The above two import declarations state that:

- We may use a class named `Account` by its simple name from `com.jdojo.chapter2` package in our source code
- We may use any classes by their simple names from `com.jdojo.util` package in our source code.

If you want to use a class named `Person` from `com.jdojo.common` package in a Java source code, you need to include one of the following two import declarations in your source code.

```
import com.jdojo.common.Person;
```

or,

```
import com.jdojo.common.*;
```

The following import declarations do not include classes in the package `com` or `com.jdojo`.

```
import com.jdojo.chapter2.Account;
import com.jdojo.chapter2.*;
```

You might think that you may have some kind of import declaration like:

```
import com.*.*;
```

that would let you use all classes whose first part of package declaration is `com`. Java does not support this type of wild card use in an import declaration. You are allowed only to name one class in a package (`com.jdojo.chapter2.Account`) or all classes in a package (`com.jdojo.chapter2.*`) in an import declaration. Any other syntax (other than the two described) to import classes in your Java program will result in error.

The third part in a Java source code contains type declarations, which may contain zero or more declarations for `class`, `interface`, and/or `enum`. According to Java Language Specification, type declaration is also optional. However, if you omit this part, your Java program does not do anything. To make your Java program meaningful, you must include at least one class, interface, or enum declaration in your Java source code. We will defer the discussion of interface and enum until later chapters in this book. Let us discuss how to declare a class in a Java source code.

Class Declaration

In the simplest form, a class declaration looks like:

```
class Welcome {
    // Code for the class body goes here
};
```

Figure 2-2 shows parts of the above class declaration. A class in Java is declared by using a `class` keyword, which is followed by the name of the class. In our example, the name of the class is `Welcome`.

Figure 2-2: Parts of a class declaration in a Java source code

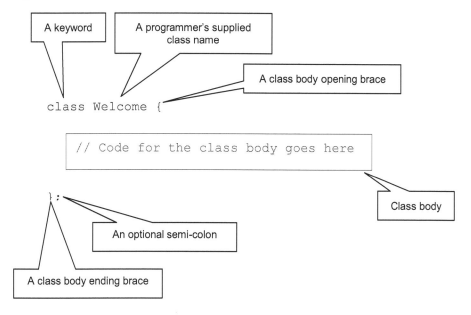

The body of a class is placed between opening and closing braces. The body of a class may be empty. However, you must include the two braces to mark the beginning and the end of a class body. Optionally, a class declaration may end with a semi-colon (;). This book will not use the optional semi-colon to end a class declaration. Before we continue the discussion of a class declaration, let us discuss the following line from the body of the class in our example.

```
// Code for the class body goes here
```

The above line is called a comment. Comments are not executable code. The Java compiler ignores them. They are included in a program to document the program's functionality and logic. There are three types of comments in a Java program.

- Single-line comment
- Multi-line comment
- Documentation comment or Javadoc comment)

The first type of comment is called a single-line comment. It starts with two forward slashes (//) followed by the comment text. For example,

```
// This is a single-line comment
package com.jdojo.chapter2; // This is also a single-line comment
```

This type of comment may start at any position in a line. The part of the line starting from two forward slashes (//) to the end of the line is considered a comment. As shown above, you can also mix Java source code, e.g., a package declaration and a comment in one line. Note that this type of comment cannot be inserted in the middle of the Java code. The following package declaration is incorrect as the package name and the semi-colon are also considered as part of the comment.

```
package // An incorrect single-line comment com.jdojo.chapter2;
```

The following line is a single-line comment. It has a valid package declaration as the comment's text. It will be treated as a comment and not as a package declaration.

```
// package com.jdojo.chapter2;
```

The second type of comment is called a multi-line comment. A multi-line comment may span multiple lines. It starts with a forward slash immediately followed by an asterisk (/*) and ends with an asterisk immediately followed by a forward slash (*/). An example of a multi-line comment in a Java source code is as follows.

```
/*
    This is a multi-line comment.
    It can span more than one line.
*/
```

The above comment can also be written using two single-line comments as follows.

```
// This is a multi-line comment.
// It can span more than one line
```

It is a programmer's personal choice, which style of comment is used in a Java program. A multi-line comment may be inserted in the middle of Java code as shown below. Compiler ignores all texts starting from /* to */.

```
package /* A correct comment */ com.jdojo.chapter2;
```

The third type of comment is called documentation (or Javadoc) comment, which is also a multi-line comment. It is used to generate documentation for Java programs. This kind of comment begins with a forward slash that is immediately followed by two asterisks (/**) and ends with an asterisk that is immediately followed by a forward slash (*/). Please refer to *Appendix- A (Vol. 3)* for more details on how to write documentation comments. The following is an example of a documentation comment.

```
/**
This is a documentation comment. A Java utility program called javadoc to
generate documentation from Java source code uses such comments.
*/
```

The simplest class declaration in a Java program may look like:

```
class Welcome { }
```

This time, we have placed the whole class declaration in one line. You can place the keyword class, the name of the class Welcome and the two braces { } in any position you want, except that you must include at least one whitespace (space, newline, tab, etc) between the keyword class and class name Welcome and you place them in order they appear. Java allows you to write source code in a freeform text format. All of the following three class declarations are the same. You can declare Welcome class in any other format other than the following three formats as long as you follow the basic syntax rules.

Class Declaration - 1	Class Declaration – 2	Class Declaration – 3
```class Welcome{ }```	```class Welcome { }```	```class Welcome { }```

This book uses the following class declaration format. The opening brace is place in the same line following the class name. The closing brace is placed in a separate line and it is aligned with the first character of the first line of the class declaration.

```
class Welcome {

}
```

The body of a class consists of four parts. All parts are optional.

- Field Declarations
- Initializers - static initializers and instance initializers
- Constructors
- Method Declarations

Java language does not impose any order in which the four parts of the body of a class may appear. We will start with method declarations and confine ourselves only to simple method declarations in this chapter. We will discuss advanced aspects of method declarations and other parts of class body declarations in the chapter on *Classes and Objects*.

Let us discuss how to declare a method for a class. You might guess that the method declaration would begin with a keyword method, as package and class declarations began with the keywords `package` and `class` respectively. However, a method declaration does not begin with a keyword `method`. In fact, `method` is not a keyword in Java language. We begin a class declaration with the keyword `class` indicating that we are going to declare a class. However, in case of a method declaration, the first thing we specify is the type of value that a method will return to its caller. Even if a method does not return anything to its caller, we must mention that fact in the beginning of the method declaration. We use the keyword `void` to indicate that a method does not return anything. The name of the method follows the return type of the method and left and right parentheses follow the method name. Like a class, a method has a body part, which is enclosed in braces. The simplest method declaration in Java looks as:

```
<<MethodReturnType>> <<MethodName>> () {
    // Body of the method goes here
}
```

The following is an example of a valid method declaration.

```
void main() {
    // Empty body of the main method
}
```

The above method declaration indicates three things.

- The method does not return anything as indicated by the keyword `void`.
- The name of the method is `main`.
- The `main` method does not do anything, as its body is empty.

The return value of a method is something, which the method returns to its caller. The caller of the method may also want to pass some values to the method. If a method requires its caller to pass some values to it, this fact must be indicated in method's declaration. The fact that you want to pass some value to a method is specified within the parentheses that follow the method name. You need to specify two things about the values you want to pass to the method.

- The type of the value you want to pass. Suppose you want to pass an integer (say 10) to the method. You need to indicate this by using a keyword `int`, which is used to indicate an integer value like 10.
- The identifier, which will hold the value you pass to the method. Identifier is a user-defined name. It is called parameter name.

If you want the `main` method to accept one integer value from its caller, its declaration will change to the one shown below.

```
void main(int num) {

}
```

Note that `num` is the identifier, which will hold the value passed to this method. Instead of `num`, you may choose to use another identifier, e.g., `num1`, `num2`, `num3`, etc. The above declaration of `main` method is read as:

> *The method main accepts one parameter of type `int` and does not return any value to its caller.*

If you want to pass two integers to the `main` method, its declaration will change to the one shown below.

```
void main(int num1, int num2) {

}
```

It is clear from the above declaration that you need to separate the parameters passed to a method by a comma (,). What will you do if you want to pass 50 integers to this method? You will end up with a method declaration like:

```
void main(int num1, int num2, ..., int num50) {

}
```

We have shown only three parameters declarations. However, when you write a Java program, you will have to type all 50 parameter declarations. Let us look for some alternate ways to passing 50 integers parameters to this method. There is one similarity among all 50 parameters that they are all of the same type – integers. No values will contain fraction like 20.11, 45.09). This similarity shared by all parameters allows us to use a magic creature in Java language, which is called an array. What is required to use array to pass 50 integer parameters to this method? When you write

```
int num
```

it means that `num` is an identifier of type `int` and it can hold one integer value. If you place two magic brackets (`[]`) after `int` as:

```
int[] num
```

it means that `num` is an array of `int` and it can hold as many integer values as you want. There is a limit for the number of integers that `num` can hold. However, that limit is very high and we will discuss that limit when we discuss arrays in details. The values stored in `num` can be accessed by using subscripts - `num[0]`, `num[1]`, `num[2]`, etc. Note that in declaring an array of type `int`, we have not mentioned the fact that we want `num` to represent 50 integers. Our modified declaration for `main` method, which can accept 50 integers, would be as follows:

```
void main(int[] num) {

}
```

How will you declare the `main` method, which will let you pass names of 50 persons? Since `int` can only be used for passing integers, we must look for some other type, which represents a text in Java language because the name of a person will be text, not an integer. There is a type `String` (note the uppercase `S` in `String`) that represents a text in Java language. Therefore, to pass 50 names to method `main` we can change its declaration as follows.

```
void main(String[] name) {

}
```

In the above declaration, we need not necessarily change the parameter name from `num` to `name`. We changed it just to make the meaning of the parameter clear and intuitive. Now let us add some

Java code in the body of the `main` method, which will print a message on the console. To print a message on the console from a Java program, you need to write the following line of code.

```
System.out.println("The message you want to print");
```

This is not the appropriate place to discuss what `System`, `out`, and `println` are all about. For now, just type in `System` (note uppercase **S** in `System`), a dot, `out`, a dot, `println` followed by two parentheses that contain the message you want to print within double quotes. We want to print a message "`Welcome to the Java world`" and our `main` method declaration will be as follows.

```
void main(String[] name) {
    System.out.println("Welcome to the Java world");
}
```

This is a valid method declaration that will print a message on console. Our next step is to compile the source code, which contains the `Welcome` class declaration, and run the `Welcome` class. However, when we run a class, the JVM looks for a method `main` in that class and the declaration of method `main` must be as follows.

```
public static void main(String[] name) {

}
```

Apart from two keywords, `public` and `static`, you should be able to understand the above method declaration, which states - "`main` is a method, which accepts an array of `String` as a parameter and returns nothing."

For now, you can think of `public` and `static` as two keywords, which must be present to declare the `main` method, because the JVM will look for them when we run our program. Note that the JVM also requires that the name of the method must be `main`. This is the reason we chose `main` as the name of the method from the very beginning of our method declaration discussion. It is just a rule imposed by the JVM to run a class that the class must have a method named `main` whose declaration must look as shown above. The final version of the source code for `Welcome` class is shown in Listing 2-1. We will save the code listed in Listing 2-1 in a file named Welcome.java.

Listing 2-1: Source code for Welcome class

```
// Welcome.java
package com.jdojo.chapter2;

class Welcome {
    public static void main(String[] args) {
        System.out.println("Welcome to the Java world.");
    }
}
```

Java compiler imposes restrictions on the file name of the source code. In our example, the name of the file in which the source code for Welcome class is saved need not be Welcome.java. You could use another file name, e.g., MyWelcome.java, JWelcome.java, etc. If you declare a class as public, the source code for that class must be saved in a file that has exactly the same name as the class. You declare a class public by using the public keyword before the class keyword in its declaration. The following snippet of code declares the Welcome class as public. For our example purpose, it does not matter if you declare the Welcome class public or not.

```
// Welcome class is public now
public class Welcome {

}
```

Every class in Java has two names – a *simple name* and a *fully qualified name*. The simple name of a class is the name that appears after the `class` keyword in the class declaration. In our example, the simple name of the class is `Welcome`. The fully qualified name of a class is its package name followed by a dot and its simple name. In our example, the fully qualified name of the class is `com.jdojo.chapter2.Welcome`.

The next question that might arise in your mind is – "What is the fully qualified name of a class, which does not have a package declaration?" The answer is simple. In such a case, the simple name and the fully qualified name of the class are the same. If we remove the package declaration part from the source code for `Welcome` class, the simple and the fully qualified names for our class will be the same and it will be `Welcome`. You might notice that the name of the class we have declared (`Welcome`) and the name of the file we saved the source code in (`Welcome`.java) exactly match (excluding the file extension *.java*). This did not happen by chance. We did select the name of our source code file as `Welcome.java` on purpose. Is it required to name the source code file the same as the name of the class? Yes, but not always. This raises another question. What should be the name of the source code file if we declare two classes in the same source code? Suppose we declare two classes `Welcome` and `Bye` in our source code. What name should we give to the source file: `Welcome.java, Bye.java` or something else? In some cases, Java forces you to keep name of class and its source code file the same. In our example, we do not need to stick to any source code file-naming rules imposed by Java. It is correct even if we name our source file as Bye.java or Test.java. However, we will continue with this example assuming that you have named the source code as `Welcome.java`.

Compiling the Source Code

Compiling Java code is the process of generating a file (or a set of files) in a special binary format called `bytecode` from the Java source code. This is accomplished using a program (usually called a compiler) *javac*, which comes with JDK from Oracle Corporation. The process of compiling Java source code has been shown in Figure 2-3. We supply the source code (in our case Welcome.java) as input to the Java compiler and it generates a new file with extension `.class`. The file with extension `.class` is called a class file. A class file is in a special format, which is called *bytecode*. Bytecode is a machine language for Java virtual machine (JVM). We will discuss more about the JVM and bytecode later in this chapter.

Figure 2-3: The process of compiling a Java source code into bytecode

Now, we will walk through the steps that are needed to compile Java source code on Windows system. For other platforms, e.g., UNIX and Mac OS X, you will need to use the file path syntax, which would be specific to those platforms.

It is assumed that you have installed JDK from Sun Microsystems on your machine. It is further assumed that you have stored your source code in a directory, which looks as follows.

```
C:\javaprograms\com\jdojo\chapter2\Welcome.java
```

To compile the `Welcome.java`, you need to open MS-DOS prompt and change the directory so that `chapter2` should be your current working directory. MS-DOS prompt should look as follows.

```
C:\javaprograms\com\jdojo\chapter2>
```

To compile `Welcome.java` execute the following command:

```
C:\javaprograms\com\jdojo\chapter2>javac Welcome.java
```

If you do not get any error message on your MS-DOS screen, it means your source code was compiled successfully and it generated a new file named `Welcome.class` in `chapter2` directory. However, if you get any error message after executing above command, there could be any of the following three reasons for getting errors.

- You have not saved the Welcome.java file in C:\javaprograms\com\jdojo\chapter2 directory.
- You may not have installed JDK on your machine.
- If you have already installed JDK, you have not added JAVA_HOME\bin directory to the PATH environment variable, where JAVA_HOME refers to the directory where you installed the JDK on your machine. If you installed JDK v1.3, by default, it is installed in C:\jdk1.3 directory and in that case, you need to add C:\jdk1.3\bin to the PATH environment variable on your machine.

If the above discussion about setting PATH environment variable did not help you compiling your source code, you can use the following command: This command assumes that you have installed JDK in `C:\jdk1.3` directory. If you have installed JDK in some other directory, you need to replace `C:\jdk1.3` in the following command with the directory path where you have installed your JDK.

```
C:\javaprograms\com\jdojo\chapter2>C:\jdk1.3\bin\javac Welcome.java
```

If you do not want to change the current working directory to `C:\javaprograms\com\jdojo\`chapter2, you can compile your source code using the full path for `Welcome.java` file as follows.

```
C:\>C:\jdk1.3\bin\javac C:\javaprograms\com\jdojo\chapter2\Welcome.java
```

It does not matter how you specify the path to the `javac` command and the Welcome.java file. If MS-DOS prompt can find them, your Java source code will be compiled successfully. Below is another way to compile your Welcome.java file. This time we assume that the javac.exe command file is in PATH and the current directory is C:\javaprograms.

```
C:\javaprograms>javac com\jdojo\chapter2\Welcome.java
```

At this point, it is assumed that you have compiled the source code in `Welcome.java` successfully, which has generated a new file named Welcome.class in `C:\javaprograms\com\jdojo\chapter2` directory.

We are ready to run our first Java program. Before we run this program, let us discuss one important point about the file name that is generated by the compiler. The name of the bytecode file (the `.class` file), which the Java compiler generated, is `Welcome.class`. Why did the compiler choose to name the class file as `Welcome.class`? We have used the word "Welcome" at three places when we wrote our source code and compiled it.

- First, we declared a class named "Welcome"
- Second, we saved the source code in a file named "Welcome" (Of course, we added .java extension to the file)
- And third, we passed Welcome.java file name to the Java compiler (`javac`) as an input to generate the bytecode

Which one of our three steps prompted Java compiler to name the generated bytecode file as `Welcome.class`? As a first guess, it appears to be the third step, which is, passing `Welcome.java` as an input file name to the Java compiler. However, our guess is wrong. It is the first step, which is declaring a class named `Welcome` in the source code `Welcome.java`, which prompted Java compiler to name the output bytecode file as `Welcome.class`. You can declare as many classes as you want in one Java source code. Suppose you declare two classes, Welcome and Bye, in `Welcome.java` file. What file name will the Java compiler choose to name the output class file? Java compiler scans the whole source code file (here, `Welcome.java`), which is supplied to it. It creates one class file for each class declared in the source code. If our `Welcome.java` file had three classes `Welcome`, `Thanks` and `Bye`, Java compiler would generate three class files - `Welcome.class`, `Thanks.class`, and `Bye.class`.

Running a Java Program

A Java program is run by a JVM. A JVM is invoked using a program called `java`, which is java.exe file installed on your machine with JDK. The `java` program accepts the fully qualified name of the Java class you want to run. Recall that a class has two names – a simple name and a fully qualified name. We use only fully qualified name while running the class. We never use the simple name of the class to run it. We are going to run `Welcome` class whose fully qualified name is `com.jdojo.chapter2.Welcome`. Use the following command at MS-DOS command prompt to run the class.

```
C:\>java com.jdojo.chapter2.Welcome
```

What happens when we use the above command? First, the JVM tries to locate the bytecode (here, `Welcome.class` file) for `com.jdojo.chapter2.Welcome` class on your machine. JVM replaces every dot (.) in the fully qualified name of the class with the file-separator character on the host system. A backslash (\) is the file-separator character on Windows and a forward slash (/) on UNIX-like operating systems. This step converts the `com.jdojo.chapter2.Welcome` class name that was passed to the JVM to `com\jdojo\chapter2\Welcome`. Note that on UNIX-like operating system, the same class name will be converted to `com/jdojo/chapter2/Welcome`.

The JVM also allows you to use a forward slash (/) in place of a dot (.) in the fully qualified name of the class to run. For example, you can also use the following command to run `Welcome` class.

```
C:\>java com/jdojo/chapter2/Welcome
```

TIP

When you use forward slashes (/) in place of dots in the fully qualified name of the class to run it, you must use only forward slashes (/) irrespective of the operating system. For example, you cannot use backslashes (\) on Windows and forward slashes (/) on UNIX.

The second step the JVM takes is to append the word ".class" to the class name thus converted. The resulting string out of the fully qualified name of the class becomes

```
com\jdojo\chapter2\Welcome.class
```

Now, the JVM looks for a `Welcome.class` file, which must be under `chapter2` directory, which in turn must be under `jdojo` directory, which in turn must be under `com` directory. The JVM is not only looking for a `Welcome.class` file, rather it is looking for a `Welcome.class` file in a directory structure like `com\jdojo\chapter2`. You may realize that there could be many directory paths on your machine, which can lead the JVM to `com\jdojo\chapter2\Welcome.class` file. Suppose you have three `Welcome.class` files on your machine as follows.

```
C:\jp1\com\jdojo\chapter2\Welcome.class
C:\jp2\com\jdojo\chapter2\Welcome.class
C:\javaprograms\com\jdojo\chapter2\Welcome.class
```

How does the JVM know which one of the three `Welcome.class` files it has to run? Here comes the concept of a mysterious (sometimes confusing and frustrating) creature, which is called the CLASSPATH environment variable. The JVM uses CLASSPATH environment variable to locate a class file on your machine. There are many questions about CLASSPATH, which might have arisen in your mind. Who defines the CLASSPATH? Where is it stored? How is it used? We will discuss all these questions and their answers one by one.

The users of the machine set CLASSPATH. It can be set permanently, temporarily or at runtime. If it is set permanently, The JVM will use it whenever it needs to locate a class file. It can be set temporarily for the duration of a MS-DOS prompt session. It can be set at runtime by using `-cp` or `-classpath` option at command line.

The value of CLASSPATH environment variable is a semi-colon separated list of directories, ZIP files, and JAR files on Windows operating system. A typical setting for CLASSPATH looks as follows.

```
SET CLASSPATH=C:\;C:\jbook;C:\javaprograms
```

Like the PATH environment variable setting, the above line, which sets CLASSPATH, appears in autoexec.bat file on Windows95/98.

On Windows NT/2000/XP/Vista, you can set the CLASSPATH environment variable using Settings >> Control Panel >> System >> Advanced Tab >> Environment Variables button. It displays "Environment Variables" dialog box as shown in Figure 2-4. Under "System Variables" group box, you should select CLASSPATH under the "Variable" column. If you do not find CLASSPATH variable, it means that it has not been set previously. If the CLASSPATH variable has not been set previously, click "New" button. Otherwise, click "Add" button. Clicking "New" or "Add" button will display a dialog box as shown in Figure 2-5 in which you would add/modify the CLASSPATH variable value.

Chapter 2. Writing Java Programs

Figure 2-4: Environment Variables dialog box on for setting the CLASSPATH environment variable on Windows NT/2000/XP/Vista

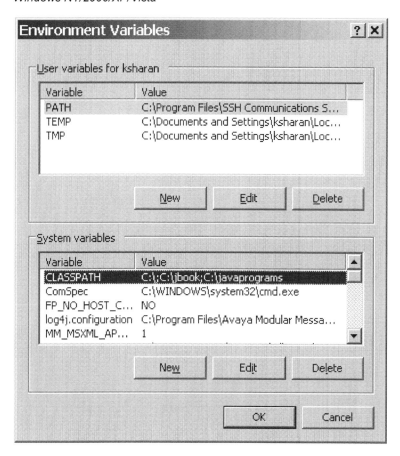

Figure 2-5: New/Edit System variable dialog box for setting the CLASSPATH environment variable on Windows NT/2000/XP/Vista

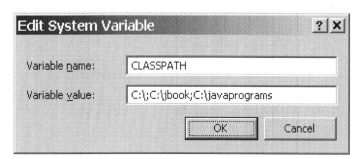

TIP

The value for CLASSPATH is a list of directories, JAR files, and ZIP files that are separated by a path-separator. The path-separator in a CLASSPATH entry is operating system dependent. On Windows operating system, the separator is a semi-colon (;). On UNIX-like operating system, e.g., Linux, Solaris, and Mac OS X, the separator is a colon (:). On Windows operating system, a CLASSPATH entry looks like "C:\;C:\jbook;C:\jp;c:\myapps.jar". On UNIX-like operating systems, a CLASSPATH entry looks like "/usr/jp/classes:/usr/myapps.jar".

You can also set CLASSPATH by typing the following command on MS-DOS prompt. However, such CLASSPATH setting is valid only for the current MS-DOS session.

```
C:\>SET CLASSPATH=C:\;C:\jbook;C:\javaprograms
```

After you have set the CLASSPATH, you can use the following command to run the `Welcome` class.

```
C:\>java com.jdojo.chapter2.Welcome
```

As we have already discussed, the JVM will convert the class name to a class file, which will be `com\jdojo\chapter2\Welcome.class`. The JVM reads the CLASSPATH value, which it will use to locate the class file. It reads the first entry from the CLASSPATH value, which is `C:\`, and concatenates the converted class name string to it (the JVM may use an extra backslash if needed to create a valid file name). In our case, the resulting string will be

```
C:\com\jdojo\chapter2\Welcome.class
```

The JVM checks if a file with above path exists on the machine. In our case, this check will fail, because we do not have a `C:\com\jdojo\chapter2\Welcome.class` file on our machine. If the JVM fails to locate a class file using an entry in the CLASSPATH, it repeats the class file search using next entry from the CLASSPATH. This process continues until the JVM locates the class file or it has exhausted all entries in the CLASSPATH. In our case, The JVM will find the class file in the third attempt. It will find the `C:\javaprograms\com\jdojo\chapter2\Welcome.class` file. This is not the end of the story. Since we passed the name `com.jdojo.chapter2.Welcome` to JVM as the name of the class to run, The JVM makes sure that `C:\javaprograms\com\jdojo\chapter2\Welcome.class`" was generated by a Java compiler for a class `Welcome`, whose package declaration was `com.jdojo.chapter2`. In our case, this criterion is fulfilled.

What does the JVM do next? Now, it looks for a method declaration in the `Welcome` class whose declaration must look as follows:

```
public static void main (String[] args)
```

If the JVM does not find a method's declaration similar to the shown above, it prints an error message on the standard error and aborts the execution. This is the reason why we declared a method `main` similar to this in our `Welcome` class. In our case, the JVM will find the correct declaration for the method `main`. It executes the body of the `main` method, which prints the following message on the console:

```
Welcome to the Java world.
```

There is another way of setting the CLASSPATH. You can set the CLASSPATH when you run your Java class. You can use `-cp` or `-classpath` option with the `java` program to set the CLASSPATH while running a Java class. For example, you can also run the `Welcome` class as follows. Note that the command is entered on the command-line in one line and not two.

```
C:\>java -cp C:\;C:\jbook;C:\javaprograms com.jdojo.chapter2.Welcome
```

or,

```
C:\>java -classpath C:\;C:\jbook;C:\javaprograms
com.jdojo.chapter2.Welcome
```

Can we run our `Welcome` class example without worrying about CLASSPATH setting? The answer is yes and no. Sometimes, CLASSPATH setting becomes a bit tricky. If you don't set any value for CLASSPATH as in

```
SET CLASSPATH=
```

The JVM uses the current working directory as the one and the only entry for the CLASSPATH. The current working directory is specified by a dot (.). Therefore, the following two CLASSPATH settings are the same for the JVM.

```
SET CLASSPATH=
```

and,

```
SET CLASSPATH=.
```

If you set some value for the CLASSPATH, you have to add a dot (.) separately to indicate that you also want to include the current working directory in the CLASSPATH. Note that you lose the default CLASSPATH setting (which is current working directory) when you set it explicitly. Suppose we have set the CLASSPATH using a command:

```
SET CLASSPATH=
```

Now, we want to run our `Welcome` class. The only thing you have to do is that you must change your working directory to `C:\javaprograms`, so that `C:\javaprograms` becomes your current working directory and using this directory, as the default entry for CLASSPATH, the JVM will find your class correctly. MS-DOS prompt should look as follows.

```
C:\javaprograms>java com.jdojo.chapter2.Welcome
```

Finally, there are some words of caution for you when you work with the CLASSPATH and the package of a class to locate the class file. The JVM uses CLASSPATH and fully qualified name of the class to locate the actual class file on the machine. However, you cannot take some part from one and add it to another even though the resulting path is the same. Always keep in mind that it is not enough for the JVM just to locate the class file. It also verifies the bytecode in class file to make sure that it contains the class definition with proper package name. Following commands are not the same. Note the use of the space in each of the command to separate the CLASSPATH value and the fully qualified name of the class.

```
C:\>java -cp C:\ javaprograms.com.jdojo.chapter2.Welcome
C:\>java -cp C:\javaprograms com.jdojo.chapter2.Welcome
C:\>java -cp C:\javaprograms\com jdojo.chapter2.Welcome
C:\>java -cp C:\javaprograms\com\jdojo chapter2.Welcome
C:\>java -cp C:\javaprograms\com\jdojo\chapter2 Welcome
```

Be careful about the CLASSPATH setting and the fully qualified name of the class you want to run. In the above examples, all the commands will look for the same class file `C:\javaprograms\com\jdojo\chapter2\Welcome.class`. However, only the second command will run successfully, because the package declaration for `Welcome` class is `com.jdojo.chapter2`.

The path of the class file is determined by the JVM on Windows as shown in Figure 2-6. On other host systems, e.g., UNIX and Mac, the JVM uses the file-separator character specific to those systems.

Figure 2-6: The process of finding a class file, when a class is run

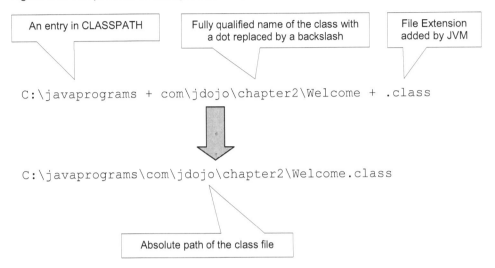

```
C:\javaprograms + com\jdojo\chapter2\Welcome + .class
```

```
C:\javaprograms\com\jdojo\chapter2\Welcome.class
```

Absolute path of the class file

Behind the Scenes

This section is aimed at answering some general questions related to compiling and running a Java program. For example, why do we compile Java source code to bytecode format before running it? What is Java platform? What is a JVM and how does it work? The detailed discussion of these topics is beyond the scope of this book. Please refer to the JVM specification for detailed discussion on any topic related to the JVM functionality. The JVM specification is available online at *http://www.oracle.com.*

Before we begin the discussion about the bytecode format and the JVM, let us look at a simple daily life example. Suppose, there is a Frenchman who can understand and speak only French and he has to communicate with three other persons - an American, a German and a Russian, and of the three knows only one language English, German and Russian respectively. How will the Frenchman communicate to the other three? There are many ways to solve this problem.

- The Frenchman may learn all three languages
- The Frenchman may hire a translator who knows all four languages
- The Frenchman may hire three translators who know French-English, French-German, and French-Russian.

There are numerous other possible solutions to this problem. Let us consider the similar problem in the context of running a Java program. The Java source code is compiled into bytecode. The same bytecode needs to be run without any modification to all operating systems. Designers of Java language chose the third option, which is to have a translator for each operating system. The translator's job is to translate the bytecode into machine code, which is native to the operating system and run the translated code. The translator is called a JVM. You need to have a JVM for each operating system. Figure 2-7 is a pictorial view of how the JVM acts as a translator between bytecode (class file) and different operating systems.

Figure 2-7: A JVM as a translator between bytecode and operating systems

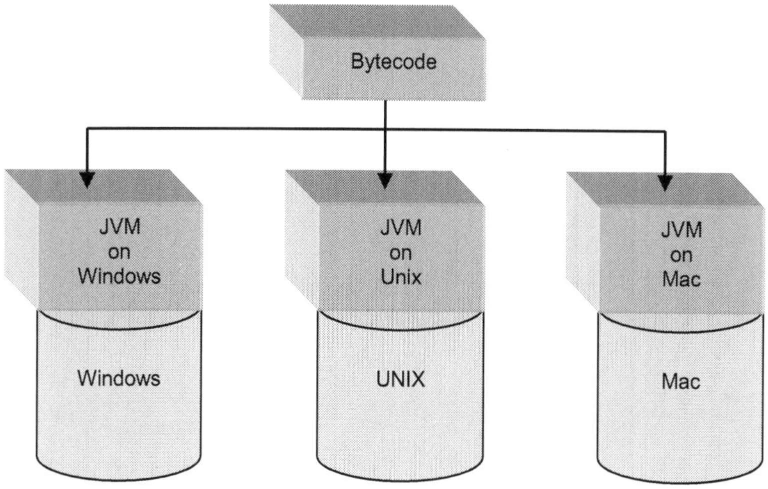

A Java program compiled into bytecode format has two advantages.

- You do not need to recompile your source code if you want to run the same compiled bytecode on other machine with a different operating system. It is also called platform independence in Java. Sometimes, it is also known as "write once run anywhere" for Java code.
- If you are running a Java program over a network, the program runs faster because of compact size of bytecode format, which results in less loading time over the network.

In order to run a Java program over the network, the size of the Java code must be compact enough to be transported over the network faster. The class file, which is generated by a Java compiler in bytecode format, is very compact. This is one of the advantages of compiling the Java source code in bytecode format. The second important advantage of using bytecode format is that it is architecture-neutral. By bytecode format being architecture-neutral, we mean if we compile a Java source code on a specific host system, say, Windows, the class file generated by the Java compiler does not have any mention or effects that it was generated on Windows host system. If you compile the same Java source code on two different host systems, e.g., Windows and UNIX, both class files generated will be the same. The class file in bytecode format cannot be directly executed on a host system because it does not have any host system specific direct instructions. In other words, we can say that bytecode is not a machine language for any specific host system. Now the question is, who understands the bytecode and who translates it into underlying host system specific language? The JVM understands bytecode formats and translates it into underlying host system specific machine language. The bytecode is the machine language for the JVM. If you compile a Java source code to generate a class file on Windows, you can run the same class file on UNIX if you have a Java platform (JVM and Java API collectively is known as Java platform) available on the machine running on UNIX. You do not need to recompile your source code to generate a new class file for UNIX, because the JVM running on UNIX can understand the bytecode you generated on Windows. This is how the concept of *"Write Once, Run Everywhere"* is implemented for a Java program.

The Java platform, also called Java runtime system, consists of two things:

- The Java virtual machine (JVM), and
- The Java Application Programming Interface (Java API)

The term JVM is used in three contexts.

- The JVM specification: It is the specification or standard of an abstract machine for which a Java compiler can generate the bytecode.
- The concrete realization of the JVM specification: If you want to run your Java program, you need to have a real JVM, which is developed using the abstract specification for a JVM. To run our Java program in previous section we used a command.

```
C:\javaprograms>java com.jdojo.chapter2.Welcome
```

    Here, `java` is a program developed fully based on the abstract specification for the JVM. Therefore, it is a concrete realization of the abstract JVM specification. This `java` program (or JVM) has been implemented completely in software. However, a JVM can be implemented in software or hardware, or a combination of both.
- A running JVM instance: You have a running JVM instance when you invoke the java program.

This book uses the term JVM for all three cases. Its actual meaning can be understood by the context of its use.

One of the jobs a JVM does is to execute the bytecode and generate machine specific instruction set for the host system. A JVM has a *classloader* and an *execution engine*. The classloader reads the content of a class file when required and loads it into memory. The job of the execution engine is to execute the bytecode.

A JVM is also called a Java Interpreter. Often, the term "Java Interpreter" is misleading, particularly to those programmers who have just started learning Java language. By the term "Java Interpreter", they conclude that the *execution engine* of a JVM interprets the bytecodes one at a time and so Java must be very slow. The name "Java Interpreter" for a JVM has nothing to do with the technique the *execution engine* uses to execute the bytecode. The actual technique, which the execution engine may opt to execute the bytecode, depends on the specific implementation of the JVM. Some *execution engines* types are – interpreter, Just-in-time compiler, and adaptive optimizer. In its simplest kind, which is interpreter, the execution engine interprets the bytecodes one at a time, and therefore it is slower. In its second kind, which is Just-in-time compiler, it compiles the whole code for a method in underlying host machine language for the first time that method is called. Then, it reuses the compiled code the next time the same method is called. This kind of *execution engine* is faster as compared with the first kind, but requires more memory to cache the compiled code. In adaptive optimizer technique, it does not compile and cache the whole bytecode; rather it does so only for the most heavily used part of the bytecode.

What is an API (**A**pplication **P**rogramming **I**nterface)? An API is a specific method made available by an operating system or by an application to the programmers for its direct use. In previous sections, we created `Welcome` class in `com.jdojo.chapter2` package, which declared a method `main`, which accepts an array of `String` as an argument and returns nothing (indicated by keyword `void`). If we expose all these pieces of information about the created package, class and method, and make it available to other programmers for use, our method `main` in the `Welcome` class is a typical, though trivial, example of an API. Generally, when we use the term API we mean a set of methods, which are available to the programmer for use. Now, it is easy to understand what Java API means. The Java API is the set of all classes and other components, which are available to programmers for use while writing Java source code. In our `Welcome` class example, we have already used one Java API. We used it inside the body of `main` method to print the message on the console. The code, which used Java API, is:

```
System.out.println("Welcome to the Java world");
```

We did not declare any method named `println` in our code. This method was made available to the JVM at run time through Java API, which is the part of Java Platform. Broadly speaking, Java API can be classified in two categories – Core API and Extension API. Every JDK must support all Core Java API. Examples of Core Java APIs are Java runtimes (e.g. Applets, AWT, I/O, etc.), JFC, JDBC, etc. Java Extension APIs are JavaMail, JNDI (Java naming and Directory Interface), JavaHelp, etc. The process of compiling and running a Java program is depicted in Figure 2-8.

Figure 2-8: All components involved in compiling and running a Java program

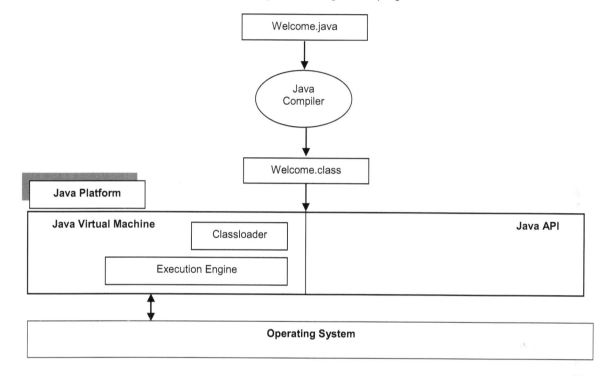

Chapter 3. Data Types

What is a Data Type?

A data type (or simply a type) is defined in terms of three components.

- A set of values (or data objects)
- A set of operations that can be applied to all values in the set
- A data representation, which determines how the values are stored

A programming language provides some pre-defined data types, which are known as built-in data types. A programming language may also let programmers define their own data types, which are known as user-defined data types.

A data type that consists of an atomic and indivisible value, and that is defined without the help of any other data types, is known as a primitive data type. User-defined data types are defined in terms of primitive data types and other user-defined data types. Typically, a programming language does not let the programmers extend or redefine primitive data types.

Java provides many built-in primitive data types such as `int`, `float`, `boolean`, `char`, etc. For example, the three components that define the `int` primitive data type in Java are as follows.

- An `int` data type consists of a set of all integers between -2147483648 and 2147483647
- Operations such as addition, subtraction, multiplication, division, comparison and many more are defined for `int` data type.
- A value of `int` data type is represented in 32-bit memory in 2's compliment form.

All three components of `int` data type are pre-defined by the Java language. You cannot extend or re-define the definition of `int` data type as a programmer. You can give a name to a value of the `int` data type as:

```
int n1;
```

The above statement states that `n1` is a name (technically called an identifier) that can be associated with one value from the set of values that defines values for `int` data type. For example, we can associate integer `1969` to the name `n1` using an assignment statement as:

```
n1 = 1969;
```

What is an Identifier?

An *identifier* in Java is a sequence of characters of unlimited length. The sequence of characters includes all Java letters and Java digits, the first of which must be a Java letter. Java uses Unicode character set. Therefore, a Java letter is a letter from any language, which is represented by

Unicode character set. For example, A-Z, a-z, _ (underscore) and $ are considered as Java letters from ASCII character set range of Unicode. Java digits include 0-9 ASCII digits and any Unicode character that denotes a digit in a language. Spaces are not allowed in an identifier. In fact, identifier is a technical term for a *name*. Therefore, identifier is simply the name given to a class, method, variable, etc. in a Java program. The name, `Welcome`, of our Java class is an example of an identifier. The names of variables `num1`, `num2`, and `str1` used in our examples are also examples of identifiers. All characters used in an identifier are important, as is their case. The names `welcome`, `Welcome`, and `WELCOME` are three different identifiers. There are three important things to remember about identifiers in Java:

- There is no limit on the number of characters used in an identifier. There can be as small an identifier as one character long, e.g., `i`, `j`, `k`, or as big as you want.
- Characters used in an identifier are drawn from Unicode character set and not only from ASCII character set.
- Identifiers are case sensitive. For example, `num` and `Num` are two different identifiers.

Examples of valid identifiers are:

```
num1       // Can use a-z and 0-9 and start with a letter
kn         // Only letters
_abc       // Can start with an underscore
_          // Can have only one letter, which is an underscore
sum_of_two_numbers // Can have letters and underscores
Outer$Inner        // Can have a-z, A-Z and $
$var               // Can also start with $
```

Examples of invalid identifiers are:

```
2num       // Cannot start with a number
my name    // Cannot have a space
num1+num2 // Cannot have + sign
num1-num2 // Cannot have hyphen or minus sign
```

Java defines a list of words called *keywords*. Keywords are words that have predefined meanings in Java and they can only be used in the contexts defined by the Java language. Keywords in Java cannot be used as identifiers. The complete list of Java keywords is listed in Table 3-1.

Table 3-1: List of keywords and reserved words in Java

abstract	continue	for	new	switch
assert	default	goto	package	synchronized
boolean	do	if	private	this
break	double	implements	protected	throw
byte	else	import	public	throws
case	enum	instanceof	return	transient
catch	extends	int	short	try
char	final	interface	static	void
class	finally	long	strictfp	volatile
const	float	Native	super	while

The two keywords, `const` and `goto`, are not currently used in Java. They are reserved keywords and they cannot be used as identifiers.

In addition to all the keywords, three words - `true`, `false`, and `null`, cannot be used as identifiers; `true` and `false` are `boolean` literals (or `boolean` constants) and `null` is a reference literal.

Data Types in Java

Before we start discussing all data types available in Java, let us take a simple example of adding two numbers. Suppose your friend asks you to add two numbers. The procedure to add two numbers will go as follows. Your friend tells you the first number. You listen to him and your brain records the number at a particular location in your memory. Of course, you do not know where the number was exactly stored in your brain's memory. Your friend tells you the second number; you listen to him; and again, your brain records it at a particular location in your memory. Now you friend asks you to add the two numbers. Your brain comes into action. It recalls (or reads) the two numbers, adds them, and you tell your friend the sum of the two numbers.

Now, if your friend wants you to tell him the difference of the same two numbers, he does not need to tell you those two numbers again. It is so, because those two numbers were stored in your memory, and your brain can recall and use them again. However, whether your brain can perform addition of those two numbers or not depends on many factors, e.g., how big those two numbers are; whether your brain can memorize (or store) those big numbers or not; whether your brain is trained to do additions or not, etc. The process of adding two numbers also depends on the type of those two numbers. Your brain will use different processes to add them depending on whether two numbers were whole numbers (e.g. 10 and 20), real numbers (e.g. 12.4 and 19.1), or the mix of whole and real numbers (e.g. 10 and 69.9). The entire process takes place in your brain without you noticing it (Maybe because you are so accustomed to doing these additions). However, when you want to do any kind of manipulation on numbers or any other types of values in a Java program, you need to specify the details about the values you want to manipulate and the procedure for manipulating those values.

Let us discuss the same example of adding two numbers in a Java program. The first thing you need to tell Java is the type of the two numbers you want to add. Let us assume that you want to add two integers that are 50 and 70. When you added two numbers by yourself, your brain gave each number a name (maybe as first number and second number). You did not notice the naming of those numbers by your brain. However, in a Java program, you have to explicitly give names (also known an *identifier)* to both numbers you want to add. Let us name our two numbers as `num1` and `num2` respectively. The following two lines in a Java program indicate the fact that there are two integers - `num1` and `num2`.

```
int num1;
int num2;
```

The `int` keyword is used to indicate that the name that follows it will represent an integer value, e.g., 10, 15, 70, 1000, etc. When the above two lines of code are executed, Java allocates two memory locations and associates the name `num1` with the first memory location and the name `num2` with the second memory location. The memory states after executions of these two lines of code have been depicted in Figure 3-1 labeled as *Memory State – I*.

Figure 3-1: Memory States in the process of adding two numbers

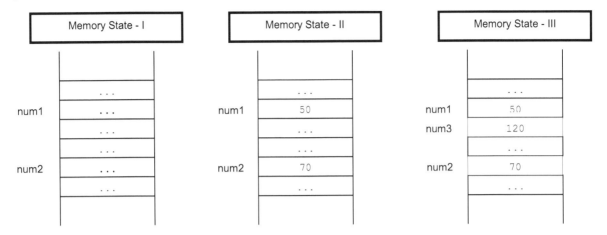

These memory locations are called variables. The names, num1 and num2, are associated with these two memory locations. Strictly speaking, num1 and num2 are two names associated with two memory locations. However, roughly speaking, we say that num1 and num2 are two variables, or num1 and num2 are two variables of int data type, or num1 and num2 are two int variables. Since we have declared num1 and num2 variables of int data type, we cannot store a real number, e.g., 10.51, at memory locations associated with any of these two variables. The following piece of code stores 50 in num1 and 70 in num2.

```
num1 = 50;
num2 = 70;
```

The memory states after execution of these two lines of code have been depicted in Figure 3-1: labeled as *Memory State-II*. Now memory location associated with num1 contains 50 and memory location associated with num2 contains 70. Now, we want to add the two numbers. Before we add the two numbers, we must allocate another memory location, which will hold the result of addition of the two numbers. We name this memory location as num3 and the following piece of code perform these tasks.

```
int num3;            // Allocate memory location num3
num3 = num1 + num2;  // Compute sum and store the result in num3
```

The memory states after execution of these two lines of code have been depicted in Figure 3-1 labeled as *Memory State-III*.

A variable has three properties.

- A memory location to hold the value
- The type of the data stored at the memory location. The data type of the variable also determines the range of the values that the memory location can hold. Therefore, the amount of memory allocated for a variable depends on its data type. For example, 32 bits of memory is allocated for a variable of int data type. In this example, each variable, num1, num2 and num3, uses 32 bits of memory.
- A name (also called *identifier*) to refer to the memory location. For example, num1, num2, and num3 are used in a Java program to refer to the three memory locations

---

Java supports two kinds of data types: They are:

- Primitive data type
- Reference data type

A variable of primitive data type holds a value whereas a variable of reference data type holds the reference to an object in memory. We will discuss one of the reference data types available in Java, `String`, in this section. `String` is a class defined in the Java library and we can use it to manipulate texts (sequence of characters). We declare a reference variable `str` of `String` type as:

```
String str;
```

A reference variable stores the reference of an object in memory. Before we assign the reference of an object to a reference variable, we need to create an object. We create an object using a `new` operator. We can create an object of String class with a text `"Hi"` as follows:

```
str = new String("Hi"); // Creates a String object and assign
                        // the reference to str
```

What happens when the above pieces of code are executed? First, memory is allocated and the name of the variable `str` is associated with that memory location as shown in Figure 3-2. This process is the same as declaring a primitive data type variable. The second piece of code creates a `String` object in memory with a text "Hi" and associates (or stores) the reference (or memory address) of that String object with variable `str`. This fact has been shown by using an arrow pointing from variable `str` to the object in memory in Figure 3-2.

Figure 3-2: Memory states using reference variables assignments

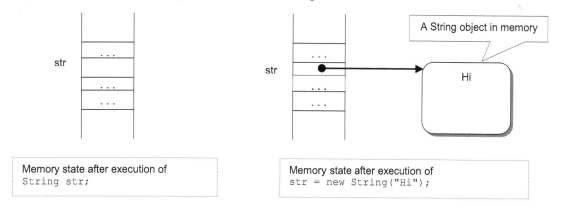

We can also assign the reference stored in one reference variable to another reference variable. In such cases, both reference variables refer to the same object in memory. This can be achieved as:

```
String str1;   // Declare String reference variable str1
String str2;   // Declare String reference variable str2

str1 = new String("Hello"); // Assign a String object "Hello" to str1
str2 = str1; // Assign the reference stored in str1 to str2
```

There is a reference constant (also known as reference literal) `null,` which can be assigned to any reference variable. If `null` is assigned to a reference variable, it means that the reference variable is not referring to an object in memory. The `null` reference literal can be assigned to `str2` as:

```
str2 = null;
```

The memory states after executions of all of the above statements are depicted in Figure 3-3.

Figure 3-3: Memory states using null in the reference variables assignments

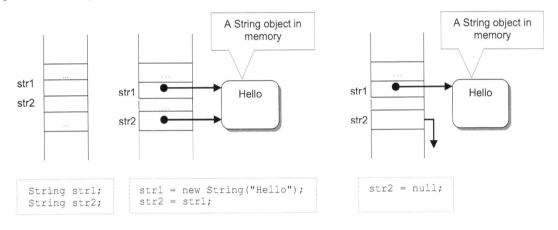

Figure 3-4: List of primitive data types in Java

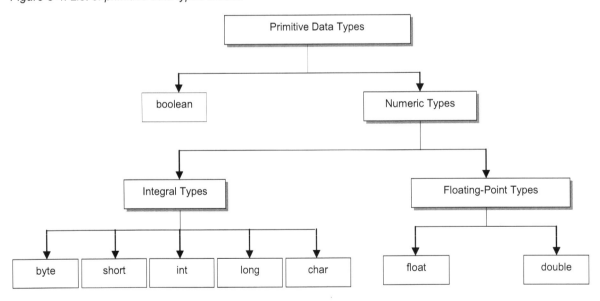

A `String` object is created using the `new` operator. However, strings are used so often in Java programs; there is a shortcut to create a string object. All string literals, sequence of characters enclosed in double quotes, are treated as `String` objects. Therefore, instead of using the `new` operator to create a `String` object, you can use string literals as shown below.

```
String str1 = "Hello";  // Assigns the reference of a String
                        // object with text "Hello" to str1
```

```
String str1 = new String ("Hello"); // Assigns the reference of a
                                     // String object with text "Hello"
                                     // to str1
```

There is a subtle difference in the above two statements, which assign a `String` object to `str1` with the same text "`Hello`".

Java has eight kinds of primitive data types. They are `byte`, `short`, `int`, `long`, `char`, `float`, `double`, and `boolean` as shown in Figure 3-4.

Integral Data Types

The int Data Type

The `int` data type is a 32-bit signed Java primitive data type. A variable of `int` data type takes 32 bits of memory. It has a range of -2,147,483,648 to 2,147,483,647 (-2^{31} to 2^{31} - 1). All whole numbers in this range are known as integer literals (or integer constants) of `int` type. For example, 10, -200, 0, 30, 19, etc. are integer literals of `int` type. An integer literal can be assigned to an `int` variable, say `num1`, as:

```
// An integer literal 21 in decimal format is assigned to num1
num1 = 21;
```

Integer literals can also be expressed in octal, hexadecimal and binary number formats. When an integer literal starts with a 0 (zero) and has at least two digits, it is considered to be in octal number format. If the above line of code is written as:

```
num1 = 021;    // 021 is in octal number format, not in decimal
```

it assigns a decimal value of 17 (021 in octal) to `num1`. The following two lines of code have the same effect of assigning a value of 17 to the variable `num1`.

```
num1 = 17;  // No leading zero, decimal number format
num1 = 021; // Leading zero, octal number format. 021 in octal is same
            // as 17 in decimal
```

Be careful while using `int` literals with a leading zero, because Java will treat these literals as in octal number format. Note that an `int` literal must have at least two digits, and must start with a zero to be treated as in the octal number format. The number 0 is treated as zero in decimal number format, and 00 is treated as zero in octal number format.

```
num1 = 0;  // Assigns zero to num1, 0 is in decimal number format
num1 = 00; // Assigns zero to num1, 00 is in octal number format
```

Note that both 0 and 00 represent the same value zero. Both statements, `num1 = 0` and `num1 = 00`, have the same effect of assigning value zero to the variable `num1`.

All `int` literals in the hexadecimal number format start with 0x or 0X, that is, zero immediately followed by an uppercase or lowercase X, and must contain at least one hexadecimal digit. Note that hexadecimal number format uses 16 digits, 0-9 and A-F (or a-f). The case of the letters A-F used as hexadecimal digits does not matter. The following are the examples of `int` literals in hexadecimal format.

```
0x123      0xdecafe      0x1A2B        0X0123
```

An `int` literal can also be represented using the binary number format. Java 7 added the support for the binary number format in `int` literals. All `int` literals in the binary number format start with 0b or 0B, that is, zero immediately followed by an uppercase or lowercase B. The following are examples of `int` literals in the binary number format.

```
0b10101      0b00011      0b10        0b00000010
```

The following assignments assign the same decimal number 51966 to an `int` variable `num1` in four different formats.

```
num1 = 51966;        // Decimal format
num1 = 0145376;      // Octal format, starts with a 0 (zero)
num1 = 0xCAFE;       // Hexadecimal format, starts with 0x
num1 = 0b1100101011111110; // Binary format starts with 0b
```

Java has a class named **Integer** (Note the upper case `I` in `Integer`), which defines two constants to represent maximum and minimum values for `int` data type. `Integer.MAX_VALUE` and `Integer.MIN_VALUE` constants represent the maximum and the minimum values for `int` data type. For example,

```
int max = Integer.MAX_VALUE; // Assigns maximum int value to max
int min = Integer.MIN_VALUE; // Assigns minimum int value to min
```

The long Data Type

The `long` data type is a 64-bit signed Java primitive data type. It is used when the result of calculations on whole numbers may exceed the range of `int` data type. Its range is -9223372036854775808 to 9223372036854775807 (-2^{63} to 2^{63} - 1). All whole numbers in the range of `long` are called integer literals of `long` type. 51 is an integer literal, but of what type, `int` or `long`? An integer literal of type `long` always ends with L (or lowercase l). This book uses L to mark the end of integer literal of `long` type, because l (lowercase L) is often confused with 1 (digit one) in print. Following are the examples of integer literal of `long` type.

```
0L        401L      -3556L        89898L          -105L
```

Note that 25L is an integer literal of `long` type, whereas 25 is an integer literal of `int` type. Integer literals of `long` type can also be expressed in octal number format or hexadecimal number format. For example,

```
long num1;
num1 = 25L;    // Decimal format
num1 = 031L;   // Octal format
num1 = 0X19L;  // Hexadecimal format
```

When a `long` literal is assigned to a variable of type `long`, Java compiler checks the value being assigned and makes sure that it is in the range of the `long` data type, otherwise it generates a compile time error. For example

```
long num1 = 9223372036854775808L; // One more than maximum positive
                                  // value for long. This will generate
                                  // a compiler error
```

Since `int` data type has a lower range than `long` data type, the value stored in an `int` variable can always be assigned to a `long` variable.

```
int num1 = 10;
long num2 = 20;    // OK to assign int literal 20 to a long variable num2
num2 = num1;       // OK to assign an int to long
```

The assignment from `int` to `long` is valid, because all values that can be stored in an `int` variable can also be stored in a `long` variable. However, the reverse is not true. You cannot simply assign the value stored in a `long` variable to an `int` variable. There is a possibility of value overflow in these cases. For example,

```
int num1 = 10;
long num2 = 2147483655L;
```

Now if you assign the value of `num2` to `num1` as:

```
num1 = num2;
```

the value stored in `num2` cannot be stored in `num1`, because the data type of `num1` is `int` and the value of `num2` falls outside the range the `int` data type can handle. To ignore such errors inadvertently, Java does not allow you to write code as follows:

```
// Compiler error. long to int assignment is not allowed in Java
num1 = num2;
```

Even if the value stored in a `long` variable is well within the range of the `int` data type, the assignment from `long` to `int` is not allowed as shown in the following example.

```
int num1 = 5;
long num2 = 25L;
num1 = num2;   // Compiler error. Even if num2's value is 25 which
               // is within range of int.
```

If you want to assign the value of a `long` variable to an `int` variable, you have to explicitly mention this fact in your code, so that Java makes sure you are aware that there may be data overflow. You do this using "cast" in Java as:

```
num1 = (int)num2;  // Now it is ok because of the cast "(int)"
```

By writing `(int)num2`, you are instructing Java to treat the value stored in `num2` as an `int`. At runtime, Java will use only the 32 least significant bits of `num2`, and assign the value stored in those 32 bits to `num1`. If `num2` has a value, which is outside the range of the `int` data type, you would not get the same value in `num1`.

Java has a class `Long` (Note the upper case L in `Long`), which defines two constants to represent maximum and minimum values of `long` data type. `Long.MAX_VALUE` and `Long.MIN_VALUE` represent the maximum and minimum values for `long` data type. For example,

```
long max = Long.MAX_VALUE;
long min = Long.MIN_VALUE;
```

The byte Data Type

The `byte` data type is an 8-bit signed Java primitive integer data type. Its range is -128 to 127 (-2^7 to 2^7 - 1). This is the smallest integer data type available in Java. Generally, `byte` variables are used when a program uses a large number of variables whose values fall in the range of `byte` data type (-128 to 127) or when dealing with binary data in a file and over the network. Unlike `int` and `long` literals, there are no `byte` literals. However, you can assign any `int` literal that falls in the range of `byte` (-128 to 127) to a `byte` variable. For example,

```
byte b1 = 125;
byte b2 = -11;
```

If you assign an `int` literal to a `byte` variable and the value is outside the range of the `byte` data type (outside -128 to 127), Java generates a compiler error. The following piece of code will produce a compiler error.

```
byte b3 = 150; // Error. 150 is an int literal greater than 127
```

Note that you can only assign an `int` literal between -128 and 127 to a `byte` variable. However, this does not imply that you can also assign the value stored in an `int` variable, which is in the range of -128 to 127, to a `byte` variable. The following piece of code will generate a compiler error, because it assigns the value of an `int` variable, `num1`, to a `byte` variable, `b1`.

```
int num1 = 15;
byte b1 = 15; // OK. Assignment of int literal (-128 to 127) to byte.
b1 = num1;    // Compiler error, even though num1 has a value of 15
              // which is in the range -128 and 127.
```

Java does not allow you to assign the value of a variable of a higher range data type to the variable of a lower range data type, because there is a possible loss of precision in making such an assignment. To make such an assignment from `int` to `byte`, you must use cast, as we did in the case of `long` to `int` assignment. The assignment of `num1` to `b1` can be rewritten as:

```
b1 = (byte)num1;    // Ok
```

After the above cast from `int` to `byte`, Java compiler would not complain about the `int` to `byte` assignment. If `num1` holds a value that cannot be correctly represented in 8-bit `byte` variable `b1`, the higher order bits (9th to 32nd) of `num1` are ignored and the value represented in the lower 8 bits is assigned `b1`. In such a case of `int` to `byte` assignment, the value assigned to the destination `byte` variable may not be the same as the value of the source `int` variable if the value of the source variable falls outside the range of `byte` data type. However, irrespective of the value in the source `int` variable, the destination `byte` variable will always have a value between -128 and 127. Since `long` is also a bigger data type than `byte`, you need to use explicit cast if you want to assign the value of `long` variable to a `byte` variable. For example,

```
byte b4 = 10;
long num3 = 19L;

b4 = (byte)num3;    // OK because of cast
b4 = 19L;           // Error. Cannot assign long literal to byte
b4 = (byte)19L;     // OK because of cast
```

It is true that both 19 and 19L represent the same number, nineteen, in Java. However, to the Java compiler, they are different. 19 is an int literal, i.e., its data type is int, whereas 19L is a long literal, i.e., its data type is long. Java allows you to assign only int literal between -128 and 127 to a byte variable. Generally, we use cast from int to byte or long to byte only when we already know that an int variable or a long variable has a value, which is in the range of the byte data type.

Java has a class Byte (Note the upper case B in Byte), which defines two constants to represent maximum and minimum values of the byte data type. Byte.MAX_VALUE and Byte.MIN_VALUE represent the maximum and minimum values for byte data type. For example,

```
byte max = Byte.MAX_VALUE;
byte min = Byte.MIN_VALUE;
```

The short Data Type

The short data type is a 16-bit signed Java primitive integer data type. Its range is -32768 to 32767 (or -2^{15} to $2^{15} - 1$). Generally, short variables are used when a program uses a large number of variables whose values fall in the range of short data type (-32768 to 32767), or when dealing with data in a file, which can be easily handled using short data type. Unlike int and long literals, there is no short literal. However, you can assign any int literal that falls in the range of short (-32768 to 32767) to a short variable. For example,

```
short s1 = 12905;   // ok
short s2 = -11890;  // ok
```

The value of a byte variable can always be assigned to a short variable because the range of the byte data type falls within the range of the short data type. All other rules for assignment of a value from int or long variable to a short variable are same as that for the byte variable. Following snippet of code illustrates the assignment of byte, int and long values to short variables.

```
short s1 = 15;   // ok
byte b1 = 10;    // ok
s1 = b1;         // ok

int num1 = 10;        // ok
s1 = num1;            // Compiler error
s1 = (short)num1;     // ok because of cast from int to short
s1 = 35000;           // Compiler error. int literal outside short range

long num2 = 555L;     // ok
s1 = num2;            // Compiler error
s1 = (short)num2;     // ok because of the cast from long to short
s1 = 555L;            // Compiler error
s = (short)555L;      // ok because of the cast from long to short
```

Java has a class `Short` (Note the upper case `S` in `Short`), which defines two constants to represent maximum and minimum values of `short` data type. `Short.MAX_VALUE` and `Short.MIN_VALUE` represent the maximum and minimum values for `short` data type. For example,

```
short max = Short.MAX_VALUE;
short min = Short.MIN_VALUE;
```

The char Data Type

The `char` data type is a 16-bit unsigned Java primitive data type. It is used to represent a Unicode character in a Java program. Please refer to the *Character Encodings* section later in this chapter for more details on the Unicode character set. Note that `char` is an unsigned data type. Therefore, a `char` variable cannot have a negative value. The range of the `char` data type is the same as the range of the Unicode set, i.e., 0 to 65,535. Java has character literals that can be expressed in the following different ways. Note that a character literal represents a value of the `char` data type. Java 7 supports Unicode 6.0.

char literal format #1

A character literal can be expressed as a character enclosed in single quotes, e.g., `'A'`, `'f'`, and `'9'`. Note that a character must be enclosed in single quotes to become a character literal in this form. If you enclose a character in double quotes, e.g., "B", it becomes a `String` literal, not a character literal. Therefore, 'B' is a character literal, whereas "B" is a `String` literal. There is another big difference between a character literal and a `String` literal. A character literal of this form must consist of exactly one character, whereas a `String` literal may consist of zero, one or more characters. For example, "A", "ABC" and "" are `String` literals. A `String` literal can never be assigned to a `char` variable, even if the `String` literal consists of exactly one character. In fact, the assignment of a `String` literal to a `char` variable is not allowed, because of the rule that a value of a reference data type can never be assigned to a variable of a primitive data type. All `String` literals represent objects of `String` class in Java and hence, they are of reference data type, whereas character literals represent a value of `char` Java primitive data type. Therefore, `String` (a reference data type) to `char` (a primitive data type) assignment is not allowed. The use of character literals of this type has been illustrated as follows.

```
char c1 = 'A';
char c2 = 'L';
char c3 = '5';
char c4 = '/';
```

char literal format #2

A character literal can also be expressed as a *character escape sequence*. A character escape sequence consists of a backslash (\) immediately followed by a character, and it is enclosed in single quotes. There are eight predefined character escape sequences in Java, which can be used in a Java program. They are listed in Table 3-2.

According to the list of character literals, a single quote character in Java is represented by `'\''` and not as `'''`. It is important to note that a backslash character is represented as `'\\'`, not as `'\'`; a forward slash is represented as `'/'`, not as `'\/'`. A character literal expressed in the form of a *character escape sequence* consists of two characters - a backslash and a character following the backslash. However, it is considered as only one character. There are only eight character escape sequences in Java. You cannot define your own character escape sequences. Examples of character escape sequences are:

```
char c1 = '\n'; // Assigns linefeed to c1
char c2 = '\"'; // Assigns double quote to c2
char c3 = '\a'; // Compiler error. Invalid character escape sequence
```

Table 3-2: List of character escape sequences

Character Escape Sequence	Description
'\n'	A linefeed
'\r'	A carriage return
'\f'	A form feed
'\b'	A backspace
'\t'	A tab
'\\'	A backslash
'\"'	A double quote
'\''	A single quote

char literal format #3

A character literal can also be expressed as a *Unicode escape sequence*. A Unicode escape sequence is expressed in the form '\uxxxx', where \u (a backslash immediately followed by a lowercase u) denotes the start of the Unicode escape sequence, and xxxx represents exactly four hexadecimal digits. In fact, xxxx, the four hexadecimal digits, represents the Unicode integer code for the character you want to express in Unicode escape sequence. The Unicode character A has the code value of 65 (in decimal). The value 65 in decimal can be represented in hexadecimal as 41. So, the character A can be expressed in Unicode escape sequence as '\u0041'. Note that, in Unicode escape sequence, exactly four hexadecimal digits must follow \u and that is why, we added 00 before 41 to make it 0041. The following snippet of code assigns the same character A to char variables c1 and c2.

```
char c1 = 'A';
char c2 = '\u0041';  // Same as c2 = 'A'
```

char literal format #4

All Unicode characters can be expressed as Unicode escape sequence in the range of '\u0000' and '\uFFFF'. A Unicode escape sequence may use uppercase or lowercase letters A-F to represent a hexadecimal number. Therefore, '\u002a' and '\u002A' represent the same Unicode character, which is an asterisk (*). 42 is the Unicode decimal code value of asterisk. The hexadecimal equivalent of decimal 42 is 002A. Note that \u, the start of Unicode escape sequence, cannot be replaced by \U. The following snippet of code has some more examples of using Unicode escape sequence as character literals.

```
char c3 = '\u002A';  // Assign asterisk character to c3
char c4 = '\u002a';  // Assign asterisk character to c4
char c4 = '\U002a';  // Compiler error. Must start with \u, not \U
char c5 = '\u20B9';  // Assign Indian currency symbol to c5
```

A character literal can also be expressed as an *octal escape sequence*. An octal escape sequence is expressed in the form `'\nnn'` where n is an octal digit (0-7). You might guess that the range of characters represented in octal escape sequence form would be `'\000'` to `'\777'`. If you guessed so, there is a disappointing news for you. The maximum octal value you can use in octal escape sequence to represent a character in Java is `'\377'`, not `'\777'`. The octal number 377 is the same as the decimal number 255. Therefore, using octal escape sequence, you can represent characters whose Unicode code range from 0 to 255 decimal integers. We have already seen that any Unicode character (code range 0 to 65535) can be represented as a Unicode escape sequence (`'\uxxxx'`) in Java. Why does Java have another octal escape sequence, which is a subset of Unicode escape sequence? Java has the octal escape sequence to represent a character for compatibility with other languages, which use 8-bit unsigned chars to represent a character. Unlike a Unicode escape sequence, where you are always required to use four hexadecimal digits, in octal escape sequence you can use one, two, or three octal digits. Therefore, an octal escape sequence may take on any form `'\n'`, `'\nn'`, or `'\nnn'`, where n is one of the octal digits 0, 1, 2, 3, 4, 5, 6, and 7. Some examples of octal escape sequence are as follows.

```
char c1 = '\52';
char c2 = '\141';
char c3 = '\400';   // Compiler error. Octal 400 is Out of range
char c4 = '\42';
char c5 = '\10';    // Same as '\n'
```

You can also assign an int literal to a char variable if int literal falls in the range 0-65535. When you assign an int literal to a char variable, the char variable represents the character whose Unicode code is equal to the value represented by that int literal. The Unicode code for the character a (lowercase A) is 97 (in decimal). The decimal value 97 is represented as 141 in octal and 61 in hexadecimal. You can represent the Unicode character a in three different forms in Java: `'a'`, `'\141'` and `'\u0061'`. You can also use int literal 97 to represent the Unicode character a as:

```
char c1 = 97; // Same as c1 = 'a', or c1 = '\141', or c1 = '\u0061'
```

A byte variable takes 8 bits and a char variable takes 16 bits. Even if the byte data type has smaller range than the char data type, you cannot assign a value stored in a byte variable to a char variable. The reason is that byte is a signed data type, whereas char is an unsigned data type. If the byte variable has a negative value, say -15, it cannot be stored in a char variable without losing the precision. In such a case, you need to use an explicit cast. The following snippet of code illustrates all possible cases of assignment from char to other integral data type and vice-versa.

```
byte b1 = 10;
short s1 = 15;
int num1 = 150;
long num2 = 20L;
char c1 = 'A';

// byte and char
b1 = c1;        // Error
b1 = (byte)c1;// Ok
c1 = b1;        // Error
c1 = (char)b1;// Ok
```

```
// short and char
s1 = c1;            // Error
s1 = (short)c1;     // Ok
c1 = s1;            // Error
c1 = (char)s1;      // Ok

// int and char
num1 = c1;          // Ok
num1 = (int)c1;     // Ok. But, cast is not required. Use num1 = c1
c1 = num1;          // Error
c1 = (char)num1;    // Ok
c1 = 255;           // Ok. 255 is in the range of 0-65535
c1 = 70000;         // Error. 70000 is out of range 0-65535
c1 = (char)70000;   // Ok. But, will lose the original value

// long and char
num2 = c1;          // Ok
num2 = (long)c1;    // Ok. But, cast is not required. Use num2 = c1
c1 = num2;          // Error
c1 = (char)num2;    // Ok
c1 = 255L;          // Error. 255L is long literal
c1 = (char)255L;    // Ok. But use c1 = 255 instead
```

The boolean Data Type

The `boolean` data type has only two valid values - `true` and `false`. These two values are called `boolean` literals. You can use `boolean` literals as:

```
boolean done;  // Declare a boolean variable named done
done = true;   // Assign true to status
```

One important point to note is that a `boolean` variable cannot be cast to any other data type and vice-versa. Java does not specify the size of the `boolean` data type. Its size is left up to the JVM implementation. Typically, a value of a `boolean` data type is stored in a byte.

Floating-Point Data Types

A number, which contains a fractional part, is known as a real number, e.g., 3.25, 0.49, and -9.19. A computer stores every number, real or integral, in binary format, which consists of only 0s and 1s. Therefore, it is necessary to convert a real number, e.g., 3.45, to its binary representation using 0 and 1 before it can be stored in computer memory. Similarly, it must be converted back to a real number after its binary representation is read from computer memory. When the real number 3.45 is converted to its binary representation, the computer must also store the position of the decimal point within the number, that is, there are two digits (4 and 5) after the decimal point and one digit (3) before the decimal point. There can be two strategies to store a real number in the computer memory.

- Store only the binary representation of the number and assume that there are always a fixed number of digits before and after the point. A point is called a *decimal point* in decimal representation of a number and a *binary point* in binary representation. The type of representation in which the position of the point is always fixed in a number is known as *fixed-point* number format.

- Store the binary representation of the real number and store the position of the point in the real number. Since the number of digits before and after the point can vary in this kind of representation of the real number, we say that the point can `float` and hence this kind of representation is called floating-point format.

The floating-point representations are slower and less accurate than the fixed-point representations. However, the floating-point representations can handle a larger range of numbers with the same computer memory as compared to the fixed-point representations.

Java supports the floating-point number format. It is important to note that not all real numbers have exact binary representations, and therefore those real numbers are represented as its floating-point approximations. Java uses IEEE 754 Floating-Point standard to store real numbers. IEEE is acronym for *Institute of Electrical and Electronic Engineer* Java has two floating-point primitive data types: `float` and `double`.

The float Data Type

The `float` data type uses 32 bits to store a floating-point number in IEEE 754 standard format. It can represent a number as small as 1.4×10^{-45} in magnitude and as big as 3.4×10^{38} (approx.). This range includes only magnitude and it could be either positive or negative. Here, 1.4×10^{-45} is the smallest positive number greater than zero that can be stored in a `float` variable. A floating-point number represented in 32 bits according to IEEE 754 standard is also known as *single-precision floating-point number*. All real numbers, which end with f or F are called `float` *literals*. A `float` literal always ends with f or F. A `float` literal can be expressed in the following two formats:

- A decimal number with an optional decimal point. For example,

   8F, 8.F, 8.0F, 3.51F, 0.29F, -455.78F, 0F, 0.0F, -0.0F, 16.78f

- A real number 3.25 is also written using exponential forms such as 32.5×10^{-1} or 0.325×10^{1}. In Java, such real numbers can be represented as `float` literals using scientific notation. In scientific notation, the number 32.5×10^{-1} is written as $32.5E-1$ and, to make it a `float` literal, it is written as $32.5E-1F$ or $32.5E-1f$. All of the following `float` literals denote the same real number 32.5.

   3.25F   32.5E-1F   0.325E+1F   0.325E1F   0.0325E2F   0.0325e2F
   3.25E0F

The `float` data type defines two zeros: +0.0F (or 0.0F) and -0.0F. However, for the comparison purposes, both +0.0F and -0.0F are considered equal. And, `float` data type also defines two infinities: *Positive Infinity* and *Negative Infinity*. For example, the result of the division of 2.5F by 0.0F is a `float` positive infinity whereas the result of division of 2.5F by -0.0F is a `float` negative infinity. The result of some of the operations on `float` is not defined; for example dividing 0.0F by 0.0F is indeterminate and such a result is represented by a special value of the `float` data type, called NaN (Not-a--Number). Java has a `Float` class (Note the upper case F in `Float`), which defines three constants that represent positive infinity, negative infinity and NaN of the `float` data type. Table 3-3 lists these three `float` constants and their meanings. The table also lists two constants, which represent the maximum and minimum (greater than zero) `float` values that can be stored in a `float` variable.

Table 3-3: float constants defined in the Float class

float Constants	Meaning
`Float.POSITIVE_INFINITY`	Positive infinity of type float
`Float.NEGATIVE_INFINITY`	Negative infinity of type float
`Float.NaN`	Not a Number of type float
`Float.MAX_VALUE`	Largest positive value that can be represented in a float variable. This is equal to 3.4×10^{38} (approx.)
`Float.MIN_VALUE`	The smallest positive value greater than zero that can be represented in a float variable. This is equal to 1.4×10^{-45}.

The value of all integral types `int`, `long`, `byte`, `short` and `char` can be assigned to a variable of `float` data type without using explicit cast. For example,

```
int num1 = 15000;
float salary = num1;             // Ok. int variable to float
salary = 12455;                  // Ok. int literal to float
float bigNum = Float.MAX_VALUE;  // Assigns maximum float value
bigNum = 1226L;                  // Ok, long literal to float
float justAChar = 'A';           // Ok. Assigns 65.0F to justAChar
float fInf = Float.POSITIVE_INFINITY; // Ok. Assigns positive
                                 // infinity to fInf variable
float fNan = Float.NaN; // Ok. Assigns Not-a-Number to fNan variable

float fTooBig = 3.5E38F; // Compiler error. Cannot assign a float
                         // literal to a float variable greater than
                         // the maximum value of float(3.4E38F approx)

float fTooSmall = 1.4E-46F;  // Compiler error. Cannot assign a float
                             // literal to a float variable less than
                             // the minimum value (greater than zero)
                             // of float 1.4E-45F
```

A float value must be cast before it is assigned to a variable of any integral data type int, long, byte, short or char. For example,

```
int num1 = 10;
float salary = 10.0F;
num1 =  salary;         // Error. Cannot assign float to int
num1 = (int)salary;     // Ok
```

As it has already been mentioned, most floating-point numbers are approximations of their corresponding real numbers. The assignment of `int` and `long` to `float` may result in loss of precision. Let us consider the following piece of code.

```
int num1 = 1029989998; // Store an integer in num1
float num2 = num1;     // Assign the value stored in num1 to num2
int num3 = (int)num2;  // Assign the value stored in num2 to num3
```

We expect that the value stored in num1 and num3 should be same. But, they are not the same, because the value stored in num1 cannot be stored exactly in a floating-point format in the float variable num2. Be careful while assigning integers to float and vice-versa in your Java programs.

The double Data Type

The double data type uses 64 bits to store a floating-point number in IEEE 754 standard format. It can represent a number as small as 4.9×10^{-324} in magnitude and as big as 1.7×10^{308} (approx.). This range includes only magnitude and it could be either positive or negative. Here, 4.9×10^{-324} is the smallest positive number greater than zero that can be stored in a double variable. A floating-point number represented in 64 bits according to IEEE 754 standard is also known as a *double-precision floating-point number*. All real numbers are called double *literals*. A double literal may optionally end with d or D, e.g., 19.27d. However, the suffix d or D is optional as a part of double literal. That is, both 19.27 and 19.27d represent the same double literal. This book uses double literals without suffix d or D. A double literal can be expressed in the following two formats:

- A decimal number with an optional decimal point. For example,

  8D, 8., 8.0, 8.D, 78.9867, 45.0

  Note that 8 is an int literal, whereas 8D, 8.0 , and 8.0 are double literals.

- A real number 3.25 is also written as 32.5×10^{-1} or 0.325×10^{1} in exponential forms. In Java, such real numbers can be represented as double literals using scientific notation. In scientific notation, the number 32.5×10^{-1} is written as 32.5E-1, which is a double literal. However, you may optionally add a suffix D or d, e.g., 32.5E-1D. All of the following double literals denote the same real number 3.25.

3.25	32.5E-1	0.325E+1	0.325E1	0.0325E2	0.0325e2
3.25E0	3.25D	32.5E-1D	0.325E+1d	0.325E1d	0.0325E2d

The data type double defines two zeros: +0.0 (or 0.0) and -0.0. For the comparison purposes, both +0.0 and -0.0 are considered equal. The double data type defines two infinities: *Positive Infinity* and *Negative Infinity*. For example, the result of the division of 2.5 by 0.0 is a positive infinity double whereas the result of division of 2.5 by -0.0 is a negative infinity double. The result of some of the operations on double is not defined; for example, dividing 0.0 by 0.0 is indeterminate, and such a result is represented by a special value of double data type, called NaN (Not a Number). Java has a class Double (Note uppercase D in Double), which defines three constants to represent positive infinity, negative infinity and NaN of double data type. Table 3-4 lists these three double constants and their meanings. Table 3-4 also lists two constants, which represent the maximum and minimum (greater than zero) double values that can be represented in a double variable.

Table 3-4: double constants in Double class

double Constants	Meaning
Double.POSITIVE_INFINITY	Positive infinity of type double
Double.NEGATIVE_INFINITY	Negative infinity of type double
Double.NaN	Not a Number of type double

Double.MAX_VALUE	Largest positive value that can be represented in a double variable. This is equal to 1.7×10^{308} (approx.)
Double.MIN_VALUE	The smallest positive value greater than zero that can be represented in a double variable. This is equal to 4.9×10^{-324}.

The value of all integral types (`int`, `long`, `byte`, `short`, `char`) and `float` can be assigned to a variable of `double` data type without using explicit cast. For example,

```
int num1 = 15000;
double salary = num1;            // Ok. int to double assignment
salary = 12455;                  // Ok. int literal to double
double bigNum = Double.MAX_VALUE;// Assigns maximum double value
bigNum = 1226L;                  // Ok, long literal to double
double justAChar = 'A';          // Ok. Assigns 65.0 to justAChar

// Ok. Assigns positive infinity to dInf variable
double dInf = Double.POSITIVE_INFINITY;

// Ok. Assigns Not-a-Number to dNan variable
double dNan = Double.NaN;

/* Compiler error. Cannot assign a double literal to a double variable
   greater than the maximum value of double (1.7E308 approx)
*/
double dTooBig = 1.8E308;

/* Compiler error. Cannot assign a double literal to a double variable
   less than the minimum value (greater than zero) of double 4.9E-324 */
double dTooSmall = 4.9E-325;
```

A `double` value must be cast to integral type before it is assigned to a variable of any integral data type `int`, `long`, `byte`, `short` or `char`. For example,

```
int num1 = 10;
double salary = 10.0;
num1 = salary;         // Compiler Error. Cannot assign double to int
num1 = (int)salary;    // Now Ok.
```

Underscores in Numeric Literals

Beginning from Java 7, you can use any number of underscores between two digits in numeric literals. For example, the `int` literal `1969` can be written as `1_969`, `19_69`, `196_9`, `1___969`, or any other forms using underscores between two digits. The use of underscores is also allowed in octal, hexadecimal, and binary formats of numeric literals. Big numbers are harder to read without any punctuation marks (e.g., a comma as a thousand-separator). Use of underscores in big numbers makes them easier to read. The following examples show the valid uses of underscores in numeric literals.

```
int x1 = 1_969;        // Underscore in deciaml format
int x2 = 1__969;       // Multiple consecutive underscores
```

```
int x3 = 03_661;                // Underscore in octal literal
int x4 = 0b0111_1011_0001;      // Underscore in binary literal
int x5 = 0x7_B_1;               // Underscores in hexadecimal literal
byte b1 = 1_2_7;
double d1  = 1_969.09_19;       // Underscores in double literal
```

Underscores are allowed in numeric literals only between digits. This means that you cannot use underscores in the beginning or end of a numeric literal. You cannot use underscores with prefixes, e.g., `0x` for hexadecimal format and `0b` for binary format, and suffixes such as `L` for long literal and `F` for float literal. The following examples show the invalid uses of underscores in numeric literals.

```
int y1 = _1969;         // Error. Underscore in the beginning
int y2 = 1969_;         // Error. Underscore in the end
int y3 = ox_7B1;        // Error. Underscore after prefix 0x
int y4 = o_x7B1;        // Error. Underscore inside prefix 0x
long z1 = 1969_L;       // Error. Underscore with suffix L
double d1 = 1969_.0919; // Error. Underscore before decimal
double d1 = 1969._0919; // Error. Underscore after decimal
```

TIP

You can write the `int` literal, `1969`, in octal format as `03661`. The zero in the beginning of an `int` literal in the octal format is considered a digit and not a prefix. It is allowed to use underscores after the first zero in the `int` literal in the octal format. You can write `03661` as `0_3661`.

Character Encodings

A character is the basic unit of a writing system, e.g., a letter of English alphabet, and an ideograph of an ideographic writing system such as Chinese and Japanese ideographs. Characters are identified in their written form by their shape, also known as glyph. However, the identification of a character with its shape is not precise and it depends on many factors, for example, a hyphen is identified as a minus sign in a mathematical expression; some Greek and Latin letters have the same shapes, but are considered different characters in two written scripts. Computers understand only numbers, more precisely, only bits "0" and "1". Therefore, it was necessary to convert, with the advent of computers, the characters into codes (or bit combinations) inside the computer's memory, so that the text (sequence of characters) could be stored and reproduced. However, different computers may represent different characters with the same bit combinations, which may lead to misinterpretation of text stored by one computer system and reproduced by another. Therefore, for correct exchange of information between two computer systems, it is necessary that one computer system understand unambiguously the coded form of the characters represented in bit combination produced by another computer system and vice-versa. Before we begin our discussion of some widely used character encodings, it is necessary to understand some commonly used terms.

An *abstract character is* a unit of textual information, for example, Latin capital letter A ('A').

A *character repertoire* is defined as the set of characters to be encoded. A character repertoire can be fixed or open. In the case of a fixed repertoire once the set of characters to be encoded is decided, it is never changed; whereas in open character repertoire a new character may be added.

A *coded character set* is defined as a mapping from a set of non-negative integers (also known as code positions, code points, code values, character number, and code space) to the set of abstract characters. The integer that maps to a character is called the *code point* for that character and the character is called *encoded character*. A coded character set is also called a "character encoding", "coded character repertoire", "character set definition", or "code page". Figure 3-5 depicts two different coded character sets; both of them have the same character repertoires, which are the sets of three characters 'A', 'B' and 'C', and the same code points, which are the set of two non-negative integers 1, 2 and 3.

Figure 3-5: Coded Character Sets

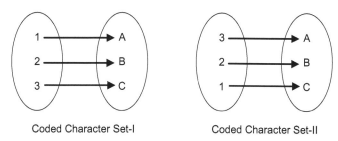

Coded Character Set-I   Coded Character Set-II

Therefore, to define a coded character set you need to specify three things:

- A set of code points
- A set of characters
- The mapping between the set of code points and the set of characters

The number of bits used to represent a character determines how many distinct characters can be represented in a coded character set. Some widely used coded character sets are as follows.

ASCII

ASCII, the American Standard Code for Information Interchange, is a 7-bit coded character set. ASCII has 2^7 or 128 code points and so it represents 128 distinct characters whose numeric value range from 0 (binary 0000000) to 127 (binary 1111111). There are two characters, NUL and DELETE, in ASCII, which are represented by code points "0000000" and "1111111" respectively. There are historical reasons to assign code points of "0000000" and "1111111" to the characters NUL and DELETE in ASCII. It was common to use punched paper tapes to store data for processing by the time ASCII was developed. A "1" bit was used to represent a hole on the paper tape whereas a "0" bit the absence of a hole. Since a row of seven "0" bits would be indistinguishable from blank tape, the coding "0000000" would have to represent a NUL character, i.e., absence of any effect. Since holes, once punched, could not be erased but an erroneous character could always be converted into "111111", this bit pattern was adopted as DELETE character. ASCII uses the first 32 bit combinations (or code points) to represent control characters. This range includes the NUL character, but not the DELETE character. Therefore, it leaves 95 (128 - 32(Control Characters) -1(DELETE) = 95) bit combinations for printing characters. All printing characters are arranged in an order that could be used for sorting purposes. The SPACE character is normally sorted before any other printing character. Therefore, the SPACE character is allocated the first position among the printing characters. The code point for SPACE character in ASCII is 32, i.e., "1100000". The code point range - 48 to 57 represents 0 to 9 digits, 65 to 90 represents 26 uppercase letters A to Z, and 97 to122 represents 26 lowercase letters a to z. Appendix-B has the complete list of ASCII character set. Modern computers use an 8-bit combination, also known as a *byte*, as the smallest unit for storage. Therefore, on modern computers, a 7-bit ASCII character uses 8 bits (or 1 byte) of memory of which the most significant bit is always set to "0", for example, SPACE is stored as "01100000", DELETE is stored as "0111111".

8-bit Character Sets

The ASCII character set worked fine for the English language. Representing the alphabets from other languages, e.g., French and German, led to the development of an 8-bit character set. An 8-bit character set defines 2^8 (or 256) character positions whose numeric values range from 0 to 255. The bit combination for an 8-bit character set ranges from "00000000" to "11111111". The 8-bit character set is divided into two parts. The first part represents characters, which are the same as in ASCII character set. The second part introduces 128 new characters. The first 32 positions in the second part are reserved for control characters. Therefore, there are two control character areas in an 8-bit character set: 0 -32 and 128-159. Since SPACE and DELETE characters are already defined in the first part, an 8-bit character set can accommodate 192 printing characters (95 + 97) including SPACE. ISO Latin-I is one of the examples of an 8-bit character set.

Even an 8-bit character set is not large enough to accommodate most of the alphabets of all languages in the world. This lead to the development of a bigger (may be the biggest) character set, which is known as the Universal Character Set (UCS).

Universal Multiple-Octet Coded Character Set (UCS)

The Universal Multiple-Octet Coded Character Set, simply known as UCS, is intended to provide a single coded character set for the encoding of written forms of all the languages of the world and of a wide range of additional symbols that may be used in conjunction with such languages. It is intended not only to cover languages in current use, but also languages of the past and such additions as may be required in the future. The UCS uses a 4-octet (1 octet is 8 bits) structure to represent a character. However, the most significant bit of the most significant octet is constrained to be "0", which permits its use for private internal purposes in a data processing system. The remaining 31 bits allow us to represent more than two thousand million characters. The four octets are named as:

- The Group-Octet or G,
- The Plane-Octet or P,
- The Row-Octet or R, and
- The Cell-Octet or C

G is the most significant octet and C is the least significant octet. So, the whole code range for UCS is viewed as a 4-dimensioanal structure composed of

- 128 groups
- 256 planes in each group
- 256 rows in each plane
- 256 cells in each row

Two hexadecimal digits (0-9, A-F) specify the values of any octet. The values of G are restricted to the range 00-7F. The plane with G=00 and P=00 is known as *Basic Multilingual Plane* (BMP). The row of BMP with R=00 represents the same set of characters as 8-bit ISO Latin-I. Therefore, the first 128 characters of ASCII, ISO Latin-1 and BMP with R=00 match. Characters 129th to 256th of

ISO Latin-I and that of BMP with R=00 match. This makes UCS compatible with the existing 7-bit ASCII and 8-bit ISO Latin-I. Further, BMP has been divided into 5 zones.

- **A-zone:** It is used for alphabetic and symbolic scripts together with various symbols. The code position available for A-zone ranges 0000-4DFF. The code positions 0000-001F and 0080-009F are reserved for control characters. The code position 007F is reserved for the DELETE character. Thus, it has 19903 code positions available for graphics characters.

- **I-zone:** It is used for Chinese/Japanese/Korean unified ideographs. Its range is 4E00-9FFF, i.e., 20992 code positions are available in this zone.

- **O-zone:** It is used for Korean Hangul syllabic scripts and for other scripts. Its range is A000-D7FF, i.e., 14336 code positions are available in this zone.

- **S-zone:** It is reserved for use with transformation format UTF-16. The transformation format UTF-16 will be described shortly. Its range is D800-DFFF, i.e., 2048 code positions are available in this zone

- **R-zone:** It is known as restricted zone. It can be used only in special circumstances. One of the uses of this zone is for specific user-defined characters. However, in this case an agreement is necessary between the sender and the recipient to communicate successfully. Its range is E000-FFFD, i.e., 8190 code positions are available in this zone.

UCS is closely related to another popular character set, called *Unicode*, which has been prepared by the Unicode Consortium. Unicode uses 2-octet (16 bits) coding structure and hence it can accommodate 2^{16} (= 65536) distinct characters. The Unicode can be considered as the 16-bit coding of the BMP of UCS. These two character sets, Unicode and UCS, were developed and maintained by two different organizations. However, they cooperate to keep Unicode and UCS compatible. If a computer system uses the Unicode character set to store some text, each character in the text has to be allocated 16 bits even if all characters in the text are from ASCII character set. Note that the first 128 characters of Unicode match with that of ASCII and a character in ASCII can be represented only in 8-bits. So, to use 16 bits to represent all characters in Unicode will be wasteful of computer memory. An alternative would be to use 8 bits for all characters from ASCII and 16 bits for characters outside the range of ASCII. However, this method of using different bits to represent different characters from Unicode has to be consistent and uniform, resulting in no ambiguity when data is stored or interchanged between different computer systems. This issue led to the development of *character encoding method.* Currently, there are four character-encoding methods specified in ISO/IEC 10646-I.

- UCS-2
- UCS-4
- UTF-16
- UTF-8

UCS-2

This is a 2-octet BMP form of encoding method, which allows the use of two octets to represent a character from the BMP. This is a fixed-length encoding method. That is, each character from BMP is represented exactly by two octets.

UCS-4

This encoding method is also called 4-octet canonical form of encoding which uses four octets for every character in UCS. This is also a fixed-length encoding method.

UTF-16 (UCS Transformation Format 16)

Once characters outside the BMP are used, UCS-2 encoding method cannot be applied to represent them. In this case, the encoding must switch over to use UCS-4, which will just double the use of resources, e.g., memory, network bandwidth, etc. The transformation format UTF-16 has been designed to avoid such a waste of memory and other resources, which would have resulted using UCS-4 encoding method. The UTF-16 is a variable-length encoding method. In UTF-16 encoding method UCS-2 is used for all characters within BMP and UCS-4 is used for encoding the characters outside BMP.

UTF-8 (UCS Transformation Format 8)

This is a variable-length encoding method, which may use 1 to 6 octets to represent a character from UCS. All ASCII characters are encoded using 1-octet. In UTF-8 format of character encoding, characters are represented using one or more octets as shown in Table 3-5.

Table 3-5: List of legal UTF-8 Sequences

No. of Octets	Bit Patterns Used	UCS Code
1	Octet 1: 0xxxxxxx	00000000-0000007F
2	Octet 1: 110xxxxx Octet 2: 10xxxxxx	00000080-000007FF
3	Octet 1: 1110xxxx Octet 2: 10xxxxxx Octet 3: 10xxxxxx	00000800-0000FFFF
4	Octet 1: 11110xxx Octet 2: 10xxxxxx Octet 3: 10xxxxxx Octet 4: 10xxxxxx	00010000-001FFFFF
5	Octet 1: 111110xx Octet 2: 10xxxxxx Octet 3: 10xxxxxx Octet 4: 10xxxxxx Octet 5: 10xxxxxx	00200000-03FFFFFF
6	Octet 1: 1111110x Octet 2: 10xxxxxx Octet 3: 10xxxxxx Octet 4: 10xxxxxx Octet 5: 10xxxxxx Octet 6: 10xxxxxx	04000000-7FFFFFFF

The "x" in Table 3-5 indicates either a "0" or a "1". Note that in UTF-8 format an octet that starts with a "0" bit indicates that it is representing an ASCII character. An octet starting with "110" bits combinations indicates that it is the first octet of the 2-octet representation of a character and so on. Also note that, in the case an octet is a part of a multi-octet character representation, the octet other than the first one starts with "10" bits pattern. Security checks can be easily implemented for UTF-8 encoded data. UTF-8 octet sequences, which do not conform to the octet-sequences shown in Table 3-5, are considered as illegal.

Java and Character Encodings

Java stores and manipulates all characters and strings as *Unicode characters.* In serialization and byte codes, Java uses the *UTF-8* encoding of the Unicode character set. All implementations of Java virtual machine are required to support the character encoding methods as shown in Table 3-6.

Table 3-6: List of the supported Character Encodings by a JVM

Character Encoding	Description
ASCII	7-bit ASCII, (Also known as ISO646-US, the Basic Latin block of the Unicode character set)
ISO-8859-1	ISO Latin Alphabet No. 1 (also known as ISO-LATIN-1)
UTF-8	Eight-bit Unicode Transformation Format
UTF-16BE	Sixteen-bit Unicode Transformation Format, big-endian byte order. Big-endian is discussed later in this chapter in detail
UTF-16LE	Sixteen-bit Unicode Transformation Format, little-endian byte order. Little-endian is discussed later in this chapter in detail
UTF-16	Sixteen-bit Unicode Transformation Format, byte order specified by a mandatory initial byte-order mark (either order accepted on input, big-endian used on output)

Java supports UTF-8 format with two significant modifications as discussed below.

- Java uses 16 bits to represent a NUL character in a class file whereas standard UTF-8 uses only 8 bits. This compromise has been made to make it easier for other languages to parse a Java class file where a NUL character is not allowed within a string. However, in some cases Java uses standard UTF-8 format to represent NUL character. Those cases will be explained at appropriate places in this book.
- Java recognizes only 1-octet, 2-octet and 3-octet UTF-8 formats whereas standard UTF-8 format may use 1-octet, 2-octet, 3-octet, 4-octet, 5-octet and 6-octet sequences. This is because Java supports Unicode character set and all characters from Unicode can be represented in 1-, 2- or 3-octet formats of UTF-8.

When you compile the Java source code, by default, Java compiler assumes that the source code file has been written using the platform's default encoding (also known as *local codepage or native encoding*). The platform's default character encoding is Latin-I on Windows and Solaris and MacRoman on Mac. Note that Windows does not use true Latin-I character encoding. It uses a variation of Latin-I that includes fewer control characters and more printing characters .You can specify a file-encoding name (or *codepage* name) to control how the compiler interprets characters beyond the ASCII character set. At the time of compiling your Java source code, you can pass the character-encoding name used in your source code file to Java compiler. The following command tells Java compiler (`javac`) that the Java source code `Test.java` has been written using a traditional Chinese encoding named `Big5`. Now, Java compiler will convert all characters encoded in `Big5` to Unicode.

```
javac -encoding Big5 Test.java
```

Java Development Kit (JDK) includes `native2ascii` tool, which can be used to convert files, which contain other character encoding into files containing Latin-1 and/or Unicode-encoded characters. The general syntax of using native2ascii tool is:

```
native2ascii option inputfile outputfile
```

For example, the following command converts all characters in source.java file into Unicode-encoded character and places the output in destination.java file assuming that the source.java files has been written using the platform's default encoding.

```
native2ascii source.java destination.java
```

The following command converts all characters in source.java file into Unicode-encoded character and places the output in destination.java file. It is assumed that that the source.java files has been written using Chinese Big5 encoding.

```
native2ascii -encoding Big5 source.java destination.java
```

The following command performs the reverse operation, that is, converts a file source.java with Latin-1 and/or Unicode-encoded characters to a file destination.java with native-encoded characters

```
native2ascii -reverse source.java destination.java
```

The `native2ascii` tool uses standard output for output if the *outputfile* name is omitted. It uses standard input for input if the *inputfile* name is omitted too.

Java Compiler and Unicode Escape Sequence

Recall that any Unicode character in a Java program can be expressed in the form of a Unicode escape sequence. For example, the character `'A'` can be replaced by `'\u0041'`. First, Java compiler converts every occurrence of a Unicode escape sequence to a Unicode character. A Unicode escape sequence starts with \u and is followed by four hexadecimal digits e.g. \uxxxx, where x is a hexadecimal digit. However, `\\u0041` is not a Unicode escape sequence. To make `uxxxx` a valid part of a Unicode escape sequence, it must be preceded by odd number of backslashes, because two contiguous backslashes (\\) represent one backslash character in Java. Therefore, `"\\u0041"` represents a six characters string composed of characters `'\'`, `'u'`, `'0'`, `'0'`, `'4'` and `'1'`. However, `\\\u0041` represents two-character string (`"\A"`). Sometimes, inappropriate use of Unicode escape sequence in Java source code may result in a compiler error. Let us consider the following declaration of a `char` variable.

```
char c = '\u000A';
```

The programmer intends to initialize the variable c with a linefeed character whose Unicode escape sequence is \u000A. When the above piece of code is compiled, the Java compiler will convert \u000A into an actual Unicode character and the above piece of code will be spread across two lines as follows.

```
char c = '
    ';   // After actual linefeed is inserted
```

Since a character literal cannot continue in two lines, the above piece of code generates compiler error. The correct way to initialize the variable c would be to use character escape sequence \n as:

```
char c = '\n'; // Correct
```

In character and string literals, the linefeed and carriage return should always be written as \n and \r respectively, not as \u000A and \u000D. Even a line of comment may generate a compiler error, if you do not use the linefeed and carriage return characters correctly. Suppose you commented the above wrong declaration of char variable as:

```
// char c = '\u000A';
```

Even if the above line is a comment line, it will generate compiler error, because it would be converted to two lines before compilation, as shown below.

```
// char c = '
';
```

The second line, which contains, ';, causes the compiler error. The multi-line comment syntax would not generate a compiler error in such a case as

```
/* char c = '\u000A'; */
```

would be converted to

```
/* char c = '
'; */
```

which is a valid multi-line comment.

Binary Representation of Integers

Computers use the binary number system to work with data. All data in binary system is stored using 1's and 0's. Character 1 or 0 is called a bit (short for **b**inary dig**it**) and it is the smallest unit of information a computer can work with. A group of 8 bits is called a byte or octet. Half a byte i.e. a group of four bits is called a nibble. A computer uses data bus, a pathway, to send data from one part of the computer system to another. How much information can be moved from one part to another in a computer system at one time depends on the bit-width of the data bus. The bit-width of data bus on a particular computer is also known as *word-size* for that computer and information contained in one word-size is simply referred to as a *word*. Therefore, a word may refer to 16-bit or 32-bit or another bit-width depending on a particular computer's architecture. The long and double data types in Java take 64-bits. On a computer with word-size of 32 bits, these two data types are not treated atomically. For example, to write a value in a variable of `long` data type two write actions are performed, one for each 32-bit half.

A decimal number can be converted to binary using the following steps.

- Divide the decimal number successively by 2
- After each division, record the remainder. This will be 1 or 0.
- Continue step-1 through step-2 until the result of the division is 0 (zero)
- Binary number is formed writing digits in remainder column from bottom to top.

For example, the binary representation of decimal number 13 can be computed as shown in Table 3-7.

Table 3-7: Decimal to Binary conversion

Number	Divided by 2	Result	Remainder
13	13/2	6	1
6	6/2	3	0
3	3/2	1	1
1	1/2	0	1

The binary representation of decimal number 13 is 1101. A `byte` variable in Java occupies one byte, i.e., 8 bits. The value 13 in a `byte` variable is stored as 00001101. Note that four zeros are added in front of the binary representation of 13 (1101), because a `byte` variable always occupies 8 bits irrespective of the value that it contains. The rightmost bit in a byte or a word is known as *least significant bit (LSB)* and the leftmost bit as *most significant bit (MSB)*. The MSB and LSB have been for the binary representation of 13 has been shown in Figure 3-6

Figure 3-6: MSB and LSB in a binary number

Each bit in a binary number is assigned a weight, which is a power of 2. A binary number can be converted to its decimal equivalent by multiplying each bit in the binary number by its weight and summing up the results. For example, 1101 in binary can be converted to its decimal equivalent as follows.

$$(1101)_2 = 1 \times 2^0 + 0 \times 2^1 + 1 \times 2^2 + 1 \times 2^3$$
$$= 1 + 0 + 4 + 8$$
$$= (13)_{10}$$

The negative of an integral number is stored as its 2's complement. Let us discuss complement of a number in a given number system. Every number system has a base, also known radix. For example, radix is 10 for decimal number system, 2 for binary number system and 8 for octal number system. We will use symbol R for radix, which will refer to the radix of a number system under discussion. Every number system defines two types of complements:

- Diminished radix complement (also known as (R-1)'s complement)
- Radix complement (also known as R's complement)

Therefore, for decimal number system, we have 9's complement and 10's complement; for octal number system, we have 7's and 8's complements, and for binary number system, we have 1's and 2's complements.

Diminished Radix Complement: Let N be a number in a number system of radix R and n is the total number of digits in the number N. The diminished radix complement or (R-1)'s complement of the number N is defined as $(r^n - 1) - N$. In decimal number system the 9's complement of a number is $(10^n - 1) - N$. Since 10^n consists of 1 followed by n zeros $(10^n - 1)$ consists of n 9s. Therefore, 9's complement of a number can be computed simply by subtracting each digit in the number from 9. For example, 9's complement of 5678 is 4321 and 9's complement of 894542 is 105457. In binary number system the 1's complement of a binary number is given by $(2^n - 1) - N$. Since 2^n in binary number system consists of 1 followed by n zeros $(2^n - 1)$ consists of n 1s. For example, 1's complement of 10110 (Here, n is 5) can be computed as $(2^5 - 1) - 10110$, which is 11111 - 10110 (2^5-1 is 31 which 11111 in binary). Therefore, 1's complement of a binary number can be computed simply by subtracting each digit in the number from 1. A binary number consists of 0s and 1s. When we subtract 1 from 1 we get 0 and when we subtract 0 from 1 we get 1. Therefore, 1's complement of a binary number can be computed just by inverting the bits of the number i.e. by changing 1 to 0 and 0 to 1. For example, 1's complement of 10110 is 01001 and 1's complement of 0110001 is 1001110. Similarly, in other number system (R-1)'s complement of a number is computed by subtracting each digit of the number from the maximum digit value of that number system. For example, the maximum digit value in octal number system is 7 and therefore, 7's complement of an octal number is computed by subtracting each digit of that number from 7. For hexadecimal number system, the maximum digit value is 15 represented by F. For example,

7's complement of 56072 octal number is: 21705
15's complement of 6A910F hexadecimal number is: 956EF0

Radix complement: Let N is a number in a number system of radix R and n is the total number of digits in the number N. The radix complement or R's complement of the number N is defined as $r^n - N$. For N = 0, the R's complement is defined as zero. It is evident from the definition of R's and (R-1)'s complement that R's complement of a number is computed by adding 1 to (R-1)'s complement of that number. Therefore, 10's complement of a decimal number is obtained by adding 1 to its 9's complement and 2's complement of a binary number is obtained by adding 1 to its 1's complement. Therefore, 2's complement of 10110 is 01001 + 1, which is 01010. By carefully looking at the procedure to compute 2's complement of a binary number you can observe that 2's complement of a binary number can be computed just by looking at the binary number and there is no need to do any paper and pencil work. Simple procedure to compute 2's complement of a binary number can be described as:

- Start from right end of the binary number
- Write down all digits unchanged until you encounter the first 1 bit
- Subsequently invert the bits to get the 2's complement of the binary number.

For example, let us compute 2's complement of 10011000. Start from right end and write down all digits unchanged until the first 1 bit. Since the fourth digit from right is 1, we will write first four digits unchanged, which is 1000. Now, invert the bits starting from fifth bit from right, which will give 01101000. This procedure to compute 2's complement of a binary number has been depicted in Figure 3-7.

Figure 3-7 Computing 2's complement of a binary number

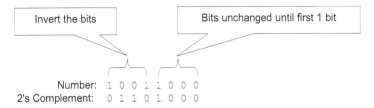

All negative integers (`byte`, `short`, `int` and `long`) are stored as their 2's complement forms in memory. Let us consider two `byte` variables in Java as:

```
byte bPos = 13;
byte bNeg = -13;
```

The `bPos` is stored in memory as 00001101. The 2's complement of 00001101 is computed as 11110011. Therefore, `bNeg`, which is -13, is stored as 11110011.

Binary Representation of Floating-Point Numbers

It is important to note that any binary floating-point system can represent only a finite number of floating-point values in exact form. All other values must be approximated by the closest representable value. The IEEE 754-1985 is the most widely accepted floating-point standard in the computer industry, which specifies the format and the method to represent binary floating-point numbers. The goal of the IEEE standard, which is designed for engineering calculations, is to maximize accuracy (to get as close as possible to the actual number). Precision refers to the number of digits that you can represent. The IEEE standard attempts to balance the number of bits dedicated to the exponent with the number of bits used for the fractional part of the number, to keep both accuracy and precision within acceptable limits. This section describes IEEE 754-1985 standard for binary floating-point format in general and points out how Java supports this standard.

A floating-point number has four parts:

- Sign
- Significand (also known as mantissa)
- Base (also known as radix)
- Exponent

The floating-point number 19.25 can be represented with all its four parts as:

```
+19.25 x 10⁰
```

Here,

        Sign is + (Positive)
        Significand is 19.25
        Base is 10, and
        Exponent is 0.

The number 19.25 can also be represented in many other forms as shown below. We will omit the positive sign of the number, that is, +19.25 will be written as 19.25.:

```
19.25 x 10⁰,
1.925 x 10¹,
0.1925 x 10²,
192.5 x 10⁻¹, or
1925 x 10⁻²
```

Therefore, a floating-point number can be represented in infinite number of ways. A floating-point number represented in base 10 is said to be in *normalized* form if its significand satisfies the following rule.

```
0.1 <= significand < 1
```

According to the above rule, the representation 0.1925×10^2 is the normalized form of 19.25. The floating-point number 19.25 (base 10) can be written as 10011.01 in binary form (base 2). The floating-point number 19.25 can be rewritten in many different binary forms. Some of the alternate binary representations of decimal 19.25 are as follows.

```
10011.01 x 2⁰
1001.101 x 2¹
100.1101 x 2²
1.001101 x 2⁴
100110.1 x 2⁻¹
1001101 x 2⁻²
```

Note that in binary form the base is 2. When the binary point is shifted to left by one digit, the exponent is incremented by one. When the binary point is shifted to right by one digit, the exponent is decremented by one. A floating-point number in a binary form is normalized if its significand satisfies the following condition.

```
1 <= significand < 2
```

That is, if the significand of a binary floating-point number is of the form `1.bbbbbbb...`, where b is a bit (0 or 1) the binary floating-point number is said to be in normalized form. Therefore, 1.001101×2^4 is the normalized form of binary floating-point number 10011.01. In other words, a normalized binary floating-point number starts with a bit 1 immediately followed by binary point. The floating-points, which are not normalized, are called *denormalized* floating-point numbers. A denormalized floating-point number is also called *denormal* or *subnormal*. All floating-point numbers cannot be represented in a normalized form. There could be two reasons why a floating-point number cannot be represented in a normalized form.

- The number does not contain any bit as 1. Example of this is 0.0. Since 0.0 does not have any bit set as 1, it cannot be represented in normalized form.

- Computers use a fixed number of bits to store the sign, significand, and exponent of a binary floating-point number. If the exponent of a binary floating-point number is the minimum exponent allowed by the computer storage format and the significand is less than 1, such a binary floating-point number cannot be normalized before storing it in computer. For example, suppose that -126 is the minimum exponent value that can be stored in a given storage format for a binary floating-point number. Now, if the binary floating-point number is 0.01101×2^{-126}, this number cannot be normalized before storing it in computer. The normalized form of this number will be 1.101×2^{-128}. However, the given storage format allows minimum exponent as -126 (We have assumed this number -126 for this example). Therefore, the exponent -128 ($-128 < -126$) cannot be stored in the given storage format and that is why 0.01101×2^{-126} cannot be stored in computer in the normalized form.

Why do we need to normalize a binary floating-point number before storing it in memory? Following are the advantages of normalizing floating-point numbers before storing them in memory.

- The normalized representation is unique.
- Since binary point in a binary floating-point number can be placed anywhere in the number, you must store the position of binary point in number. By normalizing the number, we always place the binary point after the first 1 bit, and, hence, we need not store the position of the binary point. This saves memory and time to store one extra piece of information.
- Two normalized binary floating-point numbers can be compared easily by comparing their signs, significands and exponents.
- In a normalized form, the significand can use all its storage bits to store significant digits (bits). For example, if we allocate only five bits to store significand of a binary floating-point number, for the number 0.0010110×2^{10} only 0.00101 part of the significand will be stored. However, if we normalize this number as 1.0110×2^{7}, significand can be stored fully in the five bits.
- In normalized form, the significand always starts with 1 bit. Therefore, we can omit this leading 1 bit while storing the significand in memory. While reading back the normalized number, we can always add the leading 1 bit. This omitted bit is called the "hidden bit" and it gives one extra bit of precision.

IEEE 754 -1985 standard defines four floating-point formats as follows.

- 32-bit single-precision floating-point format
- 64-bit double-precision floating-point format
- Single-extended floating-point format
- Double-extended floating-point format

Java uses IEEE 32-bit single-precision floating-point format to store the values of `float` data type. It uses 64-bit double-precision floating-point format to store the values of `double` data type.

We will discuss only IEEE 32-bit single-precision floating-point format. The difference between single-precision floating-point format and other formats are the total number of bits used to store the binary floating-point numbers and the distribution of number of bits among sign, exponent and significand. The difference among all IEEE formats will be shown at the end of the discussion in a tabular form.

32-bit Single-Precision Floating-Point Format

This format uses 32 bits to store a binary floating-point number. A binary floating-point number is of the following form.

```
Sign * Significand * 2 Exponent
```

Since the base is always 2, this format does not store the value of the base. The 32 bits are distributed as follows.

- 1 bit to store the sign
- 8 bits to store the exponent
- 23 bits to store the significand

The layout for the single-precision floating-point format is shown in Table 3-8.

Table 3-8: IEEE Single-precision format layout

1-bit Sign	8-bit Exponent	23-bit Significand
s	eeeeeeee	fffffffffffffffffffffff

Sign

IEEE single-precision floating-point format uses 1 bit to store the sign of the number. The sign bit of 0 (zero) indicates positive number whereas 1 (one) indicates negative number.

Exponent

IEEE single-precision floating-point format uses 8 bits to store the exponent. The exponent can be positive or negative. The range of the exponent value that can be stored in 8-bit is -127 to 128. Now, there must be a mechanism to represent the sign of the exponent. Note that the 1-bit sign field in the above layout shown in Table 3-8 stores the sign of the floating-point number and not the sign of the exponent of the floating-point number. To store the sign of the exponent, we can use the sign-magnitude method, where 1 bit is used to store the sign and the remaining 7 bits to store the magnitude of the exponent. We can also use 2's complement method to store the negative exponent as is used to store integers. However, IEEE does not use either of these two methods to store the exponent of the binary floating-point numbers. IEEE used biased representation of the exponent to store the exponent value.

What is bias and what is biased exponent? Bias is a constant value, which is 127 for IEEE 32-bit single-precision format. The bias value is added to the exponent before storing it in memory. This new exponent, after adding a bias, is called *biased exponent*. Therefore, the biased exponent is computed as:

```
Biased Exponent = Exponent + Bias
```

For example, 19.25 can be written in normalized binary floating-point format as: $1.001101 * 2^4$

Here, the exponent value is 4. However, the exponent value stored in memory will be biased exponent, which will be computed as:

```
Biased Exponent = Exponent + Bias
               = 4 + 127 (Single-precision format)
               = 131
```

Therefore, for 1.001101×2^4 the exponent will be stored as 131, which is the biased exponent and not the actual exponent, which is 4. While reading back the exponent of a binary floating-point number, we must subtract the bias value for that format to get the real exponent value. Why does IEEE use biased exponent? The advantage of using biased exponent is that positive floating-point numbers can be treated as integers for comparison purposes.

Suppose E is the number of bits used to store the exponent value in a given floating-point format. The value of bias for that format can be computed as:

```
Bias = 2^(E - 1) - 1
```

The exponent ranges from -127 to 128 for single-precision format. Therefore, the biased exponent ranges from 0 to 255. Two extreme exponent values (-127 and 128 for unbiased and 0 and 255 for biased) are used to represent special floating-point numbers e.g. zero, infinities, NaNs and denormalized numbers. The exponent range -126 to 127 (biased 1 to 254) is used to represent normalized binary floating-point numbers.

Significand

IEEE single-precision floating-point format uses 23 bits to store the significand. The number of bits used to store the significand is called the precision of that floating-point format. Therefore, you might have guessed that the precision of floating-point numbers stored in single-precision format is 23. However, this is not true. We need to discuss the format in which the significand is stored before we conclude about the precision of this format. The significand of a floating-point number is normalized before it is stored in memory. The normalized significand is always of the form:
```
1.fffffffffffffffffffffff
```

Here, an `f` denotes a bit 0 or 1 for fractional part of significand. Since the leading 1 bit is always present in the normalized form of significand, we need not store this leading 1 bit in memory. Therefore, while storing the normalized significand, we can use all 23 bits to store the fractional part of the significand. In fact, by not storing the leading 1 bit of a normalized significand gives us one extra bit of precision. This way, we represent 24 digits (1 leading bit + 23 fraction bits) in just 23 bits. Thus, for normalized significand the precision of a floating-point number in IEEE single-precision format is 24.

```
Actual Significand: 1.fffffffffffffffffffffff (24 digits)
Stored Significand:   fffffffffffffffffffffff (23 digits)
```

If we always represent the significand of a binary floating-point number in normalized form, there is a gap around zero on number line. The minimum number in magnitude that can be represented in IEEE single-precision format can be computed as follows.

Sign: It can be 0 or 1 denoting positive or negative number. For this example, we will assume sign bit as 0 to indicate positive number.

Exponent: The minimum exponent value is -126. Recall that the exponent values -127 and 128 are reserved to represent special floating-point numbers. The minimum biased exponent will be

-126 + 127 = 1. The binary representation of the biased exponent 1 in 8-bit is 00000001.

Significand: The minimum value of significand in normalized form will consist of leading 1 bit and all 23 fraction bits set to 0 as: 1.00000000000000000000000

If we combine the binary representation of a normalized floating-point number with minimum possible values for exponent and significand, the actual number stored in computer will look like the one shown below.

Sign	Exponent	Significand
0	00000001	00000000000000000000000
1-bit	8-bit	23-bit

The value of minimum floating-point number in decimal is 1.0×2^{-126}. Therefore, 1.0×2^{-126} is the first representable normalized number after zero leaving a gap around zero on number line.

Therefore, if we store only normalized floating-point number using IEEE single-precision format, all numbers less than 1.0×2^{-126} in magnitude must be rounded to zero. This will cause a serious problem while dealing with tiny numbers in a program. In order to store numbers smaller than 1.0×2^{-126} the numbers must be denormalized.

Special Floating-Point Numbers

This section describes special floating-point numbers and their representation using IEEE single-precision format.

Signed Zeros

IEEE floating-point format allows for two zeros +0.0 (or 0.0) and -0.0. Zero is represented by the minimum exponent value i.e. -127 for single-precision format. The significand is 0.0 for zero. Since the sign bit can be 0 or 1, there are two zero: +0.0 and -0.0. The binary representations of zeros in single-precision format are as follows.

Number	Sign	Exponent	Significand
0.0	0	00000000	00000000000000000000000
-0.0	1	00000000	00000000000000000000000

For all comparison purposes, +0.0 and -0.0 are considered equal. Therefore, the expression 0.0 == -0.0 always returns true. Why does IEEE define two zeros, if they are considered equal in comparison? The sign of zero is used to determine the result of an arithmetic expression involving multiplication and division. The result of 3.0 * 0.0 is positive zero (0.0), whereas the result of 3.0 * (-0.0) is negative zero (-0.0). For a floating-point number num with the values ±Infinity the relation 1/(1/num) = num holds true only because of two signed zeros.

Signed Infinities

IEEE floating-point format allows for two infinities: positive infinity and negative infinity. The sign bit represents the sign of infinity. The maximum exponent value 128 (biased exponent 255) for single-precision format and zero significand represent the infinity. The maximum biased value 255 can be represented in 8-bit with all bits set to 1 as 11111111. The binary representations of infinities in single-precision format are as follows.

Number	Sign	Exponent	Significand
+Infinity	0	11111111	00000000000000000000000
-Infinity	1	11111111	00000000000000000000000

NaN

NaN stands for "Not-a-Number". NaN is the result of arithmetic operations that do not have meaningful result e.g. diving zero by zero, square root of a negative number, adding -Infinity to +Infinity, etc. NaN is represented by maximum exponent value (128 for single-precision format) and non-zero significand. Sign bit is not interpreted for NaN. What happens when NaN is one of the operands in an arithmetic expression? For example, what is the result of NaN + 100 ? Should the execution of an arithmetic expression involving NaNs be stopped or, continued? There are two types of NaNs:

- Quiet NaN
- Signaling NaN

A quiet NaN, when encountered as an operand in an arithmetic expression, quietly (i.e. without raising any trap or exception) produces another quiet NaN as the result. IN case of quiet NaN the expression NaN + 100 will result in another quiet NaN. The most significant bit in significand is set to 1 for quiet NaN.

Number	Sign	Exponent	Significand
Quiet NaN	s	11111111	1bbbbbbbbbbbbbbbbbbbbbb

Here, s and b indicate a bit 0 or 1.

When a signaling NaN is encountered as an operand in an arithmetic expression, an invalid operation exception is signaled and a quiet NaN is delivered as the result. Signaling NaNs are generally used to initialize the uninitialized variables in a program so that when a variable are not initialized before they are used, errors can be signaled. The most significant bit of the significand is set to 0 for a signaling NaN.

Number	Sign	Exponent	Significand
Signaling NaN	s	11111111	0bbbbbbbbbbbbbbbbbbbbbb

Here, s and b indicate a bit 0 or 1.

IEEE defines $2^{24} - 2$ distinct NaNs for single-precision format and $2^{53} - 2$ distinct NaNs for double-precision format. However, Java has only one `NaN` for its `float` data type and one `NaN` for `double` data type. Java always uses quiet `NaN`.

Denormals

When the biased exponent is 0 and the significand is non-zero, it denotes a denormalized number. The following bit pattern is used to represent a denormalized number in single-precision format.

Sign	Exponent	Significand
s	000000000	fffffffffffffffffffffff

Here, s denotes a sign bit, which can be 0 for positive number and 1 for negative number. The exponent bits are all zero. At least one of the bits in significand denoted by `f` is 1. The decimal value of the denormalized number represented in the above pattern is computed as:

$$(-1)^s * 0. \text{ fffffffffffffffffffffff} * 2^{-126}$$

Suppose we want to store a number 0.25×2^{-128} in single-precision format. If we write this number in normalized form after converting 0.25 in binary, it can be written as:

$$1.0 \times 2^{-130}.$$

However, the minimum exponent allowed for single-precision format is -126. Therefore, this number cannot be stored in normalized form in single-precision format. The exponent is kept as -126 and binary point is shifted to left resulting in denormalized form as: 0.0001×2^{-126}.

The above number is stored in single-precision format as follows.

Number	Sign	Exponent	Significand
0.0001×2^{-126}	0	00000000	00010000000000000000000000

It seems that for the number 0.0001×2^{-126}, the biased exponent should be computed as $-126 + 127 = 1$ and the exponent bits should be `00000001`. However, this is not true. For denormalized numbers the exponent is stored as all `0` bits, and while reading it back, it is interpreted as -126. This is so because we need to distinguish between normalized and denormalized numbers while reading back the floating-point numbers, and for all denormalized numbers, there is no leading 1-bit in significand. The denormalized numbers fill the gap around zero on the number line, which would have been there if we had stored only normalized numbers.

Rounding Modes

Not all real numbers can be exactly represented in binary floating-point format in finite number of bits. Therefore, real numbers that cannot be exactly represented in a binary floating-point format must be rounded. There are four rounding modes:

- Round toward zero
- Round toward positive infinity
- Round toward negative infinity
- Round toward nearest

Round toward Zero

This rounding mode is also called truncation or chop mode. In this rounding mode, the total number of bits (or digits) that is retained from the original number is the same as the number of bits available to store the floating-point number in the given format. The rest of the bits in the original number are ignored. This rounding mode is called "Rounding toward zero", because it has the effect of making the rounded result closer to zero. Some examples of rounding towards zero are shown below.

Original Number	Available Number of Binary Points	Rounded Number
1.1101	2	1.11
-0.1011	2	-0.10
0.1010	2	0.10
0.0011	2	0.00

Round toward Positive Infinity

In this rounding mode, numbers are rounded to a value closer to the positive infinity. Some examples of rounding towards positive infinity are shown below.

Original Number	Available Number of Binary Points	Rounded Number
1.1101	2	10.00
-0.1011	2	-0.10
0.1010	2	0.11
0.0011	2	0.01

Round toward Negative Infinity

In this rounding mode, numbers are rounded to a value closer to the negative infinity. Some examples of rounding towards negative infinity are shown below.

Original Number	Available Number of Binary Points	Rounded Number
1.1101	2	1.11
-0.1011	2	-0.11
0.1010	2	0.10
0.0011	2	0.00

Round toward Nearest

In this rounding mode, the rounded result is the nearest representable floating-point number. In case of a tie, that is, if there are two representable floating-point numbers, which are equally near to the original number, the result is the one, which has its least significant, bit zero. In other words, in case of a tie, the rounded result is the even number. The system, which implements IEEE floating-point standards, has this mode as the default rounding mode. IEEE standard states that the system should also allow users to select one of the other three rounding modes. Java uses this mode as the default rounding mode for floating-point numbers. Java does not allow users (that is, programmers) to select any other rounding modes. Some examples of rounding towards nearest are shown below.

Original Number	Available Number of Binary Points	Rounded Number
1.1101	2	1.11
-0.1011	2	-0.11
0.1010	2	0.10
0.0011	2	0.01

Floating-Point Exceptions

The IEEE floating-point standard defines several exceptions that occur when the result of a floating-point operation is unacceptable. Exceptions can be ignored, in which case some default action is taken, such as returning a special value. When trapping is enabled for an exception, an error is signaled whenever that exception occurs. Floating point operations can lead to any of the following five types of floating point exceptions:

Division by Zero Exception

This exception happens when a non-zero number is divided by floating point zero. If no trap handler is installed, infinity of appropriate sign is delivered as the result.

Invalid Operation Exception

Invalid operation exception occurs when the operand is invalid for an operation being performed. If no trap handler is installed, quiet NaN is delivered as the result. Following are some of the operations, which raise invalid exception:

- Square root of negative number
- Division of zero by zero or of infinity by infinity
- Multiplication of zero and infinity
- Any operation on a signaling NaN
- Subtracting infinity from infinity
- When a quiet NaN is compared with the > or < relational operators

Overflow Exception

This exception occurs when the result of any floating-point operation is too large in magnitude to fit in the intended destination format. For example, when you multiply `Float.MAX_VALUE` by 2 and try to assign the result in a `float` variable. If no trap handler is installed, the result to be delivered depends on the rounding mode and the sign of the intermediate result.

- If the rounding mode is "Round toward Zero", the result of overflow is the largest finite number that can be represented in that format. The sign of the result is same as the sign of the intermediate result.
- If the rounding mode is "Round toward Positive Infinity", the negative overflow results in the most negative finite number for that format and the positive overflow results in the most positive finite number for that format.
- If the rounding mode is "Round toward Negative Infinity", the negative overflow results in negative infinity and the positive overflow results in the most positive finite number for that format.
- If the rounding mode is "Round toward nearest", the overflow results in infinity. The sign of the result is same as the sign of the intermediate result.

However, if trap handler is installed, the result delivered to the trap handler in case of overflow is determined as follows. The infinitely precise result is divided by 2^t and rounded before delivering it to the trap handler. The value of t is 192 for single-precision format, 1536 for double-precision format, and $3 \times 2^{n-1}$ for extended format, where n is the number of bits used to represent the exponent.

Underflow Exception

This exception occurs when the result of an operation is too small to be represented as a normalized `float` in its format. If trapping is enabled, the floating-point-underflow exception is signaled. Otherwise, the operation results in a denormalized `float` or zero. Underflow can be abrupt or gradual. If the result of an operation is less than the minimum value that can be represented in normalized form in the format, the result could be delivered as zero or a denormalized number. In case of abrupt underflow, the result is zero. In case of gradual underflow, the result is a denormalized number. The IEEE default is gradual underflow (denormalized numbers). Java supports gradual underflow.

Inexact Exception

This exception is signaled if the rounded result of an operation is not identical to the infinitely precise result. Inexact exceptions are quite common. 1.0 / 3.0 is an inexact operation. Inexact exceptions also occur when the operation overflows without an overflow trap.

Java and IEEE Floating-Point Standards

Java follows a subset of the IEEE-754 standard. Following are some of the differences between IEEE floating-point standard and their Java implementations.

- Java does not signal the IEEE exceptions.

- Java has no signaling `NaN`.
- Java uses "Round toward nearest" mode to round the inexact results. However, Java rounds towards zero when converting a floating value to an integer. Java does not provide the user-selectable rounding modes for floating-point computations: up, down, or towards zero.
- IEEE defines (2^{24} - 2) `NaNs` for single-precision format and (2^{53} - 2) `NaNs` for double-precision format. However, Java defines only one `NaN` for each of these two formats.

Table 3-9 IEEE formats' parameters

	Width in bits	Exponent Width in bits	Precision	Maximum Exponent	Minimum Exponent	Exponent Bias
Single-precision	32	8	24	127	-126	127
Double-precision	64	11	53	1023	-1022	1023
Single-extended	>= 43	>= 11	>= 32	>= 1023	<= -1022	Unspecified
Double-extended	>= 79	>= 15	>= 64	>= 16383	<= -16382	Unspecified

Little-Endian and Big-Endian

These two terms are related to the direction of bytes in a word within CPU architecture. Computer memory is referenced by addresses that are positive integers. It is 'natural' to store numbers with the least significant byte coming before the most significant byte in the computer memory. Sometimes, computer designers prefer to use a reversed order version of the representation. The 'natural' order, where less significant byte comes before more significant byte in memory is called Little-endian, many vendors like IBM, CRAY and Sun preferred the reverse order that, of course, is called Big-endian. For example, the 32-bit hex value 0x45679812 would be stored in memory as follows:

```
Address        00   01   02   03
----------     --   --   --   --
Little-endian  12   98   67   45
Big-endian     45   67   98   12
```

Difference in endian-ness can be a problem when transferring data between two machines. Table 3-10 lists some vendors, their `float` type and endian-ness on their machines. Everything in Java binary format files is stored in Big-endian order. This is sometimes called network order. This means if you use only Java, all files are done the same way on all platforms Mac, PC, Solaris, etc. You can freely exchange binary data electronically without any concerns about endian-ness. The problem comes when you must exchange data files with some program not written in Java that uses little-endian order, most commonly C on the PC. Some platforms use big-endian order internally (Mac, IBM 390); some uses little-endian order (Intel). Java hides that internal endian-ness from you.

Table 3-10 Vendors, float types and endian-ness

Vendor	Float Type	Endian-ness
ALPHA	DEC/IEEE	Little-endian
IBM	IBM	Big-endian
MAC	IEEE	Big-endian
SUN	IEEE	Big-endian
VAX	DEC	Little-endian
PC	IEEE	Little-endian

Chapter 4. Operators

What is an Operator?

An operator is a symbol that performs a specific kind of operation on one, two, or three operands, and produces a result. The type of the operator and its operands determines the kind of operation performed on the operands, and the type of the result produced. Operators in Java can be categorized based on two criteria:

- The number of operands they operate on, and
- The type of operation they perform on the operands

An operator is called unary, binary, or ternary depending on the number of operands it operates on. If an operator operates on one operand, it called a *unary operator*. If an operator operates on two operands, it called a *binary operator*. If an operator operates on three operands, it called a *ternary operator*.

A unary operator can use postfix or prefix notation. In the postfix notation, the unary operator appears after its operand as:

```
operand operator   // Postfix notation
```

For example,

```
num++;    // num is an operand and ++ is a Java unary operator
```

In a prefix notation, the Java unary operator appears before its operand as:

```
operator operand   // Prefix notation
```

For example,

```
++num;   // ++ is a Java unary operator and num is an operand
```

The use of binary operators uses infix notation, that is, the operator appears in between the two operands as:

```
operand1 operator operand2   // Infix notation
```

For example,

```
10 + 15;   // 10 is operand1, + is a binary operator, 15 is operand2
```

Ternary operator also uses infix notation as:

```
operand1 operator1 operand2 operator2 operand3 // Infix notation
```

Here, `operator1` and `operator2` make one ternary operator.

For example,

```
/* isSunday is the first operand, ? is the first part of ternary
   operator, holiday is the second operand, : is the second part of
   ternary operator, noHoliday is the third operand
*/
isSunday ? holiday : noHoliday;
```

An operator is called an *Arithmetic* operator, a *Relational* operator, a *Logical* operator, or a *Bitwise* operator, depending on the kind of operation it performs on its operands. There is a big list of operators in Java. This chapter discusses most of the Java operators. Some of the operators will be discussed in other chapters in this book.

Assignment Operator (=)

An assignment operator (=) is used to assign a value to a variable. It is a binary operator. It takes two operands. The value of the right-hand operand is assigned to the left-hand operand. The left-hand operand must be a variable. For example,

```
int num;
num = 25;
```

Here, `num = 25` uses the assignment operator =. In this example, `25` is the right-hand operand. `num` is the left-hand operand, which is a variable. Java ensures that the value of the right-hand operand of assignment operator (=) is assignment compatible to the data type of the left-hand operand. If the type of the value represented by the right-hand operand is not assignment compatible to the data type of the variable as the left-hand operand, the Java compiler generates an error at compile time. In case of the reference variables, you may be able to compile the source code and get runtime error if the object represented by the right-hand operand is not assignment compatible to the reference variable as the left-hand operand. For example, the value of type `byte`, `short` and `char` are assignment compatible to `int` data type, and hence the following snippet of code is valid.

```
byte b = 5;
char c = 'a';
short s = -200;
int i = 10;

i = b; // Ok. byte, b, is assignment compatible to int, i.
i = c; // Ok. char, c, is assignment compatible to int, i.
i = s; // Ok. short, s, is assignment compatible to int, i.
```

However, `long` to `int` and `float` to `int` assignments are not compatible and hence the following uses of assignment operator are incorrect in Java and produce compiler error.

```
long big = 524L;
float f = 1.19F;
int i = 15;

i = big;  // Compiler error. long to int, assignment incompatible
```

```
i = f;    // Compiler error. float to int, assignment incompatible
```

In such a case where the right-hand operand's value is not assignment compatible with the left-hand variable's data type, the value of the right-hand operand must be cast to appropriate type. The above piece of code, which uses assignment operators, can be rewritten with cast as follows.

```
i = (int)big; // Ok
i = (int)f;   // Ok
```

An *expression* is a series of variables, operators, and method calls, constructed according to the syntax of the Java programming language that evaluates to a single value. For example, `num = 25` is an expression. The expression, which uses the assignment operator, also has a value. The value of the expression is equal to the value of the right-hand operand. Consider the following piece of code in Java, assuming that num is an `int` variable.

```
num = 25;
```

Here, `num = 25` is called an expression and `num = 25;` is called a statement. The expre4ssion, `num = 25`, does two things.

- Assigns the value `25` to the variable `num`, and
- Produces a value `25`, which is equal to the value of the right-hand operand of assignment operator.

The second effect, producing a value, of using the assignment operator in an expression may seem strange at this point. You may wonder what happens to the value 25 produced by the expression `num = 25`. Do we ever use the value returned by an expression? The answer is yes. We do use the value returned by an expression. Let us consider the following expression, which uses chained assignment operator, assuming that num1, and num2 are `int` variables.

```
num1 = num2 = 25;
```

What happens when the above piece of code is executed? First, the part of the expression `num2 = 25` is executed. As mentioned earlier, there will be two effects of the execution of this expression.

- It will assign a value of `25` to `num2`, and
- It will produce a value of `25`. In other words, you can say that after assigning the value `25` to `num2`, the expression `num2 = 25` is replaced by a value `25` which changes the main expression `num1 = num2 = 25` to `num1 = 25`.

Now, the expression `num1 = 25` is executed and the value 25 is assigned to num1 and the value produced, which is 25, is ignored. This way you can assign the same value to more than one variable in a single expression. There can be any number of variables used in such a chained assignment expression, for example:

```
num1 = num2 = num3 = num4 = num5 = num6 = 219;
```

Suppose that there are two `int` variables `num1` and `num2`. The following assignment, `num1 = num2`, assigns the value `200` stored in `num2` to `num1`.

```
int num1 = 100;    // num1 is 100
```

```
int num2 = 200;     // num2 is 200
num1 = num2;    // num1 is 200. num2 is 200
num2 = 500;     // num2 is 500. num1 is still 200
```

When we say `num1 = num2`, the value stored in `num2` is copied to `num1` and both `num1` and `num2` maintain their own copy of the same value `200`. Later on, when `num2 = 500` is executed, the value of only `num2` changes to `500`. But, the value of `num1` remains the same as `200`. Now suppose there are two reference variable, `ref1` and `ref2`, which refer to, two different objects of the same class. If we write:

```
ref1 = ref2;
```

The effect of the expression, `ref1 = ref2`, is that both reference variables, `ref1` and `ref2`, now, refer to the same object in memory - the object which was being referred to by `ref2`. After this assignment, both reference variables, `ref1` and `ref2`, are equally capable of manipulating the object in memory. The changes made to the object in memory by reference variable `ref1` will be observed by `ref2` also and vice-versa. The chapter on *Classes and Objects* discusses more about reference assignments.

Declaration, Initialization and Assignment

Before a variable of any type is used in a Java program, it must be declared and must have a value assigned to it. Suppose you want to use an `int` variable named `num1`. First, you must declare it as:

```
int num1;       // Declaration of a variable num1
```

A value can be assigned to a variable after it is declared or at the time of declaration itself. When a value is assigned to a variable after it has been declared, it is known as *assignment*. The following piece of code declares an `int` variable `num2` and assigns 50 to it.

```
int num2;       // Declaration of a variable num2
num2 = 50;      // Assignment
```

When a value is assigned to a variable at the time of declaration itself, it is known as *initialization*. The following code declares an `int` variable num3 and initializes it to a value 100.

```
int num3 = 100;     // Declaration of variable num3 and initialization
```

You can declare more than one variable of the same type in one declaration by separating each variable name by a comma as follows.

```
// Declaration of three variables num1, num2 and num3 of type int
int num1, num2, num3;
```

You can also declare more than one variable in one declaration, and initialize some or all of them as:

```
// Declaration of variables num1, num2 and num3. Initialization of only
// num1 and num3.
int num1 = 10, num2, num3 = 200;
```

```
// Declaration and initialization of variables num1, num2 and num3
int num1 = 10, num2 = 20, num3 = 30;
```

Java would not let you use a variable unless it has been assigned a value after it is declared - either through the process of initialization or assignment. Java implicitly initializes variables declared in a particular context and so you do not have to initialize variable declared in those contexts before you use them. Variables declared in other contexts must be initialized, or assigned a value, before they are used, if Java does not initialize them implicitly. We will discuss the implicit initialization of a variable by Java in the chapter on *Classes and Objects*. It is a good programming practice to initialize a variable at the time of its declaration.

Arithmetic Operators

Table 4-1 lists all arithmetic operators in Java. All arithmetic operators listed in Table 4-1 can only be used with numeric type operands. That is, both operands to arithmetic operators must be one of types - `byte`, `short`, `char`, `int`, `long`, `float` and `double`. These operators cannot have operands of `boolean` primitive type and reference type. The following sections describe arithmetic operators in details.

Addition Operator (+)

The addition operator (+) is used in the form:

```
operand1 + operand2
```

The addition arithmetic operator (+) is used to add two numeric values represented by the two operands, for example, 5 + 3 results in 8. The operands to the addition operator (+) may be any numeric literals, numeric variables, numeric expressions, or method calls. Every expression involving addition operator (+) has a data type. The data type of the expression is determined according to one of the four following rules.

- If one of the operands is of `double` data type, the other operand is converted to `double` data type and the whole expression is of type `double`. Otherwise,
- If one of the operands is of `float` data type, the other operand is converted to `float` data type and the whole expression is of type `float`. Otherwise,
- If one of the operands is of `long` data type, the other operand is converted to `long` data type and the whole expression is of type `long`. Otherwise,
- If none of the above three rules applies, all operands are converted to `int`, provided they are not already of `int` type, and the whole expression is of type `int`.

Table 4-1: List of arithmetic operators in Java

Operators	Description	Type	Usage	Result
+	Addition	Binary	2 + 5	7
−	Subtraction	Binary	5 − 2	3
+	Unary plus	Unary	+5	Positive five. Same as 5

-	Unary minus	Unary	-5	Negative of five
*	Multiplication	Binary	`5 * 3`	15
/	Division	Binary	`5 / 2`	2
			`6 / 2`	3
			`5.0 / 2.0`	2.5
			`6.0 / 2.0`	3.0
%	Modulus	Binary	`5 % 3`	2
++	Increment	Unary	`num++`	Evaluates to the value of num, increment num by 1
--	Decrement	Unary	`num--`	Evaluates to the value of num, decrement num by 1
+=	Arithmetic *compound-assignment*	Binary	`num += 5`	Adds 5 to the value of num and assigns the result to num. If num is 10, the new value of num will be 15.
-=	Arithmetic *compound-assignment*	Binary	`num -= 3`	Subtracts 3 from the value of num and assigns the result to num. If num is 10, the new value of num will be 7.
*=	Arithmetic *compound-assignment*	Binary	`num *= 15`	Multiplies 15 to the value of num and assigns the result to num. If num is 10, the new value of num will be 150
/=	Arithmetic *compound-assignment*	Binary	`num /= 5`	Divides the value of num by 5 and assigns the result to num. If num is 10, the new value of num will be 2.
%=	Arithmetic *compound-assignment*	Binary	`num %= 5`	Calculates the remainder of num divided by 5 and assigns the result to num. If num is 12, the new value of num will be 2.

These four rules, which determine the data type of the expression involving addition operator, have some important implications. Let us consider a `byte` variable b1, which is assigned a value of 5 as shown in the following piece of code.

```
byte b1;
b1 = 5;
```

However, you get a compiler error when you try to assign the same value 5 to a `byte` variable `b1` as shown in the following snippet of code.

```
byte b1;
byte b2 = 2;
byte b3 = 3;

b1 = b2 + b3; // Compiler error. Trying to assign 5 to b1
```

Why does the above snippet of code result in a compiler error? Do the expressions `b1 = 5` and `b1 = b2 + b3` not have the same effect of assigning 5 to the variable b1? Yes, the effect would be the same, that is, both expressions `b1 = 5` and `b1 = b2 + b3` will assign the same value 5 to b1. However, the rules that govern the assignment operation are different in these two cases. In the expression, `b1 = 5`, the assignment is governed by the rule that any `int` literal between -128 and 127 can be assigned to a `byte` variable. Since 5 is between -128 and 127, so the assignment `b1 = 5` is valid. The second assignment, `b1 = b2 + b3`, is governed by the fourth rule for the determination of the data type of an arithmetic expression, which uses addition operator (+). Since both operands in expression `b2 + b3` are of `byte` types, the operands `b1` and `b2` are first converted to `int` data type, and then the expression, `b2 + b3`, becomes of `int` type. Since the data type of `b1` is `byte`, which is smaller than the `int` data type of the expression `b2 + b3`, the assignment `b1 = b2 + b3`, that is, `int` to `byte` is not compatible, and that is why it generates an error. In such a case, you need to cast the result of the right-hand expression (here, `b2 + b3`) to the data type of the left-hand operand (here, `byte`).

```
b1 = (byte)(b2 + b3);    // Ok now
```

Beginners may try to write the above statement of code as:

```
b1 = (byte) b2 + b3;     // Error again
```

In fact, the two expressions `(byte)(b2 + b3)` and `(byte)b2 + b3` are not the same. In the expression `(byte) (b2 + b3)`, first `b2` and `b3` are promoted to `int` data type, and then addition is performed, which results in a value 5 of `int` data type. Then, the `int` value 5 is cast to `byte` and assigned to `b1`. In the expression `(byte)b2 + b3`, first `b2` is cast to `byte`. Note that this cast is redundant since `b2` is already of type `byte`. Then, both b2 and b3 are promoted to `int` data type and the whole expression `(byte)b2 + b3` is of type `int`. Since `int` to `byte` assignment is not permitted in Java, the expression `(byte)b2 + b3` would not compile. The error produced by the second expression `(byte)b2 + b3` raises an interesting question. Why did Java not first compute `b2 + b3` in `(byte)b2 + b3` and then applied `(byte)` to the result? Since there were two operations to be done by Java (in expression `(byte)b2 + b3`), one being the cast to `byte` and another being the addition of b2 and `b3`, Java did cast on `b2` first and the addition second. The decision, to perform the cast first and then the addition in expression `(byte)b2 + b3`, was not arbitrary. In fact, each operator in Java has a precedence order. The operator, which has higher precedence, is evaluated first and the operator having lower precedence order is evaluated afterwards. The cast operator `(byte)` has higher precedence than the addition operator (+).This is why `(byte)b2` was evaluated first in `(byte)b2 + b3`. You can always override the precedence of operators using parentheses and that is what we did by placing `b2 + b3` in parentheses in expression `(byte)(b2 + b3)`. Let us consider another example.

```
byte b1;
b1 = 3 + 2; // Will this line of code compile?
```

Will the expression, `b1 = 3 + 2`, compile? If we apply the fourth rule for determining the data type of this expression, it should not compile. Because 3 and 2 are `int` literals, that is, they are of type `int`. So, the expression `3 + 2` is of type `int`. Since `int` is not assignment compatible to `byte`, the expression `b1 = 3 + 2` should give an error. However, our assumption is wrong and the expression `b1 = 3 + 2` will compile fine. In this case, the assignment proceeds as follows. The operands 3 and 2 of the addition operator (+) in the expression `3 + 2` are `int` literals, that is, they are constants, and their values are known at compile time. The expression `3 + 2` can be computed at compile time itself. Therefore, Java compiler computes the result of the expression `3 + 2` at the time of compilation and replaces `3 + 2` by its result 5. So, the expression `b1 = 3 + 2` is replaced by `b1 = 5` by Java compiler. Now you can see why Java didn't give any error for this expression. Since the `int` literal 5 is in the range `-128` to `127`, `b1 = 5` is valid assignment according to the rule of assignment of `int` literal to a `byte` variable. However, if you try to write an expression as `b1 = 127 + 10`, certainly it would not compile because the result of `127 + 10`, which is `137` is out of range for a `byte` data type. Here are the final words on the data type conversion of the operands and the determination of the type of the expression involving addition operator (+).

```
var = operand1 + operand2;
```

If `operand1` and `operand2` are compile-time constants, the result of `operand1 + operand2` determines whether the above assignment is valid. If the result of `operand1 + operand2` is in the range for the data type of the variable `var`, the above expression will compile. Otherwise, a compiler error is generated. If either `operand1` or `operand2` is a variable (that is, the value of either `operand1` or `operand2` cannot be ascertained at compile time), the data type of the expression is determined according to one of the four rules discussed in the beginning of this section. Following are the examples of correct and incorrect use of addition operator (+). The comments along with the code indicate the correct and incorrect use of the addition operator (+).

```
byte b1 = 2;
byte b2 = 3;
short s1 = 100;
int i = 10;
int j = 12;
float f1 = 2.5F;
double d1 = 20.0;

b1 = 15 + 110;      // Ok. 125 is in the range -128 and 127
b1 = i + 5;         // Error. Data type i + 5 is int and int to byte
                    // assignment is not permitted

b1 = (byte)(i + 5); // OK

// Error. s1 is promoted to int and s1 + 2 is of data type int. int to
// byte assignment is not permitted
b1 = s1 + 2;

// Error. b2 is promoted to float and f1 + b2 is of data type float.
// float to byte assignment is not permitted
b1 = f1 + b2;

// Error. f1 is promoted to double and f1 + d1 is of data type double
b1 = f1 + d1;

// Ok. i is promoted to float and i + f1 is of data type float
f1 = i + f1;

// Error. i is promoted to double and i + d1 is of data type double.
// double to float assignment is not permitted
f1 = i + d1;

f1 = (float)(i + d1); // OK

// Error. 2.0 and 3.0 are of type double and so that the result of
// 2.0 + 3.2 is 5.2, which is also of type double. double to float
// assignment is not permitted.
f1 = 2.0 + 3.2;

// Ok. 2.0F and 3.2F are of type float and so that the result of
// 2.0F + 3.2F, which is 5.2F is of type float.
f1 = 2.0F + 3.2F;
```

```
// Ok. j is promoted to float and f1 + j is of data type float. Float
// to double assignment is permitted
d1 = f1 + j;
```

Subtraction Operator (-)

The subtraction operator (-) is used in the form:

```
operand1 - operand2
```

The subtraction operator (-) is used to compute the difference of two numbers, for example $5 - 3$ results in 2. All rules that we discussed about the numeric data conversion of the operands and the determination of the data type of the expression involving the addition operator (+) are also applicable for an expression involving subtraction operator (-). Following are the examples that use subtraction operator (-).

```
byte b1 = 5;
int i = 100;
float f1 = 2.5F;
double d1 = 15.45;

// Ok. 200 -173 will be replaced by 27 and b1 = 27
// is ok because 27 is in the range -128 and 127
b1 = 200 - 173;

// Error. i - 27 is of type int. int to byte assignment is not allowed
b1 = i - 27;

b1 = (byte)(i -27);   // OK

// Error. b1 is promoted to float and b1 - f1 is of
// type float. float to int assignment is not allowed
i = b1 - f1;

i = (int)(b1 - f1);     // Ok.

// Ok. i - b1 is of type int and int to float assignment is allowed
f1 = i - b1;

// Error. d1 - i is of type double, and double to float assignment is
// not allowed
f1 = d1 - i;

f1 = (float)(d1 - i);   // Ok.
```

Multiplication Operator (*)

The multiplication operator (*) is used in the form:

```
operand1 * operand2
```

The multiplication operator (*) is used to compute the product of two numbers, for example, `7 * 3` results in `21`. All rules that we discussed about the numeric data conversion of the operands and the determination of the data type of the expression involving the addition operator (+) are also applicable for an expression involving the multiplication operator (*). The following are examples of using the multiplication operator (*).

```
byte b1 = 5;
int i = 10;
float f1 = 2.5F;
double d1 = 15.45;

// Ok. 20 * 6 will be replaced by 120 and b1 = 120
// is ok because 120 is in the range -128 and 127
b1 = 20 * 6;

// Error.  i * 12 is of type int. int to byte assignment is not allowed
b1 = i * 12;

b1 = (byte)(i * 12);    // OK

// Error. b1 is promoted to float and b1 * f1 is of
// type float. float to int assignment is not allowed
i = b1 * f1;

i = (int)(b1 * f1);     // Ok

// Ok. i * b1 is of type int and int to float assignment is allowed
f1 = i * b1;

// Error. d1 * i is of type double and double to float assignment
// is not allowed
f1 = d1 * i;

f1 = (float)(d1 * i);   // Ok.
```

Division Operator (/)

The division operator (/) is used in the form:

```
operand1 / operand2
```

The division operator (/) is used to compute the quotient of two numbers, for example `5.0/2.0` results in `2.5`. All rules we discussed about the numeric data conversion of the operands and the determination of the data type of the expression involving the addition operator (+) are also valid for expression involving division operator (/).

There are two types of division - *Integer division* and *Floating-point division*. If both the operands of the division operator (/) are integers, i.e., `byte`, `short`, `char`, `int` or `long`, the usual division operation is carried out and the result is truncated towards zero to represent an integer. For example, if you write an expression `5/2` the division yields `2.5` and the fractional part `0.5` is ignored and the result of `5/2` is 2. Following examples illustrate the integer division.

```
int num;
num = 5/2;      // Assigns 2 to num
```

```
num = 5/3;      // Assigns 1 to num
num = 5/4;      // Assigns 1 to num
num = 5/5;      // Assigns 1 to num
num = 5/6;      // Assigns 0 to num
num = 5/7;      // Assigns 0 to num
```

In all the above examples, the value assigned to the variable num is an integer. The result is an integer in all cases not because the data type of variable num is `int`. The result is integer because both the operands of division operator (/) are integers. Since the data type of both operands is `int` the whole expression, e.g., `5/3` is of type `int`. Since fractional portion (e.g. 0.5, .034) cannot be stored in an `int` data type, the fractional part is ignored and the result is always an integer. If either or both of the operands of the division operator (/) are `float` or `double` type, floating-point division is performed and the result is not truncated. For example:

```
float f1;

// 15.0F and 4.0F are of float type. So, the expression 15.0F/4.0F is
// of type  float. The result 3.75F is assigned to f1
f1 = 15.0F/4.0F;

// 15 is of type int and 4.0F is of type float. So, the expression
// 15/4.0F is of type float. The result 3.75F is assigned to f1
f1 = 15/4.0F;

// Error. 15.0 is of type double and 4.0F is of float type. So, the
// expression 15.0/4.0F is of type double. The result 3.75 is of
// type double and cannot be assigned to f1
f1 = 15.0/4.0F;

f1 = (float)(15.0/4.0F); // Ok. 3.75F is assigned to f1

// 15 and 4 are of int type. The expression 15/4 is of type int and so,
// integer division is performed. The result 3 is assigned to f1,
// because int to float assignment is allowed
f1 = 15/4;
```

What happens when you try to divide a number (integer or floating-point) by 0 (zero)? The result of dividing a number by zero depends on the type of division, which could be integer division or floating-point division. If integer division is performed on the number, dividing by zero results in a runtime error. If you write an expression `3/0` in a Java program, it compiles fine, but will give error when this expression is executed at runtime. For example:

```
int i = 2;
int j = 5;
int k = 0;
i = j/k;  // Runtime error. Divide by zero
i = 0/0;  // Runtime error. Divide by zero
```

If either of the operands of the division operator is a floating-point number, floating-point division is performed and the result of dividing a number with zero is not an error. If the dividend (in 7/2, 7 is the dividend and 2 is the divisor) is a non-zero number in a floating-point divide- by-zero operation, the result is a *positive infinity* or a *negative infinity*. If the dividend is a floating-point zero (e.g. 0.0 or 0,0F), the result is `NaN`. For example:

```
float f1 = 2.5F;
```

```
double d1 = 5.6;

f1 = 5.0F/0.0F;      // Float.POSITIVE_INFINITY is assigned to f1
f1 = -5.0F/0.0F;     // Float.NEGATIVE_INFINITY is assigned to f1
f1 = -5.0F/-0.0F;    // Float.POSITIVE_INFINITY is assigned to f1
f1 = 5.0F/-0.0F;     // Float.NEGATIVE_INFINITY is assigned to f1
d1 = 5.0/0.0;        // Double.POSITIVE_INFINITY is assigned to d1
d1 = -5.0/0.0;       // Double.NEGATIVE_INFINITY is assigned to d1
d1 = -5.0/-0.0;      // Double.POSITIVE_INFINITY is assigned to d1
d1 = 5.0/-0.0;       // Double.NEGATIVE_INFINITY is assigned to d1

// 5.0F is of type float and 0 is of type int, so 5.0F/0 is of type
// float. Float.POSITIVE_INFINITY is assigned to f1
f1 = 5.0F/0;

// Compiler error. 5.0F is of type float and 0.0 is of type double,
// so 5.0F/0.0 is of type double. double to float assignment is not
// allowed
f1 = 5.0F/0.0;

f1 = (float)(5.0F/0.0); // f1 is assigned Float.POSITIVE_INFINITY

f1 = 0.0F/0.0F;      // Assigns Float.NaN to f1
d1 = 0.0/0.0;        // Assigns Double.NaN to d1
d1 = -0.0/0.0;       // Assigns Double.NaN to d1
```

Note that there are two infinities - positive and negative, for each floating-point numbers - `float` and `double`, in Java, whereas there is only one `NaN` for `float` and `double`.

Modulus Operator (%)

The modulus operator (%) is used in the form:

```
operand1 % operand2
```

The modulus operator (%) is also known as the *remainder operator*. The modulus operator (%) performs division on the right-hand operand by its left-hand operand and returns the remainder of that division operation, for example `7%5` evaluates to `2`. All rules that we discussed about the numeric data conversion of the operands and the determination of the data type of the expression involving the addition operator (+) are also applicable for expressions that involves the modulus operator (%). Since the use of the modulus operator (%) involves a division operation, there are some special rules, which decide the result of a modulus operation. If both operands of the modulus operator are integers, the following rules are applied to compute the result.

- It is a runtime error if the right-hand operand is zero. For example,

  ```
  int num;
  num = 15 % 0;        // Runtime error
  ```

- If the right-hand operand is not zero, the sign of the result is the same as the sign of the left-hand operand. For example,

  ```
  int num;
  num = 15 % 6;   // Assigns 3 to num
  ```

```
num = -15 % 6;  // Assigns -3 to num
num = 15 % -6;  // Assigns 3 to num
num = -15 % -6;// Assigns -3 to num because left-hand operand
               // is -15, which is negative
num = 5 % 7;    // Assigns 5 to num
num = 0 % 7;    // Assigns 0 to num
```

- If either operand of the modulus operator is a floating-point number, the following rules are applied to compute the result.
- The operation never results in an error even if the right-hand operand is a floating-point zero.
- The result is NaN if either operand is NaN. For example,

```
float f1;
double d1;
f1 = Float.NaN % 10.5F;      // Assigns Float.NaN to f1
f1 = 20.0F % Float.NaN;      // Assigns Float.NaN to f1
f1 = Float.NaN % Float.NaN;  // Assigns Float.NaN to f1

// Compile-time error. The expression is of type double
// and double to float assignment is not allowed
f1 = Float.NaN % Double.NaN;

d1 = Float.NaN % Double.NaN; // Assigns Double.NaN to d1
```

- If the right-hand operand is zero, the result is `NaN`. For example,

```
float f1;
f1 = 15.0F % 0.0F;    // Assigns Float.NaN to f1
```

- If the left-hand operand is infinity, the result is NaN. For example,

```
float f1;
f1 = Float.POSITIVE_INFINITY % 2.1F; // Assigns Float.NaN to f1
```

- If none of the above rules applies, the modulus operator returns the remainder of the division of the left-hand operand and the right-hand operand. The sign of the result is the same as the sign of the left-hand operand. For example,

```
float f1;
double d1;
f1 = 15.5F % 6.5F;    // Assigns 2.5F to f1
d1 = 5.5 % 15.65;     // Assigns 5.5 to d1
d1 = 0.0 % 3.78;      // Assigns 0.0 to d1
d1 = 85.0 % Double.POSITIVE_INFINITY;   // Assigns 85.0 to d1
d1 = -85.0 % Double.POSITIVE_INFINITY;  // Assigns -85.0 to d1
d1 = 85.0 % Double.NEGATIVE_INFINITY;   // Assigns 85.0 to d1
d1 = -85.0 % Double.NEGATIVE_INFINITY;  // Assigns -85.0 to d1
```

Unary Plus Operator (+)

The unary plus operator (+) is used in the form:

```
+operand
```

The `operand` must be a primitive numeric type. If the `operand` is of type `byte`, `short`, or `char`, the unary plus operator promotes it to `int` type. Otherwise, there is no effect of using this operator. For example, if there is an `int` variable `num`, which has a value of 5, `+num` still has the same value 5. The following example illustrates the use this operator.

```
byte b1 = 10;
byte b2 = 5;

b1 = b2;  // Ok. byte to byte assignment

/* Compiler error. b2 is of type byte. But, use of unary plus operator
   (+) on b2 promoted its type to int. Therefore, +b2 is of type int.
   However, int (+b2) to byte (b1) assignment is not allowed.
*/
b1 = +b2;

b1 = (byte) +b2;    // Ok
```

Unary Minus Operator (-)

The unary minus operator (-) is used in the form:

```
-operand
```

The unary minus operator arithmetically negates the value of its operand. The `operand` must be a primitive numeric type. If the type of the `operand` is `byte`, `short`, or `char`, it promotes the operand to the `int` type. The following example illustrates the use the unary minus operator.

```
byte b1 = 10;
byte b2 = 5;

b1 = b2;  // Ok. byte to byte assignment

// Compiler error. b2 is of type byte. But, use of unary minus operator
// (-) on b2 promoted its type to int. So -b2 is of type int. But, int
// (-b2) to byte (b1) assignment is not allowed.
b1 = -b2;

b1 = (byte) -b2;    // Ok
```

Compound Arithmetic Assignment Operators

Each of the five basic arithmetic operators (+, -, *, / and %) has a corresponding compound arithmetic assignment operator. These operators can better be explained with an example. Suppose you have two variables `num1` and `num2` declared as follows.

```
int num1 = 100;
byte num2 = 15;
```

If you want to add the value of `num1` to `num2`, you would write code as:

```
num2 = (byte)(num2 + num1);
```

You need to cast the result of `num2 + num1` to `byte` because the data type of the expression is `int`. The same effect can be rewritten using compound arithmetic operator (+=) as follows.

```
num2 += num1;        // Adds the value of num1 to num2
```

A compound arithmetic assignment operator is used in the following form:

```
operand1 op= operand2
```

Here, `op` is one of the arithmetic operators `+`, `-`, `*`, `/`, and `%`. `operand1` and `operand2` are of primitive numeric data types, where `operand1` must be a variable. The above expression is equivalent to the following expression.

```
operand1 = (Type of operand1) (operand1 op operand2)
```

For example,

```
int i = 100;
i += 5.5;        // Assigns 105 to i
```

is equivalent to:

```
i = (int)(i + 5.5);      // Assigns 105 to i
```

There are two advantages of using the compound arithmetic assignment operators.

- The `operand1` is evaluated only once. For example, in `i += 5.5`, the variable `i` is evaluated only once, whereas in `i = (int) (i + 5.5)`, the variable `i` is evaluated twice.
- The result is automatically cast to type of operand1 before assignment. The cast may result in a narrowing conversion or an identity conversion. In the above example the cast is a narrowing conversion. The expression `i + 5.5` is of type `double` and the result of this expression is cast to `int`. So, the result `double 105.5` is converted to `int 105`. If we write an expression like `i += 5`, the equivalent expression will be `i = (int)(i + 5)`. Since the type of expression `i + 5` is already `int` the casting the result to `int` again is an identity conversion.

The compound assignment operator += can also be applied to String variable. In such case, the `operand1` must be of type String and the `operand2` may be of any type including `boolean`. For example,

```
String str1 = "Hello";
str1 = str1 + 100; // Assigns "Hello100" to str1
```

can be rewritten as:

```
str1 += 100;         // Assigns "Hello100" to str1
```

Note that only += operator can be used with left-hand operand as a String variable.

The following are the examples of using compound assignment operator. In the following examples each use of compound assignment operator is independent of the effects of its previous use. In all cases, it has been assumed that the values of the variables remain the same, as the values assigned to them at the time of their declarations.

```
int i = 110;
float f = 120.2F;
byte b = 5;
String str = "Hello";
boolean b1 = true;

i += 10;  // Assigns 120 to i
i += b1;  // Compiler error. boolean type cannot be used with +=
          // unless left-hand operand (here i) is a String variable

i -= 15;  // Assigns 95 to i. Assuming i was 110
i *= 2;   // Assigns 220 to i. Assuming i was 110
i /= 2;   // Assigns 55 to i. Assuming i was 110
i /= 0;   // Run-time error. Divide by zero error.
f /= 0.0; // Assigns Float.POSITIVE_INFINITY to f
i %= 3;   // Assigns 2 to i. Assuming i is 110

str += " How are you"; // Assigns "Hello How are you" to str
str += f;     // Assigns "Hello120.2" to str. Assuming  str was "Hello"
b += f;       // Assigns 125 to b. Assuming b was 5, f was 120.2
str += b1;    // Assigns "Hellotrue" to str. Assuming str was "Hello"
```

Increment (++) and Decrement (--) Operators

The increment operator (++) is used with a variable of numeric data type to increment its value by 1, whereas the decrement operator (--) is used to decrement the value by 1. In this section, we will discuss only the increment operator. However, the same discussion applies to decrement operator with the only difference that in case of increment operator the operand's value is incremented by 1 and in case of decrement operator the operand's value is decremented by 1.

Suppose there is an int variable i declared as:

```
int i = 100;
```

To increment the value of i by 1, you can use either one of the three following expressions.

```
i = i + 1;    // Assigns 101 to i
i += 1;       // Assigns 101 to i
i++;          // Assigns 101 to i
```

The increment operator ++ can also be used in a more complex expression as:

```
int i = 100;
int j = 50;
j = i++ + 15; // Assigns 115 to j and i becomes 101
```

The expression, i++ + 15, is evaluated as follows.

- The value of i is evaluated and the right-hand expression becomes 100 + 15.

- The value of `i` in memory is incremented by 1. So, at this stage the value of the variable `i` in memory is `101`.
- The expression `100 + 15` is evaluated and the result `115` is assigned to `j`.

There are two kinds of increment operator (++):

- Post-fix increment operator, e.g., `i++`
- Pre-fix increment operator, e.g., `++i`

When ++ appears after its operand, it is called post-fix increment operator. When ++ appears before its operand, it is called pre-fix increment operator. The only difference in using post-fix and pre-fix increment operator is the order of use of the current value of its operand and the increment in its operand's value. The post-fix increment uses the current value of its operand first, and then increments the operand's value, as we saw in the expression `j = i++ + 15`. Since `i++` uses post-fix increment operator, first, the current value of `i` is used to compute the value of expression `i++ + 15` (e.g. `100 + 15`). So, the value assigned to `j` is `115`. And, then, the value of `i` is incremented by `1`. The result would be different if the above expression is rewritten using pre-fix increment operator as:

```
int i = 100;
int j = 50;
j = ++i + 15;  // Assigns 116 to j and i becomes 101
```

In this case, the expression, `++i + 15`, is evaluated as follows.

- Since `++i` uses pre-fix increment operator, first the value of `i` is incremented in memory by 1. Therefore, the value of `i` is `101`.
- The current value of `i`, which is `101` is used in the expression and the expression becomes `101 + 15`.
- The expression `101 + 15` is evaluated and the result `116` is assigned to `j`.

Note the subtle difference in `++i` and `i++` when used in a complex expression. Note that after evaluation of both expressions `i++ + 15` and `++i + 15`, the value of `i` is the same, which is `101`. However, the values assigned to `j` differ. If you are using the increment operator ++ in a simple expression as in `i++` or `++I`, you cannot observe any difference in using post-fix or pre-fix operator because you are not using the value of the operand of ++ to compute the value of any other expression.

There is a puzzle for Java beginners. The puzzle includes the use of increment operator as follows.

```
int i = 15;
i = i++;  // What will be the value of i after this assignment?
```

Guess, what will be the value of `i` after `i = i++` is executed? If your guess is 16, you are wrong. Here is the explanation how the expression, `i = i++`, is evaluated.

- First `i++` is evaluated. Since `i++` uses post-fix increment operator the current value of `i` is used in the expression. The current value of `i` is `15`. So, the expression becomes
- i = 15.

- Now the value of i is incremented by 1 in memory as the second effect of i++. So, at this stage the value of i is 16 in memory.
- Now the expression i = 15 is evaluated and the value 15 is assigned to i. So, the value of the variable i in memory is 15 and that is the final value. In fact, variable i observed a value equal to 16 in the previous step, but this step overwrote that value with 15. So, the final value of the variable i after i = i++ is executed will be 15 not 16.

In the above example, the order of operations is important. It is important to note that in case of i++ the value of the variable i is incremented as soon as the current value of i is used in the expression. To make this point more clear let us consider the following example.

```
int i = 10;
i = i++ + i;        // Assigns 21 to i
i = 10;
i = ++i + i++;      // Assigns 22 to i
```

There are also post-fix and pre-fix decrement operators e.g. i--, --i. The following are examples of using post-fix and pre-fix decrement operators.

```
int i = 15;
int j = 16;
i--;
--i;
i = 10;
i = i--;        // Assigns 10 to i
i = 10;
j = i-- + 10;  // Assigns 20 to j and 9 to i
i = 10;
j = --i + 10;  // Assigns 19 to j and 9 to i
```

There are two important points to remember about the use of increment and decrement operators.

- The operand of the increment and decrement operators must be a variable. For example, the expression 5++ is wrong because ++ is being used with an operand 5, which is a constant not a variable.
- The result of the expression using ++ or -- operator is a value not a variable. For example, i++ evaluates to a value so we cannot use i++ as the left-hand of an assignment operator or where a variable is required. For example,

```
int i = 10;

// Compiler error. i++ evaluates to a value so it cannot be used as
// a left-hand operand with an assignment operator
i++ = i + 10;
```

String Concatenation Operator (+)

The + operator is overloaded. An operator is said to be overloaded if it is used to perform more than one function. So far, we have seen its use as an arithmetic addition operator to add two numbers, for example, in the expression 3 + 5. It can also be used to concatenate two strings.

Two strings, say `"abc"` and `"xyz"`, can be concatenated using + operator as `"abc"` + `"xyz"` to produce a new string `"abcxyz"`. Another example of string concatenation is:

```
String str1 = "Hello";
String str2 = " Alekhya";
String str3;
str3 = str1 + str2;     // Assigns "Hello Alekhya" to str3
```

The string concatenation operator is also used to concatenate a string and a primitive or a reference data type value. We will discuss only concatenation of string and primitive data types in this section. We will cover the concatenation of any reference data type and string in the chapter on *Classes and Objects*. When either operand of + is a string, it performs string concatenation. When both operands of + are numeric, it performs number addition. Let us consider the following snippet of code.

```
int num = 26;
String str1 = "Alphabets";
String str2 = num + str1;    // Assigns "26Alphabets" to str2
```

When the expression, `num + str1`, is executed, + acts as a string concatenation operator, because its right-hand operand `str1` is a String. Before `num` and `str1` are concatenated, `num` is replaced by its string representation, which is `"26"`. Now, the expression becomes `"26"` + `str1`, which results in `"26Alphabets"`. Table 4-2 lists the string representations of the values of primitive data types in Java.

Table 4-2: String representations of the values of primitive data types

Data Type	Value	String representation
`int, short, byte, long`	`1678`	`"1678"`
	`0`	`"0"`
`char`	`'A'`	`"A"`
	`'\u0041'` (Unicode escape sequence)	`"A"`
`boolean`	`true`	`"true"`
	`false`	`"false"`
`float`	`2.5`	`"2.5"`
	`0.0F`	`"0.0"`
	`-0.0F`	`"-0.0"`
	`Float.POSITIVE_INFINITY`	`"Infinity"`
	`Float.NEGATIVE_INFINITY`	`"-Infinity"`
	`Float.NaN`	`"NaN"`
`double`	`89.12`	`"89.12"`
	`0.0`	`"0.0"`
	`-0.0`	`"-0.0"`
	`Double.POSITIVE_INFINITY`	`"Infinity"`
	`Double.NEGATIVE_INFINITY`	`"-Infinity"`
	`Double.NaN`	`"NaN"`

If a `String` variable contains a `null` reference, the concatenation operator + uses string `"null"` in place of the `null` reference. The following examples illustrate the uses of string representations of the values of primitive data types in string concatenation.

```
boolean b1 = true;
boolean b2 = false;
int num = 365;
double d = -0.0;
char c = 'A';
String str1;
String str2 = null;

str1 = b1 + " friends";      // Assigns "true friends" to str1
str1 = b2 + " identity";     // Assigns "false identity" to str1

// Assigns "null and void" to str1. Since str2 is null, it is
// replaced by a string "null" by the concatenation operator
str1 = str2 + " and void";

str1 = num + " days";        // Assigns "365 days" to str1
str1 = d + " zero";          // Assigns "-0.0 zero" to str1

str1 = Double.NaN + " is absurd"; // Assigns "NaN is absurd" to str1

str1 = c + " is a letter";   // Assigns "A is a letter" to str1
str1 = "This is " + b1;      // Assigns "This is true" to str1

// Assigns "Beyond Infinity" to str1
str1 = "Beyond " + Float.POSITIVE_INFINITY
```

It may be, sometimes, confusing to determine the result of an expression which uses more than one + operator and strings. What will be the result of the expression `12 + 15 + " men"`? Will the result be `"1215 men"` or `"27 men"`? The key to finding the correct answers in such cases is to find which + is arithmetic operator and which + is string concatenation operator. If both the operands are numeric, the + operator performs addition. If either operand is a string, the + operator performs string concatenation. The execution of an expression proceeds from left to right unless overridden by using parentheses. So, in the expression `12 + 15 + " men"`, the first + from left performs addition on `12` and `15`, which results in `27`. After this step, the expression reduces to `27 + " men"`. Now, the + operator performs a string concatenation, because the right-hand operand, `" men"` is a string and it results in `"27 men"`. Let us consider the following piece of code.

```
int num1 = 12;
int num2 = 15;
String str1 = " men";
String str2;
```

Now, we want to create a string "1215 men" using the three variables `num1`, `num2` and `str1` and the + operator and we want to assign that string to `str2`. If we write as:

```
str2 = num1 + num2 + str1;
```

a string "27 men" will be assigned to `str2`. One of the solutions is to place `num2 + str1` in parentheses as:

```
str2 = num1 + (num2 + str1); // Assigns "1215 men" to str2
```

Since the expression in parentheses is evaluated first, the expression `(num2 + str1)` will be evaluated first to reduce the expression to `num1 + "15 men"`, which in turn will evaluate to `"1215 men"`. Another option is to place an empty string in the beginning of the expression as:

```
str2 = "" + num1 + num2 + str1;   // Assigns "1215 men" to str1
```

In the above case, `"" + num1` is evaluated first, and it results in `"12"`, which reduces the expression to `"12" + num2 + str1`. Now, `"12" + num2` is evaluated, which results in `"1215"`. Now, the expression is reduced to `"1215" + " men"`, which results in the string `"1215 men"`. You may also place an empty string between `num1` and `num2` in the expression to get the result as:

```
str2 = num1 + "" + num2 + str1;   // Assigns "1215 men" to str2
```

Sometimes, the string concatenation is trickier than you might think. Let us consider the following piece of code.

```
int num = 15;
boolean b = false;
String str1 = "faces"
String str2;

str2 = b + num + str1;  // Will generate a compiler error
```

The last line in the above snippet of code will generate compiler error. What is wrong with the statement? You were expecting a string `"false15faces"` to be assigned to `str2`. Weren't you? Let us analyze the expression `b + num + str1`. Is the first + operator from left an arithmetic operator or a string concatenation operator? For a + operator to be a string concatenation operator, it is necessary that at least one of its operands is a string. Since neither `b` nor `num` is a string, the first + operator from left in `b + num + str1` is not a string concatenation operator. Is it an arithmetic addition operator? Its operands are of type `boolean` (b) and `int` (num). We have learned that an arithmetic addition operator (+) cannot have a `boolean` operand. So, the presence of a `boolean` operand in the expression `b + num` caused the compiler error. A `boolean` cannot be added to a number. However, the + operator works on a `boolean` as a string concatenation operator if another operand is a string. To correct the above compiler error, we can rewrite the expression in a number of ways as shown below.

```
str2 = b + (num + str1);   // Ok. Assigns "false15faces" to str2
str2 = "" + b + num + str1; // Ok. Assigns "false15faces" to str2
str2 = b + "" + num + str1; // Ok. Assigns "false15faces" to str2
```

We use `println()` and `print()` method to print a message on the standard output as follows.

```
System.out.println("Prints a new line at the end of text");
System.out.print("Does not print a new line at the end of text");
```

If you use the `System.out.println()` method to print a text on the console, after printing the text, it also prints a new line character at the end of the text. The only difference between using the `System.out.println()` method and the `System.out.print()` method is that the former prints a new line at the end of the text, whereas the latter does not. The `println()` and `print()` methods are overloaded. Until now, we have seen their use only with string arguments. You can pass any Java data type argument to these two methods. The following snippet of code illustrates how to pass Java primitive types as arguments to these methods.

```
int num = 156;

// Prints 156 on the console
System.out.println(num);

// Prints, Value of num = 156, on the console
System.out.println("Value of num = " + num);

// Prints a new line character on the console
System.out.println();
```

Listing 4-1 has a complete program to demonstrate uses of arithmetic operators and string concatenation operator.

Listing 4-1: An example of using Java operators

```java
// ArithOperator.java
package com.jdojo.chapter4;

class ArithOperator {
    public static void main ( String[] args ) {
        int num = 120;
        double realNum = 25.5F;
        double veryBigNum = 25.8 / 0.0;
        double garbage = 0.0 / 0.0;
        boolean test = true;

        // Print the value of num
        System.out.println ("num = " + num);

        // Print the value of realNum
        System.out.println ("realNum = " + realNum);

        // Print the value of veryBigNum
        System.out.println ("veryBigNum = " + veryBigNum);

        // Print the value of garbage
        System.out.println ("garbage = " + garbage);

        // Print the value of test
        System.out.println ("test = " + test);

        // Print the maximum value of int type
        System.out.println ("Maximum int = " + Integer.MAX_VALUE);

        // Print the maximum value of double type
        System.out.println ("Maximum double = " + Double.MAX_VALUE);

        // Print the sum of two numbers
        System.out.println ("12.5 + 100 = " + (12.5 + 100));

        // Print the difference of two numbers
        System.out.println ("12.5 - 100 = " + (12.5 - 100));

        // Print the multiplication of two numbers
        System.out.println ("12.5 * 100 = " + (12.5 * 100));
```

```
        // Print the result of division
        System.out.println ("12.5 / 100 = " + (12.5 / 100));

        // Print the result of modulus
        System.out.println ("12.5 % 100 = " + (12.5 % 100));

        // Print the result of string concatenation
        System.out.println ("\"abc\" + \"xyz\" = " + "\"" +
                            ("abc" + "xyz") + "\"");

    }
}
```

```
Output:

num = 120
realNum = 25.5
veryBigNum = Infinity
garbage = NaN
test = true
Maximum int = 2147483647
Maximum double = 1.7976931348623157E308
12.5 + 100 = 112.5
12.5 - 100 = -87.5
12.5 * 100 = 1250.0
12.5 / 100 = 0.125
12.5 % 100 = 12.5
"abc" + "xyz" = "abcxyz"
```

Relational Operators

Table 4-3 lists all relational operators available in Java.

Table 4-3: List of relational Operators in Java

Operators	Meaning	Type	Usage	Result
==	Equal to	Binary	3 == 2	false
!=	Not equal to	Binary	3 != 2	true
>	Greater than	Binary	3 > 2	true
>=	Greater than or equal to	Binary	3 >= 2	true
<	Less than	Binary	3 < 2	false
<=	Less than or equal to	Binary	3 <= 2	false

All relational operators are binary operators. That is, they take two operands. The result produced by a relational operator is always a `boolean` value: `true` or `false`.

Equality Operator (==)

The equality operator (==) is used in the form:

```
operand1 == operand2
```

The operands used with the equality operator (==) can be of primitive data types or of reference data types. However, you cannot use both types of operands with the same equality operator. If the operands to == are of primitive types, it returns `true` if the both operands represent the same value; otherwise it returns `false`. If the operands to == are of reference types, it returns `true` if the both operands refer to the same object in memory; otherwise it returns `false`. If both the operands to == operator are primitive types, both must be of either numeric type or `boolean` type. The mix of numeric and `boolean` types is not allowed with == operator. Suppose there is an `int` variable `i` declared as follows.

```
int i = 10;
```

Now `i == 10` will test whether `i` is equal to 10 or not. Since `i` is equal to `10`, the expression `i == 10` will evaluates to `true`. Let us consider another example which uses == operator.

```
int i;
int j;
int k;
boolean b;

i = j = k = 15; // Assign 15 to i, j and k
b = (i == j == k); // Compiler error
```

In the above example we tried to test, whether the three variables `i`, `j` and `k` have the same value and the expression `(i == j == k)` resulted in error. Why did we get compiler error in expression `(i == j == k)`? The expression `(i == j == k)` is evaluated as follows.

- First, `i == j` is evaluated in expression `i == j == k`. Since both `i` and `j` have the same value, which is `15` the expression `i == j` returns `true`.
- After step1 the expression `i == j == k` becomes `true == k`. This is an error because the operands of == operator are of `boolean` and `int` types. The rule about the types of operands of the equality operator (==) is: "Both operands must be either `boolean` types, or numeric types, or reference types".

The following rules apply when the operands of the equality operator are floating-point types.

- Both negative zero (-0.0) and positive zero (0.0) are considered equal. Note that -0.0 and 0.0 are stored differently in memory. For example,

  ```
  double d1 = 0.0;
  double d2 = -0.0;
  boolean b;
  b = (d1 == d2); // Assigns true to b
  ```

- Positive and negative infinities are considered unequal. For example,

  ```
  double d1 = Double.POSITIVE_INFINITY;
  double d2 = Double.NEGATIVE_INFINITY;
  ```

```
boolean b;
b = (d1 == d2); // Assigns false to b
```

- If either operand is NaN the equality test returns `false`. For example,

```
double d1 = Double.NaN;
double d2 = 5.5;
boolean b;

b = (d1 == d2); // Assigns false to b
```

Note that even if both the operands are NaN the equality operator will return false as:

```
d1 = Double.NaN;
d2 = Double.NaN;

b = (d1 == d2); // Assigns false to b
```

How do you test whether the value stored in a `float` or `double` variable is `NaN` or not? If you write the following piece of code to test for the value of a `double` variable d1 being NaN, it will always return `false`.

```
double d1 = Double.NaN;
boolean b;

b = (d1 == Double.NaN); // Assigns false to b. Incorrect way
```

`Float` and `Double` classes have an `isNaN()` method, which accepts a `float` and a `double` argument respectively. It returns `true` if the argument is `NaN`, Otherwise, it returns `false`. For example, to test if d1 is `NaN`, the above expression can be rewritten using `isNaN()` method of the `Double` class as:

```
double d1 = Double.NaN;

// Assigns true to b. Correct way to test for NaN value
b = Double.isNaN(d1);
```

You should not use == operator to test two strings for equality. For example,

```
String str1 = new String("Hello");
String str2 = new String("Hello");
boolean b;

b = (str1 == str2);    // Assigns false to b
```

The `new` operator always creates a new object in memory. Therefore, str1 and str2 refer to two different objects in memory and this is why `str1 == str2` evaluates to `false`. It is true that both `String` objects in memory have the same text. Whenever == operator is used with reference variables it always compares the references of the objects its operands are referring to. To compare the text represented by two `String` variables str1 and str2, you should use the `equals()` method of the `String` class as:

```
// Assigns true to b because str1 and str2 have the same text "Hello"
```

```
b = str1.equals(str2);

// Assigns true to b because str1 and str2 have the same text "Hello"
b = str2.equals(str1);
```

We will discuss more about strings comparisons in the chapter on *Strings and Dates* in this book.

Inequality Operator (!=)

The inequality operator (!=) is used in the form:

```
operand1 != operand2
```

The inequality operator (!=) returns `true` if `operand1` and `operand2` are not equal. Otherwise, it returns `false`. The rules for the data types of the operands of inequality (!=) operator are the same that of equality operator (==). That is, both operands of the inequality operator must be either primitive types or reference types. If both operands are of primitive types, both must be either numeric or `boolean` types. For example,

```
int i = 15;
int j = 10;
int k = 15;
boolean b;
b = (i != j);          // Assigns true to b
b = (i != k);          // Assigns false to b
b = (true != true);    // Assigns false to b
b = (true != false);   // Assigns true to b
```

If either operand is `NaN` (`float` or `double`), inequality operator returns `true`. If d1 is a floating-point variable (`double` or `float`), d1 == d1 returns `false` and d1 != d1 returns `true` if and only if d1 is `NaN`.

Greater than Operator (>)

The greater than operator (>) is used in the form:

```
operand1 > operand2
```

The greater than operator returns true if the value of `operand1` is greater than the value of `operand2`. Otherwise, it returns `false`. The greater than operator can be used only with primitive numeric data types. If either of the operand is `NaN` (`float` or `double`), the greater than operator returns `false`. For example,

```
int i = 10;
int j = 15;
double d1 = Double.NaN;
boolean b;

b = (i > j);   // Assigns false to b
b = (j > i);   // Assigns true to b
```

```
// Compiler error. > can't be used with boolean operands
b = (true > false);

b = ( d1 > Double.NaN ); // Assigns false to b

String str1 = "Hello";
String str2 = "How is Java?";

// Compiler error. > can't be used with reference type operands str1
// and str2
b = (str1 > str2);
```

If you want to test if the number of characters in `String str1` is greater than that of str2, you should use the `length()` method of the `String` class. The `length()` method of `String` class returns the number of characters in a string. For example,

```
i = str1.length(); // Assigns 5 to i. "Hello" has 5 characters

b = (str1.length() > str2.length()); // Assigns false to b
b = (str2.length() > str1.length()); // Assigns true to b
```

Greater than or Equal to Operator (>=)

The greater than or equal to operator (>=) is used in the form:

```
operand1 >= operand2
```

The greater than or equal to operator returns `true` if the value of `operand1` is greater than or equal to the value of `operand2`. Otherwise, it returns `false`. The greater than or equal to operator can be used only with primitive numeric data types. If either of the operand is `NaN` (`float` or `double`), greater than or equal to operator returns `false`. For example,

```
int i = 10;
int j = 10;
boolean b;

b = (i >= j); // Assigns true to b
b = (j >= i); // Assigns true to b
```

Less than Operator (<)

The less than operator (<) is used in the form:

```
operand1 < operand2
```

The less than operator returns `true`, if `operand1` is less than `operand2`. Otherwise, it returns `false`. The less than operator can be used only with primitive numeric data types. If either operand is `NaN` (`float` or `double`), the less than operator returns `false`. For example,

```
int i = 10;
int j = 15;
```

```
double d1 = Double.NaN;
boolean b;

b = (i < j);  // Assigns true to b
b = (j < i);  // Assigns false to b

// Compiler error. < can't be used with boolean operands
b = (true < false);

b = (d1 < Double.NaN); // Assigns false to b
```

Less than or Equal to Operator (<=)

The less than or equal to operator (<=) is used in the form:

```
operand1 <= operand2
```

The less than or equal to operator returns `true` if the value of `operand1` is less than or equal to the value of `operand2`. Otherwise, it returns `false`. The less than or equal to operator can be used only with primitive numeric data types. If either of the operand is `NaN` (`float` or `double`), less than or equal to operator returns `false`.

For example,

```
int i = 10;
int j = 10;
int k = 15;
boolean b;

b = (i <= j); // Assigns true to b
b = (j <= i); // Assigns true to b
b = (j <= k); // Assigns true to b
b = (k <= j); // Assigns false to b
```

Boolean Logical Operators

Table 4-4 lists boolean logical operators that are available in Java. All boolean logical operators can be used only with `boolean` operand(s). Subsequent sections will explain the usage of these operators in details.

Table 4-4: List of boolean logical operators

Operators	Meaning	Type	Usage	Result
!	Logical NOT	Unary	!true	false
&&	Short-circuit AND	Binary	true && true	true
&	Logical AND	Binary	true & true	true
||	Short-circuit OR	Binary	true || false	true
|	Logical OR	Binary	true | false	true

^	Logical XOR(Exclusive OR)	Binary	`true ^ true`	`false`
&=	AND assignment	Binary	`test &= true`	
|=	OR assignment	Binary	`test |= true`	
^=	XOR assignment	Binary	`test ^= true`	

Logical NOT Operator (!)

The logical NOT operator (!) is used in the form:

```
!operand
```

The logical NOT operator returns true if operand is false, and false if operand is true. For example,

```
int i = 10;
int j = 15;
boolean b;

b = !true;     // Assigns false to b
b = !false;    // Assigns true to b

boolean b1 = true;
b = !b1;       // Assigns false to b
b = !(i > j);  // Assigns true to b , because i > j returns false
```

Suppose you want to change the value of a boolean variable b to true if its current value is false, and to false if its current value is true. This can be achieved as:

```
b = !b; // Assigns true to b if it was false and false if it was true
```

Logical Short-Circuit AND Operator (&&)

The logical short-circuit AND operator (&&) is used in the form:

```
operand1 && operand2
```

The logical short-circuit AND operator returns true if both operands are true. If either operand is false, it returns false. It is called short-circuit AND operator because if operand1 (the left-hand operand) evaluates to false, it does not evaluate operand2 (the right-hand operand) and immediately returns false. For example,

```
int i = 10;
int j = 15;
boolean b;

b = (i > 5 && j > 10);  // Assigns true to b
```

In the above expression i > 5 is evaluated first and it returns true. Since the left hand operand evaluated to true, the right hand operand is also evaluated. The right-hand operand j > 10 is evaluated, which also returns `true`. Now, the expression is reduced to `true && true`. Since both operands to `&&` operator are `true`, it returns `true`. Consider another example as:

```
int i = 10;
int j = 15;
boolean b;

b = (i > 20 && j > 10);      // Assigns false to b
```

The expression, `i > 20`, returns `false`. So, the expression reduces to `false && j > 10`. Since the left-hand operand to `&&` operator is `false`, the right-hand operand `j > 10` is not evaluated and `&&` returns `false`. However, there is no way to prove in the above example that the right-hand operand to `&&`, which is `j > 10`, was not evaluated. Let us consider another example to prove this point. We have already discussed the assignment operator (=). If `num` is a variable of type int, `num = 10` returns a value equal to 10.

```
int num = 10;
boolean b;

b = ((num = 50) > 5);   // Assigns true to b
```

Note the use of parentheses in the above example. In the expression `((num = 50) > 5)`, the expression, `num = 50`, is executed first. It assigns `50` to `num` and returns `50` reducing the expression to `(50 > 5)`, which in turn returns `true`. If you use the value of `num` after the expression, `num = 50`, is executed, its value will be `50`. Keeping this point in mind let us consider the following snippet of code.

```
int i = 10;
int j = 10;
boolean b;

b = (i > 5 && ((j = 20) > 15));

System.out.println("b = " + b);
System.out.println("i = " + i);
System.out.println("j = " + j);
```

The above piece of code will print:

```
b = true
i = 10
j = 20
```

Because the left-hand operand, which is `i > 5` evaluated to `true`, the right-hand operand `((j = 20) > 15)` was evaluated and the variable `j` was assigned a value of 20. If we change the above piece of code, so that the left-hand operand evaluates to `false`, the right-hand operand would not be evaluated and the value of `j` will remain 10. The changed piece of code is as follows.

```
int i = 10;
int j = 10;
boolean b;

b = (i > 25 && ((j = 20) > 15)); // ((j = 20) > 5) is not evaluated
                                 // because i > 25 returns false
```

```
System.out.println ("b = " + b);
System.out.println ("i = " + i);
System.out.println ("j = " + j); // Will print j = 10
```

The above piece of code will print:

```
b = false
i = 10
j = 10
```

Logical AND Operator (&)

The logical AND operator (&) is used in the form:

```
operand1 & operand2
```

The logical AND operator returns true if both operands are true. If either operand is false, it returns false. The logical AND operator (&) works the same as the logical short-circuit AND operator (&&) with one difference. The logical AND operator (&) evaluates its right-hand operand even if its left-hand operand evaluates to false. For example,

```
int i = 10;
int j = 15;
boolean b;

b = (i > 5 & j > 10);            // Assigns true to b
b = (i > 25 & ((j = 20) > 15));  // ((j = 20) > 5) is evaluated even
                                 // if i > 25 returns false
System.out.println ("b = " + b);
System.out.println ("i = " + i);
System.out.println ("j = " + j);  // Will print j = 20
```

The above piece of code will print:

```
b = false
i = 10
j = 20
```

Logical Short-Circuit OR Operator (| |)

The logical short-circuit OR operator (||) is used in the form:

```
operand1 || operand2
```

The logical short-circuit OR operator returns true if either operand is true. If both operands are false, it returns false. It is called a short-circuit OR operator, because if operand1 (the left-hand operand) evaluates to true, it does not evaluate operand2 (the right-hand operand) and immediately returns true. For example,

```
int i = 10;
```

```
int j = 15;
boolean b;

b = (i > 5 || j > 10);  // Assigns true to b
```

In the above expression, `i > 5` is evaluated first, and it returns `true`. Since the left-hand operand evaluated to `true`, the right hand operand is not evaluated, and the expression (`i > 5 || j > 10`) returns `true`. Consider another example as:

```
int i = 10;
int j = 15;
boolean b;

b = (i > 20 || j > 10);     // Assigns true to b
```

The expression, `i > 20`, returns `false`. So, the expression reduces to `false || j > 10`. Since the left-hand operand to `||` is `false`, the right-hand operand `j > 10` is evaluated, which returns `true` and the entire expression returns `true`.

Logical OR Operator (|)

The logical `OR` operator (|) is used in the form:

```
operand1 | operand2
```

The logical `OR` operator returns `true` if either operand is `true`. If both operands are `false`, it returns `false`. The logical `OR` operator (|) works the same as the logical short-circuit `OR` operator (||) with one difference. The logical `OR` operator (|) evaluates its right-hand operand even if its left-hand operand evaluates to `true`. For example,

```
int i = 10;
int j = 15;
boolean b;

b = (i > 5 | j > 10);  // Assigns true to b
```

The above expression, `i > 5`, is evaluated first and it returns `true`. Even if the left-hand operand `i > 5` evaluates to `true`, the right-hand operand, `j > 15`, is still evaluated, and the whole expression, (`i > 5 | j > 10`), returns `true`.

Logical XOR Operator (^)

The logical `XOR` operator (^) is used in the form:

```
operand1 ^ operand2
```

The logical `XOR` operator (^) returns `true` if `operand1` and `operand2` are different. That is, it returns `true` if one of the operands is `true`, but not both. If both operands are the same, it returns `false`. For example,

```
int i = 10;
boolean b;

b = true ^ true;        // Assigns false to b
b = true ^ false;       // Assigns true to b
b = false ^ true;       // Assigns true to b
b = false ^ false;      // Assigns false to b
b = (i > 5 ^ i < 15);   // Assigns false to b
```

Compound Boolean Logical Assignment Operators

We have only three compound boolean logical assignment operators. Note that Java does not have any operators like `&&=` and `||=`. These operators are used in the form:

```
operand1 op= operand2
```

The `operand1` must be a `boolean` variable and `op` may be `&`, `|`, or `^`. The above form is equivalent to writing.

```
operand1 = operand1 op operand2
```

Table 4-5 shows the compound logical assignment operators and their equivalents.

Table 4-5: Compound Logical Assignment Operators and their equivalents

Expression	is equivalent to
operand1 &= operand2	operand1 = operand1 & operand2
operand1 |= operand2	operand1 = operand1 | operand2
operand1 ^= operand2	operand1 = operand1 ^ operand2

If both operands evaluate to `true`, `&=` returns `true`. Otherwise, it returns `false`. For example,

```
boolean b = true;
b &= true;      // Assigns true to b
b &= false;     // Assigns false to b
```

If either operand evaluates to `true`, `!=` returns `true`. Otherwise, it returns `false`. For example,

```
boolean b = false;
b |= true;      // Assigns true to b
b |= false;     // Assigns false to b
```

If both operands evaluate to different values, that is, one of the operands is `true` but not both, `^=` returns `true`. Otherwise, it returns `false`. For example,

```
boolean b = true;
b ^= true;      // Assigns false to b
b ^= false;     // Assigns true to b
```

Ternary Operator (? :)

Java has one conditional operator. It is called ternary operator. It takes three operands. It is used in the form:

```
boolean-expression ? true-expression : false-expression
```

Two symbols, "?" and ":", make the ternary operator. If `boolean-expression` evaluates to true, it evaluates `true-expression`; otherwise, it evaluates `false-expression`. Suppose you have three integer variables - `num1`, `num2`, and `minNum`. You want to assign `minNum` the minimum of `num1` and `num2`. You can use ternary operator to accomplish this task as follows.

```
int num1 = 50;
int num2 = 25;
int minNum;

// Assigns num2 to minNum, because num2 is less than num1
minNum = (num1 < num2 ? num1 : num2);
```

Operators Precedence

Consider the following piece of code.

```
int result;
result = 10 + 8 / 2;    // What will be the value assigned to result?
```

What will be the value assigned to the variable `result` after the last statement in the above piece of code is executed? Will it be 9 or 14? It depends on the operation that is done first. It will be 9 if the addition `10 + 8` is performed first. It will be `14` if the division `8/2` is performed first. All expressions in Java are evaluated according to operator precedence hierarchy, which establishes the rules that govern the order in which expressions are evaluated. Operators, which have higher precedence, are evaluated first and the operators, which have lower precedence, are evaluated afterwards. If operators have the same precedence, the expression is evaluated from left to right. Multiplication, division and remainder operators have higher precedence than addition and subtraction operators do. So, in the above expression 8/2 is evaluated first which reduces the expression to 10 + 4, which in turn results in 14. Consider the following expression.

```
result = 10 * 5 / 2;
```

The expression, `10 * 5 / 2`, uses two operators - multiplication operator and division operator. Since both operators have the same precedence, the expression is evaluated from left to right. First, the expression, `10 * 5`, is evaluated, and then the expression, `50 / 2`, is evaluated. The whole expression evaluates to `25`. If you wanted to perform division first, you must use parentheses. Parentheses have the highest precedence and therefore, the expression within parentheses is evaluated first. We can rewrite the above piece of code using parentheses as:

```
result = 10 * (5 / 2); // Assigns 20 to result. Why?
```

You can also use nested parentheses. In nested parentheses, the innermost parentheses' expression is evaluated first. Table 4-6 lists all Java operators in their precedence order. Operators in the same level have the same precedence. Table 4-6 lists some of the operators we have not discussed yet. We will discuss those operators later in this chapter or in other chapters in this book.

Table 4-6: Java operators and their precedence

Order of Precedence	Level	Operator Symbol	Action Performed
Highest	1	++	Pre-or-post increment
		--	Pre-or-post decrement
		+, -	Unary plus, unary minus
		~	Bitwise complement
		!	Logical Not
		(type)	cast
	2	*, /, %	Multiplication, division, remainder
	3	+, -	Addition, subtraction
		+	String concatenation
	4	<<	Left shift
		>>	Signed right shift
		>>>	Unsigned right shift
	5	<	Less than
		<=	Less than or equal
		>	Greater than
		>=	Greater than or equal
		instanceof	Type comparison
	6	==	Equal in value
		!=	Not equal to
	7	&	Bitwise AND
		&	Logical AND
	8	^	Bitwise XOR
		^	Logical XOR
	9	|	Bitwise OR
		|	Logical OR
	10	&&	Logical short-circuit AND
	11	||	Logical short-circuit OR
	12	?:	Ternary operator
	13	=	Assignment
Lowest		+=, -=, *=, /=, %=, <<=, >>=, >>>=, &=, |=, ^=	Compound assignment

Bitwise Operators

Bitwise operators are listed in Table 4-7.

Table 4-7: List of bitwise operators

Operators	Meaning	Type	Usage	Result
&	Bitwise AND	Binary	25 & 24	24
|	Bitwise OR	Binary	25 | 2	27
^	Bitwise XOR	Binary	25 ^ 2	27
~	Bitwise NOT (1's complement)	Unary	~25	-26
<<	Left shift	Binary	25 << 2	100
>>	Signed right shift	Binary	25 >> 2	6
>>>	Unsigned right shift	Binary	25 >>> 2	6
&=, !=, ^=, <<=, >>=, >>>=	Compound assignment Bitwise operators	Binary		

All bitwise operators work with only integers. The bitwise AND (&) operator operates on corresponding bits of its two operands and returns 1 if both bits are 1 and 0 otherwise. Note that the bitwise AND (&) operates on each bit of the respective operands and not on the operands as a whole. Following is the result of all bit combination using bitwise AND (&) operator.

```
1 & 1 = 1
1 & 0 = 0
0 & 1 = 0
0 & 0 = 0
```

Consider the following piece of code in Java.

```
int i = 13 & 3;
```

The value of 13 & 3 is computed as follows. The 32 bits have been shown in 8 bits chunk just for clarity. In memory, all 32 bits are contiguous.

```
13        ----     00000000  00000000 00000000 00001101
 3        ----     00000000  00000000 00000000 00000011
-----------------------------------------------------------------
13 & 3    ----     00000000  00000000 00000000 00000001 (Equal to decimal 1)
```

Therefore, 13 & 3 results in 1, which is assigned to i in the above piece of code.

The bitwise OR (|) operates on corresponding bits of its operands and returns 1 if either bit is 1 and 0 otherwise. Following is the result of all bit combination using bitwise OR (|) operator.

```
1 | 1 = 1
1 | 0 = 1
0 | 1 = 1
```

```
0 | 0 = 0
```

The value of 13 | 3 can be computed as follows. The result of 13 | 3 is 15.

```
13          ----      00000000 00000000 00000000 00001101
 3          ----      00000000 00000000 00000000 00000011
-------------------------------------------------------------------
13 | 3                00000000 00000000 00000000 00001111 (Equal to decimal 15)
```

The bitwise XOR (^) operates on corresponding bits of its operands and returns 1 if only one of the bits is 1. Otherwise, it returns 0. Following is the result of all bit combination using bitwise XOR (^) operator.

```
1 ^ 1 = 0
1 ^ 0 = 1
0 ^ 1 = 1
0 ^ 0 = 0
```

The value of 13 ^ 3 can be computed as follows. The result of 13 | 3 is 14.

```
13        ---- 00000000 00000000 00000000 00001101
 3        ---- 00000000 00000000 00000000 00000011
-------------------------------------------------------------------
13 ^ 3    ---- 00000000 00000000 00000000 00001110  (Equal to decimal 14)
```

The bitwise NOT (~) operates on each bit of its operand. It inverts the bits, that is, 1 is changed to 0 and 0 is changed to 1. The bitwise NOT operator (~) is also called bitwise complement operator. It computes 1's complement of its operand. Following is the result of all bit combination using bitwise NOT (~) operator.

```
~1 = 0
~0 = 1
```

The value of ~13 can be computed as follows. The result of ~13 is -14.

```
13      ----      00000000 00000000 00000000 00001101
-------------------------------------------------------------------
~13     ----      11111111 11111111 11111111 11110010   (Equal to decimal -14)
```

The bitwise left shift operator (<<) shifts all the bits to the left by the number of bits specified as its right-hand operand. It inserts zeros at the lower order bits. The effect of shifting 1 bit to right is same as multiplying the number by 2. Therefore, 9 << 1 will produce 18 , whereas 9 << 2 produces 36. The procedure to compute 13 << 4 can be depicted as shown in Figure 4-1.

Figure 4-1: Computing 13 << 4

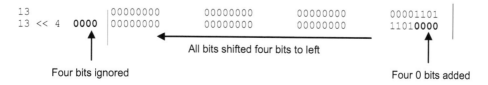

What is the result of 13 << 35? You might have guessed zero. However, this is not true. In fact, only 32 bits are used to represent 13 (13 is considered as `int` literal and `int` occupies 32 bits). Therefore, you can shift all bits to the left only by 31 bits in an `int`. If the left-hand operand of bitwise left shift operator (<<) is int, only five lower order bits' value of the right-hand operand is used as the number of bits to shift each bit in the right-hand operand. For example, in 13 << 35 the right-hand operand (35) can be represented in binary as follows.

000000000000000000000000000**100011**

The five lower order bits in 35 is **00011,** which is equal to 3. Therefore, when you say 13 << 35, it is equivalent to saying 13 << 3. For all *positive right-hand operand* of bitwise left shift operator (<<) you can take modulus of the right-hand operand with 32 and that is the final number of bits that each bit in the left-hand operand will be shifted to left. Therefore, 13 << 35 can be considered as `13 << (35 % 32)` which is same as `13 << 3`. If the left-hand operand is long, the first six lower order bits' value of the right-hand operand is used as the number of bits to shift each bit in the right-hand operand. For example,

```
long  val = 13;
long result;
result = val << 35;
```

Since `val` is a `long` variable, six lower order bits of 35, which is 100011 (decimal 35) will be used as the number to shift all bits of `val` to the left.

Figure 4-2: Computing 13 >> 4 and -13 >> 4

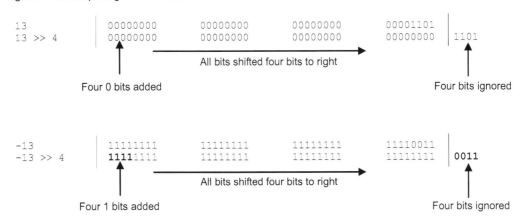

The bitwise signed right shift operator (>>) shifts all the bits to the right by the number specified as its right-hand operand. If the most significant digit of the left-hand operand is 1 (for negative numbers), all higher order bits are filled with 1s after the shift operation. If the most significant bit is 0 (for positive numbers), all higher order bits are filled with 0s. Because the sign bit after right shift operation (>>) remains the same, it is called signed right shift operator. For example, 13 >> 4 results in zero as depicted in Figure 4-2. Also note that in case of -13 >> 4 all four higher order bits are filled with 1s because in -13 the most significant digit is 1. The result of `-13 >> 4` is `-1`.

The unsigned right shift operator (>>>) works exactly same as the signed right shift operator (>>) with only one difference. It always fills the higher order bits with zero. The result of 13 >>> 4 is zero whereas the result of -13 >>> 4 is 268435455 as shown below. There is no unsigned left shift operator.

```
13                  00000000  00000000  00000000 00001101
13 >>> 4            00000000  00000000  00000000 00000000    1101

-13                 11111111  11111111  11111111 11110011
-13 >>> 4           00001111  11111111  11111111 11111111    0011
```

A compound bitwise assignment operator is used in the following form:

```
operand1 op= operand2
```

Here, `op` is one of the bitwise operators &, |,^, <<, >> and >>>. `operand1` and `operand2` are of primitive integral data type where `operand1` must be a variable. The above expression is equivalent to the following expression.

```
operand1 = (Type of operand1) (operand1 op operand2)
```

Assuming that there are two `int` variables: `i` and `j`, Table 4-8 lists the equivalent expression for compound bitwise assignment operators.

Table 4-8: List of compound bitwise assignment operators

Expression	is equivalent to
i &= j	i = i & j
i |= j	i = i | j
i ^= j	i = i ^ j
i <<= j	i = i << j
i >>= j	i = i >> j
i >>>= j	i = i >>> j

Chapter 5. Statements

What is a Statement?

A statement specifies an action in a Java program.

Types of Statements

Statements in Java can be broadly classified into the following three categories.

* Declaration Statement
* Expression Statement
* Control Flow Statement

Declaration Statement

This kind of statement is used to declare a variable. We have already been using this type of statements. For example,

```
int num;
int num2 = 100;
String str;
```

Expression Statement

An expression with a semi-colon (;) at the end is called an expression statement. However, not all Java expressions can be converted to expression statements by appending a semi-colon (;) to them. If i and j are two int variables, i + j is an arithmetic expression. However, i + j; (i + j with a semi-colon) is not a valid expression statement in Java. Only the following four kinds of expressions can be converted to expression statements by appending a semi-colon (;) to them.

* Increment and decrement expression. For example,

  ```
  num++;
  ++num;
  num--;
  --num;
  ```

* Assignment expression. For example,

  ```
  num = 100;
  ```

```
num *= 10;
```

- Object creation expression. For example,

```
new String("This is a text");
```

Note that the above statement creates a new object of the String class. However, the new object's reference is not stored in any reference variable. Therefore, the above statement is not useful. In some cases, we, however, use such an object creation statement.

- Method invocation expression

We invoke the method println() to print a text on console. When we use the println() method without semi-colon at the end, it is an expression. When we add a semi-colon (;) at the end of the method call, it becomes a statement. For example,

```
System.out.println("This is a statement");
```

Control Flow Statement

By default, all statements in a Java program are executed in the order they appear in the program. However, you can change the order of execution of statements in a Java program using control flow statements. Sometimes, you may want to execute a statement or a set of statements only if a particular condition is true. Sometimes, you may want to execute a set of statements repeatedly for a certain number of times or as long as a particular condition is true. All of these are possible in Java using control flow statements. if statement and for statement are examples of control flow statements in Java.

A Block Statement

A block statement is a sequence of zero or more Java statements enclosed in braces. A block statement is generally used to group together several statements so that they can be used in a situation that only calls for a single statement. In some situations, you can use only one statement in Java. If you want to use more than one statement, you can create a block statement placing all your statements inside braces. You can use that block statement in place of one statement. You can think of a block statement as a compound statement, which is treated as one statement. The examples of block statements are:

```
{    // Start of a block statement. Block statement starts with {

    int num1 = 20;
    num1++;

}    // End of the block statement. Block statement ends with }


{
  // Another valid block statement with no statements inside
}
```

All the variables declared in a block statement can only be used within that block. In other words, you can say that all variables declared in a block have local scope. Let us consider the following piece of code.

```
int num1;

// Start a block statement
{
    int num2;  // Declare an int variable. We say that
               // num2 is a local variable for this block

    num2 = 200;   // num2 is local to this block statement
                  // and so can be used inside this block

    num1 = 100;   // We can use num1 here because it is declared
                  // outside the block and before the start of block
}
// End of the block statement

num2 = 50;    // Compiler error. num2 has been declared inside a
              // block and so it cannot be used outside that block
```

You can also nest a block statement inside another. All the variables declared in enclosing block (outer block) are available to the enclosed block (inner block). However, the variables declared in enclosed block are not available in enclosing block. For example,

```
// Start of the outer block
{
    int num1 = 10;

    // Start of the inner block
    {
        // num1 is available here because we are in inner block
        num1 = 100;

        int num2 = 200;    // Declared inside inner block

        num2 = 678;    // OK. num2 is local to inner block
    }
    //End of the inner block

    num2 = 200;    // Compiler error. num2 is local to the inner block.
                   // So, it cannot be used outside the inner block.

}
//End of the outer block
```

One important thing to remember about nested block statement is that you cannot define a variable with the same name inside an inner block if a variable with the same name has already been defined in outer block. This is because the variables declared in the outer block can always be used inside the inner block and if you declare a variable with the same name inside inner block, there is no way for Java to differentiate between these two variables inside the inner block. Following piece of code is incorrect.

```
int num1 = 10;
{
```

```
      // Compiler error. num1 is already in scope. Cannot re-declare num1
      float num1 = 10.5F;

      float num2 = 12.98F;    // OK

      {
          // Compiler error. num2 is already in scope, i.e., you can use
          // num2 already define in the outer block, but cannot re-
          // declare it.
          float num2;
      }
}
```

The if-else Statement

The format of an `if-else` statement is:

```
if (condition)
     statement1
else
     statement2
```

The `condition` must be a `boolean` expression. That is, it must evaluate to `true` or `false`. If the `condition` evaluates to `true`, `statement1` is executed. Otherwise, `statement2` is executed. The `else` part is optional. You may write a statement as:

```
if (condition)
     statement1
```

Suppose there are two `int` variables `num1` and `num2`. You want to add `10` to `num2` if `num1` is greater than `50`. Otherwise, you want to subtract `10` from `num2`. You can write this logic in Java using an `if-else` statement as follows.

```
if (num1 > 50)
     num2 = num2 + 10;
else
     num2 = num2 - 10;
```

The execution of the above `if-else` statement is shown diagrammatically in Figure 5-1.

Suppose you have three `int` variables `num1`, `num2`, and `num3`. You want to add `10` to `num2` and `num3` if `num1` is greater than `50`. Otherwise, you want to subtract `10` from `num2` and `num3`. You may try to write a piece of code using `if-else` statement to implement this as follows.

```
if (num1 > 50)
     num2 = num2 + 10;
     num3 = num3 + 10;
else
     num2 = num2 - 10;
     num3 = num3 - 10;
```

Figure 5-1: Execution of an if-else statement

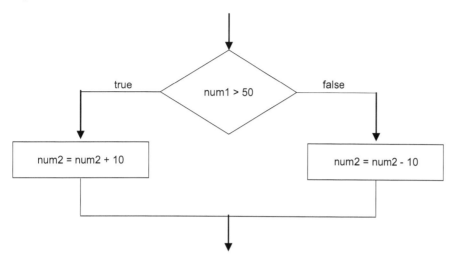

The above piece of code will generate a compiler error. What is wrong with this code? You can place only one statement between `if` and `else` in an `if-else` statement. This is the reason, the statement `num3 = num3 + 10;` caused the compiler error. In fact, you can always associate only one statement with the `if` part in an `if-else` statement or in a simple `if` statement. This is also true for the `else` part in an `if-else` statement. You can always associate only one statement with the `else` part in an `if-else` statement. In the above piece of code, only `num2 = num2 - 10;` is associated with the `else` part and the last statement `num3 = num3 - 10;` is not associated with the `else` part of the `if-else` statement. However, we want to execute two statements when `num1` is greater than `50` or not. In this case, you need to use a block statement as:

```
if (num1 > 50) {
    num2 = num2 + 10;
    num3 = num3 + 10;
}
else {
    num2 = num2 - 10;
    num3 = num3 - 10;
}
```

The `if-else` statement can be nested as shown below.

```
if (num1 > 50) {
    if (num2 < 30) {
        num3 = num3 + 130;
    }
    else {
        num3 = num3 - 130;
    }
}
else {
    num3 = num3 = 200;
}
```

Sometimes, it is confusing to determine which `else` goes with which `if` in an `if-else` statement. Consider the following piece of code.

```
int i = 10;
int j = 15;

if (i > 15)
if (j == 15)
    System.out.println("Thanks");
else
    System.out.println("Sorry");
```

What will be the output when the above snippet of code is executed? Will it print "Thanks", or "Sorry", or nothing? If you guessed that it would not print anything, you already understand `if-else` association. You can apply a simple rule to find out which `else` goes with which `if` in an `if-else` statement. Start with the "else" and move up. If you do not find any other "else", the first "`if`" you find goes with the "else" you started with. If you find one "else" in moving up before you found any "`if`", the second "`if`" goes with the "else" you started with and so on. In the above piece of code, starting with "else" the first "`if`" we find is "`if (j == 15)`" and so the "else" goes with this "`if`". The above piece of code can be rewritten as:

```
int i = 10;
int j = 15;

if (i > 15) {
    if (j == 15) {
        System.out.println("Thanks");
    }
    else {
        System.out.println("Sorry");
    }
}
```

Since `i` is equal to 10 the expression, `i > 15`, will return `false` and, hence, the control would not enter the `if` statement at all. Therefore, there would not be any output.

Note that the `condition` expression in an `if` statement must be of the `boolean` type. Therefore, if you want to compare two `int` variables, `i` and `j`, for equality, your `if` statement must look like:

```
if (i == j)
    statement
```

You cannot write an `if` statement as:

```
if (i = 5)     // Compiler error
    statement
```

The above `if` statement would not compile because `i = 5` is an assignment expression and it evaluates to an `int` value 5. The condition expression must return a `boolean` value: `true` or `false`. Therefore, assignment expression cannot be used as a condition expression in an `if` statement except when you are assigning a `boolean` value to a `boolean` variable as:

```
boolean b;
if (b = true)        // Always returns true
```

```
statement
```

Here, the assignment expression, `b = true`, always returns `true` after assigning `true` to b. In this case, the use of assignment expression in `if` statement is allowed, because the data type of expression, `b = true`, is `boolean`.

You can use ternary operator in place of simple `if-else` statement. Suppose, if a person is male, you want to set the title to "Mr.", otherwise to "Ms." .You can accomplish this using an `if-else` statement and as well as using a ternary operator as shown below.

```
String title = "";
boolean isMale = true;

// Using an if-else statement
if (isMale)
    title = "Mr.";
else
    title = "Ms.";

// Using a ternary operator
title = (isMale ? "Mr." : "Ms.");
```

You can see the difference in using the `if-else` statement and the ternary operator. The code is compact if you use the ternary operator. However, you cannot use the ternary operator in place of all `if-else` statements. You can use the ternary operator in place of the `if-else` statement only when `if` and `else` parts in the `if-else` statement contain only one statement and both statements return the same type of value. Since the ternary operator is an operator, it can be used in expressions. Suppose you want to assign the minimum of i and j to k. You can do this in the declaration statement of the variable k as follows.

```
int i = 10;
int j = 20;
int k = (i < j ? i : j); // Use of ternary operator in initialization
```

The same can be achieved using an `if-else` statement as shown below.

```
int i = 10;
int j = 20;
int k;

if (i < j)
    k = i;
else
    k = j;
```

Another difference in using a ternary operator and an `if-else` statement is that you can use an expression, which uses a ternary operator as an argument to a method. However, you cannot use an `if-else` statement as an argument to a method. Suppose you have a `calc()` method that accepts an `int` as an argument. You have two integers: `num1` and `num2`. If you want to pass the minimum of the two integers to the `calc()` method, you would write the code as shown below.

```
// Use of an if-else statement
if (num1 < num2)
    calc(num1);
```

```
else
    calc(num2);

// Use of a ternary operator
calc(num1 < num2 ? num1 : num2)
```

Suppose you want to print a message, "k is 15" if the value of an `int` variable `k` is equal to `15`. Otherwise, you want to print a message, "k is not 15". You can print the message using ternary operator writing one line of code as follows.

```
System.out.println(k == 15 ? "k is 15" : "k is not 15");
```

The switch Statement

The general form of a switch statement is:

```
switch (switch-expression) {
    case label1:
        statements

    case label2:
        statements

    case label3:
        statements

    default:
        statements
}
```

The switch-expression must evaluate to a type: `byte`, `short`, `char`, `int`, `enum`, or `String`. The `enum` type (shorthand for enumerated type) is introduced to Java 5. Please refer to the chapter on *Enum* for details on how to use an `enum` type in a `switch` statement. Java 7 added the support for `String` type in a switch statement. Please refer to the chapter on *Strings and Dates* for details on how to use strings in a switch statement. The `label1`, `label2`, etc. are compile-time constant expressions whose values must be in the range of the type of the switch-expression. A switch statement is evaluated as follows.

- switch-expression is evaluated
- If the value of the switch-expression matches any of the case labels, the execution starts from there and executes all statements for that case label and the following case label or default label.
- If the value of the switch-expression does not match any of the case labels, execution starts at the statement following the default label and all the statements following that default label and subsequent case labels, if any, are executed.

For example,

```
int i = 10;
switch (i) {
    case 10:  // Found the match
        System.out.println("Ten"); //Execution starts here
```

```
        case 20:
            System.out.println("Twenty");
        default:
            System.out.println ("No-match");
}
```

```
Output:

Ten
Twenty
No-match
```

The value of i is 10. The execution starts at the first statement following `case 10:` and falls through `case 20:` and `default` labels executing the statements under these labels. If we change the value of i to 50, there would not be any match in case labels and the execution will start at the first statement after default label, which will print `"No-match"`. The following example illustrates this logic.

```
int i = 50;
switch (i) {
    case 10:
        System.out.println("Ten");
    case 20:
        System.out.println("Twenty");
    default:
        System.out.println("No-match"); // Execution starts here
}
```

```
Output:

No-match
```

The default label may not be the last label to appear in the switch statement. For example,

```
int i = 50;
switch (i) {
    case 10:
        System.out.println("Ten");
    default:
        System.out.println("No-match"); // Execution starts here
    case 20:
        System.out.println("Twenty");

}
```

```
Output:

No-match
Twenty
```

Since the value of i is 50, which does not match any of the case labels, the execution starts at the first statement after default label. The control falls through the subsequent label `case 20:` and executes the statement following this case label, which prints `"Twenty"`. Generally, we want to print "Ten" if the value of i is 10 and "Twenty" if the value of i is 20. If the value of i is not 10 or 20, we want to print "No-match". This is possible using a new statement inside switch statement. This new statement is called break statement. As soon as a break statement is executed inside a switch statement, the control is transferred outside the switch statement. For example,

```
int i = 10;
switch (i) {
    case 10:
        System.out.println("Ten");
        break;    // Transfers control outside switch statement
    case 20:
        System.out.println("Twenty");
        break;    // Transfers control outside switch statement
    default:
        System.out.println("No-match");
        break;    // Transfers control outside switch statement
                  // This break statement is not necessary
}
```

```
Output:

Ten
```

Note the use of e break statement in the above snippet of code. In fact, the execution of a break statement inside a switch statement stops the execution of the switch statement and transfers control to the first statement, if any, following the switch statement. In the above snippet of code, the use of a break statement inside the default label is not necessary because the default label is the last label in the switch statement and the execution of the switch statement will stop after that anyway. However, it is recommended to use a break statement even inside the last label because it avoids errors if you add labels to your existing switch statement later.

The value of the constant expressions used as case labels must be in the range of the data type of switch-expression. Keeping in mind that the range of byte data type in Java is -128 to 127, the following code would not compile because the second case label is 150, which is outside the range of the byte data type.

```
byte b = 10;

switch (b) {
    case 5:
        b++;
    case 150:       // Compiler error. 150 is greater than 127
        b--;
    default:
        b = 0;
}
```

Two case labels in a switch statement cannot be the same. The following piece of code would not compile because case label 10 is repeated.

```
int num = 10;

switch (num) {
```

Chapter 5. Statements

```
        case 10:
              num++;
        case 10:          // Compiler error. Duplicate case label 10
              num--;
        default:
              num = 100;
}
```

It is important to note that the labels for each case in a switch statement must be a compile-time constant. That is, the value of the labels must be known at compile time. Otherwise, a compiler error occurs. For example, the following code would not compile.

```
int num1 = 10;
int num2 = 10;

switch (num1) {
      case 20:
            System.out.println("num1 is 20");

      case num2:     // Compiler error. num2 is a variable and can't
                     // be used as a label
            System.out.println("num1 is 10");
}
```

You can say that the value of num2 is 10 when the switch statement will be executed. However, all variables are evaluated at runtime. The values of variables are not known at compile-time. Therefore, the case num2: causes the compiler error. This is necessary because Java makes sure at compile time itself that all case labels are within the range of the data type of the switch-expression. If they are not, statements following those case labels will never get executed at runtime.

The default label is optional. There can be at most one default label in a switch statement.

A switch statement is a clear way of writing an if-else statement, if the condition-expression in a if-else statement compares the value of the same variable for equality. For example, the following if-else and switch statement accomplish the same thing.

```
// Using an if-else statement
if (i == 10)
      System.out.println("i is 10");
else if (i == 20)
      System.out.println("i is 20");
else
      System.out.println("i is neither 10 nor 20");

// Using a switch statement
switch (i) {
      case 10:
            System.out.println("i is 10");
            break;
      case 20:
            System.out.println("i is 20");
            break;
      default:
            System.out.println("i is neither 10 nor 20");
}
```

The for Statement

A `for` statement is an iteration statement (also called a `for-loop` statement), which is used to loop through a statement for a number of times based on some conditions. The general form of a `for-loop` statement is:

```
for (Initialization; Condition-expression; Expression-list)
    Statement
```

The initialization, condition-expression, and expression-list are separated by a semi-color (`;`). A `for-loop` statement consists of the following four parts.

- Initialization
- Condition-expression
- Statement
- Expression-list

First, the initialization part is executed. Then, the condition-expression is evaluated. If the condition-expression evaluates to `true`, the statement associated with the `for-loop` statement is executed. After that, all expressions in the expressions list are evaluated. Again, condition-expression is evaluated and if it evaluates to `true`, statement associated with the `for-loop` statement is executed and then, the expression list and so on. This loop of execution is repeated until condition-expression evaluates to `false`. The execution of a `for-loop` statement is depicted in Figure 5-2.

Figure 5-2: Execution of a for statement

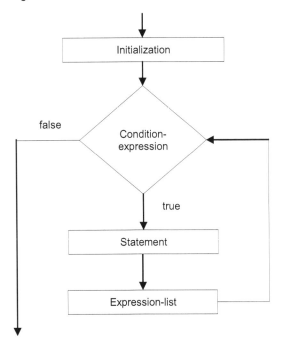

For example, the following `for-loop` statement will print all integers between 1 and 10.

```
for(int num = 1; num <= 10; num++)
    System.out.println(num);
```

First, `int num = 1` is executed, which declares an `int` variable `num` and initializes it to 1. It is important to note that any variable declared in the initialization part of the `for-loop` statement can only be used within that `for-loop` statement. Then, condition-expression (`num <= 10`) is evaluated, which is 1 <= 10. It evaluates to `true` for the first time. Now, the statement associated with the `for-loop` statement is executed, which prints the current value of `num`. Finally, the expression in the expression-list, `num++`, is evaluated, which increments the value of `num` by 1. At this point, the value of `num` becomes 2. The condition-expression 2 <= 10 is evaluated again, which returns `true`, and the current value of `num` is printed. This process continues until the value of `num` becomes 10 and it is printed. After that, `num++` sets the value of `num` to 11, and the condition-expression 11 <= 10 returns `false`, which stops the execution of the `for-loop` statement.

All three parts, initialization, condition-expression, and expression-list, in a `for-loop` statement are optional. Note that the fourth part, Statement, is not optional. Therefore, if you do not have a statement to execute in a `for-loop` statement, you must use an empty block statement or a semi-colon in place of a statement. A semi-colon is also treated as a statement called an empty statement or a null statement. An infinite loop using a `for-loop` statement in Java can be written as follows.

```
for( ; ; ) {  // An infinite loop
}
```

Or,

```
for( ; ; );   // An infinite loop. Note a semi-colon as a statement
```

The detailed discussion of each part of a `for-loop` statement follows.

Initialization

The initialization part of a for-loop statement can have a variable declaration statement, which may declare one or more variables of the same type, or it can have a list of expression statements separated by a comma. Note that the statements used in the initialization part do not end with a semi-colon. The following snippet of code shows the initialization part in a for-loop statement.

```
// Declares two variables i and j of the same type int
for(int i = 10, j = 20; ; );

// Declares one double variable salary
for(double salary = 3455.78F; ; );

// Attempts to declare two variables of diffenet types
for(int i = 10, double d1 = 20.5; ; ); // Error

// Uses an expression i++
int i = 100;
for(i++; ; ); // OK

// Uses an expression to print a message on the console
for(System.out.println("Hello"); ; );      // OK

// Uses two expressions: to print a message and to increment num
int num = 100;
for(System.out.println("Hello"), num++; ; );
```

You can declare a new variable in the initialization part of a `for-loop` statement. However, you cannot re-declare a variable, which is already in scope.

```
int i = 10;
for (int i = 0; ; ); // Error. Cannot re-declare i
```

You can re-initialize the variable `i` in the `for-loop` statement as shown below.

```
int i = 10;    // Initialize I to 10
i = 500;       // Value of i changes here to 500

// Other statements go here...

for (i = 0; ; ); // Reinitialize i to zero inside the for-loop loop
```

Condition-expression

The condition-expression must evaluate to a `boolean` value - `true` or `false`. Otherwise, a compiler error occurs. The condition-expression is optional. If it is omitted, a `boolean` value `true` is assumed as a condition-expression, which results in an infinite loop unless a `break` statement is used to stop the loop. The following two `for-loop` statements result in infinite loops and they are the same.

Infinite loop - I

```
for( ; ; );    // Implicitly condition-expression is true
```

Infinite loop - II

```
for( ; true; );    // Explicit true is used here
```

A `break` statement is used to stop the execution of a `for-loop` statement. When a `break` statement is executed, the control is transferred to the next statement, if any, after the `for-loop` statement. We can rewrite the `for-loop` statement to print all integers between 1 and 10 using a `break` statement as follows.

```
for(int num = 1;  ; num++) {     // No condition-expression
    System.out.println(num);     // Print the number
    if (num == 10) {
        break;   // Break out of loop when i is 10
    }
}
```

The above `for-loop` statement prints the same integers as the previous `for-loop` statement did. However, the latter is not recommended, because we are using a `break` statement instead of using the condition-expression to break out of the loop. It is a good programming practice to use condition-expression to break out of a `for-loop`.

Expression-list

This part is optional. It may contain one or more expressions separated by a comma (,). Only those types of expressions can be used in this part, which can be converted to a statement by appending a semi-colon at the end. Please refer to the discussion on the expression-statement in the beginning of this chapter for more details. We can rewrite the same example of printing all integers between 1 and 10 as follows.

```
for(int num = 1; num <= 10; System.out.println(num), num++);
```

Note that the above `for-loop` statement uses two expressions in expression-list part, which are separated by a comma (,). A `for-loop` statement gives you more power to write compact code. You can rewrite the above `for-loop` statement to make it more compact and accomplish the same task as follows.

```
for(int num = 1; num <= 10; System.out.println(num++));
```

Note that we combined the two expressions in the expression-list into one. We used `num++` as the argument to the `println()` method, so it prints the value of `num` first and increments its value by 1 afterwards. Can you predict the output of the above `for-loop` statement if we replace `num++` by `++num`?

You can also use nested `for-loop` statement, that is, a `for-loop` statement inside another `for-loop` statement. Suppose you want to print a 3×3 (read as three by three) matrix as follows.

```
11    12    13
21    22    23
31    32    33
```

The code to print the a 3×3 matrix can be written as:

```
// Outer for-loop statement
for(int i = 1; i <= 3; i++ ) {
    // Inner for-loop statement
    for(int j = 1; j <= 3; j++ ) {
        System.out.print(i + "" + j);

        // Print a tab after each column value
        System.out.print("\t");
    }

    System.out.println();   // Prints a new line
}
```

The above piece of code can be explained using the following steps.

1. The execution starts in the initialization part (`int i = 1`) of the outer `for-loop` statement where `i` is initialized to 1.
2. The condition expression for the outer `for-loop` statement (`i <= 3`) is evaluated for `i` equal to 1, which is true.
3. The statement part of the outer `for-loop` starts with an inner `for-loop` statement.
4. Now `j` is initialized to 1.
5. The condition expression for the inner `for-loop` statement (`j <= 3`) is evaluated for `j` equal to 1, which is true.
6. The block statement associated with the inner `for-loop` statement is executed, which prints 11 and a tab.
7. The expression-list of the inner `for-loop` statement (`j++`) is executed, which increments the value of `j` to 2.

8. The condition expression for the inner `for-loop` statement (`j <= 3`) is evaluated for `j` equal to 2, which is true.
9. The block statement associated with the inner `for-loop` statement is executed, which prints 12 and a tab. At this stage the printed text is:
   ```
   11 12
   ```
10. The expression-list of the inner `for-loop` statement (`j++`) is executed, which increments the value of `j` to 3.
11. The condition expression for the inner `for-loop` statement (`j <= 3`) is evaluated for `j` equal to 3, which is `true`.
12. The block statement associated with the inner `for-loop` statement is executed, which prints 13 and a tab. At this stage the printed text is:
    ```
    11 12 13
    ```
13. The expression-list of the inner `for-loop` statement (`j++`) is executed, which increments the value of `j` to 4.
14. The condition expression for the inner `for-loop` statement (`j <= 3`) is evaluated for `j` equal to 4, which is false. At this stage, the inner `for-loop` is finished.
15. The last statement of the block statement for outer `for-loop` statement, which is `System.out.println()`, is executed, which prints a new line.
16. The expression-list of the outer `for-loop` statement (`i++`) is executed, which increment the value if `i` to 2.
17. Now the inner `for-loop` statement is started afresh with the value of `i` equal to 2. This sequence of steps is also executed for `i` equal to 3. When `i` becomes 4, the outer `for-loop` statement exits, and at this time, the printed matrix will be:

    ```
    11 12 13
    21 22 23
    31 32 33
    ```

Note that this snippet of code also prints a tab character after 13, 23, and 33, which is not necessary. It also prints a new line at the end of the last line, which is also not necessary. The goal was to show you how to use a nested `for-loop` statement. It is left to you to modify the code so that it would not print the unnecessary tabs and new line characters. One important point to note is that the variable `j` is created every time the inner `for-loop` statement is started and it is destroyed when inner `for-loop` statement exits. Therefore, the variable `j` is created and destroyed three times. You cannot use the variable `j` outside the inner `for-loop` statement, because it has been declared inside the inner `for-loop` statement and its scope is local to that inner `for-loop` statement.

The for-each Statement

Java 5 introduced an enhanced for-loop, which is called for-each loop. It is used for iterating over elements of arrays and collections. Please refer to the chapters on *Arrays* and *Collections* for more detailed explanation of the for-each loop. The general syntax for a for-each loop is as follows.

```
for(Type element : your_collection_or_array) {
    /* This code will be executed once for each element in your
       collection/array. Each time this code is executed, the element
       variable holds the reference of the current element in the
       collection/array
    */
}
```

The following snippet of code prints all elements of an `int` array `numList`.

```java
int[] numList = {10, 20, 30, 40};

for(int num : numList) {
    System.out.println(num);
}
```

```
Output:

10
20
30
40
```

The while Statement

A `while` statement is another iteration (or, loop) statement, which is used to execute a statement repeatedly as long as a condition is true. A `while` statement is also known as a `while-loop` statement. The general form of a `while-loop` statement is:

```java
while (Condition-expression)
    Statement
```

The *condition-expression* must be a `boolean` expression and the *statement* can be a simple statement or a compound block statement. The *condition-expression* is evaluated first. If it returns `true`, the *statement* is executed. Again, the *condition-expression* is evaluated. If it returns `true`, the *statement* is executed. This loop continues until the *condition-expression* returns false. Unlike the `for-loop` statement, the *condition-expression* in a `while-loop` statement is not optional. For example, to make a while statement infinite loop you need to use the `boolean` literal `true` as the *condition-expression* as:

```java
while (true)
    System.out.println ("This is an infinite loop");
```

In general, a `for-loop` statement can be converted to a `while-loop` statement. However, not all `for-loop` statements can be converted to `while-loop` statements. The conversion between a `for-loop` and a `while-loop` statement is shown below.

A for-loop statement:

```java
for (Initialization; Condition-expression; Expression-list )
    Statement
```

Equivalent while-loop statement:

```java
Initialization
while (Condition-expression) {
    Statement
    Expression-list
}
```

We can print all integers between 1 and 500 using a `while-loop` as shown below.

```
int i = 1;
while (i <= 10) {
    System.out.println(i);
    i++;
}
```

The above code can also be rewritten as:

```
int i = 0;
while (++i <= 10) {
    System.out.println(i);
}
```

Or,

```
int i = 1;
while (i <= 10) {
    System.out.println(i++);
}
```

A `break` statement is used to exit the loop in a `while-loop` statement.. We can rewrite the above example using a `break` statement as follows. Note that the following piece of code is written only to illustrate the use of a `break` statement in a `while-loop` and this is not a good example of using a `break` statement.

```
int i = 1;
while (true) {              // Cannot exit the loop from here
    if (i <= 10) {
        System.out.println(i);
        i++;
    }
    else {
        break;          // Exit the loop
    }
}
```

The do-while Statement

The `do-while` statement is another iteration statement. It is similar to the `while-loop` statement with one difference. The statement associated with a `while-loop` statement may not be executed even once if the condition-expression evaluates to false for the first time. However, the statement associated with a `do-while` statement is executed at least once. The general form of a do-while statement is:

```
do
  Statement
while (Condition-expression);
```

Note that the `do-while` statement ends with a semi-colon (;). The *condition-expression* must be a `boolean` expression. The *statement* can be a simple statement or a compound block statement.

The *statement* is executed first. Then, the *condition-expression* is evaluated. If it evaluates to `true`, the *statement* is executed again. This loop continues until the *condition-expression* valuates to `false`. Like in a `for-loop` and a `while-loop`, a `break` statement may be used to exit a `do-while` loop. A `do-while` loop can compute the sum of integers between 1 and 10 as shown below.

```
int i = 1;
int sum = 0;
do {
    sum = sum + i;      // Better use sum += i
    i++;
}
while (i <= 10);

// Print the result
System.out.println("Sum = " + sum);
```

The break Statement

A `break` statement is used to exit from a block. There are two forms of the break statement.

Form -1: Unlabeled break statement:

```
break;
```

Form-2: Labeled break statement:

```
break label;
```

We have already seen the use of unlabeled form of the `break` statement inside `switch`, `for-loop`, `while-loop`, and `do-while` statements. An unlabeled `break` statement transfers control out of a `switch`, `for-loop`, `while-loop`, and `do-while` statement in which it appears. In case of nested statements of these four kinds, if an unlabeled `break` statement is used inside the inner statement, it transfers control only out of the inner statement and not out of outer one For example, you want to print the lower half of the 3x3 matrix as follows.

```
11
21   22
31   32   33
```

To print only the lower half of the 3x3 matrix we can write a snippet of code as follows.

```
for(int i = 1; i <= 3; i++) {
    for(int j = 1; j <= 3; j++) {
        System.out.print ( i + "" + j);
        if (i == j) {
            break;          // Exit the inner for loop
        }
        System.out.print("\t");
    }
    System.out.println();
}
```

The `break` statement has been used inside the inner `for-loop` statement. When the value of the outer loop counter (`i`) becomes equal to the value of the inner loop counter (`j`), the `break` statement is executed, and the inner loop exits. If you want to exit from the outer `for-loop` statement from inside the inner `for-loop` statement, you have to use a labeled `break` statement. A label in Java is any valid Java identifier followed by a colon (`:`). The following are some valid labels in Java.

```
label1:
alabel:
Outer:
Hello:
IamALabel:
```

Let us use a labeled break statement in the above example and see the result.

```
outer:    // Defines a label named outer
for(int i = 1; i <= 3; i++ ) {
    for(int j = 1; j <= 3; j++ ) {
        System.out.print(i + "" + j);
        if (i == j) {
            break outer;   // Exit the outer for loop
        }
        System.out.print("\t");
    }
    System.out.println();
}
// The outer label ends here
```

The output of the above snippet of code will be 11. Why did it print only one element of the 3x3 matrix? This time, we have used a labeled `break` statement inside the inner for statement. When `i == j` evaluates to `true` for the first time, the labeled `break` statement is executed. It transfers control out of the block, which has been labeled as `outer`. Note that the `outer` label appears just before the outer `for-loop` statement. Therefore, the block associated with the label `outer` is the outer `for-loop` statement. A labeled statement can be used not only inside `switch`, `for-loop`, `while-loop`, and `do-while` statements. It can be used with any kind of a block statement. The following is a trivial example of a labeled `break` statement.

```
blockLabel:
{
    int i = 10;
    if (i == 5) {
        break blockLabel;      // Exits the block
    }

    if (i == 10) {
        System.out.println(" i is not five");
    }
}
```

One important point to remember about a labeled `break` statement is that the label used with the `break` statement must be the label for the block in which that labeled `break` statement is used. Following example illustrates an incorrect use of a labeled `break` statement.

```
lab1:
{
    int i = 10;
    if (i == 10)
        break lab1;    //Ok. lab1 can be used here
}


lab2:
{
    int i = 10;
    if (i == 10)
        break lab1;    // A compiler error. lab1 cannot be used here,
                       // because this block is not associated with
                       // lab1 label. We can use only lab2 in this block
}
```

The continue Statement

A `continue` statement can only be used inside `for-loop`, `while-loop` and `do-while` statements. There are two forms of the `continue` statement.

Form-1: Unlabeled continue statement:

```
continue;
```

Form-2: Labeled continue statement:

```
continue label;
```

When a `continue` statement is executed inside a `for-loop`, the rest of the statements in the loop are skipped and the expressions in the expression-list are executed. You can print all odd integers between 1 and 10 using a `for-loop` statement as shown below.

```
for (int i = 1; i < 10; i += 2) {
    System.out.println(i);
}
```

In the above `for-loop` statement, we increment the value of i by 2 in the expression-list. We can rewrite the above `for-loop` statement using a `continue` statement as shown below.

```
for(int i = 1; i < 10; i++) {
    if (i % 2 == 0) {
        continue;
    }
    System.out.println(i);
}
```

The expression i % 2 returns zero for the values of i that are multiple of 2, and the expression i % 2 == 0 returns `true`. In such cases, the `continue` statement is executed and the last statement `System.out.println(i)` is skipped. The increment statement `i++` is executed after the `continue` statement is executed. The above snippet of code is certainly not the best example of using a `continue` statement. However, it serves the purpose of illustrating its use.

When an unlabeled `continue` statement is executed inside a `while-loop` or `do-while` loop, the rest of the statements in the loop is skipped and the condition-expression is evaluated for the next iteration. For example, the following snippet of code will print all odd integers between 1 and 10, using a `continue` statement inside a `while-loop`.

```
int i = 1;

while (i < 10) {
    if (i % 2 == 0) {
        i++;
        continue;
    }
    System.out.println(i);
    i++;
}
```

The main difference in using a `continue` statement inside a `for-loop` and a `while-loop` is the place where the control is transferred. Inside a `for-loop` the execution of a `continue` statement transfers the control to the expression-list and condition-expression is evaluated for the next iteration. However, in a `while-loop` the execution of a `continue` statement transfers the control to condition-expression, which is evaluated for the next iteration. This is why a `for-loop` statement cannot always be converted to a `while-loop` statement without modifying some logic.

An unlabeled `continue` statement always continues the innermost `for-loop`, `while-loop`, and `do-while` loop. If you are using nested loop statements, you need to use a labeled `continue` statement to continue in the outer loop. For example, we can rewrite the snippet of code which prints lower half of the 3x3 matrix using a `continue` statement as:

```
outer:    // The label "outer" starts here
for(int i = 1; i <= 3; i++) {
    for(int j = 1; j <= 3; j++) {
        System.out.print(i + "" + j);
        System.out.print("\t");
        if (i == j) {
            System.out.println(); // Print a new line
            continue outer;        // Continue the outer loop
        }

    }
}
// The label "outer" ends here
```

An Empty Statement

An empty statement is a semi-colon (`;`) by itself. An empty statement does nothing. If an empty statement does not do anything, why do we have it? Sometimes, a statement is necessary as a part of the syntax of a construct. However, you may not have anything meaningful, which can be used as a statement in those circumstances. In such a case, an empty statement is used. A `for-loop` must have a statement associated with it. However, to print all integers between 1 and 10 we can only *use initialization, condition-expression,* and *expression-list* parts of a `for-loop` statement. In this case, we do not have a statement to associate with the `for-loop` statement. Therefore, we use an empty statement in this case as:

```
for(int i = 1; i <= 10; System.out.println(i++))
;    // This semi-colon is an empty statement
```

Sometimes, an empty statement is used to avoid double negative logic in your code. Suppose `noDataFound` is a `boolean` variable. You may write a snippet of code as:

```
if (noDataFound)
     ;     // Empty statement
else {
      // Do some processing
}
```

The above `if-else` statement can be written without using an empty statement as:

```
if (!noDataFound) {
     // Do some processing
}
```

It is a matter of personal choice, which piece of code to use in your application. Finally, note that if you type two or more semi-colons where only one was required, it would not cause any errors, because each extra semi-colon is considered as an empty statement. For example,

```
i++;   // Ok. Here, semi-colon is part of statement
i++;;  // Still Ok. Second semi-colon is considered as empty statement
```

You cannot use an empty statement where a statement is not allowed. For example, when only one statement is allowed, adding an extra empty statement will cause an error as shown in the following snippet of code. It associates two statements, `i++;` and an empty statement (`;`), to an `if` statement, where only one statement is allowed.

```
if (i == 10)
     i++;;      // Error. Cannot use two statements with an if statement
                // because an if statement allows only one statement
else
     i--;
```

Chapter 6. Classes and Objects

What is a Class?

Classes are the basic units of programming in an object-oriented paradigm. In the chapter on *Writing Java Programs*, we looked at some elementary aspects of a class in Java, for example, using the `class` keyword to declare a class, declaring the `main()` method to run a class, etc. This chapter explains how to declare and use a class in detail.

Let us start with a simple example of a class in the real world and then build the technical concept of a class in Java. When you look around, you see a number of objects, e.g., books, computers, keyboards, tables, chairs, human beings, etc. Each object that you see belongs to a class. Ask yourself a simple question – "Who am I?" Your obvious answer would be – "I am a human being." What do you mean by saying that you are a human being? You mean that a human class exists in the world and you are one of the instances ("being") of that class. You also understand that other human beings (other instances of the human class) also exist, who are similar but not the same, to you. Both you and your friend, being the instances of the same human class, have the same properties (e.g. name, gender, height, weight, etc.) and behaviors (e.g. ability to think, talk, walk, etc.). However, the properties and behaviors differ for you and your friend in value and/or quality. For example, both you and your friend have a name and both of you have the ability to talk. However, your name may be Richard and your friend's name may be Greg (different from Richard). You may talk slowly, whereas your friend may talk fast. If we want to prepare a model for you and your friend to examine your behaviors, there are two choices.

- We can list all properties and behaviors for you and your friend separately and examine them separately as if there is no connection between you and your friend.
- We can list the properties and behaviors for you and your friend that are in common and then examine them as properties and behavior for an entity without naming you and your friend. This model assumes that all listed properties and behaviors will be present in an entity (without naming it) though they may vary from entity to entity. We may want to list all properties and behaviors for you and your friend as properties and behavior of a class, say human, and treat you and your friend as two different instances of that human class. Essentially, we have grouped together entities (e.g. you and your friend) with similar properties and behavior and called that group a class. Then we will treat all objects (e.g. you and your friend) as instances of that class.

The first approach treats each object as a separate entity. In the second approach, objects are classified based on similarity of properties and behaviors where an object always belongs to a class; class becomes the essential part of programming; and, to determine any property or behavior of an object we need to look up its class definition. For example, you are an object of the human class. Can you fly? This question can be answered by going through a series of steps. First, you need to answer the question – "What class do you belong to?" The answer is - you belong to the human class. Does the human class define a behavior such as flying? The answer is no. The human class does not define the flying behavior. Since you are an instance of the human class that does not define the flying behavior, you cannot fly. If you look carefully at the way we arrived at the answer, you would find that the question was made on an object (you), but the answer was provided by the class (human) to which the object belongs.

Classes are essential and they are basic parts of programs in object-oriented programming. Classes are used as templates to create objects. Let us discuss how to define a class. A class in Java may consist of five components.

- Fields
- Methods
- Constructors
- Static Initializers
- Instance Initializers

The fields and methods are also known as class members. Classes and interfaces can also be class members. This chapter focuses only on fields and methods. We will discuss classes and interfaces as class members in the chapter on *Inner Classes*. A class can have zero or more class members. Constructors are used to create objects of a class. You must have at least one constructor for a class. Initializers are used to initialize fields of a class. You can have zero or more initializers of static or instance types. The rest of this chapter will discuss how to declare and use the different components of a class.

Declaring a Class

The general syntax for declaring a class in Java is:

```
<<modifiers>> class <<class name>> {
    // Body of the class goes here
}
```

Here, <<modifiers>> are keywords that associates special meanings to the class declaration. A class declaration may have zero or more modifiers. The keyword class (all in lowercase) is used to declare a class. The <<class name>> is a user-defined name of the class, which should be a valid identifier in Java. Each class in Java has a body, which is specified inside a pair of braces ({ }). The body of a class contains its different components, e.g., fields, methods, etc. The following snippet of code defines a class named Human with an empty body. Note that Human class does not use any modifiers.

```
// Human.java
class Human {
    // Empty body for now
}
```

The source code for a class is saved in a text file with .java file extension. When it is compiled, the compiler generates a binary file with extension .class.

Declaring Fields in a Class

Fields of a class represent properties (also called attributes) of objects of that class. Suppose every object of human class has two properties – a name and a gender. The human class should include declarations of two fields – one to represent name and one to represent gender.

The fields are declared inside the body of the class. The general syntax to declare a field in a class is:

```
<<modifiers>> class <<ClassName>> {
    // Fields declaration
    <<modifiers>> <<data type>> <<field name>> = <<initial value>>;
}
```

A field declaration can use zero or more modifiers. The data type of the field precedes its name. Optionally, you can also initialize each field in a class with an initial value. If you do not want to initialize a field with an initial value, its declaration should end with a semi-colon after its name.

With the declaration of two fields, name and gender, the declaration of the Human class will look as:

```
//Human.java
class Human {
    String name;
    String gender;
}
```

TIP
It is a convention (not a rule or a requirement) in Java to start a class name with an uppercase letter and capitalize the subsequent words, e.g., Human, Table, ColorMonitor, etc. The name of fields and methods start with a lowercase letter and the subsequent words are capitalized, e.g., name, firstName, grandFatherName, etc.

The Human class declares two fields – name and gender. Both fields are of the String type. Every instance (or object) of the Human class will have a copy of these two fields.

Sometimes, a property belongs to the class itself and not to any particular instance of that class. For example, the count of all human beings is not a property of any specific human being. Rather, it belongs to the human class itself. The existence of the count of human beings is not tied to any specific instance of the human class, even though each instance of the human class contributes to the value of the count property. Only one copy of the class property exists irrespective of the number of instances that exists for the class. However, a separate copy of the instance property exists for each instance of a class. For example, a separate copy of the name and the gender properties exist for each instance of the Human class. You always specify name and gender of a human being. However, even if there is no instance of the Human class, we can say that the count of the Human class instances is zero.

Java lets you declare two types of fields for a class– class fields and instance fields. Class fields are also known as class variables. Instance fields are also known as instance variables. In the above snippet of code, the Human class has declared two instance variables – name and gender. Java has a different way to declare class variables. All class variables must be declared using the static keyword as a modifier. The declaration of the Human class in Listing 6-1 adds a count class variable. Note the use of the static keyword in the declaration for the count class variable.

Listing 6-1: Declaration of a Human class with one class variable and two instance variables

```
//Human.java
class Human {
    String name;   // Instance variable
```

```
String gender; // Instance variable
static long count; // Class variable
}
```

TIP

A class variable is also known as a static variable. An instance variable is also known as a non-static variable.

Creating Instances of a Class

We have a `Human` class as listed in Listing 6-1. We want to create an instance (an object) of this class. The new operator is used to create a new instance of a class. The following is the general syntax to create an instance of a class.

```
new <<Call to Class Constructor>>;
```

The `new` operator is followed by a call to the constructor of the class whose instance is being created. The `new` operator creates an instance of a class by allocating the memory on heap. The following statement creates an instance of the `Human` class.

```
new Human();
```

Here, "`Human()`" is a call to the constructor of the `Human` class. Did we add any constructor to our `Human` class? No. We have not added any constructor to our `Human` class. We have added only three fields to it. How can we use a constructor for a class that we have not added? When you do not add any constructors to a class, the Java compiler adds one for you. The constructor that is added by the Java compiler is called a default constructor. The default constructor accepts no arguments. The name of the constructor of a class is the same as the class name. We will discuss constructors in details later in this chapter.

What happens when an instance of a class is created using the `new` operator? The `new` operator allocates memory for each instance field of the class. Recall that class variables are not allocated memory when an instance of the class is created. Figure 6-1 depicts an instance of the `Human` class in memory. The figure shows that memory is allocated for instance variables – `name` and `gender`. You can create as many instances of the `Human` class as you want. Each time you create an instance of the `Human` class, Java runtime allocates memory for `name` and `gender` instance variables. How much memory is allocated for an instance of the `Human` class? The simple answer is that we do not know exactly how much memory is used by a `new` instance of a class in Java. In fact, you do not need to know how much memory is needed to create an instance of a class in Java. Java runtime takes care of memory allocation as well as de-allocation automatically for you.

Figure 6-1: An instance of the Human class in memory created by the "new Human()" instance creation expression.

Now, we want to move a step forward and want to assign values to `name` and `gender` instance variables for the newly created instance of the `Human` class. Can we assign values to `name` and `gender` instance variables of the newly created instance of the `Human` class? The answer is no. We cannot access `name` and `gender` instance variables in memory even though they exist in memory. To access instance variables of an instance of a class, we must have its reference (or handle). The expression "`new Human()`" creates a new instance of the `Human` class in memory. The newly created instance is like a balloon filled with Helium gas left in the air. When you release a Helium filled balloon in the air, you lose control of the balloon. If you attach a string to the balloon before releasing it in the air, you can control the balloon using the string. Similarly, if you want to have control (or access) to an instance of a class in memory, you must store the reference of that instance in a reference variable. You control a balloon with a string; you control a television with a remote controller. Therefore, the type of controlling device you need to use depends on the type of the object that you want to control. Similarly, you need to use different types of reference variables to refer to (or to handle, or to work with) instances of different classes in memory. The name of a class defines a new reference type in Java. A variable of a specific reference type can store the reference of an instance of the same reference type in memory. Suppose we want to declare a reference variable, which will store a reference of an instance of the `Human` class, we will declare the variable as:

```
Human jack;
```

Here, `Human` is the class name, which is also a reference type, and `jack` is a variable of that type. In other words, `jack` is a reference variable of `Human` type. The `jack` variable can be used to store a reference of an instance of the `Human` class in memory.

The `new` operator allocates the memory for a new instance of a class and returns the reference (or indirect pointer) to that instance. We need to store the reference that is returned by the new operator in a reference variable as:

```
jack = new Human();
```

Note that `jack` itself is a variable and it will be allocated memory separately. However, the memory location for `jack` variable will store the reference of the memory location of the newly created instance of the `Human` class. Figure 6-2 depicts the memory state when a reference variable `jack` is declared and when an instance of the `Human` class is created and its reference is assigned to `jack` variable.

Figure 6-2: Memory states when a reference variable is declared and when a reference variable is assigned the reference of an instance of a class

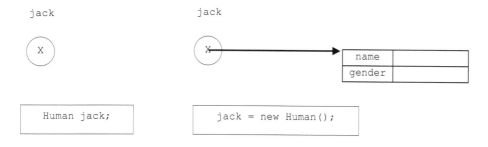

Now, you can think of the `jack` variable as a remote controller for a `Human` instance in memory. You can refer to the `Human` instance in memory using the `jack` variable. We will discuss how to use a reference variable in the next section. You can also combine the above two statements into one as shown below.

```
Human jack = new Human();
```

The null Reference Type

Every class in Java defines a new reference type. Java has a special reference type, which is called null type. It has no name. Therefore, you cannot define a variable of null reference type. The null reference type has only one value defined by Java, which is `null` literal. It is simply – `null`. The null reference type is assignment compatible with any other reference type. That is, you can assign a `null` value to a variable of any reference type. Practically, a `null` value stored in a reference type variable means that the reference variable is referring to no object. You can think of storing a `null` to a reference variable as a string with no balloon attached to it, where balloon is a valid object and string is a reference variable. For example, you can write code as:

```
// Assign null value to john
Human john = null;  // john is not referring to any object
john = new Human(); // Now, john is referring to a valid Human object
```

You can use a `null` literal with comparison operators to check for equality and inequality as:

```
if (john == null) {
    // john is referring to null. Cannot use john for anything
}

if (john != null) {
    // Do something with john
}
```

Note that `null` is a literal of null type. Java does not let you mix reference types and primitive types. You cannot assign `null` value to a primitive type variable. The following assignment statement will generate a compiler error.

```
// Compiler error. A reference type value, null,
// cannot be assigned to a primitive type variable num
int num = null;
```

Since a `null` value (or any reference type value) cannot be assigned to a primitive type variable, Java compiler does not allow you to compare a primitive value to a `null` value. The following comparison will generate a compiler error. In other words, you can compare a reference type only with reference types, and a primitive type only with primitive types.

```
// Compiler error
// Cannot compare primitive type to reference type
if (num == null) {
  // do something
}
```

Using Dot Notation to Access Fields of a Class

We use dot notation to refer to instance variables. The general form of the dot notation syntax is:

```
<<Reference Variable Name>>.<<Instance Variable Name>>
```

For example, you can use `jack.name` to refer to the `name` instance variable of the instance to which `jack` reference variable is referring. If you want to assign a value to the `name` instance variable, you can use:

```
jack.name = "Jack Parker";
```

The following statement assigns the value of the `name` instance variable of the instance of the `Human` class whose reference is stored in the `jack` reference variable to `String` variable `aName`.

```
String aName = jack.name;
```

How do we refer to class variables in our code? We have two ways to refer to a class variable in our code using dot notation.

- You can refer to a class variable using the name of the class as:

  ```
  <<Class Name>>.<<Class Variable Name>>
  ```

  For example, you can use `Human.count` to refer to the `count` class variable of the `Human` class. To assign a new value, say 101, to the `count` class variable you can write:

  ```
  Human.count = 101;
  ```

  To read the value of the `count` class variable into a variable called `population`, you can use:

  ```
  long population = Human.count;
  ```

- You can also use a reference variable to refer to the class variable of a class. For example, you can use `jack.count` to refer to the `count` class variable of the `Human` class. You can use the following statement to assign value, say 101, to the `count` class variable.

  ```
  jack.count = 101;
  ```

  The following statement reads the value of the `count` class variable into a variable called `population`.

  ```
  long population = jack.count;
  ```

Both of the above statements assume that `jack` is a reference variable of `Human` type and it refers to a valid `Human` instance.

TIP

You can use the class name or a reference variable of the class type to refer to a class variable. Since the class variable belongs to the class and it is shared by all instances of the class, it is logical to refer to it using the class name. However, you always use a reference variable of a class type to refer to the instance variables.

It is time to see the use of fields in the `Human` class. Listing 6-2 has a complete program that demonstrates how to access class variables and instance variables of a class. The following statement needs some explanation.

```
// Increase count by one
Human.count++;
```

It uses the increment operator (++) on the `count` class variable. After the `count` class variable is incremented by 1, we read and print its value. The output shows that after incrementing its value by 1, its value becomes 1. It means that its value was zero before the `Human.count++` statement was executed. However, we have never set its value to zero. Its declaration was as follows.

```
static long count;
```

When the `count` class variable was declared as shown above, it was initialized to zero by default. In fact, all fields of a class (class variables and instance variables) are initialized to a default value, if you do not assign an initial value to them. We will discuss the initialization of fields of a class in details in the next section.

Listing 6-2: A test class to demonstrate how to access (read/write) class variables and instance variables of a class

```
// FieldAccessTest.java
package com.jdojo.chapter6;

class FieldAccessTest {
    public static void main(String[] args) {
        // Create an instance of Human class
        Human jack = new Human();

        // Increase count by one
        Human.count++;

        // Assign values to name and gender
        jack.name = "Jack Parker";
        jack.gender = "Male";

        // Read and print the values of name, gender and count
        String jackName = jack.name;
        String jackGender = jack.gender;
        long population = Human.count;

        System.out.println("Name: " + jackName);
```

```
            System.out.println("Gender: " + jackGender);
            System.out.println("Population: " + population);

            // Change the name
            jack.name = "Jackie Parker";

            // Read and print the changed name
            String changedName = jack.name;
            System.out.println("Changed Name: " + changedName);
        }
    }
```

```
Output:

Name: Jack Parker
Gender: Male
Population: 1
Changed Name: Jackie Parker
```

Default Initialization of Fields

All fields of a class, static as well as non-static, are initialized to a default value. The default value of a field depends on its data type.

- A numeric type field (byte, short, char, int, long, float, and double) is initialized to zero.
- A boolean field is initialized to false.
- A reference type field is initialized to null.

According to the above rules for default initial value for the fields of a class, the fields of Human class will be initialized as follows.

- The count class variable is initialized to zero because it is of numeric type. This is the reason, Human.count++ evaluated to 1 (0 + 1 = 1) as shown in the output of Listing 6-2.
- The name and gender instance variables are of String type, which is a reference type. They are initialized to null. Note that a copy of name and gender fields exists for every object of the Human class, and each copy of name and gender is initialized to null.

If you consider the above default initialization of the fields of the Human class, it behaves as if we have declared the Human class as shown below. The effects of declaring the Human class as shown below and as shown in Listing 6-1 are the same.

```
class Human {
    String name = null;
    String gender = null;
    static long count = 0;
}
```

Listing 6-3 demonstrates the default initialization of primitive and reference type fields of a class. The DefaultInit class includes only instance variables. The class fields are initialized with the same default value as the instance fields. If you declare all fields of the `DefaultInit` class as `static`, the output will be the same.

Listing 6-3: Default initialization of class fields

```
// DefaultInit.java
package com.jdojo.chapter6;

class DefaultInit {
    byte b;
    short s;
    int i;
    long l;
    float f;
    double d;
    boolean bool;
    String str;

    public static void main(String[] args) {
        // Create an object of DefaultInit class
        DefaultInit obj = new DefaultInit();

        // Print the default values for all instance variables
        System.out.println("byte is initialized to: " + obj.l);
        System.out.println("short is initialized to: " + obj.s);
        System.out.println("int is initialized to: " + obj.i);
        System.out.println("long is initialized to: " + obj.l);
        System.out.println("float is initialized to: " + obj.f);
        System.out.println("double is initialized to: " + obj.d);
        System.out.println("boolean is initialized to: " + obj.bool);
        System.out.println("String is initialized to: " + obj.str);
    }
}
```

```
Output:

byte is initialized to: 0
short is initialized to: 0
int is initialized to: 0
long is initialized to: 0
float is initialized to: 0.0
double is initialized to: 0.0
boolean is initialized to: false
String is initialized to: null
```

Access Level Modifiers for a Class

In Listing 6-1, we created the `Human` class in `com.jdojo.chapter6` package. We used the `Human` class in Listing 6-2 to create its object in the `FieldAccessTest` class, which is in the same package as the `Human` class. We had no problem in compiling and running the following statement in Listing 6-2.

```
Human jack = new Human();
```

Let us create a class called `ClassAccessTest` in `com.jdojo.common` package. Note that the package for the `ClassAccessTest` class is different from the package for the `Human` class. The code for the `ClassAccessTest` class is shown below.

```
// ClassAccessTest.java
package com.jdojo.common;

public class ClassAccessTest {
    public static void main(String[] args) {
        Human jack;
    }
}
```

The code for the `ClassAccessTest` class is very simple. It does only one thing – declares a reference variable of `Human` type in its `main()` method. Let us compile the `ClassAccessTest` class. Oops! We got a compiler error. The error is:

```
"ClassAccessTest.java": cannot find symbol; symbol  : class Human,
location: class com.jdojo.common.ClassAccessTest at line 6, column 5
```

If you read the compiler error carefully, you will find that the compiler is complaining about the type `Human` in the following variable declaration.

```
Human jack;
```

The compiler is stating that it could not find the definition of the term `Human`. What is wrong in the `ClassAccessTest` class with the `jack` variable declaration? When you refer to a class by its simple name the compiler looks for that class declaration in the same package where the referring class is. In our case, the referring class `ClassAccessTest` is in the `com.jdojo.common` package and it uses the simple name, `Human`, to refer to the `Human` class. Therefore, the compiler looks for the `Human` class in the `com.jdojo.common` package. That is, the compiler is looking for the `com.jdojo.common.Human` class declaration, which we do not have. This is the reason we received the compiler error when we attempted to compile the `ClassAccessTest` class. By using the simple name `Human` in `ClassAccessTest`, we meant to refer to the `Human` class in `com.jdojo.chapter6` package and not in `com.jdojo.common` package. If we had the `Human` class in the `com.jdojo.common` package, our code for `ClassAccessTest` would have compiled. Let us assume that we do not have a `com.jdojo.common.Human` class and we want to fix the compiler error. The above compiler error can be fixed by using the fully qualified name of the `Human` class as shown below.

```
// ClassAccessTest.java
package com.jdojo.common;

public class ClassAccessTest {
    public static void main(String[] args) {
        com.jdojo.chapter6.Human jack;
    }
}
```

Let us compile `ClassAccessTest` class. Oops! We get a compiler error again. However, this time the compiler error is different.

```
"ClassAccessTest.java": com.jdojo.chapter6.Human is not public in
com.jdojo.chapter6; cannot be accessed from outside package at line 6,
column 24
```

This time, the compiler is not saying that it does not understand what Human type is. It is saying that it knows what com.jdojo.chapter6.Human type is; however, it is accessible only inside the com.jdojo.chapter6 package in which it has been declared. In other words, Human type is not accessible inside the com.jdojo.common package. Here comes the concept of the access-level for a class.

When you declare a class, you can also specify whether the class can be accessed (or used, or referred to) from any package in the application, or only from within the package in which it has been declared. For example, you can specify in the declaration of the Human class whether it can be accessed only within the com.jdojo.chapter6 package or from any package including the com.jdojo.common package. The general syntax specifying access-level for a class is:

```
<<access level modifier>> class <<class name>> {
    // Body of the class goes here
}
```

There are only two valid values for <<access level modifier>> in a class declaration – no value and public.

- No value: It is the same as the absence of <access level modifier>>. It is also known as package-level access level. If the class has package level access, it can be accessed only within the package in which it has been declared. The Human class in Listing 6-1 has package-level access. This is the reason why we were able to use (or access) the Human class in the FieldAccessTest class in Listing 6-2. Note that the Human class and the FieldAccessTest class are in the same package and both have package-level access. Therefore, they can refer to each other.

  The Human class is in the com.jdojo.chapter6 package and it has package-level access. Therefore, it cannot be accessed from any other package, e.g., com.jdojo.common. This is the reason, we received the compiler error when we tried to compile the ClassAccessTest class.

- public: If public access level modifier is used for a class, it can be accessed from any package in the application. If we want the Human class to be accessible from any package (e.g. com.jdojo.common), we need to declare it as public.

Let us redefine our Human class as shown in Listing 6-4. This time, we have specified its access level as public, so it is accessible from any package.

Listing 6-4: Redefined Human class with the public access level modifier

```
// Human.java
package com.jdojo.chapter6;

public class Human {
    String name;        // Instance variable
    String gender;      // Instance variable
    static long count;  // Class variable
}
```

Recompile the `Human` class, and then compile the `ClassAccessTest` class. This time, the `ClassAccessTest` class compiles without any errors.

TIP
What does it mean when we state that a class is accessible from a package? A class defines a new reference type. A reference type can be used to declare a variable. When we state that a class is accessible in a package, it means that we can use the class name as a reference type, e.g., to declare a variable, in the code that resides in that package.

Import Declarations

We have learned the following two rules from discussion in the previous section.

- You must declare a class `public` to use it in a package other than the package in which it is declared.
- You need to use the fully qualified name of a class to use it in a package other than the one in which it is declared. If you are using a class in the same package in which it is declared, you can use its simple name.

There is no alternative to the first rule. That is, a class must be declared `public` if it needs to be accessible from outside its package. However, there is another way to deal with the second rule. You can refer to a class by its simple name outside its package by using an import declaration. An import declaration is used to import a class into a compilation unit from outside the package of the compilation unit. Technically speaking, an import declaration is used to import any type into a compilation unit and not just a class. Import declarations appear just after the package declaration and before the first type declaration in a compilation unit. Figure 6-3 shows the place where import declarations appear in a compilation unit. Note that you can have multiple import declarations in a compilation unit.

Figure 6-3: The structure of a compilation unit in Java

An import declaration in a compilation unit lets you use the simple name of a class instead of its fully qualified name. If the class, which you are referring in your code, exists in the same package, you can always use its simple name. However, if the class that you are referring to exists in another package, you can use the fully qualified name of the class, or you can use an import declaration to use its simple name. This section mentions importing only class types. However, the same rules apply for importing any other types, e.g., interface types, annotation types, or enum types. Since we have covered only class type up to this chapter, we will not mention any other types in discussion in this section. When we use a phrase "import a class" in this section, it means "import a type".

There are two types of `import` declarations:

- Single-type-import declaration
- Import-on-demand declaration

Single-Type-Import Declaration

This type of `import` declaration is used to import a single type (e.g. a class) from a package. It is of the form:

```
import <<fully qualified name of a type>>;
```

For example, you would use the following import declaration to import the `Human` class from the `com.jdojo.chapter6` package.

```
import com.jdojo.chapter6.Human;
```

A single-type-import declaration imports only one type from a package. If you want to import more than one type (e.g. three classes) from a package, or from different packages, you need to use a separate import declaration for each type. The following import declarations import class `Class11` from `pkg1` package, `Class21` and `Class22` from `pkg2` package and `Class33` from `pkg3` package.

```
import pkg1.Class11;
import pkg2.Class21;
import pkg2.Class22;
import pkg3.Class33;
```

Let us revisit the `com.jdojo.common.ClassAccessTest` class, which resulted in a compiler error.

```
// ClassAccessTest.java
package com.jdojo.common;

public class ClassAccessTest {
    public static void main(String[] args) {
        Human jack;
    }
}
```

We received a compiler error when we used the simple name of the `Human` class, because the compiler could not find a `Human` class in the `com.jdojo.common` package. We had resolved this error by using the fully qualified name of the `Human` class as:

```
// ClassAccessTest.java
package com.jdojo.common;

public class ClassAccessTest {
    public static void main(String[] args) {
        com.jdojo.chapter6.Human jack;
    }
}
```

We have another way to resolve this error, which is by using a single-type-import declaration. We can import the `com.jdojo.chapter6.Human` class and then use its simple name. The modified `ClassAccessTest` class declaration is as follows.

```
// ClassAccessTest.java - Modified version
package com.jdojo.common;

import com.jdojo.chapter6.Human; // Import Human class

public class ClassAccessTest {
    public static void main(String[] args) {
        Human jack;    // Use simple name of Human class
    }
}
```

The modified version as mentioned-above of the `ClassAccessTest` class compiles fine. When the compiler comes across the simple name of `Human` class in the statement

```
Human jack;
```

it goes through all import declarations to resolve the simple name to a fully qualified name. When the compiler tries to resolve the simple name `Human`, it finds the import declaration – `import com.jdojo.chapter6.Human`, which imports a `Human` class. The Java compiler assumes that you intended to use the `com.jdojo.chapter6.Human` class, when you used the simple name `Human` in the above statement. The compiler replaces the above statement by the following statement.

```
com.jdojo.chapter6.Human jack;
```

TIP

Import declarations let you use simple name of a type in your code, thus making your code more readable. When you compile your code, the compiler replaces the simple name of a type with its fully qualified name. It uses import declarations for converting simple names to their fully qualified name of the type. It is to be emphasized that using import declarations in your Java program does not affect the size of your compiled code or runtime performance of your Java program. Using import declarations in a Java program is just a way to use the simple names of classes in your source code. The compiler will resolve those simple names using the import declarations and replace the simple names with their corresponding fully qualified names.

There are many subtle points to remember while using import declarations. We will discuss them shortly.

Import-on-Demand Declaration

Sometimes, you may need to import multiple types from a package. You need to use as many single-type-import declarations as the number of types you need to import from a package. An import-on-demand declaration is used to import multiple types from a package using one `import` declaration. The syntax for an import-on-demand declaration is:

```
import <<package name>>.*;
```

Here, the package name is followed by a dot and an asterisk (*). For example, the following import-on-demand declaration imports all types (that includes all classes) from `com.jdojo.chapter6` package.

```
import com.jdojo.chapter6.*;
```

Sometimes, the use of an asterisk in an import-on-demand declaration leads to wrong assumption about the types that are imported. Suppose there are two classes `C1` and `C2`. They are in packages `p1` and `p1.p2` respectively. That is, their fully qualified names are `p1.C1` and `p1.p2.C2`. You may write an import-on-demand declaration as

```
import p1.*;
```

thinking that it will import classes, `p1.C1` and `p1.p2.C2`. However, this assumption is wrong. The declaration

```
import p1.*;
```

imports all types only from `p1` package. It will not import the `p1.p2.C2` class, because `C2` class is not in `p1` package. Rather, it is in `p2` package, which is a sub-package of `p1`. The asterisk at the end of an import-on-demand declaration means all types only from the specified package. The asterisk does not mean sub-packages and types inside those sub-packages. Sometimes, programmers attempt to use multiple asterisks in an import-on-demand declaration thinking that it will import types from all sub-packages too.

```
import p1.*.*; // Compiler error
```

The above import-on-demand declaration results in a compiler error because it uses multiple asterisks. It does not follow the syntax for an import-on-demand declaration. In an import-on-demand declaration, the declaration must end with a dot followed by only one asterisk (.*).

If you want to import both classes , `C1` and `C2,` you need to use two import-on-demand declarations as shown below.

```
import p1.*;
import p1.p2.*;
```

We can rewrite our previous example of `ClassAccessTest` using an import-on-demand declaration as follows.

```
// ClassAccessTest.java - Modified version uses import-on-demand
package com.jdojo.common;

// Import all types from com.jdojo.chapter6 package, which
// also includes the Human class
import com.jdojo.chapter6.*;

public class ClassAccessTest {
    public static void main(String[] args) {
        Human jack;    // Use simple name of Human class
    }
}
```

When the compiler tries to resolve the simple name Human in the above code, it will use import-on-demand declaration to see if a Human class exists in com.jdojo.chapter6 package. In fact, the asterisk in the import declaration will be replaced by Human and then the compiler checks if the com.jdojo.chapter6.Human class exists. Suppose we have two classes in com.jdojo.chapter6 package, which are named Human and Table. The following code will compile with one import-on-demand declaration.

```
// ClassAccessTest.java - Modified version uses import-on-demand
package com.jdojo.common;

// Import all types from com.jdojo.chapter6 package, which also
// includes Human and Table classes
import com.jdojo.chapter6.*;

public class ClassAccessTest {
    public static void main(String[] args) {
        Human jack; // Use simple name of Human class
        Table t1;   // Use simple name Table
    }
}
```

The one import-on-demand declaration in the above code has the same effect as two single-type-import declaration shown below.

```
import com.jdojo.chapter6.Human;  // Import Human class
import com.jdojo.chapter6.Table;  // Import Table class
```

Which type of import declaration is better to use in your Java program – single-type-import or import-on-demand? It is simple to use import-on-demand declaration. However, it is not readable. Let us look at the following code that compiles fine. Assume that class A and B are not in the com.jdojo.chapter6 package.

```
// ImportOnDemandTest.java
package com.jdojo.chapter6;

import p1.*;
import p2.*;

public class ImportOnDemandTest {
    public static void main(String[] args) {
        A a; // Declare a variable of class A type
        B b; // Declare a variable of class B type
```

```
        }
}
```

Can you tell, by looking at the above code, the fully qualified names of the class A and the class B? Is class A in p1 package or p2 package? It is impossible to tell just by looking at the code the package to which class A and B belong, because we have used import-on-demand declarations. Let us rewrite the above code using single-type-import declarations as follows.

```
// ImportOnDemandTest.java
package com.jdojo.chapter6;

import p1.A;
import p2.B;

public class ImportOnDemandTest {
    public static void main(String[] args) {
        A a; // Declare a variable of class A type
        B b; // Declare a variable of class B type
    }
}
```

Now, you can tell that class A is in the package p1 and class B is in the package p2 by looking at the import declarations. Single-type-import declaration makes it easy for the reader of your code to know which class is being imported from which package. It also makes it easy to know the number and name of the classes used from other packages in your program. This book uses single-type-import declaration in all examples, except in examples where we discuss import-on-demand declaration.

Even though you are advised to use single-type-import declaration in your programs, you need to know some tricky uses and implications of using single-type-import declaration and import-on-demand declaration in a program. Subsequent sections will discuss them in detail.

Import Declarations and Type Search Order

Import declarations are used to resolve simple names of types to their fully qualified names during program compilation. The Java compiler uses predefined rules to resolve the simple names. Suppose the following statement appears in a Java program that uses a simple name A as:

```
A var;
```

The Java compiler must resolve the simple name, A, to its fully qualified name during the compilation process. It searches for a type referenced in a program (e.g. class A) in the following order.

- The current compilation unit
- Single-type-import declarations
- Types declared in the same package
- Import-on-demand declarations

The above list of type search is not complete. If a type has nested types, the nested type is searched before looking in the current compilation unit. We will discuss nested type, when we discuss inner classes later in this book.

Let us discuss the rules for a type search using some examples. Suppose you have a Java source file (a compilation unit) as `B.java` whose content is as follows. Note that the file `B.java` contains declarations for two classes – A and B.

```
// B.java
package p1;

class B {
    A var;
}
class A {
    // Code goes here
}
```

Class B refers to class A with its simple name when it declares an instance variable `var` of type A. When `B.java` file is compiled, the compiler will look for a type with the simple name A in the current compilation unit (`B.java` file). It will find a class declaration whose simple name is A in the current compilation unit. The simple name A will be replaced with its fully qualified name `p1.A`. Note that both classes A and B are declared in the same compilation unit and therefore, they are in the same package p1. The class B definition will be changed as follows by the compiler.

```
package p1;

class B {
    p1.A var; // A has been replaced by p1.A by compiler
}
```

Suppose you wanted to use class A from package p2 in the previous example. That is, there is a class p2.A and you wanted to declare the instance variable `var` of type p2.A in class B instead of p1.A. Let us try to solve it by importing class `p2.A` using a single-type-import declaration as shown below.

```
// B.java - Includes a new import declaration
package p1;

import p2.A;

class B {
    A var; // We want to use p2.A when we use A
}
class A {
    // Code goes here
}
```

When you compile the modified `B.java` file, you would get the following compilation error.

```
"B.java": p1.A is already defined in this compilation unit at line 2,
column 1
```

What is wrong with our modified `B.java` source code? When we remove the single-type-import declaration from it, it compiles fine. It means it is the single-type-import declaration that is causing the problem. Before we resolve this compiler error, we need to learn about a new rule about single-type-import declarations. The rule is:

It is a compile time error to import more than one type with the same simple name using multiple single-type-import declarations.

Suppose you have two classes, p1.A and p2.A. Note that both classes have the same simple name A. However, they are in two different packages. According to the above rules, if you want to use the two classes, p1.A and p2.A, in the same compilation unit then you cannot use two single-type-import declarations as shown below.

```
// Test.java
package pkg;

import p1.A;
import p2.A; // Compiler error.

class Test {
    A var1;   // Which A to use p1.A or p2.A?
    A var2;   // Which A to use p1.A or p2.A?
}
```

The reason behind this rule is that the compiler has no way to know which class (p1.A or p2.A) to use when you use simple name A in your code. Java might have solved this issue by using the first imported class or last imported class. However, it might introduce some subtle bugs in your program inadvertently. Java decided to nip the problem in the bud by giving you a compiler error when you import two classes with the same simple name, so you cannot make silly mistakes like this and end up spending hours resolving such issues.

Let us go back to our problem of importing p2.A class in a compilation unit, which already declares a class A. The following code gave us a compiler error.

```
// B.java - Includes a new import declaration
package p1;

import p2.A;

class B {
    A var1; // We want to use p2.A when we use A
}
class A {
    // Code goes here
}
```

We have used only one single-type-import declaration, and not two, in the above code. Why did we get an error? When you declare more than one class in the same compilation unit, most likely, they are closely related and they would refer to each other. You need to think as if Java imports each of the classes (truly speaking, any types and not just classes) declared in the same compilation unit using single-type-import declarations. You can think of the above code being transformed by Java as shown below.

```
// B.java - Includes a new import declaration
package p1;

import p1.A; // Think of it being added by Java
import p1.B; // Think of it being added by Java
import p2.A;
```

```
class B {
    A var; // We want to use p2.A when we use A
}

class A {
    // Code goes here
}
```

Can you see the problem now? The class A has been imported twice – one by Java and one by you, and this is the reason you got an error when you attempted to compile this code. So, how do you refer to p2.A in your code anyway? It is simple. Use the fully qualified name p2.A whenever you want to use p2.A in your compilation unit as shown below.

```
// B.java - Uses fully qualified name p2.A in class B
package p1;

class B {
    p2.A var; // Use fully qualified name of A
}
class A {
    // Code goes here
}
```

TIP

It is a compile-time error to import a type using a single-type-import declaration into a compilation unit, if a type with the same simple name exists in the same compilation unit.

Let us resolve the compiler error with the code, which needs to use classes from different packages with the same simple name. The code is shown below.

```
// Test.java
package pkg;

import p1.A;
import p2.A; // Compiler error.

class Test {
    A var1;   // Which A to use p1.A or p2.A?
    A var2;   // Which A to use p1.A or p2.A?
}
```

We can resolve the compiler error in the above code using any of the following two methods.

- Remove both import declarations and always use the fully qualified name of class A in the code. The modified code would look as follows:

```
// Test.java
package pkg;

class Test {
    p1.A var1; // Use p1.A
    p2.A var2; // Use p2.A
```

```
    }
```

- Use only one import declaration to import class A from one package, say p1, and use the fully
  qualified name of class A from other package p2. The modified code would look as follows.

```
// Test.java
package pkg;

import p1.A;

class Test {
    A var1;     // Refers to p1.A
    p2.A var2; // Use fully qualified name p2.A
}
```

TIP

If you want to use multiple classes in a compilation unit with the same simple name, but from
different packages, you can import a maximum of only one class. For the rest of the classes, you
must use the fully qualified name. You have another option of using the fully qualified name for all
classes and not importing any of them.

Let us discuss some of the rules about using import-on-demand declarations. The compiler uses
the import-on-demand declarations in resolving a simple name of a type after it has used all other
means to resolve the simple name. It is correct to import a class with the same simple name using
a single-type-import declaration as well as an import-on-demand declaration. In such a case, the
single-type-import declaration is used. For example, suppose we have three classes – p1.A, p2.A,
and p2.B. Suppose we have a compilation unit as follows.

```
// C.java
package p3;

import p1.A;
import p2.*;

class C {
    A var; // Will always use p1.A
}
```

In the above code, class A has been imported twice – once using simple type import declaration
from package p1, and once using import-on-demand declaration from package p2. The simple
name A inside the body of class C is resolved to p1.A, because a single-type-import declaration
always takes precedence over an import-on-demand declaration. Once the compiler finds a class
using a single-type-import declaration, it stops the search there without looking for that class using
any import-on-demand declarations.

Let us change the import declarations in the above code to use import-on-demand declarations as
follows.

```
// C.java
package p3;

import p1.*;
import p2.*;
```

```
class  C {
    A var; // Error. Which A to use p1.A or p2.A?
}
```

Compilation of class C generates the following error.

```
"C.java": reference to A is ambiguous, both class p2.A in p2 and class
p1.A in p1 match at line 8, column 5
```

The error message is loud and clear. When the compiler finds a class using an import-on-demand declaration, it tries all import-on-demand declarations. If it finds the class with the same simple name using multiple import-on-demand declarations, it generates an error, because it is not sure which class the code should use. You can resolve the above compiler error in several ways: use two single-type-import declarations, use one single-type-import and one import-on-demand declaration, or use fully qualified names for both classes.

Here is the list of some more rules about import declarations.

- Duplicate single-type-import and import-on-demand declarations are ignored. The following code is fine.

  ```
  // D.java
  package p4:

  import p1.A;
  import p1.A; // Ignored. Duplicate import declaration
  import p2.*;
  import p2.*; // Ignored. Duplicate import declaration

  class D {
     // Code goes here
  }
  ```

- It is legal, though not needed, to import classes from the same package using single-type-import declarations or import-on-demand declaration. The following code imports class F from the same package p5. Note that all classes declared in the same package are always imported by Java automatically. In such a case, the import declaration is ignored.

  ```
  // E.java
  package p5:

  import p5.F; // Will be ignored

  class E {
     // Code goes here
  }

  // F.java
  package p5:

  import p5.*; // Will be ignored

  class F {
  ```

```
        // Code goes here
    }
```

Automatic Import Declarations

We have been using the `String` class and the `System` class by their simple names and we never cared to import them in any of our programs. The fully qualified names of these classes are – `java.lang.String` and `java.lang.System`. Java always imports all types declared in the `java.lang` package automatically. Think of the following import-on-demand declaration being added to your source code before compilation.

```
import java.lang.*;
```

This is the reason why we were able to use the simple names of `String` and `System` classes in our code without importing them. You can use any types from the `java.lang` package by their simple names in your programs.

It is not an error to use an import declaration to import types from `java.lang` package. They will be simply ignored by the compiler. The following code will compile without any errors.

```
package p1;

import java.lang.*;   // Will be ignored because it is automatic

public class G {
    String anythingGoes; // refers to java.lang.String
}
```

You need to be careful when using the simple name of a type, which is the same as a type defined in `java.lang` package. Suppose there is a `p1.String` class declared as follows.

```
// String.java
package p1;

public class String {
    // Code goes here
}
```

Suppose you have a `Test` class in the same package `p1` as:

```
// Test.java
package p1;

public class Test {
    // Which String class will be used - p1.String or java.lang.String
    String myStr;
}
```

Which `String` class is referred in the `Test` class – `p1.String` or `java.lang.String`? It will refer to `p1.String` and not `java.lang.String`, because the package of the compilation unit (which is `p1` in this case) is searched before any import declarations to resolve the simple names of types. The compiler finds the `String` class in the package `p1`. It will not search `java.lang` package for the `String` class. If you wanted to use the `java.lang.String` class in the above code, you must use its fully qualified name as shown below.

```
// Test.java
package p1;

public class Test {
    java.lang.String s1;      // Use java.lang.String
    p1.String s2;             // Use p1.String
    String s3;                // Will use p1.String
}
```

Static Import Declarations

Java 5 introduced a new type of import declaration called a *static import* declaration. A static import declaration does what its name suggests. It imports `static` members (`static` variables/methods) of a type into a compilation unit. We learned about `static` variable (or class variable) in previous sections. We will discuss `static` methods in the next section. A static import declaration also comes in two flavors – single-static-import declaration and static-import-on-demand declaration. A single-static-import declaration imports one static member from a type. A static-import-on-demand declaration imports all static members of a type. Note that the static member being imported by static import declaration must be accessible to the program importing them. The general syntax of static import declaration is as follows.

Single-static-import declaration:

```
import static <<package name>>.<<type name>>.<<static member name>>;
```

Static-import-on-demand declaration:

```
import static <<package name>>.<<type name>>.*;
```

Let us discuss some examples of static import declarations. We have been printing messages on the standard output using the `System.out.println()` method. `System` is a class in `java.lang` package that has a `static` variable named `out`. When we use `System.out`, we are referring to that `static` variable `out` of the `System` class. We can use a `static` import declaration in our program to import the `out` static variable from the `System` class as follows.

```
import static java.lang.System.out;
```

Now, our program does not need to qualify the `out` variable with the `System` class name as `System.out`. Rather, it can use the name `out` to mean `System.out` in our program. The compiler will use the `static` import declaration to resolve the name, `out`, to `System.out`.

Listing 6-5 demonstrates how to use a static import declaration. It imports the out `static` variable of `System` class. Note that the `main()` method uses `out.println()` method and not `System.out.println()`. The compiler will replace the `out.println()` call with the `System.out.println()` call.

Listing 6-5: Using static import declarations

```
// StaticImportTest.java
package com.jdojo.chapter6;

import static java.lang.System.out;

public class StaticImportTest {
    public static void main(String[] args) {
        out.print("Hello static import!");
    }
}
```

```
Output:

Hello static import!
```

TIP
An import declaration imports a type name and it lets you use the type's simple name in your program. What an import declaration does with a type, a `static` import declaration does with a `static` member of a type. A `static` import declaration lets you use the name of a `static` member (`static` variable/method) of a type without qualifying it with the type name.

Let us look at another example of static import declarations. The `Math` class in the `java.lang` package has many utility constants and static methods. For example, it has a class variable named `PI`, whose value is equal to `22/7` (the mathematic pi). If you want to use any of the static variables or methods of the `Math` class, you will need to qualify them with the class name `Math`. For example, you would refer to `PI` static variable as `Math.PI` and the `sqrt()` method as `Math.sqrt()`. You can import all static members of the `Math` class using the following static-import-on-demand declaration.

```
import static java.lang.Math.*;
```

After you have imported all static members of the `Math` class in your program, you can use the name of the static member without qualifying them with the class name `Math`. Listing 6-6 demonstrates using the `Math` class by importing its `static` members.

Listing 6-6: Using static imports to import multiple static members of a type

```
// StaticImportTest2.java
package com.jdojo.chapter6;

import static java.lang.System.out;
import static java.lang.Math.*;

public class StaticImportTest2 {
    public static void main(String[] args) {
        double radius = 2.9;
        double area = PI * radius * radius;

        out.println("Value of PI is: " + PI);
        out.println("Radius of circle: " + radius);
```

```
            out.println("Area of circle: " + area);
            out.println("Square root of 2.0: " + sqrt(2.0));
        }
    }
```

```
Output:

Value of PI is: 3.141592653589793
Radius of circle: 2.9
Area of circle: 26.420794216690158
Square root of 2.0: 1.4142135623730951
```

Following are some important rules that you need to know about static import declaration.

Static Import Rule #1

If two static members with the same simple name are imported – one using single-static-import declaration and other using static-import-on-demand declaration, the one imported using single-static-import declaration takes precedence. Suppose there are two classes - `p1.C1` and `p2.C2`. Both classes have a static method named `m1`. The following code will use `p1.C1.m1()` method because it is imported using single-static-import declaration.

```
// Test.java
package com.jdojo.chapter6;

import static p1.C1.m1; // Imports C1.m1() method
import static p2.C2.*;   // Imports C2.m1() method too

public class Test {
    public static void main(String[] args) {
        m1();    // C1.m1() will be called
    }
}
```

Static Import Rule #2

Using single-static-import declaration to import two static members with the same simple name is not allowed. The following static import declarations generate an error, because both of them import the static member with the same simple name `m1`.

```
import static p1.C1.m1;
import static p1.C2.m1; // Error
```

Static Import Rule #3

If a static member is imported using a single-static-import declaration and there exists a static member in the same class with the same name, the static member in the class is used. Below is the code for two classes, `p1.A` and `p2.Test`. The `Test` class imports the `static` method `test()` from class `p1.A` using a single-static-import declaration. The `Test` class also defines a `static` method `test()`. When we use the simple name, `test`, to call the `test()` method inside the `main()` method of the `Test` class, it refers to `p2.Test.test()` method and not the one imported by the `static` import.

There is a hidden danger in using static import declarations in such cases. Suppose you did not include `test()` static method in the `p2.Test` class. Therefore, in the beginning, `test()` method call will call `p1.A.test()` method. Later, you include a `test()` method in the `Test` class and your `test()` method call will start calling `p2.Test.test()` instead of `p1.A.test()` method., which will introduce hard to find bugs in your program.

```java
// A,java
package p1;

public class A {
    public static void test() {
        System.out.println("p1.A.test()");
    }
}

// Test.java
package p2;

import static p1.A.test;

public class Test {
    public static void main(String[] args) {
        test(); // Will use p2.Test.test() method and not
                // p1.A.test() method
    }
    public static void test() {
        System.out.println("p1.Test.test()");
    }
}
```

```
Output:

p1.Test.test()
```

TIP
It may seem that static imports help you use simple names of static members from other classes in a program to make the program simpler to write and read. However, static imports may introduce subtle bugs in your programs, which may be hard to debug. It is suggested that you should not use static imports at all, or use in very rare circumstances.

Declaring Methods of a Class

A method in a Java class defines the behavior of the objects of that class or the behavior of the class itself. A method is a named block of code. A method can be invoked to execute its code. The code that invokes the method is called the *caller* of the method. Optionally, a method may accept some input values from its caller and may return a value to its caller. The list of input values that a method accepts is known as parameters. A method may have zero number of parameters. If a method has zero parameters, we say that method does not have any parameters or method does not accept any parameters. A method is always defined inside the body of a class. To keep our sample code simple, we will show a method as an isolated block of code in this section. We will show a method inside a class body when we discuss a complete example.

The general syntax for a method declaration is of the form:

```
<<modifiers>> <<return type>> <<method name>> (<<parameters list>>)
<<throws clause>> {

    // Body of the method goes here

}
```

Here, <<modifiers>> is an optional list of modifiers; <<return type>> is the data type of the value returned from the method; <<method name>> is the name of the method. The method name is followed by a pair of opening and closing parentheses. Optionally, you can specify one or more parameters to the method within its opening and closing parentheses. Parameters are separated by a comma. The closing parenthesis may be optionally followed by a throws clause. Finally, you specify the code for the method inside opening and closing braces. Note that four parts in a method declaration are mandatory and they are – the return type, method name, a pair of opening and closing parentheses and a pair of opening and closing braces. Let us discuss each part in a method declaration in detail. We will discuss modifiers in various sections of this chapter and subsequent chapters in this book. We will discuss throws clause in the chapter on exception handling. The following is an example of a method, which is named add, which accepts two integers - n1 and n2, as parameters and returns their sum.

```
int add(int n1, int n2) {
    int sum = n1 + n2;
    return sum;
}
```

The return type of a method is the data type of the value that the method will return when it is invoked. It could be a primitive data type, e.g., int, double, boolean, etc., or a reference type, e.g., Human. Sometimes, a method does not return a value to its caller. The void keyword is used as the return type of a method to indicate that the method does not return any value to the caller. In the above example, the add method returns the sum of two integers, which will be an integer. This is the reason its return type is specified as int.

The method name must be a valid Java identifier. Conventionally, a Java method starts with a lowercase and subsequently a word cap is used. For example, getName, setName, getHumanCount, and createHuman are valid method names. In the above example, add is the name of the method.

A method may accept input values from its caller. A method's parameter is used to accept an input value from a method's caller. A method's parameter consists of two parts – a data type and a variable name. In fact, a method's parameter is a variable declaration. The variables are used to hold the input values that are passed from the method's caller. A comma is used to separate two parameters of a method. In the above example, the add method declares two parameters - n1 and n2. Both parameters are of int data type. When the add method is called, the caller must pass two values of int data type. The first value, which is passed from the caller, is stored in n1 parameter, and the second value, which is passed from the caller, is stored in n2 parameter. The parameters, n1 and n2, are also known as formal parameters.

A method is uniquely identified by its signature in a particular context. The signature of a method is the combination of its name and its parameter's number, types and order. Modifiers, return type and parameter names of a method are not part of its signature. Table 6-1 lists some examples of method declarations and their signatures. Most often, you will have situations where you need to understand whether two methods have the same signature or not. It is very important to understand that the type and order of the method's parameters are part of its signature. For example, `double add(int n1, double d1)` and `double add(double d1, int n1)` have different signatures, because the order of their parameters differs even though the number and types of parameters are the same.

Table 6-1: Examples of method's declarations and their signatures

Method Declaration	Method Signature
`int add(int n1, int n2)`	`add(int, int)`
`int add(int n3, int n4)`	`add(int, int)`
`public int add(int n1, int n2)`	`add(int, int)`
`public int add(int n1, int n2) throws OutofRangeException`	`add(int, int)`
`void process(int n)`	`process(int)`
`double add(int n1, double d1)`	`add(int, double)`
`double add(double d1, int n1)`	`add(double, int)`

TIP

The signature of a method identifies the method uniquely within a class. Therefore, it is not allowed to have more than one method in a class with the same signature.

Finally, the code for the method is specified in the method's body, which is enclosed in braces. How do we execute the code for the method? Executing the code for a method is also called "calling a method" or "invoking a method". A method is invoked using its name with the values for its parameters, if any, within parentheses. To call our add method, we need to use the following statement.

```
add(10, 12);
```

The above call to the `add` method passes 10 and 12 as the values for the two parameters of the `add` method - `n1` and `n2` respectively. The two values, 10 and 12, that are used to call the add method are called actual parameters. Java copies the actual parameters to the formal parameters before it executes the code inside the body of the method. In the above call to the `add` method, 10 will be copied to `n1`, and 12 will be copied to `n2`. You can refer to the formal parameter names as variables having actual parameter values inside the method's body. You can see `n1` and `n2` being treated as variables in the following statement in the `add` method.

```
int sum = n1 + n2;
```

A `return` statement is used to return a value from a method. It starts with the `return` keyword. If a method returns a value, the `return` keyword must be followed by an expression, which evaluates to the value being returned. If the method does not return a value, its return type is specified as `void`. If the method's return type is `void`, the method does not have to include a `return` statement. If a method with a `void` return type does include a `return` statement, the `return` keyword must not be followed by any expression. In such cases, the `return` keyword is immediately followed by a semi-colon to mark the end of the statement. Here are the two flavors of the `return` statement.

```
/* If a method returns a value, <<an expression>> must evaluate to
   a data type, which is an assignment compatible with the specified
```

```
     return type of the method
*/
return <<an expression>>;
```

or

```
// If method's return type is void
return;
```

What does a `return` statement do? As its name suggests, it returns the control to the caller of the method. If it has an expression, it evaluates the expression and returns the value of the expression to the caller. If a `return` statement does not have an expression, it simply returns the control to its caller. A `return` statement is the last statement that is executed in a method's body. You can have multiple `return` statements in a method's body. However, at most, only one `return` statement may be executed for a method call.

Our add method returns the sum of two of its parameters. How do we capture the returned value of a method? A method call itself is an expression whose data type is the return type of the method and it evaluates to the returned value from the method call. For example, if we write a statement

```
add(10, 12);
```

`add(10, 12)` is an expression and its data type is `int`. At runtime, it will be evaluated to an `int` value of 22, which is the value returned from the add method. To capture the value of a method call, you can use the method call expression anywhere you can use a value. For example, the following snippet of code assigns the value returned from the add method to a variable call `sum`.

```
int sum = add(10, 12); // sum variable will be assigned 22
```

Let us turn our attention to a method, which does not return a value. We specify `void` as the return type for such a method. Let us consider the following method declaration for a method named `printPoem`.

```
void printPoem() {
    System.out.println("He that is down needs fear no fall,");
    System.out.println("he that is low no pride;");
    System.out.println("he that is humble ever shall");
    System.out.println("have God to be his guide.");
}
```

The `printPoem` method specifies `void` as its return type, which means that it does not return a value to its caller. It does not specify any parameters, which means it does not accept any input values from its caller. If you need to call the `printPoem()` method, you need to write the following statement.

```
printPoem();
```

TIP
When we refer to a method in our discussion in this book, we use the method name followed by a pair of opening and closing parentheses. For example, we will refer to our `add` method as `add()` and `printPoem` method as `printPoem()`. Sometimes, we need to refer to the formal parameters of the method to make the meaning of the method clear. In those cases, we may just use the data

---

type of the formal parameters, e.g., `add(int, int)`, to refer to `add(int n1, int n2)` method. No matter what convention we use to refer to a method in our discussion, the convention will be made clear in the context in which it is referred

Since the `printPoem` method does not return any value, you cannot use a call to this method as part of any expression, where a value is expected. For example, the following statement results in a compiler error.

```
int x = printPoem(); // Compiler error
```

When a method's return type is `void`, it is not necessary to use a `return` statement, because you do not have a value to return from the method. Recall that a `return` statement does two things – evaluates its expression, if any, and returns the control to the caller by ending the execution in the method's body. Even if you do not return a value from a method, you can still use a `return` statement in a method's body, simply to end the execution of the method. Let us add a parameter to the `printPoem` method to allow the caller to pass the stanza number that it wants to print. The modified method declaration is as follows.

```
void printPoem(int stanzaNumber) {
    if (stanzaNumber < 1 || stanzaNumber > 2) {
        System.out.println("Cannot print stanza #" + stanzaNumber);
        return; // end the method call
    }

    if (stanzaNumber == 1) {
        System.out.println("He that is down needs fear no fall,");
        System.out.println("he that is low no pride;");
        System.out.println("he that is humble ever shall");
        System.out.println("have God to be his guide.");
    }
    else if (stanzaNumber == 2) {
        System.out.println("I am content with what I have,");
        System.out.println("little be it or much;");
        System.out.println("and, Lord, contentment still I crave,");
        System.out.println("because thou savest such.");
    }
}
```

The modified `printPoem` method knows how to print stanza #1 and stanza #2. If its caller passes a stanza number outside this range, it prints a message and ends the method call without printing any stanza. This is accomplished by using a `return` statement in the first `if` statement. We could have written the above `printPoem()` method without writing any return statement as follows.

```
void printPoem(int stanzaNumber) {
    if (stanzaNumber == 1) {
        // Print stanza #1
    }
    else if (stanzaNumber == 2) {
        // Print stanza #2
    }
    else {
        System.out.println("Cannot print stanza #" + stanzaNumber);
    }
}
```

A `return` statement in the body of a method is used to return a value to the caller of the method. It ends the code execution in the method. If a method has a return type other than `void`, the method execution must end normally by executing a `return` statement with an expression. If a method specifies its return type as `void`, its execution may end normally by executing the last statement in the method's body, which is not necessarily a `return` statement. A method with its return type as `void` may also end its execution normally by executing a `return` statement, which has no expression. A method with a return type may end its execution abnormally without executing a `return` statement. In such cases, the method will throw an exception. The Java compiler will force you to include a `return` statement in the body of a method, which specifies a return type in its declaration. However, if a compiler determines that a method has specified a return type, but it always ends its execution abnormally, e.g., by throwing an exception, you do not need to include a `return` statement in the method's body. For example, the following method declaration is valid. Do not worry about the `throw` and `throws` keywords at this time. We will cover them in the chapter on *Exception Handling*.

```
int aMethod() throws Exception {
    throw new Exception("Do not call me...");
}
```

Local Variables

A variable declared inside a method, a constructor, or a block, is called a local variable. We will discuss constructors shortly. A local variable declared in a method exists only for the duration the method is being executed. Because a local variable exists only for a temporary duration, it cannot be used outside the method, the constructor, or the block in which it is declared. The formal parameters for a method are treated as local variables. They are initialized with the actual parameter values when the method is invoked, and before the method's body is executed. You need to observe the following rules about the usage of local variables.

Rule 1

Local variables are not initialized by default, except array's elements. We will discuss arrays in detail in the chapter on *Arrays*. Note that this rule is the opposite of the rule for instance/class variable's initialization. When an instance/class variable is declared, it is initialized with a default value. Consider the following partial definition of add method.

```
int add(int n1, int n2) {
    int sum;
    // What is the value of sum? We do not know, because it
    // is not initialized yet

    // More code goes here...
}
```

Rule 2

This rule is an offshoot of the first rule. A local variable cannot be accessed in the program until it is assigned a value. The following snippet of code will generate a compiler error, because it tries to print the value of the local variable, sum, before it is assigned a value. Note that Java runtime has to read the value of the sum variable before it prints its value.

```java
int add(int n1, int n2) {
    int sum;
    System.out.println(sum);// Compiler Error. Cannot read sum
                            // variable because it is not assigned
                            // a value yet.
}
```

The following snippet of code will compile fine, because the local variable sum is initialized before it is read.

```java
int add(int n1, int n2) {
    int sum = 0 ;
    System.out.println(sum); // Ok. Will print 0
}
```

Rule 3:

A local variable can be declared anywhere in the body of a method. However, it must be declared before it is used. The implication of this rule is that you do not need to declare all local variables at the start of the method body. It is a good practice to declare a variable closer to its use.

Rule 4

A local variable hides the name of an instance variable and a class variable with the same name. Let us discuss this rule in detail. Every variable, irrespective of its type, has a scope. Sometimes, the scope of a variable is also known as its visibility. The scope of a variable is the part of the program where the variable can be referred to with its simple name. The scope of a local variable declared in a method is the part of the method body that follows the variable declaration. The scope of a local variable declared in a block is the rest of the block that follows the variable declaration. The scope of the formal parameters of a method is the entire body of the method. It means that the name of the formal parameters of a method can be used throughout the body of that method. For example,

```java
int sum(int n1, int n2) {
    // n1 and n2 can be used here
}
```

The scope of an instance variable and a class variable is the entire body of the class. For example, the instance variable n1 and the class variable n2 can be referred to with its simple name anywhere in the class NameHidingTest1 as shown below.

```java
class NameHidingTest1 {
    int n1 = 10;          // Instance variable
    static int n2 = 20;   // Class variable

    // m1 is a method
    void m1() {
        // n1 and n2 can be used here
    }

    int n3 = n1;   // n1 can be used here
```

```
    }
```

What happens when two variables, say one instance variable and one local variable, are in the scope in the same part of a program? Let us consider the following code for the `NameHidingTest2` class.

```
class NameHidingTest2 {
    int n1 = 10;  // Instance variable

    // m1 is a method
    void m1() {
        int n1 = 20; // A local variable

        // Both, instance variable and local variable, with name n1
        // are in scope here

        int n2 = n1; // What value is assigned to n2 - 10 or 20?
    }

    // Only instance variable n1 is in scope here

    int n3 = n1;   // n3 is assigned value of 10
}
```

When the `m1()` method is executed in the above code, what value will be assigned to the variable n2? Note the class declares an instance variable with the name n1, and the method `m1()` also declares a local variable with the name n1. The scope of the instance variable n1 is the entire class body, including body of the `m1()` method. The scope of the local variable n1 in the `m1()` method is the entire body of the `m1()` method. When the statement

```
int n2 = n1;
```

is executed inside the `m1()` method, two variables with the same name n1 are in scope – one has value of 10 and one has value of 20. Which n1 does the above statement refer to – n1 as the instance variable, or n1 as the local variable? When a local variable has the same name as the name of a class field, an instance/class variable, the local variable name hides the name of the class field. This is known as *name hiding*. Therefore, in the above case, the local variable name n1 hides the name of the instance variable n1 inside the `m1()` method. Therefore, the above statement will refer to the local variable n1 and not the instance variable n1. Therefore, n2 will be assigned a value of 20.

TIP
A local variable, with the same name as a class field, hides the name of the class field. In other words, when a local variable as well as a class field with the same name are in the scope, the local variable takes precedence.

The following code for the class `NameHidingTest3` clarifies a little more about the time when a local variable comes into scope. It assigns the value of the n1 variable to n2 inside the `m1()` method. We have not declared the local variable n1 at the time we assigned the value of n1 to n2. At this time, only the instance variable n1 is in scope. When we assign n1 to n3, at that time, both instance variable n1 and local variable n1, are in scope. What values are assigned to n2 and n3 depends on the name-hiding rule. When two variables with the same names are in scope, the local variable is used.

```
public class NameHidingTest3 {
    int n1 = 10;   // Instance variable n1

    public void m1() {

        // Only the instance variable n1 is in scope here

        int n2 = n1; // Assigns 10 to n2

        // Only the instance variable n1 is in scope here.
        // The local variable n2 is also in scope here, which we are
        // ignoring for our discussion for now

        int n1 = 20;   // Local variable n1

        // Both, instance variable n1 and local variable n1
        // are in scope here. We are ignoring n2 for now.

        int n3 = n1;   // Assigns 20 to n3
    }
}
```

So, does it mean that we cannot declare an instance/class variable and a local variable with the same name in Java? The answer is no. You can declare an instance/class variable and a local variable with the same name. The only thing you need to know is how to refer to the instance/class variable if its name is hidden by a local variable. We will learn about referring to the hidden instance/class variables in the next section.

Instance Method and Class Method

In the previous sections, we discussed the two types of class fields - instance variables and class variables. A class can have two types of methods – instance methods and class methods. Instance methods and class methods are also called non-static methods and `static` methods respectively. An instance method is used to implement behavior of the instances (also called objects) of a class. An instance method can only be invoked in the context of an instance of the class. A class method is used to implement a behavior for the class itself. A class method can only be invoked in the context of a class.

The `static` modifier is used to define a class method. The absence of the `static` modifier in a method declaration makes the method an instance method. The following are examples declaring some static and non-static methods.

```
// A static or class method
static void aClassMethod() {
    // method's body goes here
}

// A non-static or instance method
void anInstanceMethod() {
    // method's body goes here
```

```
}
```

Recall that separate copies of an instance variable exist for each instance of a class, whereas only one copy of a class variable of a class exists, irrespective of the existence of the number of instances (possibly zero) of the class. A `static` method is called in the context of a class. When a `static` method of a class is called, an instance of that class may not exist. Therefore, it is not allowed to refer to instance variables from a `static` method. Class variables exist as soon as the class definition is loaded into memory. The class definition is always loaded into memory before the first instance of a class is created. Note that it is not necessary to create an instance of a class to load its definition into memory. JVM guarantees that all class variables of a class exist before any instances of the class. Therefore, you can always refer to a class variable inside an instance method.

TIP

A class method (or static method) can refer to only class variables (or static variables) of the class. An instance method (non-static method) can refer to class variables as well as instance variables of the class.

Let us discuss an example shown in Listing 6-7 to demonstrate the types of class fields that are accessible inside a method. The MethodType class declares m as a `static` variable and n as a non-static variable. It declare a printM() as a `static` method and printMN() as a non-static method. Inside the printM() method, we can refer to only static variable m because a static method can refer to only static variables. If you uncomment the commented statement inside the printM() method, the code will not compile because a static method will attempt to access a non-static variable - n. The printMN() method is a non-static method and it can access both static variable m and non-static variable n. Now, we would like to invoke the printM() and printMN() methods of the MethodType class. The next section discusses how to invoke a method.

Listing 6-7: Accessing class fields from static and non-static methods

```java
// MethodType.java
package com.jdojo.chapter6;

public class MethodType {
    static int m = 100; // static variable (or class variable)
    int n = 200;        // non-static variable (or instance variable)

    // Declare a static method (or class method) printM()
    static void printM() {
        // We can refer to only static variable m in
        // this method because it is a static method
        System.out.println("printM() - m = " + m);

        //System.out.println("printM() - n = " + n); // Compiler error
    }

    // Declare a non-static method (or instance method) printMN()
    void printMN() {
        // We can refer to both static and
        // non-static variables, m and n, in this method
        System.out.println("printMN() - m = " + m);
        System.out.println("printMN() - n = " + n);
    }
```

```
}
```

Invoking a Method

Executing the code in the body of a method is called invoking (or calling) a method. Instance methods and class methods are invoked differently. An instance method is invoked on an instance of the class using dot notation as:

```
<<instance reference>>.<<instance method name>>(<<actual parameters>>)
```

Note that you must have a reference to an instance of a class before you can call an instance method of that class. For example, we can write the following code snippet to invoke the printMN() instance method of the MethodType class listed in Listing 6-7.

```
// Create an instance of MethodType class and
// store its reference in mt reference variable
MethodType mt = new MethodType();

// Invoke printMN() instance method using mt reference variable
mt.printMN();
```

To invoke a class method you use dot notation with class name. The following code snippet of code invokes the printM() class method of the MethodType class.

```
// Invoke printM() class method
MethodType.printM();
```

Since whatever belongs to a class also belongs to all instances of that class, you can also invoke a class method using a reference of an instance of that class as:

```
MethodType mt = new MethodType();
mt.printM(); // Class method invocation
```

Which is a better way to invoke a class method – using the class name or using an instance reference? Both ways do the same job. However, using the class name to invoke a class method is more intuitive than using an instance reference. This book uses a class name to invoke a class method except for the purpose of demonstrating that we can also use an instance reference to invoke a class method. Listing 6-8 demonstrates how to invoke an instance method and a class method of a class. Note that the output shows the same result when you invoke the class method printM() using the class name, or an instance reference.

Listing 6-8: Examples of invoking instance methods and class methods of a class

```
// MethodTypeTest.java
package com.jdojo.chapter6;

public class MethodTypeTest {
    public static void main(String[] args) {
        // Create an instance of MethodTYpe class
        MethodType mt = new MethodType();

        System.out.println("Invoking instance method...");
```

```
        // Invoke instance method
        mt.printMN();

        System.out.println("\nInvoking class method" +
                        " on class name...");

        // Invoke class method using class name
        MethodType.printM();

        System.out.println("\nInvoking class method" +
                        " on an instance...");

        // Invoke class method using instance reference
        mt.printM();
    }
}
```

```
Output:

Invoking instance method...
printMN() - m = 100
printMN() - n = 200

Invoking class method on class name...
printM() - m = 100

Invoking class method on an instance...
printM() - m = 100
```

The Special main() Method

We learned about declaring a method in a class in the previous section. Let us discuss the `main()` method that we have been using to run our classes. The `main()` method declaration is as follows.

```
public static void main(String[] args) {
    // Method body goes here
}
```

Two modifiers, `public` and `static`, are used in the declaration of the `main()` method. The `public` modifier makes it accessible from anywhere in the application as long as the class in which it is declared is accessible. The `static` modifier makes it a class method (or static method) so that it can be invoked using a class name. Its return type is `void`, which means it does not return a value to its caller. Its name is `main` and it accepts one parameter of type `String` array (`String[]`). Note that we have been using `args` as the name of its parameter. However, you can use any parameter name as you wish. For example, you can declare main method as `public static void main(String[] myParameters)`, which is the same as declaring the `main()` method as shown above. Whatever parameter name you choose, you will need to use the same name in the body of the method if you need to refer to the parameter passed to this method.

What is special about the declaration of a `main()` method in a class? You run a Java application by passing a class name to the `java` command. For example, you would use the following command to run the `MethodTypeTest` class.

```
java com.jdojo.chapter6.MethodTypeTest
```

When the above command is executed, the JVM (the `java` command essentially starts a JVM) finds and loads the `MethodType` class definition in memory. Then, it looks for a method declaration, which is declared as `public` and `static`, returns `void` and has a method argument as `String` array. If it finds the `main()` method declaration, it invokes it. If it does not find the `main()` method, it does not know where to start the application and it throws an error stating that no `main()` method was found.

Why do we need to declare the `main()` method as `static`? The `main()` method serves as the entry point for a Java application. It is invoked by the JVM when we run a class. The JVM does not know how to create an instance of a class. It needs a standard way to start a Java application and by specifying all details about a `main()` method and making it `static` provides the JVM a standard way to start a Java application. By making the `main()` method `static`, The JVM can invoke it using the class name, which is passed on the command line.

What will happen if you do not declare the `main()` method as `static`? If you do not declare the `main()` method as `static`, it will be treated as an instance method. The code will compile fine. However, you will not be able to run the class, which has its `main()` method declared as an instance method.

Can you have more than one `main()` method in a class? The answer is yes. You can have multiple methods in a class, which can be named `main` as long as they do not have the same signature. The following declaration for the `MultipleMainMethod` class, which declares three `main()` methods, is valid. The first `main()` method, which is declared as `public static void main(String[] args)` may be used as the entry point for a Java application when the `Test` class is run. The other two `main()` methods have no special significance as far as the JVM is concerned.

```
// MultipleMainMethod.java
package com.jdojo.chapter6;

public class MultipleMainMethod {
    public static void main(String[] args) {
        // May be used as application entry point
    }

    public static void main(String[] args, int a) {
        // Another main() method
    }

    public int main() {
        // Another main() method
        return 0;
    }
}
```

Is it required for each class in Java to have a `main()` method? The answer is no. It is required that you declare a `public static void main(String[] args)` method in a class if you want to run that class. If you have a Java application, you will need to have a `main()` method, at least in one class, so you can start you application by running that class. All other classes that are used in the application, but not used to start the application, do not need to have a `main()` method.

Can you invoke the `main()` method in your code? Or, can it be invoked only by the JVM? The `main()` method is invoked by JVM when you run a class. Apart from that, you can treat the `main()` method as any other class method. Programmers have a general (and wrong) impression that the `main()` method can only be invoked by a JVM. However, that is not true. It is true that the `main()` method is generally (but not necessarily) invoked by a JVM to start a Java application. However, it does not have to be invoked (at least theoretically) only by a JVM. Here is an example that shows how the `main()` method can be invoked like any other class method. Listing 6-9 has the definition of the `MainTest1` class, which declares a `main()` method. Listing 6-10 has the definition of the `MainTest2` class, which declares a `main()` method. The `main()` method of the `MainTest2` class invokes the `main()` method of the `MainTest1` class using the following code.

```
MainTest1.main(null);
```

Note that the `main()` method of the `MainTest1` class accepts a `String` array as its parameter and the above statement passes `null` as the actual value for that parameter. We will discuss arrays in detail in the chapter on *Arrays*. We run the `MainTest2` class as:

```
java com.jdojo.chapter6.MainTest2
```

The JVM will invoke the `main()` method of the `MainTest2` class, which in turn invokes the `main()` method of the `MainTest1` class. The output in Listing 6-10 confirms this. You can also let the JVM invoke the `main()` method of the `MainTest1` class by running the `MainTest1` class as:

```
java com.jdojo.chapter6.MainTest1
```

TIP

The `main()` method in a class, which is declared as `public static void main(String[] args)`, has a special meaning only when the class is run by the JVM. It serves as an entry point for the Java application. Otherwise, the `main()` method is treated the same as any other class methods in a class.

Listing 6-9: A MainTest1 class, which declares a main() method

```java
// MainTest1.java
package com.jdojo.chapter6;

public class MainTest1 {
    public static void main(String[] args) {
        System.out.println("Inside main() method of MainTest1 " +
                           "class.");
    }
}
```

Listing 6-10: A MainTest2 class, which declares a main() method, which in turn calls the main() method of the MainTest1 class.

```java
// MainTest2.java
package com.jdojo.chapter6;
```

```
public class MainTest2 {
    public static void main(String[] args) {
        MainTest1.main(null);
    }
}
```

```
Output:

Inside main() method of MainTest1 class.
```

What is this?

Java has a keyword – this. It is a reference to the current instance of a class. It can be used only in the context of an instance. It can never be used in the context of a class, because it means the current instance, and no instance exists in the context of a class. The keyword this is used in many contexts. We will cover most of its uses in this chapter, not necessarily in this section. However, you need to note that when the keyword, this, appears in Java code, it means the current instance for which the code is being executed.

Let us consider the following snippet of code that declares a class ThisTest1.

```
public class ThisTest1 {
    int varA = 555;
    int varB = varA;        // Assign value of varA to varB
    int varC = this.varA;   // Assign value of varA to varC
}
```

The ThisTest1 class declares three instance variables – varA, varB and varC. The instance variable varA is initialized to 555. The instance variable varB is initialized to the value of varA, which is 555. The instance variable varC is initialized to the value of varA, which is 555. Note the difference in initialization expressions for varB and varC. We used unqualified varA when we initialized varB. We used this.varA when we initialized varC. However, the effect is the same. Both varB and varC are initialized with the value of varA. When we use this.varA, it means the value of varA for the current instance, which is 555. In this simple example, it was not necessary to use the keyword this. In the above case, the unqualified varA refers to the varA for the current instance. However, there are some cases where you must use the keyword this. We will discuss such cases shortly.

Since the use of the keyword this is illegal in the context of a class, you cannot use it when you initialize a class variable as shown below.

```
// Would not compile
public class ThisTest2 {
    static int varU = 555;
    static int varV = varU;
    static int varW = this.varU;  // Compiler error
}
```

When you compile the code for the class ThisTest2, you receive the following compiler error.

```
"ThisTest2.java": non-static variable this cannot be referenced from a
static context at line 4, column 21
```

The compiler error is loud and clear that you cannot use the keyword `this` in a static context. Note that static and non-static words are synonymous with class and instance words in Java. Static context is the same as class context and non-static context is the same as instance context. The above code can be corrected by removing the qualifier `this` from the initialization expression for `varW` as follows.

```
public class CorrectThisTest2 {
    static int varU = 555;
    static int varV = varU;
    static int varW = varU;
}
```

You can also qualify a class variable with a class name as shown below in `CorrectThisTest3` class.

```
public class CorrectThisTest3 {
    static int varU = 555;
    static int varV = varU;
    static int varW = CorrectThisTest3.varU;
}
```

TIP
Most of the time, you can use the simple name of instance and class variables within the class in which they are declared. You need to qualify an instance variable with the keyword `this` and a class variable with the class name only when the instance variable or the class variable is hidden by another variable with the same name.

Let us consider the following snippet of code for the `ThisTest3` class.

```
public class ThisTest3 {
    int varU = 555;
    static int varV = varU;   // Compiler error
    static int varW = varU;   // Compiler error
}
```

When you compile the `ThisTest3` class, you will receive the following compiler error.

```
"ThisTest3.java": non-static variable varU cannot be referenced from a
static context at line 3, column 21
"ThisTest3.java": non-static variable varU cannot be referenced from a
static context at line 4, column 21
```

The compiler error is the same in kind, although differently phrased, compared to the compiler error we received for the `ThisTest2` class. Last time, it complained about using the keyword `this`. This time, it complained about using the instance variable `varU`. Both, the keyword `this` and the `varU`, exist in the context of an instance. They do not exist in the context of a class. Whatever exists in the context of an instance cannot be used in the context of a class. However, whatever exists in the context of a class can always be used in the context of an instance. The instance variable declaration and initialization occurs in the context of an instance. In the `ThisTest3` class, varU, is an instance variable, and it exists only in the context of an instance. The varV and varW in ThisTest3 class are class variables and they exist only in the context of a class. This is the reason why the compiler complained, when we attempted to compile the ThisTest3 class, stating that varU, which exists in the context of an instance, cannot be used to initialize varV and varW, which exist in the context of a class.

Let us consider the code for the ThisTest4 class as shown in Listing 6-11. It declares an instance variable, num, and an instance method printNum(). In the printNum() instance method, it prints the value of the instance variable, num. In its main() method, it creates an instance of the ThisTest4 class, and invokes the printNum() method on it. The output of the ThisTest4 class shows the expected result.

Listing 6-11: An example of using the simple name of an instance variable in an instance method

```java
// ThisTest4.java
package com.jdojo.chapter6;

public class ThisTest4 {
    int num = 1982;  // An instance variable

    void printNum() {
        System.out.println("Instance variable num: " + num);
    }

    public static void main(String[] args) {
        ThisTest4 tt4 = new ThisTest4();
        tt4.printNum();
    }
}
```

```
Output:

Instance variable num: 1982
```

Let us modify the printNum() method of the ThisTest4 class, so it accepts a parameter of int data type. Let us name the parameter num. Listing 6-12 has the modified code for the printNum() method as part of the ThisTest5 class. The output of the ThisTest5 class indicates that the printNum() method is using its parameter num when we use the simple name, num, inside its body. This is an example of name hiding, where the local variable (method parameter is considered as local variable) num hides the name of the instance variable num inside the printNum() method's body. In the printNum() method, the simple name num refers to its parameter num and not the instance variable num. In this case, you must use the keyword this to qualify the num variable, if you want to refer to the num instance variable inside the printNum() method. Using this.num is the only way you can refer to the instance variable from inside the printNum() method, as long you keep the parameter name as num. Another way is to rename the parameter to something other than num, e.g., numParam or newNum.

Listing 6-12: Variables name hiding

```java
// ThisTest5.java
package com.jdojo.chapter6;

public class ThisTest5 {
    int num = 1982;  // An instance variable
```

```
    void printNum(int num) {
        System.out.println("Parameter num: " + num);
        System.out.println("Instance variable num: " + num);
    }

    public static void main(String[] args) {
        ThisTest5 tt5 = new ThisTest5();
        tt5.printNum(1969);
    }
}
```

```
Output:

Parameter num: 1969
Instance variable num: 1969
```

Listing 6-13 shows how to use the keyword `this` to refer to the `num` instance variable inside the `printNum()` method. The output of this listing shows the expected result. If you do not want to use the keyword `this`, you can rename the parameter name of the `printNum()` method as shown below. Once you rename the parameter to something other than `num`, the `num` instance variable is no longer hidden inside the body of the `printNum()` method, and therefore, you can refer to it using its simple name.

```
void printNum(int numParam) {
    System.out.println("Parameter num: " + numParam);
    System.out.println("Instance variable num: " + num);
}
```

You can still use the keyword `this` to refer to the instance variable `num` inside the `printNum()` method even if it is not hidden as shown below. However, using the keyword `this` in the following case is a matter of choice and not a requirement.

```
void printNum(int numParam) {
    System.out.println("Parameter num: " + numParam);
    System.out.println("Instance variable num: " + this.num);
}
```

Listing 6-13: Using the this keyword to refer to an instance variable, whose name is hidden by a local variable

```
// ThisTest6.java
package com.jdojo.chapter6;

public class ThisTest6 {
    int num = 1982;  // An instance variable

    void printNum(int num) {
        System.out.println("Parameter num: " + num);
        System.out.println("Instance variable num: " + this.num);
    }

    public static void main(String[] args) {
        ThisTest6 tt6 = new ThisTest6();
        tt6.printNum(1969);
```

```
        }
}
```

In the previous example, we have seen that use of the keyword `this` is necessary to access instance variables, when the instance variable name is hidden. We can avoid using the keyword `this` in such circumstances by renaming the variable that hides the instance variable name, or renaming the instance variable itself. Sometimes, it is easier to keep the variable names the same, as they represent the same thing. This book uses the convention of using the same name for instance variables and local variables, if they represent the same thing in a class. For example, the following code is very common. The `Student` class declares an instance variable named `id`. In its `setId()` method, it also names the parameter `id`, and uses `this.id` to refer to the instance variable in its body. It also uses `this.id` to refer to the instance variable id in its `getId()` method. Note that there is no name hiding occurring in the `getId()` method and you could use the simple name, `id`, which means the instance variable, `id`.

```
public class Student {
    private int id;  // Instance variable

    public void setId(int id) {
        this.id = id;
    }

    public int getId() {
        return this.id;
    {
}
```

We will discuss the use of the keyword `this` again, in this chapter and subsequent chapters. Table 6-2 lists the parts of a class, the context in which they occur, and the permitted use of the keyword `this`, the instance variable and the class variable. We have not yet covered all parts of a class that are listed in Table 6-2. We will cover them in this chapter.

Table 6-2: The context type and allowed use of the keyword this, an instance variable, and a class variable

Part of a Class	Context (Instance/Class)	Can use this keyword?	Can use instance variable?	Can use class variable?
Instance variable initialization	Instance	Yes	Yes	Yes
Class variable initialization	Class	No	No	Yes
Instance initializer	Instance	Yes	Yes	Yes
Class initializer (Also called static initializer)	Class	No	No	Yes
Constructor	Instance	Yes	Yes	Yes
Instance method (Also called non-static method)	Instance	Yes	Yes	Yes

Class method (Also called static method)	Class	No	No	Yes

The keyword `this` is a `final` (a constant is called `final` in Java, because Java uses the `final` keyword to declare a constant) reference to the current instance of the class in which it appears. Since it is `final`, you cannot change its value. Since `this` is a keyword, you cannot declare a variable named `this`. The following code will generate a compiler error.

```
public class ThisError {
    void m1() {
        int this = 10;// Error cannot name a variable as this
        this = null;  // Compiler error. Cannot assign a value to this
                      // because it is a constant
    }
}
```

You can also use the keyword `this` to qualify an instance method name although using the keyword `this` to refer to an instance method is never required. The following code shows the `m1()` method invoking the `m2()` method using the keyword `this`. Note that both methods are instance methods and they could use the simple name to invoke each other or use the `this` keyword as a qualifier.

```
public class ThisTestMethod {
    void m1() {
        // Invoke m2() method
        this.m2(); // same as - m2();
    }

    void m2() {
        // do something
    }
}
```

Access Levels for Class Members

We have covered access levels for a class, which can be public or default (or package level). This section discusses access levels for class members – fields and methods. The access level for a class member determines what area of the program can access (use or refer to) it. One of the following four access level modifiers can be used for a class member.

- `public`
- `private`
- `protected`
- Default or package-level access

Three out of four types of access levels for a class member are specified using one of the three keywords – `public`, `private`, or `protected`. The fourth type of access level is called the default access level (or package-level access), and it is specified by using no access modifiers. That is, the absence of any of the three access level modifiers, `public`, `private`, or `protected`, specifies package-level access.

If a class member is declared as public, using the `public` keyword, it can be accessed from anywhere in Java code, provided the class itself is accessible.

If a class member is declared as private, using the `private` keyword, it can be accessed only within the body of the declaring class, and nowhere else.

If a class member is declared as protected, using the `protected` keyword, it can be accessed from the same package or from descendants of the class, even if the descendants are in a different package. We will discuss the protected access level in detail in the chapter on *Inheritance*.

If you do not use any access level modifier for a class member, it has package-level access. A class member with package-level access can be accessed from the same package.

Access levels for a class member can be listed from the most restrictive to the least restrictive as – `private`, package-level, `protected` and `public`. Table 6-3 summarizes the four access levels for a class member.

Table 6-3: List of access levels for class members

Access Level for Class Member	Accessibility
private	Only within the same class
package-level	In the same package
protected	Same package or descendant in any package
public	Everywhere

The following is a sample class that declares many class members with different access levels.

```java
// AccessLevelSample.java
package com.jdojo.chapter6;

// Class AccessLevelSample has public access level
public class AccessLevelSample {
    private int num1;    // private access
    int num2;            // package-level access
    protected int num3;  // protected access level
    public int num4;     // public access level

    public static int count = 1; // public access level

    // m1() method has private access level
    private void m1() {
        // Code goes here
    }

    // m2() method has package-level access
    void m2() {
        // Code goes here
    }

    // m3() method has protected access level
    protected void m3() {
        // Code goes here
```

```
    }

    // m4() method has public access level
    public void m4() {
        // Code goes here
    }

    // doSomething() method has private access level
    private static void doSometing() {
        // Code goes here
    }
}
```

Note that access levels can be specified for both instance and static members of a class. It is a convention to specify the access level modifier as the first modifier in the declaration. If you declare a static field for a class, which is public, you should use the `public` modifier first, and then the static modifier, as a convention. For example, both of the following declarations for an instance variable, num, are valid.

```
// Declaration #1
public static int num; // Conventionally used

// Declaration #2
static public int num; // Technically correct. Conventionally not used
```

Let us discuss some examples of using the access level modifiers for class members, and their effects. Consider the code for the `AccessLevel` class as shown in Listing 6-14. It has four instance variables – v1, v2, v3 and v4, and four instance methods – m1(), m2(), m3(), and m4(). Four different access level modifiers have been used for instance variables and instance methods. We have chosen to use instance variables and methods in this example. However, the same access level rules apply to class variables and class methods. The code for `AccessLevel` class compiles without any errors. Note that no matter what the access level for a class member is, it is always accessible inside the class in which it is declared. This can be proved by the fact that we have accessed (read their values) all instance variables, which have different access levels, inside all four methods.

Listing 6-14: An AccessLevel class with class members having different access levels

```
// AccessLevel.java
package com.jdojo.chapter6;

public class AccessLevel {
    private int v1 = 100;
    int v2 = 200;
    protected int v3 = 300;
    public int v4 = 400;

    private void m1() {
        System.out.println("Inside m1().");
        System.out.println("v1 = " + v1 + ", v2 = " + v2 +
                            ", v3 = " + v3 + ", v4 = " + v4);
    }

    void m2() {
        System.out.println("Inside m2()");
        System.out.println("v1 = " + v1 + ", v2 = " + v2 +
```

```
                                  ", v3 = " + v3 + ", v4 = " + v4);
    }

    protected void m3() {
        System.out.println("Inside m3()");
        System.out.println("v1 = " + v1 + ", v2 = " + v2 +
                              ", v3 = " + v3 + ", v4 = " + v4);
    }

    public void m4() {
        System.out.println("Inside m4()");
        System.out.println("v1 = " + v1 + ", v2 = " + v2 +
                              ", v3 = " + v3 + ", v4 = " + v4);
    }
}
```

Let us consider an `AccessLevelTest1` class as shown in Listing 6-15.

Listing 6-15: A test class, which is in the same package as the AccessLevel class

```
// AccessLevelTest1.java
package com.jdojo.chapter6;

public class AccessLevelTest1 {
    public static void main(String[] args) {
        AccessLevel al = new AccessLevel();

        //int a = al.v1; // compiler error
        int b = al.v2;
        int c = al.v3;
        int d = al.v4;

        System.out.println("b = " + b + ", c = " + c +
                              ", d = " + d);

        //al.m1(); // Compiler error
        al.m2();
        al.m3();
        al.m4();

        // Modify the values of instance variables
        al.v2 = 20;
        al.v3 = 30;
        al.v4 = 40;

        System.out.println("\nAfter modifying v2, v3 and v4");

        al.m2();
        al.m3();
        al.m4();
    }
}
```

```
Output:

b = 200, c = 300, d = 400
```

```
Inside m2(): v1 = 100, v2 = 200, v3 = 300, v4 = 400
Inside m3(): v1 = 100, v2 = 200, v3 = 300, v4 = 400
Inside m4(): v1 = 100, v2 = 200, v3 = 300, v4 = 400

After modifying v2, v3 and v4
Inside m2(): v1 = 100, v2 = 20, v3 = 30, v4 = 40
Inside m3(): v1 = 100, v2 = 20, v3 = 30, v4 = 40
Inside m4(): v1 = 100, v2 = 20, v3 = 30, v4 = 40
```

Two classes, `AccessLevel` and `AccessLevelTest1`, are in the same `com.jdojo.chapter6` package. `AccessLevelTest1` can access all class members of the `AccessLevel` class, except the ones, which have been declared `private`, because they are in the same package. You cannot access the instance variable `v1` and the instance method `m1()` of the `AccessLevel` class from the `AccessLevelTest1` class, because their access level is `private`. If you uncomment the two statements in the `AccessLevelTest1` class, which attempts to access the `private` instance variable `v1` and the `private` instance method `m1()` of the `AccessLevel` class, you would receive the following compiler error.

```
"AccessLevelTest1.java": v1 has private access in
com.jdojo.chapter6.AccessLevel at line 7, column 16
"AccessLevelTest1.java": m1() has private access in
com.jdojo.chapter6.AccessLevel at line 12, column 8
```

The `AccessLevelTest1` class reads the values of the instance variables of the `AccessLevel` class, as well as modifies them. You must note one thing that even though we cannot access the `private` instance variable `v1` and the `private` method `m1()` of the `AccessLevel` class from the `AccessLevelTest1` class, we are able to print the value of the `private` instance variable `v1` as shown in the output. An access level modifier for a class member specifies who can access them directly. If a class member is not accessible directly, it might be accessible indirectly. In our example, the instance variable `v1` and the instance method `m1()` are not directly accessible from outside the class `AccessLevel`. However, they may be indirectly accessible from outside the `AccessLevel` class. Indirect access to an inaccessible class member is usually given by providing another method, which is accessible from outside, and accessing the inaccessible class member through the accessible method. Suppose we want the outside world to read and modify the value of the otherwise inaccessible `private` instance variable `v1`. We need to add two `public` methods – `getV1()` and `setV1()`, to `AccessLevel` class and these two methods will read and modify the value of the `v1` instance variable. Our modified `AccessLevel` class would look as follows.

```
public class AccessLevel {
    private int v1;

    // Other code goes here

    public int getV1() {
        return this.v1;
    }

    public void setV1(int v1) {
        this.v1 = v1;
    }
}
```

Now, even if the private instance variable `v1` is not directly accessible from outside `AccessLevel` class, it is made indirectly accessible through `public` methods - `getV1()` and `setV1()`.

Let us consider another test class as shown in Listing 6-16. Note that the `AccessLevelTest2` class in the `com.jdojo.chapter6.p1` package, which is different from the `com.jdojo.chapter6` package in which the `AccessLevel` class exists. The code for the `AccessLevelTest2` class is similar to the code for the `AccessLevelTest1` class, except for the fact that most of the statements have been commented. Note that you need to use an `import` statement to import the `AccessLevel` class from the `com.jdojo.chapter6` package, so you can use its simple name inside the `main()` method. In the `AccessLevelTest1` class, it was not necessary to import the `AccessLevel` class, because they are in the same package. The `AccessLevelTest2` class can access only the `public` members of the `AccessLevel` class, because it is in a different package than the `AccessLevel` class. This is the reason the uncommented statements access only the `public` instance variable `v4` and the `public` method `m4()`. Note that even if only the `v4` instance variable is accessible, we are able to print the values of `v1`, `v2` and `v3` as well, by accessing them indirectly through the public method `m4()`.

Listing 6-16: A test class, which is in a different package from the AccessLevel class

```java
// AccessLevelTest2.java
package com.jdojo.chapter6.p1;

import com.jdojo.chapter6.AccessLevel;

public class AccessLevelTest2 {
    public static void main(String[] args) {
        AccessLevel al = new AccessLevel();

        //int a = al.v1; // compiler error
        //int b = al.v2; // compiler error
        //int c = al.v3; // compiler error
        int d = al.v4;

        System.out.println("d = " + d);

        //al.m1(); // Compiler error
        //al.m2(); // compiler error
        //al.m3(); // compiler error
        al.m4();

        // Modify the values of instance variables
        //al.v2 = 20;  // Compiler error
        //al.v3 = 30;  // compiler error
        al.v4 = 40;

        System.out.println("\nAfter modifying v4...");
        //al.m2();  // Compiler error
        //al.m3();  // Compiler error
        al.m4();
    }
}
```

```
Output:

d = 400
Inside m4(): v1 = 100, v2 = 200, v3 = 300, v4 = 400

After modifying v4...
```

```
Inside m4(): v1 = 100, v2 = 200, v3 = 300, v4 = 40
```

Let us consider a trickier situation as shown in Listing 6-17. Note that there is no access level modifier used for the `AccessLevel2` class, which gives it a package-level access by default. That is, the `AccessLevel2` class is accessible only within the `com.jdojo.chapter6` package. The `AccessLeve2` class is simple. It declares only one member, which is the `public static` variable `v1`.

Listing 6-17: A class with package-level access having a public instance variable

```java
// AccessLevel2.java
package com.jdojo.chapter6;

class AccessLevel2 {
    public static int v1 = 600;
}
```

Let us consider the class `AccessLevelTest3` shown in Listing 6-18, which is in a different package than the package of the class `AccessLevel2`.

Listing 6-18: A test class that attempts to access a public member of a class with a package-level access

```java
// AccessLevelTest3.java
package com.jdojo.chapter6.p1;

import com.jdojo.chapter6.AccessLevel2; // Compiler error

public class AccessLevelTest3 {
    public static void main(String[] args) {
        int a = AccessLevel2.v1; // Compiler error
    }
}
```

The `AccesssLeveTest3` class attempts to access the public static variable `v1` of the `AccessLevel2` class, which generates a compiler error. Did we not say that a class member with `public` access level is accessible from anywhere? Yes. We did say that. Here is the catch. Suppose you have some money in your pocket and you declare that your money is public. Therefore, anyone can have your money. However, you hide yourself so that no one can have access to you. How can anyone access your money unless you become accessible to him first? This is the case with the `AccessLevel2` class and its `public static` variable, `v1`. Compare the `AccessLevel2` class with yourself, and its `public static` variable, `v1`, with your money. The `AccessLevel2` class has package-level access. Therefore, codes only within its package (`com.jdojo.chapter6`) can access its name. Its `static` variable `v1` has the access level of `public`, which means any code can access it from any package. The `static` variable `v1` belongs to the `AccessLevel2` class. Unless the `AccessLevel2` class itself is accessible, its `static` variable, `v1`, cannot be accessed, even though it has been declared `public`. The `import` statement in Listing 6-18 will also generate a compiler error for the reason that the `AccessLevel2` class is not accessible outside its package `com.jdojo.chapter6`.

TIP

You must consider the access level of both, the class and its member, to determine whether a class member is accessible or not. The access level of a class member may make it accessible to

---

a part of a program. However, that part of a program can access the class member only if the class itself, to which the member belongs, is also accessible to that part of the program

Access Level – A Case Study

A class member can have one of the four access levels – private, protected, public, or package-level. Which access level should be used with a class member? The answer to this question depends on the member type and its purpose. Let us discuss an example of a bank account. Suppose you create a class, whose instance represents a bank account. You name the class as Account and its definition is shown as below.

```java
// Account.java
package com.jdojo.chapter6;

public class Account {
    public double balance;
}
```

What does a bank account hold at any time? It holds the balance in the account. The above definition of the Account class does just that. In the real world, a bank account can hold many more pieces of information, e.g., account number, account holder name, address, etc. We will keep our Account class simple so that we can focus on the discussion of access level. It allows its every instance to hold a numeric value in its balance instance variable. If you want to create an instance of the Account class and manipulate its balance, you can do so as shown below.

```java
// Create an account object
Account ac = new Account();

// Change the balance to 1000.00
ac.balance = 1000.00;

// Change the balance to 550.29
ac.balance = 550.29;
```

The snippet of code can be executed anywhere in a Java application because both, the Account class and its balance instance variable, are public. However, in the real world, no one would let his bank account be manipulated like this. For example, a bank may require you to have a minimum of zero balance in your account. With the above implementation, nothing stops you from executing the following statement, which reduces the balance in an account to a negative number.

```java
// Set negative balance
ac.balance = -440.67;
```

In object-oriented programming, as a rule of thumb, the pieces of information that define the state of an object should be declared private. All instance variables of a class constitute the state of objects of that class. Therefore, they should be declared private. If code outside a class is needed to have access to a private instance variable, the access should be given indirectly, by providing a method. The method should have an appropriate access level, which will allow only intended client code to access it. Let us declare the balance instance variable as private. Our modified code for the Account class is shown below.

```
// Account.java
package com.jdojo.chapter6;

public class Account {
    private double balance;
}
```

With the modified `Account` class, we can create an object of the `Account` class anywhere in a Java application.

```
// Create an account object
Account ac = new Account();
```

However, we cannot access the `balance` instance variable of the `Account` object unless we write the code inside the `Account` class itself. The following code is valid only if it is written inside the `Account` class, because the `private` instance variable `balance` cannot be accessed from outside the `Account` class.

```
// Change the balance
ac.balance = 188.37;
```

The modified version of our `Account` class is not acceptable in this form because we can create an account, but cannot read or manipulate its balance. The `Account` class must provide some interface for the outside world to access and manipulate its balance in a controlled way. For example, if you have money and want to share it with the outside world, you do not show the money to everyone and ask him to take it directly. Rather, anyone who wants your money needs to ask you (send you a message) and then, you give him your money according to your and his situations. In other words, money is your private possession and you let other access it in a controlled way by making them ask you for that money, instead of taking money directly from your pocket. Similarly, we want others to view the balance of an account, credit money to an account and debit money from an account. However, all these actions should happen through an `Account` object, rather than manipulating the balance of an account object directly. Java lets you send a message to an object by using instance methods. An object can receive a message from the outside world and it can respond differently to the same message depending on its internal state. For example, when all your money is gone, and someone asks you for money, you can respond by saying that you do not have any money. However, you responded to the same message (give me money) differently (by giving the money) when you had money.

Let us declare three public methods in the `Account` class that will serve as an interface to the outside world who wants to access and manipulate the balance of an account. The three methods would be `getBalance()`, `credit()` and `debit()`.

*   The `getBalance()` method will return the balance of an account.
*   The `credit()` method will deposit a specified amount to an account.
*   The `debit()` method will withdraw a specified amount from an account.
*   Both `credit()` and `debit()` methods will return 1 if the transaction is successful and -1 if the transaction fails.

Listing 6-19 has the code for the modified `Account` class. It has a `private` instance variable, and `public` methods that let the outside world access and modify the `private` instance variable. The `public` methods are acting like protective covers for the `private` instance variable. They let the outside world read or modify the `private` instance variable in a controlled way. For example, you cannot credit a negative amount, and a minimum of zero balance must be maintained.

Listing 6-19: A modified version of the Account class with private instance variable and public methods

```java
// Account.java
package com.jdojo.chapter6;

public class Account {
    private double balance;

    public double getBalance() {
        // Return the balance of this account
        return this.balance;
    }

    public int credit(double amount) {
        // Make sure credit amount is not negative, NaN or infinity
        if (amount < 0.0 || Double.isNaN(amount) ||
            Double.isInfinite(amount)) {
            System.out.println("Invalid credit amount: " + amount);
            return -1;
        }

        // Credit the amount
        System.out.println("Crediting amount: " + amount);
        this.balance = this.balance + amount;
        return 1;
    }

    public int debit(double amount) {
        // Make sure debit amount is not negative, NaN or infinity
        if (amount < 0.0 || Double.isNaN(amount)
                      || Double.isInfinite(amount)) {
            System.out.println("Invalid debit amount: " + amount);
            return -1;
        }

        // Make sure minimum balance of zero is maintained
        if (this.balance < amount) {
            System.out.println("Insufficient fund. " +
                                "Debit attempted: " + amount);
            return -1;
        }

        // Debit the amount
        System.out.println("Debiting amount: " + amount);
        this.balance = this.balance - amount;
        return 1;
    }
}
```

Let us test our modified `Account` class. The test code is shown in Listing 6-20. It creates an object of the `Account` class and attempts various operations on it using its `public` methods. The result has been shown in the output. The result indicates that this is an improved `Account` class, which protects an account object from being manipulated incorrectly. You can also note that by making instance variables `private` and allowing access to them through `public` methods lets you enforce your business rules. If you expose the instance variables, you cannot enforce any business rules that control its valid values, because anyone can modify it without any restrictions.

Chapter 6. Classes and Objects

Listing 6-20: A test class to test the Account class behavior

```java
//AccountTest.java
package com.jdojo.chapter6;

public class AccountTest {
    public static void main(String[] args) {
        Account ac = new Account();
        double balance = ac.getBalance();
        System.out.println("Balance = " + balance);

        // Credit and debit some amount
        ac.credit(234.78);
        ac.debit(100.12);

        balance = ac.getBalance();
        System.out.println("Balance = " + balance);

        // Attempt to credit and debit invalid amounts
        ac.credit(-234.90);
        ac.debit(Double.POSITIVE_INFINITY);

        balance = ac.getBalance();
        System.out.println("Balance = " + balance);

        // Attempt to debit more than the balance
        ac.debit(2000.00);

        balance = ac.getBalance();
        System.out.println("Balance = " + balance);
    }
}
```

```
Output:

Balance = 0.0
Crediting amount: 234.78
Debiting amount: 100.12
Balance = 134.66
Invalid credit amount: -234.9
Invalid debit amount: Infinity
Balance = 134.66
Insufficient fund. Debit attempted: 2000.0
Balance = 134.66
```

One important point to keep in mind when you design a class is its maintainability. By keeping all instance variables `private` and allowing access to them through `public` methods makes your code ready for future changes. For example, suppose we started with a zero minimum balance for an account. We have deployed the `Account` class in the production environment and it is being used at many places in the application. Now, we want to implement a new business rule that states that every account must have a minimum balance of 100. It is easy to make this change. Just change the code for the `debit()` method and you are done. Recompile the modified `Account` class and deploy it again. You do not need to make any changes to the client codes that are calling the `debit()` method of the `Account` class. Note that we need a little more work with the

`Account` class to fully enforce the rule of a minimum balance of 100. When an account is created, the balance is zero by default. To enforce this new minimum balance rule at the time an account is created, we will need to know about constructors of a class. We will discuss constructors later in this chapter.

Another option for the access level for the `balance` instance variable in the `Account` class is to give it a package-level access. Recall that a package-level access is given to a class member by using no access modifier in its declaration. If the `balance` instance variable has package-level access, it is a little better than giving it `public` access, because it is not accessible from everywhere. However, it can be accessed and manipulated directly by any code inside the same package in which the `Account` class has been declared. We all understand that letting any code access the `balance` instance variable directly from outside the `Account` class is not acceptable. Additionally, if we declare the method of the `Account` class to have package-level access, they can be used only inside the same package in which the `Account` class has been declared. We want objects of the `Account` class to be manipulated from anywhere in the application using its methods. Therefore, we cannot declare the methods or the instance variable of the `Account` class to have package-level access. When do we declare a class and/or a class member to have package-level access? Typically, a package-level access is used for a class and its member when the class has to serve as a helper class or internal implementation for other classes in a package.

When do we use a `private` access level for class members? We have already seen the benefits of using the `private` instance variables for the `Account` class. The `private` access level for instance variables provides data hiding, where the internal state of the object is protected from outside access. An instance method for a class defines a behavior for its objects. If a method is used only internally within a class, and no outside codes have any business knowing about it, the method should have a `private` access level. Let us go back to our `Account` class. We have the same code to validate the amount that is passed to `credit()` and `debit()` methods of the `Account` class. We can move the code that validates the amount to a method called `isValidAmount()` and make it a `private` method. The `isvalidAmount()` method is used internally by the `Account` class. It checks if an amount being used for credit or debit is not a negative number, not a `NaN` and not infinity. These three criteria for a number to be a valid number apply only to the `Account` class, and no other class needs to be using them. This is the reason we need to declare this method private. Declaring it `private` has another advantage. In the future, we may make a rule that you must credit or debit a minimum of 10 from any account. At that time, we could just change the `private isValidAmount()` method and we are done. If we had made this method `public`, it would affect all the client code, which was using it to validate an amount. We may not want to change the criteria for a valid amount globally. To keep the effect of a change localized in a class, when the business rules change, we must implement a method as private. We can implement this logic in our `Account` class as follows. Only changed code is shown below.

```
// Account.java
package com.jdojo.chapter6;

public class Account {
    // Other code goes here

    public int credit(double amount) {
        // Make sure credit amount is valid
        if (!this.isValidAmount(amount, "credit")) {
          return -1;
        }
        // Other code goes here
    }
```

```java
    public int debit(double amount) {
        // Make sure debit amount is valid
        if (!this.isValidAmount(amount, "debit")) {
          return -1;
        }

        // Other code goes here
    }

    // Use a private method to validate credit/debit amount
    private boolean isValidAmount(double amount, String operation) {
        // Make sure amount is not negative, NaN or infinity
        if (amount < 0.0 || Double.isNaN(amount)
                         || Double.isInfinite(amount)) {

          System.out.println("Invalid " + operation +
                                " amount: " + amount);
          return false;
        }

        return true;
    }
}
```

You may argue that you might have implemented the `credit()` method (`debit()` method as well) in a simpler way using the following logic.

```java
if (amount >= 0)  {
    this.balance = this.balance + amount;
    return 1;
}
else {
    // Print an error message here
    return -1;
{
```

You could use the simpler logic to implement the `credit()` method, which checks if the amount is valid, instead of checking if the amount is invalid. We did not use this logic, because we wanted to demonstrate, in the same example, how to use a `private` method. Sometimes, we write more code to drive home a point in the discussion of a specific topic.

Now, we are left with the `protected` access level modifier. When do we declare a class member as `protected`? A class member with the `protected` access-level can be accessed in the same package and in the descendant class, even if the descendant class is not in the same package. We will discuss how to create a descendant class and the use of the `protected` access level in the chapter on *Inheritance*.

Parameter Passing Mechanisms

This section discusses the different ways of passing parameters to a method that are used in different programming languages. We will not discuss anything that is specific to Java in this section. Rather, we will discuss parameters passing mechanisms that may apply to any programming language and not necessarily to Java. The syntax or symbols used in this section may not be supported by Java. This section is important to programmers in understanding the memory states in the process of a method call, when different mechanism are used to pass parameters to a method. If you are an experienced programmer, who knows about different ways of parameter passing mechanisms, you may skip this section. The next section will discuss the parameter passing mechanism in Java.

The following are some of the mechanisms to pass parameters to a method.

- Pass by value
- Pass by constant Value
- Pass by reference
- Pass by reference value
- Pass by result
- Pass by result value
- Pass by name
- Pass by need

A variable has three components – a name, a memory address (or a location) and data. The name of a variable is a logical name that is used in a program to refer to its data. Data is stored at the memory address that is associated with the variable name. The data stored at the memory address is also known as the value of the variable. Suppose you have a variable named `id` of `int` data type whose value is `785`, which is stored at the memory address `131072`.You may declare and initialize the `id` variable as follows.

```
int id = 785;
```

You can visualize the relationship between the variable name, its memory address and the data stored at the memory address for `id` variable as depicted in Figure 6-4.

Figure 6-4: Relationship between a variable name, a memory address, and the value stored at that memory address.

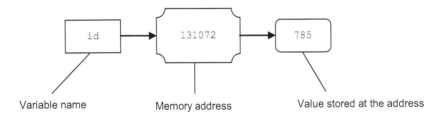

In the above example, we see that the actual data of the variable `id` is stored at the memory address. You can also store a data at a memory address, which is not the actual value for the variable; rather it is the memory address of the location where the actual value is stored. In this case, the value stored at the first memory address is a reference to the actual data stored at some other memory address, and such a value is known as a *reference* or a *pointer*. If a variable stores the reference to some data, it is called a reference variable. Contrast the phrases – "variable" and "reference variable". A variable stores the actual data itself. A reference variable stores the reference (or memory address) of the actual data. Figure 6-5 depicts the difference between a variable and a reference variable. Here, `idRef` is a reference variable and `id` is a variable. Both variables, `id` and `idRef`, are allocated memory separately. The actual value of `785` is stored at the memory location of `id` variable, which is `131072`. However, the memory location (`262144`) of `idRef` stores the address of `id` variable (or address or memory location, where `785` is stored). We can get to the value `785` in memory using either of the variables – `id` or `idRef`. The operation to get the actual data that a reference variable refers to is called *dereferencing*.

Figure 6-5: Difference between a variable and a reference variable

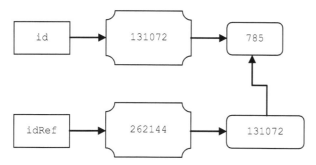

A method (also called function or procedure in some programming languages) can optionally accept parameters from its caller. A method's parameters allow data sharing between the caller context and the method context. There are many mechanisms that are in practice to pass the parameters to a method. The following sections discuss some of the commonly used parameter passing mechanisms.

Pass By Value

It is the simplest parameter passing mechanism to understand. However, it is not necessarily the most efficient and the easiest to implement in all situations. When a method is called, the values of the actual parameters are copied to the formal parameters. When the method execution starts, two copies of the value exist in memory – one copy for the actual parameter and one copy for the formal parameter. Inside the method, the formal parameter operates on its own copy of the value. Any changes made to the value of the formal parameter do not affect the value of the actual parameter. Figure 6-6 depicts the memory state when a method is called using pass by value mechanism. It is to be emphasized that once the formal parameter gets its value, which is a copy of the actual parameter, the two parameters have nothing to do with each other. The formal parameter is discarded at the end of the method call. However, the actual parameter persists in the memory after the method call ends. How long the actual parameter persists in the memory depends on the context of the actual parameter.

Figure 6-6: Memory states for actual and formal parameters when a method is call

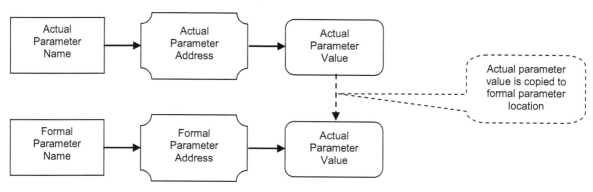

Let us consider the following code for the `increment()` method, which accepts one parameter of `int` data type and increments it by 2.

```
// Assume that num is passed by value
void increment(int num) {
    // #2
    num = num + 2;
    // #3
}
```

Suppose we call the `increment()` method with the following snippet of code.

```
int id = 57;
// #1
increment(id);
// #4
```

We have labeled four points of executions in the code as #1, #2, #3 and #4. Table 6-4 describes the memory states for the actual parameter and the formal parameter, before, after and when the `increment()` method is invoked. Note that the formal parameter `num` no longer exists in memory at #4.

Table 6-4: Description of memory states for actual and formal parameters when the increment() method is called and the parameter is passed by value

Point of Execution	Memory State of Actual Parameter id	Memory State of Formal Parameter num
#1	The id variable exists in memory and its value is 57.	The num variable does not exist at this point.
#2	The id variable exists in memory and its value is 57.	The formal parameter, num, has been created in memory. The value of the actual parameter id has been copied to the address associated with num variable. At this point, num holds the value of 57.
#3	The id variable exists in memory and its value is 57.	At this point, num holds value of 59.
#4	The id variable exists in memory and its value is 57.	The formal parameter, num, does not exist in memory at this point because method call is over.

All local variables, including formal parameters, are discarded when a method invocation is over. You can observe that incrementing the value of the formal parameter inside the `increment()` method was practically useless because it can never be communicated back to the caller's environment. If you want to send back one value to the caller environment, you can use a `return` statement in the method body to do that. The following is the code for the `smartIncrement()` method, which returns the incremented value to the caller.

```
// Assume that num is passed by value
int smartIncrement(int num) {
    num = num + 2;
    return num;
}
```

You will need to use the following snippet of code to store the incremented value that is returned from the method in `id` variable.

```
int id = 57;
id = smartIncrement(id);  // store the returned value to id
// At this point id has a value of 59
```

Note that *pass by value* lets you pass multiple values from the caller environment to the method using multiple parameters. However, it lets you send back only one value as the returned value from the method. If you just consider the parameters in a method call, *pass by value* is a one-way communication. It lets you pass information from the caller to the method using parameters. However, it does not let you pass back information to the caller through the parameters. Sometimes, you may want to send multiple values from a method to the caller's environment through the parameters to the method. In those cases, you need to consider different ways to pass parameters to the method. *Pass by value* mechanism is of no help in such situation.

A method that is used to swap two values does not work when the parameters are passed by values. Consider the following code for a classical `swap()` method.

```
// Assume that x and y are passed by value
void swap(int x, int y) {
    int temp = x;
    x = y;
    y = temp;
}
```

You can call the above `swap()` method using the following snippet of code.

```
int u = 75;
int v = 53;
swap(u, v);
//At this point, u and v will be still 75 and 53 respectively
```

By this time, you should be able to figure out why the values of u and v were not swapped when they were passed to the `swap()` method. When the `swap()` method was called, the values of u and v were copied to locations of x and y formal parameters respectively. Inside the `swap()` method, the values of the formal parameters, x and y, were swapped and the values of actual parameters, u and v, were not touched at all. When the method call was over, the formal parameters, x and y, were discarded.

Advantages of using *pass by value* are as follows.

- It is easy to implement.
- If the data being copied is a simple value, it is faster.
- The actual parameters are protected from any side effects when they are passed to the method.

Disadvantages of using *pass by value* are as follows.

- If the actual parameter is a complex data, e.g., a large object, it may be difficult, if not impossible, to copy the data to another memory location.
- Copying a large amount of data takes memory space and time, which may slow down the method call

---

Pass By Constant Value

Pass by constant value is essentially the same mechanism as *pass by value* with one difference that the formal parameters are treated as constants and hence cannot be changed inside the method's body. The values of actual parameters are copied to the formal parameters as it is done in *pass by value*. You can only read the value of formal parameters inside the method's body if they are passed by constant value.

Pass By Reference

It is important that you do not get confused with two phrases – "reference" and "pass by reference". A reference is a piece of information (typically a memory address) that is used to get to the actual data stored at some other location. *Pass by reference* is a mechanism to pass information from a caller's environment to a method using formal parameters.

In *pass by reference*, the memory address of the actual parameter is passed and the formal parameter is mapped (or associated) with the memory address of the actual parameter. This technique is also known as *aliasing* where multiple variables are associated with the same memory location. The formal parameter name is an alias for the actual parameter name. When a person has two names, no matter which of the two names you use, you are referring to the same person. Similarly, when a parameter is passed by reference, no matter which name you use in the code (the actual parameter name or the formal parameter name), you are referring to the same memory location and hence the same data.

In *pass by reference*, if the formal parameter is modified inside the method, the actual parameter sees the modification instantaneously. Figure 6-7 depicts the memory state for actual and formal parameters when a parameter to a method is passed by reference. Many books use the phrase "pass by reference". However, they do not mean the one we are discussing in this section. They really mean "pass by reference value", which we will discuss in the next section. Note that, in *pass by reference*, we do not allocate separate memory for the formal parameter. Rather, we just associate the formal parameter name to the same memory location of the actual parameter.

Figure 6-7: Memory states of actual and formal parameters when the parameters are passed by reference

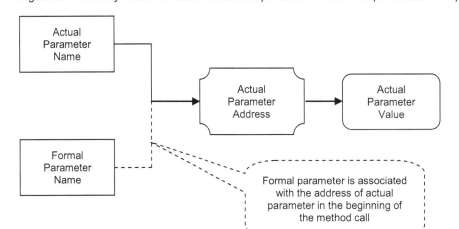

Let us do our `increment()` method call exercise again. This time, we assume that the `num` parameter is passed by reference.

```
// Assume that num is passed by reference
void increment(int num) {
    // #2
    num = num + 2;
    // #3
}
```

We will call the `increment()` method with the following snippet of code.

```
int id = 57;
// #1
increment(id);
// #4
```

Table 6-5 describes the memory states for the actual parameter and formal parameter, before, after, and during the `increment()` method's invocation. Note that at #4, the formal parameter, `num`, no longer exists in memory and still, the actual parameter `id` has the value of 59 after the method call is over.

Table 6-5: Description of memory states for actual and formal parameters when the increment() method is called and the parameter is passed by reference

Point of Execution	Memory State of Actual Parameter id	Memory State of Formal Parameter num
#1	The id variable exists in memory and its value is 57.	The num variable does not exist at this point.
#2	The id variable exists in memory and its value is 57.	The formal parameter's name, num, has been associated with the memory address of actual parameter id. At this point, num refers to value of 57, which is exactly the same as what id refers to.
#3	The id variable exists in memory and its value is 59. Inside method, we used the formal parameter name, num, to increment the value by 2. However, id and num are two names for the same memory location and therefore, the value of id is also 59.	At this point, num holds value of 59.
#4	The id variable exists in memory and its value is 59.	The formal parameter name, num, does not exist in memory at this point, because method call is over.

Pass by reference allows you to have a two-way communication between the caller environment and the called method. You can pass multiple parameters by reference to a method and the method can modify all parameters. All modifications to formal parameters are reflected back to the caller's environment instantaneously. It lets you share multiple pieces of data between the two environments.

The classical `swap()` method example works when its parameters are passed by reference. Consider the following `swap()` method's definition.

```
// Assume that x and y are passed by reference
```

```
void swap(int x, int y) {
    int temp = x;
    x = y;
    y = temp;
}
```

You can call the above `swap()` method using the following snippet of code.

```
int u = 75;
int v = 53;
swap(u, v);
//At this point, u and v will be 53 and 75 respectively.
```

Let us consider the following snippet of code for a method name `getNumber()`.

```
// Assume that x and y are passed by reference
int getNumber(int x, int y) {
    int x = 3;
    int y = 5;
    int sum = x + y;
    return sum;
}
```

Suppose we call the `getNumber()` method as follows.

```
int w = 100;
int s = getNumber(w, w);
// What is value of s at this point - 200, 8, 10 or something else?
```

When the `getNumber()` method returns, what value will be stored in the variable `s`? Note that both parameters to the `getNumber()` method are passed by reference and we pass the same variable, `w`, for both parameters in our call. When the `getNumber()` method starts executing, the formal parameters, `x` and `y`, are aliases to the same actual parameter `w`. When you use `w`, `x` or `y`, you are referring to the same data in memory. Before adding `x` and `y`, and storing the result in `sum` local variable, the method sets the value of `y` to 5, which makes all `w`, `x` and `y` have a value of 5. When `x` and `y` are added inside the method, both x and y refer the value 5. The `getNumber()` method returns 10.

Let us consider another call to the `getNumber()` method as a part of an expression as follows.

```
int a = 10;
int b = 19;
int c = getNumber(a, b) + a;
// What is value of c at this point?
```

It is little trickier to predict the value of `c` in the above snippet of code. You will need to consider the side effect of the `getNumner()` method call on the actual parameters. The `getNumber()` method will return 8, and it will also modify the value of `a` and `b` to 3 and 5 respectively. A value of 11 (8 + 3) will be assigned to c. Consider the following statement in which we have changed the order of operand for addition operator.

```
int a = 10;
int b = 19;
```

```
int d =  a + getNumber(a, b);
// What is value of d at this point?
```

The value of d will be 18 (10 + 8). The local value of 10 will be used for a. You need to consider the side effects on actual parameters by a method call if the parameters are passed by reference. You would have thought that two expressions – getNumber(a, b) + a and a + getNumber(a, b) would give the same result. However, when the parameters are passed by reference, the result may not be the same as explained above.

The advantages of using *pass by reference* are:

- It is more efficient, compared to *pass by value*, as actual parameters values are not copied.
- It lets you share more than one piece of values between the caller and the called method environments.

The disadvantages of using *pass by reference* are:

- It is potentially dangerous if the modification made to the actual parameters inside the called method is not taken into consideration by the caller.
- The program logic is not simple to follow, because of the side effects on the actual parameters through formal parameters.

Pass By Reference Value

The mechanism of passing parameters to a method using *pass by reference value* is different from *pass by reference*. However, the effect of using *pass by reference value* is the same as using *pass by reference*. In *pass by reference value*, the reference of the actual parameter is copied to the formal parameter. The formal parameter uses a dereferencing mechanism to access the actual parameter's value. The modification made by the formal parameters inside the method is immediately visible to the actual parameters, as is also the case in *pass by reference*. Figure 6-8 depicts the memory states for the actual and formal parameters when the *pass by reference value* mechanism is used.

Figure 6-8: Memory states for actual and formal parameters when a method call is made using pass by reference value mechanism

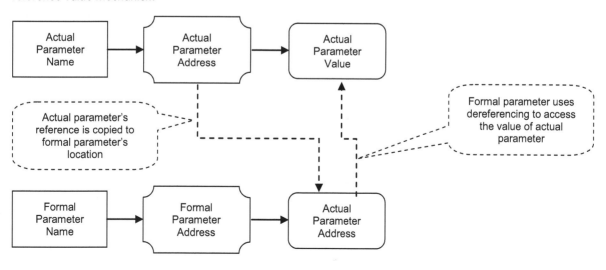

There is an important difference between *pass by reference* and *pass by reference value*. In *pass by reference value*, the reference of the actual parameter is copied to the formal parameter as part of the method call. However, you can change the formal parameter to refer to a different location in memory inside the method, which will not make the actual parameter refer to the new location in memory. Once you change the reference stored in the formal parameter, any changes made to the value stored at the new location will not change the value of the actual parameter.

Our discussions and examples referring to the side effects and memory states for *pass by reference* also apply to the *pass by reference value* mechanism. Most of the programming languages simulate the *pass by reference* mechanism using *pass by reference value*.

Pass by Constant Reference Value

Pass by constant reference value is essentially the same as *pass by reference value* with one difference. The formal parameter is treated as a constant inside the method body. That is, the formal parameter holds the copy of the reference held by the actual parameter throughout the execution of the method. The formal parameter cannot be modified inside the method's body to hold reference of data other than what actual parameter is referencing.

Pass by Result

You can think of *pass by result* as the opposite way of *pass by value*. In *pass by value*, the value of the actual parameter is copied to the formal parameter. In *pass by result*, the value of the actual parameter is not copied to the formal parameter. The formal parameter is considered an uninitialized local variable when the method execution starts. During method execution, the formal parameter is assigned a value. At the end of the method execution, the value of the formal parameter is copied back to the actual parameter.

Figure 6-9 depicts the memory state for the actual and formal parameters when pass by result mechanism of parameter passing is used. Sometimes, the formal parameters are also known as OUT parameters when pass by result mechanism is used to pass them to a method. They are called OUT parameters, because they are used to co*py out* value from the method to the caller's environment. Sometimes, the formal parameters are known as IN parameters if they uses pass by value mechanism because they are used to *copy in* the value of the actual parameter.

Figure 6-9: Memory states for actual and formal parameters when pass by result parameter passing mechanism is used

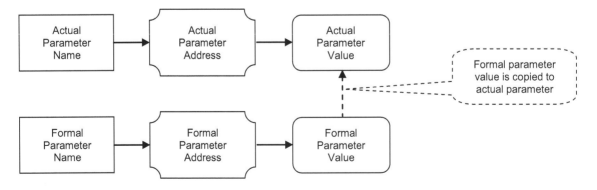

Chapter 6. Classes and Objects

Pass by Value Result

It is also known as *pass by copy-restore*. It is a combination of *pass by value* and *pass by result* (hence the name is *"pass by value result"*). It is also known as IN-OUT way of passing parameters. When a method is called, the value of the actual parameter is copied to the formal parameter. During the execution of the method, the formal parameter operates on its own local copy of data. When the method call is over, the value of the formal parameter is copied back to the actual parameter. This is the reason it is also called *pass by copy restore*. It copies the value of the actual parameter in the beginning and restores the value of formal parameter in the actual parameter at the end of the call. Figure 6-10 depicts the memory state of actual and formal parameters when *pass by value result* mechanism is used to pass parameters.

It achieves the effect of *pass by reference* in a different way. In *pass by reference*, any modification made to the formal parameter is visible to the actual parameter immediately. In *pass by value result*, any modification to the formal parameter is visible to the actual parameter only when the method call returns. If the formal parameter, which uses *pass by value result*, is modified multiple times inside a method, only the final modified value will be seen by the actual parameter.

Figure 6-10: Memory states for actual and formal parameters when pass by result parameter passing mechanism is used

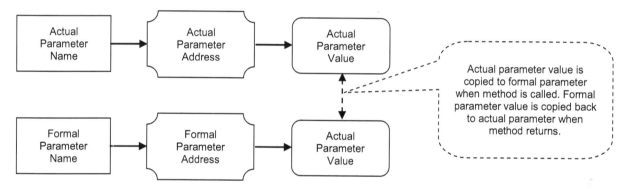

Pass by value result is used to simulate *pass by reference* in distributed applications. Suppose you make a remote method call, which executes on a different machine. The reference (memory address) of the actual parameter, which exists in one machine, will not make any sense in the machine on which the remote method is executed. In such cases, the client application sends a copy of the actual parameter to the remote machine. The value copied to the formal parameter is on the remote machine. The formal parameter operates on the copy. When the remote method call returns, the value of the formal parameter on the remote machine is copied back to the actual parameter on the client machine. This gives the client code the functionality of passing parameters by reference to remote methods that run on another machine.

Pass By Name

Typically, the actual parameter expression is evaluated before its value/reference is passed to a method. In *pass by name*, the actual parameter's expressions are not evaluated when a method is called. The formal parameter's name inside the body of the method is substituted textually with the expressions of their corresponding actual parameters. Actual parameters are evaluated each time they are encountered during the execution of the method and they are evaluated with respect to the caller's context. If there is a name conflict between the local variables in the method and the actual parameter expression during substitution, local variables are renamed so that they have unique names.

Pass by name is implemented using *thunks*. A thunk is a piece of code that computes and returns the value of an expression in a specific context. A thunk is generated for each actual parameter and its reference is passed to the method. At each use of a formal parameter, a call to thunk is made, which evaluates the actual parameter in the caller context.

The advantage of *pass by name* is that the actual parameters are never evaluated unless they are used in the method during the method's execution. This is also known as lazy evaluation. Contrast it with *pass by value* mechanism, where actual parameters are always evaluated before they are copied to the formal parameter. This is called eager evaluation. The disadvantage of *pass by name* is that the actual parameters are evaluated every time the corresponding formal parameters are used inside the method's body. It is also harder to follow the logic of a method if it uses *pass by name* formal parameter, which can also have side effects.

Let us consider the following method `squareDivide()`.

```
int squareDivide(int x, int y) {
    int z =  x * x/y * y;
    return z;
}
```

Consider the following snippet of code that calls the `squareDivide()` method;

```
squareDivide((4+4), (2+2));
```

You can visualize the execution of the above call as if you have written the `squareDivide()` method as follows. Note that the actual argument expressions `(2+2)` and `(4+4)` are evaluated multiple times inside the method's body.

```
int squareDivide() {
    int z = (4+4)*(4+4)/(2+2)*(2+2);
    return z;
}
```

Pass by Need

It is similar to *pass by name* with one difference. In *pass by name*, actual parameters are evaluated each time they are used in the method. In *pass by need*, the actual parameters are evaluated only once upon their first use. When a thunk for an actual parameter is called the first time, it evaluates the actual parameter expression, caches the value and returns it. When the same thunk is called again, it simply returns its cached value, rather than re-evaluating the actual parameter expression again.

Parameter Passing Mechanisms in Java

Java supports two kinds of data types – primitive data type and reference data type. A primitive data type is a simple data structure and it has only one value associated with it. A reference data type is a complex data structure and it represents an object. A variable of a primitive data type stores the value directly at its memory address. Suppose we have a variable, `id`, which is of `int` data type as follows. Further suppose, it has been assigned a value of `754` and its memory address is `131072`.

```
int id = 754;
```

Figure 6-11 shows the memory state of `id` variable. The value `754` is directly stored at the memory address `131072`, which is associated with the `id` variable name. What happens if we execute the following statement, which assigns a new value of `351` to the `id` variable?

```
id = 351;
```

When a new value `351` is assigned to the `id` variable, the old value of `754` is replaced with the new value `351` at the memory address as shown in Figure 6-12.

Figure 6-11: The memory state for an id variable when its value is 754.

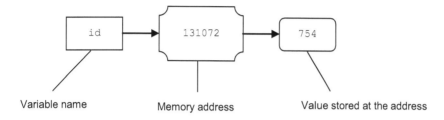

Figure 6-12: The memory state for an id variable, when a new value of 351 is assigned to it

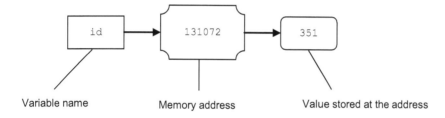

Things are different when you work with objects and reference variables. Let us consider the `Car` class as shown in Listing 6-21. It has three instance variables – `model`, `year` and `price`, which have been given initial values of "`Unknown`", `2000` and `0.0` respectively.

Listing 6-21: Car class with three public instance variables

```
// Car.java
package com.jdojo.chapter6;

public class Car {
    public String model = "Unknown";
    public int year     = 2000;
    public double price = 0.0;
}
```

When you create an object of a reference type, the object is created on the heap at a specific memory address. Let us create an object of the `Car` class as follows.

```
new Car();
```

Figure 6-13 shows the memory state when the above statement is executed to create a `Car` object. We assume that the memory address at which the object is created is `262144`. You can see that when an object is created, memory is allocated for all of its instance variables and they are initialized. In this case, `model`, `year` and `price` of the new `Car` object have been initialized properly as shown in the figure.

Figure 6-13: Memory state when a Car object is created using the new Car() statement

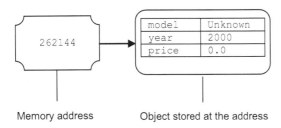

Memory address   Object stored at the address

At this point, there is no way to refer to the newly created `Car` object from a Java program even though it exists in memory. The `new` operator (as used in `new Car()`) returns the memory address of the object it creates. In our case, it will return `262144`. Recall that the memory address of the data (`Car` object in our case) is also called reference of that data. Now onwards, we will say that the `new` operator in Java returns reference to the object it creates instead of saying that it returns the memory address of the object it creates. Both mean the same thing. However, Java uses the term "reference", which has a more generic meaning than "memory address". In order to access the newly created `Car` object, we must store its reference in a reference variable. Recall that a reference variable stores the reference to some data, which is stored somewhere else. All variables that you declare of reference type are reference variables in Java. A reference variable in Java can store a `null` reference, which means that it refers to nothing. Consider the following snippet of code that performs different things on reference variable.

```
Car myCar = null;    // #1
myCar = new Car();   // #2
Car xyCar = null;    // #3
xyCar = myCar;       // $4
```

When the statement labeled #1 is executed, memory is allocated for `myCar` reference variable, say at memory address `8192`. The `null` value is a special value, typically memory address of zero, which is stored at the memory address of `myCar` variable. Figure 6-14 depicts the memory state for `myCar` variable when it is assigned a `null` reference.

Figure 6-14: Memory state for myCar variable, when "Car myCar = null" statement is executed

The execution of statement labeled #2 is a two step process. First, it executes "`new Car()`" part of the statement to create a new `Car` object. Suppose the new `Car` object is allocated at memory address of 9216. The "`new Car()`" expression returns the reference of the new object, which is `9216`. In the second step, the reference of the new object is stored in `myCar` reference variable.

The memory state for `myCar` reference variable and the new `Car` object after the statement labeled #2 is executed has been shown in Figure 6-15. Note that the memory address of new `Car` object (`9216`) and the value of `myCar` reference variable match at this point. You do not need to worry about the numbers used in this example for memory addresses. We just made up some numbers to drive home the point how the memory addresses are used internally. Java does not let you access the memory address of an object or a variable. Java lets you access/modify the state of objects through reference variables.

Figure 6-15: Memory states for myCar reference variable and the new Car object when "myCar = new Car()" statement is executed

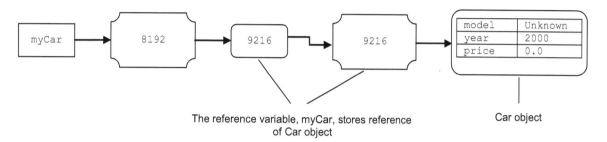

The reference variable, myCar, stores reference
of Car object

Car object

Statement labeled #3 is similar to statement labeled #1. The memory state for `xyCar` reference variable is shown in Figure 6-16 assuming that `10240` is the memory address for `xyCar` reference variable.

Figure 6-16: Memory state of xyCar reference variable.

It is interesting to note the memory state when the statement labeled #4 is executed. The statement reads as follows.

```
xyCar = myCar;   // #4
```

Recall that a variable name has two things associated with it – a memory address and a value stored at that memory address. The memory address (or location) is also known as its `lvalue` whereas the value stored at its memory address is also called `rvalue`. When a variable is used to the left of an assignment operator (`xyCar` in statement labeled #4), it refers to its memory address. When a variable is used to the right of assignment operator (`myCar` in statement labeled #4), it refers to its value (`rvalue`) stored at its memory address. The statement labeled #4 can be read as follows.

```
xyCar = myCar;                                  // #4
At lvalue of xyCar store rvalue of myCar;       // #4 - another way
At memory address of xyCar store value of myCar // #4 - another way
```

Therefore, when we execute the statement "`xyCar = myCar`", it reads the value of `myCar`, which 9216, and stores it at the memory address of `xyCar`. The reference variable `myCar` stores a reference to a `Car` object. The assignment like "`xyCar = myCar`" does not copy the object to

---

which `myCar` refers. Rather, it copies the value stored in `myCar` (a reference to the `Car` object) to `xyCar`. When the assignment, "`xyCar = myCar`" is complete, reference variables, `myCar` and `xyCar`, have reference to the same `Car` object in memory. At this point, only one `Car` object exists in memory. Figure 6-17 shows the memory state when statement labeled #4 is executed. At this time, you can use reference variables, `myCar` or `xyCar`, to access the `Car` object in memory. The following snippet of code will access the same object in memory.

```
myCar.model = "Civic LX";    // Use myCar to change model
myCar.year  = 1999;          // Use myCar to change year
xyCar.price = 16000.00;      // Use xyCar to change the price
```

After executing the above three statements, `model`, `year` and `price` will be changed for the `Car` object and the memory state will look as shown in Figure 6-18.

Figure 6-17: Memory state showing myCar and xyCar referencing the same Car object in memory.

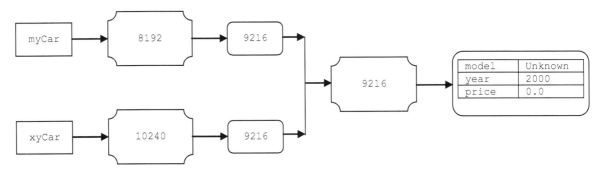

Figure 6-18: Memory state showing myCar and xyCar referencing the same Car object in memory after myCar and xyCar have been used to change the state of the Car object

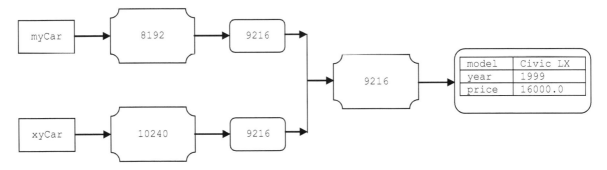

At this point, two reference variables, `myCar` and `xyCar`, and one `Car` object exist in memory. Both reference variables are referencing the same `Car` object. Let us execute the following statement and label it as #5.

```
myCar = new Car();   // #5
```

The above statement will create a new `Car` object in memory with initial values for its instance variables and assign the reference of the new `Car` object to `myCar` reference variable. The `xyCar` reference variable still references the `Car` object it was referencing before. Suppose the new `Car` object has been allocated at memory address `5120`. The memory state for two reference variables, `myCar` and `xyCar`, and two `Car` objects is shown in Figure 6-19.

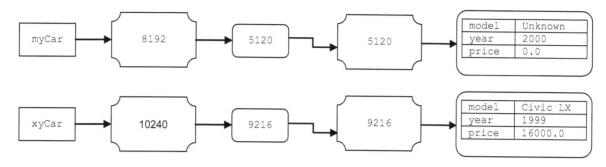

Let us make one more change and set the xyCar reference variable to null as shown below.

```
xyCar = null;  // #6
```

Figure 6-20 shows the memory state after the above statement #6 is executed. Now xyCar reference variable stores a null reference and it no longer refers to any Car object. The Car object with "Civic LX" model is not being referenced by any reference variable. Now, we cannot access this Car object at all in our program because we do not have a reference to it. In Java terminology, the Car object with "Civic LX" model is not reachable. When an object in memory is not reachable, it becomes eligible for garbage collection. Note that the Car object with the "Civic LX" model is not destroyed (or de-allocated) immediately after xyCar is set to null. It stays in memory until the garbage collector runs and makes sure that it is not reachable. Please refer to the chapter on *Garbage Collection* for more details on how an object's memory is de-allocated.

Figure 6-20: Memory state of reference variables, myCar and xyCar and two Car objects after xyCar has been assigned a null reference.

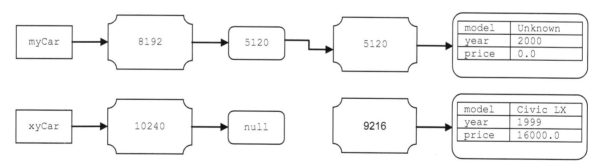

We have covered enough background about variables types and how they work in Java. It is time to discuss the parameter passing mechanism in Java. In brief, we can state:

All parameters in Java are passed by value.

This brief statement causes lots of confusion. Does it mean that when a parameter is a reference type, a copy of the object the actual parameter refers to is made and assigned to the formal parameter? It is important to elaborate on the phrase – "All parameters in Java are passed by value" with examples. Even veteran Java programmers have problems in understanding parameter passing mechanism in Java. To be more elaborate, Java supports the following four types of parameter passing mechanisms.

- Pass by value
- Pass by constant value
- Pass by reference value
- Pass by constant reference value

Note that all four ways of passing parameters in Java includes the word "value". This is the reason why many books on Java summarize them as: "Java passes all parameters by value." Please refer to the previous section for more details for the above-mentioned four types of parameter passing mechanisms.

The first two types – *pass by value* and *pass by constant value* apply to parameters of primitive data types. The last two types – *pass by reference value* and *pass by constant reference value* apply to the parameters of reference type.

When a formal parameter is of primitive data type, the value of the actual parameter is copied to the formal parameter. Any changes made to the formal parameter's value inside the method's body will change only the copy of the formal parameter and not the value of the actual parameter. Now you can tell that swap() method to swap two primitive values will not work in Java. Listing 6-22 demonstrates that swap() method cannot be written in Java, because primitive type parameters are passed by value. The output shows that the x and y formal parameters of the swap() method receive the values of a and b. The values of x and y are swapped inside the method, which does not affect the values of actual parameters a and b at all.

Listing 6-22: An unsuccessful attempt to write a swap() method to swap values of two primitive types in Java

```
// BadSwapTest.java
package com.jdojo.chapter6;

public class BadSwapTest {
    public static void swap(int x, int y) {
        System.out.println("#2: x = " + x + ", y = " + y);

        int temp = x;
        x - y;
        y = temp;

        System.out.println("#3: x = " + x + ", y = " + y);
    }

    public static void main(String[] args) {
        int a = 19;
        int b = 37;

        System.out.println("#1: a = " + a + ", b = " + b);

        // Call swap() method to swap values of a and b
        BadSwapTest.swap(a, b);

        System.out.println("#4: a = " + a + ", b = " + b);
    }
}
```

```
Output:

#1: a = 19, b = 37
```

```
#2: x = 19, y = 37
#3: x = 37, y = 19
#4: a = 19, b = 37
```

A primitive type parameter is passed by value. However, you can modify the value of the formal parameter inside the method without affecting the actual parameter value. Java also lets you use *pass by constant value*. In this case, the formal parameter cannot be modified inside the method. The formal parameter is initialized with the value of the actual parameter by making a copy of the actual parameter and then it is a constant value, which can only be read. You need to use the `final` keyword in the formal parameter declaration to indicate that you mean to pass the parameter by constant value. Any attempt to change the value of a parameter, which uses pass by constant value, results in a compiler error. Listing 6-23 demonstrates how to use pass by constant value mechanism to pass the parameter x to the `test()` method. Any attempt to change the value of the formal parameter x inside the `test()` method will result in a compiler error. If you uncomment the "x = 10;" statement inside the `test()` method, you would get the following compiler error.

```
Error(10):   final parameter x may not be assigned
```

We have passed two parameters, x and y, to the `test()` method. The parameter y is passed by value and hence it can be changed inside the method. This can be confirmed by looking at the output of Listing 6-23.

Listing 6-23: An example of pass by constant value.

```java
// PassByConstantValueTest.java
package com.jdojo.chapter6;

public class PassByConstantValueTest {
    // x uses pass by constant value and y uses pass by value
    public static void test(final int x, int y) {
        System.out.println("#2: x = " + x + ", y = " + y);

        // Uncommenting following statement will generate a compiler
        // error
        // x = 79; // Cannot change x. It is passed by constant value

        y = 223; // Ok to change y

        System.out.println("#3: x = " + x + ", y = " + y);
    }

    public static void main(String[] args) {
        int a = 19;
        int b = 37;

        System.out.println("#1: a = " + a + ", b = " + b);

        PassByConstantValueTest.test(a, b);

        System.out.println("#4: a = " + a + ", b = " + b);
    }
}
```

```
Output:
```

```
#1: a = 19, b = 37
#2: x = 19, y = 37
#3: x = 19, y = 223
#4: a = 19, b = 37
```

Let us discuss the parameter passing mechanism for reference type parameters. Java lets you use *pass by reference value* and *pass by constant reference value* mechanisms to pass reference type parameters to a method. When a parameter is passed by reference value, the reference stored in the actual parameter is copied to the formal parameter. When the method starts executing, both, the actual parameter and the formal parameter, reference the same object in memory. If the actual parameter has a `null` reference, the formal parameter will contain the `null` reference. You can assign a reference to another object to the formal parameter inside the method's body. In this case, the formal parameter starts referencing the new object in memory and the actual parameter still references the object it was referencing before the method call. Listing 6-24 demonstrates the pass by reference mechanism in Java. It creates a `Car` object inside the `main()` method and stores the reference of the `Car` object in `myCar` reference variable.

```
// Create a Car object and assign its reference to myCar
Car myCar = new Car();
```

It modifies the model, year and price of the newly created `Car` object using `myCar` reference variable.

```
// Change model, year and price of Car object using myCar
myCar.model = "Civic LX";
myCar.year  = 1999;
myCar.price = 16000.0;
```

The message labeled #1 in the output shows the state of the `Car` object. The `myCar` reference variable is passed to the `test()` method using the following call.

```
PassByReferenceValueTest.test(myCar);
```

Since the type of the formal parameter `xyCar` in the `test()` method is `Car`, which is a reference type, Java uses the *pass by reference value* mechanism to pass the value of `myCar` actual parameter to `xyCar` formal parameter. When `test(myCar)` method is called, Java copies the reference of the `Car` object stored in `myCar` reference variable to the `xyCar` reference variable. When the execution enters the `test()` method's body, `myCar` and `xyCar` reference the same object in memory. At this time, there is only one `Car` object in memory and not two. It is very important to understand that the `test(myCar)` method call did not make a copy of the `Car` object referenced by `myCar` reference variable. Rather, it made a copy of the reference (memory address) of the `Car` object referenced by `myCar` reference variable, which is the actual parameter, and copied that reference to `xyCar` reference variable, which is the formal parameter. The fact that both, `myCar` and `xyCar`, reference the same object in memory is indicated by the message labeled #2 in the output, which is printed using `xyCar` formal parameter inside the `test()` method..

Now we create a new `Car` object and assign its reference to the `xyCar` formal parameter inside the `test()` method.

```
// Let us make xyCar refer to a new Car object
xyCar = new Car();
```

At this point, there are two `Car` objects in memory. The `xyCar` formal parameter references the new `Car` object and not the one whose reference was passed to the method. Note that the actual parameter, `myCar`, still references the `Car` object that we had created in the `main()` method. The fact that `xyCar` formal parameter references the new `Car` object is indicated by the message labeled #3 in the output. When the `test()` method call returns, the `main()` method prints details of the `Car` object being referenced by `myCar` reference variable.

TIP

When a reference type parameter is passed to a method in Java, the formal parameter can access the object exactly the same way the actual parameter can access the object. The formal parameter can modify the object by directly changing the values of the instance variables or by calling methods on the object. Any modification made on the object through the formal parameter is immediately visible through the actual parameter, because both hold the reference to the same object in memory. The formal parameter itself can be modified to reference another object (or the `null` reference) inside the method.

Listing 6-24: An example of pass by reference value

```java
// PassByReferenceValueTest.java
package com.jdojo.chapter6;

public class PassByReferenceValueTest {
    public static void main(String[] args) {
        // Create a Car object and assign its reference to myCar
        Car myCar = new Car();

        // Change model, year and price of Car object using myCar
        myCar.model = "Civic LX";
        myCar.year  = 1999;
        myCar.price = 16000.0;

        System.out.println("#1: model = " + myCar.model +
                            ", year = "   + myCar.year +
                            ", price = "  + myCar.price);

        PassByReferenceValueTest.test(myCar);

        System.out.println("#4: model = " + myCar.model +
                            ", year = "   + myCar.year +
                            ", price = "  + myCar.price);
    }

    public static void test(Car xyCar) {
        System.out.println("#2: model = " + xyCar.model +
                            ", year = "   + xyCar.year +
                            ", price = "  + xyCar.price);

        // Let us make xyCar refer to a new Car object
        xyCar = new Car();

        System.out.println("#3: model = " + xyCar.model +
                            ", year = "   + xyCar.year +
                            ", price = "  + xyCar.price);
    }
```

}

If you do not want the method to change the reference type formal parameter to reference a different object than the one referenced by the actual parameter, you can use *pass by constant reference value* mechanism to pass that parameter. If you use the keyword `final` in the reference type formal parameter declaration, the parameter is passed by constant reference value and the formal parameter cannot be modified inside the method. The following declaration of the `test()` method declares the `xyzCar` formal parameter as `final` and it is passed by constant reference value. The method attempts to change the `xyzCar` formal parameter by assigning a `null` reference to it and then by assigning a reference to a new `Car` objects. Both of these assignment statements will generate a compiler error.

```
// xyzCar is passed by constant reference value
// because it is declared final
void test(final Car xyzCar) {
    // Can read object referenced by xyzCar
    String model = xyzCar.model;

    // Can modify object referenced by xyzCar
    xyzCar.year = 2001;

    /* Cannot modify xzyCar. That is, xyzCar must reference the object
       what the actual parameter is referencing at the time this method
       is called. You cannot even set it to null reference.
    */
    xyzCar = null;         // Compiler error. Cannot modify xyzCar
    xyzCar = new Car();    // Compiler error. Cannot modify xyzCar
}
```

Let us discuss one more example on parameter passing mechanism in Java. Consider the following code for the `changeString()` method.

```
public static void changeString(String s2) {
    // #2
    s2 = s2 + " there";
    // #3
}
```

Consider the following snippet of code that calls the `changeString()` method.

```
String s1 = "hi";
// #1
changeString(s1);
// #4
```

What will be the content of `s1` at #4? `String` is a reference type in Java. At #1, `s1` is referencing a `String` object whose content is "hi". When `changeString(s1)` method is called, `s1` is passed to s2 by reference value. At #2, s1 and s2 are referencing the same String object in memory whose content is "hi". When s2 = s2 + " there" statement is executed, two things happens. First, s2 + " there" expression is evaluated, which creates a new String object in memory with content of "hi there" returns its reference. The reference returned by s2 + " there" expression is assigned to s2 formal parameter. At this time, there are two String objects in memory – one with content "hi" and another with content "hi there". At #3, the actual parameter s1 is referencing the String object with content "hi" and the formal parameter s2 is referencing the String object with content "hi there". When the changeString() method call is over, the formal parameter s2 is discarded. Note that the String object with content "hi there" still exists in memory after the changeString() method call is over. Only the formal parameter is discarded when a method call is over and not the object to which the formal parameter was referencing. At #4, the reference variable s1 still refers to the String object with content "hi". Listing 6-25 has complete code that attempts to modify a formal parameter of String type.

TIP

A String object is an immutable object meaning that its content cannot be changed after it is created. If you need to change the content of a String object, you must create a new String object with a new content. We will learn more about immutable objects later in this chapter.

Listing 6-25: Another example of pass by reference value parameter passing in Java

```java
// PassByReferenceValueTest2.java
package com.jdojo.chapter6;

public class PassByReferenceValueTest2 {
    public static void changeString(String s2) {
        System.out.println("#2: s2 = " + s2);
        s2 = s2 + " there";
        System.out.println("#3: s2 = " + s2);
    }

    public static void main(String[] args) {
        String s1 = "hi";
        System.out.println("#1: s1 = " + s1);
        PassByReferenceValueTest2.changeString(s1);
        System.out.println("#4: s1 = " + s1);
    }
}
```

```
Output:

#1: s1 = hi
#2: s2 = hi
#3: s2 = hi there
#4: s1 = hi
```

Constructors

Declaring a Constructor

A constructor is a named block of code that is used to initialize an object of a class immediately after it is created. The structure of a constructor looks similar to the structure of a method. However, the similarity between the two stops right there in their looks. They are two different things and they are used for different purposes. The general syntax for a constructor declaration is:

```
<<Modifiers>> <<Constructor Name>>(<<parameters list>>) throws
<<Exceptions list>> {
    // Body of constructor goes here
}
```

The declaration of a constructor starts with modifiers. A constructor can have its access modifier as `public`, `private`, `protected` or package-level (no modifier). The constructor name is the same as the simple name of the class. Note that Java is case sensitive and constructor name must match the simple name of the class exactly. The constructor name is followed by a pair of opening and closing parentheses, which may include parameters. Optionally, the closing parenthesis may be followed by the keyword `throws`, which in turn is followed by a comma-separated list of exceptions. We will discuss the use of the keyword `throws` in the chapter on *Exception Handling*. The body of the constructor where you place your code is enclosed in braces. If you compare the syntax to declare a method with the syntax to declare a constructor, you would find that they are almost the same. It is suggested to keep the method declaration in mind when learning about constructor declaration, because most of the things are similar. The following code shows an example of declaring a constructor for a class `Test`. Figure 6-21 shows the anatomy of the constructor.

```
// Test.java
package com.jdojo.chapter6;

public class Test {

    public Test() {
        // Code goes here
    }
}
```

Figure 6-21: Anatomy of the constructor for the Test class

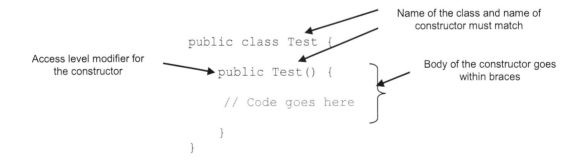

The name of the constructor must match the simple name of the class verbatim. Note that a class has two names – a simple name and a fully qualified name. In the above example, the simple name of the class is `Test` and its fully qualified name is `com.jdojo.chapter6.Test`. The name of a constructor must match the simple name of the class, e.g., `Test` and not its fully qualified name `com.jdojo.chapter6.Test`.

There is a significant difference between a method declaration and a constructor declaration. A constructor declaration does not have a return type. Recall that a method declaration must have a return type. If a method does not want to return any value, it must indicate so by specifying `void` as its return type. A constructor does not specify a return type at all. You cannot even specify `void` as a return type for a constructor. Consider the following declaration of class `Test2`.

```
public class Test2 {
    public void Test2() {    // It is method and not a constructor
        // Code goes here
    }
}
```

Does the class `Test2` declare a constructor? The answer is no. The class `Test2` does not declare a constructor. Rather, what you may be looking at is a method declaration, which has the same name as the class. It is a method declaration because it specifies a return type of `void`. Note that a method name could also be the same as the class name as shown above. However, just the name itself does not make a method or a constructor. If a construct name is the same as the simple name of the class, it could be a method or a constructor. If it specifies a return type, it is a method. If it does not specify a return type, it is a constructor.

When do we use a constructor? We use a constructor with the `new` operator to initialize an instance (or an object) of a class at the time the new instance is created. Note that it is the job of the `new` operator to create an object of a class and not the job of a constructor. Sometimes, the phrase, "create" and "initialize", are used interchangeably in the context of a constructor. However, you need to be clear about the difference in creating and initializing an object. The following statement uses a constructor of the `Test` class to initialize an object of the `Test` class.

```
Test t = new Test();
```

Figure 6-22 shows the anatomy of the above statement. The `new` operator is followed by the call to the constructor. The `new` operator along with the constructor call, for example "`new Test()`", is called instance (or object) creation expression. An instance creation expression creates an object in memory, executes the code in the body of the specified constructor and then returns the reference of the new object that it creates.

Figure 6-22: Anatomy of a constructor call with the new operator.

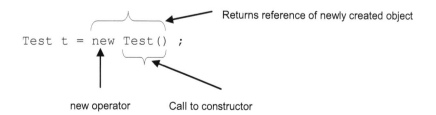

We have covered enough theories for declaring a constructor. It is time to see a constructor in action. Listing 6-26 has code for the Cat class. It declares a constructor. Inside the constructor's body, it prints a message "Meow..." to the standard output. Listing 6-27 has code for the CatTest class, which creates two Cat objects in its main() method. Note that you always use an object creation expression to create a new object of the Cat class. It is up to you to store the reference of the new object in a reference variable. The first Cat object is created and its reference is not stored. The second Cat object is created and its reference is stored in a reference variable c.

Listing 6-26: A Cat class, which declares a constructor, which prints a meow message on the standard output

```java
// Cat.java
package com.jdojo.chapter6;

public class Cat {
    public Cat() {
        System.out.println("Meow...");
    }
}
```

Listing 6-27: A test class that creates two Cat objects

```java
// CatTest.java
package com.jdojo.chapter6;

public class CatTest {
    public static void main(String[] args) {
        // Create a Cat object and ignore its reference
        new Cat();

        // Create another Cat object and store its reference in c
        Cat c = new Cat();
    }
}
```

```
Output:

Meow...
Meow...
```

Overloading a Constructor

A class can have more than one constructor. If a class has multiple constructors, they are called overloaded constructors. Since the name of the constructor must be the same as the simple name of the class, there is a need to differentiate one constructor from another. The rules for overloaded constructors are the same as for overloaded methods. If a class has multiple constructors, all of them must differ from the others in the number, order or type of parameters. The following code declares two constructors for the Dog class. Listing 6-28 has code for the Dog class, which declares two constructors. One constructor accepts no parameters and another accepts a String parameter.

Listing 6-28: A Dog class with two constructors – one with no parameter and one with a String parameter

```java
// Dog.java
package com.jdojo.chapter6;
```

```java
public class Dog {
    // Constructor #1
    public Dog() {
        System.out.println("A dog is created.");
    }

    // Constructor #2
    public Dog(String name) {
        System.out.println("A dog named " + name + " is created.");
    }
}
```

If a class declares multiple constructors, you can use any of them to create an object of that class. For example, the following two statements create two objects of the Dog class.

```java
Dog dog1 = new Dog();
Dog dog1 = new Dog("Cupid");
```

The first statement uses the constructor with no parameters and the second one uses the constructor with a String parameter. If you use a constructor with parameters to create an object, the actual parameter's order, type and number must match the formal parameter's order, type and number. Listing 6-29 has the complete code that creates two Dog objects using different constructors. When you run the DogTest class, the output will indicate that different constructors are called when two Dog objects are created in its main() method.

TIP

A constructor is called once per object creation expression. You can execute the code for one constructor only once in the process of an object creation. If the code for a constructor is executed, N times, it means N number of objects of that class will be created and you must use N number of object creation expressions to do that. However, when an object creation expression calls a constructor, the called constructor may call another constructor from its body. We will cover this scenario where one constructor calls another later in this section.

Listing 6-29: A test class to test the constructors of the Dog class

```java
// DogTest.java
package com.jdojo.chapter6;

public class DogTest {
    public static void main(String[] args) {
        Dog d1 = new Dog();             // Uses Constructor #1
        Dog d2 = new Dog ("Canis"); // Uses Constructor #2
    }
}
```

```
Output:

A dog is created.
A dog named Canis is created.
```

Writing Code for a Constructor

So far, we have written trivial code in constructors. What kind of code should you write in a constructor? The purpose of a constructor is to initialize the instance variables of the newly created object. Inside a constructor, you should restrict yourself only to write code that initializes instance variables of the object. An object is not fully created, when a constructor is called. The object is still in the process of creation. If you write some processing logic in a constructor assuming that a full blown object exists in memory, sometimes you may get unexpected results.

Let us create another class to represent a dog object. We will call this class `SmartDog` as shown in Listing 6-30. The `SmartDog` class looks a little bigger. However, its logic is very simple. The following are the main points in the `SmartDog` class that you need to understand.

- It declares two instance variables - `name` and `price`. The `name` instance variable stores the name of a smart dog. The `price` instance variable stores the price for which it can be sold.
- It declares two constructors. The first constructor has no parameters. It initializes the name and price instance variables to "Unknown" and `0.0` respectively. When you use the first constructor to create an object of the `SmartDog` class, for example `new SmartDog()`, the `name` and `price` for that object are initialized to "Unknown" and 0.0 respectively by the constructor. The second constructor accepts two parameters, which are named `name` and `price`. It initializes the `name` and `price` instance variables to whatever values are passed to the two parameters. Note the use of the keyword `this` inside the constructors. The keyword `this` refers to the object for which the constructor's code is executing. The use of the keyword `this` is not necessary in the first constructor. However, you must use the keyword `this` to refer to instance variables in the second constructor, because the names of the formal parameters hide the name of the instance variables.
- The instance method `bark()` prints a message on the standard output with the name of the smart dog.
- The `setName()` and `getName()` methods are used to set and get the name of the smart dog. The `setPrice()` and `getPrice()` methods are used to set and get the price of the smart dog.
- The `printDetails()` method prints the `name` and `price` of a smart dog. If the price for a smart dog is not set to a positive value, it prints the price as `Free`.

Listing 6-30: A SmartDog class that declares two constructors to initialize instance variables differently

```java
// SmartDog.java
package com.jdojo.chapter6;

public class SmartDog {
    private String name;
    private double price;

    public SmartDog() {
        // Initialize name to Unknown and price to 0.0
        this.name = "Unknown";
        this.price = 0.0;

        System.out.println("Using SmartDog() constructor");
    }

    public SmartDog(String name, double price) {
        // Initialize name and price to specified name and price
        this.name = name;
```

```
            this.price = price;

            System.out.println("Using SmartDog(String, double)" +
                               " constructor");
    }

    public void bark() {
        System.out.println(name + " is barking...");
    }

    public void setName(String name) {
        this.name = name;
    }

    public String getName() {
        return this.name;
    }

    public void setPrice(double price) {
        this.price = price;
    }

    public double getPrice() {
        return this.price;
    }

    public void printDetails(){
        System.out.print("Name: " + this.name );
        if (price > 0.0) {
            System.out.println(", price: " + this.price );
        }
        else {
            System.out.println(", price: Free" );
        }
    }
}
```

The two constructors of the SmartDog class initialize instance variables (or state of the object) in their bodies. They do not include any other processing logic. Listing 6-31 has the code for the SmartDogTest class that demonstrates how the two constructors initialize the instance variables.

Listing 6-31: A test class to demonstrate the use of the SmartDog class

```
// SmartDogTest.java
package com.jdojo.chapter6;

public class SmartDogTest {
    public static void main(String[] args)  {
        // Create two SmartDog objects
        SmartDog sd1 = new SmartDog();
        SmartDog sd2 = new SmartDog("Nova", 219.2);

        // Print details about them
        sd1.printDetails();
        sd2.printDetails();

        // Make them bark
```

```
        sd1.bark();
        sd2.bark();

        // Change the name and price of Unknown dog
        sd1.setName("Opal");
        sd1.setPrice(321.80);

        // Print details again
        sd1.printDetails();
        sd2.printDetails();

        // Make them bark one more time
        sd1.bark();
        sd2.bark();
    }
}
```

```
Output:

Using SmartDog() constructor
Using SmartDog(String, double) constructor
Name: Unknown, price: Free
Name: Nova, price: 219.2
Unknown is barking...
Nova is barking...
Name: Opal, price: 321.8
Name: Nova, price: 219.2
Opal is barking...
Nova is barking...
```

Calling a Constructor from another Constructor

A constructor may call another constructor of the same class. Let us consider the following `Test` class. It declares two constructors –one accepts no parameters and one accepts an `int` parameter.

```
public class Test {
    Test() {
    }

    Test(int x) {
    }
}
```

Suppose we want to call the constructor with an `int` parameter from the constructor with no parameter. Our first attempt, which is wrong, would be as follows.

```
public class Test {
    Test() {
        // Call another constructor
        Test(103); // compiler error
    }
```

```
    Test(int x) {
    }
}
```

The above code does not compile. Java has a special way to call a constructor from another constructor. You must use the keyword `this` as if it is the name of the constructor to call a constructor from inside another constructor. The following code calls the constructor with an int parameter from the constructor with no parameter using the statement, "`this(103);`". This is another use of `this` keyword.

```
public class Test {
    Test() {
        // Call another constructor
        this(103); // OK. Note the use of this keyword
    }

    Test(int x) {
    }
}
```

There are two rules about calling a constructor from another constructor. These rules are there to ensure that one constructor's code is executed once and only once during the process of an object creation of a class.

- If a constructor calls another constructor, it must be the first executable statement in the constructor's body. This makes it easy for the compiler to check that a constructor has been called and it has been called only once. For example, the following code will generate a compiler error because a call to the constructor with an `int` parameter, `this(k)`, is the second statement inside the constructor's body and not the first statement.

  ```
  public class Test {
      Test() {
          int k = 10;      // First statement
          this(k);         // Second statement. Compiler error
      }

      Test(int x) {
      }
  }
  ```

  An attempt to compile the code for the above `Test` class will generate the following error message.

  ```
  Error(4):  call to this must be first statement in constructor
  ```

- A constructor cannot call itself, because it will result in a recursive call. In the following code for the `Test` class, both constructors attempt to call themselves.

  ```
  public class Test {
      Test() {
          this();
      }

      Test(int x ) {
          this(10);
  ```

```
        }
    }
```

An attempt to compile the above code for the `Test` class will result in the following error. One error message is generated for each attempt to call the constructor itself.

```
Error(2):   recursive constructor invocation
Error(6):   recursive constructor invocation
```

Typically, you create overloaded constructors for a class when you have many ways to initialize an object of a class. Let us consider the `SmartDog` class shown in Listing 6-30. Two constructors give us two ways to initialize a new `SmartDog` object. The first one initializes the `name` and the `price` with default values of "Unknown" and `0.0`. The second constructor lets us initialize `name` and `price` with the value supplied by the caller. Sometimes, you may perform some logic to initialize the object inside a constructor. Letting you call another constructor from a constructor allows you to write such logic only once. We can make use of this feature for our `SmartDog` class as shown below.

```java
// SmartDog.java
package com.jdojo.chapter6;

public class SmartDog {
    private String name;
    private double price;

    public SmartDog() {
        // Call another constructor with "Unknown" and 0.0 as
        // parameters
        this("Unknown", 0.0);

        System.out.println("Using SmartDog() constructor");
    }

    public SmartDog(String name, double price) {
        // Initialize name and price to specified name and price
        this.name = name;
        this.price = price;

        System.out.println("Using SmartDog(String, double) " +
                           "constructor");
    }

    // Rest of code remains the same
}
```

Note that we changed the code only inside the constructor that accepts no parameters. Instead of setting the default values for `name` and `price` in the first constructor, we called the second constructor with the default values as parameters from the first one.

Using a return Statement inside a Constructor

A constructor cannot have a return type in its declaration. It means a constructor cannot return any value. Recall that a `return` statement is of two types – one with a return expression and one without a return expression. The `return` statement without a return expression simply returns the control to the caller without returning any value. You can use a `return` statement without a return expression inside a constructor body. When a return statement in a constructor is executed, the control returns and the rest of the constructor's code is not executed. The following code shows you an example of using a `return` statement in a constructor. If the parameter `x` is a negative number, the constructor simply executes a `return` statement to end the call to the constructor. Otherwise, it performs some logic.

```
public class Test {
    public Test(int x) {
        if (x < 0) {
            return;
        }

        // Perform some logic here
    }
}
```

Access Level Modifier for a Constructor

The access level for a constructor determines which part of the program can use that constructor in an object creation expression to create an object of that class. You can specify one of the four access levels for a constructor – `public`, `private`, `protected` and package-level. The following code declares four constructors for the `Test` class. Comments for each constructor explain its access level.

```
// Class Test has public access level
public class Test {
    // Constructor #1 - Package-level access
    Test() {
    }

    // Constructor #2 - public access level
    public Test(int x) {
    }

    // Constructor #3 - private access level
    private Test(int x, int y) {
    }

    // Constructor #4 - protected access level
    protected Test(int x, int y, int z){
    }
}
```

The effect of these access levels is exactly the same as their effect for a method. A constructor with a `public` access level can be used in any part of the program. A constructor with `private` access level can be used only inside the same class in which it is declared. A constructor with `protected` access level can be used in any part of the program in the same package in which its class is declared and inside any descendant class in any package. A constructor with package-level access can be used inside the same package in which its class is declared.

You can specify `public` or package-level access level for a class. A class defines a new reference type, which you can use to declare a reference variable. The access level of a class determines in which part of the program the name of the class can be used. Usually, you use the name of a class in a cast or in a reference variable declaration as shown below.

```
// Test class name is used to declare the reference variable t
Test t;

// Test class name is used to cast the reference variable xyz
Test t2 = (Test)xyz;
```

Let us discuss the different combinations of access levels for a class and its constructor and its effect in a program. Consider the following code that declares a class T1 with public access level and it has a constructor, which also has a public access level.

```
// T1.java
package com.jdojo.chapter6.p1;

public class T1 {
    public T1() {
    }
}
```

Since the class T1 has a public access level, you can declare a reference variable of type T1 as shown below anywhere in the program.

```
// Code inside any package
T1 t;
```

Since the constructor for the class T1 has a public access level, you can use that constructor in an object creation expression in any package as:

```
// Code inside any package
new T1();
```

You can combine the above two statements into one in any package as:

```
// Code inside any package
T1 t = new T1();
```

Let us consider the following code for the class T2, which has a public access level and has a constructor with a private access level.

```
// T2.java
package com.jdojo.chapter6.p1;

public class T2 {
    private T2() {
    }
}
```

Since the class T2 has a public access level, you can use its name to declare a reference variable in any package. The constructor for the class T2 has a private access level. The implication of having a private constructor is that you cannot create an object of the T2 class outside the T2 class itself. Recall that a private method, field, or a constructor cannot be used outside the class in which it is declared. Therefore, the following code will not compile unless it appears inside the T2 class.

```
// Code not inside T2 class
new T2(); // Compiler error
```

You may ask a very legitimate question. What is the use of the T2 class if we cannot create its object outside of the T2 class? Here are the possible situations where you can declare a constructor private and still create and use objects of the class.

- A constructor is used to create an object of a class. You may want to restrict the number of objects that can be created from a class. The only way you can restrict the number of objects of a class is by having the full control on its constructors. If you declare all constructors of a class to have the private access level, you have the full control on how the objects of that class will be created. Typically, you include one or more public static methods in that class, which create and/or return an object of that class. If you design a class so that only one object of the class may exist, it is called a *Singleton Pattern*. The following code is a version of the T2 class that is based on the singleton pattern. It declares a private static reference variable called instance, which holds the reference of the T2 class object. Note that the T2 class uses its own private constructor to create an object. Its public static getInstance() method returns the lone object of the class. More than one object of the T2 class cannot exist.

```
// T2.java
package com.jdojo.chapter6.p1;

public class T2 {
    private static T2 instance = new T2();

    private T2() {
    }

    public static T2 getInstance() {
        return T2.instance;
    }
    // Other code goes here
}
```

You can use the T2.getInstance() method to get the reference of an object of the T2 class. Internally, the T2 class does not create a new object every time you call the T2.getInstance() method. Rather, it returns the same object reference for all calls to this method.

```
T2 t1 = T2.getInstance();
T2 t2 = T2.getInstance();
```

- Sometimes, you want a class to have only static members. It may not make sense to create an object of such a class. For example, the java.lang.Math class declares its constructor as private. The Math class contains static variables and static methods to perform numeric operations. It does not make sense to create an object of the Math class.
- You can also declare all constructors of a class as private to prevent inheritance. Inheritance lets you define a class by extending the definition of another class. If you do not want anyone else to extend your class, one way to achieve that is to declare all constructors of your class as private. However, the obvious way to prevent your class from being extended is to declare it final. We will discuss inheritance in detail in the chapter on *Inheritance*.

Let us consider the class `T3` whose constructor has `protected` access level as shown below.

```java
// T3.java
package com.jdojo.chapter6.p1;

public class T3 {
    protected T3() {
    }
}
```

A constructor with `protected` access level can be used anywhere in the same package or inside a descendant class in any package. The class `T3` is in the `com.jdojo.chapter6.p1` package. You can write the following statement anywhere in `com.jdojo.chapter6.p1` package, which creates an object of the `T3` class.

```java
// Anywhere in com.jdojo.chapter6.p1 package
new T3();
```

We will cover inheritance in detail later. However, to complete the discussion of a `protected` constructor, we will use inheritance in the example below. If you do not follow the discussion, you can skip this discussion. Things about inheritance will be clearer when we discuss it in the chapter on *Inheritance*. You inherit (or extend) a class using the keyword `extends`. The following code creates a `T3Child` class by inheriting it from the `T3` class.

```java
// T3Child.java
package com.jdojo.chapter6.p2;

import com.jdojo.chapter6.p1.T3;

public class T3Child extends T3 {
    public T3Child() {
        super(); // Call T3() constructor
    }
}
```

The `T3` class is called the parent class of the `T3Child` class. An object of a child class cannot be created, until the object of its parent class is created. Note the use of the `super()` statement inside `T3Child()` constructor's body. The statement `super()` calls the `protected` constructor of the `T3` class. We use the `super` keyword to call the parent class constructor as we use keyword `this` to call another constructor of the same class. You cannot call the `protected` constructor of `T3` directly as

```java
new T3()
```

outside `com.jdojo.chapter6.p1` package. Note that the `T3Child` class is not in the same package as the `T3` class. To use a `protected` constructor outside its class package, you must inherit a class from its class and then use the `super` keyword to call it.

Consider the `T4` class with a constructor having package-level access. Recall that using no access level modifier (public, private or protected) gives package-level access.

```java
// T4.java
package com.jdojo.chapter6.p1;
```

```
public class T4 {
    T4() {
    }
}
```

You can use `T4`'s constructor to create its object anywhere in the `com.jdojo.chapter6.p1` package. Sometimes, you need a class that works as a helper class for other classes in a package. Objects of these classes need to be created only within the package. You can specify package-level access for constructors of such helper classes.

Default Constructor

The primary goal of declaring a class is to create its object. You need a constructor to create an object of a class. The necessity to have a constructor for a class is so obvious that the Java compiler adds a constructor to your class if you do not declare one. The constructor that is added by the Java compiler is called the *default constructor*. The default constructor does not have any parameters. Sometimes, the default constructor is also called a *no-args constructor*. The access level of the default constructor is the same as the access level of the class.

The classes that we have been working with are called top-level classes. You can also declare a class within another class, which is called an inner class. Please refer to the chapter on *Inner Classes* for details. A top-level class can have `public` or package-level access. However, an inner class can have `public`, `private`, `protected`, or package-level access. The Java compiler adds a default constructor for a top-level class as well as a nested class. A default constructor for a top-level class can have either `public` or package-level access depending on the access level of the class. However, a default constructor for an inner class can have access level of `public`, `private`, `protected` or package-level depending on its class access level. Table 6-6 shows some examples of classes and addition of default constructors to them by the Java compiler. When the Java compiler adds a default constructor, it also adds a statement – `super()` to call the no-args constructor of the parent class. Sometime, the call to the parent's no-args constructor inside the default constructor may cause your class not to compile. Please refer to the chapter on *Inheritance* for complete discussion on this topic.

Table 6-6: Examples of classes for which a default constructor is added by the Java compiler

Source Code for Your Class	Compiled Version of Your Class	Comments

`public class Test {`
 	
`}`
	`public class Test {`
	`    public Test() {`
	`    }`
	`}`
		The compiler adds a default constructor with public access level.

`class Test {`
 	
`}`
	`class Test {`
	`    Test() {`
	`    }`
	`}`
		The compiler adds a default construct with package-level access.

`public class Test {`
`  Test() {`
`  }`
`}`
	`public class Test {`
	`  Test() {`
	`  }`
	`}`
		The `Test` class already had a constructor. The compiler does not add any constructor.

`public class Test {`	`public class Test {`	The `Test` class already

``public Test(int x) {
}
}```	```public Test(int x) {
}
}```	had a constructor. The compiler does not add any constructor.
``public class Test {
private class Inner {
}
}```	```public class Test {
public Test() {
}
private class Inner {
private Inner(){
}
}
}```	Test is a public top-level class and Inner is a private inner class. The compiler adds a public default constructor for the Test class and a private default constructor for the Inner class.

TIP

It is a good programming practice to add a constructor explicitly in your source code, rather than letting the compiler add a default constructor for your class. The story of constructors is not over yet. We will revisit constructors in the chapter on *Inheritance*.

A static Constructor

Constructors are used in the context of the creating a new object; hence, it is consider as part of the object context and not the class context. You cannot declare a constructor static. The keyword this, which is a reference to the current object, is available inside the body of a constructor as it is available inside the body of an instance method.

Instance Initialization Block

We have seen that a constructor is used to initialize an instance (or object) of a class. An instance initialization block (simply instance initializer) is also used to initialize an object of a class. Why does Java provide you two constructs to perform the same thing? Not all classes in Java can have a constructor. Is it not a surprise for you to know that not all classes can have constructors? We did not mention this fact in the previous section, when we discussed constructors. Briefly, we mentioned inner classes, which are different from top-level classes. We will discuss one more type of class in the chapter on *Inner Classes*, which is called an *anonymous* class. As the name suggests, an anonymous class does not have a name. Recall that a constructor is a named block of code, whose name is the same as the simple name of the class. Since an anonymous class cannot have a name, it cannot have a constructor either. How will you initialize an object of an anonymous class? You can use an instance initializer to initialize an object of an anonymous class. The use of an instance initializer to initialize an object is not limited only to anonymous class. Any type of class can use it to initialize its object.

An instance initializer is simply a block of code (Recall that a block of code is a sequence of legal Java statements enclosed within braces) inside the body of a class, but outside any methods or constructors. Instance initializer does not have a name. Its code is simply placed inside an opening brace and a closing brace. The following code snippet shows how to declare an instance initializer for the Test class. Note that an instance initializer is executed in instance context and the keyword this is available inside the instance initializer.

```
public class Test {
```

```
    private int num;

    // Instance initializer
    {
        this.num = 101;

        // Other code for instance initializer goes here
    }

    // Other code for Test class goes here
}
```

You can have multiple instance initializer blocks for a class. All instance initializers for a class are executed automatically in textual order for every object that is created. Codes for all instance initializers are executed before the body of any constructor is executed. Listing 6-32 demonstrates the sequence in which the constructor and instance initializers are executed.

Listing 6-32: Example of using instance initializer

```java
// InstanceInitializer.java
package com.jdojo.chapter6;

public class InstanceInitializer {
    {
        System.out.println("Inside instance initializer 1.");
    }

    {
        System.out.println("Inside instance initializer 2.");
    }

    public InstanceInitializer() {
        System.out.println("Inside no-args constructor.");
    }

    public static void main(String[] args) {
        InstanceInitializer ii = new InstanceInitializer();
    }
}
```

```
Output:

Inside instance initializer 1.
Inside instance initializer 2.
Inside no-args constructor.
```

TIP

An instance initializer cannot have a `return` statement. It cannot throw checked exceptions unless all declared constructors list those checked exceptions in their `throws` clause. An exception to this rule is made in the case of an anonymous class, because it does not have a constructor. An instance initializer of an anonymous class may throw checked exceptions.

static Initialization Block

It is also known as a `static` initializer. It is similar to an instance initialization block. It is used to initialize a class. In other words, you can initialize class variables inside a `static` initializer block. An instance initializer is executed once per object. However, a static initializer is executed only once for a class, when its definition is loaded into JVM. To differentiate it from an instance initializer, you need to use the `static` keyword in the beginning of its declaration. You can have multiple static initializers in a class. All static initializers are executed in textual order in which they appear. Listing 6-33 has code that demonstrates when a `static` initializer is executed. You may be confused when you look at the output of Listing 6-33. It shows that the `static` initializer has run even before the first message is displayed in the `main()` method. You get the output when you run the `StaticInitializer` class using the following command.

```
java com.jdojo.chapter6.StaticInitializer
```

The `java` command must load the definition of the `StaticInitializer` class before it can execute its `main()` method. When the definition of the `StaticInitializer` class is loaded into memory at that time, the class is initialized and its static initializer is executed. This is the reason you see the message from static initializer before you see the message from the `main()` method. Note that instance initializer is called twice because we create two objects of the `StaticInitializer` class.

Listing 6-33: An example of using a static initializer in a class

```java
// StaticInitializer.java
package com.jdojo.chapter6;

public class StaticInitializer {
    private static int num;

    // A static initializer
    static {
        num = 1245;
        System.out.println("Inside static initializer.");
    }

    // An instance initializer
    {
        System.out.println("Inside instance initializer.");
    }

    // Constructor
    public StaticInitializer() {
        System.out.println("Inside constructor.");
    }

    public static void main(String[] args) {
        System.out.println("Inside main() #1. num: " + num);
        StaticInitializer si; // Declare a reference variable
        System.out.println("Inside main() #2. num: " + num);
        new StaticInitializer();
        System.out.println("Inside main() #3. num: " + num);
        new StaticInitializer();
    }
}
```

```
Output:

Inside static initializer.
Inside main() #1. num: 1245
Inside main() #2. num: 1245
Inside instance initializer.
Inside constructor.
Inside main() #3. num: 1245
Inside instance initializer.
Inside constructor.
```

TIP

A `static` initializer cannot throw checked exceptions and it cannot have a `return` statement.

The final Keyword

The `final` keyword is used in many contexts in a Java program. It takes on different meanings in different contexts. However, as its name suggests, its primary meaning is the same in all contexts. Its primary meaning is:

The construct with which the final keyword is associated does not allow modifying or replacing its original value or definition.

If you remember the primary meaning of the `final` keyword, it will help you understand its specialized meaning in a specific context. The `final` keyword can be used in the following three contexts.

- A variable declaration
- A class declaration
- A method declaration

In this section, we will discuss the use of the `final` keyword only in the context of a variable declaration. The chapter on *Inheritance* discusses its use in the context of class and method declarations in detail. However, we will describe its meaning in all three contexts briefly in this section.

If a variable is declared `final`, it can be assigned a value only once. That is, the value of a `final` variable cannot be modified once it has been set. If a class is declared `final`, it cannot be extended (or subclassed). If a method is declared `final`, it cannot be redefined (overridden or hidden) in the subclasses of the class that contains the method.

Let us discuss the use of the `final` keyword in a variable declaration. In our discussion, a variable declaration means the declaration of a local variable, a formal parameter of a method/constructor, an instance variable and a class variable. To declare a variable as `final`, you need to use the `final` keyword in the variable's declaration. The following snippet of code declares four `final` variables – YES, NO, MSG, and `act`.

```
final int YES = 1;
final int NO = 2;
```

```
final String MSG = "Good bye";
final Account act = new Account();
```

You can set the value of a `final` variable only once. Attempting to set the value of a `final` variable the second time will generate a compiler error.

```
final int x = 10;
int y = 101 + x; // Reading x is ok

x = 17; // Compiler error. Cannot change value of final variable
        // once it is set
```

There are two ways to initialize a `final` variable. You can initialize a `final` variable at the time of its declaration. You can also defer initializing the `final` variable. Until what time you can defer the initialization of a `final` variable depends on the variable type. However, you must initialize the `final` variable before it is read. If you do not initialize a `final` variable at the time of its declaration, such a variable is known as a *blank final* variable. Let us go through examples of each type of variable and how to declare them `final`.

```
final int multiplier; // Blank final variable

//Do something here...

multiplier = 3; // Set the value of multiplier first time

int value = 100 * multiplier; // Ok to read multiplier
```

final Local Variables

You can declare a local variable as `final`. If you declare a local variable as a blank final variable, you must initialize it before using. You will receive a compiler error if you try to change the value of the `final` local variable the second time. The following snippet of code uses `final` and blank `final` local variables in the `test()` method. The comments in the code explain what you can do with `final` variables at what point in code.

```
public static void test() {
    int x = 4;       // A variable
    final int y = 10; // A final variable. Cannot change y here onward
    final int z; // A blank final variable
    x = x + y;

    // Cannot read z because it is not initialized yet

    // Initialize the blank final variable z
    z = 87;

    // Can read z now. Cannot change the value of z here onwards

    x = x + y + z;

    // Perform other logic here...
}
```

final Parameters

You can also declare a `final` formal parameter for a method or a constructor. A formal parameter is initialized automatically with the value of the actual parameter when the method or the constructor is invoked. Therefore, you cannot change the value of a `final` formal parameter inside the method's or the constructor's body. The following snippet of code shows the `final` formal parameter x for the `test2()` method.

```
public void test2(final int x) {
    // Can read x, but cannot change it
    int y = x = 11;

    // Perform other logic here...
}
```

final Instance Variables

You can declare a `final` instance variable. You can also declare a blank `final` instance variable. An instance variable is a part of an object's state. A `final` instance variable indicates the part of the object's state that does not change after the object is created. A blank `final` instance variable must be initialized when an object is created. The following rules apply for initializing a blank `final` instance variable.

- It must be initialized in one of the instance initializers or all constructors. The following rules expand on this rule.
- If it is initialized in an instance initializer, it should not be initialized again in any other instance initializers.
- If it is initialized in an instance initializer, it should not be initialized in any of the constructors.
- If it is not initialized in any of the instance initializers, it makes sure it is initialized only once, when any of the constructors is invoked. This rule can be broken into two sub-rules. As a rule of thumb, a blank `final` instance must be initialized in all constructors. If we follow this rule, a blank `final` instance variable will be initialized multiple times if a constructor calls another constructor. To avoid multiple initialization of a blank `final` instance variable, it should not be initialized in a constructor if the first call in the constructor is a call to another constructor, which initializes the blank `final` instance variable.

The above rules for initializing a blank final instance variable may seem complex. However, it is simple to understand if you remember only one rule that a blank final instance variable must be initialized once and only once when any of its constructors is invoked to create an object. All of the above described rules are to ensure that this one rule is followed.

Let us consider different scenarios of initializing `final` and blank `final` instance variables. We do not have anything to discuss about `final` instance variable as shown below where x is a `final` instance variable for the `Test` class. The `final` instance variable x has been initialized at the time of its declaration and its value cannot be changed.

```
public class Test {
    private final int x = 10;
}
```

The following code shows a `Test2` class with a blank final instance variable y.

```
public class Test2 {
    private final int y;// A blank final instance variable
}
```

You get a compiler error if you attempt to compile the above definition of the Test2 class, because the blank final instance variable y is never initialized. Note that the compiler will add a default constructor for the Test2 class, but it will not even attempt to initialize the blank final instance variable y. The following code for the Test2 class will compile, because it initializes y in an instance initializer.

```
public class Test2 {
    private final int y;

    {
        y = 10; // Initialized in an instance initializer
    }
}
```

The following code would not compile, because it initializes y more than once inside two instance initializers.

```
public class Test2 {
    private final int y;

    {
        y = 10; // Initialized in an instance initializer
    }

    {
        y = 10; // Initialized in another instance initializer
    }
}
```

The above code may seem legal to you. However, it is not legal code, because two instance initializers are initializing y, even though both of them sets y to the same value 10. The rule is about number of times a blank final instance variable should be initialized, irrespective of the value being used for its initializations. Since all instance initializers are executed when an object of the Test2 class is created, y will be initialized twice, which is not legal.

The following code for the class Test2 with two constructors would compile. It initializes the blank final instance variable y in both constructors. It may seem that y is being initialized twice –once in each constructor. Note that y is an instance variable and one copy of y exists for each object of the Test2 class. When an object of the Test2 class is created, it will use one of the two constructors and not both. Therefore, for each object of the Test2 class, y will be initialized only once.

```
public class Test2 {
    private final int y;
    public Test() {
        y = 10; //Initialize y
    }

    public Test(int z) {
        y = z; //Initialize y
    }
```

```
}
```

Below is the modified code for the `Test2` class, which presents a tricky situation. Both constructors initialize the blank `final` instance variable `y`. The tricky part is that the no-args constructor calls another constructor.

```
public class Test2 {
    private final int y;

    public Test() {
        this(20); // Call another constructor
        y = 10;   // Initialize y
    }

    public Test(int z) {
        y = z; // Initialize y
    }
}
```

The above code for the `Test2` class would not compile. The compiler generates an error message, which reads as: *variable y might already have been assigned*. Let us consider creating an object of the `Test2` class as:

```
Test2 t = new Test2(30);
```

There is no issue in creating an object of the `Test2` class by invoking the one-arg constructor. The blank `final` instance variable `y` is initialized only once. Let us create an object of the `Test2` class:

```
Test2 t2 = new Test2();
```

When the no-args constructor is used to create an object, it calls the one-arg constructor, which will initialize y to `20`. The no-args constructor initializes `y` again to 10, which is the second time initialization for `y`. For this reason, the above code for the `Test2` class would not compile. You will need to remove the initialization of `y` from no-args constructor and the code would compile. The following is the modified code for the `Test2` class that would compile.

```
public class Test2 {
    private final int y;

    public Test() {
        this(20); // Another constructor will initialize y
    }

    public Test(int z) {
        y = z; // Initialize y
    }
}
```

final Class Variables

You can declare a class variable (static variable) as `final`. You can also declare a blank `final` class variable. You must initialize a blank `final` `static` variable in one of the `static` initializers.

If you have more than one `static` initializer for a class, you must initialize all the blank `final` `static` variables only once in one of the `static` initializers. The following code for the `Test3` class shows how to deal with a `final static` variable. It is customary to use all uppercase letters to name `static final` variables. It is also a way to define constants in Java program. The Java class library has numerous examples where it defines `public static final` variables to use them as constants.

```java
public class Test3 {
    public static final int YES = 1;
    public static final int NO = 2;
    public static final String MSG;

    static {
        MSG = "I am a blank final static variable";
    }
}
```

final Reference Variables

Primitive type as well as reference type variables can be declared `final`. The primary meaning of the `final` keyword is the same in both cases. That is, the value stored in a `final` variable cannot be changed once it has been set. We will look at the `final` reference variable in a little more detail in this section. A reference variable stores the reference of an object. A `final` reference variable means that once it references an object (or `null`), it cannot be modified to reference another object. Consider the following statement.

```java
final Account act = new Account();
```

Here, `act` is a final reference variable of `Account` type. It is initialized at the time of its declaration. At this time, `act` is referencing an object in memory. Now, we cannot make the `act` variable to reference another object in memory. That is, we cannot assign a new reference to the `act` variable. The following statement generates a compiler error.

```java
act = new Account(); // Compiler error. Cannot change act
```

A common misconception arises in this case. Mistakenly, programmers believe that the `Account` object that is referenced by the `act` reference variable cannot be changed. The declaration statement of the `act` reference variable as `final` has two things. Here, `act` is a reference variable, which is `final`, and there is an `Account` object in memory whose reference is stored in `act` variable. It is the `act` reference variable that cannot be changed, not the `Account` object it is referencing. If the `Account` class allows you to change the state of its object by letting you modify its instance variables directly or indirectly, you can still do so. The following are valid statements, which modify the `balance` instance variable of an `Account` object.

```java
act.deposit(2001.00); // Modifies state of Account object
act.debit(2.00);      // Modifies state of Account object
```

If you do not want an object of a class to be modified after it is created, you need to include that logic in its design, which does not let any of its instance variables be modified after the object is created. Such objects are called immutable objects. We will discuss how to design a class for an immutable object in the next section. A class whose objects' state cannot be changed after creation is called an immutable class. Objects of an immutable class are called immutable objects.

Compile-time vs. Runtime final Variables

We use `final` variables to essentially define constants. This is the reason why `final` variables are also called constants. If the value of a `final` variable can be computed by the compiler at compile-time, such a variable is a compile-time constant. If the value of a `final` variable cannot be computed by the compiler, it is a runtime `final` variable. The values of all blank final variables are not known until runtime. References are not computed until runtime. Therefore, all blank final variables and final reference variables are runtime constants.

Java performs an optimization when you use compile-time constants in an expression. It replaces the compile-time constant with its value. Suppose you have a class called `Constants` as shown below. It declares a `MULTIPLIER` `static final` variable.

```
public class Constants {
    public static final int MULTIPLIER = 12;
}
```

Consider the following statement;

```
int x = 100 * Constants.MULTIPLIER;
```

When you compile the above statement, the Java compiler will replace `Constants.MULTIPLIER` with its value 12 and your statement is compiled as:

```
int x = 100 * 12;
```

Now, `100 * 12` is also a compile-time constant expression. The Java compiler will replace it with its value `1200` and your original statement will be compiled as:

```
int x = 1200;
```

There is one downside of this compiler optimization. If you change the value of the `MULTIPLIER` `final` variable in the `Constants` class, you must recompile all the classes that refer to the `Constants.MULTIPLIER` variable.

What is a varargs Method?

Varargs is shorthand for variable-length arguments. The varargs feature was introduced in Java 5. It lets you declare a method or constructor that accepts a variable number of arguments (or parameters). We will use only the term "method" in our discussion of varargs. However, the discussion also applies to constructors. The number of arguments a method accepts is called its *arity*. A method that accepts variable-length arguments is called a *variable-arity method* or *varargs method*. You may wonder how a varargs method looks. Let us discuss how a non-varargs method works before we look at a varargs method.

Let us consider the following code for a `MathUtil` class that declares a `max()` method. The `max()` method has two parameters of `int` data type. It computes the maximum of its two arguments and returns it.

```
public class MathUtil {
    public static int max(int x, int y) {
```

```
        int max = x;
        if (y > max) {
            max = y;
        }
        return max;
    }
}
```

There is nothing extraordinary going on in the `MathUtil` class or in its `max()` method. Suppose you want to compute the maximum of two integers, say 12 and 18, you would invoke the `max()` method as:

```
int max = MathUtil.max(12, 18);
```

There is no surprising thing going on in the above statement. When the above statement is executed, 18 will be assigned to the variable `max`. Suppose we want to compute the maximum of three integers. Our existing `max()` method with two arguments cannot be used to compute the maximum of three integers. It is designed to accept two integer arguments and it will only accept two integer arguments. You cannot invoke `max()` method as `MathUtil.max(10, 8, 18)`. Since we want to compute the maximum of three integers, we will overload the `max()` method and create another version of it, which will accept three integer arguments. Here is the newer version of our `MathUtil` class. We call it `MathUtil2`.

```
public class MathUtil2 {
    public static int max(int x, int y) {
        int max = x;
        if (y > max) {
            max = y;
        }
        return max;
    }

    public static int max(int x, int y, int z) {
        int max = x;
        if (y > max) {
            max = y;
        }

        if (z > max) {
            max = z;
        }
        return max;
    }
}
```

You can compute maximum of two and three integers as:

```
int max1 = MathUtil2.max(12, 18);
int max2 = MathUtil2.max(10, 8, 18);
```

Adding a `max()` method with three `int` arguments did solve the problem temporarily. The real problem still remains. We will have to add a `max()` method with all possible number of integer arguments. If we want to compute maximum of four integers, we will need another `max()` method with four integer arguments. You would agree that no programmer would like to write a `max()` method where he will have to keep adding a newer version.

Before Java 5, when the number of arguments of a method was not known at design time, you would declare the method argument as an array of `int` as shown below. We will discuss arrays in details in the chapter on *Arrays*.

```
public class MathUtil3 {
    public static int max(int[] num) {
        /* Must check for zero element in num here */
        int max = Integer.MIN_VALUE;
        for(int i = 0; i < num.length; i++) {
            if (num[i] > max) {
                max = num[i];
            }
        }
        return max;
    }
}
```

We can write the following snippet of code that will compute the maximum of two and three integers using the `MathUtil3.max()` method.

```
int[] num1 = new int[] {10, 1} ;
int max1 = MathUtil3.max(num1);

int[] num2 = new int[] {10, 8, 18} ;
int max2 = MathUtil3.max(num2);
```

We can pass an arbitrary number of integers to the `MathUtil3.max()` method, which will compute the maximum value. In a sense, we have a way to pass an arbitrary number of arguments to a method. What bothers programmers is the way the method needs to be called when its argument type is an array. You must create an array object and package the values of all its elements when you need to call the method with an array argument. The issue here is not the code inside the `max(int[] num)` method. Rather, it is the client code that calls this method.

Varargs comes to our rescue. It will let us declare a `max()` method, which can accept any number of integer arguments including zero arguments. The beauty of a varargs method is in the simpler client code that calls the method. So, how do we declare a varargs method? It is very simple to declare a varargs method. All you need to do is to add an ellipsis (or triple-dot like `...`) after the data type of the method's argument. The following snippet of code shows a `max()` method declaration with one variable-length argument, `num`, which is of `int` data type. Note the placement of ellipsis after the data type `int`.

```
public static int max(int... num) {
    // Code goes here
}
```

Adding whitespaces before and after ellipsis is optional. All of the following varargs method declarations are valid. They use different whitespaces before and after ellipsis.

```
public static int max(int... num)    // A space after
public static int max(int ... num)   // A space before and after
public static int max(int...num)     // No space before and after
```

```
public static int max(int ...
num) // A space before and a newline after
```

A varargs method can have more than one argument. The following snippet of code shows that aMethod() accepts three arguments, one of which is a variable-length argument.

```
public static int aMethod(String str, double d1, int...num) {
    // Code goes here
}
```

There are two restrictions for a varargs method.

- A varargs method can have a maximum of one variable-length argument. The following declaration for m1() method is invalid, because it declares two variable-length arguments – n1 and n2.

  ```
  // Invalid declaration
  void m1(String str, int...n1, int...n2) {
      // Code goes here
  }
  ```

- The variable-length argument of a varargs method must be the last argument in the argument list. The following declaration for m2() method is invalid, because the variable-length argument n1 is not declared as the last argument.

  ```
  // Invalid declaration
  void m2(int...n1, String str) {
      // Code goes here
  }
  ```

  We can fix the above declaration by moving the argument n1 to the last as follows.

  ```
  void m2(String str, int...n1) {
      // Code goes here
  }
  ```

Let us rewrite our max() method to make it a varargs method as shown below.

```
public class MathUtil4 {
    public static int max(int...num) {
        int max = Integer.MIN_VALUE;
        for(int i = 0; i < num.length; i++) {
            if (num[i] > max) {
                max = num[i];
            }
        }
        return max;
    }
}
```

You almost always have a loop inside a varargs method that processes the list of arguments for the variable-length argument. The length property gives you the number of values that were passed for the variable-length argument. For example, num.length in max() varargs method will give you the number of integers that were passed in to the method. To get the nth value in the variable-length argument you need to use `varArgsName[n-1]`. For example, `num[0]`, `num[1]` and `num[n-1]` will contain the first, the second and the nth value passed in for `num` variable-length argument. If you just want to process all values passed in for a variable-length argument, you can use a simpler loop, a foreach loop, which was introduced to Java 5. You can rewrite the code for `max()` method using foreach loop as follows.

```
public static int max2(int...num) {
    int max = Integer.MIN_VALUE;
    for(int currentNumber : num) {
        if (currentNumber > max) {
            max = currentNumber;
        }
    }
    return max;
}
```

The body of the `MathUtil4.max()` method is exactly the same as if `num` argument is declared as an `int` array. We are right in thinking so. The Java compiler implements a variable-length argument of a method using an array. The above declaration of the `MathUtil4.max()` method is changed by the compiler. The declaration part `max(int...num)` is changed to `max(int[] num)`, when you compile the source code for the `Mathutil4` class. So, the real code for inside a varargs method is the same if the argument is a variable-length argument or an array argument. What benefit do we get using a variable-length argument? The benefit of using a variable-length argument in a method comes from the elegant way of calling the method. You can call the `MathUtil4.max()` method as follows.

```
int max1 = MathUtil4.max(12, 8);
int max2 = MathUtil4.max(10, 1, 30);
```

You can use zero or more arguments for a variable-length argument in a method. The following code is a valid call to the `max()` method.

```
int max = MathUtil4.max();   // Passing no argument is ok
```

What will be returned by calling the `MathUtil4.max()` method with no argument? If you look at the method's body, it will return `Integer.MIN_VALUE`, which is -2147483648. Practically, a call to the `max()` method without at least two arguments is not a valid call. We must check for invalid number of arguments when a method is a varargs method. We do not get a problem of invalid number of arguments for non-varargs methods, because the compiler will force you to use exact number of arguments. Listing 6-34 shows the code for the `max()` method that also checks for invalid number of arguments. If the number of integers passed to the method is less than two, it throws an exception. Otherwise, it returns the maximum integer in the list.

Listing 6-34: A utility class to compute maximum of some specified integers using a varargs method

```
public class MathUtil5 {
    public static int max(int... num) {
        if (num.length < 2) {
            String msg = "max() requires at least two arguments.";
            throw new IllegalArgumentException(msg);
        }

        int max = Integer.MIN_VALUE;
        for(int i = 0; i < num.length; i++) {
```

```
            if (num[i] > max) {
                max = num[i];
            }
        }
        return max;
    }
}
```

You can pass any number of integers when you call the `MathUtil5.max()` method. All of the following statements are valid.

```
int max1 = MathUtil5.max(12, 8);        // will return 12
int max2 = MathUtil5.max(10, 1, 30);    // will return 30
int max3 = MathUtil5.max(11, 3, 7, 37); // will return 37
```

If you call the `MathUtil5.max()` method with no arguments or one argument, it will throw an exception.

```
int max1 = MathUtil5.max();    // Will throw exception
int max2 = MathUtil5.max(10);  // Will throw exception
```

Overloading a Varargs Method

The same overloading rules for methods also apply to a varargs method. You can overload a method with a variable-length argument as long as the parameters for the methods differ in type, order or number. For example, the following is a valid example of an overloaded `max()` method.

```
public class MathUtil6 {
    public static int max(int x, int y) {
        // Code goes here
    }

    public static int max(int...num) {
        // Code goes here
    }
}
```

Consider the following snippet of code, which calls the overloaded method `MathUtil6.max()` with two arguments.

```
int max = MathUtil6.max(12, 13); // which max() will be called?
```

The `MathUtil6` class has two `max()` methods. One method accepts two `int` parameters and another method accepts a variable-length `int` parameter. In the above case, Java will call the `max(int x, int y)` version of the `max()` method. First, Java attempts to find a method declaration using an exact match for the number of parameters. If it does not find an exact match, it looks for a match using variable-length parameters.

TIP

If a varargs method is overloaded, Java uses the more specific version of the method instead of using a varargs method. Java uses varargs method as the last resort to resolve a method call.

Sometimes, a call to an overloaded varargs method may cause confusion to the Java compiler. The overloading of the method itself may be valid. However, the call to it may cause an issue. Consider the following snippet of code for the `MathUtil7` class, which is a valid example of method overloading

```java
public class MathUtil7 {
    public static int max(int...num) {
        // Code goes here
    }

    public static int max(double...num) {
        // Code goes here
    }
}
```

Which version of the `max()` method will be called when the following statement is executed.

```java
int max = MathUtil7.max(); // Which max() to call?
```

The above statement will generate a compiler error stating that the call to `MathUtil7.max()` method is ambiguous. Java allows you to pass zero or more values for a variable-length argument. In the above statement, both method `max(int...num)` and `max(double...num)` qualify for the `MathUtil7.max()` call and the compiler cannot decide which one to call. You may find many other instances where a call to an overloaded varargs method results in an ambiguous method call and the compiler generates an error.

Varargs Methods and the main() Method

Recall that if you want to run your class, you need to declare a `main()` method in it with a `String` array as its argument. The signature for the `main()` method must be `main(String[] args)`. A varargs method is implemented by the Java compiler using an array. If your method signature is `m1(XXX...args)`, it is changed to `m1(XXX[] args)` by the compiler. Now you can declare the `main()` method of your class using older notation that uses `String` array or using newer notation that uses varargs. The following declaration of `main()` method for the `Test` class is valid. You will be able to run the `Test` class using the `java` command.

```java
public class Test {
    public static void main(String...args)  {
        System.out.println("Hello from varargs main()...");
    }
}
```

Chapter 7. Object and Objects Classes

The java.lang.Object Class

Java has an `Object` class in the `java.lang` package. You do not need to use an `import` statement to use its simple name in a Java program, because all classes from `java.lang` package are imported automatically in a compilation unit. It is the superclass of all classes in Java. All Java classes, which are included in the Java class library and those you create, extend the `Object` class directly or indirectly. All Java classes are a subclass of the `Object` class and the `Object` class is the superclass of all classes. Note that the `Object` class itself does not have a superclass.

Classes in Java are arranged in a tree-like hierarchical structure, where the `Object` class is at the root. We will discuss class hierarchy in detail in the chapter on *Inheritance*. We will discuss some details of the `Object` class in this chapter. Here are two important rules about `Object` class. We will not explain the reasons behind these rules here. The reasons why we could do these things with the `Object` class will be clear after you read the chapter on *Inheritance*.

Rule 1

A reference variable of the `Object` class can hold a reference of an object of any class. As any reference variable can store a `null` reference, so can a reference variable of `Object` type. Consider the following declaration of a reference variable `obj` of `Object` type.

```
Object obj;
```

You can assign a reference of any object in Java to `obj` reference variable. All of the following statements are valid.

```
// Can assign the null reference
obj = null;

// Can assign a reference of an object of the Object class
obj = new Object();

// Can assign a reference of an object of the Account class
Account act = new Account();
obj = act;

// Can assign a reference of object of any class
// Assume that AnyClass is a class that exists
obj = new AnyClass();
```

The opposite of the above rule is not true. You cannot assign a reference of an object of the `Object` class to a reference variable of any other type. The following statement is not valid.

```
// Cannot assign a reference of an Object to an Account type
// reference variable
Account act = new Object(); // A compiler error
```

Sometimes, you may store the reference of an object of a specific type, say `Account` type, in a reference variable of `Object` type, and later you would like to assign the same reference back to a reference variable of `Account` type. You can do so by using a cast as shown below.

```
Object obj2 = new Account();
Account act = (Account)obj2; // Must use cast
```

Sometimes, you may not be sure that a reference variable of the `Object` class holds a reference to an object of a specific type. In those situations, you need to use the `instanceof` operator to test if a reference variable holds a reference of an object of a specific class. The left operand of the `instanceof` operator is a reference variable and its right operand is a class name. If its left operand is a reference of its right operand type, it returns `true`. Otherwise, it returns `false`. Refer to the chapter on *Inheritance* for more detailed discussion on the `instanceof` operator.

```
Object obj;
Cat c;

// Do something here and store a reference in obj...

if (obj instanceof Cat) {
    //If we get here then obj holds a reference of
    // a Cat object for sure
    c = (Cat)obj;
}
```

You will need to make use of this rule when you have a method, which accepts a parameter of the `Object` class. You can pass a reference of an object of any class for a parameter of the `Object` class. Consider the following snippet of code that shows a method declaration.

```
public void m1(Object obj) {
    // Code goes here
}
```

You can call `m1()` method in a number of different ways as:

```
m1(null);            // Pass null reference
m1(new Object());    // Pass a reference of an object of the Object class
m1(new AnyClass());  // Pass a reference of an object of AnyClass class
```

Rule 2

The `Object` class has nine methods, which are available to be used in all classes in Java. We can categorize methods of the `Object` class into two types.

- In the first category are the methods that have been implemented by the `Object` class and you are supposed to use them without re-implementing them. You cannot re-implement (technical term for re-implement is override) these methods in any class you create. Their implementation is `final`. Methods that fall into this category are `getClass()`, `notify()`, `notifyAll()` and `wait()`.

- In the second category are the methods that have a default implementation in the `Object` class and you can customize their implementation by re-implementing them in your class. Methods that fall into this category are `toString()`, `equals()`, `hashCode()`, `clone()` and `finalize()`.

A Java programmer must understand the proper use of all of the methods in the `Object` class. We will discuss all methods of the `Object` class in detail except `notify()`, `notifyAll()` and `wait()` methods. These methods are used in threads synchronization. We will discuss them in the chapter on *Threads*. Table 7-1 lists all methods of the `Object` class with a brief description. The "Yes" in the "Implemented" column in the table indicates that the `Object` class has implementation for the method, which can be used without writing any code. The "No" in this column means that you must implement the method before using it. The "Yes" in the "Customizable" column in the table indicates that you can re-implement the method to customize it. The "No" in this column indicates that the `Object` class has implemented the method and its implementation is `final`.

Table 7-1: List of methods of the Object class with their brief description.

Method	Implemented	Customizable	Description
`public String toString()`	Yes	Yes	It returns a string representation of an object. Typically, it is used for debugging purpose.
`public boolean equals(Object obj)`	Yes	Yes	It is used to compare two objects for equality.
`public int hashCode()`	Yes	Yes	It returns a hash code (an integer) value of an object.
`protected Object clone() throws CloneNotSupportedException`	No	Yes	It is used to make a copy of an object.
`protected void finalize() throws Throwable`	No	Yes	It is called by the garbage collector before an object is destroyed.
`public final Class getClass()`	Yes	No	It returns a reference to the Class object of the object.
`public final void notify()`	Yes	No	Notifies one thread in the wait queue of the object.
`public final void notifyAll()`	Yes	No	Notifies all threads in the wait queue of the object.

`public final void wait() throws InterruptedException`
 	
`public final void wait(long timeout) throws InterruptedException`
 	
`public final void wait(long timeout, int nanos) throws InterruptedException`
	Yes	No	Makes a thread wait in the wait queue of the object.

To re-implement a method of the `Object` class in your class, you need to declare the method the same way as it has been declared in the `Object` class and then write your own code in its body. There are more rules to re-implement a method of the `Object` class in your class. We will cover all rules in the chapter on *Inheritance*. You can re-implement the `toString()` method of the `Object` class in your class, say `Test`, as shown below.

```
public class Test {
    // Re-implement toString() method of the Object class
    public String toString() {
        return "Here is a string";
    }
}
```

We will discuss six methods of the `Object` class in detail in the next sections.

What is the Class of an Object?

Every object you create in a Java program belongs to a class. You define a class in source code, which is compiled into a binary format (usually a class file with the *.class* extension). Before a class is used at runtime, its binary representation is loaded into JVM. The loading of the binary representation of a class into JVM is handled by an object, which is called a *class loader*. Typically, multiple class loaders are used in a Java application to load different types of classes. Technically, a class loader is an instance of the class `java.lang.ClassLoader`. Java lets you create your own class loader by extending the `ClassLoader` class. Typically, you do need to create your own class loader. The Java runtime will use its built-in class loaders to load your classes.

A class loader reads the binary format of the class definition into JVM. The binary class format may be loaded from any accessible location, e.g., a local file system, a network, a database, etc. Then, it creates an object of the `java.lang.Class` class, which represents the binary representation of the class in JVM. Note the uppercase `C` in the class name `java.lang.Class`. The binary format of the class definition may be loaded multiple times in the JVM by different class loaders. A class inside a JVM is an identified by the combination of its fully qualified name and its class loader. Typically, the binary definition of a class is loaded only once in a JVM.

TIP

You can think of an object of the `Class` class as a runtime descriptor of the source code of a class. Your source code for a class is represented by an object of the `Class` class at runtime.

The `getClass()` method of the `Object` class returns the reference of the `Class` object. Since the `getClass()` method is declared and implemented in the `Object` class, you can use this method on a reference variable of any type. The following snippet of code shows how to get the reference of the `Class` object for a `Cat` object.

```
Cat c = new Cat();
Class catClass = c.getClass();
```

By default, the binary class definition is loaded only once, and there is only one `Class` object that represents a class at runtime. We are not considering those cases where you have written code to load the same class more than once. If you use the `getClass()` method on different objects of the same class, you will get the reference to the same `Class` object. Consider the following snippet of code.

```
Cat c2 = new Cat();
Cat c3 = new Cat();

Class catClass2 = c2.getClass();
Class catClass3 = c3.getClass();
```

Here, `c2` and `c3` are two objects of the same `Cat` class. Therefore, `c2.getClass()` and `c3.getClass()` return the reference of the same `Class` object, which represents the `Cat` class in the JVM. The expression, `catClass2 == catClass3`, will evaluate to `true`.

The `Class` class has many useful methods. We will discuss most of its method in the chapter on *Reflection*. You can use its `getName()` method to get the fully qualified name of the class. You can use its `getSimpleName()` to get the simple name of the class. For example,

```
String fullName = catClass.getName();
String simpleName = catClass.getSimpleName();
```

Computing Hash Code of an Object

A hash code is an integer value that is computed for a piece of information using an algorithm. A hash code is also known as a *hash sum*, a *hash value*, or simply a *hash*. The algorithm to compute an integer from a piece of information is called a *hash function*.

The definition of a hash code involves three things – a piece of information, an algorithm, and an integer value. You have a piece of information. You apply an algorithm to that piece of information to produce an integer value. The integer value that you get is the hash code for the piece of information you had. If you change the piece of information or the algorithm, the computed value (the hash code) may or may not change. Figure 7-1 depicts the process of computing the hash code. Computing a hash code is a one-way process. Getting the original piece of information from a hash code is not an easy task and it is not the goal of the hash code computation either.

Figure 7-1: Process of computing a hash code

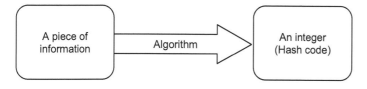

The piece of information that could have (or could be used to generate) a hash code could be an arbitrary sequence of bytes, characters, numbers, or a combination of them. For example, you may want to compute the hash code for a string `"Hello"`. How does a hash function look like? The hash function may be as simple as the following function, which returns the integer zero for all input data.

```
int myHashFunction(your input data) {
    return 0;  // Always return zero
}
```

The above hash function fits the definition of a hash function although it is not a practically good hash function. Writing a good hash function is not an easy task. You need to consider a number of things about the input data before you can write a good hash function.

Why do we need a hash code? It is needed for efficient retrieval of the piece of information (or data associated with it) when the piece of information is stored in a hash based collection (or container). Before a piece of information is stored in a container, its hash code is computed and then it is stored at a location (also called a bucket), which is based on its hash code. When you want to retrieve the piece of information, its hash code is used to find its location in the container making the retrieval of the information faster. It is worth noting that an efficient retrieval of information using hash codes is based on distribution of the hash code values value over a range. If the hash codes that are generated are not uniformly distributed, the retrieval of information may not be efficient. In the worst case, the retrieval of information using hash codes may be as bad as a linear search through all elements stored in the container. If we use a hash function as shown above, all elements in the container will be stored in the same bucket, which will require searching through all elements. Using a good hash function so that it gives you uniformly distributed hash codes is critical in implementing an efficient hash based container for fast data retrieval.

What is the use of a hash code in Java? Java uses hash codes for the same reason described above – to efficiently retrieve data from hash based collections. If the objects of your class are not used as keys in a hash based collection, e.g., `Hashtable`, `HashMap`, etc., you may not even worry about hash codes for your objects at all.

We can also compute a hash code for an object in Java. In case of an object, the pieces of information that will be used to compute the hash code are the pieces of information that make up the state of an object. Java designers considered the hash code for an object so important that they have provided a default implementation to compute the hash code for an object in the `Object` class. The `Object` class has a `hashCode()` method that returns an `int`, which is the hash code of an object. The default implementation in the `Object` class returns the hash code, which is computed by converting the memory address of the object into an integer. Since the `hashCode()` method is defined in the `Object` class, it is available in all classes in Java. However, you are free to override the implementation of the `hashCode()` method for your class. Here are the rules that you must follow when you override the `hashCode()` method in your class. Suppose there are two object references `x` and `y`.

- If `x.equals(y)` returns `true`, `x.hashCode()` must return an integer, which is equal to `y.hashCode()`. That is, if two objects are equal using the `equals()` method, they must have the same hash codes.
- If `x.hashCode()` is equal to `y.hashCode()`, it is not necessary that `x.equals(y)` returns `true`. That is, if two objects have the same hash codes using the `hashCode()` method, they do not have to be equal using the `equals()` method.
- If the `hashCode()` method is called on the same object multiple times in the same execution of a Java application, it must return the same integer value. If the pieces of information that are used in the `equals()` method to compare two objects change, the `hashCode()` method should return a different integer value in the same execution of the Java application.

The `hashCode()` and the `equals()` methods (discussed later) are closely tied. If your class overrides any of these two methods, it must override both of them for the objects of your class to work correctly in hash-based collections. Another rule that you need to observe is that you should use only those instance variables to compute the hash code for an object, which are also used in `equals()` method to check for equality.

If your class is mutable, you should not be using objects of your class as keys in hash-based collections such as `Hashtable`, `HashMap`, etc. If the object, which has been used as a key, changes afterwards, you will not be able to locate the object in the collection as locating an object in a hash based collection is based on its hash code. In such cases, you will have stranded objects in the collection, which cannot be reached.

How should you implement a `hashCode()` method for a class? Here are some guidelines to write the logic for the `hashCode()` method for your class, which is reasonable for most of the purposes.

- Start with a prime number, say 37.

  ```
  int hash = 37;
  ```

- Compute the hash code value for each instance variable of primitive data types separately using the following logic. Note that you need to use only those instance variables in the hash code computation, which are also part of `equals()` method comparison logic. Let us store the result of this step in an `int` variable `code`. Let us assume that `value` is the name of the instance variable.

  For `byte`, `short`, `int`, `char` (Unicode value) data types, use their integer value as:

  ```
  code = (int)value;
  ```

  For `long` data type, use the XOR for two halves of 64-bit as.

  ```
  code = (int)(value ^ (value >>> 32));
  ```

  For `float` data type, convert its floating-point values to equivalent integer value using

  ```
  code = Float.floatToIntBits(value)
  ```

  For `double` data type, convert its floating-point value to `long` using the `doubleToLongBits()` method of the `Double` class and then convert the long value to an `int` value using the procedure as described above for the `long` data type.

  ```
  long longBits = Double.doubleToLongBits(value);.
  code = (int)(longBits ^ (longBits >>> 32));
  ```

  For `boolean` data type, use 1 for `true` and 0 for `false`.

  ```
  code = (value? 1: 0)
  ```

- For a reference instance variable, use 0 if it is `null`. Otherwise, call its `hashCode()` method to get its code. Suppose `ref` is the name of the reference variable.

  ```
  code = (ref == null?0:ref.hashCode());
  ```

  Compute the hash code using the following formula. Using 57 in the formula is an arbitrary decision. Any other prime number, say 47, will work fine.

  ```
  hash = hash * 57 + code;
  ```

- Repeat the above three steps for all instance variables you want to include in your `hashCode()` computation.
- Finally, return the value contained in the `hash` variable from your `hashCode()` method.

The above method is one of the many ways and not the only way to compute the hash code of an object in Java. You can use any other method to compute the hash code for objects of your class. Consult a good textbook on computing hash codes, if you need a stronger hash function. All primitive wrapper classes and `String` class in Java override the `hashCode()` method and provides reasonably good implementations of hash functions.

TIP

Java 7 added a utility class `java.lang.Objects`. It contains a `hash()` method that computes the hash code for any number of values of any type. From Java 7, you are advised to use the `Objects.hash()` method to compute the hash code of an object. Please refer to *The Objects Class* section later in this chapter for more details on the `hash()` method of the `Objects` class.

The following snippet of code shows one of the possible implementations of the `hashCode()` method for the `Book` class, which has five instance variables – `title`, `author`, `pageCount`, `hardCover` and `price`. The implementation uses all five instance variables to compute the hash code for a `Book` object. You must also implement the `equals()` method for the `Book` class, which must use all the five instance variables to check if two `Book` objects are equal. You need to make sure that the `equals()` method and the `hashCode()` method use the same set of instance variables in their logic. Suppose we add one more instance variable to the `Book` class. Let us call it `ISBN`. Since `ISBN` identifies a book uniquely, we might use only the `ISBN` instance variable to compute its hash code and to compare for equality with another `Book` object. Therefore, in this case, we will use only ISBN instance variable in the `hashCode()` and `equals()` methods.

```java
// Book.java
package com.jdojo.chapter7;

public class Book {
    private String title;
    private String author;
    private int pageCount;
    private boolean hardCover;
    private double price;

    // Other code goes here

    // Must implement the equals() method too.

    public int hashCode() {
        int hash = 37;
        int code = 0;

        // use title
        code = (title == null ? 0 : title.hashCode());
        hash = hash * 57 + code;

        // use author
        code = (author == null ? 0 : author.hashCode());
        hash = hash * 57 + code;

        // Use pageCount
        code = pageCount;
        hash = hash * 57 + code;
```

```
        // Use hardCover
        code = (hardCover ? 1 : 0);
        hash = hash * 57 + code;

        // Use price
        long priceBits = Double.doubleToLongBits(price);
        code = (int)(priceBits ^ (priceBits >>> 32));
        hash = hash * 57 + code;

        return hash;
    }
}
```

TIP

There are some misconceptions about the hash code of an object in Java. Programmers think that the hash code uniquely identifies an object and it must be a positive integer. However, this is not true. The hash code does not identify an object uniquely. Two distinct objects may have the same hash codes. A hash code does not have to be a positive number either. It could be any integer value – positive as well as negative. There is also confusion about the usage of hash codes. It is used solely for the purpose of efficient retrieval of information from a hash-based collection. If your objects are not used as keys in a hash based collection and you do not override the `equals()` method in your class, you do not need to worry about the `hashCode()` method in your class at all. Most likely, it will be overriding the `equals()` method that will prompt you to override the `hashCode()` method for your class. If you do not override and provide correct implementation of `hashCode()` and `equals()` methods in your class at the same time, the objects of your class would not behave properly in hash based collections. The Java compiler or the Java runtime will never give you any warnings or errors about incorrect implementations of these two methods in your class.

Comparing Objects for Equality

Every object in this universe is different from all other objects, so is every object in a Java program different from all other objects. All objects have a unique identity. The memory address at which an object is allocated can be treated as its identity, which will make it always unique. Two objects are the same if they have the same identity (or reference in Java terminology). Consider the following snippet of code.

```
Object obj1;
Object obj2;

// Do something...
if (obj1 == obj2) {
    // obj1 and obj2 are the same object based on identity
}
else {
    // obj1 and obj2 are different objects based on identity
}
```

The above code uses identity comparison to test for equality of `obj1` and `obj2`. It compares the references of two objects to test if they are equal or not. Sometimes, you want to treat two objects equal if they have the same state based on some or all of their instance variables. If you want to compare two objects of your class for equality based on criteria other than their references (identities), your class needs to re-implement the `equals()` method of the `Object` class. The default implementation of the `equals()` method in the `Object` class compares the references of the object being passed as the parameter and the object on which it is called. If the two references are equal, it returns `true`. Otherwise, it returns `false`. In other words, the `equals()` method in the `Object` class performs identity based comparison for equality. The implementation of the `equals()` method in the `Object` class is as follows. Recall that the keyword `this` inside an instance method of a class refers to the reference of the object on which that instance method is called.

```java
public boolean equals(Object obj) {
    return (this == obj);
}
```

Consider the following snippet of code. It compares some `Point` objects using the equality operator (==), which always compares the references of its two operands. It also uses the `equals()` method of the `Object` class to compare the same two references. The output shows that the result is the same. Note that our `Point` class does not have an `equals()` method. When we call the `equals()` method on a `Point` object, the `equals()` method's implementation of the `Object` class is used.

```java
Point pt1 = new Point(10, 10);
Point pt2 = new Point(10, 10);
Point pt3 = new Point(12, 19);
Point pt4 = pt1;

System.out.println("pt1 == pt1: " + (pt1 == pt1));
System.out.println("pt1.equals(pt1): " + pt1.equals(pt1));

System.out.println("pt1 == pt2: " + (pt1 == pt2));
System.out.println("pt1.equals(pt2): " + pt1.equals(pt2));

System.out.println("pt1 == pt3: " + (pt1 == pt3));
System.out.println("pt1.equals(pt3): " + pt1.equals(pt3));

System.out.println("pt1 == pt4: " + (pt1 == pt4));
System.out.println("pt1.equals(pt4): " + pt1.equals(pt4));
```

```
Output:

pt1 == pt1: true
pt1.equals(pt1): true
pt1 == pt2: false
pt1.equals(pt2): false
pt1 == pt3: false
pt1.equals(pt3): false
pt1 == pt4: true
pt1.equals(pt4): true
```

In practice, two points are considered the same if they have the same (x, y) co-ordinates. If we want to implement this rule of equality (based on equality of co-ordinates of `Point` objects) for our `Point` class, we must re-implement the `equals()` method as shown in Listing 7-1. We call our new `Point` class as `SmartPoint`. Java advises you to re-implement `hashCode()` and `equals()` methods together, if any one of them is re-implemented in your class. The Java compiler would not complain if you re-implement the `equals()` method and not the `hashCode()` method in your class. However, you will get unpredictable results when you use the objects of your class in hash-based collections.

The only requirement that you have for a `hashCode()` method is that if the `m.equals(n)` method returns `true`, `m.hashCode()` must return the same value as `n.hashCode()`. Since our `equals()` method uses (x, y) co-ordinates to test for equality, we return the sum of x and y co-ordinates from the `hashCode()` method, which fulfills the technical requirement. Practically, you need to use a good hashing algorithm to compute a hash value for a `Point` object and return that value from the `hashCode()` method.

Listing 7-1: A SmartPoint class that re-implements equals() and hashCode() methods

```java
// SmartPoint.java
package com.jdojo.chapter7;

public class SmartPoint {
    private int x;
    private int y;

    public SmartPoint(int x, int y) {
        this.x = x;
        this.y = y;
    }

    // Re-implement equals() method
    public boolean equals(Object otherObject) {
        // Are the same?
        if (this == otherObject) {
            return true;
        }

        // Is otherObject a null reference?
        if (otherObject == null) {
            return false;
        }

        // Do they belong to the same class?
        if (this.getClass() != otherObject.getClass()) {
            return false;
        }

        // Get the reference of otherObject in a SmartPoint variable
        SmartPoint otherPoint = (SmartPoint)otherObject;

        // Do they have the same x and y co-ordinates
        boolean isSamePoint = (this.x == otherPoint.x &&
                               this.y == otherPoint.y);

        return isSamePoint;
    }

    // Re-implement hashCode() method of Object class, which is
    // a requirement when you re-implement equals() method
    public int hashCode() {
        return (this.x + this.y);
```

```
        }
}
```

We have written a few lines of codes in the `equals()` method of the `SmartPoint` class. We will go through the logic one by one. First, we need to check if the object passed to the `equals()` method is the same as the object on which the method is called. If two objects are the same, we consider them equal by retuning `true`. This is accomplished by the following code.

```
// Are they the same?
if (this == otherObject) {
    return true;
}
```

If the parameter being passed to the `equals()` method is a `null` reference, the two objects cannot be the same. Note that the object on which the method is called can never be a `null` reference, because you cannot call a method on a `null` reference. Java runtime will throw runtime exception when an attempt is made to call a method on a `null` reference. The following code makes sure that we are comparing two non-null objects.

```
// Is otherObject a null reference?
if (otherObject == null) {
    return false;
}
```

The parameter type of the `equals()` method is `Object`. This means that any type of object reference can be passed to the `equals()` method. For example, you can use `apple.equals(orange)`, where `apple` and `orange` are references to an `Apple` object and an `Orange` object respectively. In our case, we want to compare only a `SmartPoint` object to another `SmartPoint` object. To make sure that the objects being compared are of the same class, we need the following code. If someone calls the `equals()` method with a parameter, which is not a `SmartPoint` object, our `equals()` method will return `false`.

```
// Do they have the same class?
if (this.getClass() != otherObject.getClass()) {
    return false;
}
```

At this point, we are sure that someone is trying to compare two non-null `SmartPoint` objects, which have different identity (references). Now we would like to compare the (x, y) co-ordinates of two `SmartPoint` objects. To access the x and y instance variables of the `otherObject` formal parameter, we must cast it to a `SmartPoint` object. The following statement does it.

```
// Get the reference of otherObject in a SmartPoint variable
SmartPoint otherPoint = (SmartPoint)otherObject;
```

At this point, it is just the matter of comparing the values of x and y instance variables of the two `SmartPoint` objects. If they are the same, we consider two objects the same by returning `true`. Otherwise, two objects are not the same and we return `false`. This is accomplished by the following code.

```
// Do they have the same x and y co-ordinates
boolean isSamePoint = (this.x == otherPoint.x && this.y == otherPoint.y);
return isSamePoint;
```

It is time to test our re-implementation of the `equals()` method in the `SmartPoint` class. Listing 7-2 is our test class for the `SmartPoint` objects. You can observe in the output that we have two ways of comparing two `SmartPoint` objects for equality. The equality operator (==) compares them based on identity and the `equals()` method compares them based on values of the (x, y) co-ordinates. Note that if (x, y) co-ordinates are the same for two `SmartPoint` objects, the `equals()` method returns `true`.

Listing 7-2: A test class to demonstrate the difference between identity comparison and state comparison for SmartPoint objects

```java
// SmartPointTest.java
package com.jdojo.chapter7;

public class SmartPointTest {
    public static void main(String[] args)  {
        SmartPoint pt1 = new SmartPoint(10, 10);
        SmartPoint pt2 = new SmartPoint(10, 10);
        SmartPoint pt3 = new SmartPoint(12, 19);
        SmartPoint pt4 = pt1;

        System.out.println("pt1 == pt1: " + (pt1 == pt1));
        System.out.println("pt1.equals(pt1): " + pt1.equals(pt1));

        System.out.println("pt1 == pt2: " + (pt1 == pt2));
        System.out.println("pt1.equals(pt2): " + pt1.equals(pt2));

        System.out.println("pt1 == pt3: " + (pt1 == pt3));
        System.out.println("pt1.equals(pt3): " + pt1.equals(pt3));

        System.out.println("pt1 == pt4: " + (pt1 == pt4));
        System.out.println("pt1.equals(pt4): " + pt1.equals(pt4));
    }
}
```

```
Output:

pt1 == pt1: true
pt1.equals(pt1): true
pt1 == pt2: false
pt1.equals(pt2): true
pt1 == pt3: false
pt1.equals(pt3): false
pt1 == pt4: true
pt1.equals(pt4): true
```

There are some specifications for implementing the `equals()` method in your class so that your class will work correctly when used with other areas (e.g. hash-based collections) of Java. It is the responsibility of the class designer to enforce these specifications. If your class does not conform to these specifications, The Java compiler or Java runtime will not generate any errors. Rather, objects of your class will behave incorrectly. For example, you will add your object to a collection, but may not be able to retrieve it. Here are specifications for the `equals()` method's implementation. Assume that `x`, `y`, and `z` are non-null references of three objects.

- **Reflexivity**: It should be reflexive. The expression, `x.equals(x)`, should return `true`. That is, an object must be equal to itself.

- **Symmetry**: It should be symmetric. If `x.equals(y)` returns `true`, `y.equals(x)` must return `true`. That is, if x is equal to `y`, `y` must be equal to x.
- **Transitivity**: It should be transitive. If `x.equals(y)` returns `true` and `y.equals(z)` returns `true`, `x.equals(z)` must return `true`. That is, if x is equal to `y` and `y` is equal to z, x must be equal to z.
- **Consistency**: It should be consistent. If `x.equals(y)` returns `true`, it should keep returning `true` until state of x or y is modified. If `x.equals(y)` returns `false`, it should keep returning `false` until state of x or y is modified.
- **Comparison with null reference:** An object of any class should not be equal to a `null` reference. The expression, `x.equals(null)`, should always return `false`.
- **Relationship with hashCode() method:** If `x.equals(y)` returns `true`, `x.hashCode()` must return the same value as `y.hashCode()`. That is, if two objects are equal according to `equals()` method, they must have the same hash code values returned from their `hashCode()` methods. However, the opposite may not be true. If two objects have the same hash code, that does not mean that they must be equal according to `equals()` method. That is, if `x.hashCode()` is equal to `y.hashCode()`, that does not imply that `x.equals(y)` will return `true`.

Our `SmartPoint` class satisfies all six rules for `equals()` and `hashCode()` methods. It was fairly easy to implement the `equals()` method for the `SmartPoint` class. It has two primitive type instance variables and we used both of them in comparison for equality.

There are no rules as to how many of instance variables should be used to compare for equality of two objects of a class. It all depends on the use of the class. For example, if you have an `Account` class, the account number itself may be sufficient in your case to compare for the equality of two `Account` objects. However, make sure you use the same instance variables in the `equals()` method to compare for equality and in the `hashCode()` method to compute hash code value. If your class has reference instance variables, you may call their `equals()` methods from inside the `equals()` method of your class. Listing 7-3 shows how to use a reference instance variable comparison inside the `equals()` method. The `SmartCat` class has a name instance variable, which is of type `String`. The `String` class has its own version of the `equals()` method implementation that compares two strings, character-by-character. The `equals()` method of the `SmartCat` class calls the `equals()` method on the `name` instance variables to check if two names are the same. Similarly, it makes use of the `hashCode()` method's implementation in the `String` class in its `hashCode()` method.

Listing 7-3: A SmartCat class that demonstrates how to use reference instance variables' equals() and hashCode() method to write logic for the equals() and hashCode() methods of a class

```java
// SmartCat.java
package com.jdojo.chapter7;

public class SmartCat {
    private String name;

    public SmartCat(String name) {
        this.name = name;
    }

    // Re-implement equals() method
    public boolean equals(Object otherObject) {
        // Are they the same?
        if (this == otherObject) {
```

```
                return true;
        }

        // Is otherObject a null reference?
        if (otherObject == null) {
            return false;
        }

        // Do they belong to the same class?
        if (this.getClass() != otherObject.getClass()) {
            return false;
        }

        // Get the reference of otherObject is a SmartCat variable
        SmartCat otherCat = (SmartCat)otherObject;

        // Do they have the same names
        boolean isSameName = (this.name == null? otherCat.name == null
                                :this.name.equals(otherCat.name) );

        return isSameName;
    }

    // Re-implement hashCode() method of Object class, which is
    // a requirement when you re-implement equals() method
    public int hashCode() {
        return (this.name == null? 0: this.name.hashCode());
    }
}
```

String Representation of an Object

An object is represented by its state, which is the combination of values of all its instance variables at a point in time. Sometimes, it is helpful, usually in debugging, to represent an object in a string form. What should be in the string that represents an object? The string representation of an object should contain enough information about the state of the object and it should be readable. The toString() method of the Object class lets you write your own logic to represent the object of your class in a string form. The Object class has default implementation of its toString() method. It returns a string of the following format.

```
<<fully qualified class name>>@<<hash code of object in hexadecimal>>
```

Consider the following snippet of code and its output.

```
// Create two objects
Object obj = new Object();
IntHolder intHolder = new IntHolder(234);

// Get string representation of objects
String objStr = obj.toString();
String intHolderStr = intHolder.toString();

// Print the string representations
```

```
System.out.println(objStr);
System.out.println(intHolderStr);
```

Output: (You may get a different output after the @ symbol)

```
java.lang.Object@360be0
com.jdojo.chapter7.IntHolder@45a877
```

Note that our IntHolder class does not have a toString() method. Still, we were able to call the toString() method using the intHolder reference variable, because all methods in the Object class are available in all classes automatically. However, you may notice that the string representation that is returned from toString() method for IntHolder object is not so useful. It does not give you any clues as to what is the state of the IntHolder object. Let us re-implement the toString() method in our IntHolder class. We will call the new class SmartIntHolder. What should our toString() method return? An object of SmartIntHolder represents an integer value. It would be good just to return the stored integer value as a string. You can convert an integer value, say 123, into a String object using the valueOf() static method of the String class as:

```
String str = String.valueOf(123); // str contains 123 as a string
```

Listing 7-4 has the complete code for our SmartIntHolder class. The following snippet of code shows you how to use the toString() method of the SmartIntHolder class.

```
// Create an object of SmartIntHolder class
SmartIntHolder intHolder = new SmartIntHolder(234);
String intHolderStr = intHolder.toString();
System.out.println(intHolderStr);

// Change the value in SmartIntHolder object
intHolder.setValue(8967);
intHolderStr = intHolder.toString();
System.out.println(intHolderStr);
```

Output:

```
234
8967
```

Listing 7-4:Re-implementing toString() method of the Object class in the SmartIntHolder class

```
// SmartIntHolder.java
package com.jdojo.chapter7;

public class SmartIntHolder {
    private int value;

    public SmartIntHolder(int value) {
        this.value = value;
    }

    public void setValue(int value) {
        this.value = value;
```

```
    }

    public int getValue() {
        return value;
    }

    // Re-implement toString() method of the Object class
    public String toString() {
        // Return the stored value as string
        String str = String.valueOf(this.value);
        return str;
    }
}
```

There is no special technical requirement for re-implementing the `toString()` method in your class. You need to make sure it is declared `public`, its return type is `String`, and it does not accept any parameters. You should return a string from this method that returns a human readable text, to give an idea about the state of the object at the time this method is called. It is recommended to re-implement the `toString()` method of the `Object` class in every class you create.

Suppose you have a `Point` class to represent a 2D point as shown in Listing 7-5. An object of `Point` class holds the x and y co-ordinates of a point. An implementation of the `toString()` method in the `Point` class may return a string of the form `(x, y)`, where x and y are the co-ordinates of the point.

Listing 7-5: A Point class whose object represents a 2-D point

```
// Point.java
package com.jdojo.chapter7;

public class Point {
    private int x;
    private int y;

    public Point(int x, int y) {
        this.x = x;
        this.y = y;
    }

    // Re-implement toString() method of Object class
    public String toString() {
        String str = "(" + x + ", " + y + ")";
        return str;
    }
}
```

The `toString()` method of a class is very important and Java provides you with easy ways to use it. In fact, Java calls the `toString()` method of an object automatically for you in situations when it needs a string representation of your object. Two such situations that are worth mentioning are:

- A string concatenation expression involving a reference of an object.
- Calls to `System.out.print()` and `System.out.println()` methods with an object reference as a parameter.

When you concatenate a string with an object as in

```
String str = "Hello" + new Point(10, 20);
```

then the Java will call the `toString()` method on the `Point` object and concatenate its return value to "Hello" string. The above statement will assign "Hello(10, 20)" string to the `str` variable. The above statement is the same as the one shown below.

```
String str = "Hello" + new Point(10, 20).toString();
```

You use the string concatenation operator (+) to concatenate data of different types. First, Java gets the string representation of all data before concatenating them. Calling the `toString()` method of an object automatically for you in a concatenation expression helps you save some typing. If the object reference that is used in concatenation is a `null` reference, Java uses "null" string as its string representation. The following snippet of code makes the call to the `toString()` method on object references clear. You may observe that the result is the same when we use the object's reference by itself, or we call its `toString()` method in a string concatenation expression. Similarly, when we use `System.out.println(pt)`, Java automatically calls the `toString()` method on the `pt` reference variable.

```
Point pt = new Point(10, 12);

String str1 = "Test " + pt;
String str2 = "Test " + pt.toString();

// str1 and str 2 will have the same content
System.out.println(pt);
System.out.println(pt.toString());
System.out.println(str1);
System.out.println(str2);
```

```
Output:

(10, 12)
(10, 12)
Test (10, 12)
Test (10, 12)
```

The following snippet of code shows the effect of using a `null` reference in a string concatenation expression and in the `System.out.println()` method call. Java uses a string, "null", as the string representation for a `null` reference. Note that you cannot use `pt.toString()` when pt is holding a `null` reference. The call to any method on a `null` reference will generate a runtime exception.

```
// Set pt to null
Point pt = null;
String str3 = "Test " + pt;
System.out.println(pt);
System.out.println(str3);
//System.out.println(pt.toString()); // Will generate runtime exception
```

```
Output:
```

```
null
Test null
```

Cloning an Object

Java does not provide an automatic mechanism to clone (or make a copy) an object. Recall that when you assign a reference variable to another reference variable, only the object's reference is copied, not the object's content. Cloning an object means copying the content of the object bit-by-bit. If you want objects of your class to be cloned, you must re-implement the `clone()` method in your class that is declared in the `Object` class. Once you re-implement the `clone()` method in your class, you should be able to clone objects of your class by calling the `clone()` method. The declaration of the `clone()` method in the `Object` class is as follows.

```
protected Object clone() throws CloneNotSupportedException
```

There are a few things you need to observe about the declaration of the `clone()` method in the `Object` class.

- It is declared `protected`. Therefore, you will not be able to call it from the client code. The following code is not valid.

  ```
  Object obj = new Object();
  Object clone = obj.clone(); // Error. Cannot access
                              // protected clone() method
  ```

  This means that you need to declare the `clone()` method `public` in your class if you want the client code to clone objects of your class.

- Its return type is `Object`. It means you will need to cast the returned value of the `clone()` method. Suppose `MyClass` is a cloneable. Then, your code will look as:

  ```
  MyClass mc = new MyClass();
  MyClass clone = (MyClass)mc.clone(); // Need to use cast
  ```

Cloning of an object requires deep knowledge about the object structure, the amount of memory it takes, etc. You do not need to know any internal details about an object to clone it. The `clone()` method in the `Object` class has all the code that is needed to clone an object. All you need is to call it from the `clone()` method of your class. It will make a bitwise copy of the original object and return the reference of the clone.

The `clone()` method in the `Object` class throws `CloneNotSupportedException`. It means when you call the `clone()` method of the `Object` class, you need to place the call in a `try-catch` block. We will learn more about the `try-catch` block in the chapter on *Exception Handling*. You have the option not to throw `CloneNotSupportedException` from the `clone()` method of your class. The following snippet of code is placed inside the `clone()` method of your class, which calls the `clone()` method of the `Object` class using `super` keyword.

```
YourClass obj = null;
try {
```

```
    // Call clone() method of the Object class using super.clone()
    obj = (YourClass)super.clone();
}
catch (CloneNotSupportedException e){
    e. printStackTrace();
}
return obj;
```

One important thing that you must do is add "implements Cloneable" clause in your class declaration. Cloneable is an interface declared in the java.lang package. We will learn about interface in the chapter on *Interface* later in this book. For now, just add this clause in your class declaration. Otherwise, you will get a runtime error when you call the clone() method on the objects of your class. Your class declaration must look like:

```
public class MyClass implements Cloneable {
  // Code for your class goes here
}
```

Listing 7-6 has code for the DoubleHolder class. It overrides the clone() method of the Object class. The comments in the clone() method explains what the code is doing. The clone() method of DoubleHolder class does not have a throws clause as the clone() method of the Object class. When you override a method, you have an option to drop the throws clause that is declared in the superclass.

Listing 7-6: A DoubleHolder class with cloning capability

```
// DoubleHolder.java
package com.jdojo.chapter7;

public class DoubleHolder implements Cloneable {
    private double value;

    public DoubleHolder(double value) {
        this.value = value;
    }

    public void setValue(double value) {
        this.value = value;
    }

    public double getValue() {
        return this.value;
    }

    public Object clone() {
        DoubleHolder copy = null;
        try {
            // Call Object's class clone() method, which will do a
            // bit-by-bit copy and return the reference of the clone
            copy = (DoubleHolder)super.clone();
        }
        catch (CloneNotSupportedException e) {
            // If anything goes wrong during cloning then
            // print the error details
            e.printStackTrace();
```

```
        }
        return copy;
    }
}
```

Once your class implements the `clone()` method correctly, cloning an object of your class is as simple as calling the `clone()` method. The following snippet of code shows you how to clone an object of the `DoubleHolder` class. Note that you must use cast to cast the returned reference from the `dh.clone()` method call to the `DoubleHolder` type.

```
DoubleHolder dh = new DoubleHolder(100.00);

// Clone dh. Must use cast
DoubleHolder dhClone = (DoubleHolder)dh.clone();
```

At this point, there are two separate objects of the `DoubleHolder` class. The `dh` reference variable references the original object and `dhClone` reference variable references the copy of the original object. The original as well as the cloned object hold the same value of `100.00`. However, they have separate copies of the value. If you change the value in original object, e.g., `dh.setValue(200)`, the value in the cloned object remains unchanged. Listing 7-7 shows you how to use the `clone()` method to clone an object of the `DoubleHolder` class. The output proves that once you clone an object, there are two separate objects in memory.

Listing 7-7: A test class to demonstrate object cloning

```
// CloningTest.java
package com.jdojo.chapter7;

public class CloningTest {
    public static void main(String[] args)  {
        DoubleHolder dh = new DoubleHolder(100.00);

        // Clone dh
        DoubleHolder dhClone = (DoubleHolder)dh.clone();

        // Print the values in original and clone
        System.out.println("Original:" + dh.getValue());
        System.out.println("Clone :" + dhClone.getValue());

        // Change the value in original and clone
        dh.setValue(200.00);
        dhClone.setValue(400.00);

        // Print the values in original and clone again
        System.out.println("Original:" + dh.getValue());
        System.out.println("Clone :" + dhClone.getValue());
    }
}
```

```
Output:

Original:100.0
Clone :100.0
Original:200.0
Clone :400.0
```

From Java 5, you need not specify the return type of the `clone()` method in your class as the `Object` type. You can specify the return type of your class in the `clone()` method's declaration. This will not force the client code to use a cast when it call the `clone()` method of your class. The following snippet of code shows the changed code for the `DoubleHolder` class, which will compile only in Java 5 or later. It declares `DoubleHolder` as the return type of the `clone()` method and uses a cast in the `return` statement.

```
// DoubleHolder.java
package com.jdojo.chapter7;

public class DoubleHolder implements Cloneable {
    // The same code goes here as before...

    public DoubleHolder clone() {
        Object copy = null;
        // The same code goes here as before...
        return (DoubleHolder)copy;
    }
}
```

With the above declaration for the `clone()` method, you can write code to clone an object as follows. Note that no cast is needed anymore.

```
DoubleHolder dh = new DoubleHolder(100.00);
DoubleHolder dhClone = dh.clone();// Clone dh. No cast is needed
```

An object may be composed of another object. In such cases, two objects exist in memory separately – a contained object and a container object. The container object stores the reference of the contained object. When you clone the container object, the reference of the contained object is cloned. After cloning is performed, there are two copies of the container object and both of them have references to the same contained object. This is called a shallow cloning, because references are copied and not the objects. The `clone()` method of the `Object` class makes only shallow cloning. Figure 7-2 shows the memory state of a compound object, where an object contains a reference of another object. Figure 7-3 shows the memory state when a compound object is cloned using a shallow cloning. You may notice that in shallow cloning the contained object is shared by the original compound object and the cloned compound object.

When the contained objects are copied rather than their references during cloning of a compound object, it is called deep cloning. You must clone all the objects referenced by all reference variables of an object to get a deep cloning. A compound object may have multiple levels of chaining of contained objects. For example, the container object may have a reference of another contained object, which in turn has a reference of another contained object and so on. Whether you will be able to perform a deep cloning of a compound object depends on many factors. If you have a reference of a contained object, it may not support cloning and in that case, you have to be content with shallow cloning. You may have a reference of a contained object, which itself is a compound object. However, the contained object supports only shallow cloning and in that case again, you will have to be content with shallow cloning. Let us look at examples of shallow cloning and deep cloning.

If the reference instance variables of an object store references to immutable objects, you do not need to clone them. That is, if the contained objects of a compound object are immutable, we do not need to clone the contained objects. In this case, shallow copy of the immutable contained objects is fine. Recall that immutable objects cannot be modified after they are created. An immutable object's references can be shared by the multiple objects without any side effects. This is one of the benefits of having immutable objects. If a compound object contains some references to mutable objects and some to immutable objects, you must clone the referenced mutable objects to get a deep copy.

Figure 7-2: A compound object. The container object stores a reference of another object (Contained object)

Figure 7-3: Memory state after the container object is cloned using a shallow cloning

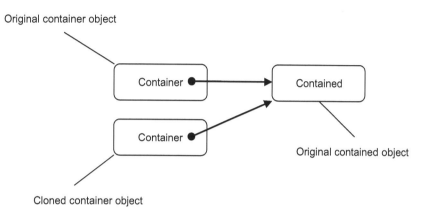

Listing 7-8 has code for the `ShallowClone` class. An object of the `ShallowClone` class is composed of an object of the `DoubleHolder` class. The code in the `clone()` method of the `ShallowClone` class is the same as for the `clone()` method of the `DoubleHolder` class. The difference lies in the type of instance variables that are used for the two classes. The `DoubleHolder` class has an instance variable of primitive type `double`, whereas the `ShallowClone` class has an instance variable of reference type `DoubleHolder`. When the `ShallowClone` class calls the `clone()` method of the `Object` class (using `super.clone()`), it receives a shallow copy of itself. That is, it shares the `DoubleHolder` object used in its instance variable with its clone. Listing 7-9 has test cases to test an object of the `ShallowClone` class and its clone. The output shows that after you make a clone, changing the value through the original object also changes the value of the cloned object. This is so, because the `ShallowClone` object stores the value in another object of the `DoubleHolder` class, which is shared by both the cloned and the original objects.

Listing 7-8: A ShallowClone class that supports shallow cloning

```
// ShallowClone.java
package com.jdojo.chapter7;

public class ShallowClone implements Cloneable {
    private DoubleHolder holder = new DoubleHolder(0.0);

    public ShallowClone(double value) {
        this.holder.setValue(value);
    }

    public void setValue(double value) {
        this.holder.setValue(value);
```

```
        }

    public double getValue() {
        return this.holder.getValue();
    }

    public Object clone() {
        ShallowClone copy = null;
        try {
            copy = (ShallowClone)super.clone();
        }
        catch (CloneNotSupportedException e) {
            e.printStackTrace();
        }
        return copy;
    }
}
```

Listing 7-9: A test class to demonstrate the shallow copy mechanism

```
// ShallowCloneTest.java
package com.jdojo.chapter7;

public class ShallowCloneTest {
    public static void main(String[] args)  {
        ShallowClone sc = new ShallowClone(100.00);
        ShallowClone scClone = (ShallowClone)sc.clone();

        // Print the value in original and clone
        System.out.println("Original:" + sc.getValue());
        System.out.println("Clone :" + scClone.getValue());

        // Change the value in original and it will change the
        // value for clone too because we have done shallow cloning
        sc.setValue(200.00);

        // Print the value in original and clone
        System.out.println("Original:" + sc.getValue());
        System.out.println("Clone :" + scClone.getValue());
    }
}
```

```
Output:

Original:100.0
Clone :100.0
Original:200.0
Clone :200.0
```

In a deep cloning, you need to clone all objects referenced by all reference instance variables of an object. You must perform a shallow cloning before you can perform a deep cloning. The shallow cloning is performed by calling the `clone()` method of the `Object` class. Then, you will need to write code to clone all reference instance variables. Listing 7-10 has code for the `DeepClone` class, which performs the deep cloning. If you compare the code in the `clone()` method of

`ShallowClone` and `DeepClone` classes, you will find that for deep cloning we had to write only one extra line of code. The extra line of code is:

```
// Need to clone the holder reference variable too
copy.holder = (DoubleHolder)this.holder.clone();
```

What will happen if the `DoubleHolder` class is not cleanable? In that case, you would not be able to write the above statement to clone the `holder` instance variable. You could have cloned the holder instance variable as follows.

```
// Need to clone the holder reference variable too
copy.holder = new DoubleHolder(this.holder.getValue());
```

The goal is to clone the `holder` instance variable and it does not have to be done by calling its `clone()` method. Listing 7-11 shows how our `DeepClone` class works. Compare its output with the output of the `ShallowCloneTest` class and you will see the difference.

Listing 7-10: A DeepClone class that performs deep cloning

```java
// DeepClone.java
package com.jdojo.chapter7;

public class DeepClone implements Cloneable {
    private DoubleHolder holder = new DoubleHolder(0.0);

    public DeepClone(double value) {
        this.holder.setValue(value);
    }

    public void setValue(double value) {
        this.holder.setValue(value);
    }

    public double getValue() {
        return this.holder.getValue();
    }

    public Object clone() {
        DeepClone copy = null;
        try {
            copy = (DeepClone)super.clone();

            // Need to clone the holder reference variable too
            copy.holder = (DoubleHolder)this.holder.clone();
        }
        catch (CloneNotSupportedException e) {
            e.printStackTrace();
        }

        return copy;
    }
}
```

Listing 7-11: A test class to test deep cloning of objects

```java
// DeepCloneTest.java
```

```
package com.jdojo.chapter7;

public class DeepCloneTest {
    public static void main(String[] args)  {
        DeepClone sc = new DeepClone(100.00);
        DeepClone scClone = (DeepClone)sc.clone();

        // Print the value in original and clone
        System.out.println("Original:" + sc.getValue());
        System.out.println("Clone :" + scClone.getValue());

        // Change the value in original and it will not change the
        // value for clone because we have done deep cloning
        sc.setValue(200.00);

        // Print the value in original and clone
        System.out.println("Original:" + sc.getValue());
        System.out.println("Clone :" + scClone.getValue());
    }
}
```

```
Output:

Original:100.0
Clone :100.0
Original:200.0
Clone :100.0
```

TIP

Using the `clone()` method of the `Object` class is not the only way to make a clone of an object. You can use other methods to clone an object. You may provide a copy constructor, which accepts an object of the same class, and creates a clone of that object. You may provide a factory method in your class, which may accept an object and returns its clone. Another way to clone an object is to serialize it and then deserialized it. We will discuss the serialization of objects in the chapter on *Input/Output*. Using serialization to clone an object is slower.

Finalizing an Object

Sometimes you obtain references to some resources when an object is created and you want to hold onto those resources while the object is alive. You want to release the resources when the object is destroyed. Java provides you with a way to perform resource release or some other type of cleanup, when an object is about to be destroyed. In Java, you create objects. However, you cannot destroy objects. The JVM keeps running a low priority special task called *Garbage Collector* to destroy all objects that are no longer referenced. The garbage collector gives you a chance to execute your custom code before an object is destroyed.

The `Object` class has a `finalize()` method, which is declared as follows.

```
protected void finalize() throws Throwable{ ... }
```

The `finalize()` method in the `Object` class does not do anything. You need to override the `finalize()` method of the `Object` class in your class. The `finalize()` method of your class will be called by the garbage collector before an object of your class is destroyed. Listing 7-12 has code for the `Finalize` class. It overrides the `finalize()` method of the `Object` class and prints a message on the standard output. You can perform any cleanup logic in this method. The code in the `finalize()` method is also called *finalizer*.

Listing 7-12: A Finalize class that overrides the finalize() method of the Object class

```java
// Finalize.java
package com.jdojo.chapter7;

public class Finalize {
    private int x;

    public Finalize(int x) {
        this.x = x;
    }

    public void finalize() {
        System.out.println("Finalizing " + this.x);

        // Perform any cleanup work here...
    }
}
```

The garbage collector calls the finalizer for each object only once. The running of a finalizer for an object by a garbage collector does not necessarily mean that the object will be immediately destroyed after the finalizer call is over. An object's finalizer is run when the garbage collector determines that no reference exists for the object. However, an object may pass its own reference to some other part of the program when its finalizer is run. This is the reason why the garbage collector checks one more time after it runs an object's finalizer to make sure that no references exists for that object and then it destroys (de-allocates memory) the object. The order in which finalizers are run and the time at which they are run are not specified. It is not even guaranteed that a finalizer will run at all. This makes it undependable for a programmer to write cleanup logic in the `finalize()` method. There are better ways to perform cleanup logic, for example, using a `try-finally` block. It is suggested not to depend on the `finalize()` method in your Java program to clean up your resources.

Listing 7-13 has code that tests the finalizers for our `Finalize` class. It creates 20000 objects of the `Finalize` class without storing their references. It is important that you do not store the references of the objects you create. As long as you hold the reference of an object, it will not be destroyed and its finalizer will not be run. You can see from the output that only three objects got a chance to run their finalizers before the program finished. You may get no output at all or a different output. If you do not get any output, you can try by increasing the number of objects to create from 20000 to 50000 or more. The garbage collector will destroy objects when it feels it is running low in memory. You may need to create more objects to trigger garbage collection, which in turn will run finalizers of your objects.

Listing 7-13: A test class to test the finalizer for the Finalize class objects

```java
// FinalizeTest.java
package com.jdojo.chapter7;

public class FinalizeTest {
    public static void main(String[] args) {
```

```
        // Create many objects
        for(int i = 0; i < 20000; i++) {
            new Finalize(i);
        }
    }
}
```

```
Output: (You may get different output or no output at all.)

Finalizing 15247
Finalizing 15248
Finalizing 15246
```

Immutable Objects

An object, whose state cannot be changed after it is created, is called an *immutable* object. A class whose objects are immutable is called an *immutable* class. On the other hand, if an object's state can be changed (or mutated) after it has been created, it is called a *mutable* object, and its class is called a *mutable* class.

Before we go into details of creating and using immutable objects, let us define the word "immutability". Values of all instance variables of an object define the state of an object. There are two views of the object's state – internal and external. The internal state of the object is defined by the actual values of its instance variables at a point in time. The external state of the object is defined by the values that the users (or clients) of the object see at a point in time. When we state that an object is immutable, we must be specific about which state of the object we mean to be immutable – internal state or external state or both. Typically, when we use the phrase "immutable object" in Java, we mean external immutability. In an external immutability, an object may change its internal state after its creation. However, the change in its internal state is not visible to external users. Its users do not see any changes in its state after its creation. In an internal immutability, the state of an object does not change after it is created. If an object is internally immutable, it is also externally immutable. We will have examples of both external and internal immutable objects.

Using immutable objects has several advantages over using mutable objects. An immutable object can be shared by different areas of a program without worrying about its state changes. Testing an immutable class is easy. An immutable object is inherently thread-safe. You do not have to synchronize access to your immutable object from multiple threads, since its state does not change. Please refer to the chapter on *Thread* for more details on thread synchronization. It does not have to be copied and passed to another area of the program in the same Java application, because its state does not change. You can just pass its reference and that serves as its copy. Its reference can be used to access its content. Avoiding copying is a big performance advantages as it saves both, time and space.

Let us start with a mutable class whose object's state can be modified after it is created. Listing 7-14 has code for IntHolder class.

Listing 7-14: An example of a mutable class, whose object's state can be changed after creation

```
// IntHolder.java
package com.jdojo.chapter7;

public class IntHolder {
    private int value;
```

```
    public IntHolder(int value) {
        this.value = value;
    }

    public void setValue(int value) {
        this.value = value;
    }

    public int getValue() {
        return value;
    }
}
```

The `value` instance variable defines the state of an `IntHolder` object. We create an object of the `IntHolder` class as:

```
IntHolder holder = new IntHolder(101);
int v = holder.getValue(); // will return 101
```

At this time, the `value` instance variable of `holder` object holds `101`, which defines its state. We can get the value held in the object using its `getValue()` method as shown above. We can change its state by using the `setValue()` method as:

```
holder.setValue(505);
int w = holder.getValue(); // will return 505
```

At this point, the `value` instance variable of the `holder` object has changed from `101` to `505`. That is, the state of the object has changed. The change in state was facilitated by the `setValue()` method. Objects of the `IntHolder` class are examples of mutable objects.

Let us make the `IntHolder` class immutable. All we need to do is to remove the `setValue()` method from it and then it becomes an immutable class. Let us call our immutable version of the `IntHolder` class as `IntWrapper` as shown in Listing 7-15.

Listing 7-15: An example of an immutable class whose object's state cannot be changed after creation

```
// IntWrapper.java
package com.jdojo.chapter7;

public class IntWrapper {
    private final int value;

    public IntWrapper(int value) {
        this.value = value;
    }

    public int getValue() {
        return value;
    }
}
```

This is how we create an object of the `IntWrapper` class.

```
IntWrapper wrapper = new IntWrapper(101);
```

At this point, the `wrapper` object holds an integer value of `101` and there is no way to change it. Therefore, `IntWrapper` class is an immutable class and its objects are immutable objects. You might have noticed that two changes were made to the `IntHolder` class to convert it to the `IntWrapper` class. The `setValue()` method was removed and the `value` instance variable was made `final`. In this case, it was not necessary to make the `value` instance variable in `IntWrapper` class as `final`. Even if it is not `final`, objects of `IntWrapper` class will be immutable because there is no way to change it after it is created. The use of the `final` keyword makes your intention clear to the reader of your class and it protects the `value` instance variable from being changed inadvertently. It is a good practice (use it as a rule of thumb) to declare all instance variables that define the immutable state of an object as `final` so that Java compiler will enforce the immutability during compile time. The objects of `IntWrapper` class are immutable internally as well as externally. There is no way to change its state once it is created.

Let us create a variation of `IntWrapper` class, which is immutable externally, but not internally. Let us call it `IntWrapper2`. It is listed in Listing 7-16. It adds another instance variable called `halfValue`, which will hold the half value of the value that is passed to the constructor. It is a trivial example. However, it serves the purpose to explain what we mean by externally and internally immutable objects. Suppose (just for the sake of this discussion) that computing half of an integer is a very costly process and we do not want to compute it in the constructor of the `IntWrapper2` class. The `halfValue` instance variable is initialized to the maximum integer value, which works as a flag to know that we have not computed the half value of the integer yet. We have added a `getHalfValue()` method, which checks if we have already computed the half value. For the first time, it will compute the half value and cache it in `halfValue` instance variable. From the second time onward, it will simply return the cached half value.

The question is, "Is an `IntWrapper` object immutable?" The answer is yes and no. It is internally mutable. However, it is externally immutable. Once it is created, its client will see the same return value from its `getValue()` and `getHalfValue()` methods. However, its state (`halfValue` to be specific) changes once in its lifetime when the `getHalfValue()` method is called the first time. However, this change is not visible to the clients of the object. This method returns the same value on all subsequent calls. Objects like `IntWrapper2` objects are called immutable objects. Recall that typically an immutable object means externally immutable.

The `String` class in the Java class library is an example of an immutable class. It uses the caching technique as discussed for `IntWrapper2` class. `String` class computes hash code for its content when its `hashCode()` method is called the first time and caches the value. Thus, a `String` object changes its state internally, but not for its client. You will not come across the phrase – "A `String` object in Java is externally immutable and internally mutable". Rather, you will come across the phrase like - "A `String` object in Java is immutable". You should understand that it means `String` objects are at least externally immutable.

Listing 7-16: An example of an externally immutable object, whose state changes internally over time, while, externally, its state remains the same

```
// IntWrapper2.java
package com.jdojo.chapter7;

public class IntWrapper2 {
    private final int value;
    private int halfValue = Integer.MAX_VALUE;

    public IntWrapper2(int value) {
```

```
            this.value = value;
        }

        public int getValue() {
            return value;
        }

        public int getHalfValue() {
            // Compute half value if it is not already computed
            if (this.halfValue == Integer.MAX_VALUE) {
                // Cache the half value for future use
                this.halfValue = this.value / 2;
            }
            return this.halfValue;
        }
}
```

Listing 7-17 shows a tricky situation where an attempt has been made to create an immutable class. The IntHolderWrapper class has no method that can directly let you modify the value stored in its valueHolder instance variable. It seems to be an immutable class.

Listing 7-17: An unsuccessful attempt to create an immutable class

```
// IntHolderWrapper.java
package com.jdojo.chapter7;

public class IntHolderWrapper {
    private final IntHolder valueHolder;

    public IntHolderWrapper(int value) {
        this.valueHolder = new IntHolder(value);
    }

    public IntHolder getIntHolder() {
        return this.valueHolder;
    }

    public int getValue() {
        return this.valueHolder.getValue();
    }
}
```

Listing 7-18 has a test class that shows that the IntHolderWrapper class is mutable. The two calls to its getValue() method return different values. The culprit is its getIntHolder() method. It returns the instance variable valueHolder, which is a reference variable. Note that the valueHolder instance variable represents an object of the IntHolder class, which makes up the state of an IntHolderWrapper object. If the object that valueHolder reference variable references is changed, the state of IntHolderWrapper is changed, too. Since the IntHolder object is a mutable object, we should not return its reference to the client from the getIntHolder() method. The following two statements change the state of the object from the client code. Note that the designer of the IntHolderWrapper class missed the point when he returned the valueHolder reference, that even though there is no direct way to change the state of a IntHolderWrapper class, it can be changed indirectly.

```
IntHolder holder = ihw.getIntHolder(); // Got hold of instance variable
```

```
holder.setValue(207);    // Change the state by changing
                         // the instance variable's state
```

Listing 7-18: A test class to test immutability of the IntHolderWrapper class

```java
// BadImmutableTest.java
package com.jdojo.chapter7;

public class BadImmutableTest {
    public static void main(String[] args) {
        IntHolderWrapper ihw = new IntHolderWrapper(101);

        int value = ihw.getValue();
        System.out.println("#1 value = " + value);

        IntHolder holder = ihw.getIntHolder();
        holder.setValue(207);

        value = ihw.getValue();
        System.out.println("#2 value = " + value);
    }
}
```

```
Output:

#1 value = 101
#2 value = 207
```

So, how do we correct the problem with the `IntHolderWrapper` class? We want it to be an immutable class. The solution is easy. In the `getIntHolder()` method, make a copy of the `valueHolder` object and return the reference of the copy instead of the instance variable itself.. This way, if the client changes the value, it will be changed only in client's copy and not in the copy held by `IntHolderWrapper` object. Listing 7-19 has the corrected immutable version of the `IntHolderWrapper` class, which we call `IntHolderWrapper2`.

Listing 7-19: A modified version of the IntHolderWrapper class, which is immutable

```java
// IntHolderWrapper2.java
package com.jdojo.chapter7;

public class IntHolderWrapper2 {
    private final IntHolder valueHolder;

    public IntHolderWrapper2(int value) {
        this.valueHolder = new IntHolder(value);
    }

    public IntHolder getIntHolder() {
        // Make a copy of valueHolder
        int v = this.valueHolder.getValue();
        IntHolder copy = new IntHolder(v);

        // Return the copy instead of the original
        return copy;
    }
```

```
    public int getValue() {
        return this.valueHolder.getValue();
    }
}
```

At first, it may seem to be an easy task to create an immutable class. However, it may prove to be a little trickier than you think. We have covered some of the cases in this section. Here is another case where you need to be careful. Suppose you have designed an immutable class, which has a reference type instance variable. Suppose it accepts the initial value of its reference type instance variable in one of its constructors. If the instance variable's class is a mutable class, you must make a copy of the parameter passed to its constructor and store the copy in the instance variable. The client code that passes the object's reference in the constructor may change the state of this object through the same reference later. Listing 7-20 shows how to implement the second constructor for the `IntHolderWrapper3` class correctly. It has the incorrect version of the implementation for the second constructor commented.

Listing 7-20: Using a copy constructor to correctly implement an immutable class

```
// IntHolderWrapper3.java
package com.jdojo.chapter7;

public class IntHolderWrapper3 {
    private final IntHolder valueHolder;

    public IntHolderWrapper3(int value) {
        this.valueHolder = new IntHolder(value);
    }

    public IntHolderWrapper3(IntHolder holder) {
        // Must make a copy of holder parameter and
        // store it in the instance variable
        int v = holder.getValue();
        this.valueHolder = new IntHolder(v);

        /* Following implementation is incorrect.
           Client code will be able to change the
           state of the object using holder reference later
        */
        //this.valueHolder = holder; // do not use it
    }
    // Rest of the code goes here...
}
```

The Objects Class

Java 7 added a new utility class in the `java.util` package for working with objects. The new class is called `Objects`, which consists of many `static` methods. Most of the methods of the `Objects` class deal with `null` values gracefully. Table 7-2 lists methods of the `Objects` class with their descriptions. Listing 7-21 demonstrates how to use some of the methods of this class.

Table 7-2: List of methods of the java.util.Objects class

Method	Description
`public static <T> int compare(T a, T b, Comparator<? super T> c)`	It returns 0 if both arguments are identical. Otherwise, it returns the value of `c.compare(a, b)`. It returns 0, if both arguments are `null`.
`public static boolean deepEquals(Object a, Object b)`	It returns `true`, if both arguments are deeply equal. Otherwise, it returns `false`. It returns `true`, if both arguments are `null`.
`public static boolean equals(Object a, Object b)`	It returns `true`, if both arguments are equal. Otherwise, it returns `false`. It returns `true`, if both arguments are `null`.
`public static int hash(Object... values)`	It generates hash code for all the input values. It can be used to compute the hash code for an object, which is based on the multiple instance fields. If a single object reference is passed to this method, the returned hash code value is not equal to the hash code value returned from the object's `hashCode()` method. Suppose `obj` is an object reference. Then, `obj.hashCode()` is not equal to `Objects.(obj)`.
`public static int hashCode(Object o)`	It returns the hash code value of the object. If the argument is `null`, it returns 0.
`public static <T> T requireNonNull(T obj)`	It checks if the argument is not `null`. If the argument is `null`, it throws a `NullPointerException`. This method is designed for validating parameters of methods and constructors.
`public static <T> T requireNonNull(T obj, String message)`	This version of the method lets you specify the message for the `NullPointerException` that is thrown, when the argument is `null`.
`public static String toString(Object o)`	If the argument is `null`, it returns a "null" string. For a non-null argument, it returns the value returned by calling the `toString()` method on the argument.
`public static String toString(Object o, String nullDefault)`	If the first argument is `null`, it returns the specified second argument. For a non-null first argument, it returns the value returned by calling the `toString()` method on the first argument.

Listing 7-21: A test class to demonstrate the use of the methods of the Objects class

```
// ObjectsTest.java
package com.jdojo.chapter7;

import java.util.Objects;
```

```java
public class ObjectsTest {
    public static void main(String[] args) {
        // Compute hash code for two integers, a char and a string
        int hash = Objects.hash(10, 8900, '\u20b9', "Hello");
        System.out.println("Hash Code is " + hash);

        // Test for equality
        boolean isEqual = Objects.equals(null, null);
        System.out.println("null is equal to null: " + isEqual);

        isEqual = Objects.equals(null, "XYZ");
        System.out.println("null is equal to XYZ: " + isEqual);

        // toString() method test
        System.out.println("toString(null) is " +
                            Objects.toString(null));
        System.out.println("toString(null, \"XXX\") is " +
                            Objects.toString(null, "XXX"));

        // requireNonNull() method test
        try {
            printName("Doug Dyer");
            printName(null);
        }
        catch(NullPointerException e) {
            System.out.println(e.getMessage());
        }
    }

    public static void printName(String name) {
        // Test name for not null
        Objects.requireNonNull(name, "Name is required");
        System.out.println("Name is " + name);
    }
}
```

```
Output:

Hash Code is 79643668
null is equal to null: true
null is equal to XYZ: false
toString(null) is null
toString(null, "XXX") is XXX
Name is Doug Dyer
Name is required
```

Chapter 8. AutoBoxing

What is Autoboxing and Unboxing?

AutoBoxing and Unboxing is a new feature that was added to Java 5. It is implemented completely in the compiler. Before we define autoboxing/Unboxing, let us discuss one example, which is valid whether you use Java 5 or not. The example is trivial, but it serves the purpose of demonstrating the pain you had to go through before Java 5, when you were working with conversion between primitive types to their wrapper objects and vice-versa.

Suppose you have a method that accepts two `int` values, adds them, and returns an `int` value as the result. You might say, "What is the big deal about this method?" It should be as simple as shown below.

```
// Only method code is shown
public static int add(int a, int b) {
    return a + b;
}
```

The method can be used as:

```
int a = 200;
int b = 300;
int result = add(a, b); // result will get a value of 500
```

And, you are right that there is no big deal about this method at all. Let us add a little bit of a twist to the logic. Think about the same method working with `Integer` objects instead of `int` values. Here is the code for the same method.

```
public static Integer add(Integer a, Integer b) {
    int aValue = a.intValue();
    int bValue = b.intValue();
    int resultValue = aValue + bValue;
    Integer result = new Integer(resultValue);

    return result;
}
```

Did you notice the complexity that is involved when we changed the same method to use `Integer` objects? We had to perform three things to add two `int` values in the `Integer` objects.

- Unwrap the methods arguments, `a` and `b`, from `Integer` objects to `int` values using their `intValue()` method as:

  ```
  int aValue = a.intValue();
  int bValue = b.intValue();
  ```

- Perform the addition of two `int` values.

```
int resultValue = aValue + bValue;
```

- Wrap the result into a new Integer object and return the result.

```
Integer result = Integer.valueOf(resultValue);
return result;
```

Listing 8-1 has the complete code to demonstrate the use of the `add()` method, which performs addition on two `int` values using `Integer` objects. You can realize the amount of code you need to write just to add two `int` values. You may realize that wrapping an `int` value to an `Integer` object and unwrapping an `Integer` object to an `int` value is just a pain for Java developers. Java designers realized it (though too late) and they have automated this wrapping and unwrapping process for you.

Listing 8-1: Adding two int values using Integer objects

```java
// MathUtil.java
package com.jdojo.chapter8;

public class MathUtil {
    public static Integer add(Integer a, Integer b) {
        int aValue = a.intValue();
        int bValue = b.intValue();
        int resultValue = aValue + bValue;
        Integer result = Integer.valueOf(resultValue);
        return result;
    }

    public static void main(String[] args) {
        // We have 3 int values and need to use MathUtil.add() method
        // to add them and store result in kValue int variable
        int iValue = 200;
        int jValue = 300;
        int kValue; // will hold result as int

        // Box iValue and jValue into Integer objects
        // because add() method accepts Integer objects
        Integer i = Integer.valueOf(iValue);
        Integer j = Integer.valueOf(jValue);

        // Store returned value of add() method in an Integer object k
        Integer k = MathUtil.add(i, j);

        // Unbox Integer object's int value into kValue int variable
        kValue = k.intValue();

        // Display the result using int variables
        System.out.println(iValue + " + " + jValue + " = " + kValue);
    }
}
```

The automatic wrapping from a primitive data type (`byte`, `short`, `int`, `long`, `float`, `double`, `char` and `boolean`) to its corresponding wrapper object (`Byte`, `Integer`, `Long`, `Float`, `Double`,

`Character` and `Boolean`) is called *autoboxing*. The reverse, unwrapping from wrapper object to its corresponding primitive data type, is called *autounboxing*.

With autoboxing/unboxing in Java 5, the following code is valid.

```
Integer n = 200; // boxing
int a = n;       // unboxing
```

Java compiler will replace the above code with the following.

```
Integer n = Integer.valueOf(200);
int a = n.intValue();
```

The code in the `main()` method of the `MathUtil` class listed in Listing 8-1 can be rewritten as follows. The boxing and unboxing are done for us automatically.

```
int iValue = 200;
int jValue = 300;
int kValue = MathUtil.add(iValue, jValue);
System.out.println(iValue + " + " + jValue + " = " + kValue);
```

TIP
Autoboxing/Unboxing is performed when you compile the code. The JVM is completely unaware of the boxing and unboxing performed by the compiler.

Beware of null values

Autoboxing/unboxing does save you from writing additional lines of codes. It also makes your code look neater. However, it does come with some surprises too. One of the surprises is a getting `NullPointerException` where you would not expect it to happen. Primitive types cannot have a `null` value assigned to them, whereas reference types can have a `null` value. The boxing and unboxing happens between primitive types and reference types. Look at the following lines of code.

```
Integer n = null; // n can be assigned a null value
int a = n; // will throw NullPointerException at run time
```

In the above snippet of code, suppose you do not control the assignment of `null` to n. You might get a `null Integer` object as a result of a method call, e.g., `int a = getSomeValue()`, where `getSomeValue()` returns an `Integer` object. A `NullPointerException` in such places may be a surprise for you. However, it will happen, because `int a = n` is converted to `int a = n.intValue()` and n is `null` in this case. This surprise is the part of advantage you get from autoboxing/unboxing and you need to just be aware of it.

Overloaded Methods and Autoboxing/Unboxing

You have a few surprises when you call an overloaded method and want to rely on autoboxing/unboxing feature. Suppose you have two methods in a class as:

```
public void test(Integer iObject) {
    System.out.println("Integer=" + iObject);
}

public void test(int iValue) {
    System.out.println("int=" + iValue);
}
```

Suppose you make a call to the `test()` method as:

```
test(101);
test(new Integer(101));
```

Which of the following will be the output?

```
int=101
Integer=101
```

or

```
Integer=101
int=101
```

The rule for a method invocation that uses autoboxing/unboxing follows a two steps process.

- If the actual argument being passed is a primitive type (as in `test(10)`):
    - Try to find a method with the primitive type argument. If there is no exact match, try widening the primitive type to find a match.
    - If the previous step fails, box the primitive type and try to find a match.
- If the actual argument being passed is a reference type (as in `test(new Integer(101))`:
    - Try to find a method with the reference type argument. If there is match, call that method. In this case, a match does not have to be exact. It should follow the subtype and super type assignment rule.
    - If the previous step fails, unbox the reference type to the corresponding primitive type and try to find an exact match, or widen the primitive type and find a match.

If you apply the above rules to our test cases, it will print as follows.

```
int=101
Integer=101
```

Suppose we have two methods as follows.

```
public void test(Integer iObject) {
    System.out.println("Integer=" + iObject);
}

public void test(long iValue) {
    System.out.println("long=" + iValue);
}
```

What will be printed if we use the following code?

```
test(101);
test(new Integer(101));
```

It will print:

```
long=101
Integer=101
```

The first call of `test(101)` will try to find an exact match for an `int` argument. It does not find a method `test(int)`, and so it widens the `int` data type, finds a match `test(long)`, and calls this method.

Suppose we have two methods as follows.

```
public void test(Long lObject) {
   System.out.println("Long=" + lObject);
}

public void test(long lValue) {
   System.out.println("long=" + lValue);
}
```

What will be printed if we execute the following code?

```
test(101);
test(new Integer(101));
```

It will print:

```
long=101
long=101
```

Are you surprised by looking at the output? Apply the rules that we have listed and you will find that the above output followed those rules. Call to `test(101)` is clear, because it widens 101 from `int` type to `long` and it executes `test(long)` method. To call `test(new Integer(101))`, it looks for a method `test(Integer)` and it does not find one. Note that a reference type is never widened. That is, an `Integer` type is never widened to `Long` type. Therefore, it unboxes `Integer` to `int` type and looks for `test(int)` method, which it does not find. Now, it widens `int` type and it finds `test(long)` and executes it.

We will have one more surprise. Consider the following two methods.

```
public void test(Long lObject) {
    System.out.println("Long=" + lObject);
}

public void test(Object obj) {
    System.out.println("Object=" + obj);
}
```

What will be printed when we execute the following code?

```
test(101);
test(new Integer(101));
```

This time, you will get the following output.

```
Object=101
Object=101
```

Does it make sense? Not really. Here is the explanation. When it calls `test(101)`, it has to box `int` to an `Integer`, because there is no match for `test(int)`, even after widening the `int` value. So, `test(101)` becomes `test(Integer.valueOf(101))`. Now, it does not find any `test(Integer)` either. Note that `Integer` is a reference type and it inherits the `Number` class, which in turn inherits the `Object` class. Therefore, an `Integer` is always an `Object`, and Java allows you to assign an object of subtype (`Integer`) to a variable of super type (`Object`). This is the reason why the `test(Object)` is called in this case. The second call, `test(new Integer(101))`, works the same way. It tries for `test(Integer)` method. When it does not find it, the next match for it is `test(Object)` based on the subtype and super type assignment rule for reference types.

Comparison Operators and AutoBoxing/Unboxing

We will discuss comparison operations: ==, >, >=, <, <=. Only == (logical equality operator) can be used with both reference type and primitive types. Other operators must be used only with primitive types.

Let us discuss the easy ones first (>, >=, < and <=). If a numeric wrapper object is used with these comparison operators, it must be unboxed and the corresponding primitive type used in comparison. Let us consider the following snippet of code.

```
Integer a = 100;
Integer b = 100;
System.out.println("a : " + a);
System.out.println("b : " + b);
System.out.println("a > b: " + (a > b));
System.out.println("a >= b: " + (a >= b));
System.out.println("a < b: " + (a < b));
System.out.println("a <= b: " + (a <= b));
```

```
Output:

a : 100
b : 100
a > b: false
a >= b: true
a < b: false
a <= b: true
```

There is no surprise in the above output. If you mix the two types, reference and primitive, with these comparison operators, you still get the same result. First, the reference type is unboxed and a comparison with the two primitive types takes place. For example,

```
if (101 > new Integer(100)) {
    // Do something
}
```

is converted to

```
if(101 <= (new Integer(100)).intValue()) {
    // Do something
}
```

Now, let us discuss `==` operator and autoboxing rules. If both operands are primitive types, they are compared as primitive types using a value comparison. If both operands are reference types, their references are compared. In these two cases, no autoboxing/unboxing takes place. When one operand is a reference type and another is a primitive type, the reference type is unboxed to a primitive type and a value comparison takes place. Let us have examples of each type.

Consider the following snippet of code. It is an example of using both primitive type operands for the `==` operator.

```
int a = 100;
int b = 100;
int c = 505;
System.out.println(a == b); // will print true
System.out.println(a == c); // will print false
```

Consider the following snippet of code where no autoboxing/unboxing takes place. Here, `aa ==` `bb` and `aa == cc` compare the references of `aa`, `bb` and `cc` and not their values. Every object created with the `new` operator has a unique reference.

```
Integer aa = new Integer(100);
Integer bb = new Integer(100);
Integer cc = new Integer(505);
System.out.println(aa == bb); // will print false
System.out.println(aa == cc); // will print false
```

Let us have a surprise and consider the following snippet of code. This time, we are relying on autoboxing.

```
Integer aaa = 100; // Boxing - Integer.valueOf(100)
Integer bbb = 100; // Boxing - Integer.valueOf(100)
Integer ccc = 505; // Boxing - Integer.valueOf(505)
Integer ddd = 505; // Boxing - Integer.valueOf(505)
System.out.println(aaa == bbb); // will print true
System.out.println(aaa == ccc); // will print false
System.out.println(ccc == ddd); // will print false
```

We used `aaa`, `bbb`, `ccc`, and `ddd` as reference types. How `aaa == bbb` is `true`, whereas `ccc == ddd` is `false`? All right. This time, there is no surprise coming from the autoboxing feature. Rather, it is coming from the `Integer.valueOf()` method. For all values between −128 and 127, the `Integer` class caches `Integer` objects references. The cache is used when you call its `valueOf()` method. For example, if you call `Integer.valueOf(100)` twice, you get the reference of the same `Integer` object from the cache that represents the `int` value of 100. However, if you call `Integer.valueOf(n)`, where n is outside the range −128 to 127, a new object is created for every call. This is the reason, `aaa` and `bbb` have the same reference from the cache, whereas `ccc` and `ddd` have different references. The wrapper class Byte, Short, Character and Long also cache object reference whose −128 to 127 primitive value range.

Collections and Autoboxing/Unboxing

Autoboxing/unboxing helps us working with collections. Collections work only with reference types. You cannot use primitive types in collections. If you want to store primitive types in a collection, you must wrap the primitive value before storing it, and unwrap it after retrieving it. Suppose you have a `List` and you want to store integers in it. This is how you would do it.

```
List list = new ArrayList();
list.add(new Integer(101));
Integer a = (Integer)list.get(0);
int aValue = a.intValue();
```

We are back to square one. The `add()` and `get()` methods of `List` interface work with `Object` type, and we had to resort to wrapping and unwrapping the primitive types again. The autoboxing/unboxing may help us in wrapping the primitive type to a reference type, and the above code may be rewritten as:

```
List list = new ArrayList();
list.add(101);    // autoboxing will work here
Integer a = (Integer)list.get(0);
int aValue = a.intValue();
//int aValue = list.get(0); // autounboxing won't compile
```

Since the return type of the `get()` method is the `Object` type, in our case, the last statement in the above snippet of code would not work. Note that autounboxing happens from a primitive wrapper type (e.g. `Integer`) to its corresponding primitive type (e.g. `int`). If you try to assign an `Object` reference type to an `int` primitive type, the autounboxing does not happen. In fact, your code would not even compile, because `Object` to `int` conversion is not allowed.

```
List<Integer> list = new ArrayList<Integer>();
list.add(101);              // autoboxing will work
int aValue = list.get(0); // autounboxing will work too
```

Specifying the `Integer` type in angle brackets (`<Integer>`), while creating the `List` object, tells the compiler that the `List` will hold object of only `Integer` type. This gives the compiler freedom to wrap and unwrap our primitive `int` values while we work with the `List` object. Please refer to the chapter on *Generics* for more details.

Chapter 9. Exception Handling

What is an Exception?

An exception is a condition that may arise during execution of a Java program when a normal path of execution is not defined. For example, a Java program may encounter a numeric expression that attempts to divide an integer by zero. Such a condition may occur during the execution of the following snippet of code.

```
int x = 10, y = 0, z;
z = x/y;
```

The statement, z = x/y, attempts to divide x by y. Since the value of y is zero, the result of x/y is not defined in Java. Note that dividing a floating--point number by zero, for example 9.5/0.0, is infinity in Java. However, dividing an integer by zero, for example, 9/0 is not defined. In generic terms, the abnormal condition, such as dividing an integer by zero, in Java is described as:

   An error occurs when a Java program attempts to divide an integer by zero.

However, the Java programming language uses a different phrase to describe this error condition. In Java, it is said.

   An exception is thrown when a Java program attempts to divide an integer by zero.

Practically, both statements mean the same thing. It means that an abnormal condition in a program has occurred. Let us move on to the next step after the abnormal condition has occurred. We need to handle such an abnormal condition in our program. One of the ways to handle such an abnormal condition is to check for all possibilities that may lead to an abnormal condition before performing the action. We may rewrite our code as follows.

```
int x = 10, y = 0, z;

if (y == 0) {
    // Report the abnormal/error condition here
}
else {
    // Perform division here
    z = x/y;
}
```

You may observe that the above snippet of code does two things – handles error condition and performs the intended action. It has mixed the code for performing error handling and performing the action. One line of code (z = x/y) has become at least five lines of code. This is a simple example, and you may not fully realize the real problem when the error handling code is mixed with the actual code that performs the actions. To make the problem with the above approach to handle errors clear, let us consider another example. Suppose we want to write Java code that will update an employee's salary. An employee's records are stored in a database. The pseudo code to update an employee's salary might look as follows.

```
Connect to database
Fetch the employee record
Update the employee salary
Commit the changes
```

The actual code would perform the above-mentioned four actions to update the salary of an employee in the database. Any of the four actions may result in error. For example, you may not be able to connect to the database because it is down; you may not be able to commit the changes, because of some problems. You need to perform error checking after an action is performed and before a subsequent action is started. The pseudo code with error checking may look as follows.

```
Connect to database
if (connected to database successfully) {
    Fetch the employee record
    if (employee record fetched) {
        Update the employee salary
        if (update is successful) {
            Commit the changes
            if (commit was successful ) {
            // Employee salary was saved successfully
            }
            else {
                // Error. Save failed
            }
        }
        else {
            // Error. Salary could not be updated
        }
    }
    else {
        // Error. Employee record does not exist
    }
}
else {
    // Error. Could not connect to database
}
```

You may observe that when we added error handling to our four lines of pseudo code, the code bloated to over twenty lines. The worse thing about the above code is that the code that performs the action has been cluttered with error handling code. It has also introduced many nested `if-else` statements resulting in spaghetti code.

In the last two examples, we saw that the way of handling errors that uses `if-else` statements is not elegant and maintainable. Java has a better way to handle errors by separating the code that performs actions from the code that handles errors. In Java, we use the phrase "exception" instead of "error" to indicate an abnormal condition in a program. The phrase "exception handling" is used instead of the phrase "error handling". In general, we say that an error occurs and you handle it. In Java, we say that an exception is thrown and you catch it. This is the reason why, sometimes, an *exception handling* is also called *catching an exception*. The code that handles the exception is known as an exception handler. We could rewrite the above pseudo code using Java syntax (not full-fledged Java code though) as follows.

```
try {
    Connect to database
    Fetch employee record
    Update employee salary
```

```
        Commit the changes
}
catch(DbConnectionException e1){
        // Handle Db Connection exception here
}
catch(EmpNotFoundException e2){
        // Handle employee not found exception here
}
catch(UpdateFailedException e3){
        // Handle update failed exception here
}
catch(CommitFailedException e4){
        // Handle commit failed exception here
}
```

You do not need to understand the above pseudo code fully. We will discuss all details later in this chapter. You need to observe the structure of the code, which allows for separation of the code that performs the actions from the code that handles the exceptions. The code that performs actions is placed inside a `try` block and the code that handles the exception is placed inside a `catch` block. You will observe that this code is much better in terms of elegance and maintainability compared to the previous attempt in which we had to write many `if-else` statements to achieve the same.

TIP
In Java, an exception is thrown and it is caught. Catching an exception is the same as handling the exception. The code that performs the action may throw an exception and the code that handles the exception catches the thrown exception. This style of exception handling allows you to separate the code that performs actions from the code that handles the exceptions that may arise while performing the actions.

Exception is an Object

The exception handling mechanism in Java lets you separate action-performing code from exception handling code. Now the obvious question would be – "How does the exception handling part of the code know about the exceptional condition, e.g., the exception type, the action that caused the exception, etc.?" There must be a link between the point where the exception occurs and the point where it is handled. When an exception occurs, Java creates an object with all pieces of information about the exception (e.g. type of exception, line number of code that caused the exception, etc.) stored in that object and passes it to the appropriate exception handling code. The word "exception" is used to mean one of two things – the exceptional condition, or the Java object to represent the exceptional condition. The meaning of the "exception" word will be clear from the context in which it is used.

When we talk about throwing an exception, we are talking about three things.

- Occurrence of an exceptional condition
- Creation of a Java object to represent the exceptional condition
- Throwing (or passing) the exception object to the exception handler

The throwing of an exception is the same as passing an object reference to a method. Here, you may imagine the exception handler as a method that accepts a reference of an exception object.

The exception handler catches the exception object and takes appropriate action. You can think of catching an exception by the exception handler as a method call, where the exception object's reference is the actual parameter to the method. Java also lets you create your own object that represents an exception and then throw it.

TIP

An exception handler is similar to a method, which accepts the reference of an exception object as its parameter. The body of an exception handler may use its parameter to know the details of the exceptional condition that occurred. Throwing an exception is similar to calling a method (exception handler) using the exception object as the actual parameter.

Using a try-catch Block

Before we discuss the `try-catch` block, let us write a Java program that attempts to divide an integer by zero as shown in Listing 9-1.

Listing 9-1: A Java program that attempts to divide an integer by zero

```java
// DivideByZero.java
package com.jdojo.chapter9;

public class DivideByZero {
    public static void main(String[] args) {
        int x = 10, y = 0, z;
        z = x/y;
        System.out.println("z = " + z);
    }
}
```

```
Output:

Exception in thread "main" java.lang.ArithmeticException: / by zero
    at com.jdojo.chapter9.DivideByZero.main(DivideByZero.java:7)
```

The output of Listing 9-1 is not what we were expecting. It indicates an exception has occurred when we ran the `DivideByZero` class. The output contains four pieces of information.

- It includes the name of the thread in which the exception occurred. The name of the thread is "main". We will learn about thread and the name of a thread name in detail in the chapter on *Threads*.
- It includes the type of the exception that has occurred. The type of an exception is indicated by the name of the class. In this case, java.lang.ArithmeticException is the name of the class of the exception. The Java runtime creates an object of this class and passes its reference to the exception handler.
- It includes a message that describes the exceptional condition in the code that caused the error. In this case, the message is "/ by zero" (read as "divide by zero").
- It includes the location at which the exception occurred. If you read the second line in the output, you would find that it states that the exception has occurred inside the `main()` method of the `com.jdojo.chapter9.DivideByZero` class. The source code is contained in the `DivideByZero.java` file. The line number in the source code that caused the exception is 7.

Chapter 9. Exception Handling

You may notice that in just two lines of output Java runtime has printed enough pieces of information to help you track down the error in your code.

When the statement (z = x/y) in line number 7 is executed, Java runtime detects the exceptional condition, which is an attempt to divide an integer by zero. It creates a new object of class `java.lang.ArithmeticException` with all relevant pieces of information about the exception and then throws (or passes) this object to an exception handler. Who caught (or handled) the exception in our case? We did not specify any exception handler in our code. In fact, we do not even know how to specify an exception handler at this point. Since we did not specify an exception handler in this case, Java runtime handled the exception for us. Does Java runtime handle all exceptions that are thrown in a Java program? The answer is yes. Java runtime handles all exceptions in a Java program. However, Java runtime handles an exception only when you have not handled it yourself. First, it gives you a chance to handle any exceptions that occur in your program. If you do not handle the exception, the Java runtime handles it for you.

If an exception occurs and the Java runtime does not find a programmer defined exception handler to handle it, such an exception is called an *uncaught exception*. All uncaught exceptions are handled by the Java runtime. Since an uncaught exception is always handled by Java runtime, why even worry about providing any exception handler in our program? We do have a point here. Why do we need to worry about doing something, which would be done by the Java runtime for us? If you are too lazy to clean up your own mess (handling your own error condition), there is bad news for you. You should not expect too much from the Java runtime. Sometimes, you may not like the way Java runtime handles all uncaught exceptions. It catches the uncaught exception, prints the error stack on standard error, and halts your Java application. It means, if you let the Java runtime handle all your exceptions, your program stops executing at the point where the exception occurs. However, this is not what you always want to do. Sometimes, after you handle the exception, you may want to proceed with executing the rest of your program rather than halting the program. When we ran the `DivideByZero` class, the expression x/y in the statement z =x/y resulted in an exception. Java did not finish executing the statement $z=x/y$. Sometimes, this situation is phrased as – "The statement $z=x/y$ finished abnormally." Java runtime handled the exception, but it stopped executing the whole program. This is the reason you do not see the output of the following statement in your program.

```
System.out.println("z = " + z);
```

Now, you know that letting the Java runtime handle your exception is not always a good idea. If you want to handle exceptions yourself, you need to place your code in a `try` block. A `try` block looks as:

```
try {
    // Code for the try block goes here
}
```

A `try` block starts with the keyword `try`, which is followed by an opening brace and a closing brace. The code for the `try` block is placed inside the opening and the closing braces.

A `try` block cannot be used by itself. It must be followed by one or more `catch` blocks, or one `finally` block, or a combination of both. To handle an exception that might be thrown by the code inside a `try` block, we need to use a `catch` block. One catch block is used to handle only one type of exception. The syntax for a `catch` block is similar to the syntax for a method. The syntax for a `catch` block is:

```
catch (ExceptionClassName parameterName) {
    // Exception handling code goes here
```

```
}
```

Note that a `catch` block declaration looks like a method declaration. It starts with the keyword `catch`, which is followed by a pair of parentheses. Within the parentheses, you declare a parameter, as you do in a method. The parameter type is the name of the exception class that it is supposed to catch. The `parameterName` is a user given name. Parentheses are followed by an opening brace and a closing brace. The exception handling code is placed within the opening and closing braces. When an exception is thrown the reference of the exception object is copied to the `parameterName`. You can use the `parameterName` to get information from the exception object. It is like a formal parameter of a method. Unlike a method, you can have one, and only one, parameter to a `catch` block. To handle multiple exceptions, you needed a separate `catch` block for each exception before Java 7. Java 7 lets you catch multiple exceptions in one `catch` block.

You can associate one or more `catch` blocks to a `try` block. The general syntax for a `try-catch` block is as follows. The following snippet of code shows a `try` block, which has three `catch` blocks associated with it. You can associate as many `catch` blocks to a `try` block as you want.

```java
try {
    // Your code that may throw an exception goes here
}
catch (ExceptionClass1 e1){
    // Handle exception of ExceptionClass1 type
}
catch (ExceptionClass2 e2){
    // Handle exception of ExceptionClass2 type
}
catch (ExceptionClass3 e3){
    // Handle exception of ExceptionClass3 type
}
```

Let us use a `try-catch` block to handle the possible divide by zero exception in our code. Listing 9-2 has code that uses a `try-catch` block to handle `ArithmeticException`.

Listing 9-2: A program, which attempts to divide an integer by zero inside a try block and handles the exception in a catch block

```java
// DivideByZeroWithTryCatch.java
package com.jdojo.chapter9;

public class DivideByZeroWithTryCatch {
    public static void main(String[] args) {
        int x = 10, y = 0, z;
        try {
            z = x / y;
            System.out.println("z = " + z);
        }
        catch(ArithmeticException e) {
            // Get the description of the exception
            String msg = e.getMessage();

            // Print a custom error message
            System.out.println("An error has occurred. Error is: "
                                + msg);
        }
```

```
            System.out.println("At the end of the program.");
    }
}
```

```
Output:

An exception has occurred. Error is: / by zero
At the end of the program.
```

The output of Listing 9-2 is nicer, compared to the output of Listing 9-1. It tells us exactly what happened when the program was executed. You will also notice that the program did not terminate when the exception occurred. This time, we handled the exception, and this is the reason the program continued. The program also printed "At the end of the program" message.

Figure 9-1: Transfer of control when an exception occurs in a try block

```
        Some statements go here...
        try {
            try-statement-1;
            try-statement-2;
            try-statement-3;
        }
        catch(Exception1 e1) {
            catch-statement-11;
            catch-statement-12;
        }
        catch(Exception2 e2) {
            catch-statement-21;
            catch-statement-22;
        }
        catch(Exception3 e3) {
            catch-statement-31;
            catch-statement-32;
        }
        statement-1;
        more statements go here...
```

You need to understand very precisely the flow of control when an exception is thrown in a `try` block. First, Java runtime creates an object of the appropriate class to represent the exception that has occurred. The first catch block that follows the `try` block is checked. If the exception object can be assigned to the exception parameter declared for that `catch` block, the parameter of the `catch` block is assigned the reference of the exception object, and the control is transferred to the body of the catch block. When the `catch` block finishes executing its body, the control is transferred to the point following the `try-catch` block. It is very important to note that after executing the `catch` block the control is not transferred back to the `try` block. The control is transferred to the code that follows the `try-catch` block. If a `try` block has many `catch` blocks associated with it, a maximum of one `catch` block is executed. Figure 9-1 shows the transfer of control in a typical Java program when an exception occurs in a `try` block. It assumes that when `try-statement-2` is executed, it throws an exception of type `Exception2`. When the exception is thrown, the control is transferred to the second `catch` block, and `catch-statement-21` and `catch-statement-22` are executed. After `catch-statement-22` is executed, control is transferred outside the `try-catch` block, and `statement-1` starts executing. It is very important to understand that `try-statement-3` is never executed when `try-statement-2` throws an exception. Among three `catch` blocks, a maximum of one will be executed when a statement inside the `try` block throws an exception.

Exception Classes in Java

The Java class library contains many exception classes. Figure 9-2 shows a few exception classes. Note that the `Object` class does not belong to the family of exception classes. It is shown here as an ancestor of the `Throwable` class in its inheritance hierarchy. The exception class hierarchy starts at the `java.lang.Throwable` class. Recall that the `Object` class is the superclass for all classes in Java. It is also the superclass of the `Throwable` class. This is the reason why Figure 9-2 shows the `Object` class at the top of the class hierarchy. It is to be emphasized that the Java exception class family starts at the `Throwable` class and not at the `Object` class.

Figure 9-2: A few classes in the exception class hierarchy

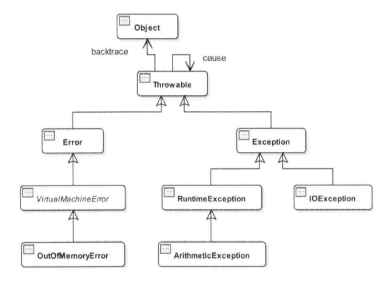

When an exception is thrown, it must be an object of the `Throwable` class, or any of its subclasses. The parameter of the `catch` block must be of type `Throwable`, or one of its subclasses, e.g., `Exception`, `ArithmeticException`, `IOException`, etc. The following `catch` blocks are not valid `catch` blocks, because their parameters are not a `Throwable`, or a subclass of `Throwable`.

```
// Compiler error
catch(Object e1) {
    // Object class is not an exception class
}

// Compiler error
catch(String e1) {
    // String class is not an exception class
}
```

The following `catch` blocks are valid, because they specify exception types as parameter, which are the `Throwable` class or its subclass.

```
catch(Throwable t) {
    // Throwable class is a valid exception class
}

catch(Exception e) {
    // Exception class is a valid exception class because it is
    // a subclass of Throwable class
}

catch(IOException t) {
    // IOException class is a valid exception class because it is
    // a subclass of Throwable class
}

catch(ArithmeticException t) {
    // ArithmeticException class is a valid exception class because
    // it is a subclass of Throwable class
}
```

The `Throwable` class, or a class below it in the class hierarchy is a valid exception class and it can be specified as the parameter type for a `catch` block. Note that you can also create your own exception class by inheriting your class from one of the exception classes. Figure 9-2 shows only a few of the hundreds of exception classes that are available in Java class library. We will discuss in detail how to inherit a class from another class in the chapter on *Inheritance*. We will present an example of a user-defined exception class later in this chapter.

Arranging Multiple catch Blocks

We have already discussed in the chapter on *The Object Class* that a reference variable of `Object` class can refer to any type of object in Java. Assuming `AnyClass` is a class, the following is a valid statement.

```
Object obj = new AnyClass();
```

The rule behind the above assignment is that the reference of an object of a class can be assigned to a reference variable of its own type or its superclass. Since the `Object` class is the superclass (direct or indirect) of all classes in Java, it is valid to assign a reference of any object to a reference variable of the `Object` class. This assignment rule is not limited to just a reference variable of the `Object` class. It is a rule in Java that can apply to any object. It is stated as:

A reference variable of class T can refer to an object of class S if S is the same as T or S is a subclass of T. The following statements are always valid in Java assuming S is a subclass of T.

```
T t1 = new T();
T t2 = new S();
```

Now, you can see that the rule about any object's reference being stored in a reference variable of `Object` type is implied in the above rule. We will elaborate on this rule in the chapter on *Inheritance*.

Let us apply this assignment rule to the exception class hierarchy. Since the `Throwable` class is the superclass (direct or indirect) of all exception classes, a reference variable of `Throwable` class can refer to an object of any exception class. All of the following statements are valid in Java.

```
Throwable e1 = new Exception();
Throwable e2 = new IOException();
Throwable e3 = new RuntimeException();
Throwable e4 = new ArithmeticException();
```

With this rule of assignment in mind, let us consider the following try-catch block.

```
try {
    statement1;
    statement2; // Exception of class MyException is thrown here
    statement3;
}
catch (Exception1 e1) {
    // Handle Exception1
}
catch (Exception2 e2) {
    // Handle Exception2
}
```

When the above snippet of code is executed, the `statement2` in the `try` block throws an exception of the `MyException` type. Suppose the Java runtime creates an object of `MyException` as:

```
new MyException();
```

Now, the Java runtime selects the appropriate `catch` block, which can catch the exception object. It starts looking for the appropriate `catch` clock sequentially starting from the first catch block that is associated with the `try` block. The process to check if a `catch` block can handle an exception is very simple. Take the parameter type and parameter name of the catch block and place them to the left of an assignment operator and place the exception object that is thrown to the right. If the statement that is thus formed is a valid Java statement, that `catch` block will handle the exception. Otherwise, Java runtime will repeat this check with the next `catch` block. To check if the first `catch` block can handle the `MyException` in the above snippet of code, Java will form the following statement.

```
// Catch parameter declaration = thrown exception object reference
Exception1 e1 = new MyException();
```

The above statement is a valid Java statement only if the `MyException` class is a subclass of the `Exception1` class, or `MyException` and `Exception1` are the same class. If the above statement is valid, Java runtime will assign the reference of `MyException` object to `e1`, and then execute the code inside the first `catch` block. If the above statement is not a valid statement, Java runtime will apply the same check for the second `catch` block by using the following statement.

```
// Catch parameter declaration = thrown exception object reference
Exception2 e2 = new MyException();
```

Chapter 9. Exception Handling

The above statement is a valid only if the `MyException` class is a subclass of the `Exception2` class, or `MyException` and `Exception2` classes are the same class. If the above statement is a valid statement, Java runtime will assign the reference of the `MyException` object to `e2` and execute the code inside the second `catch` block. If the above statement is not valid, Java runtime did not find a matching `catch` block for the exception that was thrown in the `try` block. In this case, a different execution path is chosen, which we will discuss shortly.

Typically, you add a `catch` block to a `try` block for every type of exception that can be thrown from the `try` block. Suppose there is a `try` block and it can throw three kinds of exceptions, which are represented by three classes – `Exception1`, `Exception2`, and `Exception3`. Suppose `Exception1` is the superclass of `Exception2`, and `Exception 2` is the superclass of `Exception3`. The class hierarchy for the three exception classes is shown in Figure 9-3. Consider the following `try-catch` block.

```
try {
    // Exception1, Exception2 or Exception 3 could be thrown here
}
catch (Exception1 e1) {
    // Handle Exception1
}
catch (Exception2 e2) {
    // Handle Exception2
}
catch (Exception3 e3) {
    // Handle Exception3
}
```

Figure 9-3: The class hierarchy for Exception1, Exception2, and Exception3 exception classes

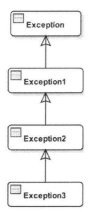

If you apply the steps to find an appropriate `catch` block, you would find that the above snippet of code would always execute the first `catch` block, irrespective of the type of exception thrown (`Exception1`, `Exception2`, or `Exception3`) from the `try` block. This is so, because `Exception1` is the direct/indirect superclass of `Exception2` and `Exception3`. The above snippet of code shows a logical mistake on part of the programmer. The Java compiler is designed to handle this kind of logical mistake that you might make. You must follow the following rule for arranging multiple `catch` blocks for a `try` block.

Multiple catch blocks for a try block must be arranged from the most specific exception type to the most generic exception type. Otherwise, a compile-time error occurs. The first catch block should handle the most specific exception type and the last catch block should handle the most generic exception type.

The following snippet of code uses a valid sequence of multiple `catch` blocks. The `ArithmeticException` class is a subclass of the `RuntimeException` class. If both of these exceptions are handled in `catch` blocks for the same `try` block, the most specific type, which is `ArithmeticException`, must appear before the most generic type, which is `RuntimeException`.

```
try {
    // Do something, which might throw Exception
}
catch(ArithmeticException e1) {
    // Handle ArithmeticException first
}
catch(RuntimeException e2) {
    // Handle RuntimeException after ArithmeticException
}
```

Checked and Unchecked Exceptions

Before we start discussing checked and unchecked exceptions, let us look at a Java program that reads a character from the standard input. We have been using the `System.out.println()` method to print messages on the standard output, which is typically the console. You can use the `System.in.read()` method to read a byte from standard input, which is typically the keyboard. It returns the value of the byte as an `int` between 0 and 255. It returns −1 if the end of input is reached. The following code shows the code that reads a byte from the standard input and returns it as a character. It assumes that the language you are using has all alphabets whose Unicode values are between 0 and 255. The `readChar()` method has the main code. To read a character from the standard input, you will need to use the `ReadInput.readChar()` method.

```
// ReadInput.java
package com.jdojo.chapter9;

public class ReadInput {
    public static char readChar() {
        char c = '\u0000';
        int input = System.in.read();
        if (input != -1) {
            c = (char)input;
        }
        return c;
    }
}
```

Let us try to compile the `ReadInput` class. Oops! The compiler could not compile `ReadInput` class. It generated the following error message.

```
"ReadInput.java": unreported exception java.io.IOException; must be
caught or declared to be thrown at line 7, column 31
```

The compiler error is pointing to the line number 7 in the source code, which is as follows.

```
int input = System.in.read();
```

There is something missing in this statement. The compiler error also tells us that there is an uncaught exception, which must be caught or declared. We do understand about catching an exception using a `try-catch` block. However, we do not understand about declaring an exception. We will learn about declaring an exception in the next section. In fact, the `System.in.read()` method call may throw `java.io.IOException`. The compiler error is telling us to place this method call in a `try-catch` block so that we can handle the exception. If we do not catch this exception, we need to include in the declaration of the `readChar()` method that it might throw the `java.io.IOException`. Did we not learn in the previous sections that Java runtime handles all uncaught exceptions? Yes. We did. Why can the Java runtime not handle `java.io.IOException` in this case? Here comes the concept of checked and unchecked exceptions. We need to learn about them to understand this compiler error.

Three kinds of exceptional conditions may occur in a Java program. They are:

- In this category, we have exceptions that have a higher potential to occur and you can handle the exception. For example, when you read from a file, it is more likely that an I/O error may occur. It is better to handle these kinds of exceptions in your program. Classes in the exception class hierarchy (refer to Figure 9-2), which are subclasses of the `Exception` class, including the `Exception` class itself, and excluding `RuntimeException` and all its subclasses, fall into this category. If a method or constructor may throw an exception of this category, you must take an appropriate action to handle that exception in your code, which calls the method or the constructor. What is that "appropriate action" that you need to take to handle these kinds of exceptions? You may take one of the following two actions.

  You can place the code that can throw the exception in a `try-catch` block. One of the `catch` blocks must be capable of handling the type of exception that may be thrown.

  You can specify in the method/constructor declaration that it may throw an exception. You accomplish this by using a `throws` clause in the method/constructor declaration.

- In this category, we have exceptions that may occur during the course of the execution of a Java program, and there is little you can do to handle the exception. For example, you would receive the `java.lang.OutOfMemeoryError` exception when Java runtime is out of memory. You cannot do anything to recover from an out of memory error. It is better for you to let the application crash and then look at the ways to manage the memory more efficiently in your program. Classes in the exception class hierarchy (refer to Figure 9-2), which are subclasses of the `Error` class, and the `Error` class itself, fall into this category of exception. If a piece of code may throw an exception of this category, the Java compiler does not insist on taking an action on your part. If an exception of this kind is thrown at runtime, The Java runtime will handle it for you by displaying a detailed error message, and halting the application.

- In this category, we have exceptions that may occur at runtime, and you may be able to recover from the exceptional condition if you handle them yourself. There are numerous exceptions in this category. However, if you feel that it is more likely that an exception of this kind may be thrown, you should handle it in your code. If you attempt to handle them by using `try-catch` blocks, your code tends to clutter. Classes in the exception class hierarchy (refer to Figure 9-2), which are subclasses of the `RuntimeException` class, and the `RuntimeException` class itself, fall into this category of exceptions. If a piece of code may throw an exception of this category, the Java compiler does not insist on any action on your part. If an exception of this kind is thrown at runtime, The Java runtime will handle it for you by displaying a detailed error message and halting the program.

Exceptions in the first category are known as checked exceptions. The `Throwable` class also falls under checked exceptions. The `Throwable` class, the `Exception` class and subclasses of the `Exception` class, excluding the `RuntimeException` class and its subclasses, are called checked exceptions. They are called checked exceptions because the Java compiler checks that they are handled in the code.

All exceptions that are not checked exceptions are called unchecked exceptions. The `Error` class, all subclasses of the `Error` class, the `RuntimeException` class, and all its subclasses, are unchecked exceptions. They are called unchecked exceptions because the Java compiler does not check if they are handled in the code. However, you are always free to handle the unchecked exceptions. The program structure for handling a checked or an unchecked exception is the same. The difference between them is in the way the compiler forces (or does not force) you to handle them in the code.

Let us fix the compiler error for our `ReadInput` class. Now we know that `java.io.IOException` is a checked exception and the compiler will force us to handle it. We will handle it by using a `try-catch` block. Listing 9-3 shows the code for the `ReadInput` class. This time we have handled the `IOException` in its `readChar()` method and the code will compile fine.

Listing 9-3: A ReadInput class whose readChar() method reads one character from the standard input

```
// ReadInput.java
package com.jdojo.chapter9;

import java.io.IOException;

public class ReadInput {
    public static char readChar() {
        char c = '\u0000';
        int input = 0;
        try {
            input = System.in.read();
            if (input != -1) {
                c = (char)input;
            }
        }
        catch (IOException e) {
            System.out.print("IOException occurred while" +
                            " reading input.");
        }
        return c;
    }
}
```

How do we use the `ReadInput` class? You can use it the same way you use other classes in Java. You need to call the `ReadInput.readChar()` `static` method if you want to capture the first character entered by the user. Listing 9-4 has code that shows how to use the `ReadInput` class. It prompts the user to enter some text. The first character of the entered text is shown on the standard output.

Listing 9-4: A program to test the ReadInput class

```java
// ReadInputTest.java
package com.jdojo.chapter9;

public class ReadInputTest {
    public static void main(String[] args) {
        System.out.print("Enter some text and press Enter key: ");
        char c = ReadInput.readChar();
        System.out.println("First character you entered is: " + c);
    }
}
```

```
Output:

Enter some text and press Enter key: Hello
First character you entered is: H
```

Checked Exception - Catch or Declare

If a piece of code may throw a checked exception, you must do one of the following two things.

- Handle the checked exception by placing the piece of code inside a `try-catch` block.
- Specify in your method/constructor declaration that it throws the checked exception.

The call to the `System.in.read()` method in the `readChar()` method of the `ReadInput` class (see Listing 9-3) throws a checked exception of `java.io.IOException` type. We applied the first option in this case and handled the `IOException` by placing the call to the `System.in.read()` method in a `try-catch` block

Let us assume that we are writing a method `m1()` for a class that has three statements. Suppose three statements may throw checked exceptions of types `Exception1`, `Exception2`, and `Exception3` respectively. The code for the `m1()` method is shown below.

```java
// Will not compile
public void m1() {
    statement-1; // May throw Exception1
    statement-2; // May throw Exception2
    statement-3; // May throw Exception3
}
```

You cannot compile the code for the `m1()` method in the above form. You must either handle the exception using a `try-catch` block or include in its declaration that it may throw the three checked exceptions. If you want to handle the checked exceptions in the `m1()` method's body, your code may look as follows.

```java
public void m1() {
    try {
        statement-1; // May throw Exception1
        statement-2; // May throw Exception2
        statement-3; // May throw Exception3
```

```
    }
    catch(Exception1 e1) {
        // Handle Exception1 here
    }
    catch(Exception2 e2) {
        // Handle Exception2 here
    }
    catch(Exception3 e3) {
        // Handle Exception3 here
    }
}
```

The above code assumes that when one of the three exceptions is thrown, you do not want to execute the remaining statements. If you want to use a different logic, you might need more than one `try-catch` block. For example, if your logic states that you must attempt to execute all three statements, even if the previous statement throws an exception, your code would look as follows.

```
public void m1() {
    try {
        statement-1; // May throw Exception1
    }
    catch(Exception1 e1) {
        // Handle Exception1 here
    }

    try {
        statement-2; // May throw Exception2
    }
    catch(Exception2 e2) {
        // Handle Exception2 here
    }

    try {
        statement-3; // May throw Exception3
    }
    catch(Exception3 e3) {
        // Handle Exception3 here
    }
}
```

The second way to get rid of the compiler error is to specify in the `m1()` method's declaration that it throws three checked exceptions. This is accomplished by using a `throws` clause in the `m1()` method's declaration. The general syntax for a `throws` clause for a method/constructor is as follows.

```
<<modifiers>> <<return type>> <<method name>>(<<params>>) throws <<List
of Exceptions>> {
    // Method body goes here
}
```

The `throws` keyword is used to specify a `throws` clause. The `throws` clause is placed after the closing parenthesis of the method's parameters list. The `throws` keyword is followed by a comma-separated list of exception types. Recall that an exception type is nothing but the name of a Java class, which is in the exception class hierarchy. We can specify a `throws` clause in the declaration of the `m1()` method as follows.

```
public void m1() throws Exception1, Exception2, Exception3 {
    statement-1; // May throw Exception1
    statement-2; // May throw Exception2
    statement-3; // May throw Exception3
}
```

You can also apply a mixture of two options when a piece of code throws more than one checked exception. You can handle some of them using a `try-catch` block, and declare some of them using a `throws` clause in method's declaration. The following code handles `Exception2` using a `try-catch` block and uses a `throws` clause to declare exceptions `Exception1` and `Exception3` in method's declaration.

```
public void m1() throws Exception1, Exception3 {
    statement-1; // May throw Exception1

    try {
        statement-2; // May throw Exception2
    }
    catch(Exception2 e){
        // Handle Exception2 here
    }

    statement-3; // May throw Exception3
}
```

Let us get back to our `ReadInput` class example. Listing 9-3 fixed the compiler error for the `ReadInput` class using the first option, which added a `try-catch` block. Let us use the second option to fix the compiler error for the `ReadInput` class. We will include a `throws` clause to the `readChar()` method's declaration. Listing 9-5 has another version of the `ReadInput` class, which is called `ReadInput2`. Note that `ReadInput2` class does not use a `try-catch` block inside its `readChar()` method's body. Rather, it specifies a `throws` clause in the `readChar()` method's declaration.

Listing 9-5: Another version of the ReadInput class, which specifies a throws clause in the readChar() method's declaration instead of handling the exception using a try-catch block

```
// ReadInput2.java
package com.jdojo.chapter9;

import java.io.IOException;

public class ReadInput2 {
    public static char readChar() throws IOException {
        char c = '\u0000';
        int input = 0;
        input = System.in.read();
        if (input != -1) {
            c = (char)input;
        }
        return c;
    }
}
```

The following code for the `ReadInput2Test` class tests the `readChar()` method of the `ReadInput2` class.

```
// ReadInput2Test.java
package com.jdojo.chapter9;

public class ReadInput2Test {
    public static void main(String[] args) {
        System.out.print("Enter some text and then " +
                            "press Enter key: ");
        char c = ReadInput2.readChar();
        System.out.print("The first character you entered is: " + c);
    }
}
```

Let us compile the `ReadInput2Test` class. Oops! Compiling the `ReadInput2Test` class generates the following error.

```
Error(6,11): unreported exception: class java.io.IOException; must be
caught or declared to be thrown
```

The compiler error may not be very clear to you at this point. The `readChar()` method of the `ReadInput2` class declares that it may throw an `IOException`. The `IOException` is a checked exception. Therefore, the following piece of code in the `main()` method of `ReadInput2Test` may throw a checked `IOException`.

```
char c = ReadInput2.readChar();
```

Recall the rules about handling the checked exceptions, which we mentioned in the beginning of this section. If a piece of code may throw a checked exception, you must use one of the two options – place that piece of code inside a `try-catch` block to handle the exception, or specify the checked exception using a `throws` clause in the method's or constructor's declaration. Now, we must apply one of the two options for the `ReadInput2.readChar()` method's call in the `main()` method. Listing 9-6 uses the first option and places the call to `ReadInput2.readChar()` method inside a `try-catch` block. Note that we have placed three statements inside the `try` block, which is not necessary. We needed to place only codes inside the `try` block that may throw the checked exception.

Listing 9-6: A program to test the ReadInput2.readChar() method

```
// ReadInput2Test2.java
package com.jdojo.chapter9;

import java.io.IOException;

public class ReadInput2Test2 {
    public static void main(String[] args) {
        char c = '\u0000';
        try {
            System.out.print("Enter some text and then " +
                                "press Enter key:");
            c = ReadInput2.readChar();
            System.out.println("The first character you " +
                                "entered is: " + c);
        }
        catch(IOException e) {
            System.out.println("Error occurred while reading input.");
        }
```

```
        }
    }
```

We can also use the second option to fix the compiler error in the `ReadInput2Test` class. Listing 9-7 has the code that uses the second option. It includes a `throws` clause with `IOException` for the `main()` method. Can we run the `ReadInput2Test3` class as we have been running other classes using the `java` command? You can run the `ReadInput2Test3` class the same way you run other classes in Java. The requirement to run a class is that it should include a `main()` method, which is declared as "`public static void main(String[] args)`". The requirement does not specify anything about a `throws` clause. A `main()` method, which is used to run a class as a starting point, may or may not contain a `throws` clause.

Listing 9-7: A program to test the ReadInput2.readChar() method

```java
// ReadInput2Test3.java
package com.jdojo.chapter9;

import java.io.IOException;

public class ReadInput2Test3 {
    public static void main(String[] args) throws IOException {
        char c = '\u0000';
        System.out.print("Enter some text and then " +
                        "press Enter key: ");
        c = ReadInput2.readChar();
        System.out.print("The first character you entered is: " + c);
    }
}
```

Suppose we run the `ReadInput2Test3` class and the call to the `System.in.read()` method in the `readChar()` method of the `ReadInput2` class throws an `IOException`. How will the `IOException` be handled and who will handle it? When an exception is thrown in a method's body, Java runtime checks if the code that throws the exception is inside a `try-catch` block. If the exception throwing code is inside a `try-catch` block, the Java runtime looks for the `catch` block that can handle the exception. If it does not find a `catch` block that can handle the exception, or the method call is not inside a `try-catch` block, the exception is propagated up the method call stack. That is, the exception is passed to the caller of the method. In our case, the exception is not handled in the `readChar()` method of the `ReadInput2` class. Its caller is the piece of code in the `main()` method of the `ReadInput2Test2` class. In this case, the same exception is thrown at the point, where the `ReadInput2.readChar()` method call is made inside the `ReadInput2Test2.main()` method. Java runtime applies the same checks to handle the exception.. If we run the `ReadInput2Test2` class and an `IOException` is thrown, Java runtime finds that the call to `ReadInput2.readChar()` is inside a `try-catch` block, which can handle the `IOException`. Therefore, it will transfer the control to the `catch` block, which handles the exception, and the program continues in the `main()` method of the `ReadInput2Test2` class. It is very important to understand that the control does not go back to the `ReadInput2.readChar()` method after it throws an exception and the exception is handled inside the `ReadInput2Test2.main()` method.

When we run the `ReadInput2Test3` class, the call to the `ReadInput2.readChar()` method is not inside a `try-catch` block. In this case, Java runtime will have to propagate the exception up the method call stack. The `main()` method is the beginning of the method call stack for a Java application. This is the method where all Java application starts. If the `main()` method throws an exception, the Java runtime handles it. Recall that if the Java runtime handles an exception for you, it prints the call stack details on the standard error, and exits the application.

Recall that a `catch` block with an exception type can handle an exception of the same type, or any of its subclass type. For example, a `catch` block with `Throwable` exception type is capable of handling all types of exceptions in Java, because the `Throwable` class is the superclass of all exception classes. This concept is also applicable to the `throws` clause. If a method throws a checked exception of `Exception1` type, you can mention `Exception1` type in its `throws` clause or any of the superclass of `Exception1`. The reasoning behind this rule is that if a caller of the method handles an exception, which is the superclass of `Exception1`, it can also handle the exception type of `Exception1` type.

TIP

The Java compiler forces you to handle a checked exception either by using a `try-catch` block or by using a `throws` clause in the method or constructor declaration. If a method throws an exception, it should be handled anywhere in the call stack. That is, if a method throws an exception, its caller can handle it, or its caller's caller can handle, and so on. If an exception is not handled by any callers in the call stack, it is known as an uncaught exception (or an unhandled exception). An uncaught exception is finally handled by the Java runtime, which prints the exception stack trace on standard error, and exits the Java application. A different behavior may be specified for uncaught exception in a thread. Please refer to the chapter on *Threads* for more details on how to specify an exception handler for a thread. .

The Java compiler is very particular about checked exceptions being handled by programmers. If the code in a `try` block cannot throw a checked exception and its associated `catch` blocks catch a checked exception, the Java compiler will generate compiler error. Consider the following code, which uses a `try-catch` block. The `catch` block specifies an `IOException`, which is a checked exception. However, the corresponding `try` block does not throw an `IOException`.

```
// CatchNonExistentException.java
package com.jdojo.chapter9;

import java.io.IOException;

// Will not compile
public class CatchNonExistentException {
    public static void main(String[] args) {
        int x = 10, y = 0, z = 0;
        try {
            z = x / y;
        }
        catch(IOException e) {
            // Handle exception
        }
    }
}
```

When you compile the code for the `CatchNonExistentException` class, you would get the following compiler error. The error message is self-explanatory. It states that `IOException` is never thrown in the `try` block. Therefore, the `catch` block must not catch it.

```
Error(12):  exception java.io.IOException is never thrown in body of
corresponding try statement
```

One way to fix the above compiler error is to remove the `try-catch` block altogether. Below is
another interesting way (but not a good way) to mention a generic `catch` block.

```java
// CatchNonExistentException.java
package com.jdojo.chapter9;

import java.io.IOException;

// Will compile fine
public class CatchNonExistentException2 {
    public static void main(String[] args) {
        int x = 10, y = 0, z = 0;
        try {
            z = x / y;
        }
        catch(Exception e) {
            // Handle exception
        }
    }
}
```

`Exception` is also a checked exception type in Java as is `IOException`. If a `catch` block should
not catch a checked exception unless it is thrown in the corresponding `try` block, how does the
code for `CatchNonExistentException2` compile fine? Should it not generate a compiler error?
At first thought, you are right. It should fail compilation for the same reason the
`CatchNonExistentException` class had failed compilation. There are two checked exceptions
classes, which are exceptions to this rule. Those two exception classes are – `Exception` and
`Throwable`. The `Exception` class is the superclass of `IOException` and other exceptions,
which are checked exceptions. It is also the superclass of `RuntimeException` and all subclasses
of `RuntimeException`, which are unchecked exceptions. Recall the rule that a superclass
exception type can also handle a subclass exception type. Therefore, you can use the `Exception`
class to handle checked exceptions as well as unchecked exceptions. The rule of checking for
`catch` blocks for un-thrown exceptions applies only to checked exceptions. `Exception` and
`Throwable` classes in a `catch` block can handle checked as well as unchecked exceptions
because they are superclasses of both types. This is the reason why the compiler will let you use
these two checked exception types in a `catch` block, even though the associated `try` block does
not throw any checked exceptions.

TIP

All rules about the compiler check for exceptions being handled or thrown are applicable only to
checked exceptions. These rules do not apply to unchecked exceptions. For example, there may
be a `catch` block with an unchecked exception type whose corresponding `try` block may never
throw that unchecked exception. A method may have a `throws` clause that includes unchecked
exceptions. If a method specified a `throws` clause with unchecked exceptions in its declaration,
the code that calls that method does not have to handle these exceptions. In short, Java does not
force you to handle the unchecked exceptions in your code. However, you are free to handle them,
as you feel appropriate to do so.

Checked Exceptions and Initializers

You cannot throw a checked exception from a `static` initializer. If a piece of code in a `static` initializer throws a checked exception, it must be handled using a `try-catch` block inside the initializer itself. The `static` initializer is called only once for a class, and the programmer does not have a specific point in code to catch it. This is the reason why a `static` initializer must handle all possible checked exceptions that its code may throw.

```
public class Test {
    static {
        // Must use try-catch blocks to handle all checked exceptions
        // which are thrown here
    }
}
```

The rule is different for an instance initializer. An instance initializer is called as part of a constructor call for the class. An instance initializer may throw checked exceptions. However, all those checked exceptions must be included in the `throws` clause of all constructors for that class. This way, the Java compiler can make sure that all checked exceptions are taken care of by the programmers when any of the constructors are called. The following code for `Test` class assumes that the instance initializer throws a checked exception of `CException` type. The compiler will force you to add a `throws` clause with `CException` to all constructors of `Test`.

```
public class Test {
    // Instance initializer
    {
        // Throws a checked exception of type CException
    }

    // All constructors must specify that they throw CException
    // because the instance initializer throws CException.
    public Test() throws CException {
        // Code goes here
    }

    public Test(int x) throws CException {
        // Code goes here
    }

    // Rest of the code goes here
}
```

You must handle the `CException` when you create an object of the `Test` class using any of its constructors as.

```
Test t = null;
try {
    t = new Test();
}
catch (CException e) {
    // Handle exception here
}
```

If you do not handle the CException using a try-catch block, you must use a throws clause to specify that the method or constructor that uses the constructor of the Test class may throw CException.

Recall that if you do not declare a constructor for a class than the Java compiler adds a default constructor for you. If an instance initializer throws a checked exception, you must declare a constructor for your class. The compiler will add a default constructor to your class if you do not add one. However, the compiler does not add a throws clause to the default constructor, which will break the above rule. The following code will not compile.

```
public class Test123 {
    {
        // May throw CException, which is a checked exception
    }
}
```

When the Test123 class is compiled, the compiler adds a default constructor, and the class Test123 will look as follows.

```
public class Test123 {
    {
        // May throw CException, which is a checked exception
    }

    public Test123() {
        // Empty body. The compiler did not add a throws clause
    }
}
```

Note that the default constructor, which was added by the compiler, does not contain a throws clause to include CException, which is thrown by the instance initializer. This is the reason why the Test123 class will not compile. To make the Test123 class compile, you must add at least one constructor explicitly and use a throws clause to specify that it may throw CException.

Throwing an Exception

A Java exception is not something that is always thrown by the Java runtime. You can also throw an exception from your code using a throw statement. The syntax for a throw statement is:

```
throw <<A throwable object reference>>;
```

Here, throw is a keyword, which is followed by a reference to a throwable object. A throwable object is an object of a class, which is a subclass of the Throwable class, or the Throwable class itself. The following is an example of a throw statement, which throws IOException.

```
// Create an object of IOException
IOException e1 = new IOException("File not found");

// Throw the IOException
throw e1;
```

Recall that the `new` operator returns the reference of the new object. You can also create a throwable object and throw it in one statement as:

```
// Throw an IOException
throw new IOException("File not found");
```

The same rules for handling exceptions in your code apply, when you throw an exception in your code. If you throw a checked exception using a `throw` statement, you must handle it by placing the code in a `try-catch` block, or by using a `throws` clause in the method or constructor declaration that contains the `throw` statement. These rules do not apply if you throw an unchecked exception using a `throw` statement.

Creating an Exception Class

You can also create your own exception classes. Your exception class must extend (or inherit from) an existing exception class. We will cover how to extend a class in detail in the chapter on *Inheritance*. This section will discuss the necessary syntax to extend a class. The keyword `extends` is used to extend a class. The syntax to extend a class is shown below.

```
<<Class Modifiers>> class <<Class Name>> extends <<Super Class Name>> {
    // Body for <<Class Name>> goes here
}
```

Here, `<<Class Name>>` is your exception class name and `<<Super Class Name>>` is an existing exception class name, which is extended by your class.

Suppose you want to create your exception class, say `MyException`, which extends the `java.lang.Exception` class. The syntax would be as follows.

```
public class MyException extends Exception {
    // Body for MyException class goes here
}
```

How does the body of an exception class look? An exception class is like any other class in Java. Typically, you do not add any methods to your exception class. Many useful methods that can be used to query an exception object's state are declared in the `Throwable` class and you can use them without re-declaring them. Typically, you include four constructors to your exception class. All constructors will call the corresponding constructor of its superclass using the `super` keyword. Listing 9-8 shows the code for a `MyException` class with four constructors.

The first constructor creates an exception with `null` as its detail message. The second constructor creates an exception with a detailed message. The third and fourth constructors were introduced to Java 1.4. They let you create an exception by wrapping another exception with/without a detailed message.

Listing 9-8: An exception class, MyException that extends Exception class

```
// MyException.java
package com.jdojo.chapter9;

public class MyException extends Exception {
    public MyException() {
```

```
        super();
    }

    public MyException(String message) {
        super(message);
    }

    public MyException(String message, Throwable cause) {
        super(message, cause);
    }

    public MyException(Throwable cause) {
        super(cause);
    }
}
```

You can create and throw an exception of type `MyException` as:

```
throw new MyException("your message goes here");
```

You can use the `MyException` class in a `throws` clause in a method/constructor declaration or as a parameter type in a `catch` block as:

```
import com.jdojo.chapter9.MyException;
...
public void m1() throws MyException {

}

try {
    // Code for try block goes here
}
catch(MyException e) {
    // Code for catch block goes here
}
```

Table 9-1 shows some of the commonly used methods of the `Throwable` class. Note that the `Throwable` class is the superclass of all exception classes in Java. All of the methods shown in this table are available in all exception classes.

Table 9-1: A partial list of methods of the Throwable class that can be used with all exception objects

Method	Description
`public Throwable getCause()`	This method was added in Java 1.4. It returns the cause of the exception. If the cause of the exception is not set, it returns `null`.
`public String getMessage()`	It returns the detailed message of the exception.
`public StackTraceElement[] getStackTrace()`	This method was added in Java 1.4. It returns an array of stack trace elements. Each element in the array represents one stack frame. The first element of the array represents the top of the stack and the last element of the array represents the bottom of the stack.

	The top of the stack is the method/constructor where the exception object is created. The object of `StackTraceElement` class holds information such as class name, method name, file name, line number etc.
`public Throwable initCause(Throwable cause)`	It was added in Java 1.4. There are two ways to set an exception as the cause of an exception. One way is to use the constructor, which accepts the cause as a parameter. Another way is to use this method.
`public void printStackTrace()`	It prints the stack trace on the standard error stream. The output prints the description of the exception object itself as the first line and then the description of each stack frame. Printing stack trace for an exception is very useful for the debugging purpose.
`public void printStackTrace(PrintStream s)`	It prints the stack trace to the specified `PrintStream` object.
`public void printStackTrace(PrintWriter s)`	It prints the stack trace to the specified `PrintWriter` object.
`public String toString()`	It returns a short description of the exception object. The description of an exception object contains the name of the exception class and the detail message.

Listing 9-9 demonstrates the use of the `printStackTrace()` method for an exception class. The `main()` method calls the `m1()` method, which in turn calls the `m2()` method. The stack frame for this call starts with the `main()` method, which will be at the bottom of the stack. The top of the stack contains the `m2()` method. The output shows that the `printStackTrace()` method prints the stack information from top to bottom. Each stack frame contains the name of the class, the method name, the source file name, and the line number. The first line of the `printStackTrace()` method prints the class name of the exception object with the detailed message.

Listing 9-9: Printing the stack trace of an exception

```java
// StackTraceTest.java
package com.jdojo.chapter9;

public class StackTraceTest {
    public static void main(String[] args) {
        try {
            m1();
        }
        catch(MyException e) {
            e.printStackTrace();// Print the stack trace
        }
    }

    public static void m1() throws MyException {
        m2();
    }

    public static void m2() throws MyException {
        throw new MyException("Some error has occurred.");
    }
}
```

```
Output:

com.jdojo.chapter9.MyException: Some error has occurred.
        at com.jdojo.chapter9.StackTraceTest.m2(StackTraceTest.java:20)
        at com.jdojo.chapter9.StackTraceTest.m1(StackTraceTest.java:16)
        at com.jdojo.chapter9.StackTraceTest.main(StackTraceTest.java:7)
```

Listing 9-9 demonstrates how to print the stack trace of an exception on the standard error. Sometimes, you may need to save the stack trace to a file or in a database. You may need to get the stack trace information as a string in a variable. Another version of the `printStackTrace()` method lets you do this. Listing 9-10 shows how to use `printStackTrace(PrintWriter s)` method to print the stack trace of an exception object to a `String` object. The program is the same as Listing 9-9 with one difference. It stores the stack trace in a string and then prints that string on the standard output. The method `getStackTrace()` writes the stack trace to a string and returns that string. Please refer to the chapter on *Input/Output* for more details on how to use `StringWriter` and `PrintWriter` classes.

Listing 9-10: A sample program that demonstrates how to print an exception stack trace to a string object using printStackTrace(PrintWriter s) method of the Throwable class

```java
// StackTraceAsStringTest.java
package com.jdojo.chapter9;

import java.io.StringWriter;
import java.io.PrintWriter;

public class StackTraceAsStringTest {
    public static void main(String[] args) {
        try {
            m1();
        }
        catch(MyException e) {
            String str = getStackTrace(e);

            // Print the stack trace to the standard output
            System.out.println(str);
        }
    }

    public static void m1() throws MyException {
        m2();
    }

    public static void m2() throws MyException {
        throw new MyException("Some error has occurred.");
    }

    public static String getStackTrace(Throwable e) {
        StringWriter strWriter = new StringWriter();
        PrintWriter printWriter = new PrintWriter(strWriter);
        e.printStackTrace(printWriter);

        // Get the stack trace as a string
        String str = strWriter.toString();

        return str;
```

```
        }
}
```

```
Output:

com.jdojo.chapter9.MyException: Some error has occurred.
     at com.jdojo.chapter9.StackTraceAsString.m2(StackTraceAsString.java:25)
     at com.jdojo.chapter9.StackTraceAsString.m1(StackTraceAsString.java:21)
     at com.jdojo.chapter9.StackTraceAsString.main(StackTraceAsString.java:10)
```

The finally Block

In addition to associating a `catch` block, you can also associate a `finally` block to a `try` block. A `finally` block is never used by itself. It is always used with a `try` block. The syntax for using a `finally` block is:

```
finally {
    // Code for finally block goes here
}
```

A `finally` block starts with the keyword `finally`, which is followed by an opening brace and a closing brace. The code for a `finally` block is placed inside braces.

There are two possible combinations for `try`, `catch`, and `finally` blocks. They are `try-catch-finally` or `try-finally`. A `try` block may be followed by zero or more `catch` blocks. A `try` block can have a maximum of one `finally` block. A `try` block must have either a `catch` block, a `finally` block, or both. The syntax for a `try-catch-finally` block is:

```
try {
    // Code for try block goes here
}
catch(Exception1 e1) {
    // Code for catch block goes here
}
finally {
    // Code for finally block goes here
}
```

The syntax for a `try-finally` block is:

```
try {
    // Code for try block goes here
}
finally {
    // Code for finally block goes here
}
```

When you use a `try-catch-finally` block, your intention is to execute the following logic.

Let us try executing the code in the `try` block. If the code in the `try` block throws any exception, execute the matching catch block. Finally, execute the code in the `finally` block no matter how the code in the try block and in the catch blocks finish executing.

When you use a `try-finally` block, your intention is to execute the following logic.

Let us try executing the code in the `try` block. When the code in the `try` block finishes, execute the code in the `finally` block.

TIP

The code in a `finally` block is guaranteed to be executed no matter what happens in the associated `try` and/or `catch` block. There are two exceptions to this rule. The `finally` block may not execute if the thread that is executing the `try` or the `catch` block dies. A Java application may exit, for example, by calling `System.exit()` method, while executing the `try` or the `catch` block. If a Java application exits while executing `try` or `catch` block, the associated `finally` block is not executed.

Why do we need to use a `finally` block? Sometimes, you want to execute two sets of statements, say `set-1` and `set-2`. The condition is that `set-2` should be executed no matter how statements in `set-1` finish executing. For example, statements in `set-1` may throw an exception or may finish normally. You may be able to write the logic, which will execute `set-2` after `set-1` is executed, without using a `finally` block.. However, the code may not look clean. You may end up repeating the same code multiple places and writing spaghetti `if-else` statements. For example, `set-1` may use constructs, which make the control jump from one point of the program to another. It may use constructs like `break`, `continue`, `return`, `throw`, etc. If `set-1` has many points of exit, you will need to repeat the call to `set-2` before exiting at many places. It is difficult and ugly to write logic that will execute `set-1` and `set-2`. The `finally` block makes it easy to write this logic. All you need to do is to place `set-1` code in a `try` block and the `set-2` codes in a `finally` block. Optionally, you can also use `catch` blocks to handle exceptions that may be thrown from `set-1`. You can write Java code to execute `set-1` and `set-2` as follows.

```
try {
    // Execute all statements in set-1
}
catch(MyException e1) {
    // Handle any exceptions here that may be thrown by set-1
}
finally {
    // Execute statements in set-2
}
```

If you structure your code to execute `set-1` and `set-2` the way we have shown above, you get cleaner code with guaranteed execution of `set-2` after `set-1` is executed.

Typically, we use a `finally` block to write cleanup code. For example, you may obtain some resources in your program that must be released when you are done with them. A `try-finally` block lets you implement this logic. Your code structure would look like.

```
try {
    // Obtain and use some resource here
}
```

```
finally {
    // Release the resources that were obtained in the try block
}
```

You write `try-finally` blocks frequently when you write programs that perform database transactions and file input/output. You obtain and use a database connection in the `try` block and release the connection in the `finally` block. When you work with a database related program, you must release the database connection, which you obtained in the beginning, no matter what happens to the transaction. It is a similar situation as executing statements in `set-1` and `set-2` as described above.

Listing 9-11 demonstrates the use of a `finally` block in four different situations. The first `try-catch-finally` block attempts to perform divide by zero operation on an integer. The expression `x/y` throws `ArithmeticException` and control is transferred to `catch` block. The `finally` block is executed after `catch` block finishes. Note that the second message in the `try` block is not printed, because once an exception is thrown, the control jumps to the nearest matching `catch` block and the control never goes back to the `try` block again.

The second `try-catch-finally` block is an example where the `try` block finishes normally (without throwing an exception). After the `try` block finishes, the `finally` block is executed.

The third `try-finally` block is simple. The `try` block finishes normally and then the `finally` block is executed.

The fourth `try-finally` block demonstrates the exceptional case when a `finally` block is not executed. The `try` block exits the application by executing the `System.exit()` method. The application stops executing when the `System.exit()` method is called. The associated `finally` block is not executed when the application exits.

Listing 9-11: A sample program to demonstrate use of finally block

```java
// FinallyTest.java
package com.jdojo.chapter9;

public class FinallyTest {
    public static void main(String[] args) {
        int x = 10, y = 0, z;
        try {
            System.out.println("Before dividing x by y.");
            z = x / y;
            System.out.println("After dividing x by y.");
        }
        catch (ArithmeticException e) {
            System.out.println("Inside catch block - 1.");
        }
        finally {
            System.out.println("Inside finally block - 1.");
        }

        System.out.println("-----------------------------");

        try {
            System.out.println("Before setting z to 2449.");
            z = 2449;
            System.out.println("After setting z to 2449.");
```

```
        }
        catch (Exception e) {
            System.out.println("Inside catch block - 2.");
        }
        finally {
            System.out.println("Inside finally block - 2.");
        }

        System.out.println("------------------------------");

        try {
            System.out.println("Inside try block - 3.");
        }
        finally {
            System.out.println("Inside finally block - 3.");
        }

        System.out.println("------------------------------");
        try {
            System.out.println("Before executing System.exit().");
            System.exit(0);
            System.out.println("After executing System.exit().");
        }
        finally {
            // This finally block will not be executed because
            // application exits in try block
            System.out.println("Inside finally block - 4.");
        }
    }
}
```

```
Output:

Before dividing x by y.
Inside catch block - 1.
Inside finally block - 1.
------------------------------
Before setting z to 2449.
After setting z to 2449.
Inside finally block - 2.
------------------------------
Inside try block - 3.
Inside finally block - 3.
------------------------------
Before executing System.exit().
```

Re-throwing an Exception

An exception that is caught can be re-thrown. You may want to re-throw an exception for different reasons. One of the reasons to re-throw an exception could be to take an action after catching it and before propagating it up the stack. For example, you may want to log the details about the exception and then re-throw the exception to the client. Another reason that you may want to re-throw an exception is to hide the exception type/location from the client. You are not hiding the exceptional condition itself from the client. Rather, you are hiding the type of the exceptional condition. You may want to hide the actual exception type from clients for two reasons - client may not be ready to handle the exception that is thrown or the exception that is thrown does not make sense to the client. Re-throwing exception is as simple as using a `throw` statement. The following code snippet catches the exception, prints its stack trace and then re-throws the same exception. When the same exception object is re-thrown, it preserves the details of the original exception.

```
try {
    // Code that might throw MyException
}
catch(MyException e) {
    e.printStackTrace();// Print the stack trace

    // Re-throw the same exception
    throw e;
}
```

When an exception is thrown from a `catch` block, another `catch` block in the same group is not searched to handle that exception. If you want to handle the exception that is thrown from a `catch` block, you need to enclose the code that throws the exception inside another `try-catch` block. Another way to handle the exception that is thrown from a `catch` block is to enclose the whole `try-catch` block inside another `try-catch` block. The following snippet of code shows the two ways of arranging nested `try-catch` to handle `Exception1` and `Exception2`. The actual arrangement of nested `try-catch` depends on the situation at hand. If you do not enclose the code that may throw an exception inside a `try` block or the `try` block does not have a matching associated `catch` block that can catch the exception, the Java runtime will propagate the exception up the call stack.

```
// #1 - Arranging nested try-catch
try {
    // May throw Exception1
}
catch(Exception1 e1) {
    // Handle Exception1 here

    try {
        // May throw Exception2
    }
    catch(Exception2 e2) {
        // Handle Exception2 here
    }
}


// #2 - Arranging nested try-catch
try {
    try {
        // May throw Exception1
    }
    catch(Exception1 e1) {
        // Handle Exception1 here
        // May throw Exception2
    }
}
catch(Exception2 e2) {
```

```
        // Handle Exception2 here
}
```

The following snippet of code shows how to catch an exception of one type and re-throw an exception of another type. The `catch` block catches an exception of `MyException` type, prints its stack trace and then re-throws an exception of `RuntimeException` type. In the process, it loses the details of the original exception that was thrown. When the `RuntimeException` is created, it packages the information of stack frames from the point where it was created. The client gets the information about the re-thrown `RuntimeException` exception from the point it was created and not about the original `MyException` exception. In the following code, we have hidden both the type and the location of the original exception from the client.

```
try {
    // Code that might throw a MyException
}
catch(MyException e) {
    e.printStackTrace();    // Print the stack trace

    // Re-throw another type of exception
    throw new RuntimeException(e.getMessage());
}
```

You can also re-throw another type of exception and use the original exception as the cause of the new re-thrown exception. It is as if the new exception is a wrapper for the original exception. You can set the cause of an exception using one of the constructors of the new exception type that accepts a cause as a parameter or you can use the `initCause()` method to set the cause of the exception. The `initCause()` method is available from Java 1.4. Before Java 1.4, your new exception class must have a way to set a cause. The following snippet of code re-throws a `RuntimeException` setting `MyException` as its cause.

```
try {
    // Code that might throw a MyException
}
catch(MyException e) {
    e.printStackTrace();    // Print the stack trace

    // Re-throw a new exception using original exception as its cause
    throw new RuntimeException(e.getMessage(), e);
}
```

You also have the option just to hide the location of the exception from the client when you re-throw an exception. The `fillInStackTrace()` method of the `Throwable` class fills in the stack trace information to an exception object from the point where this method is called. You need to call this method on the exception you catch and want to re-throw it to hide the location of the original exception. The following snippet of code shows how to re-throw an exception by hiding the location of the original exception.

```
try {
    // Code that might throw MyException
}
catch(MyException e) {
    // Re-package the stack frames in the exception object
    e.fillInStackTrace();
    throw e; // Re-throw the same exception
}
```

Listing 9-12 demonstrates how to re-throw an exception by hiding the location of the original exception. The MyException is thrown inside the m2() method. The m1() method catches the exception, refills the stack trace and then re-throws it. The main() method receives the exception as if the exception was thrown inside the m1() method, not inside the m2() method. This is an example where the m1() method re-throws the exception to hide the original location of the exception.

Listing 9-12: Re-throwing an exception to hide the location of the original exception

```java
// RethrowTest.java
package com.jdojo.chapter9;

public class RethrowTest {
    public static void main(String[] args) {
        try {
            m1();
        }
        catch(MyException e) {
            // Print the stack trace
            e.printStackTrace();
        }
    }

    public static void m1() throws MyException {
        try {
            m2();
        }
        catch(MyException e) {
            e.fillInStackTrace();
            throw e;
        }
    }

    public static void m2() throws MyException {
        throw new MyException("Some error has occurred.");
    }
}
```

```
Output:

com.jdojo.chapter9.MyException: Some error has occurred.
    at com.jdojo.chapter9.RethrowTest.m1(RethrowTest.java:20)
    at com.jdojo.chapter9.RethrowTest.main(RethrowTest.java:7)
```

Analysis of Re-thrown Exceptions

Java 7 improved the mechanism of re-throwing exceptions. Consider the following snippet of code for a method declaration.

```java
public void test() throws Exception {
    try {
        // May throw Exception1, or Exception2
    }
```

```
    catch (Exception e) {
        // Re-throw the caught exception
        throw e;
    }
}
```

The `try` block may throw `Exception1` or `Exception2`. The `catch` block specifies `Exception` as its parameter and it re-throws the exception it catches. Prior to Java 7, the compiler sees the `catch` block throwing an exception of `Exception` type and it insists that, in the `throws` clause, the `test()` method must specify that it throws an exception of the `Exception` type or the supertype of the `Exception` type.

Since the `try` block can throw exceptions of only `Exception1` type or `Exception2` type, the `catch` block will re-throw an exception that is always of `Exception1` type or `Exception2` type. Java 7 performs this analysis, when an exception is re-thrown. It lets you specify the `throws` clause of the `test()` method accordingly. In Java 7, you can specify more specific exception types, `Exception1` and `Exception2`, in the `test()` method's `throws` clause as shown below.

```
public void test() throws Exception1, Exception2 {
    try {
        // May throw Exception1, Exception2 or Exception3
    }
    catch (Exception e) {
        // Re-throw the caught exception
        throw e;
    }
}
```

Throwing too Many Exceptions

There is no limit on the number of exception types that a method/constructor can list in its `throws` clause. However, it is better to keep the number of exceptions that a method may throw to the minimum. The client that uses a method has to deal with all the exceptions that the method may throw in one way or another. It is also important to keep in mind that a method should not throw a new type of exception once it has been designed, implemented, and released to public. If a method starts throwing a new type of exception after its public release, all client codes that call this method must change. It indicates poor design if a method throws too many exceptions or a new exception is added after its public release. You can avoid these issues with your method by catching all lower-level exceptions inside your method and then re-throwing a higher-level exception from your method. The exception that you throw may contain the lower-level exception as its cause. Note that you can include constructors to your higher-level exception class from Java 1.4 that can handle the cause of the exception for you. Prior to Java 1.4, you needed to design your exception class so that it can store the cause of the exception. Consider the following snippet of code for the `m1()` method that throws three exceptions – `Exception1`, `Exception2` and `Exception3`.

```
public void m1() throws Exception1, Exception2, Exception3 {
    // Code for m1() method goes here
}
```

You can redesign the `m1()` method to throw only one exception, say `MyException`, as follows.

```
public void m1() throws MyException {
```

```
try {
    // Code for m1() method goes here
}
catch(Exception1 e1){
    throw new MyException("Msg1", e1);
}
catch(Exception2 e2){
    throw new MyException("Msg2", e1);
}
catch(Exception3 e3){
    throw new MyException("Msg3", e1);
}
}
```

The redesigned `m1()` method throws only one exception, which is of type `MyException`. The detailed message for the exception is specific to the lower-level exception that is thrown and caught inside the method. The lower-level exception is also propagated to the client as the cause of the higher-level exception, which is always `MyException`. If the `m1()` method needs to throw a new exception in the future, you can still fit the new exception in the old design. You need to add a `catch` block to catch the new exception inside the `m1()` method and then re-throw `MyException`. This design keeps the `throws` clause of the `m1()` method stable. It also allows for more exception types to be included in its body in future.

TIP

You should not throw a generic exception from your method such as `Throwable`, `Exception`, `Error`, `RuntimeException`, etc. Similarly, you should not specify a generic exception type in a `catch` block. The purpose of exception throwing or handling is to know exactly the error condition that occurred and to take appropriate action. The appropriate action could be to try to recover from the error or pass that error on to the caller. It helps to give specific error message to the users instead of giving them a generic error message. Generating a specific error message is possible only when you handle an exception using the specific exception type.

Accessing the Stack of a Thread

Stack is an area of memory, which is used to store temporary data. It uses last-in-first-out (LIFO) style to add and remove data to it. A stack resembles a stack in everyday life, for example, a stack of books. The bottom of the stack has the first book that was placed on it. The top of the stack has the last book that was placed on it. When a book has to be removed from the stack, the last book that was placed on the stack will be removed first. This is the reason; a stack is also called last-in-first-out memory.

Figure 9-4 shows the arrangement of a stack. It shows three books placed on a stack. `Book-1` was placed first, `Book-2` second, and then `Book-3`. `Book-3`, which is added last onto the stack, represents the top of the stack. `Book-1`, which is added first onto the stack, represents the bottom of the stack. Adding an element to a stack is called a *push* operation and removing an element from a stack is called a *pop* operation. Initially, a stack is empty and the first operation is the push operation. When a stack is being discarded, it must have performed an equal number of push and pop operations so that it is empty again.

Each thread in Java is allocated a stack to store its temporary data. A thread stores the state of a method invocation onto its stack. The state of a Java method comprises the parameters values, local variables values, any intermediate computed values and its return value, if any. A Java stack consists of stack frames (or simple frames). Each frame stores the state of one method invocation. A new frame is pushed onto a thread's stack for a method invocation. A frame is popped from a thread's stack when a method completes. Suppose a thread starts at the m1() method. The m1() method calls the m2() method, which in turn calls the m3() method. When a method is invoked, a frame for that method is pushed onto the thread's stack. When the method finishes, the frame is popped. Figure 9-5 shows the frames on the stack of a thread when method m1(), m2(), and m3() are called. Note that the figures shows the frames when the method m3() is called from the method m2(), which in turn is called from the method m1().

Figure 9-4: Memory arrangement in a stack

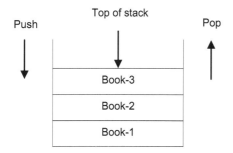

Figure 9-5: State of the stack of a thread when methods m1(). m2() and m3() are called

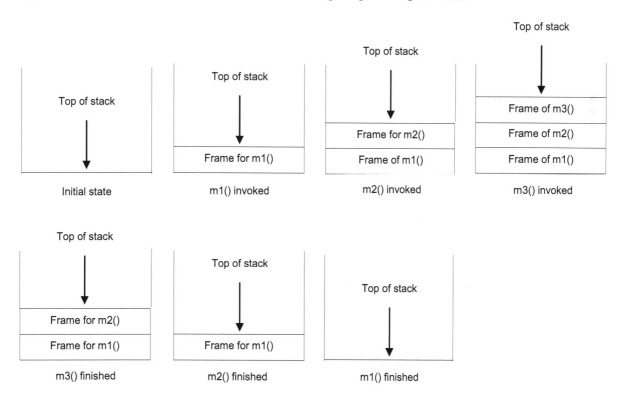

Starting from Java 1.4, you can get some pieces of information about the stack of a thread at a specific point in time. Note that the state of a thread's stack is always changing as the program executes. Therefore, you get a snapshot of the stack of a thread as it existed at the time you requested it. An object of the `java.lang.StackTraceElement` class represents a frame on the stack of a thread. You can query four pieces of information about a stack frame – class name, file name, method name and line number. To get the stack information you need to call the `getStackTrace()` method of a `Throwable` object. It returns an array of `StackTraceElement` objects. The first element of the array represents the top stack frame. The last element of the array represents the bottom stack frame. When you create an object of the `Throwable` class (or any exception class in Java), it captures the stack of the thread that is executing. Listing 9-13 demonstrates how to get to the stack frames of a thread. A `Throwable` object captures the stack of the thread at the point it is created. If you have a `Throwable` object and want to capture the snapshot of the stack of a thread at a different point where the `Throwable` object was created, you can call the `fillInStackTrace()` method of the `Throwable` class. It captures the current state of stack for the current thread at the point you call this method.

Listing 9-13: A sample program that prints the details of the stack frames of a thread.

```java
// StackFrameTest.java
package com.jdojo.chapter9;

public class StackFrameTest {
    public static void main(String[] args) {
        m1();
    }

    public static void m1() {
        m2();
    }

    public static void m2() {
        m3();
    }

    public static void m3() {
        // Create a Throwable object that will hold
        // the stack state at this point for the thread that
        // executes the following statement
        Throwable t = new Throwable();

        // Get the stack trace elements
        StackTraceElement[] frames = t.getStackTrace();

        // Print details about the stack frames
        printStackDetails(frames);
    }

    public static void printStackDetails(StackTraceElement[] frames) {
        System.out.println("Frame count: " + frames.length);

        for (int i = 0; i < frames.length; i++) {
            // Get frame details
            int frameIndex = i; // 0 means top frame
            String fileName = frames[i].getFileName();
            String className = frames[i].getClassName();
            String methodName = frames[i].getMethodName();
            int lineNumber = frames[i].getLineNumber();

            // Print frame details
```

```
                    System.out.println("Frame Index: " + frameIndex);
                    System.out.println("File Name: " + fileName);
                    System.out.println("Class Name: " + className);
                    System.out.println("Method Name: " + methodName);
                    System.out.println("Line Number: " + lineNumber);
                    System.out.println("--------------------------");
            }
        }
    }
```

```
Output:

Frame count: 4
Frame Index: 0
File Name: StackFrameTest.java
Class Name: com.jdojo.chapter9.StackFrameTest
Method Name: m3
Line Number: 21
--------------------------
Frame Index: 1
File Name: StackFrameTest.java
Class Name: com.jdojo.chapter9.StackFrameTest
Method Name: m2
Line Number: 14
--------------------------
Frame Index: 2
File Name: StackFrameTest.java
Class Name: com.jdojo.chapter9.StackFrameTest
Method Name: m1
Line Number: 10
--------------------------
Frame Index: 3
File Name: StackFrameTest.java
Class Name: com.jdojo.chapter9.StackFrameTest
Method Name: main
Line Number: 6
--------------------------
```

Now that we have access to the stack frames of a thread, you may want to know what you can do with this information. The information about a thread's stack lets you know about the location in the program where the code is executing. Typically, you log this information for debugging purpose. If you compare the `output` of the `printStackTrace()` method with the output of Listing 9-13, you would observe that they are similar, except that they print the same information in different formats.

The try-with-resources Block

Java 7 added a new construct called `try-with-resources`. Before Java 7, when you worked with a resource, e.g. a File, a SQL statement, etc., you had to use a `finally` block and write a few lines of boilerplate code to close the resource. Prior to Java 7, the typical code, to work with a resource, would look as shown below.

```
AnyResource aRes;
try {
```

```
        aRes = create the resource...;
        // Work with the resource here
    }
finally {
    // Let us try to close the resource
    try {
        if (aRes != null) {
            aRes.close(); // Close the resource
        }
    }
    catch(Exception e) {
        e.printStackTrace();
    }
}
```

With the new `try-with-resources` construct in Java 7, the above code can be written as:

```
try (AnyResource aRes = create the resource...) {
    // Work with the resource here. Your resource will be closed
    // automatically
}
```

Wow! We were able to write the same logic in just three lines of code using a `try-with-resource` construct in Java 7, what used to take sixteen lines of code before. The `try-with-resources` construct automatically closes the resources when the program exits the construct. A `try-with-resource` construct may have one or more `catch` blocks and/or a `finally` block.

On the surface, the `try-with-resources` construct is as simple as it seems in the above example. However, it comes with some subtleties that we need to discuss in detail in this section.

You can specify multiple resources in a `try-with-resources` construct. Two resources must be separated by a semi-colon. The last resource must not be followed by a semi-column. The following snippet of code shows some usage of `try-with-resources` construct to use one and multiple resources.

```
try (AnyResource aRes1 = getResource1()) {
    // Use aRes1 here
}

try (AnyResource aRes1 = getResource1();
     AnyResource aRes2 = getResource2()) {
    // Use aRes1 and aRes2 here
}
```

The resources that you specify in the `try-with-resources` construct are implicitly `final`. You can declare the resources `final`, even though it is redundant to do so as:

```
try (final AnyResource aRes1 = getResource1()) {
    // Use aRes1 here
}
```

A resource that you specify in the `try-with-resources` construct must be of the type `java.lang.AutoCloseable`. Java 7 added the `AutoCloseable` interface, which has a `close()` method. When the program exits the `try-with-resources` block, the `close()`

method of all the resources is called automatically. In the case of multiple resources, the `close()` method is called in the reverse order in which the resources are specified.

Consider a `MyResource` class as shown in Listing 9-14. It implements the `AutoCloseable` interface and provides implementation for the `close()` method. If the `exceptionOnClose` instance variable is set to `true`, its `close()` method throws a `RuntimeException`.. Its `use()` method throws a `RuntimeException`, if the `level` is zero or less. We will use the `MyResource` class to demonstrate various rules in using the `try-with-resources` construct.

Listing 9-14: An AutoCloseable resource class

```java
// MyResource.java
package com.jdojo.chapter9;

public class MyResource implements AutoCloseable {
    private int level;
    private boolean exceptionOnClose;

    public MyResource(int level, boolean exceptionOnClose) {
        this.level = level;
        this.exceptionOnClose = exceptionOnClose;
        System.out.println("Creating MyResource. Level = " + level);
    }

    public void use() {
        if (level <= 0) {
            throw new RuntimeException("Low in level.");
        }
        System.out.println("Using MyResource level " + this.level);
        level--;
    }

    @Override
    public void close() {
        if (exceptionOnClose) {
            throw new RuntimeException("Error in closing");
        }
        System.out.println("Closing MyResource...");
    }
}
```

Listing 9-15 shows a simple case of using a `MyResource` object in a `try-with-resources` construct. The output demonstrates that the `try-with-resources` construct automatically calls its `close()` method.

Listing 9-15: A simple use of MyResource object in a try-with-resources block

```java
// SimpleTryWithResource.java
package com.jdojo.chapter9;

public class SimpleTryWithResource {
    public static void main(String[] args) {
        // Create and use a resource of MyResource type
        // Its close() method will be called automatically
        try (MyResource mr = new MyResource(2, false)) {
            mr.use();
```

```
                mr.use();
            }
        }
    }
```

When a resource is being closed automatically, an exception may be thrown, If a `try-with-resources` block completes without throwing any exception and the call to the `close()` method throws the exception, the Java runtime reports the exception thrown from the `close()` method. If a `try-with-resources` block throws an exception and the call to the `close()` method also throws the exception, the Java runtime suppresses the exception thrown from the `close()` method and reports the exception thrown from the `try-with-resources` block. The following snippet of code demonstrates this rule. The third call to the `use()` method throws an exception. In this snippet of code, the automatic `close()` method call will throw a `RuntimeException`, because we pass `true` as the second argument when we create the resource. The output shows that the `catch` block received the `RuntimeException` that was thrown from the `use()` method, not from the `close()` method.

```
// Create a resource of MyResource type with two levels, which can
// throw exception on closing and use it thrice so that its use() method
// throws an exception
try (MyResource mr = new MyResource (2, true) ) {
    mr.use();
    mr.use();
    mr.use(); // Will throw a RuntimeException
}
catch(Exception e) {
    System.out.println(e.getMessage());
}
```

You can retrieve the suppressed exceptions by using the `getSuppressed()` method of the `Throwable` class, which was added in Java 7. It returns an array of `Throwable` objects. Each object in the array represents a suppressed exception. The following snippet of code demonstrates the use of the `getSuppressed()` method to retrieve the suppressed exceptions.

```
try (MyResource mr = new MyResource (2, true) ) {
    mr.use();
    mr.use();
    mr.use(); // Exception
}
```

```
catch(Exception e) {
    System.out.println(e.getMessage());

    // Display messages of supressed exceptions
    System.out.println("Suppressed exception messages are...");
    for(Throwable t : e.getSuppressed() ) {
        System.out.println(t.getMessage());
    }
}
```

```
Output:

Creating MyResource. Level = 2
Using MyResource level 2
Using MyResource level 1
Low in level.
Suppressed exception messages are...
Error in closing
```

A Multi-catch Block

Java 7 added support for a multi-catch block to handle multiple types of exceptions in a `catch` block. Suppose you want to catch three exceptions - `Exception1`, `Exception2`, and `Exception3`. Prior to Java 7, your code would look as:

```
try {
    // Code that may throw Exception1, Exception2 or Exception3
}
catch (Exception1 e1){
    // Handle Exception1
}
catch (Exception2 e2){
    // Handle Exception2
}
catch (Exception3 e3){
    // Handle Exception3
}
```

Prior to Java 7, each exception must be handled in a separate `catch` block. This resulted in code duplication. Sometimes, instead of using a separate `catch` block to catch multiple exceptions, a programmer would use one `catch` block and specify the parameter of a more generic exception type as:

```
try {
    // Code that may throw Exception1, Exception2 or Exception3
}
catch (Throwable t){
    // Handle any exception
}
```

Java 7 addresses both issues - the deficiency in Java language that did not let a programmer handle multiple exceptions in one `catch` block and the laziness of a programmer of using a

---

generic exception type to handle multiple exceptions in a `catch` block. Java 7 added support for catching multiple exceptions using a multi-catch block. You can specify multiple exceptions types in a multi-catch block. Multiple exceptions are separated by a vertical bar (|). In Java 7, the above code can be written as:

```
try {
    // May throw Exception1, Exception2 or Exception3
}
catch (Exception1 | Exception2 | Exception3  e) {
    // Handle Exception1, Exception2 and Exception3
}
```

In a multi-catch block, it is not allowed to have alternative exceptions that are related by subclassing. For example, the following multi-catch block is not allowed, because `Exception1` and `Exception2` are subclasses of `Throwable`.

```
try {
    // May throw Exception1, Exception2 or Exception3
}
catch (Exception1 | Exception2 | Throwable  e) {
    // Handle Exceptions here
}
```

The above snippet of code will generate the following compiler error.

```
error: Alternatives in a multi-catch statement
cannot be related by subclassing
                catch (Exception1 | Exception2 | Throwable  e) {
                                                 ^
  Alternative Exception1 is a subclass of alternative Throwable
1 error
```

Chapter 10. Assertions

What is an Assertion?

The literal meaning of assertion is to state something in a strong, confident, and forceful way. When you assert "something", you believe that "something" to be true. Note that asserting "something" does not make that "something" always true. Asserting "something" means that chances are very high (or you are confident) that "something" is true. Sometimes, you may be wrong and that "something" may be false, even if you assert it to be true.

The meaning of assertion in Java is similar to its literal meaning. It is a statement in Java through which a programmer states a condition to be true at a specific point in a program. Consider the following snippet of code, which has two statements with one comment in between them.

```
int x = 10 + 15;
// We assert that value of x is 25 at this point
int z = x + 12;
```

The first statement uses hard-coded two integer values, 10 and 15, and assigns their sum to the variable x. We can assert that the value of variable x will be 25 after the first statement is executed. We have used comments to make our assertion in the above case. What is the probability that the value of x will be other than 25 in the above code? You may think that the probability of x having a value other than 25 is zero. It means our assertion (just a comment in above) will be true all the time. So, what was the point in adding a comment, which asserts that the value of x is 25 when it is obvious by just looking at the code? In programming, what seems obvious at one time may not be obvious at other times. Let us consider the following snippet of code assuming that a getPrice() method exists.

```
int quantity = 15;
double unitPrice = getPrice();
// We assert that unitPrice is greater than 0.0 at this point
double totalPrice = quantity * unitPrice;
```

In the above code, we have made an assertion that the value of the variable unitPrice will be greater than 0.0 after the second statement is executed. What is the probability that the value of unitPrice will be greater than 0.0 after the second statement is executed? It is difficult to answer this question by just looking at the code. However, we assume, for the above code to work correctly, that our assertion, the value of unitPrice is greater than 0.0, must be true. Otherwise, our code will indicate a serious bug in the getPrice() method. It may be obvious for a customer that the price for an item will be always greater than zero. However, it is not so obvious to a programmer, because he has to depend on the correct implementation of the getPrice() method. If the getPrice() method has a bug, the programmer's assertion will be false. If the programmer's assertion is false, he needs to know about the failure of his assertion, and he needs to take action to fix the bug. If his assertion were false, he would not like to proceed with the price computations. He would like to halt the price computation as soon as his assertion fails. We have used a comment to state our assertion. A comment is not an executable code. Even if the value of unitPrice is not greater than zero, our comment is not going to report this error condition or halt the program. We need to use the assertion facility available from Java 1.4 in such cases to receive a detailed error message and to halt the program.

You can make an assertion in Java using `assert` statement. The syntax for an `assert` statement comes in two forms. They are:

Syntax #1

```
assert booleanAssertionExpression;
```

Syntax #2

```
assert booleanAssertionExpression : errorMessageExpression;
```

An `assert` statement starts with the `assert` keyword, which is followed by a boolean assertion expression. The boolean assertion expression is the condition that a programmer believes to be true. If the assertion expression evaluates to `true`, no action is taken. If the assertion expression evaluates to `false`, the Java runtime throws a `java.lang.AssertionError`.

The second form of the `assert` statement syntax allows you to specify a custom error message expression when the assertion error is thrown. The assertion condition and the custom message are separated by a colon (`:`). The `errorMessageExpression` does not have to be a string. It could an expression that may evaluate to any data type except the `void` data type. The Java runtime will convert the result of the error message expression to string. We can rewrite the code shown previously in this section to take advantage of the `assert` statement as follows.

```
int x = 10 + 15;
assert x == 25;    // Uses first form of assert statement
int z = x + 12;
```

Note that we have replaced the comment that the value of `x` is 25 with an `assert` statement. All you need to specify is the condition you assert (or believe) to be true. We used the first form of the `assert` statement. We did not use any custom message when our assertion fails. When assertion fails, the Java runtime provides you with all details such as line number, source code, file name, etc. about the error. In most cases, the first form of the `assert` statement is sufficient. If you think some values from the program at the time of error may help you diagnose the problem better, you should use the second form of the `assert` statement. Suppose, we want to print the value of `x` when the assertion fails, we could use the following snippet of code.

```
int x = 10 + 15;
assert x == 25: "x = " + x; // Uses the second form of assert statement
int z = x + 12;
```

If you want just the value of `x` and nothing else, you can use the following snippet of code.

```
int x = 10 + 15;
assert x == 25: x;   // Uses second form of assert statement
int z = x + 12;
```

Note that the `errorMessageExpression` in the second form of `assert` statement could be of any data type excluding `void`. The above snippet of code provides x as the value of `errorMessageExpression`, which evaluates to an `int`. Java runtime will use the string representation of the value of `x` when it throws `AssertionError`.

At this point, you may be tempted to test the `assert` statement. We need to discuss some more details before you can compile and run Java classes with the `assert` statement. However, we will use Java code with an `assert` statement as shown in Listing 10-1.

Listing 10-1: A simple test class to test the assert statement

```
// AssertTest.java
package com.jdojo.chapter10;

public class AssertTest {
    public static void main(String[] args) {
        int x = 10 + 15;
        assert x == 100:"x = " + x; // should throw AssertionError
    }
}
```

The code for the `AssertTest` class is simple. It assigns a value of 25 to the variable `x` and asserts that the value of `x` should be `100`. When you run the `AssertTest` class, you expect that it would always throws an `AssertionError`.

Compiling a Class with `assert` Statements

This section applies if you are using the Java 1.4 compiler. If you are using Java 5 or higher compiler, you can skip this section.

Assertion was introduced in Java 1.4, which also introduced `assert` as a new keyword to Java language. It was legal to use `assert` as a valid identifier up to Java 1.3. In Java 1.4 and onwards, you cannot use `assert` as an identifier, e.g., as a variable name or a method name.

The Java 1.4 compiler defaults the source code version to 1.3. It is fine to have `assert` as an identifier in Java 1.3. However, an `assert` statement will generate a compiler error when compiled with the default option of Java 1.4 compiler. If you compile the source code for the `AssertTest` class using a Java 1.4 compiler using any of the two following commands, you would receive compiler warnings and errors.

```
// Java 1.4 compiler will assume that AssertTest.java uses 1.3 source
javac AssertTest.java

// We specify explicitly that AssertTest.java uses 1.3 source
javac -source 1.3 AssertTest.java
```

The above commands will generate the following error.

```
AssertTest.java:7: warning: as of release 1.4, assert is a keyword, and
may not be used as an identifier
        assert x == 24 : "x = " + x;    // should throw AssertionError
               ^
com/jdojo/chapter10/AssertTest.java:7: ';' expected
        assert x == 24 : "x = " + x;    // should throw AssertionError
               ^
1 error
1 warning
```

The error message is loud and clear that `assert` is not recognized as a keyword by the Java 1.4 compiler in source 1.3 mode. You need to tell the Java 1.4 compiler that your source code should be treated as the source mode 1.4. The following command will compile the `AssertTest` class fine using Java 1.4 compiler.

```
javac -source 1.4 AssertTest.java
```

If you are using Java 5 or a higher version of Java, you do not need to worry the about source mode of your class during compilation. They will generate errors if `assert` is used as an identifier. They allow you to use `assert` only as a keyword to specify assertion in your program.

Testing Assertions

It is time to see `assert` statement in action. Let us try to run the `AssertTest` class using the following command.

```
java com.jdojo.chapter10.AssertTest
```

The above command finishes without any output. Did we not expect some kind of error message on the standard output? Is our assertion, `x == 100`, not false? The value of `x` is `25` and not `100`. We need to perform one more step before we can see the `assert` statement in action. Let us try the following command to run the `AssertTest` class.

```
java -ea com.jdojo.chapter10.AssertTest
```

The above command generates the following output.

```
Exception in thread "main" java.lang.AssertionError: x = 25
        at com.jdojo.chapter10.AssertTest.main(AssertTest.java:7)
```

An exception of type `java.lang.AssertionError` was generated with "x = 25" as the error message when we ran the `AssertTest` class. This is what happens when an assertion fails in your code. Java runtime throws an `AssertionError`. Since we used the second form of the `assert` statement in our code, the error message also contains our custom assertion message, which prints the value of `x`. Note that the assertion error, by default, contains the line number and the source code file name, where the assertion fails. The above error message states that the assertion failed at line number 7 in AssertFile.java source file.

So, what is the magic behind using `-ea` switch with java command? By default, `assert` statements are not executed by Java runtime. In other words, assertion is disabled by default. You must enable the assertion when you run your class, so that your `assert` statements are executed. The `-ea` switch enables the assertion at runtime. This is the reason why we received the expected error message when we used the `-ea` switch to run the `AssertTest` class. We will discuss enabling/disabling assertion in detail in the next section.

Enabling/Disabling Assertions

The goal in using assertions is to detect programmer's logic error. Typically, assertions should be enabled in development and test environments. Assertions help programmers find the location and type of problems in code quickly. Once an application is tested, it is very unlikely that the assertions will fail. Java designers kept in mind the performance penalty that you may incur by using assertions in production environment. This is the reason why assertion is disabled at runtime by default. Although it is not desirable to enable assertion in a production environment, you have options to do so if you need to.

Java provides command-line options (or switches) to enable assertions at runtime at various levels. For example, you have options to enable assertions in all user-defined classes, all system classes, all classes in a package and its sub-packages, just for one class, etc. Table 10-1 lists all switches that you can use at command-line to enable/disable assertions at runtime.

Table 10-1: Command-line switches to enable/disable assertions at runtime

Command-line Switch	Description

`-enableassertions`
`or`
`-ea`
	It is used to enable assertions at runtime for system classes as well as user-defined classes. You can pass an argument to this switch to control the level at which assertions is enabled.

`-disableassertions`
`or`
`-da`
	It is used to disable assertions at runtime for system classes as well as user-defined classes. You can pass an argument to this switch to control the level at which assertions is disabled.

`-enablesystemassertions`
`or`
`-esa`
	It is used to enable assertions in all system classes. You cannot pass any arguments to this switch.

`-disablesystemassertions`
`or`
`-dsa`
	It is used to disable assertions in all system classes. You cannot pass any arguments to this switch.

Two switches, `-ea` and `da`, let you control enabling and disabling of assertions at various levels. You can pass an argument to these switches to control the level at which assertions should be enabled or disabled. Note that you cannot pass any arguments to `-esa` and `-dsa` switches. They enable and disable assertions in all system classes. If you pass an argument to the `-ea` or `-da` switch, the switch and the argument must be separated by a colon as shown below. Table 10-2 lists the possible arguments that can be used with these switches.

```
-ea:argument
-da:argument
```

Table 10-2: List of arguments that can be passed to –ea and –da switches

Argument for –ea and –da switches	Description
`(no argument)`	It enables or disables assertions in all user-defined classes. Note that to enable/disable assertions in all system classes you need to use –esa and –dsa switches with no argument respectively.
`packageName...`	Note the three dots after the packageName. It enables/disables

	assertions in the specified packageName and any of its sub-packages. It can also be used to enable/disable assertions in system packages.
`...`	This argument value is three dots. It enables/disables assertions in the unnamed package in the current working directory
`className`	It enables/disables assertions in the specified className. It can also be used to enable/disable assertions in system classes.

The following are examples of using assertion switches with different arguments. All examples assume that you are enabling assertions when you are running the `com.jdojo.chapter10.AssertTest` class. Examples show you only how to enable assertions. By default, all assertions are disabled.

```
// Enable assertion in all system classes
java -esa com.jdojo.chapter10.AssertTest

// Enable assertion in all user-defined classes
java -ea com.jdojo.chapter10.AssertTest

// Enable assertion in com.jdojo package and its sub-packages
java -ea:com.jdojo... com.jdojo.chapter10.AssertTest

// Enable assertions in unnamed package in the current directory
java -ea:... com.jdojo.chapter10.AssertTest

// Enable assertions in com.jdojo.chapter10.AssertTest class
java -ea:com.jdojo.chapter10.AssertTest com.jdojo.chapter10.AssertTest
```

You can use multiple `-ea` or `-da` switches in one command to achieve finer granularity in enabling/disabling assertions. All switches are processed from left to right in the order they are specified.

```
// Enable assertions in p1 package and all its sub-packages and disable
// assertion for p1.p2.MyClass
java -ea:p1... -da:p1.p2.MyClass com.jdojo.chapter10.AssertTest
```

TIP
Assertions for a class are enabled or disabled when a class is loaded. The assertion status for a class cannot be changed after it is set. There is one exception to this rule. If an `assert` statement is executed before a class has been initialized, the Java runtime executes it as if assertions are enabled. This situation arises when two classes refer to each other in their `static` initializers by calling the constructors or the methods of another class.

Using Assertions

Confusion may arise as to when to use assertion in a program. An assertion is implemented in Java by adding a new class, `java.lang.AssertionError`, in the existing exception class hierarchy. Sometimes, programmers mistake an assertion as another exception. This may be true when you just look at the class hierarchy and you may say that it is just another class in the

---

existing exception class hierarchy. However, the similarity between exceptions and assertions stops right there in the class hierarchy. The main difference lies in the reason behind their usage. An exception is used to handle a user's error and business rules implementation. If it is possible to recover from exceptional conditions, you want to recover from them and proceed with the application. An assertion is used to detect programming errors made by programmers. We do not want to recover from a programming error and proceed with the application. Assertions are used to verify - what a programmer assumes about his program at a specific point in his code is true. You should never use assertion to handle a user's error or to validate data, because assertions are not meant to be enabled in production environment.

Assertions should not be used to validate data arguments for `public` methods. The following snippet of code is for a `credit()` method of the `BankAccount` class, which uses assertion to validate the amount being credited.

```
// Incorrect implementation
public void credit(double amount) {
    assert amount > 0.0 : "Invalid credit amount:" + amount;
    // Other code goes here
}
```

The code for the `credit()` method depends on enabling assertion to validate the amount of credit to an account. However, most likely the assertion will be disabled in the production environment, which will allow a credit of even a negative number. Such validations for a `public` method's arguments should be performed using exceptions as shown below.

```
// Correct implementation
public void credit(double amount) {
    if (amount <=  0.0) {
        throw new IllegalArgumentException("Invalid credit amount:" +
                                            amount);
    }
    // Other code goes here
}
```

You can use assertions to validate a method's arguments for a non-public method. A non-public method cannot be called by clients directly. If a method's parameters for a non-public method are incorrect, it indicates programmer's errors and use of assertions is appropriate.

You should not use an assertion that has side effects, e.g., an assertion that modifies the state of an object. Consider the following snippet of code in a method of a class assuming that `reComputeState()` alters the state of the object of the class.

```
assert reComputeState();
```

When the above `assert` statement is executed, it will alter the state of the object. The subsequent interaction with the object depends on its altered state. If the assertions' are disabled, the above code would not execute and the object will not behave properly.

You can use assertions to implement class invariants. Class invariants are conditions that hold true at all times about the values that determine the state of an object of a class. Class invariants may not be true for brief moments when an object is transitioning from one state to another. Suppose we have a `BankAccount` class with four instance variables – `name`, `dob`, `startDate` and `balance`. The following class invariants must be true for an object of `BankAccount` class.

- The `name` on the account must not be `null`.
- The `dob` on the account must not be `null` and must not be a date in future.
- The `startDate` on the account must not be `null`.
- The `startDate` on the account must not be before `dob`.
- The `balance` on the account must be greater than zero.

You pack all these conditions checks in one method, say `validAccount()` method.

```
private boolean validAccount() {
    boolean valid = false;

    /* Check for class invariants here. Return true if
       it is true. Otherwise, return false.
    */
    return valid;
}
```

You can use the following assertion in methods and constructors to make sure that the class invariants are enforced. We assume that the `toString()` method of the `BankAccount` class returns enough pieces of information to help the programmer debug the error.

```
assert validAccount(); this.tostring();
```

You can use the above `assert` statement in the beginning of every method and before you return from the method. You do not need to check for class invariants inside a method if it does not modify the object's state. You should use it only at the end in a constructor because class invariants will not hold when the constructor starts executing.

Checking for Assertion Status

How do you know in your program if assertion is enabled or disabled? It is easy to check for the assertion status using an `assert` statement. Consider the following snippet of code.

```
boolean enabled = false;
assert enabled = true;
// Check the value of enabled here
```

The above code uses the first form of the `assert` statement. Note that it uses the assignment operator (=) and not the equality comparison operator (==) in the expression "enabled = true". The expression "enabled = true" will assign a value of `true` to the `enabled` variable and then it will evaluate to `true`. Note that the `enabled` variable has been initialized to `false`. If assertion is enabled, `enabled` variable will have a value of `true` after the `assert` statement is executed. If assertion is disabled, the variable `enabled` will have a value of `false`. Therefore, checking for the value of `enabled` variable after the `assert` statement will give you a clue if assertions are enabled for your class or not. Listing 10-2 shows the complete code for checking if assertions are enabled for the `AssertionStatusTest` class. Note that assertion can be enabled or disabled on a class basis too. If assertions are enabled for a specific class, it does not guarantee that it is enabled for all other classes too.

Listing 10-2: A program that checks if assertion is enabled

```java
// AssertionStatusTest.java
package com.jdojo.chapter10;

public class AssertionStatusTest {
    public static void main(String[] args)  {
        boolean enabled = false;
        assert enabled = true;
        if (enabled) {
            System.out.println("Assertion is enabled.");
        }
        else {
            System.out.println("Assertion is disabled.");
        }
    }
}
```

Chapter 11. Strings and Dates

A sequence of zero or more characters is known as a string. In Java programs, a string is represented by an object of the `java.lang.String` class. The `String` class is immutable. That is, the contents of a `String` object cannot be modified after it is created. The `String` class has two companion classes, `java.lang.StringBuffer`, and `java.lang.StringBuilder`. The `StringBuilder` class was introduced in Java 5. The companion classes are mutable. You should use them when the contents of your string can be modified.

String Literals

A string literal consists of a sequence of zero or more characters enclosed in double quotes. All string literals are objects of the `String` class. Examples of string literals are:

```
""                   // An empty string
"Hello"              // A String literal consisting of 5 characters
"Just a string literal" // A String literal consisting of 21 characters
```

A string literal may be composed of more than one string literals as:

```
"Hello" + "Hi"// Composed of two string literals "Hello" and "Hi"
              // It represents one string literal "HelloHi"
```

Note that a string literal cannot be broken into two lines. For example, `"Hello"` cannot be broken as:

```
"He
llo"      // Cannot continue "He in this line. A compiler error
```

If you want to break `"Hello"` in two lines, you must break it using the + operator (string concatenation operator) as:

```
"He" +
"llo"
```

or,

```
"He"
+ "llo"
```

Another example of a multi-line string literal is:

```
"This is a big string literal" +
" and it will continue in several lines." +

" It is also valid to insert multiple new lines as we did here" +
"Adding more than one line in between two string literals " +
```

```
"is a feature of Java Language " +
" and not of string literal"
```

Escape Sequence Characters inside String Literals

A string literal is composed of characters. It is valid to use all escape characters to form a string literal. For example, to include a line feed and a carriage return characters in a string literal you will use \n and \r as shown below.

```
"\n"       // String literal with a line feed
"\r"       // String literal with a carriage return
"\n\r"     // String literal with a line feed and a carriage return
"First line.\nSecond line."  // Embedded line feed
"Tab\tSeparated\twords"      // Embedded tab escape character
"Double quote \" is here"    // Embedded double quote in string literal
```

Unicode Escapes inside String Literals

A character can also be represented as a Unicode escape in the form \uxxxx, where an x is a hexadecimal digit (0-9, A-F). In a string literal, the character A, the first uppercase English letter, can also be written as \u0041, e.g., "Apple" and "\u0041pple" are treated the same in Java. Line feed and carriage return escape characters can also be represented in Unicode escape character as \u000A and \u000D respectively. However, you cannot use Unicode escapes to embed a line feed and a carriage return characters in string literals. In other words, you cannot replace "\n" with "\u000A" and "\r" with "\u000D" in a string literal. Why is this exception? The reason is that Unicode escapes are processed in the very beginning of the compilation process resulting in the conversion of \u000A and \u000D into a real line feed, and a carriage return respectively. This violates the rule that a string literal cannot be continued in two lines. For example, in the early stages of compilation "Hel\u000Alo" is translated into the following, which is an invalid string literal and generates a compiler error.

```
"Hel
lo"
```

TIP
It is a compiler error to use Unicode escapes, \u000A and \u000D, in a string literal to represent a line feed and a carriage return respectively. You must use the escape sequence \n and \r instead.

How to Create a String Object

The String class has many constructors, which can be used to create a string object. The default constructor lets you create a String object with an empty string as its contents. For example, the following statement creates an empty String object and assigns its reference to the emptyStr variable.

```
String emptyStr = new String();
```

The `String` class has a constructor, which takes another `String` object as an argument. For example,

```
String str1 = new String();
String str2 = new String(str1);
```

Now, `str1` represents the same sequence of characters as `str2`. At this point, both `str1` and `str2` represent an empty string. You can also pass a string literal to this constructor as:

```
String str2 = new String("");
String str3 = new String("Have fun!");
```

After these two statements are executed, `str2` will refer to a `String` object with contents as an empty string (a sequence of zero characters), and `str3` will refer to a `String` object with contents as "`Have fun!`" (a sequence of nine characters).

Length of a String

The `String` class has a `length()` method that returns the number of characters in a `String` object. Note that the `length()` method returns the number of characters in a string, not the number of bytes used by the characters in a string. The return type of the method `length()` is `int`. Listing 11-1 demonstrates how to compute the length of a string. The length of an empty string is zero.

Listing 11-1: Knowing the length of a String

```java
// StringLength.java
package com.jdojo.chapter11;

public class StringLength {
    public static void main (String[] args) {
        // Create two string objects
        String str1 = new String() ;
        String str2 = new String("Hello") ;

        // Get the length of str1 and str2
        int len1 = str1.length();
        int len2 = str2.length();

        // Display the length of str1 and str2
        System.out.println("Length of \"" + str1 + "\": " + len1);
        System.out.println("Length of \"" + str2 + "\": " + len2);
    }
}
```

```
Output

Length of "": 0
Length of "Hello": 5
```

String Literals are String Objects

All string literals are objects of the `String` class. The Java compiler replaces all string literals with a reference to a `String` object. Let us consider the following statement:

```
String str1 = "Hello";
```

When the above statement is compiled, the compiler encounters the string literal `"Hello"`, and it creates a `String` object with `"Hello"` as its content. For all practical purposes, a string literal is the same as a `String` object. Wherever we can use the reference of a `String` object, we can also use a `String` literal. All methods of the `String` class can be used with `String` literals directly. For example, to compute the length of `String` literals you can write:

```
int len1 = "".length();        // len1 is equal to 0
int len2 = "Hello".length();   // len2 is equal to 5
```

A String Object is Immutable

`String` objects are immutable. That is, you cannot modify the contents of a `String` object. This leads to a good feature that strings can be shared without worrying about them getting modified. For example, if you need two objects of the `String` class with the identical content (the same sequence of characters), you can create one `String` object and can use its reference at both places. Sometimes, the immutability property of strings in Java is misunderstood by the programmers. Let us consider the following piece of code:

```
String str;
str = new String ("Just a string");
str = new String ("Another string");
```

Here, `str` is a reference variable that can refer to any string object. Note that it is a **variable** and that is why it can be assigned a reference of any string object. In other words, `str` can be changed and it is mutable. However, the string object, which `str` refers to, is always immutable. This scenario has been depicted in Figure 11-1.

Figure 11-1: String objects and String reference variables

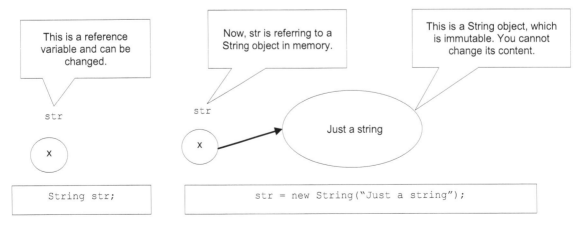

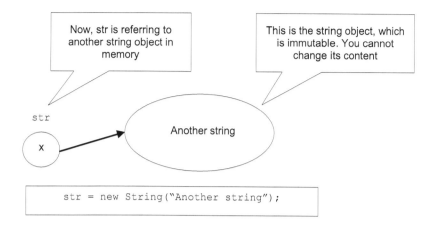

```
str = new String("Another string");
```

If you do not want str to refer to any other String object after it has been initialized, you can declare it as final as shown below.

```
final String str = new String("Now str cannot refer to other object");
str = new String("Lets  try"); // Compiler error. str is final
```

TIP

It is the String object in memory that is immutable, not the reference variable of the String type. If you want a reference variable to refer to the same String object in memory all the time, you must declare it as final.

Comparing Two Strings

You may want to compare the sequence of characters represented by two String objects. The String class overrides the equals() method of the Object class and provides its own implementation, which compares two strings for equality based on their contents. For example, you can compare two strings as:

```
String str1 = new String("Hello");
String str2 = new String("Hi");
String str3 = new String("Hello");

boolean b1, b2;

b1 = str1.equals(str2);      // false will be assigned to b1
b2 = str1.equals(str3);      // true will be assigned to b2
```

You can also compare string literals with string literals or string objects as:

```
b1 = str1.equals("Hello");   // true will be assigned to b1
b2 = "Hello".equals(str1);   // true will be assigned to b2
b1 = "Hello".equals("Hi");   // false will be assigned to b1
```

Note that the == operator always compares the references of two objects in memory. For example, str1 == str2 and str1 == str3 will return false, because str1, str2 and str3 are references of three different `String` objects in memory. Note that the `new` operator always creates a new reference in memory.

If you want to compare two strings based on the Unicode values of their characters, you can use the `compareTo()` method. Its signature is:

```
public int compareTo(String anotherString)
```

It returns an integer, which can be 0 (zero), a positive integer or a negative integer. It compares the Unicode values of the corresponding characters of two strings. If any two characters differ in their Unicode values, the method returns the difference between the Unicode values of those two characters. For example, `"a".compareTo("b")` will return `-1`. The Unicode value is 97 for `a`, and 98 for `b`. It returns the difference `97 - 98`, which is `-1`. Examples of string comparisons are:

```
"abc".compareTo("abc") will return 0
"abc".compareTo("xyz") will return -23 (value of 'a' - 'x')
"xyz".compareTo("abc") will return 23 (value of 'x' - 'a')
```

TIP

It is very important to note that the `compareTo()` method discussed here compares two strings based on the Unicode values of their characters. The comparison may not be the same as the dictionary order comparison. This is fine for English and some other languages in which the Unicode values for characters are in the same order as the dictionary order of characters. This method should not be used to compare two strings in languages where the dictionary order of characters may not be the same as their Unicode values. To perform language based string comparisons, you should use `java.text.Collator` class's `compare()` method instead. Please refer the *Locale-Insensitive String Comparison* section later in this chapter to learn how to use `java.text.Collator` class.

The program listed in Listing 11-2 demonstrates the string comparisons.

Listing 11-2: Comparing strings

```
// StringComparison.java
package com.jdojo.chapter11;

public class StringComparison {
    public static void main(String[] args) {
        String apple = new String("Apple") ;
        String orange = new String("Orange") ;

        System.out.println(apple.equals(orange));
        System.out.println(apple.equals(apple));
        System.out.println(apple == apple);
        System.out.println(apple == orange);
        System.out.println(apple.compareTo(apple));
        System.out.println(apple.compareTo(orange));
    }
}
```

Output:

Chapter 11. Strings and Dates

```
false
true
true
false
0
-14
```

The String Pool

Java maintains a pool of all string literals in order to minimize the memory usage and for better efficiency. Java creates a `String` object in the string pool for every string literal it finds in a program. When it encounters a string literal, it looks for a string object in the string pool with the identical content. If it does not find a match in the string pool, it creates a new `String` object with that content and adds it to the string pool. Finally, it replaces the string literal with the reference of the newly created `String` object in pool. If it finds a match in the string pool, it replaces the string literal with the reference of the `String` object found in the pool. Let us discuss this scenario with an example.

```
String str1 = new String("Hello");
```

When Java encounters the string literal "`Hello`" in the program, it tries to find a match in the string pool. If there is no String object with the content "`Hello`" in the string pool, a new String object with "`Hello`" content is created and added to the string pool. The string literal "`Hello`" will be replaced by the reference of that new `String` object in the string pool. Since we are using the `new` operator, Java will create another string object on the heap. Therefore, two string objects will be created in this case. Let us consider the following code.

```
String str1 = new String("Hello");
String str2 = new String("Hello");
```

How many `String` objects will be created by the above code? Suppose when the first statement is executed, "`Hello`" was not in the string pool. Therefore, the first statement will create two string objects. When the second statement is executed, the string literal "`Hello`" will be found in the string pool, and this time "`Hello`" will be replaced by the reference of the already existing object in the pool. However, Java will create a new string object, because we are using the `new` operator in the second statement. Therefore, the above two statements will create three string objects assuming that "`Hello`" was not there in the string pool. If "`Hello`" was already in the string pool when these statements started executing, only two String objects will be created. Let us consider the following statements:

```
String str1 = new String("Hello");
String str2 = new String("Hello");
String str3 = "Hello";
String str4 = "Hello";
```

What will be the value returned by `str1 == str2`? It will be `false`, because the `new` operator always creates a new object in memory and returns the reference of that object.

What will be the value returned by `str2 == str3`? It will be `false` again. This needs a little explanation. Note that the `new` operator always creates a new object. Therefore, `str2` has a reference to a new object in memory. Since "`Hello`" has already been encountered while executing the first statement, it is there in the string pool and `str3` refers to the string object with content "`Hello`" in the string pool. Therefore, `str2` and `str3` refer to two different objects and that is why `str2 == str3` returned `false`.

What will be the value returned by `str3 == str4`? It will be `true`. Note that "`Hello`" has already been in the string pool when the first statement was executed. The third statement will assign a reference of a `String` object to `str3` from the string pool. The fourth statement will assign the same object reference from the string pool to `str4`. In other words, both `str3` and `str4` are referring to the same `String` object in the string pool. Since `==` operator compares the two references, `str3 == str4` will return `true`.

Let us consider another example.

```
String s1 = "Have" + "Fun";
String s2 = "HaveFun";
```

Will `s1 == s2` return `true`? Yes, it will return `true`. When a `String` object is created in a compile-time constant expression, it is also added to the string pool. Since "`Have`" + "`Fun`" is a compile time constant expression, the resulting string "`HaveFun`" will be added to the string pool. Therefore, `s1` and `s2` will refer to the same object in the string pool.

All compile-time constant string literals are added to the string pool. Consider the following examples to clarify this rule.

```
final String constStr = "Constant"; // constStr is a constant
String varStr = "Variable";          // varStr is not a constant

// "Constant is pooled" will be added to the string pool
String s1 = constStr + " is pooled";

// Concatenated string will not be added to the string pool
String s2 = varStr + " is not pooled";
```

After executing above snippet of code, "`Constant is pooled`" `== s1` will return `true`, whereas "`Variable is not pooled`" `== s2` will return `false`.

TIP
All string literals and string literals resulting from a compile time constant expressions are added to the string pool.

You can add a `String` object to the string pool using its `intern()` method. The `intern()` method returns the reference of the object from string pool if it finds a match. Otherwise, it adds a new `String` object to the string pool and returns the reference of the new object. For example, in the previous snippet of code, `s2` refers to a `String` object, which has the content "`Variable is not pooled`". You can add this `String` object to the string pool by writing:

```
s2 = s2.intern();  // Will add the content of s2 to the string pool and
                   // return the reference of the string object from
                   // the pool
```

Now, `"Variable is not pooled" == s2` will return true, because we have already called the `intern()` method on `s2` and its content has been pooled.

TIP

The `String` class maintains a pool of strings internally. All string literals are added to the pool automatically. You can add your own strings to the pool by invoking the `intern()` method on the String objects. You cannot access the pool directly. There is no way to remove string objects from the pool.

Some Methods of String Class

This section describes some of the frequently used methods of the `String` class and their usage.

The charAt() Method

You can use the `charAt()` method If you want to get a character at a particular index from a `String` object. The index of characters in a string starts at zero as depicted in Table 11-1. Note that the index of the first character H is 0 (zero), the second character E is 1, and so on. The index of the last character O is 4, which is equal to the length of the string `Hello` minus 1.

Table 11-1: Index of a character in a String object

Index >>	0	1	2	3	4
Character >>	H	E	L	L	O

The following snippet of code will print the index value and the character at each index in string `HELLO`.

```
String str = "HELLO";

// Get the length of string
int len = str.length();

// Loop through all characters and print their indexes
for (int i = 0; i < len; i++) {
    System.out.println(str.charAt(i) + " has index " + i);
}
```

```
Output:

H has index 0
E has index 1
L has index 2
L has index 3
O has index 4
```

The equalsIgnoreCase() and equals() Methods

If you want to compare two strings ignoring their cases, you can use the `equalsIgnoreCase()` method. If you want to perform a case-sensitive comparison for equality of two strings, you need to use the `equals()` method instead.

```
String str1 = "Hello";
String str2 = "HELLO";

if (str1.equalsIgnoreCase(str2)) {
    System.out.println ("Ignoring cases str1 and str2 are equal");
}
else {
    System.out.println("Ignoring cases str1 and str2 are not equal");
}

if (str1.equals(str2)) {
    System.out.println("str1 and str2 are equal");
}
else {
    System.out.println("str1 and str2 are not equal");
}
```

```
Output:

Ignoring cases str1 and str2 are equal
str1 and str2 are not equal
```

The toLowerCase() and toUpperCase() Methods

To convert the contents of a string to lower and upper case, you can use the `toLowerCase()` and the `toUpperCase()` methods respectively. For example, `"Hello".toUpperCase()` will return a string `"HELLO"`, whereas `"Hello".toLowerCase()` will return a string `"hello"`.

Recall that `String` objects are immutable. When you use the `toLowerCase()` or `toUpperCase()` method on a `String` object, the contents of the original object is not modified. Rather, Java creates a new `String` object with the identical content as the original `String` object with the cases of the original characters changed.

The indexOf() and lastIndexOf() Methods

You can get the index of a character or a string within another string using the `indexOf()` and `lastIndexOf()` methods. For example,

```
String str = new String("Apple");

int index ;
index = str.indexOf('p');        // index will have a value of 1
index = str.indexOf("pl");       // index will have a value of 2
index = str.lastIndexOf('p');    // index will have a value of 2
index = str.lastIndexOf("pl");   // index will have a value of 2
```

```
index = str.indexOf ("k");          // index will have a value of -1
```

Note that the `indexOf()` method starts searching for the character or the string from the start of the string and returns the index of the first match, whereas the `lastIndexOf()` method matches the character or the string from the end and returns the index of the first match. If the character or string is not found in the string, these methods return −1.

The valueOf() Method

The `String` class has an overloaded `valueOf()` `static` method. You do not need a `String` object to invoke this method, because it is `static`. It can be used to get string representation of the values of any primitive data type or any object. For example,

`String.valueOf ('C')` will return "C" as a string
`String.valueOf ("10")` will return "10" as a string
`String.valueOf (true)` will return "true" as a string

The substring() Method

You can use the `substring()` method to get a sub-part of a string. This method is overloaded. One version takes the start index as the parameter and returns a substring beginning at the start index to the end of string. Another version takes the start index and the end index as parameters. It returns the substring beginning at the start index and one less than the end index. For example,

```
"Hello".substring(1) will return "ello"
"Hello".substring(1,4) will return "ell"
```

The trim() Method

You can use the `trim()` method to remove all leading and trailing whitespaces and control characters from a string. In fact, the `trim()` method removes all leading and trailing characters from the string, which have Unicode value less than `\u0020` (decimal 32). For example,

- `"   hello   ".trim()` will return "hello"
- `"hello     ".trim()` will return "hello"
- `"\n   \r \t   hello\n\n\n\r\r"` will return "hello"

Note that the `trim()` method removes only leading and trailing whitespaces. It does not remove any whitespace or control characters if they appear in the middle of the string. For example,

- `"  he\nllo   ".trim()` will return "he\nllo" because \n is inside the string
- `"h ello".trim()` will return "h ello" because the space is inside the string

The replace() Method

The `replace()` method takes an old character and a new character as arguments. It returns a new string object reference by replacing all occurrences of the old character by the new character. For example,

```
String oldStr = new String("tooth");

// o in oldStr will be replaced by e. newStr will contain "teeth"
String newStr = oldStr.replace('o', 'e');
```

The startsWith() and endsWith() Methods

These two methods take a string argument. The `startsWith()` checks if the string starts with the specified argument, whereas the `endsWith()` checks if the string ends with the specified string argument. Both methods return a `boolean` value. For example,

```
String str = "This is a Java program";

// Test str, if it starts with "This"
if (str.startsWith("This")) {
    System.out.println("String starts with This");
}
else {
    System.out.println("String does not start with This");
}

// Test str, if it ends with "program"
if (str.endsWith("program")) {
    System.out.println("String ends with program");
}
else {
    System.out.println("String does not end with program");
}
```

```
Output:

String starts with This
String ends with program
```

Strings in a switch Statement

Java 7 added support for strings in a `switch` statement. The switch-expression uses a `String` type. If the switch-expression is `null`, a `NullPointerException` is thrown. The `case` labels must be `String` literals. You cannot use `String` variables in the `case` labels. The following is an example of using a `String` in a `switch` statement, which will print "Turn on" on the standard output.

```
String status = "on";
switch(status) {
```

```
        case "on":
            System.out.println("Turn on"); // Will execute this
            break;
        case "off":
            System.out.println("Turn off");
            break;
        default:
            System.out.println("Unknown command");
            break;
}
```

The `switch` statement for strings compares the switch-expression with `case` labels as if the `equals()` method of the `String` class has been invoked. In the above example, `status.equals("on")` will be invoked to test if the first `case` block should be executed. Note that the `equals()` method of the `String` class performs case-sensitive string comparison. It means that the `switch` statement that uses strings is case-sensitive. The following `switch` statement will print "`Unknown command`" on the standard output, because the switch-expression "ON" in uppercase will not match the first `case` label "on" in lowercase.

```
String status = "ON";
switch(status) {
    case "on":
        System.out.println("Turn on");
        break;
    case "off":
        System.out.println("Turn off");
        break;
    default:
        System.out.println("Unknown command"); // Will execute this
        break;
}
```

As a good programming practice, you need to do the following two things before executing a `switch` statement with strings.

- Check if the switch-expression for the `switch` statement is `null`. If it is `null`, do not execute the `switch` statement,
- If you want to perform case-insensitive comparison in a `switch` statement, you need to convert the switch-expression to lowercase or uppercase and use lowercase or uppercase in `case` labels accordingly.

We can rewrite the above `switch` statement example as Listing 11-3, which takes care of the above two suggestions.

Listing 11-3: Using strings in a switch statement

```
// StringInSwitch.java
package com.jdojo.chapter11;

public class StringInSwitch {
    public static void main(String[] args) {
        operate("on");
        operate("off");
        operate("ON");
```

```
        operate("Nothing");
        operate("OFF");
        operate(null);
    }

    public static void operate(String status) {
        // Check for null
        if (status == null) {
            System.out.println("status cannot be null.");
            return;
        }

        // Convert to lowercase
        status = status.toLowerCase();

        switch (status) {
            case "on":
                System.out.println("Turn on");
                break;
            case "off":
                System.out.println("Turn off");
                break;
            default:
                System.out.println("Unknown command");
                break;
        }
    }
}
```

```
Output:

Turn on
Turn off
Turn on
Unknown command
Turn off
status cannot be null.
```

An Example – Testing a String for a Palindrome

A palindrome is a word, a verse, a sentence, or a number that reads the same when it is read in forward or backward direction. For example, "Able was I ere I saw Elba" and 1991 are palindromes. Let us write a method that will accept a string as an argument and test if that string is a palindrome. The method will return `true` if the string is a palindrome. Otherwise, it will return `false`. We will use some methods of the `String` class that we learned in the previous section. The following is the description of the steps to be performed inside the method.

- Let us say the number of characters in the input string is n.
- We need to compare the 1st character with the nth character, the 2nd character with the $(n-1)^{th}$ character, the 3rd character with the $(n-2)^{th}$ character, and so on. Note that if we continue the comparison, we will compare nth character with 1st one at the end. However, we have already compared these two characters at the beginning. We need to compare the

characters only half way through. If all comparisons for equality returned `true`, the string is a palindrome. Wait a minute. We did not consider the cases where the number of characters in a string could be odd or even. The middle of a string varies depending on whether the length of string is an odd number or even. For example, the middle of the string `"FIRST"` is the character `R`. What is the middle character in the string `"SECOND"`? You can say there is no middle character in the string `"second"`. For our purpose, it is interesting to note that if the number of characters in string is odd, we do not need to compare the middle character with another character.

We need to continue the character comparison up to the half of the string length if the number of characters in the string is even, and up to half of the string *length minus one* if the number of characters is odd. You can get the numbers of comparisons to be done in both the cases by dividing the length of string by 2. Note that the length of a string is an integer and if you divide an integer by 2, integer division will discard the fraction part, if any, which will take care of cases with an odd number of characters. Listing 11-4 has the complete code.

Listing 11-4: Testing a string for a palindrome

```java
//Palindrome.java
package com.jdojo.chapter11;

public class Palindrome {
    public static void main(String[] args) {
        String str1 = "hello";
        boolean b1 = Palindrome.isPalindrome(str1);
        System.out.println(str1 + " is palindrome: " + b1 );

        String str2 = "noon";
        boolean b2 = Palindrome.isPalindrome(str2);
        System.out.println(str2 + " is palindrome: " + b2 );
    }

    public static boolean isPalindrome(String inputString) {
        // Check for null argument.
        if (inputString == null) {
            throw new IllegalArgumentException();
        }

        // Get the length of string
        int len = inputString.length();

        // In case of empty string and one character strings,
        // we do not need to do any comparisions.
        // They are always palindrome
        if (len == 0 || len == 1) {
            return true;
        }

        // Convert the string into uppercase so that we can make
        // the comparisons case insensitive
        String newStr = inputString.toUpperCase();

        // Initialize the result variable to true
        boolean result = true;

        /* Do the real job now */
```

```
            // Get the number of comparison to be done
            int counter = len / 2;

            // Do the comparison
            for (int i = 0; i < counter; i++) {
                if (newStr.charAt(i) != newStr.charAt(len - 1 - i)) {
                    // It is not a palindrome
                    result = false;

                    // Exit the loop
                    break;
                }
            }

            return result;
        }
    }
```

```
Output:

hello is palindrome: false
noon is  palindrome: true
```

The StringBuffer Class

The `java.lang.StringBuffer` is a companion class of the `String` class. It is used to represent and manipulate a sequence of characters. Unlike the `String` class, the `StringBuffer` class is mutable. That is, you can change the contents of a `StringBuffer` object. You can use objects of the `StringBuffer` class, instead of the `String` class, in situations where contents of a string change frequently. Recall that because of the immutability of the `String` class, string manipulations using a `String` object result in many new `String` objects, which in turn degrade the performance. A `StringBuffer` object can be thought of as a modifiable string. It has many methods to modify its contents. There are three constructors for the `StringBuffer` class. The default constructor creates an empty `StringBuffer` object. Another constructor takes a string object as an argument. It creates a `StringBuffer` object, whose content is the same as the specified string argument. The third constructor takes an `int` value as argument. It creates an empty `StringBuffer` object whose initial capacity is the same as the specified argument. Below are some examples of creating `StringBuffer` objects.

```
// Create an empty StringBuffer with a default initial capacity of 16
// characters
StringBuffer sb1 = new StringBuffer();

// Create a StringBuffer from of a string
StringBuffer sb1 = new StringBuffer("Here is the content");

// Create an empty StringBuffer with 200 characters as the initial
// capacity
StringBuffer sb1 = new StringBuffer(200);
```

The StringBuffer class is thread-safe. Java 5 added a java.lang.StringBuilder as a replacement for the StringBuffer class. The StringBuilder class is not thread-safe. The use of the StringBuilder class is recommended over the StringBuffer class for better performance, when thread-safety is not needed. The StringBuilder class has the same set of methods as the StringBuffer class.

The append() method lets you add text to the end of the StringBuffer. It is overloaded. It takes many types of arguments. Please refer to the Java API documentation for the complete list of all overloaded append() methods. It has other methods, e.g., insert() and delete(), that let you modify its contents.

The StringBuffer class has two properties - *length* and *capacity*. At a given point in time, their values may not be the same. Its length refers to the length of its contents, whereas its capacity refers to the maximum number of characters it can hold without going for new memory allocation. Its length can be, at most, equal to its capacity. The length() and capacity() methods return its length and capacity respectively. For example,

```
StringBuffer sb = new StringBuffer(200);   // Capacity:200, length:0
sb.append("Hello");                         // Capacity:200, length:5
int len = sb.length();                      // len is assigned 5
int capacity = sb.capacity();               // capacity is assigned 200
```

Capacity of a StringBuffer is controlled by the runtime, whereas its length is controlled by the contents you place in it. Runtime adjusts the capacity as you modify its contents.

You can get the contents of a StringBuffer as a String ay using its toString() method as:

```
// Create a String object
String s1 = new String("Hello");

// Create a StringBuffer out of a String object
StringBuffer sb = new StringBuffer(s1);

// Append " Java" to the StringBuffer's content
sb.append(" Java");     // Now sb contains "Hello Java"

// Convert StringBuffer back to a String object
String s2 = sb.toString();   // s2 contains "Hello Java"
```

Unlike String, StringBuffer has a setLength() method, which takes its new length as an argument. If the new length is greater than the old length, the extra positions are filled with null characters (a null character is '\u0000'). If the new length is less than the old length, its content is truncated to fit in the new length. For example,

```
StringBuffer sb = new StringBuffer("Hello");     // Length is 5
sb.setLength(7);    // Now length is 7 with last two characters
                    // as null characters '\u0000'
sb.setLength(2);    // Now length is 2 and the content is "He"
```

The `StringBuffer` class has a `reverse()` method, which replaces its contents with the same sequence of characters, but in reverse order. Listing 11-5 illustrates the use of some of the methods of the `StringBuffer` class.

Listing 11-5: Using a StringBuffer object

```java
// StringBufferTest.java
package com.jdojo.chapter11;

public class StringBufferTest {
    public static void main(String[] args) {
        // Create an empty StringNuffer
        StringBuffer sb = new StringBuffer();
        printDetails(sb);

        // Append "blessings"
        sb.append("blessings");
        printDetails(sb);

        // Insert "Good " in the beginning
        sb.insert(0, "Good ");
        printDetails(sb);

        // Delete the first o
        sb.deleteCharAt(1);
        printDetails(sb);

        // Append " be with you"
        sb.append(" be with you");
        printDetails(sb);

        // Set the length to 3
        sb.setLength(3);
        printDetails(sb);

        // Reverse the content
        sb.reverse();
        printDetails(sb);
    }

    public static void printDetails(StringBuffer sb) {
        System.out.println("Content: \"" + sb + "\"");
        System.out.println("Length: " + sb.length());
        System.out.println("Capacity: " + sb.capacity());

        // Print an empty line to separate results
        System.out.println();
    }
}
```

```
Output:

Content: ""
Length: 0
Capacity: 16
```

```
Content: "blessings"
Length: 9
Capacity: 16

Content: "Good blessings"
Length: 14
Capacity: 16

Content: "God blessings"
Length: 13
Capacity: 16

Content: "God blessings be with you"
Length: 25
Capacity: 34

Content: "God"
Length: 3
Capacity: 34

Content: "doG"
Length: 3
Capacity: 34
```

String Concatenation Operator (+)

We often use the + operator to concatenate a string, a primitive type value or an object to another string. For example,

```
String str = "X" + "Y" + 12.56;
```

If concatenation were performed by creating intermediate string objects, the concatenation operation would create a big overhead. To optimize the string concatenation operation, Java compiler replaces the string concatenation by a statement, which uses a `StringBuffer`. Because a `StringBuffer` object is modifiable, only one `StringBuffer` object needs to be created. The compiler replaces the above statement by:

```
String str =
  new StringBuffer().append("X").append("Y").append(12.56).toString();
```

Note the use of the `toString()` method at the end of the above statement. It is used to convert the final content of a `StringBuffer` object to a string object. It is also important to note that such cascaded method calls is possible, because the `append()` method of `StringBuffer` returns a reference to itself.

Locale-Insensitive String Comparison

The `String` class compares strings based on the Unicode values of their characters. Sometimes, you may want to compare strings based on the dictionary order of their characters, rather than the order of the Unicode values of their characters. You should use the `java.text.Collator` class's `compare()` method to perform language-sensitive string comparisons. The `compare()` method takes two strings to be compared as arguments. It returns 0 if two strings are the same; 1 if the first string comes after the second string; and –1 if the first string comes before the second string. Listing 11-6 illustrates the use of the `Collator` class. The program also shows the comparison of the same two strings using the `String` class. Note that the word "cat" comes before the word "Dog" in the dictionary order. The `Collator` class uses their dictionary orders to compare them. However, the `String` class compares the Unicode value of the first character of "cat", which is 99, and the Unicode value of the first character of "Dog", which is 68. Based on these two values, 99 and 68, the `String` class determines that "Dog" comes before "cat". The output of the program confirms the two different ways of comparing strings.

Listing 11-6: Language-sensitive string comparisons

```java
// CollatorStringComparison.java
package com.jdojo.chapter11;

import java.text.Collator;
import java.util.Locale;

public class CollatorStringComparison {
    public static void main(String[] args) {
        // Create a Locale object for Spanish
        Locale spanishLocale = new Locale("es", "ES");

        // Get collator instance for Spanish
        Collator c = Collator.getInstance(spanishLocale);
        String str1  = "cat";
        String str2 = "Dog";

        int diff = c.compare(str1, str2);

        System.out.println("Comparing using Collator class:");
        print(diff, str1, str2);

        System.out.println("\nComparing using String class:");
        diff = str1.compareTo(str2);
        print(diff, str1, str2);
    }

    public static void print(int diff, String str1, String str2) {
        if (diff > 0) {
            System.out.println(str1 + " comes after " + str2);
        }
        else if (diff < 0) {
            System.out.println(str1 + " comes before " + str2);
        }
        else {
            System.out.println(str1 + " and "
                            + str2 + " are considered the same."  );
        }
    }
}
```

```
Output:
```

```
Comparing using Collator class:
cat comes before Dog

Comparing using String class:
cat comes after Dog
```

Working with Dates and Times

We will discuss three classes that deal with dates and times. They are:

- `java.util.Date`
- `java.util.Calendar`
- `java.util.GregorianCalendar`

An object of the `Date` class represents a specific instant in time. The precision of all times represented by a `Date` object is millisecond. Most of the constructors and methods of the `Date` class have been deprecated as of JDK1.1. It is recommended to use the `Calendar` and `GregorianCalendar` classes to work with dates instead of the `Date` class. Time is always included in a `Date` object. We will use the word "date" to refer to "date and time" in this section.

You may be surprised to find that a date is represented as an integer. In Java programs, date is represented as an integer, which is the number of milliseconds elapsed since midnight January 1, 1970 UTC. UTC is an acronym for Coordinated Universal Time. UT (Universal Time) is scientific name for GMT (Greenwich Mean Time). UT is based on astronomical observations, whereas UTC is based on atomic clock.

The default constructor of the `Date` class is used to create a `Date` object with the current system date and time. Note that the `Date` object thus created represents the current date and time, when it is created and not when it is used. For example, you may create a `Date` object in your program (say, at 9 AM) and use it an hour later (i.e. 10 AM). In this case, the `Date` object will represent the time 9 AM whenever it is used and not 10 AM. Listing 11-7 illustrates the use of the `Date` class. You can also get the current date and time as an integer using the `currentTimeMillis()` static method of the `java.lang.System` class.

Listing 11-7: Using the Date class

```java
// CurrentDate.java
package com.jdojo.chapter11;

import java.util.Date;

public class CurrentDate {
    public static void main (String[] args) {
        // Create a new date object
        Date currentDate = new Date();

        // Print current date
        System.out.println("Current date: " + currentDate);

        // Get the number value of current date
        long milliseconds = currentDate.getTime();
```

```
                    // Print the long value of current date
            System.out.println("Current date in milliseconds: " +
                                milliseconds);

            System.out.println("Current time using System class:" +
            System.currentTimeMillis() ) ;
        }
    }
```

```
Output:

Current date: Wed Mar 26 10:59:30 CST 2003
Current date in milliseconds: 1048697970718
Current time using System class: 1048697970796
```

Note that your output will be different when you run this program. It will print the current date on your system, when the program is executed. Also note that the times in milliseconds differ by a small amount, because of the difference in time when the `Date` object is created in program and the call to the `currentTimeMillis()` method of the `System` class is made.

The `Calendar` class is an `abstract` class. An `abstract` class cannot be instantiated. We will discuss `abstract` class in the chapter on *Inheritance.* The `GregorianCalendar` class is a concrete class, which inherits the `Calendar` class. The `Calendar` class declares some `final` `static` fields to represent date fields. For example, `Calendar.JANUARY` can be used to indicate the January month field in a date. The `GregorianCalendar` class has a default constructor, which create an object to represent the current date. You can also create a `GregorianCalendar` object to represent a specific date using its other constructors. You can also get the current date in a particular time zone. For example,

```
// Get the current date in the default time zone for your machine
GregorianCalendar currentDate = new GregorianCalendar();

// Get GregorianCalendar object representing March 26, 2003 6:30:45 AM
// Note the use of Calendar.MARCH to represent month March
GregorianCalendar someDate =
            new GregorianCalendar(2003, Calendar.MARCH, 26, 6, 30, 45 );

// Get Indian time zone, which is GMT+05:30
TimeZone indianTZ = TimeZone.getTimeZone("GMT+05:30");

// Get current date in India
GregorianCalendar indianDate = new GregorianCalendar(indianTZ);

// Get Moscow time zone, which is GMT+03:00
TimeZone moscowTZ = TimeZone.getTimeZone("GMT+03:00");

// Get current date in Moscow
GregorianCalendar moscowDate = new GregorianCalendar(moscowTZ);
```

TIP

A `Date` object contains only date and time. However, a `GregorianCalendar` object contains date, time, and a time zone.

The month part of a date ranges from 0 to 11. That is, January is 0, February is 1, and so on. It is easier to use the constants declared for months and the other date fields in the `Calendar` class rather than using their integer values. For example, you should use `Calendar.JANUARY` constant to represent the January month in your program, rather than using the integer value 0. You can get the value of a field in a date using the `get()` method passing the field as an argument.

```
// Create a GregorianCalendar object
GregorianCalendar gc = new GregorianCalendar();

// year will contain the current year value
int year = gc.get(Calendar.YEAR);

// month will contain the current month value
int month = gc.get(Calendar.MONTH);

// day will contain day of month of the current date
int day = gc.get(Calendar.DAY_OF_MONTH);

// hour will contain hour value
int hour = gc.get(Calendar.HOUR);

// minute will contain minute value
int minute = gc.get(Calendar.MINUTE);

// second will contain second values
int second = gc.get(Calendar.SECOND);
```

You can set the date interpretation to be lenient or not lenient by using the `setLenient()` method of the `GregorianCalendar` class. By default, it is lenient. If the date interpretation is lenient, a date such as "`March 35, 2003`" will be interpreted as "`April 5, 2003`". If date interpretation is not lenient, such a date will result in an error. You can also compare two dates, whether one date occurs before or after another, by using `before()` and `after()` methods. There are two methods, `add()` and `roll()`, which need special attention.

The add() method

It is used to add an amount to a particular field in a date. The amount being added may be negative or positive. Suppose, we have a date "December 1, 2003" stored in a `GregorianCalendar` object. We want to add 5 to the month field. Month field in date has a range of 0 to 11, January being 0 and December 11. If we add 5 to our date, month's field value will be 16, which is out of range. In such a case, the larger date field (here, year is larger than month) will be adjusted to accommodate the overflow. The date after adding 5 to the month field will be "May 1, 2004". The following snippet of code illustrates this.

```
// Create date object
GregorianCalendar gc =
            new GregorianCalendar(2003, Calendar.DECEMBER, 1);

// Add 5 to month field
gc.add(Calendar.MONTH, 5);   // Now gc represents "May 1, 2004"
```

This method may result in adjusting smaller fields too. Suppose, we have a date "`January 30, 2003`" stored in a `GregorianCalendar` object. We add 1 to the month field. The new month field does not overflow. However, the resulting date "February 30, 2003" is not a valid date. The day of month must be between 1 and 28 in the month of February 2003. Therefore, the day of month field is automatically adjusted and it is set to the nearest possible valid value, which is 28. The resulting date will be "February 28, 2003".

The roll() method

It works the same as the add() method, except it does not change the larger field when the field being changed overflows. It may adjust the smaller fields to make the date a valid date. It is an overloaded method. The signatures of its two versions are:

```
roll(int field, int amount)
roll(int field, boolean up)
```

The second version rolls up/down the specified field by a single unit of time, whereas the first version rolls the specified field by the specified amount. Therefore, gc.roll(Calendar.MONTH, 1) is the same as gc.roll(Calendar.MONTH, true) and gc.roll(Calendar.MONTH, -1) is the same as gc.roll(Calendar.MONTH, false). Listing 11-8 illustrates the use of some of the methods of the GregorianCalendar class.

Listing 11-8: Using the GregorianCalendar class

```
// GregorianDate .java
package com.jdojo.chapter11;

import java.util.Calendar;
import java.util.Date;
import java.util.GregorianCalendar;

public class GregorianDate {
    public static void main(String[] args) {
        GregorianCalendar gc = new GregorianCalendar();

        System.out.println("Current Date: " + getStr(gc));

        // Add 1 year
        gc.add(Calendar.YEAR, 1);
        System.out.println("After adding a year: " + getStr(gc));

        // Add 15 days
        gc.add(Calendar.DATE, 15);
        System.out.println("After adding 15 days: " + getStr(gc));

        long millis = gc.getTimeInMillis();
        Date dt = gc.getTime();
        System.out.println("Time in millis: " + millis);
        System.out.println("Time as Date: " + dt);
    }

    public static String getStr(GregorianCalendar gc) {
        int day = gc.get(Calendar.DAY_OF_MONTH);
        int month = gc.get(Calendar.MONTH);
        int year = gc.get(Calendar.YEAR);
        int hour = gc.get(Calendar.HOUR);
```

```
            int minute = gc.get(Calendar.MINUTE);
            int second = gc.get(Calendar.SECOND);

            String str = day + "/" + (month + 1) + "/" + year + " " +
                         hour + ":" + minute + ":" + second;
            return str;
        }
    }
```

Chapter 12. Formatting Objects

Java provides a rich set of formatter API that lets you format objects and values of different types in various formats. In this chapter, we will discuss how to format dates, numbers, strings and other types of objects. At the end, we will discuss the printf-style formatting in detail that was introduced in Java 5.

Formatting Dates

In this section, we will discuss how to format dates. We will also discuss how to parse a string to create a date object. You can format dates in predefined formats or formats of your choice. There are two classes to format dates:

- `java.text.DateFormat`
- `java.text.SimpleDateFormat`

If you want to format dates using a predefined format, you can use the `DateFormat` class. It is an abstract class. You cannot create an instance of this class using the `new` operator. You can call one of its `getXXXInstance()` methods, where `XXX` can be replaced by `Date`, `DateTime`, or `Time`, to get the formatter object. The actual formatted text depends on two things: style and locale. The style of formatting determines how much date information is included in the formatted text, whereas the locale determines how all pieces of information are assembled. The `DateFormat` class defines five styles and it has five constants to represent those styles. The five style constants are:

- `DateFormat.DEFAULT`
- `DateFormat.SHORT`
- `DateFormat.MEDIUM`
- `DateFormat.LONG`
- `DateFormat.FULL`

The `DEFAULT` format is the same as `MEDIUM`. Table 12-1 shows the same date formatted in different styles for locale as United States.

Table 12-1: Predefined date format styles and formatted text for locale as United States

Style	Formatted Date
DEFAULT	Mar 27, 2003
SHORT	3/27/03
MEDIUM	Mar 27, 2003
LONG	March 27, 2003
FULL	Thursday, March 27, 2003

The program listed in Listing 12-1 displays dates in short and medium formats for locales as default (which is US for JVM running this example), FRANCE and GERMANY. The program prints the current date. It will print different date, when you run this program. However, the format will be the same.

Listing 12-1: Using the predefined date formats

```java
// PredefinedDateFormats.java
package com.jdojo.chapter12;

import java.util.Date;
import java.util.Locale;
import java.text.DateFormat;

public class PredefinedDateFormats {
    public static void main(String[] args) {
        // Get current date
        Date today = new Date();

        // Print date in default locale format
        Locale defaultLocale = Locale.getDefault();

        System.out.println ("Default locale...");
        printLocaleDetails(defaultLocale);
        printDate(defaultLocale, today);

        // Print date in French format
        System.out.println ("French locale...");
        printLocaleDetails(Locale.FRANCE);
        printDate(Locale.FRANCE, today);

        // Print date in German format. We could also use
        // Locale.GERMANY instead of new Locale ("de", "DE")
        System.out.println ("German locale...");
        Locale germanLocale = new Locale ("de", "DE");
        printLocaleDetails(germanLocalc);
        printDate(germanLocale, today);
    }

    public static void printLocaleDetails (Locale locale){
        // Get the language code for the locale
        String languageCode = locale.getLanguage();

        // Get language display name
        String languageName = locale.getDisplayLanguage();

        // Get country code
        String countryCode = locale.getCountry();

        // Get country display name
        String countryName = locale.getDisplayCountry();

        // Print the locale info
        System.out.println("Language: " + languageName +
                           "(" + languageCode + "); " +
                           "Country: " + countryName +
                           "(" + countryCode + ")"   );
```

```
        }

    public static void printDate (Locale locale, Date date){
        DateFormat formatter;
        String formattedDate;

        // Get the date instance for SHORT style for locale
        formatter = DateFormat.getDateInstance(DateFormat.SHORT,
                                            locale);

        // Format the date
        formattedDate = formatter.format(date);

        // Print formatted date with country and language names
        System.out.println("SHORT: " + formattedDate);

        // Get the date instance for MEDIUM style for locale
        formatter = DateFormat.getDateInstance(DateFormat.MEDIUM,
                                            locale);

        // Format the date
        formattedDate = formatter.format(date);

        // Print formatted date with country and language names
        System.out.println("MEDIUM: " + formattedDate);

        // Print a blank line at the end
        System.out.println();
    }
}
```

```
Output:

Default locale...
Language: English(en); Country: United States(US)
SHORT: 3/27/03
MEDIUM: Mar 27, 2003

French locale...
Language: French(fr); Country: France(FR)
SHORT: 27/03/03
MEDIUM: 27 mars 03

German locale...
Language: German(de); Country: Germany(DE)
SHORT: 27.03.03
MEDIUM: 27.03.2003
```

Note that the `java.util.Locale` class has some predefined locales declared as constants. For example, you can use `Locale.FRANCE` for locale with language as "fr" and country code as "FR". Alternatively, you can create a locale object for France as:

```
Locale frenchLocale = new Locale("fr", "FR") ;
```

You need to create a `Locale` object as shown above, by supplying a two-letter lowercase language code and a two-letter uppercase country code. The `Locale` class does not declare a constant for that country. Language codes and country codes have been listed in `ISO-639 code` and `ISO-3166 code`. Some more examples of creating locales are:

```
Locale hindiIndiaLocale = new Locale("hi", "IN");
Locale bengaliIndiaLocale = new Locale("bn", "IN");
Locale thaiThailandLocale = new Locale("th", "TH");
```

To get the default locale that your JVM uses, you can use the `getDefault() static` method of the `Locale` class.

You need to use the `SimpleDateFormat` class, if you want to supply your own date formats. The `SimpleDateFormat` is also locale sensitive. Its default constructor creates a formatter with a default locale and a default date format for that locale. You can also create a formatter using other constructors where you can specify your own date format and locale. Once you have an object of the `SimpleDateFormat` class, you can call its `format()` method to format the date. If you want to change the date format for subsequent formatting, you can use the `applyPattern()` method by passing the new date format (or pattern) as an argument. For example,

```
// Create a formatter with a pattern dd/MM/yyyy. Note that uppercase
// M is used for month of year. Lowercase d denotes day in month,
// whereas uppercase D denotes day in year
SimpleDateFormat simpleFormatter = new SimpleDateFormat("dd/MM/yyyy");

// Get current date
Date today = new Date();

// Format the current date
String formattedDate = simpleFormatter.format(today);

// Print the date
System.out.println("Today is (dd/MM/yyyy): " + formattedDate);

// Change the date format. Now month will be spelled fully
// Note comma will appear as a comma and has no special interpretation
simpleFormatter.applyPattern("MMMM dd, yyyy");

// Format the current date
formattedDate = simpleFormatter.format(today);

// Print the date
System.out.println("Today is (MMMM dd, yyyy): " + formattedDate);
```

```
Output:

Today is (dd/MM/yyyy): 27/03/2003
Today is (MMMM dd, yyyy): March 27, 2003
```

Note that the output will be different when you run this code on your computer. It will print the current date in this format when you run this program provided your locale is US.

Letters that are used to create the pattern to format a date and time have been listed with their meaning in Table 12-2.

Table 12-2: List of formatting symbols for formatting date and time

Letter	Date or Time Component	Presentation	Examples
G	Era designator	Text	`AD`
Y	Year	Year	`1996; 96`
M	Month in year	Month	`July; Jul; 07`
w	Week in year	Number	`27`
W	Week in month	Number	`2`
D	Day in year	Number	`189`
d	Day in month	Number	`10`
F	Day of week in month	Number	`2`
E	Day in week	Text	`Tuesday; Tue`
a	Am/pm marker	Text	`PM`
H	Hour in day (0-23)	Number	`0`
k	Hour in day (1-24)	Number	`24`
K	Hour in am/pm (0-11)	Number	`0`
h	Hour in am/pm (1-12)	Number	`12`
m	Minute in hour	Number	`30`
s	Second in minute	Number	`55`
S	Millisecond	Number	`978`
z	Time zone	General time zone	`Pacific Standard Time; PST; GMT-08:00`
Z	Time zone	RFC 822 time zone	`-0800`

You can also embed literals inside formatted dates. Suppose you have your birth date (September 19, 1969) stored in a date object and now you want to print it as- "I was born on the Day **19** of the month **September** in **1969**". Some of the words in the message have been shown in boldface to indicate that they are coming from the date object. Others are literals and are intended to appear in the message as they are. You cannot use any alphabets a-z and A-Z as literals inside a date pattern. You need to place them inside single quotes so that they will be treated literally. First, we need a `Date` object to represent September 19, 1969. The `Date` class' constructor, which takes year, month and day, has been deprecated. We will start with the `GregorianCalendar` class and use its `getTime()` method to get a `Date` object. The following snippet of code prints this message.

```
// Create a GregorianCalendar object with September 19, 1969 as date
GregorianCalendar gc = new GregorianCalendar(1969,
Calendar.SEPTEMBER,19);

// Get date object
Date birthDate = gc.getTime();

// Create the pattern. You must place literals inside single quotes
String pattern = "'I was born on the Day' dd 'of the month' MMMM 'in '"
            + "yyyy";
```

```
// Create simple date format
SimpleDateFormat simpleFormatter = new SimpleDateFormat(pattern);

// Print the date
System.out.println(simpleFormatter.format(birthDate));
```

```
Output:

I was born on the Day 19 of the month September in 1969
```

So far, we have converted date objects into formatted text. Let us look at converting text into `Date` objects. This is accomplished by using the `parse()` method of the `SimpleDateFormat` class. The signature of the `parse()` method is:

```
public Date parse(String text, ParsePosition startPos)
```

The `parse()` method takes two arguments. The first argument is the text from which you want to extract the date. The second one is the starting position of the character in the text from where you want to start parsing. The text can have date part embedded in it. For example, you can extract two dates embedded in text – "`First date is 01/01/1995 and second one is 12/12/2001`". Since the parser does not know where the date begins in the string, you need to tell it using the `ParsePosition` object. It simply keeps track of the parsing position. There is only one constructor for the `ParsePosition` class and it takes an integer (position where parsing starts). After the `parse()` method is successful, the index for the `ParsePosition` object is set to index of the last character of the date text used plus one. Note that the `parse()` method does not use all the text passed as its first argument. It uses only the text as necessary to create a date object. Let us start with a simple example. Suppose we have a string "09/19/1969", which has a date September 19, 1969. We want to get a date object out of this string. The following snippet of code illustrates this.

```
// Our text to be parsed
String text = "09/19/1969";

// Create a pattern for our date text "09/19/1969"
String pattern = "MM/dd/yyyy";

// Create a simple date format object to represent this pattern
SimpleDateFormat simpleFormatter = new SimpleDateFormat(pattern);

// Since the date part in text "09/19/1969" start at index zero we
// create a ParsePosition object with value zero
ParsePosition startPos = new ParsePosition(0);

// Parse the text
Date parsedDate = simpleFormatter.parse(text, startPos);

// Here, parsedDate will have September 19, 1969 as date and
// startPos current index will be set to 10, which you can get
// calling startPos.getIndex() method
```

Let us parse text that is a little more complex. If the text in the previous example were "09/19/1969 Junk", we would have gotten the same result, because after reading 1969, the parser will not look at any more characters in the text. Suppose we have a text

"XX01/01/1999XX12/31/2000XX". There are two dates embedded in the text. How would you parse these two dates? Note that the first date text starts at index 2 (the first two Xs have indices 0 and 1). Once parsing is done for the first date text, the ParsePosition object used in parsing will point to the third X in the text. We just need to increment its index by two, so that it point to the first character of the second date text. The following snippet of code illustrates this.

```
// Our text to be parsed
String text = "XX01/01/1999XX12/31/2000XX";

// Create a pattern for our date text "09/19/1969"
String pattern = "MM/dd/yyyy";

// Create a simple date format object to represent this pattern
SimpleDateFormat simpleFormatter = new SimpleDateFormat(pattern);

// Set the start index at 2
ParsePosition startPos = new ParsePosition(2);

// Parse the text to get the first date (January 1, 1999)
Date firstDate = simpleFormatter.parse(text, startPos);

// Now startPos has its index set after the last character of the
// first date parsed. To set its index to the next date increment its
// index by 2
int currentIndex = startPos.getIndex();
int nextIndex = currentIndex + 2;
startPos.setIndex(nextIndex);

// Parse the text to get the second date (December 31, 2000)
Date secondDate = simpleFormatter.parse(text, startPos);
```

It is left to the readers, as an exercise, to write a program that will extract the date in a date object from the text - "I was born on the Day 19 of the month September in 1969". The date extracted should be September 19, 1969. (Hint: we already have the pattern for this text in one of the previous examples, when we worked on formatting date objects).

We will have one more example of parsing text, which contains date and time. Suppose we have a text "2003-04-03 09:10:40.325", which represents a timestamp in the format "year-month-day hour:minute:second.millisecond". We want to get the time parts of the timestamp. Listing 12-2 shows how to get time parts from this text.

Listing 12-2: Parsing a timestamp to get its time parts

```
// ParseTimeStamp.java
package com.jdojo.chapter12;

import java.util.Date;
import java.util.Calendar;
import java.text.ParsePosition;
import java.text.SimpleDateFormat;

public class ParseTimeStamp {
    public static void main(String[] args){
        String input = "2003-04-03 09:10:40. 325";
        // Prepare the pattern
        String pattern = "yyyy-MM-dd HH:mm:ss.SSS" ;
```

```
SimpleDateFormat sdf = new SimpleDateFormat(pattern);

// Parse the text into a Date object
Date dt = sdf.parse(input, new ParsePosition(0));
System.out.println(dt);

// Get the Calendar instance
Calendar cal = Calendar.getInstance();

// Set the time
cal.setTime(dt);

// Print time parts
System.out.println("Hour:" + cal.get(Calendar.HOUR));
System.out.println("Minute:" + cal.get(Calendar.MINUTE));
System.out.println("Second:" + cal.get(Calendar.SECOND));
System.out.println("Millisecond:"+
                    cal.get(Calendar.MILLISECOND));

    }
}
```

```
Output:

Thu Apr 03 09:10:40 CST 2003
Hour:9
Minute:10
Second:40
Millisecond:325
```

Formatting Numbers

In this section, we will discuss how to format numbers. We will also discuss how to parse a string to create a `Number` object. Two classes can be used to format and parse numbers. They are:

- `java.text.NumberFormat`
- `java.text.DecimalFormat`

The `NumberFormat` class is used to format a number in a particular locale's predefined format. The `DecimalFormat` class is used to format a number in a format of your choice in a particular locale. You can use a `getXXXInstance()` method of the `NumberFormat` class to get the instance of a formatter object, where `XXX` can be replaced by `Number`, `Currency`, `Integer`, or `Percent`. These methods are overloaded. If you call them without any argument, they return a formatter object for default locale for the JVM running the program. You have to call the `format()` method passing the number as an argument to get the formatted number as a string. For example,

```
NumberFormat formatter;

// Get number formatter for default locale
formatter = NumberFormatter.getNumberInstance();
```

```
// Get number formatter for French locale
formatter = NumberFormatter.getNumberInstance(Locale.FRENCH);

// Get currency formatter for German
formatter = NumberFormatter.getCurrencyInstance(Locale.GERMAN);
```

Listing 12-3 illustrates how to format numbers in default format for current locale (United States is the default locale for JVM running this example), French locale, and German locale.

Listing 12-3: Formatting numbers using default formats

```java
// DefaultNumberFormatters.java
package com.jdojo.chapter12;

import java.util.Locale;
import java.text.NumberFormat;

public class DefaultNumberFormatters {
    public static void main(String[] args){
        double value = 1566789.785 ;

        // Default locale
        printFormatted(Locale.getDefault(), value);

        // Indian locale
        // (Rupee is the Indian currency. Short form is Rs.)
        Locale indianLocale = new Locale("en", "IN");
        printFormatted(indianLocale, value);
    }

    public static void printFormatted(Locale locale, double value) {
        // Get number and currency formatter
        NumberFormat nf = NumberFormat.getInstance(locale);
        NumberFormat cf = NumberFormat.getCurrencyInstance(locale);

        System.out.println("Formatting value: " + value +
                        " for locale: " + locale);

        System.out.println("Number: "   + nf.format(value));
        System.out.println("Currency: " + cf.format(value));
        System.out.println();   // Blank line
    }
}
```

```
Output:

Formatting value: 1566789.785 for locale: en_US
Number: 1,566,789.785
Currency: $1,566,789.78

Formatting value: 1566789.785 for locale: en_IN
Number: 1,566,789.785
Currency: Rs.1,566,789.78
```

To perform more advanced formatting, you can use the `DecimalFormat` class. It allows you to supply your own format pattern. Once you create an object of the `DecimalFormat` class, you can change the format pattern using its `applyPattern()` method. You can specify different patterns for positive and negative numbers. The two patterns are separated by a semi-colon. The `DecimalFormat` class uses round to even rounding while formatting numbers. For example, if you have specified only two digits after the decimal point in your number format, `12.745` will be rounded to `12.74`, because 4 is even; `12.735` will also be rounded to `12,74`, and `12.746` will be rounded to `12.75`. You can also parse a string to a number using the `parse()` method. Note that the `parse()` method returns an object of `java.lang.Number`. You can use `XXXValue()` methods to get the primitive value, where `XXX` can be `byte`, `double`, `float`, `int`, `long`, and `short`.

Listing 12-4 illustrates the use of the `DecimalFormat` class. Note that you can also use the `parseDouble()` method of the `java.lang.Double` class to parse a string into a `double` value. However, the string has to be in the default number format. The advantage of using the `parse()` method of the `DecimalFormat` class is that the string can be in any format.

Listing 12-4: Formatting and parsing numbers

```
// DecimalFormatter.java
package com.jdojo.chapter12;

import java.text.ParsePosition;
import java.text.DecimalFormat;

public class DecimalFormatter {
    private static DecimalFormat formatter = new DecimalFormat();
    public static void main (String[] args){
        formatNumber("##.##", 12.745);
        formatNumber("##.##", 12.746);
        formatNumber("0000.0000", 12.735);
        formatNumber("#.##", -12.735);

        // Positive and negative number format
        formatNumber("#.##;(#.##)", -12.735);

        // Parse a string to decimal number
        String str = "XY4,123.983";
        String pattern = "#,###.###";
        formatter.applyPattern(pattern);

        // Create a ParsePosition object to specify the
        // first digit of number in string.
        // It is 4 in "XY4,123.983" and its index is 2
        ParsePosition pp = new ParsePosition(2);

        Number numberObject = formatter.parse(str, pp);

        double value = numberObject.doubleValue();
        System.out.println("Parsed Value is " + value);
    }

    public static void formatNumber(String pattern, double value) {
        // Apply the pattern
        formatter.applyPattern ( pattern );
```

```
            // Format the number
            String formattedNumber = formatter.format(value) ;

            System.out.println("Number:" + value +
                    ", Pattern:" + pattern +
                    ", Formatted Number:" + formattedNumber);
    }
}
```

```
Output:

Number:12.745, Pattern:##.##, Formatted Number:12.74
Number:12.746, Pattern:##.##, Formatted Number:12.75
Number:12.735, Pattern:0000.0000, Formatted Number:0012.7350
Number:-12.735, Pattern:#.##, Formatted Number:-12.74
Number:-12.735, Pattern:#.##;(#.##), Formatted Number:(12.74)
Parsed Value is 4123.983
```

Printf-style Formatting

The Big Picture

Java 5 introduced a `java.util.Formatter` class to support printf-style formatting, which is similar to the formatting supported by the `printf()` function in C programming language. If you are familiar with C programming language, it should be easier for you to understand the discussion in this section. In this section, we will use formatting string such as "%1$s", "%1$4d", etc. in our codes without explaining their meanings. You may not be able to understand them. You should ignore them for now. Just focus on the output and try to get the bigger picture of what the `Formatter` class is intended to accomplish, rather than trying to understand all details in the code. We will discuss the details of formatting texts in the next section. Let us start with a simple example as listed in Listing 12-5.

Listing 12-5: Using C's printf-style formatting in Java

```
// PrintfTest.java
package com.jdojo.chapter12;

import java.util.Date;

public class PrintfTest {
    public static void main(String[] args) {
        // Formatting strings
        System.out.printf("%1$s, %2$s, and %3$s %n", "Fu", "Hu", "Lo");
        System.out.printf("%3$s, %2$s, and %1$s %n", "Fu", "Hu", "Lo");

        // Formatting numbers
        System.out.printf("%1$4d, %2$4d, %3$4d %n", 1, 10, 100);
        System.out.printf("%1$4d, %2$4d, %3$4d %n", 10, 100, 1000);
        System.out.printf("%1$-4d, %2$-4d, %3$-4d %n", 1, 10, 100);
        System.out.printf("%1$-4d, %2$-4d, %3$-4d %n", 10, 100, 1000);

        // Formatting date and time
```

```
        Date dt = new Date();
        System.out.printf("Today is %tD %n", dt);
        System.out.printf("Today is %tF %n", dt);
        System.out.printf("Today is %tc %n", dt);
    }
}
```

```
Output: (Your output may be formatted a little differently.)

Fu, Hu, and Lo
Lo, Hu, and Fu
    1,    10,   100
   10,   100,  1000
1    , 10   , 100
10   , 100  , 1000
Today is 01/06/11
Today is 2011-01-06
Today is Thu Jan 06 15:21:31 CST 2011
```

We have been using the `System.out.println()` and `System.out.print()` methods to print texts on the standard output. In fact, `System.out` is an instance of the `java.io.PrintStream` class, which has `println()` and `print()` as two instance methods. Java 5 added two more methods, `format()` and `printf()`, to the `PrintStream` class, which can be used to write a formatted output to a `PrintStream` instance. Both `format()` and `printf()` methods of the `PrintStream` class work the same. Listing 12-5 uses `System.out.printf()` method to print the formatted text to the standard output.

Java 5 also added a `format()` static method to the `String` class, which returns a formatted string. The formatting behavior of the `format()`/`printf()` method of the `PrintStream` class and the `format()` static method of the `String` class is the same. The only difference between them is that the `format()`/`printf()` method in the `PrintStream` class writes the formatted output to an output stream, whereas the `format()` method of the `String` class returns the formatted output.

The `format()`/`printf()` method of the `PrintStream` class and the `format()` static method of the `String` class are convenience methods. These convenience methods exist to make the job of formatting a text easier for programmers. However, the real work is done by the `Formatter` class. Let us discuss the `Formatter` class in details. However, we will use these convenience methods in our examples.

A `Formatter` object lets you format text and write the formatted text to the following types of output destination.

- An `Appendable` (e.g. `StringBuffer`, `StringBuilder`, `Writer`, etc.)
- A `File`
- An `OutputStream`
- A `PrintStream`

The following snippet of code accomplishes the same thing as the code in Listing 12-5. This time, we have used a `Formatter` object to format the data. When you call the `format()` method of the `Formatter` object, the formatted text is stored in the `StringBuilder` object, `sb`, which we passed to the constructor of the `Formatter` object. When we are done with formatting all texts, we call the `toString()` method of the `StringBuilder` to get the entire formatted text.

```
// Create an Appendable data storage for our formatted output
StringBuilder sb = new StringBuilder();

// Create a Formatter that will send its output to sb
Formatter fm = new Formatter(sb);

// Formatting strings
fm.format("%1$s, %2$s, and %3$s %n", "Fu", "Hu", "Lo");
fm.format("%3$s, %2$s, and %1$s %n", "Fu", "Hu", "Lo");

// Formatting numbers
fm.format("%1$4d, %2$4d, %3$4d %n", 1, 10, 100);
fm.format("%1$4d, %2$4d, %3$4d %n", 10, 100, 1000);
fm.format("%1$-4d, %2$-4d, %3$-4d %n", 1, 10, 100);
fm.format("%1$-4d, %2$-4d, %3$-4d %n", 10, 100, 1000);

// Formatting date and time
Date dt = new Date();
fm.format("Today is %tD %n", dt);
fm.format("Today is %tF %n", dt);
fm.format("Today is %tc %n", dt);

// Display the entire formatted string
System.out.println(sb.toString());
```

If you want to write all formatted texts to a file, you can do so using the following snippet of code. You will need to handle the `FileNotFoundException`, which may be thrown from the constructor of the `Formatter` class if the specified file does not exist. When you are done with the `Formatter` object, you will need to call its `close()` method, which will close the file that it was using to output the formatted text.

```
// Let us write the formatted output to C:\xyz.text file
File file = new File("C:\\xyz.txt");
Formatter fm = null;
try {
    // Create a Formatter that will write the output a file
    fm = new Formatter(file);

    // Formatting strings
    fm.format("%1$s, %2$s, and %3$s %n", "Fu", "Hu", "Lo");
    fm.format("%3$s, %2$s, and %1$s %n", "Fu", "Hu", "Lo");

    // Format more texts here…
}
catch(FileNotFoundException e) {
    e.printStackTrace();
}
finally {
    if (fm != null) {
        fm.close();
    }
}
```

The `format()` method of the `Formatter` class is overloaded. Its declarations are as follows.

```
public Formatter format(String format, Object... args)
public Formatter format(Locale l, String format, Object... args)
```

The first version of the `format()` method uses the default locale for formatting. The second version allows you to specify a locale. The `format()`/`printf()` method of the `PrintStream` class and the `format()` method of the `String` class provide the same two versions of the `format()` method, which accept the same types of arguments. Our discussion for the `format()` method of the `Formatter` class, equally applies to these convenience methods in `PrintStream` and `String` classes.

The `Formatter` class uses the locale-specific formatting whenever it is applicable. For example, if you want to format a decimal number, say 12.89, the number is formatted as 12,89 (notice a comma between 12 and 89) in France, whereas it is formatted as 12.89 (notice a dot between 12 and 89) in United States. The locale argument of the `format()` method is used to format a text in a locale-specific format. The following snippet of code demonstrates the effects of locale-specific formatting. Note the difference in the formatted output for US and France for the same input values.

```
System.out.printf(Locale.US, "In US: %1$.2f %n", 12.89);
System.out.printf(Locale.FRANCE, "In France: %1$.2f %n", 12.89);

Date dt = new Date();
System.out.printf(Locale.US, "In US: %tA %n", dt);
System.out.printf(Locale.FRANCE, "In France: %tA %n", dt);
```

```
Output:

In US: 12.89
In France: 12,89
In US: Friday
In France: vendredi
```

The Details

Formatting data using the `Formatter` class requires two types of inputs - a format string and a list of values. A format string is the template that defines how the output will look like. It contains zero or more occurrences of fixed texts with zero or more embedded format specifiers. No formatting is applied to the fixed texts. A format specifier serves two purposes. It acts as a placeholder for the formatted data inside the format string and it specifies how the data should be formatted. Let us consider the following example. Suppose you want to print a text with the birth date of a person. An example of such a text is as shown below.

```
January 16, 1970 is John's birth day.
```

NOTE
All outputs in this section are in US locale unless specified otherwise.

In the above text, there are some fixed texts and some formatted texts whose value may change. We can convert the above text into a template as shown below.

```
<month> <day>, <year> is <name>'s birth day.
```

We have replaced the texts that may vary with placeholders that are enclosed in angle brackets, e.g. <month>, <day>, etc. We will need four input values - month, day, year, and name, to use the above template to get a formatted text. For example, if we supply the values for <month>, <day>, <year>, and <name> as "January", "16", "1970", and "John" respectively in the above template, we will get a formatted string as:

```
January 16, 1970 is John's birth day.
```

In fact, in the above example, we have just replaced the placeholders in our template with their actual values. We did not perform any formatting for the actual values. The formatting that is provided by the Formatter class works in a similar fashion. What we called a placeholder in our example is called a *format specifier* when you work with the Formatter class. What we called a template in our example is called a *format string* when you work with the Formatter class.

A format specifier always starts with a percent sign (%). We can convert our template into a format string, which can be used with the Formatter class as follows.

```
%1$tB %1$td, %1$tY is %2$s's birth day.
```

In the above format string, "%1$tB", "%1$td", "%1$tY", and %2$s" are four format specifiers, whereas " " , ", "," is ", and "'s birth day." are fixed texts.

The following snippet of code uses the above format string to print a formatted text. Note that c and "John" are the list of input values for the format string. In this case, the input value c is an instance of the Calendar class that encapsulates a date.

```
Calendar c = new GregorianCalendar(1970, Calendar.JANUARY, 16);
System.out.printf("%1$tB %1$td, %1$tY is %2$s's birth day.", c, "John");
```

Output

```
January 16, 1970 is John's birth day.
```

The general syntax for a format specifier is as follows. Except the % and <conversion> parts, all other parts are optional. Note that there is no space between any two parts of a format specifier.

```
%<argument-index$><flags><width><.precision><conversion>
```

The % (percent sign) denotes the start of a format specifier inside a format string. If you want to specify % as the part of a fixed text inside a format string, you need to use two consecutive % as %%.

The <argument-index$> denotes the index of the argument that the format specifier refers to. It consists of an integer in base-10 format followed by a $ (dollar sign). The first argument is referred to as 1$, the second as 2$, and so on. You can refer to the same argument multiple times in different format specifiers inside the same format string. It is optional.

The <flags> denotes the format of the output. It is a set of characters. What values for <flags> are valid depend on the data type of the argument that the format specifier refers to. It is optional.

The `<width>` denotes the minimum number of characters that need to be written to the output. It is optional.

Typically, the `<.precision>` denotes the maximum number of characters to be written to the output. However, its exact meaning varies depending on the value for `<conversion>`. It is a decimal integer. It starts with a dot (.). It is optional.

The `<conversion>` denotes how the output should be formatted. Its value depends on the data type of the argument, which the format specifier refers to. It is mandatory.

There are two special format specifiers – "%%" and "%n". The "%%" format specifier outputs "%" (a percent sign) and the "%n" format specifier outputs a platform-specific newline character. The following snippet of code demonstrates the use of these two special format specifiers. We have not supplied any arguments to the `printf()` method in the following code, because these two special format specifiers do not work on any arguments. Note the two newlines in the output that are generated by the two "%n" format specifiers in the format string.

```
System.out.printf("Interest rate is 10%%.%nJohn%nDonna");
```

```
Output:

Interest rate is 10%.
John
Donna
```

Referencing an Argument inside a Format Specifier

We have not covered the conversion part of the format specifier yet. For our discussion in this section, we will use 's' as the conversion character for our format specifiers. The 's' conversion formats its argument as a string. In its simplest form, we can use "%s" as a format specifier. Let us consider the following snippet of code and its output.

```
System.out.printf("%s, %s, and %s", "Ken", "Lola", "Matt");
```

```
Output:

Ken, Lola, and Matt
```

A format specifier in a format string can refer to an argument in the following three ways.

- Ordinary indexing
- Explicit indexing
- Relative indexing

When a format specifier does not specify an argument-index value (as in "%s"), it is called *ordinary indexing*. In ordinary indexing, the argument-index is determined by the index of the format specifier in the format string. The first format specifier without argument-index in a format string has index of 1, the second has index of 2 and so on. The format specifier with index 1 refers to the first argument; the format specifier with index 2 refers to the second argument and so on. Figure 12-1 shows the indices of the format specifiers and the arguments. It also shows how those indices are mapped in the above example. The first "%s" format specified refers to the first argument "Ken". The second "%s" format specified refers to the second argument "Lola". And, the third "%s" format specified refers to the third argument "Matt".

Figure 12-1: Indexes of format specifiers in a format string "%s, %s, and %s" and indexes of the arguments "Ken", "Lola", "Matt"

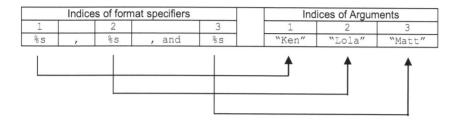

If the number of arguments is more than the number of format specifiers in the format string, the extra arguments are ignored. Consider the following snippet of code and its output. It has three format specifiers (three "%s") and four arguments. The fourth argument "Lo" is an extra argument and it is ignored silently.

```
System.out.printf("%s, %s, and %s", "Ken", "Lola", "Matt", "Lo");
```

```
Output:

Ken, Lola, and Matt
```

If a format specifier references a non-existent argument, Java runtime throws java.util.MissingFormatArgumentException. The following snippet of code will throw MissingFormatArgumentException, because the number of arguments is one less than the number of format specifiers. There are three format specifiers. However, there are only two arguments.

```
// Compiles fine, but throws runtime exception
System.out.printf("%s, %s, and %s", "Ken", "Lola");
```

Note that the last argument to the format() method of the Formatter class is a varargs argument. You can also pass an array to varargs arguments. The following snippet of code is valid even though it uses three format specifiers and only one argument of array type. The array type argument contains three values for the three format specifiers.

```
String[] names = {"Ken", "Matt", "Lola"};
System.out.printf("%s, %s, and %s", names);
```

```
Output:

Ken, Matt, and Lola
```

The following snippet of code is also valid, because it passes four values in the array type argument and it uses only three format specifiers.

```
String[] names = {"Ken", "Matt", "Lola", "Lo"};
```

```
System.out.printf("%s, %s, and %s", names);
```

```
Output:

Ken, Matt, and Lola
```

The following snippet of code is not valid, because it uses an array type argument that has only two elements and there are three format specifiers. A `MissingFormatArgumentException` will be thrown when the following snippet of code is run.

```
String[] names = {"Ken", "Matt"};
System.out.printf("%s, %s, and %s", names); // Will throw exception
```

When a format specifier specifies an argument index explicitly, it is called *explicit indexing*. Note that an argument index is specified just after the `%` (a percent sign) in a format specifier. It is an integer in decimal format (base-10 format) and it ends with $ (a dollar sign). Consider the following snippet of code and its output. It uses three format specifiers – "`%1$s`", "`%2$s`", and "`%3$s`", which use explicit indexing.

```
System.out.printf("%1$s, %2$s, and %3$s", "Ken", "Lola", "Matt");
```

```
Output:

Ken, Lola, and Matt
```

When a format specifier uses explicit indexing, it can refer to an argument at any index in the argument list using the index of the argument. Consider the following snippet of code. It has the same output as the above snippet of code. However, in this case, the values in the argument list are not in the same order. The first format specifier "`%3$s`" refers to the third argument "`Ken`", the second format specifier "`%1$s`" refers to the first argument "`Lola`" and the third format specifier "`%2$s`" refers to the second argument "`Matt`".

```
System.out.printf("%3$s, %1$s, and %2$s", "Lola", "Matt", "Ken");
```

```
Output:

Ken, Lola, and Matt
```

It is allowed to reference the same argument multiple times using explicit indexing. It is also allowed not to reference some arguments inside a format string. In the following snippet of code, the first argument "`Lola`" is not referenced and the third argument "`Ken`" is referenced twice.

```
System.out.printf("%3$s, %2$s, and %3$s", "Lola", "Matt", "Ken");
```

```
Output:

Ken, Matt, and Ken
```

There is a third way to refer to an argument inside a format specifier, which is called *relative indexing*. In relative indexing, a format specifier uses the same argument that was used by the previous format specifier. Relative indexing does not use an argument-index value. Rather, it uses

`<` character as a flag in the format specifier. Since in relative indexing, a format specifier uses the same argument that is used by the previous format specifier, it cannot be used with the first format specifier. Remember that, to use a relative indexing, there must be a previous format specifier and there is no previous format specifier for the first format specifier. Consider the following snippet of code and its output, which uses relative indexing.

```
System.out.printf("%1$s, %<s, %<s, %2$s, and %<s", "Ken", "Matt");
```

```
Output:

Ken, Ken, Ken, Matt, and Matt
```

The above snippet of code uses five format specifiers – "%1$s", "%<s", "%<s", "%2$s", and "%<s". It uses two arguments – "Ken" and "Matt". Note that it is possible to have less number of arguments than the number of format specifiers if some format specifiers use relative indexing. The first format specifier "%1$s" uses explicit indexing to references the first argument "Ken". The second format specifier "%<s" uses relative indexing (notice `<` flag) and, therefore, it will use the same argument, which was used by the previous format specifier "1$s". This way, both the first and the second format specifiers use the first argument "Ken". This is confirmed by the output that displays "Ken" as the first two names. The third format specifier "%<s" also uses relative indexing. It will use the same argument as used by the previous format specifier (the second format specifier). Since the second format specifier used the first argument "Ken", the third one will also use the same argument. This is confirmed in the output that shows "Ken" as the third name. The fourth "%2$s" format specifier uses explicit indexing to use the second argument "Matt". The fifth and the last format specifier "%<s" uses relative indexing and it will use the same argument that is used by its previous format specifier (the fourth format specifier). Since the fourth format specifier uses the second argument "Matt", the fifth format specifier will also use the second argument "Matt". This is confirmed in the output that displays "Matt" as the fifth name.

The following statement will throw `java.util.MissingFormatArgumentException` runtime exception, because it uses relative indexing for the first format specifier.

```
System.out.printf("%<s, %<s, %<s, %2$s, and %<s", "Ken", "Matt");
```

It is possible to mix all three types of indexing to reference arguments inside different format specifiers in the same format string. Consider the following statement and its output.

```
System.out.printf("%1$s, %s, %<s, %s, and %<s", "Ken", "Matt");
```

```
Output:

Ken, Ken, Ken, Matt, and Matt
```

The first format specifier uses the explicit indexing and it will use the first argument "Ken". The second and the fourth formats specifier (both "%s") use ordinary indexing. The third and the fifth format specifiers (both "%<s") use relative indexing. It is clear from the rule of relative indexing that the third format specifier and the fifth format specifier will use the same arguments as used by the second and the fourth format specifiers respectively. Which arguments will be used by the second and the fourth format specifiers? The answer is simple. When you have some format specifiers that use ordinary indexing and some explicit indexing, just for the purpose of understanding this rule, ignore the format specifiers that use explicit indexing and number the format specifiers that use ordinary indexing as 1, 2, and so on. Using this rule, we can think of the above statement the same

as shown below. Note that we have replaced the first occurrence of "%s" with %1$s" and the second occurrence of "%s" with "%2$s" as if they are using explicit indexing. This explains the output generated by the above statement.

```
System.out.printf("%1$s, %1$s, %<s, %2$s, and %<s", "Ken", "Matt");
```

TIP
When explicit indexing and ordinary indexing are mixed in a format string, the format specifiers that use ordinary indexing are numbered as 1, 2, 3 and so on from left to right. The numbering starts from 1. For example, the format string "%s, %1$s, %s, %<s, and %s" is the same as "%1$s, %1$s, %2$s, %<s, and %3$s".

Using Flags in a Format Specifier

Flags act as modifiers for the formatting rules. It modifies the formatted output. Table 12-3 lists all valid flags that can be used in a format specifier. Note that which flags can be used in a format specifier and which not, and their effects depend on many other criteria, e.g., data type of the value. Depending on the value that is formatted, it is allowed to use multiple flags in a format specifier. For example, the format specifier "%1$,0(12d" uses three flags – ',', '0', and '('. If –122899 is used as the argument by this format specifier, it will output (000122,899). The effects of using each flag will be discussed in details when we discuss formatting for different data types in the sections to follow.

Table 12-3: List of valid flags, their descriptions, and examples of their usage

Flag	Description	Examples		
		Format String	**Argument**	**Formatted Text**
'-'	The result is left justified. Note that the result is right justified when you do not use '-' flag in a format specifier.	"'%6s'"	"Ken"	' Ken'
		"'%-6s'"	"Ken"	'Ken '
'#'	The argument is formatted in alternate form depending on the conversion part of the format specifier. The example shows the same decimal number 6270185 being formatted to a hexadecimal format. When '#' flag is used, the hexadecimal number is prefixed with "0x".	"%x"	6270185	5face9
		"%#x"	6270185	0x5face9
'+'	The result contains a + sign for positive values. It applies only to numeric values.	"%d"	105	105
		"%+d"	105	+105
' '	The result contains a leading space for positive values. It applies only to numeric values.	"'% d'"	105	'105'
		"'% d'"	105	' 105'
'0'	The result is zero padded. It applies only to numeric values.	"'%6d'"	105	' 105'
		"'%06d'"	105	'000105'
','	The result contains a locale-specific grouping separator. It applied only to numeric values. For example, a comma is used as a thousand-	"%,d"	89105	89,105 (US Locale)
		"%,d"	89105	89 105

	separator in US locale, whereas a space is used in France locale.			(France locale)
`'('`	The result is enclosed in parentheses for a negative number. It applies only to numeric values.	`"%d"`	-1969	-1969
		`"%(d"`	-1969	(1969)
`'<'`	It causes the argument for the previous format specifier to be reused.	`"%s and %<s"`	"Ken"	Ken and Ken

Conversion Characters

Different conversion characters are used to format values of different data types. For example, `'s'` conversion character is used to format a value as a string. The valid values for other parts in a format specifier are also determined by the conversion character in the format specifier and the data type of the argument that the format specifier references. We can broadly classify the formatting types based on data types in four categories.

- General formatting
- Character formatting
- Numeric formatting
- Date/Time formatting

Many of the conversion characters have uppercase variants. For example, `'S'` conversion character is the uppercase variant of `'s'` conversion character. The uppercase variant of a conversion character converts the formatted output to uppercase as if `output.toUpperCase()` method was called, where `output` is the reference to the formatted output string. The following statement and its output demonstrates the effect of using the uppercase variant `'S'` of `'s'` conversion character. Note that `'s'` produces "Ken" and `'S'` produces "KEN" for the same input value "Ken"

```
System.out.printf("%s and %S", "Ken", "Ken");
```

```
Output:

Ken and KEN
```

General Formatting

The general formatting can be applied to format values of any data types. Table 12-4 has the list of conversions that are available under the general formatting category.

Table 12-4: List of conversion characters for general formatting

Conversion	Uppercase variant	Description
`'b'`	`'B'`	It produces "true" or "false" based on the value of the argument. It produces "false" for a null argument and for a boolean argument whose value is false. Otherwise, it produces "true".
`'h'`	`'H'`	It produces a string that is the hash code value in hexadecimal

		format of the argument. If the argument is `null`, it produces "null".
`'s'`	`'S'`	It produces a string representation of the argument. If the argument is `null`, it produces a "null" string. If the argument implements the java.util.`Formattable` interface, it invokes the `formatTo()` method on the argument and the returned value is the result. If the argument does not implement the java.util.Formattable interface, `toString()` method is invoked on the argument to get the result.

The general syntax for a format specifier for general formatting is as follows.

```
%<argument_index$><flags><width><.precision><conversion>
```

The width denotes the minimum number of characters to be written to the output. If the length of the string representation of the argument is less than the width value, the result will be padded with spaces. The space padding is performed to the left of the argument value. If `'-'` flag is used, space padding is performed to the right. The value of width alone does not decide the content of the result. The values of width and precision together decide the final content of the result.

The precision denotes the maximum number of characters to be written to the output. The precision is applied to the argument before the width is applied. You need to understand the consequences of applying the precision before the width. If the precision is less than the length of the argument, the argument is truncated to the length that is equal to the precision, and space padding is performed to match the length of the output to the value of the width. Consider the following snippet of code.

```
System.out.printf("'%4.1s'", "Ken");
```

```
Output:

'   K'
```

The argument's value is "Ken" and the format specifier is "%4.1s", where 4 is the width and 1 is the precision. First, the precision is applied that will truncate the value "Ken" to "K". Now, the width is applied, which states that minimum of four characters should be written to the output. However, after the precision is applied, we have only one character left. Therefore, "K" will be left padded with three spaces to match the width value of four, which is displayed in the above output.

Consider the following snippet of code.

```
System.out.printf("'%1.4s'", "Ken");
```

```
Output:

'Ken'
```

The argument's value is "Ken" and the format specifier is "%1.4s",.where 1 is the width and 4 is the precision. Since precision value 4 is greater than the length of the argument, which is 3, there is no effect of the precision. Since width value of 1 is less than the width of the result after precision is applied, there is no effect of the width value on the output.

The following are some examples of using boolean, string and hash code formatting conversions. Note that the hash code formatting conversion (`'h'` and `'H'`) outputs the hash code value of the argument in a hexadecimal format. Examples also demonstrate the effect of using the uppercase variants of the conversions.

```
// Boolean conversion
System.out.printf("'%b', '%5b', '%.3b'%n", true, false, true);
System.out.printf("'%b', '%5b', '%.3b'%n", "Ken", "Matt", "Lola");
System.out.printf("'%B', '%5B', '%.3B'%n", "Ken", "Matt", "Lola");
System.out.printf("%b %n", 1969);
System.out.printf("%b %n", new Object());
```

```
Output:

'true', 'false', 'tru'
'true', ' true', 'tru'
'TRUE', ' TRUE', 'TRU'
true
true
```

```
// String conversion
System.out.printf("'%s', '%5s', '%.3s'%n", "Ken", "Matt", "Lola");
System.out.printf("'%S', '%5S', '%.3S'%n", "Ken", "Matt", "Lola");

// Use '-' flag to left-justify the result. You must use width when
// you specify the '-' flag
System.out.printf("'%S', '%-5S', '%.3S'%n", "Ken", "Matt", "Lola");
System.out.printf("%s %n", 1969);
System.out.printf("%s %n", true);
System.out.printf("%s %n", new Object());
```

```
Output:

'Ken', ' Matt', 'Lol'
'KEN', ' MATT', 'LOL'
'KEN', 'MATT ', 'LOL'
1969
true
java.lang.Object@de6f34
```

```
// Hash Code conversion
System.out.printf("'%h', '%5h', '%.3h'%n", "Ken", "Matt", "Lola");
System.out.printf("'%H', '%5H', '%.3H'%n", "Ken", "Matt", "Lola");
System.out.printf("%h %n", 1969);
System.out.printf("%h %n", true);
System.out.printf("%h %n", new Object());
```

```
Output:

'12634', '247b34', '243'
'12634', '247B34', '243'
7b1
```

TIP

If you pass a value of a primitive type as an argument to the `format()` method of the `Formatter` class (or the `printf()` method of the `PrintStream` class), the primitive type value is converted to a reference type using an appropriate type of wrapper class using the autoboxing rule of Java 5. Please refer to the chapter on *Autoboxing* for more details. For example, the statement

```
System.out.println("%s", 1969);
```

will be converted to

```
System.out.println("%s", new Integer(1969));
```

The `Formatter` class supports custom formatting through 's' and 'S' conversions. If the argument implements `java.util.Formattable` interface, 's' conversion calls the `formatTo()` method on the argument to get the formatted result. The `formatTo()` method is passed the reference of a `Formatter` object, flags, width and precision values that are used in the format specifier. You can apply any custom logic inside the `formatTo()` method of the class to format the objects of your class.

Listing 12-6 has the code for a `FormattablePerson` class, which implements the `Formattable` interface. Our `Formattable` person has a first name and a last name. We have kept the logic inside the `formatTo()` method simple. We check for alternate flag '#'. If this flag is used in the format specifier, we format the person's name in "LastName, FirstName" format. If the alternate flag is not used, we the person's name in "FirstName LastName" format. We also support uppercase variant 'S' of 's' conversion. If 'S' conversion is used, we format the person's name in uppercase. Our logic does not use other values of the flags, width, and precision. The flags are passed in as an `int` value as bitmask. To check, if a flag was passed, you will need to use the bitwise `&` operator. The operand to be used in the bitwise `&` operator are defined by the constants defined in `java.util.FormattableFlags` class. For example, to check if the format specifier uses a left-justify '-' flag, you will need to use the following logic.

```
int leftJustifiedFlagValue = FormattableFlags.LEFT_JUSTIFY & flags;
if (leftJustifiedFlagValue == FormattableFlags.LEFT_JUSTIFY) {
    // Left-justified flag '-' is used
}
else {
    // Left-justified flag '-' is not used
}
```

Listing 12-6: Implementing a custom formatter using the Formattable interface

```
// FormattablePerson.java
package com.jdojo.chapter12;

import java.util.Formattable;
import java.util.Formatter;
import java.util.FormattableFlags;

public class FormattablePerson implements Formattable {
```

```
        private String firstName = "Unknown";
        private String lastName = "Unknown";

        public FormattablePerson(String firstName, String lastName ) {
            this.firstName = firstName;
            this.lastName = lastName;
        }

        // Other code goes here...

        public void formatTo(Formatter formatter, int flags, int width,
                             int precision) {
            String str = this.firstName + " " + this.lastName;

            int alternateFlagValue = FormattableFlags.ALTERNATE & flags;
            if (alternateFlagValue == FormattableFlags.ALTERNATE) {
                str = this.lastName + ", " + this.firstName;
            }

            // Check if uppercase variant of the conversio is being used
            int upperFlagValue = FormattableFlags.UPPERCASE & flags;
            if (upperFlagValue == FormattableFlags.UPPERCASE) {
                str = str.toUpperCase();
            }

            // Call the format() method of formatter argument so that
            // out result is stored in it and the caller will get it
            formatter.format(str);
        }
    }
}
```

We can use our `FormattablePerson` objects with format specifiers using string conversion 's' and 'S' as shown below.

```
FormattablePerson fp = new FormattablePerson("Ken", "Smith");
System.out.printf("%s %n", fp );
System.out.printf("%#s %n", fp );
System.out.printf("%S %n", fp );
System.out.printf("%#S %n", fp );
```

```
Output:

Ken Smith
Smith, Ken
KEN SMITH
SMITH, KEN
```

Character Formatting

Character formatting may be applied to the values of `char` primitive data type or `Character` objects. It can also be applied to the values of `byte`, `Byte`, `short`, `Short`, `int`, or `Integer` types if their values are valid Unicode code points. You can test if an integer value represents a valid Unicode code point by using the `isValidCodePoint(int value)` static method of the `Character` class.

The conversion character for character formatting is `c`. Its uppercase variant is `C`. The flag `#` and the precision are not supported for character formatting. The flag `-` and width have the same meaning as in the context of the general formatting. The following snippet of code demonstrates the use of character formatting.

```
System.out.printf("%c %n", 'a');
System.out.printf("%C %n", 'a');
System.out.printf("%C %n", 98);
System.out.printf("'%5C' %n", 100);
System.out.printf("'%-5C' %n", 100);
```

```
Output:

a
A
B
'    D'
'D    '
```

Numeric Formatting

The numeric formatting can be broadly classified into two categories.

- Integral number formatting
- Floating-point number formatting

Many locale-specific formatting are automatically applied when a numeric value is formatted. For example, the numeric digits that are used for number formatting are always locale-specific. If the formatted number contains a decimal separator or group separators, those separators are always replaced with locale-specific decimal separator or group separators. The following snippet of code shows the same number 1234567890 being formatted differently for three different locales – US, Indian and Thailand.

```
Locale englishUS = new Locale ("en", "US");
Locale hindiIndia = new Locale ("hi", "IN");
Locale thaiThailand = new Locale ("th", "TH", "TH");

System.out.printf(englishUS, "%d %n", 1234567890);
System.out.printf(hindiIndia, "%d %n", 1234567890);
System.out.printf(thaiThailand, "%d %n", 1234567890);
```

```
Output:

US: 1234567890

India: १२३४५६७८९०

Thailand: ๑๒๓๔๕๖๗๘๙๐
```

Integral Number Formatting

The integral number formatting deals with formatting whole numbers. It can be applied to format values of `byte`, `Byte`, `short`, `Short`, `int`, `Integer`, `long`, `Long` and `BigInteger` data types. Table 12-4 has the list of conversions that are available under integral number formatting category. The general syntax for a format specifier for integral number formatting is as follows. Note that precision part in a format specifier is not applicable to integral number formatting.

```
%<argument_index$><flags><width><conversion>
```

Table 12-5: List of conversions applicable to byte, Byte, short, Short, int, Integer, long, Long, and BigInteger data types

Conversion	Uppercase variant	Description
`d`		It formats the argument in locale-specific decimal integer (base-10). The '#' flag cannot be used with this conversion.
`o`		It formats the argument as a base-8 integer without any localization. If '#' flag is used with this conversion, the output always begins with a '0' (a zero). The '(', '+', ' ', and ',' flags cannot be used with this conversion.
`x`	`X`	It formats the argument as a base-16 integer without any localization. If '#' flag is used with this conversion, the output always begins with a "0x". When the uppercase variant 'X' is used with '#' flag, the output always begins with "0X". The '(', '+', ' ', and ',' flags cannot be used with this conversion with an argument of `byte`, `Byte`, `short`, `Short`, `int`, `Integer`, `long` and `Long` data type. The ',' flag cannot be used with this conversion with an argument of `BigInteger` data type.

The following snippet of code demonstrates the use of `d` conversion with various flags to format integers.

```
System.out.printf("'%d' %n", 1969);
System.out.printf("'%6d' %n", 1969);
System.out.printf("'%-6d' %n", 1969);
System.out.printf("'%06d' %n", 1969);
System.out.printf("'%(d' %n", 1969);
System.out.printf("'%(d' %n", -1969);
System.out.printf("'% d' %n", 1969);
```

```
System.out.printf("'% d' %n", -1969);
System.out.printf("'%+d' %n", 1969);
System.out.printf("'%+d' %n", -1969);
```

```
Output:

'1969'
'  1969'
'1969  '
'001969'
'1969'
'(1969)'
' 1969'
'-1969'
'+1969'
'-1969'
```

When conversions 'o' and 'x' are used with a negative argument of byte, Byte, short, Short, int, Integer, long and Long data type, the argument value is first converted to an unsigned number by adding a number 2^N to it, where N is the number of bits used to represent the value of the data type of the argument. For example, if the argument data type is byte, which takes 8-bit to store the value, the argument value of -X will be converted to a positive value of -X + 256 by adding 256 to it and the result contain the base-8 or base-16 equivalent of the value -X + 256. The conversions 'o' and 'x' do not transform the negative argument value to an unsigned value for a BigInteger argument type. . Consider the following snippet of code and its output.

```
byte b1 = 9;
byte b2 = -9;
System.out.printf("%o %n", b1);
System.out.printf("%o %n", b2);
```

```
Output:

11
367
```

The conversion 'o' outputs the base-8 integer 11 for s positive decimal number 9. However, when a negative decimal integer -9 is used with 'o' conversion, the negative number -9 is converted to a positive number -9 + 256 (=247). The final output contains 367, which is the base-8 equivalent of the decimal 247.

The following snippet of code shows some more examples of 'o' and 'x' conversions for int and BigInteger argument types.

```
System.out.printf("%o %n", 1969);
System.out.printf("%o %n", -1969);
System.out.printf("%o %n", new BigInteger("1969"));
System.out.printf("%o %n", new BigInteger("-1969"));

System.out.printf("%x %n", 1969);
System.out.printf("%x %n", -1969);
System.out.printf("%x %n", new BigInteger("1969"));
```

```
System.out.printf("%x %n", new BigInteger("-1969"));

System.out.printf("%#o %n", 1969);
System.out.printf("%#x %n", 1969);
System.out.printf("%#o %n", new BigInteger("1969"));
System.out.printf("%#x %n", new BigInteger("1969"));
```

```
Output:

3661
37777774117
3661
-3661
7b1
fffff84f
7b1
-7b1
03661
0x7b1
03661
0x7b1
```

Floating-Point Number Formatting

Floating-point number formatting deals with formatting numbers, which have a whole part and a fraction part. It can be applied to format values of `float`, `Float`, `double`, `Double` and `BigDecimal` data types. Table 12-6 has the list of conversions that are available under floating-point number formatting category. The general syntax for a format specifier for floating-point number formatting is as follows.

```
%<argument_index$><flags><width><.precision><conversion>
```

The precision has different meanings in the context of floating-point number formatting. Its meaning depends on the conversion character. By default, the value of precision is 6. For 'e' and 'f' conversions, the precision is the number of digits after the decimal separator. For 'g' conversion, the precision is the total number of digits in the resulting magnitude after rounding. Precision is not applicable to 'a' conversion.

If the argument value for a floating-point conversion is `NaN` or Infinity, the output contains the strings "`NaN`" and "`Infinity`" respectively.

Table 12-6: List of conversions applicable to float, Float, double, Double and BigDecimal data types

Conversion	Uppercase variant	Description
'e'	'E'	It formats the argument in a locale-specific computerized scientific notation, e.g. 1.969919e+03. The output contains one digit followed by a decimal separator, which is followed by exponent part. For example, 1969.919 will be formatted as 1.969919e+03 if the precision is 6. Precision is the number of digits after the decimal separator.

		The group separator flag ',' cannot be used with this conversion.
'g'	'G'	It formats the argument in a locale-specific general scientific notation. Depending on the value of the argument, it acts as 'e' conversion or 'f' conversion. It applies rounding to the value of the argument depending on the value of the precision. If the value after rounding is greater than or equal to 10^{-4} but less than $10^{precision}$, it formats the value as if 'f' conversion is used. If the value after rounding is less than 10^{-4} or greater than or equal to $10^{precision}$, it formats the value as if 'e' conversion is used. Note that the total number of significant digits in the result is equal to the value of the precision. By default, precision of 6 is used.
'f'		It formats the argument in a locale-specific decimal format. Precision is the number of digits after the decimal separator. The value is rounded depending on the specified value of the precision.
'a'	'A'	It formats the argument in hexadecimal exponential form. It is not applicable to the argument of `BigDecimal` type.

The following snippet of code shows how to format floating-point numbers with the default precision, which is 6.

```
System.out.printf("%e %n", 10.2);
System.out.printf("%f %n", 10.2);
System.out.printf("%g %n", 10.2);

System.out.printf("%e %n", 0.000002079);
System.out.printf("%f %n", 0.000002079);
System.out.printf("%g %n", 0.000002079);

System.out.printf("%a %n", 0.000002079);
```

```
Output:

1.020000e+01
10.200000
10.2000
2.079000e-06
0.000002
2.07900e-06
'1.97e+03'
0x1.1709e564a6d14p-19
```

The following snippet of code shows the effects of using width and precision in floating-point number formatting.

```
System.out.printf("%.2e %n", 1969.27);
System.out.printf("%.2f %n", 1969.27);
System.out.printf("%.2g %n", 1969.27);

System.out.printf("'%8.2e' %n", 1969.27);
System.out.printf("'%8.2f' %n", 1969.27);
```

```
System.out.printf("'%8.2g' %n", 1969.27);

System.out.printf("'%10.2e' %n", 1969.27);
System.out.printf("'%10.2f' %n", 1969.27);
System.out.printf("'%10.2g' %n", 1969.27);

System.out.printf("'%-10.2e' %n", 1969.27);
System.out.printf("'%-10.2f' %n", 1969.27);
System.out.printf("'%-10.2g' %n", 1969.27);

System.out.printf("'%010.2e' %n", 1969.27);
System.out.printf("'%010.2f' %n", 1969.27);
System.out.printf("'%010.2g' %n", 1969.27);
```

```
Output:

1.97e+03
1969.27
2.0e+03
'1.97e+03'
'  1969.27'
'  2.0e+03'
'   1.97e+03'
'    1969.27'
'    2.0e+03'
'1.97e+03   '
'1969.27    '
'2.0e+03    '
'001.97e+03'
'0001969.27'
'0002.0e+03'
```

The following snippet of code shows the formatting of floating-point numbers when their values are NaN or infinities.

```
System.out.printf("%.2e %n", Double.NaN);
System.out.printf("%.2f %n", Double.POSITIVE_INFINITY);
System.out.printf("%.2g %n", Double.NEGATIVE_INFINITY);
System.out.printf("%(f %n", Double.POSITIVE_INFINITY);
System.out.printf("%(f %n", Double.NEGATIVE_INFINITY);
```

```
Output:

NaN
Infinity
-Infinity
Infinity
(Infinity)
```

Formatting Date/Time

Date/time formatting deals with formatting date, time, and datetime. It can be applied to format values of `long`, `Long`, `java.util.Calandar` and `java.util.Date` types. The value in a `long`/`Long` type argument is interpreted as the milliseconds passed since January 1, 1970 midnight UTC.

The `'t'` conversion character is used to format date/time values. It has an uppercase variant `'T'`. The general syntax for a format specifier for date/time formatting is as follows. Note that precision part in a format specifier is not applicable to date/time formatting.

```
%<argument_index$><flags><width><conversion>
```

For date/time formatting, the conversion is a two-character sequence. The first character in the conversion is always `'t'` or `'T'`. The second character is called the conversion suffix, which determines the format of the date/time argument. Table 12-7, Table 12-8 and Table 12-9 lists all the conversion suffixes that can be used with `'t'`/`'T'` data/time conversion character.

Table 12-7: List of suffix characters for time formatting

Conversion Suffix	Description
`'H'`	A two-digit hour of the day for the 24-hour clock. The valid values are 00 to 23. The 00 value corresponds to midnight.
`'I'`	A two-digit hour of the day for the 12-hour clock. The valid values are 01 to 12. The 01 value corresponds to one o'clock in the morning or afternoon..
`'k'`	It behaves the same as 'H' suffix except that it does not add a leading zero to the output. Valid values are 0 to 23.
`'l'`	It behaves the same as 'I' suffix except that it does not add a leading zero. Valid values are 1 to 12.
`'M'`	A two-digit minute within an hour. Valid values are 00 to 59.
`'S'`	A two-digit second within a minute. Valid values are 00 to 60. The value 60 is a special value that is required to support leap seconds.
`'L'`	A three-digit millisecond within a second. Valid values are 000 to 999.
`'N'`	A nine-digit nanosecond within a second. The valid values are 000000000 to 999999999. The precision of the nanosecond value is dependent on the precision that is supported by the operating system.
`'p'`	It outputs a locale-specific morning or afternoon marker in lowercase. For example, for US locale, it will output "am" or "pm". If you want the output in uppercase, e.g., "AM" and "PM" for US locale, you need to use the uppercase variant 'T' as the conversion character..
`'z'`	It outputs the numeric time zone offset from GMT, e.g., +0530
`'Z'`	It is a string abbreviation of the time zone, e.g., CST, EST, IST, etc.
`'s'`	It outputs seconds since the beginning of the epoch starting at January 1, 1970 midnight UTC.
`'Q'`	It outputs milliseconds since the beginning of the epoch starting at January 1, 1970 midnight UTC.

Table 12-8: List of suffix characters for date formatting

Conversion Suffix	Description
`'B'`	Locale-specific full name of the month, e.g., "January", "February", etc. for US locale.
`'b'`	Locale-specific abbreviated month name, e.g., "Jan", "Feb", etc. for US locale.
`'h'`	Same as 'b'
`'A'`	Locale-specific full name of the day of the week, e.g., "Sunday", "Monday", etc. for US locale.
`'a'`	Locale-specific short name of the day of the week, e.g., "Sun", "Mon", etc. for US locale.
`'C'`	It divides the four-digit year by 100 and formats the result as two digits. It adds a leading zero if the resulting number is one digit. It ignores the fraction part from the result of the division by 100. Valid values are 00 to 99. For example, if the four-digit year is 2011, it will output 20; if the four-digit year is 12, it will output 00.
`'Y'`	An at least four-digit year. It adds leading zeros if the year contains less than four digits. For example, if year is 789, it will output 0789; if year is 2011, it will output 2011; if year is 20189, it will output 20189.
`'y'`	The last two digits of the year. It adds leading zero if necessary. For example, if the year is 9, it will output 09; if the year is 123, it will output 23; if the year is 2011, it will output 11.
`'j'`	A three-digit day of the year. Valid values are 000 to 366.
`'m'`	A two-digit month. Valid values are 01 to 13. The special value of 13 is required to support lunar calendar.
`'d'`	A two-digit day of the month. Valid values are 01 to 31.
`'e'`	Day of the month. Valid values are 1 to 31. It behaves the same as 'd' except that it does not add a leading zero to the output.

Table 12-9: List of suffix characters for date/time formatting

Conversion Suffix	Description
`'R'`	It formats time in 24-hour clock format as "hour:minute". Its effects is the same as using "%tH:%tM" as a format specifier. Examples are "11:23", "01:35", "21:30", etc.
`'T'`	It formats time in 24-hour clock format as "hour:minute:second". Its effects is the same as using "%tH:%tM:%tS" as a format specifier. Examples are,"11:23:10", "01:35:01", "21:30:34", etc.
`'r'`	It formats time in 12-hour clock format as "hour:minute:second morning/afternoon marker". Its effects is the same as using "%tI:%tM:%tS %Tp" as a format specifier. The morning/afternoon marker may be locale-specific. "09:23:45 AM", "09:30:00 PM", etc. are example for US locale..
`'D'`	It formats the date as "%tm/%td/%ty", e.g., "01/19/11".

'F'	It formats the date as `"%tY-%tm-%td"`, e.g., "2011-01-19".
'c'	It formats the date and time as `"%ta %tb %td %tT %tZ %tY"`, e.g. "Wed Jan 19 11:52:06 CST 2011".

The data/time conversion applies localization wherever it is applicable. The following snippet of code formats the same date and time, February 20, 2011 11:48:16 AM, in US, Indian, and Thai locales. Note the use of the `'<'` flag in the format specifier. It lets us use the argument that holds the date and time value in multiple format specifiers.

```
Locale englishUS = Locale.US;
Locale hindiIndia = new Locale ("hi", "IN");
Locale thaiThailand = new Locale ("th", "TH", "TH");

Calendar cal = new GregorianCalendar(2011, 1, 20, 11, 48, 16);

System.out.printf(englishUS, "In US: %tB %<te, %<tY %<tT %<Tp%n", cal);
System.out.printf(hindiIndia,
                "In India: %tB %<te, %<tY %<tT %<Tp%n", cal);
System.out.printf(thaiThailand,
                "In Thailand: %tB %<te, %<tY %<tT %<Tp%n", cal);
```

```
Output:

In US: February 20, 2011 11:48:16 AM
In India: फ़रवरी २०, २०११ ११:४८:१६ पूर्वाह्न
In Thailand: กุมภาพันธ์ ๒๐, ๒๐๑๑ ๑๑:๔๘:๑๖ ก่อนเ
```

The following snippet of code formats the current date and time in default locale (US in this case). You will get different output when you run the following code. It uses a long data type argument that holds a date and time. Note the effect of using the uppercase variant `'T'` as the conversion character. It formats the argument value in uppercase letters. The definition of uppercase depends on the locale that is used. If the locale does not have different uppercase and lowercase letters, the output will be the same when you use `'T'` or `'t'` as the conversion character.

```
long currentTime = System.currentTimeMillis();

System.out.printf("%tA %<tB %<te, %<tY %n", currentTime);
System.out.printf("%TA %<TB %<te, %<tY %n", currentTime);
System.out.printf("%tD %n", currentTime);
System.out.printf("%tF %n", currentTime);
System.out.printf("%tc %n", currentTime);
System.out.printf("%Tc %n", currentTime);
```

```
Output:

Thursday January 20, 2011
THURSDAY JANUARY 20, 2011
01/20/11
2011-01-20
Thu Jan 20 14:35:40 CST 2011
THU JAN 20 14:35:40 CST 2011
```

Chapter 13. Regular Expressions

What is a Regular Expression?

Let us start with an example. Suppose you have a string, which may be an email address. How would you make sure that the string is a valid email address? You would like to validate the string against some rules. For example, the string must contain an @ sign, which is preceded by some characters (at least one) and followed by a domain name. Optionally, you may specify that the text preceding the @ sign must contain only alphabets, digits, underscores and hyphens. The domain name must contain a dot. You may want to add some more validations. If you just want to check for a '@' character in a string, you can do it by calling `email.indexOf('@')`, where `email` is the reference of the string holding the email address . If you want to make sure that there is only one '@' character in the email string, you need to write some more code. In such cases, you may end up with 20 to 50, or even more lines of codes depending on the number of validations you want to perform. This is where regular expressions come in handy. It will make your email validation easy and you can accomplish it in just one line of code. Does it not sound unbelievable? Just a little while ago, you were told that you might end up with 50 lines of code. Now you are told that you could accomplish the same thing in one line of code. That is true. It can be done in one line of code. Before, we go into the details of how to do the email validation, let us list the steps needed to accomplish this task.

- To validate these kinds of strings, we need to recognize the pattern we are looking for. For example, in the simplest form of email address validation, we can state that it should consist of some text (at least one character), an @ sign followed by some text (for domain name, we are ignoring any other details for now).
- We need a way to express the recognized pattern. The regular expressions are used to describe such patterns.
- We need a program that can match the pattern against the input string. Such a program is also known as a *Regular Expression Engine*.

Suppose we want to test whether a string is of the form x@x or not, where x is any character. The strings a@a, b@f, 3@h all are of the form x@x. You can observe a pattern here. The pattern is "Any character followed by @, which is followed by any character". How do we express this pattern in Java? A . (dot) represents any character inside a regular expression. The string .@. will represent our regular expression in this case. In the string .@., dot has special meaning. It represents any character. All such characters, which have special meanings inside a regular expression, are called *metacharacters*. We will discuss metacharacters in the next section. The `String` class has a `matches()` method. It takes a regular expression as an argument and returns `true` if the whole string matches the regular expression. Otherwise, it returns `false`. The signature of this method is:

```
boolean matches(String regex)
```

The program listed in Listing 13-1 illustrates the use of the `matches()` method of the `String` class.

Listing 13-1: Matching a string against a pattern

```java
// RegexMatch.java
package com.jdojo.chapter13;

public class RegexMatch {
    public static void main(String[] args) {
        // Prepare a regular expression to represent a pattern
        String regex = ".@.";

        String str = "a@k";
        RegexMatch.matchIt(str, regex);

        str = "webmaster@jdojo.com";
        RegexMatch.matchIt(str, regex);

        str = "r@j";
        RegexMatch.matchIt(str, regex);

        str = "a%N";
        RegexMatch.matchIt(str, regex);

        str = ".@.";
        RegexMatch.matchIt(str, regex);
    }

    public static void matchIt(String str, String regex) {
        // Test for pattern match
        if (str.matches(regex)) {
            System.out.println("String " + str +
                            " matches regular expression " + regex);
        }
        else {
            System.out.println("String " + str +
                        " does not match regular expression " + regex);
        }
    }
}
```

```
Output:

String a@k matches regular expression .@.
String webmaster@jdojo.com does not match regular expression .@.
String r@j matches regular expression .@.
String a%N does not match regular expression .@.
String .@. matches regular expression .@.
```

Some important points to note are:

- The ".@." regular expression did not match "webmaster@jdojo.com", because a dot means only one character and the matches() method of the String class matches the pattern represented by the regular expression against the whole string. Note that the string "webmaster@jdojo.com" has the pattern represented by ".@.", that is, a character followed by @ and another character. However, the pattern matches a part of the string and not the whole string. The "r@j" part of "webmaster@jdojo.com" matches that pattern. We will present some examples of such cases where we will be interested in matching a pattern anywhere in a string rather than matching the whole string.

- If you want to match a '.' character in a string, you will need to escape the '.' character in your regular expression. The regular expression ".\\.." will match any string of three character in which the middle character is a '.' character. For example, The method call "a.b".matches(".\\..") will return `true`; The method call "...".matches(".\\..") will return `true`; The method calls "abc".matches(".\\..") and "aa.ca".matches(".\\..") will return `false`.

TIP

A regular expression is a way to describe a pattern in a sequence of characters. The pattern may be used to validate the sequence of characters, to search through the sequence of characters, to replace the sequence of characters matching the pattern with other sequence of characters, etc. Java added support for regular expressions from *Java2 version 1.4*. The `String` class contains some convenience methods that let you use regular expressions.

You can also replace the matching string with another string. The `String` class has two methods to do the match replacement:

- `String replaceAll(String regex, String replacementString)`: It replaces strings, which match the pattern represented by `regex`, with the `replacementString`. It returns the new string after replacement. Some examples of using the `replaceAll()` method are shown below.

```
String regex = ".@.";
String str = "webmaster@jdojo.com";
String newStr;
newStr = str.replaceAll(regex,"***");   // newStr will contain
                                        // webmaste***dojo.com

str = "A@B";
newStr = str.replaceAll(regex,"***");   // newStr will contain
                                        // ***

str = "A@BandH@G";
newStr = str.replaceAll(regex,"***");   // newStr will contain
                                        // ***and***

str = "B%T";
newStr = str.replaceAll(regex,"***");   // newStr will contain
                                        // B%T (same as original
                                        // string)
```

- `String replaceFirst(String regex, String replacementString)`: It replaces the first occurrence of the string, which matches the pattern represented by `regex`, with the `replacementString`. It returns the new string after replacement. Some examples of using the `replaceFirst()` method are as follows.

```
String regex = ".@.";
String str = "webmaster@jdojo.com" ;
String newStr;
newStr = str.replaceFirst(regex,"***");       // newStr will contain
                                              // webmaste***dojo.com

str = "A@B";
newStr = str.replaceFirst(regex,"***");       // newStr will contain
```

```
                                                // ***

    str = "A@BandH@G";
    newStr = str.replaceFirst(regex,"***");     // newStr will contain
                                                // ***andH@G

    str = "B%T";
    newStr = str.replaceFirst(regex,"***");     // newStr will contain
                                                // B%T (same as
                                                // original string)
```

Metacharacters

Metacharacters are characters with special meaning that are used in preparing regular expressions. Sometimes, metacharacters do not have any special meanings and they are treated as ordinary characters. They are treated as ordinary characters or metacharacters depending on the context in which they are used. The metacharacters supported by the regular expressions in Java are as follows.

- ((left parenthesis)
-) (right parenthesis)
- [(left bracket)
- { (left brace)
- \ (backslash)
- ^ (caret)
- $ (dollar sign)
- | (vertical bar)
- ? (question mark)
- * (asterisk)
- + (addition sign)
- . (dot or period)

Character Classes

The metacharacters, '[' and ']', (left and right brackets) are used to specify a *character class* inside a regular expression. A character class is a set of characters. The regular expression engine will attempt to match one character from the set of the character class. Note that a character class has no relation with class construct or class files in Java. The character class "[ABC]" will match a character 'A', 'B', or 'C'. For example, the string "A@V" will match the regular expression "[ABC]@."; the string "B@V" will match the regular expression "[ABC]@."; the string "C@V" will match the regular expression "[ABC]@.". The string "H@V" will not match the regular expression "[ABC]@." because '@' is not preceded by A, B, or C. As another example, to match "man" or "men" the regular expression should be "m[ae]n".

TIP
When we use the word "match", we mean that the pattern exists in a string. We do not mean that the whole string matches the pattern. For example, "WEB@JDOJO.COM" matches the pattern

---

"`[ABC]@.`", because '`@`' is preceded by '`B`' The string "`A@BAND@YEA@U`" matches the pattern "`[ABC]@.`" twice even though the string contains three '`@`' signs. The second '`@`' is not a part of the match, because it is preceded by '`D`' and not '`A`', '`B`' or '`C`'..

You can also specify a range of characters using a character class. The range is expressed using a '`-`' (dash or hyphen) character. For example, "`[A-Z]`" in a regular expression represents any uppercase English letters; "`[0-9]`" represents any digit between `0` (zero) and `9` (nine). If you use '`^`' in the beginning of a character class, it means *complement (meaning not)*. For example, "`[^ABC]`" means any character except '`A`', '`B`' and '`C`'. The character class "`[^A-Z]`" represents any character except uppercase English letters. If you use '`^`' anywhere in a character class except in the beginning, it loses its special meaning (i.e. special meaning of complement) and it matches just a '`^`' character. For example, "`[ABC^]`" will match '`A`', '`B`', '`C`', or '`^`'..

You can also include two or more ranges in one character class. For example, "`[a-zA-Z]`" matches any character '`a`' through '`z`' and '`A`' through '`Z`'. "`[a-zA-Z0-9]`" matches any character '`a`' through '`z`' (uppercase and lowercase), and any digit '`0`' through '`9`'. Some examples of character classes are listed in Table 13-1.

Table 13-1: Examples of character classes

Character Classes	Meaning	Category
`[abc]`	Character a, b or c	Simple character class
`[^xyz]`	A character except x, y and z	Complement or negation
`[a-p]`	Characters a through p	Range
`[a-cx-z]`	Characters a through c, or x through z, which would include a, b, c, x, y or z.	Union
`[0-9&&[4-8]]`	Intersection of two ranges (4, 5, 6, 7 or 8)	Intersection
`[a-z&&[^aeiou]]`	All lowercase letters minus vowels. In other words, A lower case letter, which is not a vowel. That is, all lowercase consonants.	Subtraction

Predefined Character Classes

Some frequently used pre-defined character classes that are used in a regular expression are listed in Table 13-2.

Table 13-2: List of the predefined regular expression character classes

Predefined Character Classes	Meaning
. (dot)	Any character (may or may not match line terminators)
`\d`	A digit. Same as `[0-9]`
`\D`	A non-digit. Same as `[^0-9]`
`\s`	A whitespace character. Same as `[ \t\n\x0B\f\r]`. The list includes a space,

	tab, new line, vertical tab, form feed, and carriage return characters.
`\S`	A non-whitespace character. Same as `[^\s]`
`\w`	A word character. Same as `[a-zA-Z_0-9]`. The list includes lowercase letters, uppercase letter, underscore and decimal digits.
`\W`	A non-word character. Same as `[^\w]`

If we allow all uppercase and lowercase letters, underscore and digits in our email address validations, the regular expression to validate email addresses of only three characters would be `\w@\w`. Now, we are one step ahead in our email address validation process. Instead of allowing only `A`, `B`, or `C` in the first part of email (as expressed by regular expression `[ABC]@.`), now we are allowing any word character as the first part as well as second part in email address validation.

More Powers to Regular Expressions

Until now, we have seen only three methods of the `String` class using the regular expressions. *Java2 version 1.4* added a package `java.util.regex`, which contains three classes to support the full version of regular expressions. The classes are:

- `java.util.regex.Pattern`
- `java.util.regex.Matcher`
- `java.util.regex.PatternSyntaxException`

The Pattern Class

An instance of this class holds the compiled form of a regular expression. It is an immutable class and therefore, instances of this class can be shared. It has no `public` constructor. Therefore, you cannot create its object using the `new` operator. It has an overloaded `static compile()` method, which returns a reference to a `Pattern` object.. One of the `compile()` methods must be used to get a reference of a `Pattern` object. For example,

```
// Prepare the regular expression
String regex = "[a-z]@.";

// Compile the regular expression, which in turn will create a
// Pattern object
Pattern p = Pattern.compile(regex);
```

The Matcher Class

An instance of the `Matcher` class is used to perform a match on a sequence of characters by interpreting the compiled pattern held in an instance of the `Pattern` class. It has no `public` constructor. Therefore, you cannot create its object using the `new` operator. The `matcher()` method of the `Pattern` class is used to get an instance of the `Matcher` class. Continuing with the above snippet of code, we can get the reference of a `Matcher` object as:

```
// String to perform the match
String str = "abc@yahoo.com,123@cnn.com,ksharan@jdojo.com";

// Get a matcher object using Pattern object p
Matcher m = p.matcher(str);
```

At this point, the `Matcher` object `m` has associated the pattern represented in the `Pattern` object `p` with the sequence of characters in `str`. It is ready to start the match operation. Typically, a matcher object is used to find a match in the sequence of characters. The match may succeed. If the match succeeds, you may be interested in knowing the start and the end positions of the match as well as the matching text. You can query a `Matcher` object to get all these pieces of information.

The PatternSyntaxException Class

An instance of this class represents an error in a malformed regular expression.

Methods of the Matcher Class

The find() Method

It is used to find a match for the pattern in the input sequence of characters. If the find succeeds, it returns `true`. Otherwise, it returns `false`. The first call to this method starts the search for the pattern at the beginning of the sequence of characters. If the previous call to this method was successful, the call to this method starts the search after the previous match. Typically, a call to `find()` method is used in conjunction with a while-loop to find all the matches. It is an overloaded method. Another version of this method takes an integer argument, which is the offset to start the find for a match.

The start() Method

It returns the start index of the previous match. Typically, it is used after a successful `find()` method call.

The end() Method

It returns the index of the last character in the matched text plus one. Therefore, after a successful invocation of the `find()` method, the difference between the values returned by the `end()` and `start()` method of the `Matcher` object will give you the length of the matched string. Using the `substring()` method of the `String` class, you can get the matched string as:

```
// Continued from previous fragment of code
if (m.find()){
    // str is the string we are looking into
    String foundStr = str.substring(m.start(), m.end());
```

```
            System.out.println("Found text is:" + foundStr);
}
```

The group() Method

It returns the found text by the previous successful `find()` method call. Recall that you can also get the previous matched text using the `substring()` method of the `String` class by using the start and end of the match. Therefore, the above snippet of code can be replaced by (the redundant or lengthy version has been commented for comparison purpose) the following code.

```
if (m.find()) {
    /* Following three lines are not needed any more
        int len = m.end() - m.start();
        str is the string we are looking into
        String foundStr = str.substring(start, end - start)
    */
    String foundStr = m.group();
    System.out.println("Found text is:" + foundStr);
}
```

It is recommended to use the `group()` method to get the matched text. In fact, a `Matcher` object can perform a pattern match on a `CharSequence`, which is an interface defined in the `java.lang` package. An object of any class, which implements the `CharSequence` interface, can be used with the `Pattern` and `Matcher` classes to perform a match. The `String` class implements the `CharSequence` interface. Therefore, we can use any string with the `Pattern` and `Matcher` class to perform a match. We were able to use the `substring()` method to get the matched text, because we were working with strings and the `String` class has a `substring()` method. However, not all classes implementing the `CharSequence` interface may have a `substring()` method. Therefore, you may not be able to use it to get the matched text. We have not covered interfaces yet. If you do not understand what an interface means in Java, just skip this explanation and revisit it when you learn about Interfaces in the chapter on *Interfaces*. Listing 13-2 illustrates the use of these methods. The validations for the method's arguments have been omitted for clarity. The program attempts to find the "`[abc]@.`" pattern in different strings.

Listing 13-2: Using Pattern and Matcher classes

```
// PatternMatcher.java
package com.jdojo.chapter13;

import java.util.regex.Pattern;   // Import Pattern class
import java.util.regex.Matcher;   // Import Matcher class

public class PatternMatcher {
    public static void main(String[] args) {
        String regex = "[abc]@.";

        String source = "abha@jdojo.com is a valid email address";
        PatternMatcher.findPattern(regex, source);

        source = "kelly@jdojo.com is invalid";
        PatternMatcher.findPattern(regex, source);

        source = "a@band@yea@u";
        PatternMatcher.findPattern(regex, source);
```

```
            source = "There is an @ sign here";
            PatternMatcher.findPattern(regex, source);
        }

    public static void findPattern(String regex, String source) {
        // Compile regex into a Pattern object
        Pattern p = Pattern.compile(regex);

        // Get a Matcher object
        Matcher m = p.matcher(source);

        boolean found = false ;

        // Print regex and source text
        System.out.println("\nRegex:" + regex);
        System.out.println("Text:" + source);

        // Perform find
        while (m.find()) {
            System.out.println("Matched Text:" + m.group() +
                              ", Start:" + m.start() + ", " +
                              "End:" + m.end());

            // We found at least one match
            // Set the found flag to true
            found = true;
        }

        if (!found) {
            // We did not find any match
            System.out.println("No match found");
        }
    }
}
```

```
Output

Regex:[abc]@.
Text:abha@jdojo.com is a valid email address
Matched Text:a@j, Start:3, End:6

Regex:[abc]@.
Text:kelly@jdojo.com is invalid
No match found

Regex:[abc]@.
Text:a@band@yea@u
Matched Text:a@b, Start:0, End:3
Matched Text:a@u, Start:9, End:12

Regex:[abc]@.
Text:There is an @ sign here
No match found
```

Beware of Backslashes

Beware of using backslashes in regular expressions. The character class `\w`, that is, a backslash followed by a `w` represents a word character. Recall that a backslash character is also used as a part of an escape character. Therefore, `\w` must be written as "`\\w`" as a string literal. You can also use backslash to nullify the special meaning of metacharacters. For example, `[` (left bracket) marks the beginning of a character class. What would be the regular expression, which will match a digit enclosed in brackets, e.g., `[1]`, `[5]`, etc.? Note that the regular expression `[0-9]` will match any digit. The digit may or may not be enclosed in a bracket. You may think about `[[0-9]]`. It will not give you any error message. It will not do the intended job either. You can also embed a character class within another. For example, you can write `[a-z[0-9]]` and it is same as `[a-z0-9]`. In our case, the first `[` (bracket in `[[0-9]]`) should be treated as an ordinary character and not as a metacharacter. We must use a backslash as `\[[0-9]\]`. To write this regular expression as a string literal, we need to use two backslashes as "`\\[[0-9]\\]`".

Quantifiers in Regular Expressions

You can also specify the number of times a character in a regular expression may match the sequence of characters. If we want to match all two digit integers, our regular expression would be `\d\d` (same as: `[0-9][0-9]`). What would be the regular expression, which would match any integer? We cannot write the regular expression to match any integer with the knowledge we have gained so far. We need to be able to express a pattern – "one digit or more" using a regular expression. Here comes the concept of quantifiers. All quantifiers and their meanings have been listed in Table 13-3.

Table 13-3: Quantifiers and their meaning

Quantifiers	Meaning
`*`	Zero or more times
`+`	One or more times
`?`	Once or not at all
`{m}`	Exactly m times
`{m, }`	At least m times
`{m, n}`	At least m, but not more than n times

It is important to note that quantifiers must follow a character or character class for which it specifies the quantity. The regular expression to match any integer would be `\d+`, which says that match one or more number of digits. Is our solution for matching integer correct? No. It is not. Suppose our text is "`This is text123 which contains 10 and 120`". If we run our pattern `\d+` against this string, it will match against `123,  10` and `120`. Note that `123` is not used as an integer rather it is a part of word `text123`. If we are looking for integers in a text, certainly `123` in `text123` does not qualify as an integer. We want to match all integers, which form a word in the text.

Necessity is the mother of invention. Now, we need to specify that the match should be performed only on word boundaries and not inside any text having embedded integers. This is necessary to exclude integer `123` from our previous result. The next section discusses the use of metacharacters to match boundaries.

With the knowledge we have gained in this section, let us improve our email address validation. Inside an email address, there must be one and only one @ sign. To specify one and only one character we use that character one time in the regular expression although we can use `{1}` as quantifier. For example, `X{1}` and `X` means the same thing inside a regular expression. We are fine on this account. However, our solution until now supports only one character before and after the @ sign. In reality, there can be more than one character before and after the @ sign in an email address. We can specify the pattern to validate an email address as `\w+@\w+`, which means – one or more word characters, an @ sign, and one or more word characters.

Matching Boundaries

Until now, we did not care about the location of the pattern match in the text. Sometimes, you may be interested in knowing if the match occurred in the beginning of a line. You may be interested in finding and replacing a particular match only if the match was found in a word and not as a part of any word. For example, you may want to replace word `apple` inside a string by word `orange`. Suppose your string is – `"I have an apple and five pineapples"`. Certainly, you do not want to replace all occurrences of `apple` by `orange` in this string. If you do, your new string would be: `"I have an orange and five pineoranges"`. In fact, you want the new string to be - `"I have an orange and five pineapples"`. You want to match the word `apple`, which is a standalone word and not the part of any other word. Note that the word `apple` also appears as a part of the word `pine**apple**s`.

Table 13-4 lists all boundary matchers, which can be used in a regular expression. The regular expression to match the word `apple` would be `\bapple\b`, which means – "A word boundary, the word `apple`, and a word boundary". Listing 13-3 demonstrates how to match a word boundary using a regular expression.

Table 13-4: List of boundary matchers inside regular expressions

Boundary Matchers	Meaning
^	The beginning of a line
$	The end of a line
\b	A word boundary
\B	A non-word boundary
\A	The beginning of the input
\G	The end of previous match
\Z	The end of the input but for the final terminator, if any
\z	The end of the input

Listing 13-3: Matching a word boundary

```java
// MatchBoundary.java
package com.jdojo.chapter13;
```

```
public class MatchBoundary {
    public static void main(String[] args) {
        // Prepare regular expression.
        // Use \\b to get \b inside string literal
        String regex = "\\bapple\\b";
        String replacementStr = "orange";
        String inputStr = "I have an apple and five pineapples";
        String newStr = inputStr.replaceAll(regex, replacementStr);

        System.out.println("Regular Expression: " + regex);
        System.out.println("Input String: " + inputStr);
        System.out.println("Replacement String: " + replacementStr);
        System.out.println("New String: " + newStr);
    }
}
```

```
Output:

Regular Expression: \bapple\b
Input String: I have an apple and five pineapples
Replacement String: orange
New String: I have an orange and five pineapples
```

There are two boundary matchers: ^ (beginning of a line) and \A (beginning of the input). Input string may consist of multiple lines. If the input string consists of multiple lines, \A will match the beginning of entire input string, whereas ^ will match beginning of each line in the input. For example, regular expression "^The" will match each The in input string, which is in the beginning of a line.

Groups and Back Referencing

You can treat multiple characters as a unit by using them as a group. A group is created inside a regular expression by enclosing one or more characters inside parentheses. For example, (ab), ab(z), ab(ab)(xyz), (the((is)(is))) are all examples of groups. A number is associated with each group. The group number starts at 1. The Matcher class has a method groupCount() that returns an int value, which is the total number of groups present in the pattern associated with the Matcher instance. There is a special group called group 0 (zero). It refers to the entire regular expression. The group 0 is not reported in the groupCount() method call for the Matcher object. How is each group numbered? Each left parenthesis inside a regular expression marks the start of a new group.

Table 13-5 lists some examples of how groups are numbered in a regular expression. Note that we have also listed group 0 for all regular expressions although it is not reported by the groupCount() method of the Matcher class. The last example in the list shows that the group 0 is present, even if there are no explicit groups present in the regular expression.

Table 13-5: Examples of groups in regular expressions

Regular Expression: AB(XY)
Number of groups reported by Matcher class's groupCount() method: 1

Group Number	Group Text
0	AB(XY)
1	(XY)

Regular Expression: (AB)(XY)

Number of groups reported by Matcher class's groupCount() method: 2

Group Number	Group Text
0	(AB)(XY)
1	(AB)
2	(XY)

Regular Expression: ((A)((X)(Y)))

Number of groups reported by Matcher class's groupCount() method: 5

Group Number	Group Text
0	((A)((X)(Y)))
1	((A)((X)(Y)))
2	(A)
3	((X)(Y))
4	(X)
5	(Y)

Regular Expression: ABXY

Number of groups reported by Matcher class's groupCount() method: 0

Group Number	Group Text
0	ABXY

You can also back reference group numbers in a regular expression. Suppose you want to match texts, which start with ab followed by xy, which is followed by ab. You can write a regular expression as abxyab. You can also achieve the same result by forming a group, which will contain ab and back referencing it as (ab)xy\1. Here, \1 refers to group 1, which is (ab) in our case. You can use a \2 to refer to group 2, \3 to refer to group 3 and so on. How will regular expression (ab)xy\12 be interpreted? We have used \12 as the group back reference. The regular expression engine is smart enough to detect that there is only one group in the regular expression (ab)xy\12. It uses \1 as back reference to group 1, which is (ab) and 2 as an ordinary character 2. Therefore, (ab)xy\12 is the same as abxyab2 for the matching purposes.

You can also fetch part of a matched text by using a group number in the regular expression. The group() method in the Matcher class is overloaded. We have already seen the group() method, which takes no argument. Another version of the method takes a group number as an argument and it returns the matched text by that group. Suppose we have phone numbers embedded in an input text. All phone numbers occurs as a word and are ten digits long. The first three digits is the area code. The regular expression \b\d{10}\b will match all phone numbers in the input text. However, to get the first three digits, that is the area code, we will have to write extra code. If we form a regular expression using groups, we can get the area code by referring to it by group number. The regular expression placing the first three digits of a phone number in a group would be `\b(\d{3})\d{7}\b`. If m is reference to the `Matcher` object associated with this pattern, `m.group(1)` will return the first three digits of the phone number after a successful match. You can also use `m.group(0)` to get the entire matched text. Listing 13-4 illustrates the use of groups in regular expressions to get the area code part of phone numbers. Note that `2339829` did not match the pattern, because it has only 7 digits.

Listing 13-4: Using groups in regular expressions

```
// PhoneMatcher.java
package com.jdojo.chapter13;

import java.util.regex.Pattern;
import java.util.regex.Matcher;

public class PhoneMatcher {
    public static void main(String[] args){
        // Prepare regular expression.
        // A group of 3 digits followed by 7 digits
        String regex = "\\b(\\d{3})\\d{7}\\b";
        String source = "3342449027, 2339829, and 6152534734";

        // Compile the regular expression
        Pattern p = Pattern.compile(regex);

        // Get Matcher object
        Matcher m = p.matcher(source);

        // Start matching and display the found area codes
        while(m.find()){
            /* Display the phone number and area code
               Note that group 1 captures first 3 digits of match
               whereas group 0 will have the entire phone number.
               The matched text can be obtained using m.group()
               or m.group(0)
            */
            String phone = m.group();
            String areaCode = m.group(1);
            System.out.println("Phone: " + phone +
                            ", Area Code: " + areaCode);
        }
    }
}
```

```
Output:

Phone: 3342449027, Area Code: 334
Phone: 6152534734, Area Code: 615
```

Groups are also used to format or replace the matched string with another string. Suppose we want to format all 10-digit phone numbers as (XXX) XXX-XXXX, where X denotes a digit. The format is- "The first three digits enclosed in parentheses followed by a space, followed by three digits, followed by a – (hyphen), followed by the last four digits. You may observe that we have broken the phone number into three groups – the first three digits, the next three digits and the last four digits. We need to form a regular expression using the three groups, so that we can refer to the three

matched groups by their group numbers. Our regular expression would be
`\b(\d{3})(\d{3})(\d{4})\b`. The `\b` in the beginning and in the end denotes that we are interested in matching ten digits only at word boundaries. The following snippet of code illustrates how we can display formatted phone numbers.

```
// Prepare the regular expression
String regex = "\\b(\\d{3})(\\d{3})(\\d{4})\\b";
String source = "3342449027, 2339829, and 6152534734";

// Compile the regular expression
Pattern p = Pattern.compile(regex);

// Get Matcher object
Matcher m = p.matcher(source);

// Start match and display formatted phone numbers
while(m.find()){
    System.out.println("Phone: " + m.group() + ", " +
                       "Formatted Phone: (" + m.group(1) + ") " +
                       m.group(2) + "-"  + m.group(3));
}
```

```
Output:

Phone: 3342449027, Formatted Phone: (334) 244-9027
Phone: 6152534734, Formatted Phone: (615) 253-4734
```

You can also replace all 10-digit phone numbers in the input text by formatted phone numbers. You have already learned how to replace the matched text with another text using the `replaceAll()` method of the `String` class. The `Matcher` class also has a `replaceAll()` method, which accomplishes the same thing. The problem we are facing in replacing the phone numbers by the formatted phone numbers is getting the matched parts of the matched phone numbers. In this case, the replacement text also contains the matched text. We do not know what text matched the pattern in advance. Groups come to our rescue. $n, where n is a group number, inside a replacement text refers to the matched text for group n. For example, $1 refers to the first matched group. The replacement text to replace the phone numbers with the formatted phone numbers will be ($1) $2-$3. Listing 13-5 illustrates the technique of referencing groups in a replacement text.

Listing 13-5: Back referencing a group in a replacement text

```
// MatchAndreplace.java
package com.jdojo.chapter13;

import java.util.regex.Matcher;
import java.util.regex.Pattern;

public class MatchAndreplace {
    public static void main(String[] args) {
        // Prepare the regular expression
        String regex = "\\b(\\d{3})(\\d{3})(\\d{4})\\b";
        String replacementText = "($1) $2-$3";
        String source = "3342449027, 2339829, and 6152534734";

        // Compile the regular expression
        Pattern p = Pattern.compile(regex);
```

```
                // Get Matcher object
                Matcher m = p.matcher(source);

                // Replace the phone numbers by formatted phone numbers
                String formattedSource = m.replaceAll(replacementText);

                System.out.println("Text: " + source );
                System.out.println("Formatted Text: " + formattedSource );
        }
}
```

```
Output:

Text: 3342449027, 2339829, and 6152534734
Formatted Text: (334) 244-9027, 2339829, and (615) 253-4734
```

You can also achieve the same result by using the `String` class. You do not need to use the `Pattern` and `Matcher` classes at all. The following snippet of code illustrates the same concept as above, using the `String` class instead. Note that the `String` class uses `Pattern` and `Matcher` class internally to get the result.

```
// Prepare the regular expression
String regex = "\\b(\\d{3})(\\d{3})(\\d{4})\\b";
String replacementText = "($1) $2-$3";
String source = "3342449027, 2339829, and 6152534734";

// Use replaceAll() method of String class
String formattedSource = source.replaceAll(regex, replacementText)
```

Resetting the Matcher

If you have finished matching a pattern against an input text and you want to restart matching from the beginning of the input text again, you need to use the `reset()` method of the `Matcher` class. After a call to the `reset()` method, the next call to match a pattern will start from the beginning of the input text. The `reset()` method is overloaded. Another version allows you to associate a different input text with the pattern. These two versions of `reset()` methods allow you to reuse any existing instance of the `Matcher` class if your pattern remains the same. This enhances the performance of your program by avoiding the need to recreate a new `Matcher` object to perform matches against the same pattern.

Final Words on Email Validations

Now that we have covered the major parts of regular expressions, we are ready to complete our email address validation example. Our email addresses will be validated against the following rules.

- All email addresses will be of the form `name@domain`
- The name part must start with an alphanumeric character (`a-z`, `A-Z`, `0-9`)

- The name part must have at least one character.
- The name part may have any alphanumeric character (`a-z`, `A-Z`, `0-9`), underscore, hyphen, dot
- The dot in the domain part must contain at least one dot
- The . (dot) in domain name must be preceded and followed by at least one alphanumeric character.
- We should also be able to refer to the name and the domain parts using group numbers. This validation states that we place name and domain part as groups inside the regular expression

The following regular expression will match an email address, according to the above rules. - group 1 is the name part whereas group 2 is the domain part.

```
([a-zA-Z0-9]+[\\w\\-.]*)@([a-zA-Z0-9]+\\.[a-zA-Z0-9\\-.]+)
```

The more validations you add, the more complex will be the regular expression. Readers are encouraged to add some more validations for email addresses and modify the above regular expression accordingly. This regular expression to validate an email address allows two consecutive dots in the domain part. How would you prevent that?

Advanced Regular Expression Features - Find and Replace

Find and replace is a very powerful technique supported by regular expressions in Java. Implementing the find and replace features may not be easy. Sometimes, you may be required to find a pattern and replace it depending upon the text it matches, that is, the replacement text is decided based on some conditions. The Java regular expression designer visualized this need and they have included two methods in the `Matcher` class, which let you accomplish this task. The methods are `appendReplacement()` and `appendTail()`. The signatures for these two methods are:

```
public Matcher appendReplacement(StringBuffer sb, String replacement)
public StringBuffer appendTail(StringBuffer sb)
```

Let us consider a text as follows.

```
A train carrying 125 men and women was traveling at the speed of 100
miles per hour. The train fare was 75 dollars per person.
```

We want to find all numbers in this text (e.g. 1000, 100 and 75). We want to replace numbers as follows.

```
"100" by "a hundred"
"> 100" by "more than a hundred", and
"< 100" by "less than a hundred"
```

After replacement, the above text should read as follows. The replaced texts have been shown in italics.

```
A train carrying more than a hundred men and women was traveling at the
speed of a hundred miles per hour. The train fare was less than a hundred
dollars per person.
```

To accomplish this task, we need to find all numbers embedded in the text, compare the found number with 100, and decide on the replacement text. Such a situation also arises when you find and replace text using a text editor. The text editor highlights the word you were searching for, you type in the new word and text editor does the replacement for you. You can also create a find/replace program as found in text editors using these two methods of the `Matcher` class. Typically, these two methods are used in conjunction with the `find()` method of the `Matcher` class. The steps that are performed to accomplish find and replace texts using these two methods are outlined below.

Step #1

Create a `Pattern` object by compiling the regular expression. Since we want to find all numbers our regular expression would be \b\d+\b. Note the first and last \b. They specify that we are interested in numbers only on word boundaries.

```
String regex = "\\b\\d+\\b";
Pattern p = Pattern.compile(regex);
```

Step #2

Get a `Matcher` object by associating the pattern with the text.

```
String text = "A train carrying 125 men and women was traveling"
            + " at the speed of 100 miles per hour. The train"
            + " fare was 75 dollars per person.";

Matcher m = p.matcher(text);
```

Step #3

Create a `StringBuffer` object to hold the new text

```
StringBuffer sb = new StringBuffer();
```

Step #4

Start using the `find()` method on the `Matcher` object to find a match. When you invoke the `find()` method for the first time, the number 125 will match the pattern. The text before the match has been shown in a box. The matched text has been shown in bold and the text yet to be matched has been shown in normal fonts.

A train carrying **125** men and women was traveling at the speed of 100 miles per hour. The train fare was 75 dollars per person.

At this point, we would like to prepare the replacement text depending on the matched text as:

```
String replacementText = "";

// Get the matched text. Recall that group() method returns the
// whole matched text
String matchedText = m.group();

// Convert the text into integer for comparison
int num = Integer.parseInt(matchedText);
```

```
// Prepare the replacement text
if (num == 100){
    replacementText = "a hundred";
}
else if (num < 100){
    replacementText = "less than a hundred";
}
else {
    replacementText = "more than a hundred";
}
```

Now, we will call the `appendReplacement()` method on the `Matcher` object passing an empty `StringBuffer` and `replacementText` as arguments. In this case, `replacementText` has a string "more than hundred" because the `find()` method call matched the number 125..

```
m.appendReplacement(sb, replacementText);
```

Now, it is interesting to know what the `appendReplacement()` method call does. It checks if there was a previous match. Since this is the first call to the `find()` method, there is no previous match. For the first match, it appends the text starting from the beginning of the input text until the character before the matching text. In our case, the text shown in the box is appended to the `StringBuffer`. At this point, the text in the `StringBuffer` is

```
"A train carrying "
```

Now, the `appendReplacement()` method appends the text in the `replacementText` argument to the `StringBuffer`. This will change the `StringBuffer` contents to:

```
"A train carrying more than a hundred"
```

The, `appendReplacement()` method does one more thing. It sets the append position (an internal state of the `Matcher` object) to the character position just after the first matching text. In our case, the append position will be set to the character following 125, which is the position of the following space character.

This will finish the first find and replace step. We will call the `find()` method of the `Matcher` object again. It will find the pattern, i.e., another number, which is 100. The input text can be shown as follows.

A train carrying 125 men and women was traveling at the speed of **100** miles per hour. The train fare was 75 dollars per person.

The matched text is shown in bold. The text after the first match and before the second match has been shown in a box. The text that has already been processed is shown in italics. The text that is yet to be matched is shown in normal font. We will compute the value of the replacement text using the same procedure as we did after the first match. This time, the `replacementText` will contain the string "a hundred". We call `appendReplacement()` method as follows.

```
m.appendReplacement(sb, replacementText);
```

Again, it checks if there was a previous match. Since this was the second call to the `find()` method, it will find a previous match and it will use the append position saved by the last `appendReplacement()` call as the starting position. The last character to be appended will be the character just before the second match. The text in the box shown above will be appended to the existing text in the `StringBuffer` and it will append the words "`a hundred`" to it. It will also set the append position to the character position following the number 100. At this point, the `StringBuffer` contains the following text:

```
"A train carrying more than a hundred men and women was traveling
at the speed of a hundred"
```

When we call `find()` method for the third time, it will find the number 75 and the `StringBuffer` buffer content will be as follows after the replacement. The append position will be set to the character position following the number 75.

```
"A train carrying more than a hundred men and women was traveling
 at the speed of a hundred miles per hour. The train fare was less than
 a hundred"
```

If we call the `find()` method again, this time, it will not find any match. However, the `StringBuffer` does not contain the text following the last match i.e. "`dollars per person.`". To append the text following the last match, you need to call the `appendTail()` method. It appends the text to the `StringBuffer` starting at append position until the end of the input string. The call to this method as:

```
m.appendTail(sb);
```

will modify the `StringBuffer` to :

```
"A train carrying more than a hundred men and women was traveling
at the speed of a hundred miles per hour. The train fare was less than
a hundred dollars per person."
```

What will be the content of the `StringBuffer`, if we would have called the `appendTail()` method just after the second call to the `appendReplacement()` method? The complete program has been listed in Listing 13-6..

Listing 13-6: Find and replace using regular expressions and appendReplacement() and appendTail() methods

```java
// AdvanceFindReplace.java
package com.jdojo.chapter13;

import java.util.regex.Pattern;
import java.util.regex.Matcher;

public class AdvanceFindReplace {
    public static void main (String[] args){
        String regex = "\\b\\d+\\b";
        StringBuffer sb = new StringBuffer();
        String replacementText = "";
        String matchedText = "";

        String text = "A train carrying 125 men and women" +
                        " was traveling at the speed of 100" +
                        " miles per  hour. The train" +
```

```
                          " fare was 75 dollars per person." ;

        Pattern p = Pattern.compile(regex);
        Matcher m = p.matcher(text);

        while (m.find()) {
            matchedText = m.group();

            // Convert the text into integer for comparison
            int num = Integer.parseInt(matchedText);

            // Prepare the replacement text
            if (num == 100){
                replacementText = "a hundred";
            }

            if (num < 100){
                replacementText = "less than a hundred";
            }
            else {
                replacementText = "more than a hundred";
            }

            m.appendReplacement(sb, replacementText);

        } // End of while

        // append the tail
        m.appendTail(sb);

        // Display the old and new text
        System.out.println("Old Text: " + text);

        System.out.println("New Text: " + sb.toString());

    }    // End of main method

}    // End of AdvanceFindReplace class
```

```
Output:

Old Text: A train carrying 125 men and women was traveling at the speed
of 100 miles per hour. The train fare was 75 dollars per person.
New Text: A train carrying more than hundred men and women was traveling
at the speed of more than hundred miles per hour. The train fare was less
than hundred dollars per person.
```

Chapter 14. Arrays

What is an Array?

An array is a fixed-length data structure that is used to hold more than one value of the same type. Let us consider an example, which will explain why we need an array. Suppose you have been asked to declare variables to hold employee ids of three employees. It has been stated that the employee ids will be integers. Your variable declarations to hold three integer values will look like:

```
int empId1, empId2, empId3;
```

What do you do if the number of employees increases to five? You may modify your variable declarations to:

```
int empId1, empId2, empId3, empId4, empId5;
```

What do you do if the number of employees increases to one thousand? Definitely, you would not want to declare one thousand `int` variables like `empId1, empId2...empId1000`. Even if you go for 1000 variables declarations, the resulting code would be unmanageable and clumsy. Arrays come to your rescue in such situations. Using an array, you can declare a variable of a type, which can hold as many values of that type as you want. In fact, Java has a restriction on the number of values an array can hold. An array can hold a maximum of 2147483647 values, which is the maximum value of the `int` data type. What makes a variable an array? Placing `[]` (empty brackets) after the data type or after the variable name in a variable declaration makes the variable an array. For example,

```
int empId;
```

is a simple variable declaration. Here, `int` is the data type and `empId` is the variable name. This declaration means that the `empId` variable can hold one integer value. If we place `[]` after the data type in the above declaration:

```
int[] empId;
```

then `empId` is an array variable. The above declaration is read as – "*empId is an array of int*". You can also make the `empId` variable an array as:

```
int empId[];
```

Both of the above declarations of `empId` as an array of `int` are valid. This book uses the first convention to declare an array (e.g. `int[] empId;`). We started our discussion with an example of variable declaration to hold three employee ids. Until now, we have prepared the ground to hold more than one value in one variable. That is, our `empId` variable declared as an array of `int` is capable of holding more than one `int` value. How many values can our `empId` array variable hold? The answer is we do not know yet. You cannot specify the number of values an array can hold at the time you declare the array. The subsequent sections explain how to specify the number

of values an array can hold. You can declare an array to hold multiple values of a data type –
primitive or reference. More examples of arrays declarations are shown below.

```
//salary can hold multiple float values
float[] salary;

//name can hold multiple references to String objects
String[] name;

//emp can hold multiple references to Employee objects
Employee[] emp;
```

An Array is an Object

All arrays in Java are objects. Every object belongs to a class, so does every array object. You can
create an array object using the `new` operator. We have used the `new` operator with a constructor
to create an object of a class. The name of a constructor is the same as the name of the class.
What is the name of the class of an array object? The answer to this question is not so obvious.
We will answer this question later in this chapter. For now, we will concentrate on how to create an
array object of a particular type. The array object creation expression starts with the `new` operator,
followed by the data type of the values you want to store in the array, followed by an integer
enclosed in `[]` (brackets), which is the number of values you want to store in the array. The
general syntax for array creation expression is shown below.

```
new ArrayDataType[ArrayLength];   // Creates an array object of type
                                  // ArrayDataType of ArrayLength length
```

Continuing with our discussion, we can declare an array to store five employee ids as follows.

```
new int[5];
```

In the above expression, 5 is the *length* of the array (also called the *dimension* of the array). The
word *dimension* is also used in another context. You can have an array of dimension one, two,
three, or more. An array with more than one dimension is called a multi-dimensional array. We will
cover the multi-dimensional array later in this chapter. In this book, we will refer to 5 in the above
expression as the length and not as the dimension of the array.

Note that the above expression creates an array object in memory, which allocates memory to
store 5 integers. The `new` operator returns the reference of the new object in memory. If we want to
use this object later in our code, we must store that reference in an object reference variable. The
reference variable type must match the type of object reference returned by the `new` operator. In
the above case, the `new` operator will return an object reference of `int` array type. We have
already seen how to declare a reference variable of `int` array type. It is declared as:

```
int[] empId;
```

To store the array object reference in `empId`, we can write:

```
empId = new int[5];
```

We can also combine the declaration of an array and its creation in one statement as:

```
int[] empId = new int[5];
```

How would you create an array to store 252 employee ids? You can do this as:

```
int[] empId = new int[252];
```

You can also use an expression to specify the length of an array while creating it. For example,

```
int total = 23;
int[] array1 = new int[total];       // array1 has 23 elements
int[] array2 = new int[total * 3];   // array2 has 69 elements
```

Since all arrays in Java are objects, their references can be assigned to a reference variable of `Object` type. For example,

```
int[] empId = new int[5]; // Create an array object
Object obj = empId;       // Valid assignment
```

However, if you have the reference of an array in a reference variable of `Object` type, you need to cast it to the appropriate array type before you can assign it to an array reference variable. Remember that every array in Java is an object. However, not every object in Java is necessarily an array. If you want to assign an `int` array reference stored in an `obj` reference variable to a variable of `int` array type, in the above code, you will do it as:

```
// Assume that obj has a reference of an int array. If obj does not
// have a reference to an int array, the following assignment will
// generate runtime error, but will compile fine
int[] tempIds = (int[])obj;
```

Referring to Elements of an Array

Once you create an array object using the `new` operator, you can refer to each individual element of the array using an element's index enclosed in brackets. The index for the first element of an array is 0 (zero). The index for the second element of an array is 1 and so on. The index for the last element of an array is equal to the length of the array minus 1. If you have an array of length 5, the indexes you can use to refer to array elements would be 0, 1, 2, 3 and 4. Consider the following statement:

```
int[] empId = new int[5];
```

The length of the `empId` array is 5; its elements can be referred to as `empId[0]`, `empId[1]`, `empId[2]`, `empId[3]`, and `empId[4]`. It is a runtime error to refer to a non-existing element of an array. For example, using `empId[5]` in your code will throw an exception, because `empId` has a length of 5 and `empId[5]` refers to the 6th element, which is non-existent. You can assign values to elements of an array as follows.

```
empId[0] = 10; // Assign 10 to the 1st element of empId
empId[1] = 20; // Assign 20 to the 2nd element of empId
empId[2] = 30; // Assign 30 to the 3rd element of empId
empId[3] = 40; // Assign 40 to the 4th element of empId
empId[4] = 50; // Assign 50 to the 5th element of empId
```

Table 14-1 has array's elements index, elements in memory with values and the element's syntactic notation to refer to them in program after above statements are executed.

Table 14-1: Array elements in memory for the empId array

Element's Index →	0	1	2	3	4
Element's values →	10	20	30	40	50
Element's reference →	empId[0]	empId[1]	empId[2]	empId[3]	empId[4]

If you want to assign the value of the 3rd element of the empId array to an int variable temp, you can do so as:

```
int temp = empId[2];    // Assign the value stored in 3rd element of
                        // empId array to variable temp
```

Length of an Array

An array object has a public final instance variable named length. You can use the length instance variable to get the number of elements in the array as:

```
int[] empId = new int[5];    // Create an array of length 5
int len = empId.length ;     // 5 will be assigned to len
```

Note that length is the property of the array object you create. Unless you create the array object, you cannot use its length property. Following code fragment illustrates this situation.

```
int[] salary; // salary is just a reference variable, which can
              // refer to an array of int. At this point,
              // salary is not referring to any array object

int len = salary.length;     // Runtime error. salary is not referring
                             // to any array object yet

salary = new int[1000];      // Create an int array of length 1000
                             // and assign its reference to salary

int len2 = salary.length;    // Correct. len2 has value 1000
```

Typically, when you work with arrays, you also work with loops. If you want to do any processing with all elements of an array, you execute a loop starting from index 0 (zero) to length minus 1. For example, to assign the values 10, 20, 30, 40, and 50 to the elements of the empId array of length 5, you would execute a for-loop as:

```
for (int i = 0 ; i < empId.length; i++) {
    empId[i] = (i + 1) * 10;
}
```

It is important to note that while executing the loop, the loop condition must check for array index/subscript for being less than the length of array as in "i < empId.length", because the array index starts with 0 (zero) and not 1. Another common mistake made by programmers, while processing an array using a for-loop, is to start the loop with a loop counter of 1 as opposed to 0 (zero). What will happen if we change the initialization part of the for-loop in the above code from `int i = 0` to `int i = 1`? It would not give us any errors. However, our first element `empId[0]` would not be processed and would not be assigned the value of 10 as intended.

You cannot change the length of an array after it is created. You may be tempted to modify its length property as:

```
int[] roll = new int[5]; // Create an array of 5 elements

roll.length = 10;   // Compiler error. Length property of an array is
                    // declared final. You cannot modify it.
```

You can have a zero-length array. Such an array is called an empty array. You can create an array of `int` of zero length as:

```
int[] emptyArray = new int[0];   // Create an array of length zero
int len = emptyArray.length;     // Will assign zero to len
```

TIP
In Java, array indexes are zero based. That is, the first element of an array has an index of zero. Arrays are created dynamically at runtime and their length cannot be modified after it has been created. If you feel the need to alter the length of an array, you must create a new array and copy the elements from the old array to the new array. It is valid to create an array of length zero.

Initializing Elements of an Array

Recall from the chapter on *Classes and Objects* that unlike class member variables (instance and static variables), local variables are not initialized by default. That is, you cannot access a local variable in your code unless you have assigned a value to it. The same rule applies to blank final variables. The Java compiler uses *Rules of Definite Assignment* to make sure that all variables have been initialized before their values are used in a program.

Array elements are always initialized irrespective of the scope in which the array is created. Array elements of primitive data type are initialized to the default value for their data types. For example, the elements of arrays of numeric types are initialized to zero; the elements of `boolean` arrays are initialized to `false`; the elements of a reference type arrays are initialized to `null`. The following snippet of code illustrates the array initialization. Listing 14-1 illustrates the array initialization for an instance variable and some local variables.

```
// All three elements have value of zero. intArray[0], intArray[1]
// and intArray[2] are initialized to zero by default
int[] intArray = new int[3];

// bArray[0] and bArray[1] are initialized to false
boolean[] bArray = new boolean[2];

// Example of reference type array strArray[0] and strArray[1]
// are initialized to null
String[] strArray = new String[2]
```

```
// Another example of reference type array. All 100 elements of
// person array are initialized to null
Person[] person = new Person[100];
```

Listing 14-1: Array Initialization

```java
// ArrayInit.java
package com.jdojo.chapter14;

public class ArrayInit {
    private boolean[] bArray = new boolean[3];   // An instance variable

    public ArrayInit() {
        // Display the initial value for elements of
        // instance variable bArray
        for (int i = 0; i < bArray.length; i++) {
            System.out.println("bArray[" + i + "]:" + bArray[i]);
        }
    }

    public static void main(String[] args) {
        int[] empId = new int[3];  // A local array variable
        System.out.println("int array initialization:");
        for (int i = 0; i < empId.length; i++) {
            System.out.println("empId[" + i + "]:" + empId[i]);
        }

        System.out.println("\nboolean array initialization:");
        new ArrayInit();  // Note that we are displaying initial
                          // value for bArray inside constructor

        String[] name = new String[3];   // A array local variable
        System.out.println("\nReference type array initialization:");

        for (int i = 0; i < name.length; i++) {
            System.out.println("name[" + i + "]:" + name[i]);
        }
    }
}
```

```
Output:

int array initialization:
empId[0]:0
empId[1]:0
empId[2]:0

boolean array initialization:
bArray[0]:false
bArray[1]:false
bArray[2]:false

Reference type array initialization:
name[0]:null
name[1]:null
name[2]:null
```

Be Careful with Reference Type Arrays

Array elements of a primitive type contain values of that primitive type, whereas array elements of a reference type contain the reference of objects. For example, if we have an array `empId` as:

```
int[] empId = new int[5];
```

Then, `empId[0]`,`empId[1]`...`empId[4]` contain an `int` value. However, if we have an array `name` as:

```
String[] name = new String[5];
```

Then, `name[0]`, `name[1]`...`name[4]` may contain reference of a `String` object. Note that the `String` objects, the elements of the `name` array, have not been created yet. As discussed in the previous section, all elements of the `name` array are referring to `null` at this stage. You need to create the `String` objects and assign those object references to the elements of the array one by one as:

```
name[0] = new String("name1");
name[1] = new String("name2");
name[2] = new String("name3");
name[3] = new String("name4");
name[4] = new String("name5");
```

It is a common mistake to refer to the elements of an array of reference type just after creating the array and before assigning a valid object reference to each element. The following code illustrates this common mistake.

```
String[] name = new String[5];  // Create an array of string

/* Error! Code is trying to get the length of first string stored in
   name array. It will generate runtime error because name[0] is not
   referring to any string object yet. name[0] is null at this point
*/
int len = name[0].length();

// Assign a valid string object to all elements of name array
for (int i = 0; i < name.length; i++){
    name[i] = "name" + ( i + 1 );
}

// Now you can get the length of the first element as
int len2 = name[0].length();     // Correct. len2 has value 5
```

The concept of initialization of the `String` reference type array has been depicted in Figure 14-1. This concept applies to all reference types.

Figure 14-1: Reference type array initialization

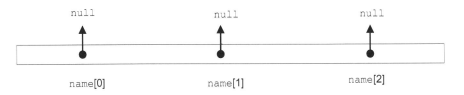

Memory state after the following statement is executed.
```
String[] name = new String[3];
```

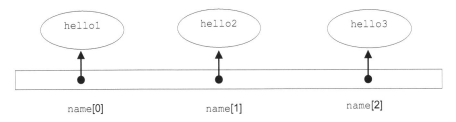

Memory state after the following statement is executed.
```
For (int i = 0; i < name.length; i++){
      name[i] = "hello" + ( i + 1 );
}
```

Explicit Array Initialization

You may want to initialize array elements with values other than the default values. You can initialize elements of an array explicitly either when you declare the array or when you create the array object using the `new` operator. The initial values for elements are separated by a comma and enclosed in braces ({}). For example,

```
int[] empId = {1, 2, 3, 4, 5};
```

The above statement creates an array of `int` of length 5, and initializes its elements to 1, 2, 3, 4, and 5. Note that you do not specify the length of an array when you specify the array initialization list at the time of the array declaration. The length of the array is the same as the number of values specified in the array initialization list. Here, length of `empId` array will be 5, because we passed 5 values in the initialization list {1, 2, 3, 4, 5}.

A comma may follow the last value in initialization list as:

```
int[] empId = {1, 2, 3, 4, 5,}; // A comma after last value 5 is valid
```

Alternatively, you can initialize the elements of an array as:

```
int[] empId = new int[]{1, 2, 3, 4, 5};
```

Note that you cannot specify the length of an array if you specify the array initialization list. The length of the array is the same as the number of values specified in the initialization list.

It is valid to create an empty array by using an empty initialization list as:

```
int[] emptyNumList = { };
```

For a reference type array, you can specify the list of objects in the initialization list. The following code fragment illustrates array initialization for `String` and `Account` types. Assume that `Account` class exists and it has a constructor, which takes account number as an argument.

```
// Create name array with two elements with text "Sara" and "Truman"
String[] name = {new String("Sara"), new String("Truman")};

// Create ac array with two object of Account type
Account[] ac = new Account[]{new Account(1), new Account(2)};
```

TIP

You can initialize the array elements at the time of declaration or at the time of creation using an array initialization list. When you use an initialization list to initialize the elements of an array, you cannot specify the length of an array. The length of the array is set to the number of values in the array initialization list.

Limitations of Using Arrays

An array in Java cannot be expanded or shrunk after it is created. Suppose you have an array of 100 elements and at some point of time, you need to keep only 15 elements. You cannot get rid of the remaining (and redundant for you) 85 elements of the array. If you need 135 elements and you have created an array of only 100 elements, you cannot append 35 more elements to it. You can deal with the first limitation (memory cannot be freed for unused array elements), if you have enough memory available to your application. However, there is no way out if you need to add more elements to an existing array. The only solution you have is to create another array of the desired length, and copy the array elements from the original array to the new array. You can copy array elements from one array to another in two ways:

- Using a loop
- Using the `arraycopy()` static method of the `java.lang.System` class

If we have an `int` array of `originalLength` length and we want to modify its length to `newLength`, we can apply the first method of copying arrays as shown in the following snippet of code.

```
int originalLength = 100;
int newLength = 15;
int[] ids = new int[originalLength];

// Do some processing here...

// Create a temporary array of new length
int[] tempIds = new int[newLength];
```

```
// While copying array elements we have to check if the new length
// is less than or greater than original length
int elementsToCopy = 0;

if (originalLength > newLength) {
    elementsToCopy = newLength;
}
else {
    elementsToCopy = originalLength;
}

// Copy the elements from original array to new array
for (int i = 0; i < elementsToCopy; i++){
    tempIds[i] = ids[i];
}

// Finally assign the reference of new array to ids
ids = tempIds;     // Now ids array has newLength length
                   // If newLength is greater than originalLength,
                   // new elements will have default values
```

Another way to copy elements of an array to another array is by using the `arraycopy()` method of the `System` class. The signature of the `arraycopy()` method is shown below.

```
public static void arraycopy(Object sourceArray,
                             int sourceStartPosition,
                             Object destinationArray,
                             int destinationStartPosition,
                             int lengthToBeCopied)
```

Here,
`sourceArray` is the reference to the source array,
`sourceStartPosition` is the starting index in source array from where the copying of elements will start,
`destinationArray` is the reference to the destination array,
`destinationStartPosition` is the start index in destination array from where new elements from source array will be copied,
`lengthToBeCopied` is the number of elements to be copied from source array to destination array.

We can replace the last for-loop, which copies array elements from ids to `tempIds`, in the above snippet of code with the code shown below:

```
// Now copy array elements using arraycopy() method
System.arraycopy (ids, 0, tempIds, 0, elementsToCopy);
```

You may observe that using the `arraycopy()` method offers more flexibility over using a for-loop. Refer to Java2 Platform online documentation at *http://www.oracle.com* for the complete documentation of the `arraycopy()` method. The objects of the two classes, `java.util.ArrayList` and `java.util.Vector`, can be used in place of an arrays, where the length of the array needs to be modified. You can think of the objects of these two classes as variable length arrays. The next section discusses these two classes in detail.

Listing 14-2 demonstrates how to copy an array using a for-loop and the `System.arraycopy()` method. An `Arrays` class is in the `java.util` package. It has many convenience methods for dealing with arrays, e.g., methods for converting elements of an array to a string format, sorting an array, etc. Listing 14-2 uses the `Arrays.toString()` static method to get the contents of an array in the string format. The `Arrays.toString()` method is overloaded and you can use it to get the contents of an array of any type in string format. In this example, we have used a for-loop and the `System.arraycopy()` method to copy arrays. However, note that using the `arraycopy()` method is much more powerful than using a for-loop. For example, the `arraycopy()` method is designed to handle copying of the elements of an array from one region to another region in the same array. It takes care of any overlap in the source and the destination regions within the array. You can use the `arraycopy()` method to copy any type of array. Our for-loop implementation to copy an array is a trivial example and it can be used only to copy `int` arrays.

Listing 14-2: Copying an array using a for-loop and the System.arraycopy() method

```java
// ArrayCopyTest.java
package com.jdojo.chapter14;

import java.util.Arrays;

public class ArrayCopyTest {
    public static void main(String[] args) {
        // Have an array with 5 elements
        int[] data = {1, 2, 3, 4, 5 };

        // Expand the data array to 7 elements
        int[] eData = expandArray(data, 7);

        // Truncate the data array to 3 elements
        int[] tData = expandArray(data, 3);

        System.out.println("Using for-loop...");
        System.out.println("Original Array: " +
                        Arrays.toString(data));
        System.out.println("Expanded Array: " +
                    Arrays.toString(eData));
        System.out.println("Truncated Array: " +
                    Arrays.toString(tData));

        // Copy data array to new arrays
        eData = new int[9];
        tData = new int[2];
        System.arraycopy(data, 0, eData, 0, 5);
        System.arraycopy(data, 0, tData, 0, 2);

        System.out.println("\nUsing System.arraycopy() method...");
        System.out.println("Original Array: " +
                        Arrays.toString(data));
        System.out.println("Expanded Array: " +
                        Arrays.toString(eData));
        System.out.println("Truncated Array: " +
                        Arrays.toString(tData));
    }

    // Uses a for-loop to copy an array
```

```
    public static int[] expandArray(int[] oldArray, int newLength) {
        int originalLength = oldArray.length;
        int[] newArray = new int[newLength];
        int elementsToCopy = 0;

        if (originalLength > newLength) {
            elementsToCopy = newLength;
        }
        else {
            elementsToCopy = originalLength;
        }

        for (int i = 0; i < elementsToCopy; i++) {
            newArray[i] = oldArray[i];
        }
        return newArray;
    }
}
```

```
Output:

Using for-loop...
Original Array: [1, 2, 3, 4, 5]
Expanded Array: [1, 2, 3, 4, 5, 0, 0]
Truncated Array: [1, 2, 3]

Using System.arraycopy() method...
Original Array: [1, 2, 3, 4, 5]
Expanded Array: [1, 2, 3, 4, 5, 0, 0, 0, 0]
Truncated Array: [1, 2]
```

ArrayList and Vector

`ArrayList` and `Vector` classes work the same way (roughly speaking). The only major difference between them is that the methods in the `Vector` class are synchronized, whereas methods in `ArrayList` are not synchronized. If your object list is accessed and modified by multiple threads simultaneously, you should use the `Vector` class, which will be slower but thread safe. Otherwise, you should use the `ArrayList` class. The big difference between arrays and `ArrayList`/`Vector` classes is that these two classes work with only objects and not with primitive data types. For example, if you need to store an `int` in an `ArrayList`/`Vector`, you must wrap it in an `Integer` object, before you could store it. All methods for these two classes accepts arguments of `Object` type whenever an element is expected in the argument and return an object of `Object` type whenever an element is returned. Therefore, most of the time, you will have to cast the element returned by methods of these classes to appropriate type.

TIP
Java 5 introduced a feature called *Autoboxing*, which relieves you of the pain of wrapping and unwrapping primitive values to objects and vice-versa when you work with collections, e.g., `ArrayList` or `Vector`. Please refer to the chapter on *AutoBoxing* for more details.

The following code fragment illustrates the use of the `ArrayList` class. Note that you need to import `java.util.ArrayList` and `java.util.Vector` classes in you programs to use the simple names `ArrayList` and `Vector` respectively.

```
// Create an ArrayList object
ArrayList ids = new ArrayList();

// Get the size of array list
int total = ids.size(); // total will be zero at this point

// Print the details of array list
System.out.println("Array List size is " + total);
System.out.println("Array List elements are " + ids);

// Add three ids 10, 20, 30 in array list. Note that we cannot add
// int values directly to array list. We must wrap them in
// primitive wrapper class Integer
ids.add(new Integer(10));
ids.add(new Integer(20));
ids.add(new Integer(30));

// Get the size of the array list
total = ids.size();      // total will be 3

// Print the details of array list
System.out.println("Array List size is " + total);
System.out.println("Array List elements are " + ids);

// Clear all elements from array list
ids.clear();

// Get the size of the array list
total = ids.size();      // total will be 0

// Print the details of array list
System.out.println("Array List size is " + total);
System.out.println("Array List elements are " + ids);
```

```
Output:

Array List size is 0
Array List elements are []
Array List size is 3
Array List elements are [10, 20, 30]
Array List size is 0
Array List elements are []
```

You can make one important observation from the above output. You can print the list of all elements in an `ArrayList` just by passing its reference to the `System.out.println()` method. The `toString()` method of the `ArrayList` class returns a string that is a comma separated string representation of its elements enclosed in brackets (`[]`).

Like arrays, `ArrayList` and `Vector` use zero based indexes. That is, the first element of `ArrayList` and `Vector` will have an index of zero. You can get the element stored at any index by using the `get()` method as:

```
// Get the element at the index 1, that is, the second element
Integer secondId = (Integer)ids.get(1);   // Must cast to Integer
                                           // because the return type of
                                           // the get() method is Object

// Get the integer value
int secondIntValue = secondId.intValue();

// Add three objects to the arraylist
ids.add(new Integer(10));
ids.add(new Integer(20));
ids.add(new Integer(30));
```

You can check if an object is one of the elements in an array list by using its `contains()` method as:

```
Integer id20 = new Integer(20);
Integer id50 = new Integer(50);

// Check if the array list contains id20 and id50
boolean found20 = ids.contains(id20);    // found20 will be true
boolean found50 = ids.contains(id50);    // found50 will be false
```

You can iterate through the elements of an `ArrayList` in one of the two ways – using a loop or using an iterator. In this chapter, we will discuss how to iterate through elements of an `ArrayList` using a for-loop. Please refer to the chapter on *Collections* to learn how to iterate through elements of an `ArrayList` (or any type of collection, e.g. a `Set`) using an iterator. The following snippet of code shows how to use a for-loop to iterate through the elements of an `ArrayList`.

```
// Get the size of the ArrayList
int total = ids.size();

Integer temp = null;

// Iterate through all elements
for (int i = 0; i < total; i++) {
    temp = (Integer)ids.get(i); // Get element at index I
    // Do some processing …
}
```

Listing 14-3 illustrates the use of a for-loop to iterate through elements of an `ArrayList`. It also shows you how to remove an element from an `ArrayList` using its `remove()` method.

Listing 14-3: Iterating through elements of an ArrayList

```java
// NameIterator.java
package com.jdojo.chapter14;

import java.util.ArrayList;

public class NameIterator {
    public static void main(String[] args) {
        ArrayList nameList = new ArrayList();

        //Add some names to it
        nameList.add("Christopher");
        nameList.add("Kathleen");
        nameList.add("Ann");

        // Get the count of names in the list
        int count = nameList.size();

        // Let us print the name list
        System.out.println("List of names...");
        for(int i = 0; i < count; i++) {
            String name = (String)nameList.get(i);
            System.out.println(name);
        }

        // Let us remove Kathleen from the list
        nameList.remove("Kathleen");

        // Get the count of names in the list again
        count = nameList.size();

        // Let us print the name list again
        System.out.println("\nAfter removing Kathleen...");
        for(int i = 0; i < count; i++) {
            String name = (String)nameList.get(i);
            System.out.println(name);
        }
    }
}
```

```
Output

List of names...
Christopher
Kathleen
Ann

After removing Kathleen...
Christopher
Ann
```

Passing an Array as a Parameter

You can pass an array as a parameter to a method or a constructor. The type of array you pass to the method must be assignment compatible to the formal parameter type. The syntax for array type parameter declaration for a method is the same as for the other data types. That is, parameter declaration should start with the array type, followed by one or more whitespaces and the argument name as:

```
modifiers returnType methodName(ArrayType argumentName, ...)
```

Some examples of method declarations with array arguments are:

```
// processSalary() has two parameters:
// 1. id is an array of int
// 2. salary is an array of double
public static void processSalary(int[] id, double[] salary) {
    // Code goes here...
}

// setAKA() has two parameters:
// 1. id is int (It is simply int type and not array of int)
// 2. aka is an array of String
public static void setAKA(int id, String[] aka) {
    // Code goes here...
}

// printStates() has one parameter:
// 1. stateNames is array of String
public static void printStates(String[] stateNames) {
    // Code goes here...
}
```

TIP

The parameter declaration for an array type in a method is specified the same way as we do an array type variable declaration. The parameter declaration of an array type must not specify the length of the array. The length of the array type parameter is determined at runtime using the actual parameter.

The following code fragment for a method mimics the `toString()` method of `ArrayList`. It accepts an `int` array and returns the comma-separated values enclosed in brackets (`[]`).

```
public static String arrayToString (int[] source){
    if (source == null) {
        return null;
    }

    // Use StringBuffer instead of String to improve
    // performance because we are doing string manipulations
    StringBuffer result = new StringBuffer("[");

    for (int i = 0; i < source.length; i++){
        if (i == source.length - 1) {
            result.append(source[i]);
```

```
            }
            else {
                result.append(source[i] + ",");
            }
        }

    result.append("]");
    return result.toString() ;
}
```

The above method may be called as:

```
int[] ids = {10, 15, 19};
String str = arrayToString(ids); // Pass ids int array to
                                 // arrayToString() method
```

Since an array is an object, the array reference is passed to the method. The method, which receives an array parameter, can modify the elements of the array. Listing 14-4 illustrates how a method can change the elements of its array parameter. This example also shows how to implement the swap() method to swap two integers using an array.

Listing 14-4: Passing an array as a method parameter

```
// Swap.java
package com.jdojo.chapter14;

public class Swap {
    public static void main(String[] args) {
        int[] num = {17, 80};

        System.out.println("Before swap");
        System.out.println("#1: " + num[0]);
        System.out.println("#2: " + num[1]);

        swap(num);

        System.out.println("\nAfter swap");
        System.out.println("#1: " + num[0]);
        System.out.println("#2: " + num[1]);
    }

    // swap method accepts an int array as argument and swaps the
    // values if array contains two values
    public static void swap (int[] source) {
        if (source != null && source.length == 2) {
            // Swap the first and the second elements
            int temp = source[0];
            source[0] = source[1] ;
            source[1] = temp ;
        }
    }
}
```

Output

```
Before swap
#1: 17
#2: 80

After swap
#1: 80
#2: 17
```

Recall that we were not able to implement a method for swapping two integers using method's parameters of primitive types. It was so, because the actual parameters' values are copied to the formal parameters for primitive data type parameters. Here, we were able to swap two integers inside the `swap()` method, because we used an array as the parameter. The array's reference is passed to the method and not the copy of the elements of the array.

There is a risk involved when an array is passed to a method. The method that receives an array as its parameter may modify the array elements, which may not be desired in some cases. In such a case, you should pass a copy of the array to the method and not the original array. The method may modify its array argument, which is a copy of original array, without affecting your original array. You can make a quick copy of your array using array's `clone()` method. The phrase *"quick copy"* warrants special attention. For primitive arrays, the cloned array will have a true copy of the original array. A new array of the same length is created and the value of each element in the original array is copied to the corresponding element of the cloned array. However, for reference type arrays, the reference of the object (not the object) stored in each element of the original array is copied to the corresponding element of the cloned array. This is known as a *shallow copy*, whereas the former type, where the object (or the value) is copied, is known as a *deep copy*. In case of a shallow copy, elements of both arrays, the original and the cloned, refer to the same object in memory. You can modify the objects using their reference stored in the original array as well as using the reference stored in the cloned array. In this case, even if you pass a copy of the original array to a method, your original array can be modified inside that method. The solution to this problem is to make a deep copy of your original array and pass the copy to the method. The following snippet of code illustrates the cloning of an `int` array and a `String` array. Note that the return type of the `clone()` method is `Object` and you need to cast the returned value to an appropriate array type.

```
// Create an array of 3 integers - 1,2,3
int[] ids = {1, 2, 3};

// Declare an array of int named clonedIds
int[] clonedIds;

// clonedIds array has the same values as ids array i.e. 1,2,3
clonedIds = (int[])ids.clone()

// Create an array of 3 strings
String[] names  = {"Lisa", "Pat", "Kathy"};

// Declare an array of String named clonedNames
String[] clonedNames ;

// clonedNames array has the reference of the same three strings as
// the names array has
clonedNames = (String[])names.clone();
```

The cloning processes for primitive array (i.e. `ids`) and reference array (e.g. `names`) have been depicted in Figure 14-2.

Figure 14-2: Difference in primitive arrays and reference arrays cloning

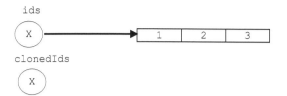

Memory state after the following statements are executed.
```
int[] ids = {1,2,3};
int[] clonedIds;
```

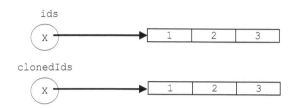

Memory state after the following statement is executed.
```
clonedIds = (int[])ids.clone();
```

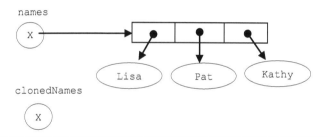

Memory state after the following statements are executed.
```
String names = {"Lisa", "Pat", "Kathy"};
String[] clonedNames;
```

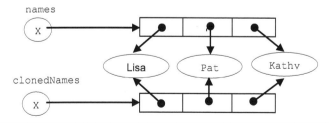

Memory state after the following statement is executed.
```
clonedNames = (String[])names.clone();
```

You may observe that when the `names` array is cloned, the `clonedNames` array elements also refer to the same `String` objects in memory. When we mention a method of modifying an array parameter passed to it, we may mean one or all of the following three things.

- Array Parameter Reference
- Elements of the Array Parameter
- The Object Referred by the Array Parameter Elements

In subsequent discussions, assume that we have a `getElements()` method that returns a `String` containing the elements of the passed array enclosed in `[]` and separated by a comma.

Array Parameter Reference

Since an array is an object in Java, a copy of its reference is passed to a method. If the method changes the array parameter, the actual parameter is not affected. For example, consider a method `tryArrayChange()` as shown below.

```java
void tryArrayChange(int[] num) {
    System.out.println("Inside method-1:" + getElements(num));

    // Create and store a new int array in num
    num = new int[] {10, 20};

    System.out.println("Inside method-2:" + getElements(num));
}
```

The following snippet of code calls the method `tryArrayChange()`:

```java
int[] origNum = {101, 307, 78};
System.out.println("Before method call:" + getElements(origNum));
tryArrayChange(origNum);
System.out.println("After method call:" + getElements(origNum))
```

```
Output:

Before method call:[101,307,78]
Inside method-1:[101, 307, 78]
Inside method-2:[10, 20]
After method call:[101,307,78]
```

You may observe that we assign a new array reference to the num method's parameter inside the method. However, it did not affect the actual parameter `origNum`.

If you do not want your method to change the array reference inside the method body, you must declare the method parameter as `final` as shown below.

```java
void tryArrayChange(final int[] num) {
    // Error. num is final and cannot be changed
    num = new int[]{10, 20};
}
```

Elements of the Array Parameter

The values stored in the elements of an array parameter can always be changed inside a method. Consider the following snippet of code, which defines two methods.

```
void tryElementChange(int[] num) {
    // If array has at least one element, store 1116
    // in its first element
    if (num != null && num.length > 0) {
        num[0] = 1116;
    }
}

void tryElementChange(String[] names) {
    // If array has at least one element, store "Twinkle"
    // in its first element
    if (names != null && names.length > 0) {
        names[0] = "Twinkle";
    }
}
```

We use the following snippet of code to test these two methods.

```
Int[] origNum = { 10, 89 , 7};
String[] origNames  = {"Mike", "John"};

System.out.println("Before method call, origNum:" +
                getElements(origNum));

System.out.println("Before method call, origNames:" +
                getElements(origNames));

tryElementChange(origNum);
tryElementChange(origNames);

System.out.println("After method call, origNum:" +
                getElements(origNum));

System.out.println("After method call, origNames:" +
                getElements(origNames));
```

```
Output:

Before method call, origNum:[10, 89, 7]
Before method call, origNames:[Mike, John]
After method call, origNum:[1116, 89, 7]
After method call, origNames:[Twinkle, John]
```

You may observe that the arrays' first element has changed after the method calls. You can change the elements of an array parameter inside a method, even if the array parameter is declared final.

The Object Referred by the Array Parameter Elements

This section applies to array parameters of only the reference type. If the array's reference type is mutable, you can change the state of the object stored in the array elements. Note that in case 2 discussed above, we discussed replacing the reference stored in the array element by a new object

---

reference. This section discusses changing the state of the object referred to by the elements of the array. Consider a class `Item` as follows.

```
public class Item {
    private double price;
    private String name;

    public Item (String name, double initialPrice) {
        this.name = name;
        this.price = initialPrice;
    }

    public double getPrice() {
        return this.price;
    }

    public void setPrice(double newPrice ) {
        this.price = newPrice;
    }

    public String toString() {
        return "[" + this.name + ", " + this.price + "]";
    }
}
```

Let us consider the following snippet of code that defines a method, which changes the object state.

```
void tryStateChange(Item[] allItems) {
    if (allItems != null && allItems.length > 0 ) {
        // Change the price of first item to 10.38
        allItems[0].setPrice(10.38);
    }
}
```

The following piece of code is used to test the above method.

```
Item[] myItems = {new Item("Pen",25.11),new Item("Pencil",0.10)};

System.out.println("Before method call #1:" + myItems[0]);
System.out.println("Before method call #2:" + myItems[1]);

tryStateChange(myItems);

System.out.println("After method call #1:" + myItems[0]);
System.out.println("After method call #2:" + myItems[1]);
```

```
Output:

Before method call #1:[Pen, 25.11]
Before method call #2:[Pencil, 0.1]
After method call #1:[Pen, 10.38]
After method call #2:[Pencil, 0.1]
```

Note that the price of the first item has been changed inside the method.

The `clone()` method can be used to make a clone of an array. For a reference array, the `clone()` method performs a shallow copy. An array should be passed to a method and returned from a method with caution. If a method may modify its array parameter and you do not want your actual array parameter to get affected by that method call, you must pass a deep copy of your array to that method.

If you store the state of an object in an array instance variable, you should think carefully before returning the reference of that array from any method. The caller of that method will get the handle of the array instance variable and will be able to change the state of the objects of that class outside the class. This situation is illustrated in following example.

```java
public class MagicNumber {
    // Magic numbers are not supposed to be changed
    // It can be look up though
    private int[] magicNumbers = {5, 11, 21, 51, 101};

    // Other codes go here...

    public int[] getMagicNumbers ( ) {
        /* Never do the following. If you do this, caller of
           this method will be able to change the magic numbers
        */
        //return this.magicNumbers;

        /* Do the following instead. In case of reference array,
           make a deep copy, and return that copy. For
           primitive array you can use clone() method
        */
        return (int[])magicNumbers.clone();
    }
}
```

You can also create an array and pass it to a method without storing the array reference in a variable. Suppose there is a method named `setNumbers(int[] nums)`, which accepts an `int` array as a parameter. You can call this method as shown below.

```java
setNumbers(new int[]{10, 20, 30});
```

Command-Line Arguments

A Java application can be launched from a command prompt, e.g., a DOS prompt in windows and a shell prompt in UNIX. It can also be launched from within a Java development environment tool, e.g., NetBeans. A java application is run at the command line as:

```
java <<optionslists>> <<classname>>
```

`<<optionslists>>` is optional. You can also pass command-line arguments to a Java application by specifying arguments after the class name as:

```
java classname <<List of Command-line Arguments>>
```

Each argument in the argument list is separated by a space. For example, the following command runs the `com.jdojo.chapter14.Test` class and passes three animal names as the command line arguments.

```
java com.jdojo.chapter14.Test Cat Dog Rat
```

What happens to these three command-line arguments when the `Test` class is run? The operating system passes the list of the arguments to the JVM. Sometimes, the operating system may expand the list of argument by interpreting its meaning and may pass a modified arguments list to the JVM. The JVM parses the argument lists. The separator used for parsing is a space. It creates an array of `String`, whose length is the same as the number of arguments in the list. It populates the `String` array with the items in the arguments list sequentially. Finally, the JVM passes this `String` array to the `main()` method of the `Test` class that you are running. This is the time when we use the `String` array argument passed to the `main()` method. If there is no command-line argument, the JVM creates a `String` array of length zero and passes it to the `main()` method. If you want to pass space-separated words as one argument, you can enclose them in double quotes. You can also avoid the operating system interpretation of special characters by enclosing them in double quotes. Let us create a class called `CommandLine` as listed in Listing 14-1.

Listing 14-5: Processing Command-line arguments inside the main() method

```
// CommandLine.java
package com.jdojo.chapter14;

public class CommandLine {
    public static void main(String[] args) {
        // args contains all command-line arguments
        System.out.println("Total Arguments:" + args.length);

        // Display all arguments
        for(int i = 0 ; i < args.length; i++) {
            System.out.println("Argument #" + (i+1) + ":" + args[i]);
        }
    }
}
```

Table 14-2 shows the command to run the `com.jdojo.chapter14.CommandLine` class and its output.

Table 14-2: Output of command-line argument program running on Windows 2000 DOS prompt

Command	Output
`java com.jdojo.chapter14.CommandLine`	`Total Arguments:0`

`java com.jdojo.chapter14.CommandLine Cat Dog Rat`	`Total Arguments:3`
	`Argument #1:Cat`
	`Argument #2:Dog`
	`Argument #3:Rat`

`java com.jdojo.chapter14.CommandLine "Cat Dog Rat"`	`Total Arguments:1` `Argument #1:Cat Dog Rat`

java com.jdojo.chapter14.CommandLine 29 Dogs	Total Arguments:2 Argument #1:29 Argument #2:Dogs

What is the use of command-line arguments? It lets you change the behavior of your program without re-compiling it. For example, you may want to sort the contents of a file in ascending or descending order. You may pass command-line arguments, which will specify sorting order. If there is no sorting order specified on the command line, you may assume ascending order by default. If you call the sorting class `com.jdojo.chapter14.SortFile`, you may run it as:

To sort `employee.txt` file in ascending order

```
java com.jdojo.chapter14.SortFile employee.txt asc
```

To sort `department.txt` file in descending order

```
java com.jdojo.chapter14.SortFile department.txt desc
```

To sort `salary.txt` in ascending order

```
java com.jdojo.chapter14.SortFile salary.txt
```

Depending on the second element, if any, of the `String` array passed to the `main()` method of the `SortFile` class, you may sort the file differently.

Note that all command-line arguments are passed to the `main()` method as `Strings`. If you pass a numeric argument, you need to convert the string argument to a number inside the `main()` method. To illustrate this numeric argument conversion let us develop a mini calculator class, which takes an expression as command-line argument and prints the result. Our min calculator supports only four basic operations: add, subtract, multiply and divide. The program is listed in Listing 14-6.

Listing 14-6: A mini command-line calculator

```
// Calc.java
package com.jdojo.chapter14;

public class Calc {
    public static void main(String[] args) {
        // Make sure we have three arguments
        // second argument has only one character to
        // indicate operation
        System.out.println(java.util.Arrays.toString(args));

        if (!(args.length == 3 && args[1].length() == 1)) {
            printUsage();
            return;    // Stop the program here
        }

        // Parse the two number operands. Place the parsing code
        // inside try-catch so that we will handle the error in
        // case both operands are not numbers
        double n1 = 0.0;
```

```java
        double n2 = 0.0;
        try {
            n1 = Double.parseDouble(args[0]);
            n2 = Double.parseDouble(args[2]);
        }
        catch (NumberFormatException e) {
            System.out.println("Both operands must be number");
            printUsage();
            return;   // Stop the program here
        }

        // Convert the operation string to char so that we can
        // use switch case statement
        char operation = args[1].charAt(0);

        double result = compute(n1, n2, operation);

        // Print the result
        System.out.println(args[0] + args[1] + args[2] +
                           "=" + result);
    }

    public static double compute(double n1, double n2, char operation)
    {
        // Initialize the result with not-a-number
        double result = Double.NaN;

        switch (operation) {
            case '+':
                result = n1 + n2;
                break;
            case '-':
                result = n1 - n2;
                break;
            case '*':
                result = n1 * n2;
                break;
            case '/':
                result = n1 / n2;
                break;
            default:
                System.out.println("Invalid operation:" + operation);
        }

        return result;
    }

    public static void printUsage() {
        System.out.println("Usage: " +
                           " java com.jdojo.chapter14.Calc expr");
        System.out.println("Where expr could be:");
        System.out.println("n1 + n1");
        System.out.println("n1 - n2");
        System.out.println("n1 * n2");
        System.out.println("n1 / n2");
        System.out.println("n1, n2 are two numbers");
    }
```

```
}
```

You may use the `Calc` class as:

```
java com.jdojo.chapter14.Calc 3 + 7
java com.jdojo.chapter14.Calc 78.9 * 98.5
```

You may get an error when you try to use * (asterisk) to multiply two numbers. The operating system may interpret it as all files names in the current directory. To avoid such errors, you can enclose the operator in double quotes or the escape character provided by your operating system as:

```
java com.jdojo.chapter14.Calc 7 "*" 8
```

TIP
If you use command-line arguments in your Java program, your program is not 100% Java. It is so, because your program does not fit in the category of "Write once, run everywhere". Some operating systems do not have a command prompt and hence you may not be able to use the command-line argument feature. Additionally, an operating system may interpret the meta-characters used in the command-line arguments differently.

Multi-Dimensional Arrays

If a data element in a list is identified using more than one dimension, you can use a multi-dimensional array to represent the list in your program. For example, a data element in a table is identified by two dimensions, row and column. You can store a tabular data in your Java program in a two dimensional array. You can declare a multi-dimensional array by using a pair of brackets ([]) for each dimension in the array declaration. For example, you can declare a two dimensional array of `int` as:

```
int[][] table;     // table can refer to any two-dimensional array
```

Here, `table` is a reference variable that can hold a reference to a two-dimensional array of `int`. Memory is allocated only for the reference variable `table` and not for any array elements at the time of declaration. The memory state after the above fragment of code is executed is depicted in Figure 14-3.

Figure 14-3: Memory state after the declaration of a two-dimensional array

table

A two-dimensional array of `int` with 3 rows and 2 columns can be created as:

```
table = new int[3][2];
```

The memory state after execution of the above snippet of code has been depicted in Figure 14-4. All elements have been shown to have a value of zero, because all elements of a numeric array are initialized to zero by default. The rules for default initialization of array elements of a multi-dimensional array are the same as that of a single dimensional array as discussed previously in this chapter.

Figure 14-4: Memory state after the creation of a two-dimensional array

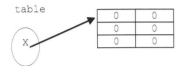

The index of each dimension in a multi-dimensional array is zero-based. Each element of the `table` array can be accessed as `table[rownumber][columnNumber]`. The row number and the column number always starts at zero. For example, we can assign a value to the first row and the second column in `table` array as:

```
table[0][1] = 32;
```

We can assign a value 71 to the third row and the first column as:

```
table[2][0] = 71;
```

The memory state after the above two assignments has been depicted in Figure 14-5.

Figure 14-5: Memory state after two assignments to the two-dimensional array elements

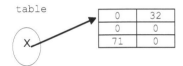

Java does not support multi-dimensional arrays in a true sense. Rather, it supports array of arrays. Using an array of arrays, you can implement the same functionality as provided by multi-dimensional arrays. When you create a two-dimensional array, the elements of the first array are of an array type, which can refer to a single dimensional array. The size of each single-dimensional array need not be the same. Considering the array of arrays concept for the `table` two-dimensional array, we can depict the memory state after array creation and assignments of two values as shown in Figure 14-6. The name of the two-dimensional array, `table`, refers to an array of three elements. Each element of the array to which `table` refers is a one-dimensional array of `int`. The data type of `table[0]`, `table[1]` and `table[2]` is an `int` array. The length of `table[0]`, `table[1]` and `table[2]` is 2.

You must specify the dimension of at least the first level array at the time you create a multi-dimensional array. For example, when you create a two-dimensional array you must specify at least the first dimension, which is the number of rows. We can achieve the same results as above code fragment as follows.

```
table = new int[3][];   // You must specify at least first dimension
                        // Number of columns is left
```

Figure 14-6: An array of arrays

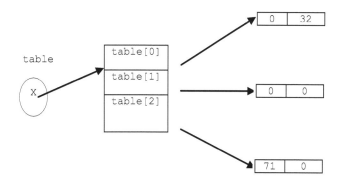

The above statement creates only first level of array. Only `table[0]`, `table[1]` and `table[2]` exist at this time. They are referring to `null`. At this time, `table.length` has a value of 3. Since `table[0]`, `table[1]` and `table[2]` are referring to `null`, you cannot use `length` attribute on them. That is, we have created three rows in a table, but we do not know how many columns each row will contain. Since `table[0]`, `table[1]` and `table[2]` are arrays of `int`, we can assign them values as:

```
table[0] = new int[2];  // Create two columns for row 1
table[1] = new int[2];  // Create two columns for row 2
table[2] = new int[2];  // Create two columns for row 3
```

We have completed the creation of the two-dimensional array, which has the three rows and each row has two columns. We can assign the values to some cells as:

```
table[0][1] = 32
table[2][0] = 71
```

It is also possible to create a two-dimensional array with different number of columns for each row. Such an array is called a *ragged* array. Listing 14-7 illustrates working with a ragged array.

Listing 14-7: An example of a ragged array

```java
// RaggedArray.java
package com.jdojo.chapter14;

public class RaggedArray {
    public static void main(String[] args) {
        // Create a two-dimensional array of 3 rows
        int[][] raggedArr = new int[3][];

        // Add 2 columns to first row
        raggedArr[0] = new int[2];

        // Add 1 column to second row
        raggedArr[1] = new int[1];

        // Add 3 columns to third row
        raggedArr[2] = new int[3];

        // Assign values to all elements of raggedArr
```

```
            raggedArr[0][0] = 1;
            raggedArr[0][1] = 2;
            raggedArr[1][0] = 3;
            raggedArr[2][0] = 4;
            raggedArr[2][1] = 5;
            raggedArr[2][2] = 6;

            // Print all elements. One row at one line
            System.out.println(raggedArr[0][0] + "\t" + raggedArr[0][1]);
            System.out.println(raggedArr[1][0]);
            System.out.println(raggedArr[2][0] + "\t" + raggedArr[2][1]
                               + "\t" + raggedArr[2][2]);
    }
}
```

```
Output

1    2
3
4    5    6
```

TIP
Java supports array of arrays, which can be used to achieve functionalities provided by multi-dimensional arrays. Multi-dimensional arrays are widely used in scientific and engineering applications. If you are using arrays in your business application program that have more than two dimensions, you may need to reconsider the choice of multi-dimensional arrays as your choice of data structure.

Accessing Elements of a Multi-Dimensional Array

Typically, a multi-dimensional array is populated using nested for loops. The number of for- loops used to populate a multi-dimensional array equals the number of dimensions in the array. For example, two for-loops are used to populate a two-dimensional array. Typically, a loop is used to access the elements' values of a multi-dimensional array. Listing 14-8 illustrates how to populate and access elements of a two-dimensional array.

Listing 14-8: Accessing elements of a multi-dimensional array

```
// MDAccess.java
package com.jdojo.chapter14;

public class MDAccess {
    public static void main(String[] args){
        int[][] ra = new int[3][];

        ra[0] = new int[2];
        ra[1] = new int[1];
        ra[2] = new int[3];

        // Populate the ragged array using for loops
        for(int i = 0; i < ra.length; i++) {
            for(int j = 0; j < ra[i].length; j++){
```

```
                    ra[i][j] = i + j;
            }
      }

      // Print the array using for loops
      for(int i = 0; i < ra.length; i++) {
            for (int j = 0; j < ra[i].length; j++){
                  System.out.print(ra[i][j] + "\t");
            }

            // Add a new line after each row is printed
            System.out.println();
      }
   }
}
```

```
Output

0    1
1
2    3    4
```

Initializing Multi-Dimensional Arrays

You may initialize the elements of a multi-dimensional array by supplying the list of values at the time of its declaration or at the time of its creation. You cannot specify the length of any dimension if you initialize the array with a list of values. The number of initial values for each dimension will determine the length of each dimension in the array. Since many dimensions are involved in a multi-dimensional array, the list of values for a level is enclosed in braces. For a two-dimensional array, the list of values for each row is enclosed in a pair of braces as:

```
int[][] arr = {{10, 20, 30}, {11, 22}, {222, 333, 444, 555}};
```

The above statement created a two-dimensional array with 3 rows. The first row contains 3 columns with values 10, 20, and 30. The second row contains two columns with values 11 and 22. The third row contains 4 columns with values 222, 333, 444, and 555. A zero-row and zero-column two-dimensional array can be created as:

```
int[][] empty2D = { };
```

Initialization of a multi-dimensional array of reference type follows the same rule. We can initialize a two-dimensional reference type arrays as:

```
String[][] acronymList = {{"JMF", "Java Media Framework"},
                          {"JSP", "Java Server Pages"},
                          {"JMS", "Java Message Service"}};
```

You can initialize the elements of a multi-dimensional array at the time you create it as:

```
int[][] arr = new int[][]{{1, 2}, {3,4,5}};
```

Enhanced for-loop for Arrays

Java 5 introduced an enhanced for-loop that lets you loop through elements of an array in a cleaner way. The enhanced for–loop is also known as for-each loop. The syntax of the for-each loop is as follows.

```
for(DataType e : array) {
    // Loop body goes here...

    // e contains one element of the array at a time
}
```

The for-each loop uses the same `for` keyword used by the basic for-loop. Its body is executed as many times as the number of elements in the `array`. The "`DataType e`" is a variable declaration, where `e` is the variable name and `DataType` is its data type. The data type of the variable `e` should be assignment-compatible with the type of the `array`. The variable declaration is followed by a colon (`:`), which is followed by the reference of the array that you want to loop through. The for-each loop assigns the value of an element of the array to the variable `e`, which you can use inside the body of the for-each loop. The following snippet of code uses a for-each loop to print all elements of an `int` array.

```
int[] numList = {1, 2, 3, 4};

for(int num : numList) {
    System.out.println(num);
}
```

```
Output:

1
2
3
4
```

We can accomplish the same thing using the basic for-loop as follows.

```
int[] numList = {1, 2, 3, 4};

for(int i = 0; i < numList.length; i++ ) {
    int num = numList[i];
    System.out.println(num);
}
```

```
Output:

1
2
3
4
```

Note that the for-each loop provides a way to loop through elements of an array, which is cleaner than the basic for-loop. However, the for-each loop is not a replacement for the basic for-loop, because you cannot use it in all circumstances. For example, if you need to get to the index of the element inside the body of the loop, the for-each loop does not provide that. If you want to modify the value of the element of the array inside the for-each loop, you cannot do that.

TIP
The for-each loop also lets you iterate over elements of any collection object that implements `java.lang.Iterable` interface. We will revisit for-each loop in the chapter on *Collections*.

Array Declaration Syntax

You can declare an array by placing brackets (`[]`) after the data type of the array or after the name of the array reference variable. For example, the following declaration

```
int[] empIds;
int[][] points2D;
int[][][] points3D;
Person[] persons;
```

are equivalent to:

```
int empIds[];
int points2D[][];
int points3D[][][];
Person persons[];
```

Java also allows you to mix two syntaxes. In the same array declaration, you can place some brackets after the data type and some after the variable name. For example, you can declare a two-dimensional array of `int` as:

```
int[] points2D[];
```

You can declare a two-dimensional and a three-dimensional array of `int` in one declaration statement as:

```
int[] points2D[], points3D[][];
```

or

```
int[][] points2D, points3D[];
```

Runtime Array Bounds Checks

Java checks array bounds for every access to an array element runtime. If the array bound is exceeded, `java.lang.ArrayIndexOutOfBoundsException` exception is thrown. The only requirement for array index values at compile time is that they must be integers. The Java compiler does not check if the value of an array index is less than zero or beyond its length. This check must be performed at runtime, before every access to an array element is allowed. Runtime array

---

bounds checks slow down the program execution for two reasons. The first reason is the cost of bound checks itself. To check the array bounds, the length of array must be loaded in memory and two comparisons (one for less than zero and one for greater than or equal to its length) must be performed. The second reason is that an exception must be thrown when the array bounds are exceeded, Java must do some housekeeping and get ready to throw an exception, if the array bounds are exceeded. Listing 14-9 illustrates the exception thrown if array bounds are exceeded. The program creates an array of int named test. Since the test array has a length of 3, the program cannot access the 4th element, i.e., test[3]. An attempt to access the fourth element will result in an ArrayIndexOutOfBoundsException exception.

Listing 14-9: Array bounds checks

```
// ArrayBounds.java
package   com.jdojo.chapter14;

public class ArrayBounds {
    public static void main(String[] args) {
        int[] test = new int[3];

        System.out.println("Assigning 12 to the first element");
        test[0] = 12; // index 0 is between 0 and 2. Ok

        System.out.println("Assigning 79 to the fourth element");
        test[3] = 12; // index 3 is not between 0 and 2.
                      // At runtime exception will be thrown

        System.out.println("We will not get here");
    }
}
```

```
Output:

Assigning 12 to the first element
Assigning 79 to the fourth element
java.lang.ArrayIndexOutOfBoundsException: 3
    at com.jdojo.chapter14.ArrayBounds.main(ArrayBounds.java:12)
Exception in thread "main"
```

It is a good practice to check for array length before accessing an array element. The fact that array bounds violation throws an exception may be misused as shown in the following snippet of code, which prints values stored in an array. The code fragment uses an infinite while–loop to print values of the elements of an array and relies on exception throwing mechanism to check for array bounds. The right way is to use a for-loop and check for array index value using length property of the array

```
// Create an array
int[] arr = new int[10];

//Populate the array here...

// Print the array. Wrong way
try {
    // Start an infinite loop. When we are done with all elements
    // an exception will be thrown and we will be in catch block
    // and hence out of loop
```

```
        int counter = 0;
        while (true) {
            System.out.println(arr[counter++]);
        }
    }
}
catch (ArrayIndexOutOfBoundsException e) {
    // We are done with printing array elements
}

// Do some processing here...
```

What is the Class of an Array Object?

Arrays in Java are objects. Since every object has a class, we must have a class for every array. All methods of `java.lang.Object` can be used on arrays of all types. Since the `getClass()` method of the `java.lang.Object` class gives the reference of the class for any object in Java, we will use this method to get the class name for all arrays. Listing 14-10 illustrates how to get the class name of an array.

Listing 14-10: Knowing the class of an array

```
// ArrayClass.java
package com.jdojo.chapter14;

public class ArrayClass {
    public static void main (String[] args){
        int[] iArr = new int[2];
        int[][] iiArr = new int[2][2];
        int[][][] iiiArr = new int[2][2][2];

        String[] sArr  = {"A", "B"} ;
        String[][] ssArr = {{"AA"}, {"BB"}} ;
        String[][][] sssArr = {} ; // 3D empty array of string

        // Print the class name for all arrays
        System.out.println("int[]:" + getClassName(iArr));
        System.out.println("int[][]:" + getClassName(iiArr));
        System.out.println("int[][][]:" + getClassName(iiiArr));
        System.out.println("String[]:" + getClassName(sArr));
        System.out.println("String[][]:" + getClassName(ssArr));
        System.out.println("String[][][]:" + getClassName(sssArr));
    }

    /* Any java object can be passed to getClassName() method.
       Since every array is also an object, we can also pass
       an array to this method.
    */
    public static String getClassName(Object obj) {
        // Get the reference of its class
        Class c = obj.getClass();

        // Get the name of the class
        String className = c.getName();
        return className;
```

```
        }
}
```

```
Output

int[]:[I
int[][]:[[I
int[][][]:[[[I
String[]:[Ljava.lang.String;
String[][]:[[Ljava.lang.String;
String[][][]:[[[Ljava.lang.String;
```

The class name of an array starts with left bracket(s) `([)`. The number of left brackets is equal to the dimension of the array. For `int` array, the left bracket(s) is followed by a character `I`. For reference type array, the left bracket(s) is followed by a character `L`, followed by the name of the class name, which is followed by a semi-colon. The class names for one-dimensional primitive array and reference type have been shown in Table 14-3.

Table 14-3: Class name of arrays

Array Type	Class Name
byte[]	[B
short[]	[S
int[]	[I
long[]	[J
char[]	[C
float[]	[F
double[]	[D
boolean[]	[Z
com.jdojo.Person[]	[Lcom.jdojo.Person;

The class names of arrays are not available at compile time for declaring or creating arrays. You must use the syntax described in this chapter to create an array. That is, you cannot write the following to create an `int` array.

```
[I myIntArray;
```

Rather, you must write to create an `int` array.

```
int[] myIntArray;
```

Array Assignment Compatibility

Data type of each element of an array is the same as the data type of the array. For example, each element of `int[]` array is of type `int`; each element of `String[]` array is of type `String`. The value assigned to an element of an array must be assignment compatible to its data type. For example, it is allowed to assign a `byte` value to an element of an `int` array, because `byte` is assignment compatible to `int`. However, it is not allowed to assign a `float` value to an element of an `int` array, because `float` is not assignment compatible to `int`.

```
byte bValue = 10;
float fValue = 10.5f;
int[] sequence = new int[10];

sequence[0] = bValue;        // Ok
sequence[1] = fValue;        // Compiler error
```

The same rule must be followed while dealing with a reference type array. If there is a reference type array of type `T`, its elements can be assigned an object reference of type `S`, if and only if, `S` is assignment compatible to `T`. The subclass object reference is always assignment compatible to the superclass. Since the `java.lang.Object` class is the superclass of all classes in Java, you can use an array of `Object` class to store objects of any class. For example,

```
Object[] genericArray = new Object[4];

genericArray[0] = new String("Hello");      // Ok

genericArray[1] = new Person("Daniel");     // Ok. Assuming Person class
                                            // exists

genericArray[2] = new Account(189);         // Ok. Assuming Account class
                                            // exists

genericArray[3] = null;                     // Ok. null can be assigned
                                            // to any reference type
```

You need to perform a cast at the time you read back the object from array as:

```
/* Compiler will flag an error for the following statement.
   genericArray is of Object type and an Object reference cannot be
   assigned to a String reference variable. Even though genericArray[0]
   contains a String object reference, we need to cast it to String as
   we do in next statement.
*/
String s = genericArray[0];             // Compiler error

String str = (String)genericArray[0];
Person p = (Person)genericArray[1];
Account a = (Account)genericArray[2];
```

If you try to cast the array element to a type, whose actual type is not assignment compatible to the new type, the `java.lang.ClassCastException` is thrown. For example, the following statement will throw the `ClassCastException` at runtime.

```
String str = (String)genericArray[1]; // Person can't be cast to String
```

The vice-versa is not true. That is, you cannot store an object reference of the superclass in an array of the subclass. The following snippet of code illustrates this.

```
String[] names = new String[3];
names[0] = new Object(); // Error. Object is superclass of String
```

```
names[1] = new Person();     // Error, Person is not subclass of String
names[2] = null;             // Ok.
```

Finally, an array reference can be assigned to another array reference of another type if the former type is assignment compatible to the latter type. For example,

```
Object[] obj = new Object[3];
String[] str = new String[2];
Account[] a = new Account[5];

obj = str;                // Ok
str = (String[]) obj;     // Ok. Because obj has String array reference

obj = a;
str = (String[]) obj;     // ClassCastException error. Because obj has
                          // reference of Account array and Account can't
                          // be converted to String

a = (Account[]) obj;      // Ok
```

Converting an ArrayList/Vector to an Array

An `ArrayList` can be used when the number of elements in the list is not precisely known. Once the number of elements in the list is fixed, you may want to convert an `ArrayList` to an array. You may do this for one of the following reasons.

- The program semantics may require you to use an array and not an `ArrayList`. For example, you may need to pass an array to a method, but you have data stored in an `ArrayList`.
- You may want to store user inputs in an array. However, you do not know the number of values the user will input. In such a case, you can store values in an `ArrayList` while accepting input from the user. At the end, you can convert the `ArrayList` to an array.
- Accessing array elements is faster than accessing `ArrayList` elements. If you have an `ArrayList` and you want to access the elements multiple times, you may want to convert the `ArrayList` to an array for better performance.

The `ArrayList` class has an overloaded method named `toArray()` as:

```
public Object[] toArray()
public Object[] toArray(Object[] a)
```

The first method returns the elements of `ArrayList` as an array of `Object`. The second method takes an array of `Object` (you can pass an array of any class though) as argument. All `ArrayList` elements are copied to that array if there is enough space and the same array is returned. If there is not enough space in the array that is passed to copy all `ArrayList` elements, a new array is created. The type of new array is the same as the passed in array. The length of the new array is equal to the size of `ArrayList`.

The above discussions and the example described in Listing 14-11 also apply to converting a `Vector` to an array.

Listing 14-11: An ArrayList to an array conversion

```java
// ArrayListToArray.java
package com.jdojo.chapter14;

import java.util.ArrayList;

public class ArrayListToArray {
    public static void main(String[] args){
        ArrayList al = new ArrayList();
        al.add("cat");
        al.add("dog");
        al.add("rat");

        // Print the content of arraylist
        System.out.println("ArrayList:" + al );

        // Create an array of same length as arraylist
        String[] s1 = new String[al.size()];

        // Copy arraylist elements to array
        String[] s2 = (String[]) al.toArray(s1);

        // Since s has enough space to copy all arraylist
        // elements, al.toArray(s) returns s itself after copying
        // all arraylist elements to it. Here, s1 == s2 is true
        System.out.println("s1 == s2:" + (s1 == s2));
        System.out.println("s1:" + getArrayContent(s1));
        System.out.println("s2:" + getArrayContent(s2));


        // Create an array of string with 1 elements, which is less
        // than size of arraylist, which is 3
        s1 = new String[1];
        s1[0] = "hello" ;  // Store hello in first element

        // Copy arraylist elements to array
        s2 = (String[]) al.toArray(s1);

        /* Since s doesn't have sufficient space to copy all
           arraylist elements, al.toArray(s) creates a new String
           array with 3 elements in it. All elements of arraylist
           are copied to new array. Finally, new array is returned.
           Here, s1 == s2 is false. s will be untouched by the
           method call
        */
        System.out.println("s1 == s2:" + (s1 == s2));
        System.out.println("s1:" + getArrayContent(s1));
        System.out.println("s2:" + getArrayContent(s2));
    }

    // Method to get the array content enclosed in square brackets
    public static String getArrayContent ( String[] s){
        StringBuffer  sb = new StringBuffer("[");
        for (int i = 0; i < s.length; i++ ){
            sb.append(s[i]);
```

```
                    // Append a comma, if needed
                    if (i != s.length - 1) {
                        sb.append (", ");
                    }
                }

            sb.append("]");
            return sb.toString();
        }
    }
```

```
Output

ArrayList:[cat, dog, rat]
s1 == s2:true
s1:[cat, dog, rat]
s2:[cat, dog, rat]
s1 == s2:false
s1:[hello]
s2:[cat, dog, rat]
```

Chapter 15. Garbage Collection

What is Garbage Collection?

Memory management is central to the development of a fast, efficient and bug free software using a programming language. Memory management involves two activities: memory allocation and memory reclamation. When a program needs memory, memory is allocated from a memory pool. When the program is finished with that memory, the memory is returned to the memory pool, so that it can be reused by some other part of the program in the future. The process of returning memory to the pool is known as *memory reclamation* or *memory recycling*. The memory allocation and reclamation can be accomplished explicitly or implicitly.

In explicit memory allocation, the programmer decides how much memory is needed. The programmer requests that amount of memory from the program runtime environment known as the *memory allocator* or simply *allocator*. An allocator allocates the requested memory and marks that memory as in-use, so it will not allocate the same memory block again. In the preceding memory allocation process, we assumed that our request for new memory block to allocator is always fulfilled. This can happen only if we have an infinite amount of memory. However, that is not the case with any computer. Some computers may have megabytes of memory; some may have gigabytes. However, there is always a limit to the memory available on a computer. If we run a program that always allocates memory blocks from the memory pool and never returns them back to the pool, we will soon run out of memory and our program will stop.

In explicit memory reclamation, the programmer decides when to return the memory to the memory-pool. The allocator is free to allocate the returned memory when it receives a new request for memory allocation. Explicit memory reclamation often leads to subtle bugs in programs. It also complicates the inter-modules interface design. Suppose there are two modules, m1 and m2, in an application. Module m1 allocates a block of memory and the reference to that memory is r1. Module m1 makes a call to module m2 passing the reference r1. Module m2 stores the reference r1 with it for future use. Which module should be responsible for reclamation of the memory referenced by r1? There could be different scenarios depending on the program flow between module m1 and m2. Suppose module m1 reclaims the memory immediately after a call to module m2. In such a case, we may come across two problems:

- At some point in the program execution, module m2 tries to access the memory using reference r1. Since module m1 has already reclaimed the memory referenced by r1, the same memory might have been reallocated by the allocator and may have entirely different data stored at that memory location. In such a case, r1 is called *dangling reference*, because it is referencing a memory location which has already been reclaimed. If you try to read data using a dangling reference, the result would be unpredictable. You cannot have a dangling reference in Java. We will discuss the memory allocation/reclamation process in Java later in this chapter.
- Module m1 may try to use reference r1 after it has reclaimed the memory referenced by r1. This will also lead to the problem of using a dangling reference.

If module m2 reclaims the memory referenced by r1, we may end up with the same dangling reference problem if any of the modules, m1 or m2, tries to use the reference r1. What happens if none of the modules reclaims the memory and never uses the reference r1 again? The memory will never be returned to the memory pool and will never be reused. This situation is known as a *memory leak,* because the allocator has no knowledge of the memory block, which is not returned to it, even though it is never used again by the program. If memory leaks happen regularly, the program will eventually run out of memory and will cease to function. If your program runs for a short time with small memory leaks, you may not even notice this bug for years or may be for the entire life of your program!

In a programming language, which allows explicit memory management, programmers spend a substantial amount of efforts in the memory management aspect of the program. In another kind of memory related problem, a programmer may allocate a big amount of memory statically, so that he can use it throughout the life cycle of the program. The static memory allocation may not always succeed, since static memory has an upper limit. The hardest part of the memory management decision is to decide when to reclaim the memory to avoid dangling references and memory leaks.

In implicit memory allocation, a programmer indicates to the runtime system that he wants to allocate the memory to store a particular type of data. The runtime system computes the memory needed to store the requested type of data and allocates it to the running program. In implicit/automatic memory reclamation, a programmer does not need to worry about memory reclamation. The runtime system will automatically reclaim all memory blocks, which will never be used by the program again. The process of automatic reclamation of unused memory is known as *Garbage Collection*. The program, which performs garbage collection, is known as *Garbage Collector* or simply *Collector*. The garbage collector may be implemented as part of the language runtime system or as an add-on library.

Memory Allocation in Java

In Java, programmers deal with objects. The memory required for an object is always allocated on heap. Memory required for an object is allocated implicitly using the `new` operator. Suppose we have a class called `Employee`. We create an object of the `Employee` class as:

```
Employee emp = new Employee();
```

Depending on the definition of the `Employee` class, Java runtime computes how much memory is needed; allocates that amount of memory on heap, and stores the reference to that memory block in the `emp` reference variable. Note that when we want to create an `Employee` object, we do not specify how much memory we need. The `new Employee()` part of the above statement indicates to Java that we want to create an object of the `Employee` class. Java queries the definition of the `Employee` class to compute the memory required to represent an `Employee` object.

Every Java object in memory has two areas: header area and data area. The object's header area stores bookkeeping information to be used by Java runtime, e.g., the pointer to the object class, information about garbage collection status of the object, locking information about the object, length of an array if the object is an array, etc. The data area is used to store the values for all instance variables of the object. The header area layout is fixed for a particular JVM implementation whereas data area layout is dependent on the object type. The Java Hotspot virtual machine uses two machine-words (on 32-bit architecture one word is 4 bytes) for the object's header. If the object is an array, it uses three machine-words for its header. One extra word in the header is used to store the array length. However, most JVMs use three-machine words for an object header. Figure 15-1 depicts the object layout for the Java Hotspot VM and the IBM VM.

Java Hotspot VM uses a variable length object header to save memory on the heap. Since most Java objects are small, one machine-word saving per object for non-array objects is a significant heap space saving. Java Hotspot VM's object header contains the following information:

classptr: This is the first machine-word in the object layout. It contains a pointer to the class information of the object. The class information includes the object's method table, object's size, pointer to a `Class` structure, which contains information about the class of the object, etc.

hash + age + lock: This is the second machine-word in the object header. It contains the object's hash code, age information and lock fields. Age information is used in the process of reclamation of the object's memory by the generational garbage collector. Generation garbage collector is a special type of garbage collector that uses object's age in its algorithm to reclaim an object's memory.

arraylength: This is the third machine-word in the object header. It is included only if the object is an array. It contains the length of the array. In this case, the object's data area contains the array elements.

Figure 15-1: The layout of an object in Java Hotspot VM and IBM VM

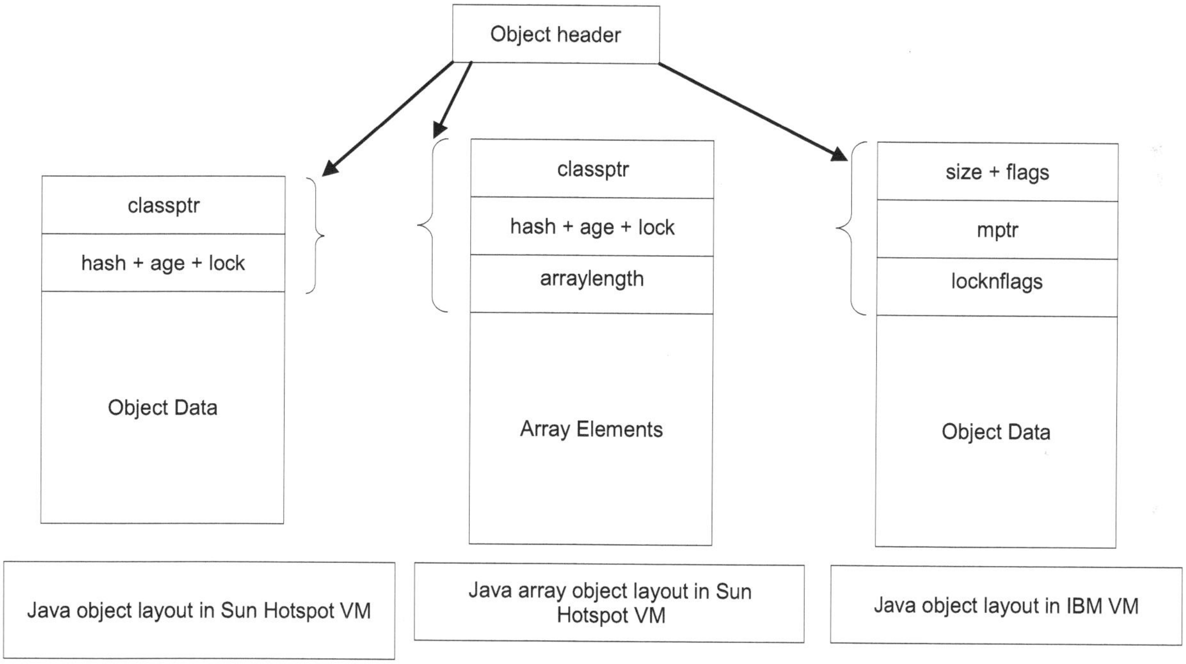

IBM VM uses three machine-words for the object header. All header fields hold the following information.

size + flags: This field is the first machine-word of the object header. This field contains the size of the object and flags to indicate different states of the object. Since the size of the object is limited and all objects start at 8 bytes boundary, some of the bits are used to store flags indicating different states of the object.

mptr: This field is the second machine-word in the object header. It can hold one of the two pieces of information depending on if the object is an array or not.

- It holds a pointer to the method block, if the object is not an array. The method block has reference to class block, which can give more information about the Java class the object belongs to.
- If the object is an array, this field holds the length of the array.

locknflags: This field is the third machine-word in the object header. It is used to hold information about the object locking and some flags. A 1-bit flag is used to indicate whether the object is an array or not. If this bit is set, *mptr* field contains the length of the array object. Another 1-bit flag is used to indicate if the object was hashed and moved. Note that objects are moved during some kind of garbage collection. Since the hash code of an object is its address in the memory and is supposed to be the same, the garbage collector that moves objects around during garbage collection uses this flag to preserve the hash code, if it was computed and used before the garbage collection.

TIP

In Java, all objects are created on heap. Java uses the `new` operator to allocate memory for an object on heap. An array's length is not a part of its class definition. It is defined at runtime. It is stored in its object header. You will not find the `length` instance variable in array's class definition when you perform introspection on an array's class.

Java does not provide any direct means to compute the size of an object. You should not write a Java program that depends on the size of the objects anyway. The size of primitive types, e.g., `int`, `long`, `double`, etc. is fixed for all JVM implementations. The layout and size of an object depends on the JVM implementation. Therefore, any code that depends on an object's size may work on one platform, not on others.

Garbage Collection in Java

The garbage collector is part of the Java platform. It runs in the background in a low priority thread. The garbage collector in Java automatically reclaims an object. However, before it reclaims the object, it makes sure that the running program in its current state will never use the object again. This way, it ensures that the program will not have any dangling references. An object, which cannot be used in future by the running program, is known as a *dead object* or *garbage*. An object, which can be used in the future by the running program, is known as a *live object*.

There are many algorithms to determine if an object is live or dead. One of the simplest, but not very efficient, algorithms is based on reference counting. The reference counting algorithm stores the count of references that refer to an object. When an object's reference is assigned to a reference variable, the reference count is incremented by 1. When a reference variable no longer refers to an object, the reference count is decremented by 1. When the reference count for an object is zero, it becomes garbage. This algorithm has a lot of overhead of updating the reference count of objects. Another type of algorithm, which is called a *tracing algorithm*, is based on the concept of a root set. A root set includes:

- Reference variables in Java stack for each thread
- Static reference variables defined in loaded classes
- Reference variables registered using the Java Native Interface (JNI)

A garbage collector, which is based on the tracing algorithm, starts traversing references starting from the root set. Objects that can be reached (or accessed) from the reference variables in the root set are known as reachable. A reachable object is considered live. A reachable object from the root set may refer to other objects. These objects are also considered as reachable. Therefore, any object that can be reached directly or indirectly from the root set reference variables is considered live. Other objects are considered dead and hence they are eligible for garbage collection.

An object may manage resources other than memory on heap. These resources may include network connections, files handles, memory managed explicitly by native codes, etc. For example, an object may open a file when it is created. File handles that can be opened simultaneously may have an upper limit depending on your operating system. When the object is garbage collected, you may want to close the file handles. The garbage collector gives the dying object a chance to perform the cleanup work. It does this by executing a predefined block of code before the memory for the dying object is reclaimed. The process of performing the cleanup work, before the object is reclaimed by the garbage collector, is known as *finalization*. The block of code that is invoked by the garbage collector to perform finalization is known as the *finalizer*. In Java, you can define a method named `finalize()` for a class, which serves as a finalizer for the objects of the class. That is, the Java garbage collector invokes the `finalize()` method of an object before it reclaims the memory occupied by the object.

Invoking Garbage Collector

Programmers have little control over the timing when the garbage collector is run. The JVM performs the garbage collection whenever it runs low in memory. The JVM tries its best to free up all unused object's memory, before it throws the `java.lang.OutOfMemoryError` error. The `gc()` method of the `java.lang.Runtime` class may be used to pass a hint to the JVM that it may run the garbage collector. The call to the `gc()` method of the `Runtime` class is just a hint to the JVM. The JVM is free to ignore the call. The Java Language API Documentation describes the behavior of a call to the `gc()` as follows.

> *"Runs the garbage collector. Calling this method suggests that the Java virtual machine expend effort toward recycling unused objects in order to make the memory they currently occupy available for quick reuse. When control returns from the method call, the virtual machine has made its best effort to recycle all discarded objects…"*

The `gc()` method of the `Runtime` class can be called as:

```
// Get the Runtime instance
Runtime rt = Runtime.getRuntime();

// Run the garbage collector
rt.gc();
```

You can combine the above two statements into one statement, if you do not intend to use the `Runtime` instance again as:

```
// Get runtime instance and run the garbage collector
Runtime.getRuntime().gc();
```

The `java.lang.System` class contains a convenience method, `gc()`, which is equivalent to executing `Runtime.getRuntime().gc()` statement. You can also use the following statement to run the garbage collector.

```
// Invoke the garbage collector
System.gc();
```

The program in Listing 15-1 demonstrates the use of the `System.gc()` method. The program creates two thousand objects of the `Object` class in the `createObjects()` method. The references for the new objects are not stored in any reference variable. That is, these objects

---

cannot be referred to again and hence, they are garbage. When we invoke the `System.gc()` method, the JVM will try to reclaim the memory used by these objects. The memory freed by the garbage collector is displayed in the output section. Note that you may get a different output, when you run this program on your machine.

Listing 15-1: Invoking garbage collection

```java
// InvokeGC.java
package com.jdojo.chapter15;

public class InvokeGC {
    public static void main(String[] args) {
        long m1, m2, m3;

        // Get runtime instance
        Runtime rt = Runtime.getRuntime();

        for(int i = 0; i < 3; i++){
            // Get free memory
            m1 =  rt.freeMemory();

            // Create some objects
            createObjects(2000);

            // Get free memory
            m2 =  rt.freeMemory();

            // Invoke garbage collection
            System.gc();

            // Get free memory
            m3 =  rt.freeMemory();

            System.out.println("m1=" + m1 + ", m2=" + m2 + ", m3=" +
                          m3 + "\nMemory freed by gc()=" + (m3 -m2));

            System.out.println("------------------------");
        }
    }

    public static void createObjects(int count) {
        for(int i = 0; i < count; i++) {
            /* Do not store new object's reference so that they are
               immediately eligible for garbage collection
            */
            new Object();
        }
    }
}
```

```
Output:

m1=1862480, m2=1846480, m3=1929680
Memory freed by gc()=83200
------------------------
m1=1927856, m2=1911856, m3=1929680
```

```
Memory freed by gc()=17824
------------------------
m1=1928496, m2=1912496, m3=1929680
Memory freed by gc()=17184
------------------------
```

In general, it is not advisable to invoke the garbage collector programmatically using the `System.gc()` method. Invoking the garbage collector has some overhead. It may slow down performance if it is invoked arbitrarily. The Java runtime takes care of reclaiming unused object's memory automatically. You may get `OutOfMemoryError` in your program. This error may be caused by many reasons. The Java runtime makes all efforts to free up memory invoking the garbage collector before throwing the `OutOfMemoryError` error. Therefore, simply invoking the garbage collector programmatically will not make this error go away. To resolve this error, you can look at the following:

- Review your program to make sure that you are not holding onto some object references, which you will never use again. Set these references to `null`, after you are done with them. Setting all references to an object to `null` makes the object eligible for the garbage collection. If you are storing large objects in `static` variables, those objects will remain in memory until the class itself is unloaded. Generally, the objects stored in `static` variables will take up memory forever. Review your program and try to avoid storing large objects in `static` variables.
- Review your code and make sure that you are not caching large amount of data in objects. You can use weak references to cache large amount of data in objects. Weak references have an advantage over regular references (regular references are also known as strong references) that the objects referenced by weak references are garbage collected, before the Java runtime throws an `OutOfMemoryError`. We will discuss weak references later in this chapter.
- If none of the above solutions work for you, you may try to adjust the heap size.

Object Finalization

Finalization is the action that is automatically performed on an object before the memory used by the object is reclaimed by the garbage collector. The block of code that contains the action to be performed is known as a *finalizer*. The `java.lang.Object` class has a `finalize()` method, which is declared as:

```
protected void finalize() throws Throwable
```

Since all Java classes inherit from the `Object` class, the `finalize()` method can be invoked on all Java objects. Any class can override and implement its own version of the `finalize()` method. The `finalize()` method serves as a finalizer for Java objects. That is, the garbage collector automatically invokes the `finalize()` method on an object, before it reclaims the object's memory. Understanding the correct use of the `finalize()` method in a class is key to writing a good Java program, which manages resources other than the heap memory. Let us first start with a simple example that demonstrates the fact that the `finalize()` method is called before an object is garbage collected. Listing 15-2 defines a method `finalize()` in the `Finalizer` class, which will be called by the garbage collector before the object of this class is garbage collected. The `finalize()` method prints a message if the object being garbage collected has an `id`, which is a multiple of `100`. The `main()` method creates five hundred objects of the `Finalizer` class and calls `System.gc()` to invoke the garbage collector. You may not see any output on your machine when you run this program, because calling `System.gc()` does not guarantee that the garbage collector will be run by the JVM.

Listing 15-2: Using the finalize() method

```java
// Finalizer.java
package com.jdojo.chapter15;

public class Finalizer {
    // id is used to identify the object
    private int id;

    // Constructor which takes id as argument
    public Finalizer(int id){
        this.id = id;
    }

    // This is the finalizer for the object. The JVM will call this
    // method, before the object is garbage collected
    public void finalize(){
        /* Just print a message indicating which
           object is being garbage collected. Print message
           when id is a multiple of 100 just to avoid bigger output
        */
        if (id % 100 == 0) {
            System.out.println ("finalize() called for " + id ) ;
        }
    }

    public static void main(String[] args) {
        // Create 500 objects of Finalizer class
        for(int i = 1; i <= 500000; i++){
            // Do not store reference to the new object
            new Finalizer(i);
        }

        // Invoke garbage collector
        System.gc();
    }
}
```

```
Output:

finalize() called for 100
finalize() called for 200
finalize() called for 300
finalize() called for 400
finalize() called for 500
more output (not shown here)...
```

When the garbage collector determines that an object is unreachable, it marks that object for finalization and places that object in a queue. If you want Java runtime to finalize all objects, which are pending for finalization, you can do so by calling the `runFinalization()` method of the `Runtime` class as:

```
Runtime rt = Runtime.getRuntime();
rt.runFinalization();
```

The `System` class has a `runFinalization()` convenience method, which is equivalent to calling the `runFinalization()` method of the `Runtime` class. It can be called as:

```
System.runFinalization();
```

Invoking the `runFinalization()` method is only a hint to the Java runtime to invoke the `finalize()` method of all objects with pending finalization. Technically, you may call the `finalize()` method on an object in your code as many times as you want. However, it is meant for the garbage collector to call an object's `finalize()` method at most one time during the lifetime of the object. The garbage collector's one time call to the `finalize()` method of an object is not affected by the fact that the `finalize()` method of the object was called programmatically before.

Programmers should not override the `finalize()` method in a class trivially. A `finalize()` method with no code, or which calls the `finalize()` method of the `Object` class, is an example of trivially overridden `finalize()` method. The `finalize()` method in the `Object` class does nothing. So, if your class is a direct subclass of the `Object` class and you do not have any meaningful code in the `finalize()` method of your class, it is better not to include the `finalize()` method in your class at all. Memory reclamation is faster and sooner for the objects, which do not have an implementation of the `finalize()` method compared to those that have an implementation of the `finalize()` method.

finally or finalize?

The time when an object is finalized is not guaranteed. That all unreachable objects will ever be finalized is also not guaranteed. In short, there is no guarantee when the `finalize()` method of an unreachable object will be called or if it will be called at all. So, what good is the `finalize()` method? The main purpose of a garbage collector in Java is to relieve the programmers from the burden of freeing the memory of an unused object to avoid the problem of memory leaks and dangling references. Its secondary job is to run the finalization on the objects with no guarantee about the timing of the finalization. As a programmer, you should not depend much on the finalization process of garbage collection in your programs. You should code the `finalize()` method with care. If you need to cleanup resources for sure when you are done with them, you should use a `try-finally` clause as:

```
try {
    // Get your resources and work with them
}
finally {
    // Release your resources
}
```

You can acquire resources and use them in a `try` block and release them in the associated `finally` block. A `finally` block is guaranteed to be executed after a `try` block is executed. This way, you can be sure that scarce resources in your program are always freed once you are done with them. However, it may not be always feasible, because of performance issues, to release resources immediately after you are done with them. For example, you may not want to open a network connection every time you need it. You may open a network connection once, use it and close it when you no longer need it. Sometimes, you may not know the exact point in program from where you will not need that network connection. In such cases, you can code the `finalize()` method as a backup to free the resources if they have not been freed yet. You can call the `finalize()` method programmatically when you know for sure that resources can be freed. The `FinalizeAsBackup` class as shown below shows the skeleton of code using such a technique. The `aMethod()` method of the class gets the resources and stores its reference in `sr` instance variables. Programmers call the `finalize()` method when he is sure that he should free the resources. Otherwise, the garbage collector will call the `finalize()` method and resources will be freed when the object is destroyed. Note that the `FinalizeAsBackup` class is a template. It contains pseudo code to explain the technique. This class will not compile.

```
// Template of a class, which uses finalize() method as a backup to
// free resources
public class FinalizeAsBackup {
    // Other codes go here
    SomeResource sr;
    public void aMethod() {
        sr = Obtain the resources here...;

        // Do some processing . . .

        // Note the conditional freeing of resources
        if (some condition is true) {
            //Free resources here calling finalize()
            this.finalize();
        }
    }

    public void finalize() {
        // Free the resources if they have not been freed yet
        if (resources not yet freed ) {
            free resources now;
        }
    }
}
```

TIP

The moral of the story about using the `finalize()` method is – use it with care and use it only as a last resort to free resources. You can use a `try-finally` block to free resources. The order in which objects are finalized is not defined. For example, if an object, `obj1`, becomes eligible for garbage collection before another object, `obj2`, it is not guaranteed that `obj1` will be finalized before `obj2`. When an uncaught exception is thrown, the main program is halted. However, if an uncaught exception in a finalizer halts the finalization of only that object, not the entire application.

Object Resurrection

Someone is about to die. God asks him for his last wish. He says, "Give me my life back". God grants his last wish and he gets back his life. When he was about to die the second time God kept quiet and let him die without asking him for his last wish. Otherwise, he would ask for his life repeatedly and he would never die. The same logic applies to an object's finalization in Java. The call to the `finalize()` method of an object is like the garbage collector asking the object for its last wish. Generally, the object responds, "I want to clean up all my mess." That is, an object responds to its `finalize()` method call by performing some cleanup work. It may respond to its `finalize()` method call by resurrecting itself by placing its reference in a reachable reference variable. Once it is reachable through an already reachable reference variable, it is back to life. The garbage collector marks an object, using the object's header bits, as finalized after it calls the object's `finalize()` method. If the same object becomes unreachable the next time during garbage collection, the garbage collector does not call the object's `finalize()` method again if the object was already finalized. The resurrection of an object is possible, because the garbage collector does not reclaim an object's memory just after calling its `finalize()` method. After calling the `finalize()` method, it just marks the object as finalized. In the next phase of the garbage collection, it determines again if the object is reachable. If the object is unreachable and finalized, only then will it reclaim the object's memory. If an object is reachable and finalized, it does not reclaim object's memory and this is a typical case of resurrection.

Resurrecting an object in its `finalize()` method is not a good programming practice. One simple reason is that if you have coded the `finalize()` method, you expect it to be executed every time an object dies. If you resurrect the object in its `finalize()` method, the garbage collector will not call its `finalize()` method again when it becomes unreachable a second time. After resurrection, you might have obtained some resources that you expect to be released in the `finalize()` method. This will leave subtle bugs in your program. It is also hard for other programmers to understand your program flow if your program resurrects objects in their `finalize()` methods. Listing 15-3 demonstrates how an object can resurrect using its `finalize()` method.

Listing 15-3: Object resurrection

```
// Resurrect.java
package com.jdojo.chapter15;

public class Resurrect {
    // Declare a static variable of Resurrect type
    private static Resurrect res = null;

    // Declare an instance variable that stores name of object
    private String name = "";

    public Resurrect(String name) {
        this.name = name;
    }

    public static void main(String[] args) {
        /* We will create objects of Resurrect class and will not
           store their references so that they are eligible for
           garbage collection immediately
        */
        for(int count = 1; count <= 1000; count++) {
            new Resurrect("Object #" + count);

            // For every 100 objects created invoke garbage·
            // collection
            if (count % 100 == 0) {
                System.gc();
                System.runFinalization();
            }
        }
    }
```

```java
    public void sayHello() {
        System.out.println("Hello from " + name);
    }

    public static void resurrectIt(Resurrect r) {
        // Set the reference r to static variable res
        // which makes it reachable as long as res is reachable
        res = r ;

        // Call a method to show that we really got the object back
        res.sayHello();
    }

    public void finalize() {
        System.out.println("Inside finalize(): " + name);

        // Resurrect this object
        Resurrect.resurrectIt(this);
    }
}
```

```
Output:  (Partial output is shown below)
...
Inside finalize(): Object #14
Hello from Object #14
...
Inside finalize(): Object #997
Hello from Object #997
```

The `Resurrect` class creates one thousand objects in its `main()` method. It does not store references of those new objects, so that they become garbage as soon as they are created. After creating one hundred new objects, it invokes the garbage collector using the `System.gc()` method. It also calls the `System.runFinalization()` method, so that the finalizers are run for garbage objects. When the garbage collector calls the `finalize()` method for an object, that object passes its reference to the `resurrectIt()` method. This method stores the dying object reference in the `static` variable `res`, which is reachable. The method `resurrectIt()` also calls the `sayHello()` method on the resurrected object to show which object was resurrected. Note that once another object resurrects itself we are overwriting the `res static` variable with the recently resurrected object reference. The previously resurrected object becomes garbage again. The garbage collector will reclaim the memory for the previously resurrected object without calling its `finalize()` method again. You may get a different output when you run the program in Listing 15-3 on your machine.

State of an Object

The state of a Java object is defined based on two criteria:

- Object's Finalization status
- Object's Reachability

Based on the finalization status, an object can be in one of the following three states:

- Unfinalized
- Finalizable
- Finalized

When an object is instantiated, it is in the unfinalized state. For example,

```
Employee john = new Employee();
```

The object referred to by the `john` reference variable is in an unfinalized state after the above statement is executed. The finalizer of an unfinalized object had never been invoked automatically by the JVM. An object becomes finalizable when the garbage collector determines that the `finalize()` method can be invoked on the object. A finalized object has its `finalize()` method invoked automatically by the garbage collector.

Based on reachability, an object can be in one of three states:

- Reachable
- Finalizer-reachable
- Unreachable

An object is reachable if it can be accessed through any chain of reference from the root set. A finalizer-reachable object can be reached through the finalizer of any finalizable object. A finalizer-reachable object may become reachable if the finalizer from which it is reachable stores its reference in an object, which is reachable. This is the situation when an object resurrects. An object may resurrect itself in its `finalize()` method or through another object's `finalize()` method. An unreachable object cannot be reached by any means.

We have nine combinations of object's states based on their finalization status and reachability status. One of the nine combinations, finalizable and unreachable, is not possible. The `finalize()` method of a finalizable object may be called in future. The `finalize()` method can still refer to the object using `this` keyword. Therefore, a finalizable object cannot also be unreachable. An object can exist in one of the following eight states.

- Unfinalized – Reachable
- Unfinalized – Finalizer-reachable
- Unfinalized – Unreachable
- Finalizable-Reachable
- Finalizable-Finalizer-reachable
- Finalized – Reachable
- Finalized – Finalizer-reachable
- Finalized – Unreachable

Weak References

The Java 2 platform introduced the concept of weak references in Java garbage collection by including a new package `java.lang.ref`. The concept of weak references in the context of garbage collection is not new to Java. It was there before, but Java included it in the Java2 platform. So far, the object references we have discussed are strong references. That is, as long as the object reference is in scope, the object it refers to cannot be garbage collected. For example, consider the following object creation and reference assignment statement:

```
Employee john = new Employee("John Jacobs");
```

Here, `john` is a reference to the object created by the expression, `new Employee("John Jacobs")`. The memory state that exists after executing the above statement is depicted in Figure 15-1.

Figure 15-2: An example of a strong reference

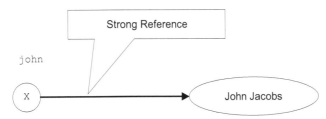

If at least one strong reference to an object exists, the garbage collector will not reclaim that object. In the previous section, we discussed the object state based on its reachability. By stating, there is a strong reference to an object; we mean that the object is reachable. With the introduction of weak references, now there are three more states of an object based on its reachability. They are:

- Softly reachable
- Weakly reachable
- Phantom reachable

Therefore, when we called an object as *reachable* in the last section, we will call it *strongly reachable* now onwards. This change in terminology is because of the introduction of three new kinds of object's reachability. Before we discuss the three new object's reachability, we need to know about the classes included in `java.lang.ref` package. There are four classes of interest. They have been shown in Figure 15-3.

Figure 15-3: Some classes in the java.lang.ref package

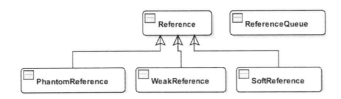

The `Reference` class is the superclass for the `SoftReference`, `WeakReference` and `PhantomReference` classes. The `Reference` class is an abstract class. Therefore, you cannot create an object of this class. Three classes, `SoftReference`, `WeakReference` and `PhantomReference`, are used to create weak references. Note that by the phrase "weak reference", we mean reference, which is not a strong reference. By the phrase `WeakReference`, we mean the class `java.lang.ref.WeakReference`. We will describe a weak reference in the following discussion in this section. The `ReferenceQueue` class is used to place the references of

`SoftReference`, `WeakReference` and `PhantomReference` objects in a queue. Let us look at different ways to create these three types of objects. Constructors for these three classes have been shown in Table 15-1.

Table 15-1: Constructors for SoftReference, WeakReference and PhantomReference classes

Class	Constructors
SoftReference	`SoftReference(Object referent)`
	`SoftReference(Object referent, ReferenceQueue q)`
WeakReference	`WeakReference(Object referent)`
	`WeakReference(Object referent, ReferenceQueue q)`
PhantomReference	`PhantomReference(Object referent, ReferenceQueue q)`

You can create objects of `SoftReference` and `WeakReference` classes using an object of any class, or using an object of any class and an object of the `ReferenceQueue` class. You must create an object of the `PhantomReference` class using an object of any class and an object of the `ReferenceQueue` class. You can create an object of the `SoftReference` class as:

```
Employee john = new Employee ("John Jacobs");
SoftReference sr = new SoftReference(john);
```

The memory state after executing the above two statements has been depicted in Figure 15-4.

Figure 15-4: An example of a soft reference

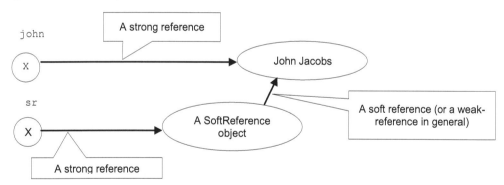

In Figure 15-4, there are two strong references and one weak reference. All three weak reference classes have two instance variables: `referent` and `queue`. We will not discuss other instance variables of these classes. They are used to hold the reference of the object and reference queue passed in to the constructors of these classes. A reference to any object stored in the `referent` instance variable of any of these three classes is known as a weak reference in general, and soft reference, weak reference or Phantom reference in particular, depending on the class being used. Therefore, the link from a soft reference object to the employee object shown in Figure 15-4 is a weak-reference. To be specific, we will call it a soft reference, because we used an object of the `SoftReference` class. Any reference that does not involve the `referent` instance variable of any of these three classes is a strong reference in Java. Therefore, `john` and `sr` are the strong references created by the above two statements.

How are weak references different from strong references? The difference lies in how the garbage collector treats them. Weak references do not prevent the objects from being collected by the garbage collector. That is, if there is a weak reference to an object, the garbage collector can still collect that object. However, if there is at least one strong reference to an object, the garbage collector will not collect that object. Before we start looking at details of how to use these three reference classes in Java programs, let us discuss the reachability of an object when these classes are involved in a program.

- *Strongly reachable:* An object is strongly reachable if it can be reached from the root set through at least one chain of references, which does not involve any weak reference objects (e.g. `WeakReference`, `SoftReference` or `PhantomReference`).
- *Softly reachable:* An object is softly reachable if it is not strongly reachable and it can be reached from the root set through at least one chain of references, which involves at least one soft reference, but no weak and phantom references.
- *Weakly reachable:* An object is weakly reachable if it is not strongly and softly reachable and it can be reached from the root set through at least one chain of references, which involves at least a weak reference and no phantom references.
- *Phantom reachable:* An object is phantom reachable if it is not strongly, softly and weakly reachable and it can be reached from the root set through at least one chain of references, which involves at least a phantom reference. A phantom reachable object is finalized, but not reclaimed.

Among three kinds of weak-references, a soft reference is considered stronger than a weak reference and a phantom reference. A weak reference is considered stronger than a phantom reference. Therefore, the rule to identify the reachability of an object is that if an object is not strongly reachable, it is as reachable as the weakest reference in the reference chain leading to that object. That is, if a chain of references to an object involves a phantom reference, the object must be phantom reachable. If a chain of references to an object does not involve a phantom reference, but it involves a weak reference, the object must be weakly reachable. If a chain of references to an object does not involve a phantom reference and a weak reference, but it involves a soft reference, the object must be softly reachable. How do we determine the reachability of an object when there is more than one chain of reference to an object? In such cases, we determine the object's reachability using all possible chains of references and use the strongest one. That is, if an object is softly reachable through one chain of references and phantom reachable through other, the object is considered softly reachable. Figure 15-5 depicts the examples of how an object's reachability is determined. The elliptical shape at the end of every reference chain represents an object. The reachability of the object has been indicated inside the elliptical shape. The rectangles denote references.

TIP

Weak references do not prevent objects from being garbage collected. To determine the reachability of an object, the garbage collector traverses all possible chain of references leading to that object from the root set. An object is as reachable as the weakest reference in a chain of references leading to that object. If there is more than one chain of references from the root set leading to an object, the strongest reachability is determined by considering all chain of references in the object's reachability.

Figure 15-5: Different kinds of object's reachability

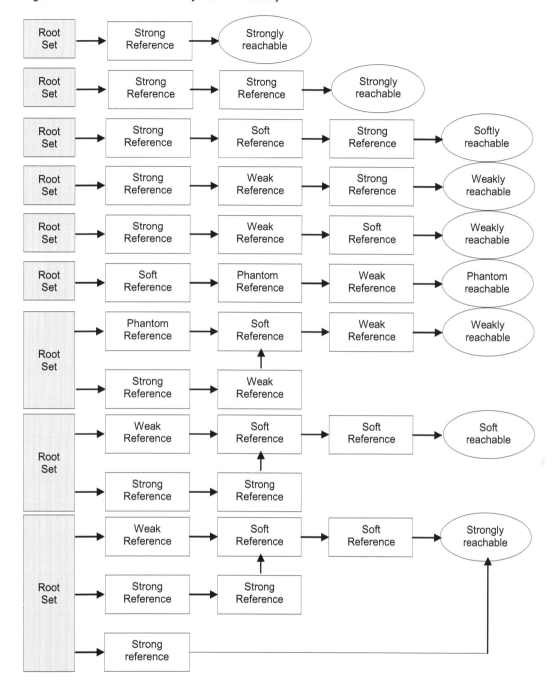

Accessing and Clearing Referent's Reference

We will use objects of a trivial class to demonstrate the use of reference classes. This class is called `BigObject` as listed in Listing 15-4. This class has a big array of `long` as an instance variable so that it uses a big chunk of memory. The `id` instance variable is used to track the objects of this class. The `finalize()` method prints a message to the console using the object's `id`.

Listing 15-4: A BigObject class, which uses big memory

```java
// BigObject.java
package com.jdojo.chapter15;

public class BigObject {
    // Declare a 16KB big array. This choice is arbitrary.
    // We just wanted to consume a large amount of memory when
    // an object of this class is created
    private long [] anArray = new long[4096];

    // Have an id to track the object
    private long id;

    public BigObject(long id) {
        this.id = id;
    }

    // Define finalize() to track the object's finalization
    public void finalize(){
        System.out.println("finalize() called for id:" + id);
    }

    public String toString() {
        return "BigObject: id = " + id;
    }
}
```

The object that we pass to the constructors of `WeakReference`, `SoftReference` and `PhantomReference` classes is called *referent*. In other words, the object referred to by the object of these three reference classes is called referent. To get the reference of the referent of a reference object you need to call the `get()` method. You need to cast the returned object reference from the `get()` method to an appropriate type, because it returns a reference of `java.lang.Object` type.. The following piece of code demonstrate the use of the `get()` method.

```java
// Create a big object with id as 101
BigObject bigObj  = new BigObject(101);

/* At this point, the big object with id 101 is strongly reachable */

// Create a soft reference object using bigObj as referent
SoftReference sr = new SoftReference(bigObj);

/* At this point, the big object with id 101 is still strongly reachable,
because bigObj is a strong reference referring to it. It also has a soft
reference referring to it.
*/

// Set bigObj to null to make the object softly reachable
bigObj = null;

/* At this point, the big object with id 101 is softly reachable,
   because  it can be reached only through a soft reference sr.
*/
```

```
// Get the reference of referent of soft reference object
BigObject referent = (BigObject)sr.get();


/* At this point, the big object with id 101 again becomes strongly
   reachable because referent is a strong reference. It also has a soft
   reference referring to it.
*/
```

Figure 15-6 depicts the memory states with all the references after we execute each statement in the snippet of code. We use the `clear()` method to clear the link between the reference (weak, soft or phantom) object and its referent. The following piece of code illustrates the use of the `clear()` method.

```
// Create a soft reference object. Use a big object
// with id 976 as its referent
SoftReference sr1 = new SoftReference(new BigObject(976));

/* At this point, the big object with id 976 is softly reachable,
   because it is reachable only through a soft reference sr
*/

// Clear the referent
sr1.clear();
```

Figure 15-6: Accessing the referent of a reference object

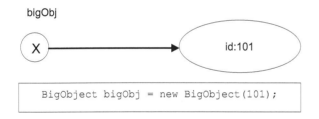

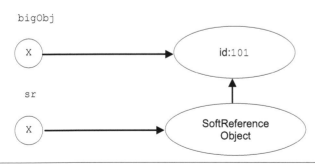

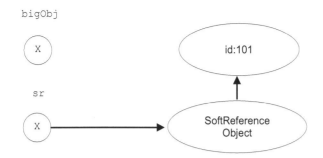

bigObj

sr

```
BigObject bigObj  = new BigObject(101);
SoftReference sr = new SoftReference(bigObj);
bigObj = null;
```

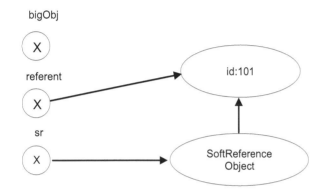

bigObj

referent

sr

```
BigObject bigObj  = new BigObject(101);
SoftReference sr = new SoftReference(bigObj);
bigObj = null;
BigObject referent = (BigObject)sr.get();
```

```
/* At this point, the big object with id 976 is unreachable (to be
   exact, it is finalizer-reachable), because we cleared the only one
   reference (soft reference) we had to the object.
*/
```

The memory state with all references, after each statement in the above code fragment is executed, has been depicted in Figure 15-7. After the referent's reference is cleared using the clear() method, the get() method returns null. The get() method of a PhantomReference object always returns null.

Figure 15-7: Clearing referent

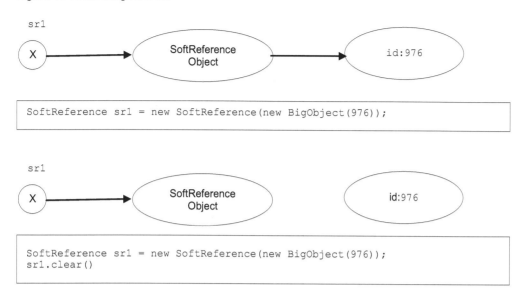

```
SoftReference sr1 = new SoftReference(new BigObject(976));
```

```
SoftReference sr1 = new SoftReference(new BigObject(976));
sr1.clear()
```

Using SoftReference Class

A softly reachable object is used to maintain memory-sensitive caches. That is, if you want to maintain a cache of objects as long as the program is not running low in memory, you can use softly reachable objects. When the program runs low in memory, the garbage collector clears the soft references to an object making the object eligible for reclamation. At that point, your program will lose some or all objects from the cache. Java does not guarantee that soft references will not be cleared if the program is not running low in memory. However, it guarantees that all soft references will be cleared before the JVM throws an OutOfMemoryError. There is also no guarantee for the order in which soft references will be cleared. However, JVM implementations are encouraged to clear the least-recently created/used soft reference first.

It is very important to note that, to take advantage of the garbage collector behavior with respect to soft references, you must not keep a strong reference to the object. As long as you keep strong references to the object, the garbage collector will not clear the soft references to it, even if the program is running low in memory. The garbage collector clears the soft reference only if an object is softly reachable. Listing 15-5 shows the wrong use of soft references to cache data. The intention of the programmer is to cache a big object with an id of 101 using a soft reference. If the program runs low in memory, the cached big object with id 101 may be reclaimed. The while-loop inside the program is trying to create many big objects to make the program run low in memory. The programmer is expecting that when this program is executed, it should reclaim memory used by the big object with id 101, before throwing an OutOfMemoryError.

Listing 15-5: An incorrect use of a soft references

```
// WrongSoftRef.java
package com.jdojo.chapter15;

import java.util.ArrayList;
import java.lang.ref.SoftReference;

public class WrongSoftRef {
    public static void main(String[] args) {
```

```
            // Create a big object with id 101 for caching
            BigObject bigObj = new BigObject(101);

            // Wrap soft reference inside a soft reference
            SoftReference sr = new SoftReference(bigObj);

            // Let us try to create many big objects storing their
            // references in an array list, just to use up big memory
            ArrayList bigList = new ArrayList();
            long counter = 102;

            while ( true ) {
                bigList.add(new BigObject(counter++) );
            }
        }
    }
}
```

```
Output:

Exception in thread "main" java.lang.OutOfMemoryError
```

The output shows that the program did not reclaim the memory used by the big object with id 101. Why did the garbage collector not behave the way it was expected to behave? We made a mistake when we wrote the code for the WrongSoftRef class. In fact, the big object with id 101 is strongly reachable, because the bigObj reference to it is a strong reference. Therefore, we must set the bigObj reference variable to null to make it softly reachable. Listing 15-6 shows the correct use of soft references. It is clear from the output that finalize() method for the big object with id 101 was called and it was reclaimed before JVM threw OutOfMemoryError. We still got a OutOfMemoryError, because we are creating many new objects inside a while-loop and all of them are strongly reachable from the array list. We proved the point that soft references are cleared and the referents are reclaimed by the garbage collector before JVM throws OutOfMemoryError.

Listing 15-6: A correct use of a soft reference

```
// CorrectSoftRef.java
package com.jdojo.chapter15;

import java.util.ArrayList;
import java.lang.ref.SoftReference;

public class CorrectSoftRef {
    public static void main(String[] args) {
        // Create a big object with id 101 for caching
        BigObject bigObj = new BigObject(101);

        // Wrap soft reference inside a soft reference
        SoftReference sr = new SoftReference(bigObj);

        // Set bigObj to null so that the big object will
        // be softly reachable and can be reclaimed, if necessary
        bigObj = null;

        // Let us try to create many big objects storing their
        // references in an array list, just to use up big memory
```

```
        ArrayList bigList = new ArrayList();
        long counter = 102;

        while (true) {
            bigList.add(new BigObject(counter++));
        }
    }
}
```

```
Output:

finalize() called for id:101
Exception in thread "main" java.lang.OutOfMemoryError
```

Listing 15-7 illustrates how to use a soft reference to implement memory-sensitive caches. It can cache up to 10 objects of the `BigObject` class with ids from 0 to 9. You can call the `createCache()` method to cache all 10 objects. To get the cached object for a given `id`, you need to call the `getObjectById()` method. If that `id` has not yet been cached or it was reclaimed by the garbage collector, this method re-caches the object with that `id` and returns the object to the caller. This example is very restrictive and its purpose is only to demonstrate the use of the `SoftReference` class to maintain a memory-sensitive cache. You can cache only objects with ids from 0 to 9. It can be modified to meet specific requirements. For example, you can use an `ArrayList` to cache the objects instead of using an array. Alternatively, you can allow storing a big object with any `id` in the array itself and search through the array for a given object when an object is required from the cache. You can use the `BigObjectCache` class as:

```
// Get the object from cache
BigObject cachedObject = BigObjectCache.getObjectById(5);

// Do some processing...

// You must set the cachedObject to null after you are done with it,
// so that the cached object becomes softly reachable and may be
// reclaimed by the garbage collector
cachedObject = null;
```

If an object with an `id` of 5 is not already in the cache, it will be cached and the new object reference will be assigned to `cachedObject`. If an object with an `id` of 5 is already in the cache, the reference of that object from the cache will be returned and assigned to `cachedObject`.

Listing 15-7: Creating a cache using soft references

```
// BigObjectCache.java
package com.jdojo.chapter15;

import java.lang.ref.SoftReference;

public class BigObjectCache {
    private static SoftReference[] cache = new SoftReference[10];

    public static BigObject getObjectById(int id) {
        // Check for valid cache id
        if (id < 0 || id >= cache.length) {
            throw new IllegalArgumentException("Invalid id");
```

```
        }

        BigObject obj = null;

        // Check if we have a cache for this id
        if (cache[id] == null) {
            // We haven't cached the object yet.
            // Cache it and return it
            obj = createCacheForId(id);
            return obj;
        }

        // Get the BigObject reference using soft reference
        obj = (BigObject)cache[id].get();

        // Make sure the object has not yet been reclaimed
        if (obj == null) {
            // Garbage collector has reclaimed the object
            // Cache it again and return the newly cached object
            obj = createCacheForId(id);
        }

        return obj;
    }

    // Create cache at once for all ids
    public static void createCache() {
        for (int i = 0; i < cache.length; i++) {
            cache[i] = new SoftReference(new BigObject(i));
        }
    }

    //Creates cache for a given id
    private static BigObject createCacheForId(int id) {
        BigObject obj = null;
        if (id >= 0 && id < cache.length) {
            obj =  new BigObject(id);
            cache[id] = new SoftReference(obj);
        }

        return obj;
    }
}
```

Using ReferenceQueue Class

An object of the `ReferenceQueue` class is used in conjunction with an object of the `SoftReference`, `WeakReference` and `PhantomReference` class, when the object needs to be notified upon its reachability change. An object of any of these reference classes can be registered with a reference queue as:

```
ReferenceQueue q = new ReferenceQueue();

SoftReference sr = new SoftReference(new BigObject(19), q);
```

```
WeakReference wr = new WeakReference(new BigObject(20), q);
PhantomReference pr = new PhantomReference(new BigObject(21), q);
```

It is optional to register the `SoftReference` and `WeakReference` objects with a reference queue. However, you must register a `PhantomReference` object with a reference queue. When a `SoftReference` or a `WeakReference` is cleared by the garbage collector, the reference of the `SoftReference` or the `WeakReference` object is appended to the reference queue. Note that it is the references of the `SoftReference` and `WeakReference` that are placed in the queue and not the reference of their referent. For example, if the garbage collector clears the soft reference to `BigObject` with `id` 19 in the above snippet of code, `sr` will be placed in the reference queue. In case of a `PhantomReference` object, when its referent becomes phantom reachable, the garbage collector places the `PhantomReference` object in the reference queue. Unlike, soft and weak reference, the garbage collector does not clear the phantom references as it places them in their reference queue. The program must clear the phantom references by calling its `clear()` method.

There are two ways to determine if a reference object has been placed in its reference queue. You can call the `poll()` or `remove()` method on a `ReferenceQueue` object, or you can call the `isEnqueued()` method on the soft, weak and phantom references. The `poll()` method removes a reference from the queue and returns it. If there is no reference available in the queue, it returns `null`. The `remove()` method works the same as the `poll()` method except that if there is no reference available in the queue, it blocks until it becomes available. The `isEnqueued()` method for soft, weak and phantom reference returns `true` if they are placed in queue. Otherwise, it returns `false`. Listing 15-8 demonstrates the use of the `ReferenceQueue` class.

Listing 15-8: Using the ReferenceQueue class

```
// ReferenceQueueDemo.java
package com.jdojo.chapter15;

import java.lang.ref.WeakReference;
import java.lang.ref.ReferenceQueue;

public class ReferenceQueueDemo {
    public static void main(String[] args) {
        // Create a reference queue
        ReferenceQueue q = new ReferenceQueue();

        // Wrap a BigObject inside a soft reference. Also
        // register the soft reference with the reference queue
        BigObject bigObj = new BigObject(131);
        WeakReference wr = new WeakReference(bigObj, q);

        // Clear the strong reference to the big object
        bigObj = null;

        // Check if weak reference has been queued
        System.out.println("Before calling gc():");
        printMessage(wr, q);

        // Invoke garbage collector. If it runs, it will
        // clear the weak reference
        System.out.println("Invoking garbage collector...");
        System.gc();
        System.out.println("Garbage collector finished...");
```

```
            // Check if weak reference has been queued
            System.out.println("After calling gc(): ");
            printMessage(wr, q);
        }

        public static void printMessage(WeakReference wr,
                                ReferenceQueue q) {

            System.out.println("wr.get()= " + wr.get());
            System.out.println("wr.isEnqueued()= " + wr.isEnqueued());
            WeakReference temp = (WeakReference)q.poll();
            if (temp == wr) {
                System.out.println("q.poll() returned wr");
            }
            else {
                System.out.println("q.poll()= " + temp);
            }
        }
    }
}
```

```
Output:

Before calling gc():
wr.get()= BigObject: id = 131
wr.isEnqueued()= false
q.poll()= null
Invoking garbage collector...
finalize() called. id:131
Garbage collector finished...
After calling gc():
wr.get()= null
wr.isEnqueued()= true
q.poll() returned wr
```

Using WeakReference Class

The only difference between a softly reachable and a weakly reachable object is that the garbage collector clears and reclaims weakly reachable objects whenever it runs, whereas it uses some algorithm to decide if it needs to clear and reclaim a softly reachable object or not. In other words, the garbage collector may or may not reclaim a softly reachable object, whereas it always reclaims a weakly reachable object.

You may not see any important use of a weak reference, because its referent is reclaimed when the garbage collector is run. Generally, weak references are not used to maintain caches. It is used to associate extra data with an object. Suppose you have a person's details and his address. If you lose his details, you will not be interested in his address. However, as long as a person's detail is accessible to you, you want to keep his address information. This kind of information can be stored using weak references and a Hashtable. Hashtable stores objects in key-value pairs. We will discuss Hashtable in detail in the chapter on *Collections*. While adding a key-value pair to a Hashtable, you need to wrap the key object in a WeakReference object. The key object and the value object are not garbage collected, when the key object is accessible or in use. When the key object is no longer in use, it will be garbage collected, because it was wrapped inside a WeakReference. At that point of time, you can remove that entry from the Hashtable, so that the value object will also be eligible for the garbage collection. A sample snippet of code using `Hashtable` and `WeakReference` object is shown below.

```
// Create a Hashtable object
Hashtable ht = new Hashtable();

// Create a reference queue, so that we can check
// when key was garbage collected
Referencequeue q = new ReferenceQueue();

// Create key and value objects
key = your key object creation logic goes here
value = your value object creation logic goes here

// Create a weak reference object using key object as referent
WeakReference wKey = new WeakReference(key, q);

// Place the key-value pair in the Hashtable. Note that we place key
// wrapped in weak reference. That is, we will use wKey as key
ht.put(wKey, value);

/* Use key and value objects in your program ...*/

// When done with key object, set key to null, so that it
// will not be strongly reachable
key = null;


// At this point if garbage collector is run, weak reference
// to key object will be cleared and the WeakReference, wr, will be
// placed in reference queue, q.


// Your logic to remove the entry for garbage collected key
// object will be as follows
if (wr.isEnqueued()) {
    // This will make value object eligible for reclamation
    ht.remove(wr);
}
```

Note that using a `WeakReference` object to associate extra information with an object using a `Hashtable` involves a little complex code and logic. The `java.util.WeakHashMap` class provides this functionality without requiring any complex logic on the part of programmers. You add the key-value object pairs to a `WeakHashMap` without wrapping the key object inside a `WeakReference`. The `WeakHashMap` class takes care of creating a reference queue and wrapping the key object inside a `WeakReference`. There is one important point to remember while using `WeakHashMap`. The key object is reclaimed when it is not strongly reachable. However, the value object is not reclaimed immediately. The value object is reclaimed after the entry is removed from the map. The `WeakHashMap` removes the entry after the weak reference to the key has been cleared and one of its method `put()`, `remove()` or `clear()` is called. Listing 15-9 demonstrates the use of `WeakHashMap`. The example uses objects of our `BigObject` class as keys as well as values. The messages in the output show when the key and value objects are reclaimed by the garbage collector.

Listing 15-9: Using a WeakHashMap

```java
// WeakHashMapdemo.java
package com.jdojo.chapter15;

import java.util.WeakHashMap;

public class WeakHashMapDemo {
    public static void main(String[] args) {
        // Create a WeakHashMap
        WeakHashMap wmap = new WeakHashMap();

        // Add two key-value pairs to WeakHashMap
        BigObject key1 = new BigObject(10);
        BigObject value1 = new BigObject(110);
        BigObject key2 = new BigObject(20);
        BigObject value2 = new BigObject(210);

        // Enter two key-value pairs in map
        wmap.put(key1, value1);
        wmap.put(key2, value2);

        // Print message
        printMessage ("After adding two entries:", wmap);

        // Invoke gc(). This gc() invocation will not reclaim
        // any of the key objects, because we are still having
        // their strong references
        System.out.println("Invoking gc() first time...");
        System.gc();

        // Print message
        printMessage ("After first gc() call:", wmap);

        // Now remove string references to keys and values
        key1 = null;
        key2 = null;
        value1 = null;
        value2 = null;

        /* Invoke gc(). This gc() invocation will reclaim
           two key objects with ids 10 and 20. However,
           the corresponding two value objects will still be strongly
           referenced by WeakHashMap internally and hence will not
           be reclaimed at this point
        */
        System.out.println("Invoking gc() second time...");
        System.gc();

        // Print message
        printMessage ( "After second gc() call:", wmap);

        /* Both keys have been reclaimed by now. Just to make value
           objects reclaimable, we will call clear() method on
           WeakHashMap. Usually, you will not call this method here
           in your program.
        */
```

```
            wmap.clear();

            // Invoke gc() so that value object will be reclaimed
            System.out.println("Invoking gc() third time...");
            System.gc();

            // Print message
            printMessage("After calling clear() method:", wmap);
        }

    public static void printMessage(String msgHeader,
                                    WeakHashMap wmap){
        System.out.println(msgHeader) ;

            // Print the size and content of map
            System.out.println("Size=" + wmap.size());
            System.out.println("Content=" + wmap);
            System.out.println();
        }
}
```

```
Output:

After adding two entries:
Size=2
Content={BigObject: id = 10=BigObject: id = 110, BigObject: id =
20=BigObject: id = 210}

Invoking gc() first time...
After first gc() call:
Size=2
Content={BigObject: id = 10=BigObject: id = 110, BigObject: id =
20=BigObject: id = 210}

Invoking gc() second time...
finalize() called. id:10
finalize() called. id:20
After second gc() call:
Size=0
Content={}

Invoking gc() third time...
finalize() called. id:110
finalize() called. id:210
After calling clear() method:
Size=0
Content={}
```

Using PhantomReference Class

Phantom references work a little different than soft and weak references. A `PhantomReference`
object must be created with a `ReferenceQueue` object. When the garbage collector determines
that there are only phantom references to an object, it finalizes the object and adds the phantom

references to their reference queues. Unlike soft and weak references, it does not clear the phantom references to the object automatically. Programs must clear the phantom reference to the object by calling the `clear()` method. A garbage collector will not reclaim the object until the program clears the phantom references to that object. Therefore, a phantom reference acts as a strong reference as long as reclaiming of objects is concerned. Why would you use a phantom reference instead of using a strong reference? A phantom reference is used to do post-finalization and pre-mortem processing. At the end of post-finalization processing, you must call the `clear()` method on the `PhantomReference` object, so that its referent will be reclaimed by the garbage collector. Unlike the `get()` method of the soft and weak references, the phantom reference's `get()` method always returns `null`. An object is phantom reachable when it has been finalized. If a phantom reference returns the referent's reference from its `get()` method, it would resurrect the referent. This is why phantom reference's `get()` method always returns `null`.

Listing 15-10 demonstrates the use of a phantom reference to do some post-finalization processing for an object. Note that the post-finalization processing cannot involve the object itself because you cannot get to the object using the `get()` method of the phantom reference.

Listing 15-10: Using PhantomReference objects

```
// PhantomRef.java
package com.jdojo.chapter15;

import java.lang.ref.ReferenceQueue;
import java.lang.ref.PhantomReference;

public class PhantomRef {
    public static void main(String[] args){
        ReferenceQueue q  = new ReferenceQueue();
        BigObject bigObject = new BigObject(1857);
        PhantomReference pr = new PhantomReference(bigObject, q);

        // You can use BigObject reference here

        // Set BigObject null, so that garbage collector will
        // find only the phantom reference to it and finalize it
        bigObject = null;

        // Invoke garbage collector
        printMessage(pr, "Invoking gc() first time:") ;
        System.gc();
        printMessage(pr, "After invoking gc() first time:");

        // Invoke garbage collector again
        printMessage(pr, "Invoking gc() second time:") ;
        System.gc();
        printMessage(pr, "After invoking gc() second time:");
    }

    public static void printMessage(PhantomReference pr, String msg){
        System.out.println(msg);
        System.out.println("pr.isEnqueued = " + pr.isEnqueued());
        System.out.println("pr.get() = " + pr.get());

        // we will check if pr is queued. If it has been
        // queued, we will clear its referent's reference
        if ( pr.isEnqueued() ) {
```

```
                    pr.clear();
                    System.out.println("Cleared the referent's reference");
                }
                System.out.println("----------------------");
            }
        }
```

```
Output:

Invoking gc() first time:
pr.isEnqueued = false
pr.get() = null
----------------------
finalize() called. id:1857
After invoking gc() first time:
pr.isEnqueued = false
pr.get() = null
----------------------
Invoking gc() second time:
pr.isEnqueued = false
pr.get() = null
----------------------
After invoking gc() second time:
pr.isEnqueued = true
pr.get() = null
Cleared the referent's reference
----------------------
```

You can also use phantom references to co-ordinate the post-finalization processing of more than one object. For example, suppose you have three objects obj1, obj2 and obj3. All of them share a network connection. When all three objects become unreachable, you would like to close the shared network connection. You can achieve this by wrapping the three objects in a phantom reference object and using the reference queue. Your program can wait on a separate thread for all three phantom reference objects to be queued. When the last phantom reference is queued, you can close the shared network connection. Post-finalization co-ordination using a phantom reference has been demonstrated in Listing 15-11. Note that the startThread() method of the PhantomRefDemo class uses a thread object and anonymous class. We have not covered these two topics yet. If you do not know about threads and anonymous classes in Java, you can refer to this example after you finish reading these two topics in this book. The remove() method blocks until there is a phantom reference in the queue.

Listing 15-11: Post-finalization co-ordination using phantom references

```java
// PhantomRefDemo.java
package com.jdojo.chapter15;

import java.lang.ref.Reference;
import java.lang.ref.PhantomReference;
import java.lang.ref.ReferenceQueue;

public class PhantomRefDemo {
    public static void main(String[] args) {
        final ReferenceQueue q = new ReferenceQueue();
        BigObject bigObject1 = new BigObject (101);
        BigObject bigObject2 = new BigObject (102);
```

```
        BigObject bigObject3 = new BigObject (103);
        PhantomReference pr1 = new PhantomReference(bigObject1, q);
        PhantomReference pr2 = new PhantomReference(bigObject2, q);
        PhantomReference pr3 = new PhantomReference(bigObject3, q);

        // This method will start a thread that will wait for the
        // arrival of new phantom references in reference queue q
        startThread(q);

        // You can use bigObject1, bigObject2 and bigObject3 here
        // Set the bigObject1, bigObject2 and bigObject3 to null
        // after using them,  so the objects they are referring to
        // may become phantom reachable
        bigObject1 = null;
        bigObject2 = null;
        bigObject3 = null;

        /* Let us invoke garbage collection in a loop. One garbage
        collection will just finalize the three big objects with ids
        101, 102 and 103. They may not be placed in a reference queue.
        In another garbage collection run, they will become phantom
        reachable and they will be placed in a queue and the waiting
        thread will remove them from the queue and will clear their
        referent's reference. Note that we exit the application when
        all three objects are cleared inside run() method of thread.
        Therefore, the following infinite loop is ok for demonstration
        purpose. If System.gc() does not invoke the garbage collector
        on your machine, you should replace the following loop with a
        loop which would create many big objects keeping their
        reference, so that the garbage collector would run.
        */
        while (true) {
            System.gc();
        }
    }

    public static void startThread(final ReferenceQueue q ) {
        // Create a thread and wait for the reference object's
        // arrival in the queue
        Thread t = new Thread(new Runnable() {
            public void run() {
                Reference r = null;
                try {
                    // Wait for first phantom reference to be
                    //queued
                    r =  q.remove();

                    // Clear the referent's reference
                    r.clear();

                    // Wait for second phantom reference to be
                    // queued
                    r = q.remove();

                    // Clear the referent's reference
                    r.clear();
```

```
                // Wait for third phantom reference to be
                // queued
                r = q.remove();

                // Clear the referent's reference
                r.clear();

                System.out.println("All three objects have" +
                                    " been queued and cleared");

                /* Typically, you will release the network
                   connection or any resources shared by three
                   objects   here…
                */

                // Exit the application
                System.exit(1);
            }
            catch (InterruptedException e) {
                System.out.println(e.getMessage());
            }
        }
    } );

    // Start the thread, which will wait for three phantom
    // references to be queued
    t.start();
    }
}
```

```
Output:

finalize() called. id:101
finalize() called. id:102
finalize() called. id:103
All three objects have been queued and cleared
```

Chapter 16. Inheritance

What is Inheritance?

Sometimes, you may need the same functionality at multiple places in your application. There are different ways to write code if the same functionality is needed at multiple places. One way is to copy the same code in all places where you need the same functionality. If you follow this logic, you need to make changes at all places when the functionality changes. Let us consider an example where we need the same functionality at three different places. Suppose we have an application that deals with three kinds of objects – planets, employees and managers. Further, suppose that all three kinds of objects have a name. We create three classes – `Planet`, `Employee` and `Manager` to represent the three kinds of objects. Each class has an instance variable - `name` and two methods, `getName()` and `setName()`. If you think about the code that is written in three classes to maintain the name of their objects, you would find that they are the same. You might have written code for one class and copied it to other two classes. You may realize the problem in maintaining this kind of code when the same code is copied multiple places. If you need to handle the name differently later, you will need to make changes at three places. Inheritance is the feature of object-oriented programming that helps in such circumstances to avoid copying the same code at multiple places thus facilitating code reuse. Inheritance also lets you customize the code without changing the existing code. Inheritance offers much more than just the code reuse and customization.

Inheritance is one of the cornerstones of object-oriented programming languages. It lets you create a new class by reusing code from an existing class. The new class is called *subclass* and the existing class is called *superclass*. A superclass contains the code that is reused and customized by the subclass. It is said that the subclass inherits the superclass. A superclass is also known as a *base* class or a *parent* class. A subclass is also known as a *derived* class or a *child* class. Technically, it may be possible to inherit a class from another existing class. However, practically it is not always a good idea to inherit a new class from any existing class. Inheritance in software development works much the same way as inheritance in normal human life. You inherit something from your parents; your parents inherit something from their parents and so on. If you look at inheritance in human lives, you would find that there exists a relationship between humans for inheritance to occur. Similarly, there exists a relationship between objects of the superclass and the subclass. The relationship that must exist between the superclass and the subclass in order for inheritance to be effective is called "*is-a*" relationship. You need to ask yourself a simple question before you should inherit a class Q from a class P - "Is an object of class P also an object of class Q?" If the answer is yes, class Q may inherit class P. Let us consider three classes – `Planet`, `Employee` and `Manager`. Let us ask the same question using these three classes one-by-one.

- Is a planet an employee? That is, does an "is-a" relationship exist between a planet and an employee. The answer is no. Is an employee a planet? The answer is no.
- Is a planet a manager? The answer is no. Is a manager a planet? The answer is no.
- Is an employee a manager? The answer is maybe. An employee may be a manager, a clerk, a programmer, or any other type of employee. However, an employee is not necessarily always a manager. Is a manager an employee? The answer is yes.

We asked six questions using the three classes. We got "yes" as the answer in only one case. This is the only case that is fit for using inheritance. The `Manager` class should inherit the `Employee` class. That is, the `Manager` class can be a subclass the of the `Employee` class. In other words, the `Employee` class can be the superclass of the `Manager` class.

How does a class inherit another class in Java? It is very simple to inherit a class from another class in Java. You need to use the `extends` keyword followed by the superclass name in the class declaration of your subclass. The general syntax is:

```
<<class modifiers>> class <<SubclassName>> extends <<SuperclassName>> {
    // Code for Subclass goes here
}
```

For example, the following code declares a class `Q`, which inherits from class `P`.

```
public class Q extends P {
    // Code for class Q goes here
}
```

You can use either the simple name or the fully qualified name of the superclass in a class declaration. If the subclass and the superclass do not reside in the same package, you may need to import the superclass name to use its simple name in the `extends` clause. Suppose the fully qualified names of class `P` and `Q` are `pkg1.P` and `pkg2.Q` respectively. The above declaration may be rewritten in one of the following two ways – one using simple name of the superclass and another using the fully qualified name of the superclass.

```
// #1 - Use the simple name of P in the extends clause
// and use an import statement
package pkg2;

import pkg1.P;

public class Q extends P {
    // Code for class Q goes here
}


// #2 - Use the fully qualified name of P.
// No need to use an import statement
package pkg2;

public class Q extends pkg1.P {
    // Code for class Q goes here
}
```

Let us look at the simplest example of inheritance in Java. Let us start with an `Employee` class as listed in Listing 16-1. It is a very simple class with one `private` instance variable, `name`, and two `public` methods, `setName()` and `getName()`. The instance variable is used to store the name for an employee and the two methods are used to read and write the `name` instance variable's value. Note that there is no special code in the `Employee` class. It is one of the simplest classes you can write in Java. It is easy to write and understand the following snippet of code that uses the `Employee` class.

```
Employee emp = new Employee();
emp.setName("John Jacobs");
String empName = emp.getName();
```

```
System.out.println("Employee Name: " + empName);
```

```
Output:

Employee Name: John Jacobs
```

Listing 16-1: An Employee class

```java
// Employee.java
package com.jdojo.chapter16;

public class Employee {
    private String name = "Unknown";

    public void setName(String name) {
        this.name = name;
    }

    public String getName() {
        return name;
    }
}
```

We want to create our Manager class by inheriting it from the Employee class. Listing 16-2 contains the code for the Manager class. Note the use of the keyword extends in Listing 16-2, which indicates that the Employee class is the superclass and the Manager class is the subclass. In other words, the Manager class inherits from the Employee class. We have not written any code for the Manager class, except its declaration. That is all we need in the Manager class for now.

Listing 16-2: A Manager class

```java
// Manager.java
package com.jdojo.chapter16;

public class Manager extends Employee {
    // No code is needed for now
}
```

Let us test our Manager class. Listing 16-3 contains the code. Even if we did not write any code for the Manager class, it works the same as the Employee class, because it inherits from the Employee class. We create a manager object by using the Manager class's constructor as:

```java
Manager mgr = new Manager();
```

After the manager object is created, the code looks similar to the one we used for dealing with an Employee object. We could use the setName() and getName() methods with the manager object, mgr, as:.

```java
mgr.setName("Leslie Zanders");
String mgrName = mgr.getName();
```

Note that the Manager class does not declare the setName() and getName() methods. Neither does it declare the name instance variable. However, it appears that all of them have been

---

declared inside the `Manager` class, because it uses the "extends Employee" clause in its declaration. When a class inherits from another class, it inherits its superclass members (instance variables, methods, etc.). There are many rules that govern inheritance. We will discuss the details of all inheritance rules one-by-one later in this chapter.

Listing 16-3: Testing the Manager class

```
// SimplestInheritanceTest.java
package com.jdojo.chapter16;

public class SimplestInheritanceTest {
    public static void main(String[] args) {
        // Create an object of Manager class
        Manager mgr = new Manager();

        // Set the name of the manager
        mgr.setName("Leslie Zanders");

        // Get the name of the manager
        String mgrName = mgr.getName();

        // Display the manager's name
        System.out.println("Manager Name: " + mgrName);
    }
}
```

```
Output:

Manager Name: Leslie Zanders
```

Object Class is the Default Superclass

If a class does not specify a superclass using the `extends` keyword in its class declaration, it inherits from the `java.lang.Object` class. For example, the following two class declarations for class `P` are the same.

```
//#1 – "extends Object" is implicitly added for class P
public class P {
    // Code for class P goes here
}

//#2 – "extends Object" is explicitly added for class P
public class P extends Object {
    // Code for class P goes here
}
```

If a class declaration does not include an `extends` clause, it inherits from the `Object` class by default. This is the reason why we have been using methods with objects of our classes, which we did not declare inside our classes. For example, the following is a valid snippet of code.

```
Employee emp = new Employee();
int hc = emp.hashCode();
String str = emp.toString();
```

Note that the `Employee` class does not specify its superclass using an `extends` clause. This means, it inherits from the `Object` class. The `Object` class declares the `hashCode()` and `toString()` methods. Since the `Employee` class inherits from the `Object` class, it can use these methods as if they have been included in its own declaration. We have been using inheritance from the very first Java program we wrote without knowing about it. This section has demonstrated the power of inheritance that comes as code reuse. We will see other benefits of inheritance later in this chapter.

Inheritance Establishes a Hierarchical Relationship

We touched upon this point in the previous section that inheritance should be used only if "is-a" relationship exists between the subclass and the superclass. A subclass can have its own subclasses, which in turn can have their own subclasses, and so on. All classes in an inheritance chain form a tree-like structure, which is known as an inheritance hierarchy or a class hierarchy. All classes above a class in the inheritance hierarchy are called ancestors for that class. All classes below a class in the inheritance hierarchy are called descendants of that class.

Java allows single inheritance for a class. That is, a class can have only one superclass (or parent). However, a class can be the superclass for multiple classes. All classes in Java have a superclass except the `Object` class. The `Object` class sits at the top of the inheritance hierarchies for all classes in Java. Figure 16-1 shows a sample inheritance hierarchy for the `Employee` class and its descendants using a UML (Unified Modeling Language) diagram. In a UML diagram, a superclass and a subclass are connected using an arrow pointing from the subclass to the superclass.

Figure 16-1: A sample inheritance class hierarchy

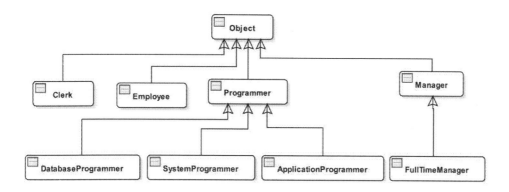

Sometimes, the term "immediate superclass" is used to mean the ancestor class, which is one level up in the inheritance hierarchy whereas the term "superclass" is used to mean an ancestor class at any level. This book uses the term "superclass" to mean ancestor of a class, which is one level up in the inheritance hierarchy. For example, `Programmer` is the superclass of `SystemProgrammer`, whereas `Programmer`, `Employee`, and `Object` are ancestors of `SystemProgrammer`. Sometimes, the term "immediate subclass" is used to mean a descendant class, which is one level down in the inheritance hierarchy, whereas the term "subclass" is used to mean a descendant class at any level. This book uses the term "subclass" to mean a descendant of a class, which is one level down in the inheritance hierarchy. For example, `Employee` is a subclass of `Object`, whereas `Clerk`, `Programmer` and `Manager` are subclasses of `Employee`. `Clerk`, `Programmer`,

`ApplicationProgrammer, SystemProgrammer, DatabaseProgrammer, Manager,`
`FullTimeManager` and `PartTimeManager` are all descendants of `Employee`. If a class is a descendant of another class, it is also a descendant of ancestor of that class. For example, all descendants of the `Employee` class are also descendants of the `Object` class. All descendants of the `Manager` class are also descendants of the `Employee` class and the `Object` class.

What is Inherited by a Subclass?

A subclass does not inherit everything from its superclass. However, a subclass can use, directly or indirectly, everything from its superclass. Let us discuss the distinction between "a subclass *inheriting* something from its superclass" and "a subclass *using* something from its superclass".

Let us take a real world example. Suppose your parent (a superclass) has money in a bank account. The money belongs to your parent. You (a subclass) need some money. If you *inherit* the money, you would just use the money at your will as if the money is yours. If you can just *use* the money, you cannot get to the parent's money directly. Rather, you need to ask your parents for money and they will give it to you. In both cases, you used your parent's money. In the case of inheritance, the money appears to be owned by you. That is, you have direct access to it. In the second case, your parent's money was available to you for use without you having direct access to it. You always had to go through your parent to use their money.

A subclass inherits non-private members of its superclass. We will discuss this rule in detail shortly. Note that constructors and initializers (static and instance) are not members of a class and therefore, they are not inherited. Members of a class are all members that are declared inside the body of the class and members that are inherited from the superclass. This definition of members of a class has trickle-down effect. Suppose there are three classes - A, B and C. The class A inherits from the `Object` class. The class B inherits from the class A, and the class C inherits from the class B. Suppose class A declares a private member `m1` and a non-private member `m2`. The members of class A are `m1`, `m2` and all inherited members of the `Object` class. Note that `m1` and `m2` members of class A are declared members, whereas others are inherited members. Members of class B will be any members that are declared in class B and all non-private members of class A. Since the member, `m1`, is declared `private` in the class A, it is not inherited by the class B. The same logic applies to the members of the class C. Note that the members of the `Object` class are inherited by class A. Members of the class A, which include its own declared members and members of the `Object` class, are inherited by the class B. Members of the class B, which include its own declared members and the members of the class A, are inherited by the class C. Note that non-private members of the `Object` class trickle down to class A, B, and C through the inheritance hierarchy. The non-private members of the class A trickle down to the class B, which in turn trickle down to the class C, through the inheritance hierarchy.

There are four access modifiers: `private`, `public`, `protected` and package-level. The absence of the `private`, `public` and `protected` access modifier is considered as the package-level access. The access level modifier of a class member determines two things.

- Who can access (or use) that class member directly
- Whether a subclass inherits that class member or not

Access modifiers are also used with non-members (e.g. constructors) of a class. In such cases, an access modifier role is only one – "who can access that non-member."

If a class member is declared `private`, it is accessible only inside the class that declares it. A `private` class member is not inherited by a subclass of that class.

A `public` class member is accessible from everywhere in an application. A subclass inherits all `public` members of its superclass.

If a class member is declared `protected`, it is accessible in the package in which it is declared. A `protected` class member is always accessible inside the body of a subclass whether the subclass is in the same package as the class or in a different package. A `protected` class member is inherited by a subclass. The `protected` access modifier is used with a class member when you want subclasses to access and inherit the class member. Note that a `protected` class member can be accessed through the package in which it is declared and inside subclasses. If you want to provide access to a class member only from inside its package, you should use package-level access modifier and not `protected` access modifier.

If a class member is declared package-level, it is accessible only inside the package in which the class is declared. A package-level class member is inherited only if the superclass and subclass are in the same package. If the superclass and the subclass are in different packages, the subclass does not inherit package-level members from its superclass.

Let us look at our example of inheritance in Listing 16-1 and Listing 16-2. The `Employee` class has three members – a `name` field, a `getName()` method, and a `setName()` method. The `name` field has been declared `private` and hence it is not accessible inside the `Manager` class, because it is not inherited. The `getName()` and `setName()` methods have been declared `public`. They are accessible from anywhere including the `Manager` class. They are inherited.

Upcasting and Downcasting

An "is-a" relationship in the real world translates into inheritance class hierarchy in software. A class is a type in Java. When we express the "is-a" relationship using inheritance, we create a subclass, which is a more specific type of the superclass. For example, a `Manager` is a specific type of `Employee`. An `Employee` is a specific type of `Object`. As we move up in the inheritance hierarchy, we move from a specific type to a more general type. How does inheritance affect the client code? In this context, the client code is any code that uses the classes in a class hierarchy. Inheritance guarantees that whatever behavior is present in a class will also be present in its subclass. A method in a class represents a behavior of the objects of that class. This means, whatever behavior a client code expects to be present in a class will also be present in the class's subclass. This leads to the conclusion that if a client code works with a class, it will also work with the class's subclass, because a subclass guarantees at least the same behaviors as its superclass. For example, the `Manager` class provides at least the same behaviors as provided by its superclass `Employee`.

Consider the following snippet of code used by a client.

```
Employee emp;
emp = new Employee();
emp.setName("Richard Castillo");
String name = emp.getName();
```

The compiler will compile the above snippet of code without any error. When the compiler comes across `emp.setName("Richard Castillo")` and `emp.getName()` calls, it checks the declared type of the `emp` variable. It finds that the declared type of `emp` variable is `Employee`. It makes sure that the `Employee` class has `setName()` and `getName()` methods that conform to the call being made. It finds that the `Employee` class does have a `setName()` method that accepts a `String` object as its parameter. It finds that the `Employee` class does have a `getName()` method that accepts no parameters and returns a `String` object. After verifying these two facts, the compiler passes the `emp.setName()` and `emp.getName()` method calls in the source code.

With the point in mind that a subclass guarantees at least the same behavior (methods) as its superclass, let us consider the following snippet of code.

```
Employee emp;
emp = new Manager();  // Manager object assigned to Employee variable
emp.setName("Richard Castillo");
String name = emp.getName();
```

The compiler will pass the above snippet of code too, even though we have changed the code this time to assign `emp` variable an object of the `Manager` class. It will pass the `setName()` and `getName()` method calls on the same basis as described in the previous case. It also passes the assignment statement:

```
emp = new Manager();
```

The compile-time type of "`new Manager()`" expression is the `Manager` type. The compile-time type (or declared type) of `emp` variable is `Employee` type. Since the `Manager` class inherits from the `Employee` class, an object of the `Manager` class "is-a" object of the `Employee` class. Simply, we say that a manager is always an employee. Such an assignment (from subclass to superclass) is called *upcasting* and it is always allowed in Java. It is also called a *widening conversion*, because an object of the `Manager` class (more specific type) is assigned to a reference variable of the `Employee` type (a more generic type). All of the following assignments are allowed and they are all examples of upcasting.

```
Object obj;
Employee emp;
Manager mgr;
PartTimeManager ptm;

// An employee is always an object
obj = emp;

// A manager is always an employee
emp = mgr;

// A part-time manager is always a manager
mgr = ptm;

// A part-time manager is always an employee
emp = ptm;

// A part-time manager is always an object
obj = ptm;
```

Use a simple rule to check if an assignment is a case of upcasting. Look at the compile-time type (declared type) of the expression on the right side of the assignment operator (e.g. `b` in `a = b`). If the compile-time type of the right hand operand is a subclass of the compile-time type of the left-hand operand, it is a case of upcasting and the assignment is safe and allowed. Upcasting is a direct technical translation of the fact that an object of a subclass "is-a" object of the superclass too.

Upcasting is a very powerful feature of inheritance. It lets you write extensible code that works with classes that exists and classes that will be added in future. It lets you code your application logic in terms of a superclass that will always work with all subclasses (existing subclasses or subclasses to be added). It lets you write generic code without worrying about a specific type (class) with which the code will be used at runtime. Listing 16-4 is a simple utility class to test our upcasting rule. It has a `printName()` static method that accepts an argument of `Employee` type. The `printName()` method uses the `getName()` method of the `Employee` class to get the name of the employee object and prints the name on the standard output.

Listing 16-4: A utility class that uses Employee type parameter in its printName() method

```java
// EmpUtil.java
package com.jdojo.chapter16;

public class EmpUtil {
    public static void printName(Employee emp) {
        // Get the name of employee
        String name = emp.getName();

        // Print employee name
        System.out.println(name);
    }
}
```

Listing 16-5 contains code to test the upcasting rule using the `EmpUtil` class. It creates two objects (`emp` and `mgr`) - one of `Employee` type and one of `Manager` class. It sets names for both objects. Finally, it calls the `printName()` method of the `EmpUtil` class to print the names of both objects. The first call to `EmpUtil.printName(emp)` is fine, because the `printName()` method accepts an `Employee` object and we have passed an `Employee` object (`emp`). The second call `EmpUtil.printName(mgr)` is fine because of the upcasting rule. The `printName(Employee emp)` accepts an `Employee` object and we were able to pass a `Manager` object (`mgr`) instead, because a manager is always an employee and upcasting rules allows the assignment of a subclass object to a variable of superclass type.

TIP

One of the main benefits of inheritance is code reuse. For example, the `Manager` class uses methods that are defined in its superclass, `Employee`, because of inheritance. Another great benefit of inheritance is that it allows you to write generic code in terms of a superclass. The `printName()` method of the `EmpUtil` class falls into the latter category. Writing code in terms of superclass has two benefits – it lets you reuse the code. The same code works (and will keep working) without any modifications with all subclasses in the class hierarchy. For example, if you create a new class `PartTimeManager` as a subclass of `Manager` class, you can still use the `printName()` method of `EmpUtil` class to print the names of part-time managers.

Listing 16-5: A test class to test the upcasting rule

```java
// UpcastTest.java
package com.jdojo.chapter16;
```

```
public class UpcastTest {
    public static void main(String[] args)  {
        Employee emp = new Employee();
        emp.setName("Ken Wood");

        Manager mgr = new Manager();
        mgr.setName("Ken Furr"); //Inheritance of setName() at work

        // Print names
        EmpUtil.printName(emp);
        EmpUtil.printName(mgr); // Upcasting at work
    }
}
```

```
Output:

Ken Furr
Ken Wood
```

Assigning a superclass reference to a subclass variable is called *downcasting* (or narrowing conversion). Downcasting is the opposite of upcasting. In upcasting, the assignment moves up the class hierarchy whereas in downcasting the assignment moves down the class hierarchy. The Java compiler cannot make sure at compiler time that downcasting is legal or not. Let us consider the following snippet of code.

```
Employee emp;
Manager mgr = new Manager();
emp = mgr;      // Ok. Upcasting
mgr = emp;      // Compiler error. Downcasting
```

The assignment, "emp = mgr", is allowed because it is a case of upcasting. However, the assignment, "mgr = emp", is not allowed because it is a case of downcasting where a variable of superclass (Employee) is being assigned to a variable of subclass (Manager). The compiler is right in assuming that every manager is an employee (upcasting). However, not every employee is a manager (downcasting). In the above snippet of code, we would like the downcasting to work, because we know for sure that emp variable holds a reference to an object of the Manager class. Java imposes an additional rule in order for your downcast to succeed at compile-time. You need to give additional assurance to the compiler that you have considered the assignment of a superclass reference to a subclass reference variable and you would like the compiler to pass it. You give this assurance to the compiler by adding a typecast to the assignment as:

```
mgr = (Manager)emp;  // OK. Downcast at work
```

The above downcasting with a typecast succeeds at compile-time. However, the Java runtime will perform an additional verification. The job of the compiler is just to make sure that the declared type of mgr variable, which is Manager, is assignment compatible with the typecast being used, which is Manager. The compiler cannot check what type of object emp variable will actually refer to at runtime. Runtime verifies the correctness of the typecast (Manager)emp in the above statement. The type of the object to which the emp variable refers at runtime is also called its runtime type. The runtime compares the runtime type of the emp variable and the Manager type (Manager type is used in the typecast). If the runtime type of emp variable is assignment compatible with the type used in typecast, the typecast succeeds at runtime. Otherwise, runtime throws the java.lang.ClassCastException.

Let us consider the following snippet of code assuming that we have a subclass of the `Manager` class, which is called `PartTimeManager`. The last assignment, which uses downcasting, succeeds at compile-time because the declared type of ptm variable and the typecast type are the same. The runtime type of `emp` is `Manager`, because the "`emp = mgr`" statement assigns a `Manager` object's reference to it. When the runtime attempts to execute the "`(PartTimeManager)emp`" part of the downcasting, it finds that the runtime type of `emp`, which is `Manager`, is not assignment compatible with the typecast type, which is `PartTimeManager`. This is the reason why the runtime will throw a `ClassCastException`.

```
Employee emp;
Manager mgr = new Manager();
PartTimeManager ptm = new PartTimeManager();
emp = mgr;  // Upcasting. OK
ptm = (PartTimeManager)emp; // Downcasting. OK at compile-time
                            // Error at runtime
```

You can think of a statement that involves a downcasting as having two parts for the verification purpose. Suppose the statement is "`a2 = (K)b2`". The compiler's job is to verify the declared type of `a2` is assignment compatible with type `K`. The runtime's job is to verify that the runtime type of `b2` is assignment compatible with type `K`. If any of the two checks fails, you get error at compile-time or runtime depending of which check fails. Figure 16-2 depicts this scenario.

Figure 16-2: Run-time and Compile-time checks made for downcasting

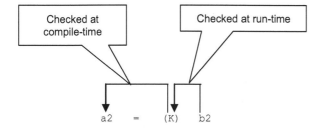

TIP
The `Object` class is at the top of every class hierarchy in Java. This allows you to assign a reference of any class type to a variable of the `Object` type. The following type of assignment is always allowed.

```
Object obj = new AnyJavaClass(); // Upcasting
```

Whether downcasting from an `Object` type to a Java class type will succeed or not depends on the downcasting rule discussed above.

The instanceof Operator

How can you be sure that a downcasting will always succeed at runtime? Java has an `instanceof` operator, which helps you in determining at runtime if a reference variable has a reference to an object of a class or its subclass. It takes two operands and it evaluates to a `boolean` value - `true` or `false`. Its syntax is:

```
<<Class Reference Variable>> instanceof <<Class Name>>
```

If <<Class Reference Variable>> refers to an object of class <<Class Name>> or any of its descendants, instanceof returns true. Otherwise, it returns false. Note that if <<Class Reference Variable>> is null, instanceof always returns false.

You should use instanceof operator before downcasting to check if the reference variable you are trying to downcast is actually of the type you expected it to be. For example, if you want to check if a variable of Employee type refers to a Manager object at runtime, you would write code as:

```
Manager mgr = new Manager();
Employee emp = mgr;

if (emp instanceof Manager) {
    // Following downcast will always succeed
    mgr = (Manager)emp;
}
else {
    // emp is not a Manager type
}
```

The instanceof operator goes through two types of checks – compile-time check and runtime check. The compiler checks if it is ever possible for the left-hand operand to refer to an object of the right-hand operand. This check may not be obvious to you at this point. The purpose of using instanceof operator is to compare the runtime type of a reference variable to another type. In short, instanceof operator compares two types. Does it ever make sense to you to compare a mango with an employee? You would say no. The compiler adds checks for this kind of illogical comparison using instanceof operator. The compiler makes sure that it is possible for the left-hand operand of the instanceof operator to hold a reference of an object of the right-hand operand type. If it is not possible, the compiler generates an error. It is easy to find out if the compiler will generate an error for using the instanceof operator or not. Consider the following snippet of code.

```
Manager mgr = null;
if (mgr instanceof Clerk) { // Compile-time error
}
```

The variable, mgr, can hold a reference of Manager type or any of its descendant type. However, it can never hold a reference of Clerk type. The Clerk type is not in the same inheritance-chain as the Manager class, although it is in the same inheritance tree. For the same reason, the following use of the instanceof operator will generate a compiler error, because the String class is not in the inheritance-chain of the Employee class.

```
String str = "test";
if (str instanceof Employee) { // Compile-time error
}
```

TIP
An object is considered an instance of a class if that object is of that class type, or its direct or indirect descendant type. You can use the instanceof operator to check if an object is an instance of a class or not.

Sometimes, you may end up writing code that uses the `instanceof` operator to test for multiple conditions at one place as shown below.

```
Employee emp;

// Some logic goes here...

if (emp instanceof Employee) {
    // Code to deal with a employee
}
else if (emp instanceof Manager) {
    // Code to deal with a manager
}
else if (emp instanceof Clerk) {
    // Code to deal with a clerk
}
```

You should avoid writing this kind of code. If you add a new subclass of Employee, you will need to add the logic for the new subclass to the above code. Usually, this kind of code indicates a design flaw. Always ask yourself the question, "Will this code keep working when I add a new class to the existing class hierarchy?" If the answer is yes, you are fine. Otherwise, reconsider your design.

The `equals()` method is the one place in which you will often end up using the `instanceof` operator. The `equals()` method is defined in the `Object` class and it is inherited by all classes in Java. It accepts an argument of `Object` type. It returns `true` if the object passed to this method and the object on which this method is called are considered equal. Otherwise, it returns `false`. Objects of each class may be compared for equality differently. For example, two employees may be considered equal if they work for the same company and in the same department and have same employee id. What happens if a `Manager` object is passed to the `equals()` method of the `Employee` class? Since a manager is also an employee, it should compare the two for equality. The following code snippet shows you a possible implementation of the `equals()` method for the `Employee` class.

```
// Employee.java
package com.jdojo.chapter16;

public class Employee {
    private String name = "Unknown";

    public void setName(String name) {
        this.name = name;
    }

    public String getName() {
        return name;
    }

    public boolean equals(Object obj) {
        boolean isEqual = false;
        // We compare objects of Employee class with
        // objects of Employee class or its descendants
        if (obj instanceof Employee) {
            // If two have same name, consider them equals
            Employee e = (Employee)obj;
```

```
            String n = e.getName();
            isEqual = n.equals(this.name);
        }

        return isEqual;
    }
}
```

After you have added the `equals()` method to the `Employee` class, you can write code like the one shown below, which compares two objects of the `Employee` type for equality based on their names. In the third comparison, we compare an `Employee` object with a `String` object, which returns `false`. Comparing an `Employee` and a `Manager` object returns `true`, because they have the same names.

```
Employee emp = new Employee();
emp.setName("John Jacobs");

Manager mgr = new Manager();
mgr.setName("John Jacobs");

System.out.println(mgr.equals(emp));              // prints - true
System.out.println(emp.equals(mgr));              // prints - true
System.out.println(emp.equals("John Jacobs"));    // prints - false
```

Binding

Classes have methods and fields; we write code to access them as follows. Assume that `myMethod()` and `xyz` are members of the `MyClass` class, which is the declared type of `myObject` reference variable.

```
MyClass myobject = get an object reference;
myObject.myMethod();   // Which myMethod() to call?
int a = myObject.xyz;  // Which xyz to access?
```

Binding is the process of identifying the accessed method's code (`myMethod()` in this case) or the field (`xyz` in this case), which will be used when the code executes. In other words, binding is a process of making a decision, which method's code or field will be accessed, when the code executes. There are two stages where the binding can happen – compile-time or runtime. When the binding occurs at compile-time, it is known as *early binding*. Early binding is also known as *static binding* or *compile-time binding*. When the binding occurs at runtime, it is known as *late binding*. Late binding is also known as *dynamic binding* or *runtime binding*.

Early Binding

Early binding is simple to understand compared to late binding. In early binding, the decision about which method code and field will be accessed is made by the compiler at compile-time. For a method call, the compiler decides which method from which class will be executed when the code having the method call is executed. For a field access, the compiler decides which field from which class will be accessed when the code having the field access is executed. Early binding is used for the following types of methods and fields of a class in Java.

- All types of fields – static and non-static.
- Static methods
- Non-static and final methods

In early binding, a method or a field is accessed based on the declared type (or compile-time type) of the variable (or expression) accessing the method or the field. For example, if early binding is used for `a2.m1()` method call, if `a2` has been declared of type `A`, `m1()` method in class `A` will be called when `a2.m1()` is executed.

Let us look at a detailed example that demonstrates the early binding rules. Let us consider two classes listed in Listing 16-6 and Listing 16-7.

Listing 16-6: An EarlyBindingSuper class that has a static field, an instance field, and a static method

```java
// EarlyBindingSuper.java
package com.jdojo.chapter16;

public class EarlyBindingSuper {
    // Instance variable
    public String str = "EarlyBindingSuper";

    // Static variable
    public static int count = 100;

    public static void print() {
        System.out.println("Inside EarlyBindingSuper.print()");
    }
}
```

Listing 16-7: An EarlyBindingSub class, which inherits from EarlyBindingSuper class and has a static field, an instance field, and a static method, which are of the same type as in its superclass

```java
// EarlyBindingSub.java
package com.jdojo.chapter16;

public class EarlyBindingSub extends EarlyBindingSuper{
    // Instance variable
    public String str = "EarlyBindingSub";

    // Static variable
    public static int count = 200;

    public static void print() {
        System.out.println("Inside EarlyBindingSub.print()");
    }
}
```

The `EarlyBindingSuper` class declares two fields – `str` and `count`. The `str` field is declared non-static (or instance) field and `count` is declared a `static` field. The `print()` method is declared `static`. The `EarlyBindingSub` class inherits from the `EarlyBindingSuper` class and it declares exactly the same types of fields and methods, which have the same names. Fields are set to different values and the method prints different message in the `EarlyBindingSub` class, so we can know which one is accessed when we execute our code. The `EarlyBindingTest` class in Listing 16-8 demonstrates the result of the early binding. It creates two objects – one of `EarlyBindingSuper` type and one of `EarlyBindingSub` type.

```
EarlyBindingSuper ebSuper = new EarlyBindingSuper();
EarlyBindingSub ebSub = new EarlyBindingSub();
```

According to early binding rules, the statements, `ebSuper.str`, `ebSuper.count`, and `ebSuper.print()`, will always access the `str` and `count` fields, and the `print()` method of the `EarlyBindingSuper` class, because we have declared `ebSuper` of type `EarlyBindingSuper`. This decision is made by the compiler, because `str` and `count` are fields and for fields, Java always uses early binding. The `print()` method is a `static` method and Java always uses early binding for `static` methods. The same rule applies when you access these members using `ebSub` variable.

The output of the following statements may not be obvious.

```
// Will access EarlyBindingSuper.str
System.out.println(((EarlyBindingSuper)ebSub).str);

// Will access EarlyBindingSuper.count
System.out.println(((EarlyBindingSuper)ebSub).count);

// Will access EarlyBindingSuper.print()
((EarlyBindingSuper)ebSub).print();
```

All of the three statements use an expression to access fields and methods. When you write `ebSub.str`, you access `str` field using `ebSub` variable directly. It is clear that `ebSub` variable is of type `EarlyBindingSub` and therefore, `ebSub.str` will access `str` field of the `EarlyBindingSub` class. When you use typecast, the compile-time type of the expression that results changes. For example, the compile-time type of `ebSub` is `EarlyBindingSub`. However, the compile-time type of the expression, `(EarlyBindingSuper)ebSub`, is `EarlyBindingSuper`. This is the reason all of the above three statements will access fields and methods from the `EarlyBindingSuper` class and not from the `EarlyBindingSub` class even though they all use the `ebSub` variable, which is of the `EarlyBindingSub` type . The output of Listing 16-8 validates our discussion about the early binding rules.

TIP

You can also access `static` fields and `static` methods of a class using the name of the class, for example, `EarlyBindingSub.str`. The early binding rules still applies and the compiler will bind the access to `static` fields and methods to the class whose name is used. Note that a class does not have to declare a field or a method to access them using the class name. A field or a method may be accessible using a class name because the class inherits it from its superclass.

Listing 16-8: A test class to demonstrate early binding for fields and methods

```
// EarlyBindingTest.java
package com.jdojo.chapter16;

public class EarlyBindingTest {
    public static void main(String[] args) {
        EarlyBindingSuper ebSuper = new EarlyBindingSuper();
        EarlyBindingSub ebSub = new EarlyBindingSub();

        // Will access EarlyBindingSuper.str
        System.out.println(ebSuper.str);
```

```java
            // Will access EarlyBindingSuper.count
            System.out.println(ebSuper.count);

            // Will access EarlyBindingSuper.print()
            ebSuper.print();

            System.out.println("----------------------------");

            // Will access EarlyBindingSub.str
            System.out.println(ebSub.str);

            // Will access EarlyBindingSub.count
            System.out.println(ebSub.count);

            // Will access EarlyBindingSub.print()
            ebSub.print();

            System.out.println("----------------------------");

            // Will access EarlyBindingSuper.str
            System.out.println(((EarlyBindingSuper)ebSub).str);

            // Will access EarlyBindingSuper.count
            System.out.println(((EarlyBindingSuper)ebSub).count);

            // Will access EarlyBindingSuper.print()
            ((EarlyBindingSuper)ebSub).print();

            System.out.println("----------------------------");

            // Assign the ebSub to ebSuper
            ebSuper = ebSub; // Upcasting

            // Now access methods and fields using ebSuper
            // variable, which is referring to a EarlyBindingSub object

            // Will access EarlyBindingSuper.str
            System.out.println(ebSuper.str);

            // Will access EarlyBindingSuper.count
            System.out.println(ebSuper.count);

            // Will access EarlyBindingSuper.print()
            ebSuper.print();
            System.out.println("----------------------------");
    }
}
```

```
Output:

EarlyBindingSuper
100
Inside EarlyBindingSuper.print()
----------------------------
EarlyBindingSub
```

```
200
Inside EarlyBindingSub.print()
-----------------------------
EarlyBindingSuper
100
Inside EarlyBindingSuper.print()
-----------------------------
EarlyBindingSuper
100
Inside EarlyBindingSuper.print()
-----------------------------
```

Late Binding

Binding for all non-static and non-final methods follows the rules of late binding. That is, if your code accesses a non-static method, which is not declared as `final`, the decision, as to which version of the method is called, is made at runtime. The version of the method that will be called depends on the runtime type of the object on which the method call is made and not on its compile-time type. Let us consider the following snippet of code, which creates an object of the `Manager` class and assigns the reference to a variable (`emp`) of the `Employee` class. The `emp` variable accesses the `setName()` method.

```
Employee emp = new Manager();
emp.setName("John Jacobs");
```

The compiler performs only one check for the `emp.setName()` method call in the above code. It makes sure that the declared type of `emp` variable, which is the `Employee` class, has a method `setName(String s)`. The compiler detects that the `setName(String s)` method in the `Employee` class is an instance method, which is not `final`. For an instance method call, the compiler does not perform binding. It will leave this work for runtime. The method call, `emp.setName("John Jacobs")`, is the case of late binding. At runtime, the JVM decides which `setName(String s)` method should be called. The JVM gets the runtime type of `emp` variable. The runtime type of the `emp` variable will be the `Manager` class, when `emp.setName("John Jacobs")` statement is looked at. The JVM traverses up the class hierarchy starting from the runtime type (that is, `Manager`) of `emp` variable looking for `setName(String s)` method definition. First, it looks at the `Manager` class and it finds that the `Manager` class does not declare a `setName(String s)` method. Now, the JVM moves one level up the class hierarchy, which is the `Employee` class. It finds that `Employee` class declares a `setName(String s)` method. Once the JVM finds a matching method definition in a class, it binds the call to that method and stops the search for the method definition. Recall that the `Object` class is always at the top of all class hierarchies in Java. The JVM continues its search for a method definition up to the `Object` class. If it does not find a matching method in the `Object` class, it throws a runtime exception.

Let us look at an example that will demonstrate the late binding process. Listing 16-9 and Listing 16-10 have code for `LateBindingSuper` and `LateBindingSub` classes respectively. The `LateBindingSub` class inherits from the `LateBindingSuper` class. It defines the same instance method `print()` as defined in the `LateBindingSuper` class. The `print()` method in both classes prints different messages so that we can see which method is being called.

Listing 16-9: A LateBindingSuper class, which has an instance method named print()

```
// LateBindingSuper.java
```

```
package com.jdojo.chapter16;

public class LateBindingSuper {
    public void print() {
        System.out.println("Inside LateBindingSuper.print()");
    }
}
```

Listing 16-10: A LateBindingSub class, which has an instance method named print()

```
// LateBindingSub.java
package com.jdojo.chapter16;

public class LateBindingSub extends LateBindingSuper{
    public void print() {
        System.out.println("Inside LateBindingSub.print()");
    }
}
```

Listing 16-11 demonstrates the result of late binding. It creates two objects – one of the LateBindingSuper class and another of the LateBindingSub class. The calls to the print() method have been labeled #1, #2, #3 and #4 so that we may refer to them in our discussion.

```
LateBindingSuper lbSuper = new LateBindingSuper();
LateBindingSub lbSub = new LateBindingSub();
```

Both variables, lbSuper and lbSub, are used to access the print() instance method. The runtime decides which version of the print() method is called. When we use lbSuper.print(), which print() method is called depends on the object to which lbSuper variable is referring to at that point in time. Recall that a reference variable of a class type may also refer to an object of any of its descendant. The lbSuper variable may refer to an object of the LateBindingSuper class or an object of the LateBindingSub class.

When the statement #1, lbSuper.print(), is ready to execute, the runtime will need to find the code for the print() method. The runtime looks for the runtime type of lbSuper variable and it finds that lbSuper variable is referring to an object of LateBindingSuper type. It looks for a print() method in the LateBindingSuper class and finds it. Therefore, the runtime binds the print() method call in the statement labeled #1 to the print() method of the LateBindingSuper class. This is confirmed by the first line in the output.

The logic for binding the print() method in the statement #2 is the same as for the statement labeled #1.

The statement #3 is tricky. When you use a typecast such as (LateBindingSuper)lbSub, the object to which lbSub refers to at runtime does not change. Using a typecast, all you say is that you want to use the object to which lbSub variable refers as an object of LateBindingSuper type. However, the object itself never changes. You can verify this by using the following code, which gets the class name of an object.

```
// Both s1 and s2 have "com.jdojo.chapter16.LateBindingSub" class name
LateBindingSub lbSub = new LateBindingSub();
String s1 = lbSub.getClass().getName();
String s2 = ((LateBindingSuper)lbSub).getClass().getName();
```

When statement #3 is ready to execute, at that time the expression with the typecast still refers to an object of LateBindingSub type, and therefore, the print() method of the LateBindingSub class will be called. This is confirmed by the third line in the output.

Let us consider two statements to discuss statement #4.

```
lbSuper = lbSub; // Upcasting
lbSuper.print(); // #4
```

The first statement assigns lbSub to lbSuper. The effect of this statement is that lbSuper variable starts referring to an object of LateBindingSub object. When the statement #4 is ready to execute, the runtime needs to find the code for the print() method. The runtime finds that the runtime type of the lbSuper variable is the LateBindingSub class. It looks for the print() method in the LateBindingSub class and finds it right there. Therefore, the statement #4 executes the print() method in the LateBindingSub class. This is confirmed by the fourth line in the output.

Listing 16-11: A test class to demonstrate early binding for fields and methods

```
// LateBindingTest.java
package com.jdojo.chapter16;

public class LateBindingTest {
    public static void main(String[] args) {
        LateBindingSuper lbSuper = new LateBindingSuper();
        LateBindingSub lbSub = new LateBindingSub();

        // Will access EarlyBindingSuper.print()
        lbSuper.print(); // #1

        // Will access EarlyBindingSub.print()
        lbSub.print();   // #2

        // Will access EarlyBindingSub.print()
        ((LateBindingSuper)lbSub).print(); // #3

        // Assign the lbSub to lbSuper
        lbSuper = lbSub; // Upcasting

        // Will access EarlyBindingSub.print() because
        // lbSuper is referring to a LateBindingSub object
        lbSuper.print(); // #4
    }
}
```

```
Output:

Inside LateBindingSuper.print()
Inside LateBindingSub.print()
Inside LateBindingSub.print()
Inside LateBindingSub.print()
```

Late binding incurs little additional performance overhead than does early binding, because the method calls are resolved at runtime. However, many techniques (e.g. virtual method table) can be used to implement late binding, so that the performance hit is minimal or negligible. However, the benefit of late binding overshadows the little performance loss. It lets you implement runtime polymorphism. Polymorphism means "many forms/meanings". When you write code like `a2.print()`, `a2` variable exhibits polymorphic behavior with respect to the `print()` method.. The same code, `a2.print()`, may call the `print()` method of the class of the `a2` variable or any of its descendant classes depending on what type of object `a2` is referring to at runtime. Inheritance and late binding lets you write polymorphic code, which is written in terms of superclass type instead of using a specific class type.

Method Overriding

Redefining an instance method in a class, which is inherited from the superclass, is called method overriding. Let us consider the following declarations of class A and class B.

```
public class A {
    public void print() {
        System.out.println("A");
    }
}

public class B extends A {
    public void print() {
        System.out.println("B");
    }
}
```

Class B is a subclass of class A. It inherits the `print()` method from its superclass. However, it redefines the same `print()` method that is already defined in class A. It is said that the `print()` method in class B overrides the `print()` method of class A. It is like class B telling class A – "Thanks for being my superclass and letting me inherit your `print()` method. However, I need to work differently. Therefore, I am going to redefine it my way, without affecting your `print()` method in any way. You can keep using your `print()` method." If a class overrides a method, it affects the overriding class and its subclasses. Consider the following declaration of class C.

```
public class C extends B {
    // Inherits B.print()
}
```

Class C does not declare any methods. What method does class C inherit: `A.print()` or `B.print()`, or both? It inherits the `print()` method from class B. A class always inherits what is available from its immediate superclass (declared in superclass or inherited by its super superclass). If a class D inherits from class C, it will inherit `print()` method of class B through class C.

```
public class D extends C {
    // Inherits B.print() through C
}
```

Let us consider two more classes E and F, which inherit from D and E respectively. Class E overrides the `print()` method of class B, which it inherited from class D.

```
public class E extends D {
    public void print() {
        System.out.println("E");
    }
}

public class F extends E {
    // Inherits E.print() through E
}
```

What will be the output of the following snippet of code? The comments in the code tell you what will be printed. Can you figure out why you get this output? There are three things at play. First, we can assign an object of a descendant of class A to a variable of class A type. This is the reason we have called `a.print()` in all statements below. Second, the `print()` method has been overridden by some of the descendants of class A in the class hierarchy. Third, late binding performs the magic of calling the appropriate `print()` method depending on the class of the object to which the variable is referring to at runtime.

```
A a = new A();
a.print();      // will print A
a = new B();
a.print();      // will print B
a = new C();
a.print();      // will print B
a = new D();
a.print();      // will print B
a = new E();
a.print();      // will print E
a = new F();
a.print();      // will print E
```

Let us consider the following definitions of two classes – S and T.

```
public class S {
    public void print() {
        System.out.println("S");
    }
}

public class T extends S {
    public void print(String msg) {
        System.out.println(msg);
    }
}
```

Does the `print()` method in class T override the `print()` method in its superclass S? The answer is no. The `print()` method in class T does not override the `print()` method in class S. This is called method overloading. Class T will now have two `print()` methods – one inherited from its superclass S, which accepts no arguments, `print()`, and one declared in it, which accepts one String argument, `print(String msg)`. However, both methods of class T have the same name, `print`. This is the reason it is called method overloading because the same method name is used more than once in the same class.

Let us discuss detailed rules about method overriding. Here are the rules when a class is said to override a method, which it inherits from its superclass.

- The method must be an instance method. Overriding does not apply to static methods.
- The overriding method must have the same name as the overridden method.
- The overriding method must have the same number of parameters of the same type in the same order as the overridden method. Java 5 has changed this rule slightly when the methods use generic types as their parameters. When the method's parameters use generic type, you need to consider the erasure of the generic type parameter and not the generic type itself when comparing with other methods to check if one overrides another. We will revisit this rule in the Behind the Scenes section to discuss it in detail with examples. For now, we will consider a method as overriding another method if they have the same number of parameters of the same type in the same order. Note that the name of the method parameter does not matter. It is the types and the orders of the parameters that matters and not their names. For example, `void print(String str)` and `void print(String msg)` are considered the same method. The different names of the parameters – `str` and `msg`, do not make them different methods.
- Before Java 5, the rule for the return type was that the return type of the overriding and the overridden methods must be the same. In Java 5, this rule remains the same for return types of primitive data types. However, it has changed for return types of reference data types. If the return type of the overridden method is a reference type, the return type of the overriding method must be assignment compatible to the return type of the overridden method. The return type of a reference type needs a little more explanation. Suppose a class has a method definition of `R1 m1()`, which is overridden by a method definition `R2 m1()`; This method overriding is allowed only if an instance of `R2` can be assigned to a variable of `R1` type without any typecast. Let us consider the following snippet of code that defines three classes P, Q, and R. Class P defines a method `getEmp()` that returns an object of `Employee` type. The `getEmp()` method of Class Q overrides `getEmp()` method of its superclass P, because it has the same name, number of parameters (zero in this case) of the same type in the same order and it has the same return type (`Employee`). The `getEmp()` method of class R also overrides `getEmp()` method of class P even though its return type (`Manager`) is different from the return type of the overridden method, which is `Employee`. The `getEmp()` method of class R overrides its superclass `getEmp()` method because an instance of `Manager` type can always be assigned to a variable of `Employee` type without any typecast.

```
public class P {
    public Employee getEmp() {
        // code goes here
    }
}

public class Q extends P {
    public Employee getEmp() {
        // code goes here
    }
}

public class R extends P {
    public Manager getEmp() {
        // code goes here
    }
}
```

- The access level of the overriding method must be at least the same or more relaxed than that of the overridden method. The three access levels are `public`, `protected` and package-level that allow for inheritance. Recall that `private` members are not inherited and hence cannot be overridden. The order of access level from the most relaxed to the strictest is `public`, `protected` and package-level. If the overridden method has `public` access level, the overriding method must have the `public` access level, because `public` is the most relaxed access level. If the overridden method has `protected` access level, the overriding method may have `public` or `protected` access level. If the overridden method has package-level access, the overriding method may have `public`, `protected` or package-level access. Table 16-1 summarizes this rule. We will discuss why this rule exists shortly.
- A method may include a list of checked exceptions in its throws clause. Although it is allowed to include an unchecked exception in the `throws` clause of a method, it is not required. In this section, we are discussing only checked exceptions. The overriding method cannot add a new exception to the list of exceptions in the overridden method. It may remove one or all exceptions or it may replace an exception with another exception, which is one of the descendants of the exception listed in the overridden method. Let us consider the following class definitions.

```
public class G {
    public void m1() throws CheckedException1, CheckedException2{
        // Code goes here
    }
}
```

If a class overrides `m1()` method of class `G`, it must not add any new checked exception to it. The following code will not compile, because it has added a new checked exception `CheckException3` in the overridden method `m1()`..

```
public class H extends G {
    public void m1() throws CheckedException1, CheckedException2,
                            CheckedException3 {
        // Code goes here
    }
}
```

The following class declarations override the `m1()` method in class `G` and they are all valid. In class `I`, the method `m1()` removes both exceptions. In class `J`, it removes one exception and keeps one. In class `K`, it keeps one and replaces the other one with a descendant type assuming that the `CheckedException22` is a descendant class of `CheckedException2`.

```
public class I extends G {
    // m1() removes all exceptions
    public void m1() throws {
        // Code goes here
    }
}

public class J extends G {
    // m1() removes one exception and keeps one
    public void m1() throws CheckedException1{
        // Code goes here
    }
}

public class J extends G {
```

```
        // m1() removes keep one and replaces one with a subclass
        public void m1() throws CheckedException1, CheckedException22{
            // Code goes here
        }
    }
```

Table 16-1: List of allowed access levels for an overriding method

Overridden Method Access Level	Allowed Overriding Method Access Level
public	public
protected	protected, package-level
package-level	public, protected, package-level

The rules about the return type and the list of exceptions of an overriding method may not be obvious. We will discuss the reasons behind these rules. There is a rule behind these rules, which is - "A variable of a class type can hold the reference of an object of any of its descendants." When you write code using the superclass type, that code must also work without any modification with objects of subclass types. Let us consider the following definition of class P assuming the EmpNotFoundException is a checked exception class.

```
public class P {
    public Employee getEmp(int empId) throws EmpNotFoundException{
        // code goes here
    }
}
```

You can write the following snippet of code.

```
P p = get an object reference of P or its descendant;
try {
    Employee emp = p.getEmp(10);
}
catch(EmpNotFoundException e) {
    // Handle exception here
}
```

There are two points that need to be considered in the above snippet of code. First, the variable p, which is of type P, can point to an object of type P or to an object of any descendant of class P. Second, when p.getEmp(10) method is called, the compiler verifies that the declared type of variable p (P class) has a getEmp() method, which accepts one parameter of type int, returns a Employee type object and throws EmpNotFoundException. These pieces of information are verified by the compiler with class P. The assumption made (and verified too) by the compiler about the getEmp() method should never be invalidated at runtime. Otherwise, it will result in a chaos. Code compiles, but might not run.

Let us consider one of the possible cases of overriding the getEmp() method as shown below.

```
public class Q extends P {
    public Manager getEmp(int empId) {
        // code goes here
    }
}
```

If the variable p is assigned an object of class Q, the code

```
Employee emp = p.getEmp(10);
```

inside the `try-catch` block is still valid. In this case, the variable p will refer to an object of class Q whose `getEmp()` method returns a `Manager` object and does not throw any exception. Returning a `Manager` object from the `getEmp()` method is fine, because we can assign a `Manager` object to the `emp` variable, which is a case of upcasting. Not throwing an exception from the `getEmp()` method is also fine, because the code was ready to handle the exception (by using a `try-catch` block) in case the exception was thrown.

What is the reason behind the access level rules for overriding methods? Note that when a variable p accesses the `getEmp()` method, the compiler verifies that the code, where `p.getEmp()` is used, has access to the `getEmp()` method of class P. If the subclasses of P reduces the access level, the same code, `p.getEmp()`, may not work at runtime, because the code executing the statement may not have access to the `getEmp()` method in the descendant of class P.

Let us consider the following definition of class Q2, which inherits from class P. It overrides the `getEmp()` method and replaces the `EmpNoFoundException` with another checked exception named `BadEmpIdException`.

```
// Won't compile
public class Q2 extends P {
    public Manager getEmp(int empId)  throws BadEmpIdException {
        // code goes here
    }
}
```

Suppose the code, which was written in terms of P type, gets a reference of a Q2 object as follows. Note that the `try-catch` block is not prepared to handle the `BadEmpIdException`, which the method `getEmp()` of the Q2 class may throw. This is the reason why declaration of class Q2 would not compile.

```
P p = new Q2();
try {
    Employee emp = p.getEmp(10);
}
catch(EmpNotFoundException e) {
    // Handle exception here
}
```

To summarize the rules of overriding, let us break down the parts of a method declaration as follows.

- Name of the method
- Number of parameters
- Type of parameters
- Order of parameters
- Return type of parameters
- Access level
- List of checked exceptions in the throws clause

The first four parts must always be the same in the overriding and the overridden methods. Before Java 5, the return type must be the same in the overriding and the overridden methods. From Java 5, if the return type is a reference type, overriding a method's return type could also be a subtype (any descendant) of the return type of the overridden method. Access level and list of exceptions in the overridden method may be thought of as its constraints. An overriding method may relax (or even remove) the constraints of the overridden method. However, an overriding method can never have more restrictive constraints than that of the overridden method.

TIP

The rules of overriding a method are complex. It may take you a long time to master them. All rules are directly supported by the compiler. If you make a mistake in the source code while overriding a method, the compiler will generate a nice (not always) error message that will give you a clue about your mistake. There is a golden rule about method overriding that helps you avoid mistakes – "Whatever code is written using the superclass type must also work with the subclass type".

Accessing Overridden Method

Sometimes, you may need to access the overridden method from a subclass. A subclass can use the `super` keyword as a qualifier to call the overridden method of the superclass. Note that the `Object` class has no superclass. It is illegal to use the `super` keyword in the `Object` class. As a programmer, you will never need to write code for the `Object` class anyway as it is part of the Java class library.

Let us consider the code for the `AOSuper` class in Listing 16-12. It has a `print()` method, which prints a message on the standard output. The code in Listing 16-13 is for `AOSub` class, which inherits from the `AOSuper` class. The `AOSub` class overrides the `print()` method of the `AOSuper` class. Note the `super.print()` method call inside the `print()` and the `callOverridenPrint` methods of the `AOSub` class. It will call the `print()` method of `AOSuper` class. The output of Listing 16-14 demonstrates that a method call with `super` qualifier calls the overridden method in superclass.

Listing 16-12: An AOSuper class

```
// AOSuper.java
package com.jdojo.chapter16;

public class AOSuper {
    public void print() {
        System.out.println("Inside AOSuper.print()");
    }
}
```

Listing 16-13: An AOSub class, which inherits from the AOSuper class

```
// AOSub.java
package com.jdojo.chapter16;

public class AOSub extends AOSuper {
    public void print() {
        // Call print() method of AOSuper class
        super.print();
```

```
        // Print a message
        System.out.println("Inside AOSub.print()");
    }

    public void callOverridenPrint() {
        // Call print() method of AOSuper class
        super.print();
    }
}
```

Listing 16-14: A test class to test a method call with the super qualifier

```
// AOTest.java
package com.jdojo.chapter16;

public class AOTest {
    public static void main(String[] args) {
        AOSub aoSub = new AOSub();
        aoSub.print();
        aoSub.callOverridenPrint();
    }
}
```

```
Output:

Inside AOSuper.print()
Inside AOSub.print()
Inside AOSuper.print()
```

You can call the overridden method of the superclass (immediate ancestor) using the super keyword. There is no way to call a method of the superclass of the superclass. Suppose there are three classes – A, B and C, where class B inherits class A, and class C inherits class B. There is no way to call methods of class A from inside class C. If class C needs to call a method of class A, you need to provide a method in class B that will call method of class A. Class C will call the method of class B, which in turn will call the method of class A.

TIP
When a method call is made using the super keyword, Java uses early binding (compile-time binding), even though the method is an instance method. Another instance when Java uses early biding for an instance method call is a private method call, because a private method cannot be invoked from outside its defining class. A private method cannot be overridden either. The super keyword refers to the instance fields and methods or constructors of the immediate ancestor of the class in which it appears.

Method Overloading

Having more than one method with the same name in the same class is called method overloading. Methods with the same name in a class could be declared methods, inherited methods or combination of both. Overloaded methods must have different number of parameters or different

---

types of parameters or both. The return type, access level and throws clause of a method play no role in making it an overloaded method. The `m1()` method of the `OME1` class is an example of an overloaded method.

```
public class OME1 {
    public void m1(int a) {
        // Code goes here
    }

    public void m1(int a, int b) {
        // Code goes here
    }

    public int m1(String a) {
        // Code goes here
    }

    public int m1(String a, int b) throws CheckedException1 {
        // Code goes here
    }
}
```

The following is an example of an incorrect attempt to overload the `m2()` method in class `OME2`. Using different names for parameters (`p1` and `p2`) does not make the `m2()` method overloaded. The code for the `OME2` class would not compile, because it has a duplicate declaration for the `m2()` method. Both methods have the same number and type of parameters, which makes it not overloaded.

```
// Won't compile
public class OME2 {
    public void m2(int p1) {
        // Code goes here
    }

    public void m2(int p2) {
        // Code goes here
    }
}
```

The order of the parameters may play a role in making a method overloaded. The `m3()` method of the `OME3` class is overloaded, because parameter types are different. Both methods have one parameter of type `int` and another of type `double`. However, they are in a different order.

```
public class OME3 {
    public void m3(int p1, double p2) {
        // Code goes here
    }

    public void m3(double p1, int p2) {
        // Code goes here
    }
}
```

Use a simple rule to check if two methods can be termed as an overloaded method. List the name of the methods and the type of their parameters from left to right separated by a comma (you can use any other separator.). If the two methods of a class having the same name give you different lists, they are overloaded. Otherwise, they are not overloaded. If we make such lists for `m1()`, `m2()` and `m3()` methods in class `OME1`, `OME2` and `OME3` classes, we will come up with the following results. You can realize that the results for the `m2()` method in class `OME2` are the same for both versions and hence `OME2.m2()` is not overloaded. Table 16-2 lists some important differences between method overriding and method overloading.

```
// Method list for m1 in class OME1 - Overloaded
m1,int
m1,int,int
m1,String
m1,String,int

// Method list for m2 in class OME2 - Not Overloaded
m2,int
m2,int

// Method list for m3 in class OME3 - Overloaded
m3,int,double
m3,double,int
```

Table 16-2: Some important differences between method overriding and method overloading.

Method Overriding	Method Overloading
Overriding involves inheritance and at least two classes.	Overloading has nothing to do with inheritance. Overloading involves only one class.
It occurs when a class defines a method with the same name, the same number of parameters of the same type in the same order as defined by its superclass.	It occurs when a class defines more than one method with the same name. All methods with the same name must differ at least in one respect from others - the number of parameters, their types or orders.
The return type of the overriding method must be assignment substitutable with the return type of the overridden method.	Return types of overloaded methods do not play any roles in overloading
The overriding method cannot have additional throws clause than the overridden method. It can have the same or less restrictive list of exceptions as the overridden method.	Throws clauses of overloaded methods do not play any roles in overloading.
Overriding applies only to instance (non-static) methods.	Any method (static or non-static) can be overloaded.

Method overloading is another kind of polymorphism where the same method name has different meanings. Method overloading is bound at compile-time as opposed to method overriding that is bound at runtime. Note that the compiler only resolves the version of the overloaded methods that will be called. If the overloaded method is an instance method, which code will be executed is still determined at runtime using late binding. The compiler determines which version of the overloaded method will be called matching the actual parameters with the formal parameters of the overloaded methods.

For an overloaded method call, the compiler chooses the most specific method. If it does not find an exact matching method, it will try to look for a more generic version by converting the actual parameter type to a more generic type using the rules of automatic type widening. Listing 16-15 demonstrates how the compiler chooses an overloaded method. Note that the compiler knows only the compile-time type (the declared type) of the actual and the formal parameters. Let us look at `ot.add(f1, s2)` method call. The types of actual parameters are `float` and `short`. There is no `add(float, short)` method in the `OverloadingTest` class. The compiler tries to widen the type of the first argument to a `double` data type and it finds a match based on the first parameter - `add(double, double)`. Still, the second parameter type does not match – the actual type is `short` and the formal type is `double`. Java allows automatic widening from `short` to `double`. The compiler converts the `short` type to the `double` type and binds `add(f1, s2)` call to `add(double, double)` method. When `ot.test(mgr)` is called, the compiler looks for an exact match and, in this case, it finds one, `test(Manager m)`, and binds the call to this version of the `test()` method. Suppose the `test(Manager m)` method is not present in the `OverloadingTest` class. The compiler will bind `ot.test(mgr)` call to `test(Employee e)` method because a `Manager` type can be widened (using upcasting) to `Employee` type automatically.

Listing 16-15: A test program that demonstrates how the compiler chooses the most specific method from several versions of an overloaded method

```java
// OverloadingTest.java
package com.jdojo.chapter16;

public class OverloadingTest {
    public double add(int a, int b) {
        System.out.println("Inside add(int a, int b)");
        double s = a + b;
        return s;
    }

    public double add(double a, double b) {
        System.out.println("Inside add(double a, double b)");
        double s = a + b;
        return s;
    }

    public void test(Employee e) {
        System.out.println("Inside test(Employee e)");
    }

    public void test(Manager e) {
        System.out.println("Inside test(Manager m)");
    }

    public static void main(String[] args) {
        OverloadingTest ot = new OverloadingTest();

        int i = 10;
        int j = 15;
        double d1 = 10.4;
        double d2 = 2.5;
        float f1 = 2.3F;
        float f2 = 4.5F;
        short s1 = 2;
        short s2 = 6;

        ot.add(i, j);
        ot.add(d1, j);
```

```
        ot.add(i, s1);
        ot.add(s1, s2);
        ot.add(f1, f2);
        ot.add(f1, s2);

        Employee emp = new Employee();
        Manager mgr = new Manager();
        ot.test(emp);
        ot.test(mgr);

        emp = mgr;
        ot.test(emp);
    }
}
```

```
Output:

Inside add(int a, int b)
Inside add(double a, double b)
Inside add(int a, int b)
Inside add(int a, int b)
Inside add(double a, double b)
Inside add(double a, double b)
Inside test(Employee e)
Inside test(Manager m)
Inside test(Employee e)
```

Sometimes, overloaded methods and automatic type widening may confuse the compiler resulting in a compiler error. Consider Listing 16-16 for an Adder class with an overloaded add() method.

Listing 16-16: The Adder class, which has overloaded add().method

```
// Adder.java
package com.jdojo.chapter16;

public class Adder {
    public double add(int a, double b) {
        return a + b;
    }

    public double add(double a, int b) {
        return a + b;
    }
}
```

Listing 16-17: Testing add() method of the Adder class

```
// AdderTest.java
package com.jdojo.chapter16;

public class AdderTest {
    public static void main(String[] args) {
        Adder a = new Adder();
        double d = a.add(2, 3); // Compiler error
    }
}
```

An attempt to compile the `AdderTest` class as listed in Listing 16-17 generates the following error.

```
"AdderTest.java": reference to add is ambiguous, both method
add(int,double) in com.jdojo.chapter16.Adder and method add(double,int)
in com.jdojo.chapter16.Adder match at line 7, column 18
```

The error message states that compiler is not able to decide which one of the two `add()` methods in the `Adder` class to call for `a.add(3, 7)` method invocation. The compiler is confused in deciding: "Should it widen the `int` type of 3 to make it `double` type 3.0 and call the `add(double, int)` or should it widen the `int` type of 7 to make it `double` type 7.0 and call the `add(int, double)`?" In situations like this, you need to help the compiler by using a typecast as follows.

```
double d1 = a.add((double)2, 3); // OK. Will use add(double, int)
double d2 = a.add(2, (double)3); // OK. Will use add(int, double)
```

Inheritance and Constructors

An object has two things: state and behavior. Instance variables in a class represent the state of its objects. Instance methods represent the behavior of its objects. Each object of a class maintains its own state. When you create an object of a class, memory is allocated for all instance variables declared in the class and all instance variables declared in its ancestors at all levels Our `Employee` class declares a `name` instance variable. When we create an object of the `Employee` class, the memory is allocated for its `name` instance variable. When an object of the `Manager` class is created, memory is allocated for the `name` field that is present in its superclass `Employee`. After all, a manager has a similar state as that of an employee. A manager behaves similar to an employee. Let us look at an example. Consider two classes: `U` and `V` as shown below. Figure 16-3 depicts the memory allocation when objects of class `U` and `V` are created. When an object of class `U` is created, memory is allocated only for the instance variables that are declared in class `U`. When an object of class `V` is created, memory is allocated for all instance variables in class `U` and class `V`.

```
public class U {
    private int id;
    protected String name;
}

public class V extends U{
    protected double salary;
    protected String address;
}
```

Figure 16-3: Memory allocation for an object includes all instance variable of the class and all its ancestors

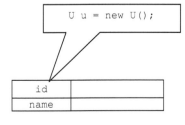

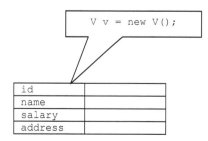

Let us get to the main topic of discussion for this section – constructors. Constructors are not members of a class and they are not inherited by subclasses. What is the purpose of having constructors? Constructors are used to initialize the instance variables. When you create an object of a class, the object contains instance variables from the class and all of its ancestors. To initialize the instance variables of ancestor classes the constructors of ancestor classes must be called. Let us consider the following two classes – CSuper and CSub as shown in Listing 16-18 and Listing 16-19. The CTest class in Listing 16-20 is used to create an object of the CSub class.

Listing 16-18: A CSuper class with a no-args constructor

```
// CSuper.java
package com.jdojo.chapter16;

public class CSuper {
    public CSuper() {
        System.out.println("Inside CSuper() constructor.");
    }
}
```

Listing 16-19: A CSub class, which inherits from the CSuper class and has a no-args constructor

```
//CSub.java
package com.jdojo.chapter16;

public class CSub extends CSuper {
    public CSub() {
        System.out.println("Inside CSub() constructor.");
    }
}
```

Listing 16-20: A test class, which demonstrates that constructors for all ancestors are called when an object of a class is created starting at the top of the class hierarchy and going down

```
// CTest.java
package com.jdojo.chapter16;

public class CTest {
    public static void main(String[] args) {
        CSub cs = new CSub();
    }
}
```

```
Output:

Inside CSuper() constructor.
Inside CSub() constructor.
```

The output of the CTest class shows that the constructor of the CSuper class is called first and then the constructor of the CSub class. In fact, the constructor of the Object class is called, before the constructor of the CSuper class. We cannot print the fact the constructor of the Object class is called, because the Object class is not our class, and therefore, we cannot modify it. The question is – "How does the constructor of the CSuper class get called?" The answer to this question is based on the rule that when an object of a class is created, memory is allocated for all instance variables including instance variables in all its ancestor classes. Instance variables for all classes must be initialized by calling their constructors. The compiler helps us to enforce this rule to the most extent. The compiler injects the call to the immediate ancestor's no-args constructor as the first statement in every constructor you add to your class. We need to introduce a new keyword – super. The keyword `super` refers to the immediate ancestor of a class. It is used in different contexts. If it is followed by parentheses, it refers to the constructor of the superclass. If superclass constructor accepts parameters, you can pass the list of parameters within parentheses similar to a method call. The following are examples of calling constructor of a superclass.

```
// Call no-args constructor of superclass
super();

// Call superclass constructor with a String argument
super("Hello");

// Call superclass constructor with two double arguments
super(10.5, 89.2);
```

You can call constructor of the superclass explicitly or let the compiler inject the call to the no-args constructor for you. When you compile the CSuper and CSub class, the compiler modifies their constructor's code, which look as shown in Listing 16-21 and Listing 16-22.

Listing 16-21: Compiler injection of a super() call to call the immediate ancestor's no-args constructor

```
// CSuper.java
package com.jdojo.chapter16;

public class CSuper {
    public CSuper() {
        super();  // Injected by the compiler
        System.out.println("Inside CSuper() constructor.");
    }
}
```

Listing 16-22: Compiler injection of a super() call to call the immediate ancestor's no-args constructor

```
//CSub.java
package com.jdojo.chapter16;

public class CSub extends CSuper {
    public CSub() {
        super();  // Injected by the compiler
        System.out.println("Inside CSub() constructor.");
    }
}
```

TIP

The `super` keyword refers to the immediate ancestor of a class. You can refer only to the immediate ancestor (or superclass) from inside a class using the `super` keyword. You cannot jump two or more levels up in the class hierarchy. The `super` keyword is used to refer to constructors, fields, or methods of the superclass. You can call superclass constructors using the `super` keyword only as the first statement inside a constructor. The `Object` class is at the top of all class hierarchies in Java and it has no superclass. Therefore, the `super` keyword cannot be used inside the `Object` class.

You can also call the no-args constructor or any other constructors of the superclass explicitly as the first statement in constructor of your class. The compiler injects the no-args constructor call only if you have not added one explicitly. Let us try to improve our `Employee` and `Manager` classes. Let us add a constructor to the `Employee` class that accepts the name of the employee as its parameter. We will call the new class `Employee2` as shown in Listing 16-23.

Listing 16-23: Employee2 class, which is a modified version of the original Employee class. It has added a constructor that accepts a String argument

```
// Employee2.java
package com.jdojo.chapter16;

public class Employee2 {
    private String name = "Unknown";

    public Employee2(String name) {
        this.name = name;
    }

    public void setName(String name) {
        this.name = name;
    }

    public String getName() {
        return name;
    }
}
```

Let us call our new `Manager` class `Manager2`, which inherits from the `Employee2` class.

```
//Manager2.java
package com.jdojo.chapter16;

// Won't compile
public class Manager2 extends Employee2 {
    // No code for now
}
```

The above code for the `Manager2` class does not compile. It generates the following compiler error.

```
Error(4,23): constructor Employee2() not found in class
com.jdojo.chapter16.Employee2
```

We have not added any constructor for the `Manager2` class. Therefore, the compiler will add a no-args constructor for it. It will also try to inject a `super()` call as the first statement inside the no-args constructor, which will call the no-args constructor of the `Employee2` class. However, the `Employee2` class does not have a no-args constructor. This is the reason why we get the error, when we attempt to compile the `Manager2` class. The code for the `Manager2` class looks as follows, after it is modified by the compiler. You may observe that the `super()` call is invalid, because the `Employee2` class does not have a no-args constructor.

```
/* Code for Manager2 class after compiler injects a no-args constructor
   with a call to super()
*/
```

```
package com.jdojo.chapter16;

// Won't compile
public class Manager2 extends Employee2 {
    // Injected by the compiler
    public Manager2() {
        super();  // Calls the nonexistent no-args constructor
                  // of Employee2 class
    }
}
```

So, how do we fix the `Manager2` class? There are many ways to fix it. Some of the ways you can fix the `Manager2` class are as follows.

- Add a no-args constructor to the `Employee2` class as:

```
public class Employee2 {
    // No args constructor
    public Employee2() {
    }

    // all other code for class remains the same
}
```

After adding a no-args constructor to the `Employee2` class the code for the `Manager2` class will compile fine.

- Add a no-args constructor to the `Manager2` class and explicitly call the constructor of the `Employee2` class with a `String` argument as:

```
public class Manager2 extends Employee2 {
    public Manager2() {
        // Call constructor of Employee2 class explicitly
        super("Unknown");
    }
}
```

- Add a constructor to the `Manager2` class, which accepts a `String` argument and pass the argument value to the `Employee2` class constructor. This way, you can create a `Manager` by passing the name of the `Manager` as a parameter to its constructor.

```
public class Manager2 extends Employee2 {
    public Manager2(String name) {
        //Call constructor of Employee2 class explicitly
        super(name);
    }
}
```

Normally, the third option is used where you would provide a way to create an object of the `Manager2` class with manager's name. Note that `Manager2` class does not have access to the `name` instance variable of the `Employee2` class. Still, you can initialize the `name` instance variable in the `Employee2` class from the `Manager2` class using the `super` keyword and invoking the constructor of the `Employee2` class. Listing 16-24 has the complete code for the `Manager2` class

---

that will compile. Listing 16-25 has code to test the `Manager2` class and its output shows that it works as expected.

TIP
Every class must call the constructor of its superclass from its constructors directly or indirectly. If the superclass does not have a no-args constructor, you must call any other existing constructors of the superclass explicitly as we have done in Listing 16-24.

Listing 16-24: A Manager2 class that has a constructor that accepts a String argument. It calls the constructor of the Employee2 class explicitly.

```java
// Manager2.java
package com.jdojo.chapter16;

public class Manager2 extends Employee2 {
    public Manager2(String name) {
        super(name);
    }
}
```

Listing 16-25: A test class to test the Manager2 class

```java
// Manager2Test.java
package com.jdojo.chapter16;

public class Manager2Test {
    public static void main(String[] args) {
        Manager2 mgr = new Manager2("John Jacobs");
        String name = mgr.getName();
        System.out.println("Manager name: " + name);
    }
}
```

```
Output:

Manager name: Leslie Zanders
```

We need to discuss a few more rules about using the constructors of a superclass from a subclass. Let us consider the following definition of two classes – X and Y, which are in two different packages.

```java
// X.java
package com.jdojo.chapter16.pkg1;

public class X {
    // X() has package-level access
    X() {
    }
}

// Y.java
package com.jdojo.chapter16.pkg2;
```

```
import com.jdojo.chapter16.pkg1.X;

public class Y extends X {
    public Y() {
    }
}
```

The code for class Y would not compile. It generates a compiler error as follows.

```
Error(7):  X() is not public in com.jdojo.chapter16.pkg1.X; cannot be
accessed from outside package
```

The error states that the no-args constructor in class X has a package-level access. Therefore, it cannot be accessed from class Y, which is in a different package. We received this error because the compiler will modify class Y definition as follows.

```
// Compiler modified version of class Y
// Y.java
package com.jdojo.chapter16.pkg2;

import com.jdojo.chapter16.pkg1.X;

public class Y extends X {
    public Y() {
        super(); // Injected by compiler to call X() constructor
    }
}
```

The no-args constructor of class X has a package-level access. Therefore, it can only be accessed from com.jdojo.chapter16.pkg1 package. How do we fix class Y? It is tricky to suggest a solution in such cases. The solution depends on the design that is used behind the creation of class X and class Y. However, for the class Y to compile, you must create a constructor for the class X, which has public or protected access, so that it can be accessed from class Y.

Here is another rule for using constructors along with inheritance. The superclass constructor must be called explicitly or implicitly from inside the constructor of a class using the super keyword. However, the access to a superclass constructor from a class is controlled by the access level of the constructor of the superclass. Sometimes, consequences of the access level of the constructors of a class could be that it cannot be accessed at all. Consider the following definition of the class called NoSubclassingAllowed.

```
public class NoSubclassingAllowed {
    private NoSubclassingAllowed() {
    }
    // Other code go here
}
```

Note that NoSubclassingAllowed has explicitly declared a private constructor. A private constructor cannot be accessed from anywhere including any of its subclasses. Note that, for a subclass to exist, it must be able to call at least one of the constructors of its superclass. This concludes that the NoSubclassingAllowed class cannot be inherited by any class. This is one of the ways to disable inheritance for a class. The following code will not compile, which tries to subclass the NoSubclassingAllowed class, which has no accessible constructors. One thing you may notice is that no one can create an object of the NoSubclassingAllowed class, because its constructor is not accessible from outside. Classes like this one provide methods that create its object and return it to the caller. This is also a way to control and encapsulate object creation of a class.

```
// Won't compile.
public class LetUsTryInVain extends NoSubclassingAllowed {
}
```

TIP

You can prevent subclassing of a class by declaring all of its constructors as `private`. Usually, you declare all constructors of a class as `private` to control the object creation of that class, for example, a singleton class for which you want only one object to exist in a JVM. An inner class, which is discussed in the chapter in *Inner Classes*, has access to `private` constructors of its enclosing class. In that case, it is possible to subclass a class even if all its constructors are declared private. The following code is a valid. Here X is the enclosing class and Y is an inner class. Class X is also superclass of class Y.

```
public class X {
        private X() {
        }

        class Y extends X {      // Subclassing X is OK here
        }
}
```

Recall that you can call a constructor of a class from another constructor of the same class using the `this` keyword and this call must be the first statement in the constructor's body. When you look at the rule to call another constructor of the same class and constructor of the superclass, you would find that both state that the call must be the first statement inside the body of the constructor. The result of these two rules is that from one constructor either you can use `this()` to call another constructer of the same class or `super()` to call a constructor of the superclass, but not both. This rule also ensures that the constructor of the superclass is always called once and only once.

Method Hiding

A class also inherits all non-private static methods (also called class methods) from its superclass. Redefining an inherited static method in a class is known as method hiding. The redefined static method in a subclass is said to hide the static method of its superclass. Recall that redefining a non-static method (also called instance method) in a class is called method overriding. Listing 16-26 has the code for class `MHidingSuper`, which has a `static print()` method. Listing 16-27 has the code for a `MHidingSub` class that inherits from the `MHidingSuper` class. It redefines the `print()` method, which hides the `print()` method in the `MHidingSuper` class. The `print()` method in `MHidingSub` is an example of method hiding.

Listing 16-26: A MHidingSuper class that has a static method

```
// MHidingSuper.java
package com.jdojo.chapter16;

public class MHidingSuper {
```

```
    public static void print() {
        System.out.println("Inside MHidingSuper.print()");
    }
}
```

Listing 16-27: A MHidingSub class that inherits from the MHidingSuper and hides the print() of its superclass

```
// MHidingSub.java
package com.jdojo.chapter16;

public class MHidingSub extends MHidingSuper {
    public static void print() {
        System.out.println("Inside MHidingSub.print()");
    }
}
```

All the rules about the redefined method - name, access level, return types, and exception, for method hiding are the same as for method overriding. Please refer to the *Method Overriding* section in this chapter for more detailed discussion on these rules. One rule that is different for method hiding is the binding rule. Early binding is used for `static` methods. Based on the compile-time type of the expression, the compiler determines at compile-time what code will be executed at runtime for a `static` method call. Note that you can use the class name as well as a reference variable to invoke a `static` method. There is no ambiguity about method binding, when you use a class name to invoke a `static` method. The compiler binds the `static` method that is defined (or redefined) in the class. If a class does not define (or redefine) the `static` method, the compiler binds the method that the class inherits from its superclass. If the compiler does not find a defined/redefined/inherited method in the class, it generates an error.

Listing 16-28: A test class to demonstrate method hiding

```
// MHidingTest.java
package com.jdojo.chapter16;

public class MHidingTest {
    public static void main(String[] args) {
        MHidingSuper mhSuper = new MHidingSub();
        MHidingSub mhSub = new MHidingSub();

        System.out.println("#1");

        // #1
        MHidingSuper.print();
        mhSuper.print();

        System.out.println("\n#2");

        // #2
        MHidingSub.print();
        mhSub.print();
        ((MHidingSuper)mhSub).print();

        System.out.println("\n#3");

        // #3
        mhSuper = mhSub;
        mhSuper.print();
```

```
            ((MHidingSub)mhSuper).print();
    }
}
```

```
Output:

#1
Inside MHidingSuper.print()
Inside MHidingSuper.print()

#2
Inside MHidingSub.print()
Inside MHidingSub.print()
Inside MHidingSuper.print()

#3
Inside MHidingSuper.print()
Inside MHidingSub.print()
```

Listing 16-28 has the code that demonstrates the early binding rules for method hiding for `static` methods of a class. The test code has three sections labeled #1, #2 and #3. Let us discuss how early binding is performed by the compiler in each section.

```
// #1
MHidingSuper.print();
mhSuper.print();
```

The first call, `MHidingSuper.print()`, is made using a class name. The compiler binds this call to execute the `print()` method of the `MHidingSuper` class. The second call, `mhSuper.print()`, is made using the reference variable `mhSuper`. The compile-time type (or declared type) of `mhSuper` variable is `MHidingSuper`. Therefore, the compiler binds this call to execute the `print()` method of the `MHidingSuper` class.

```
// #2
MHidingSub.print();
mhSub.print();
((MHidingSuper)mhSub).print();
```

The first two calls in the section #2 are similar to the two calls in the section #1. They are bound to the `print()` method of the `MHidingSub` class. The third call, `((MHidingSuper)mhSub).print()`, needs a little explanation. The compile-time type of the `mhSub` variable is `MHidingSub`. When we use a typecast, `(MHidingSuper)`, on the `mhSub` variable, the compile-time type of the expression, `(MHidingSuper)mhSub`, becomes `MHidingSuper`. When we call the `print()` method on this expression, the compiler binds it to its compile-time type, which is `MHidingSuper`. Therefore, the third method call in section #2 is bound to the `print()` method of the `MHidingSuper` class.

```
// #3
mhSuper = mhSub;
mhSuper.print();
((MHidingSub)mhSuper).print();
```

The first statement in section #3 assigns a reference of MHidingSub object to the mhSuper reference variable. After the first statement is executed, mhSuper variable is referring to an object of the MHidingSub class. When the first call to the print() method is made in section #3, the compiler looks at the compile-time type (or declared type) of mhSuper variable, which is MHidingSuper type. Therefore, the compiler binds the call, mhSuper.print(), to the print() method of the MHidingSuper class. The second call to the print() method is bound to the print() method of the MHidingSub class, because the typecast, (MHidingSub), makes the type of the entire expression as MHidingSub.

TIP

A static method of a class cannot hide an instance method of its superclass. If you want to invoke a hidden method of the superclass from inside a class, you need to qualify the hidden method call with the superclass name. For example, if you want to call the print() method of the MHidingSuper class from inside the MHidingSub class, you need to use MHidingSuper.print(). Inside the MHidingSub class, the call to the print() method, without using the class name or a variable, refers to the hiding method print() of the MHidingSub class.

Field Hiding

A field declaration (static or non-static) in a class hides the inherited field declaration in its superclass with the same name. The type of the field and its access level are not considered in the case of field hiding. Field hiding occurs solely based on the field name. Early binding is used for field access. That is, the compiler-time type of the class is used to bind the field access. Consider the following declaration of two classes – G and H.

```
public class G {
    protected int x = 200;
    protected String y = "Hello";
    protected double z = 10.5;
}

public class H extends G{
    protected int x = 400;        // Hides x in class G
    protected String y = "Bye";   // Hides y in class G
    protected String z = "OK";    // Hides z in class G
}
```

The field declarations x, y and z in the class H hide the inherited fields x, y and z from the class G. It is to be emphasized that the same field name in a class alone hides a field of its superclass. Data types of the hidden and the hiding fields are immaterial. For example, the data type of z in class G is double, whereas data type of z in class H is String. Still, the field z in class H hides the field z in class G. The simple names of fields x, y and z in class H refer to the hiding fields and not inherited ones. Therefore, if you use the simple name x in class H, it refers to the field x declared in class H and not in class G. If you want to refer to the field x in class G from inside class H, you need to use super keyword, e.g., super.x.

Let us consider a detailed example of field hiding. In Listing 16-29, the FHidingSuper class declares two fields – num and name. In Listing 16-30, the FHidingSub class inherits from the FHidingSuper class and it inherits the num and name fields from it. The print() method of the

---

FHidingSub class prints the values of the num and name fields. The print() method uses simple names of num and name fields and they refer to the inherited fields from the FHidingSuper class. When you run the FHidingTest class in Listing 16-31, the output shows that the FHidingSub class really inherits num and name fields from its superclass.

Listing 16-29: FHidingSuper class with two protected instance fields

```java
// FHidingSuper.java
package com.jdojo.chapter16;

public class FHidingSuper {
    protected int num = 100;
    protected String name = "John Jacobs";
}
```

Listing 16-30: FHidingSub class, which inherits from FHidingSuper class and inherits two fields- num and name

```java
// FHidingSub.java
package com.jdojo.chapter16;

public class FHidingSub extends FHidingSuper {
    public void print() {
        System.out.println("num: " + num);
        System.out.println("name: " + name);
    }
}
```

Listing 16-31: A test class to demonstrate field's inheritances

```java
// FHidingTest.java
package com.jdojo.chapter16;

public class FHidingTest {
    public static void main(String[] args) {
        FHidingSub fhSub = new FHidingSub();
        fhSub.print();
    }
}
```

```
Output:

num: 100
name: John Jacobs
```

Let us consider the definition of class FHidingSub2 listed in Listing 16-32. It inherits from the FHidingSuper class. It declares two fields - num and name, which have the same names as the two fields declared in its superclass. This is a case of field hiding. The num and name fields in FHidingSub2 hide the num and name fields that are inherited from the FHidingSuper class. When the num and name fields are used by their simple names inside the FHidingSub2 class, they refer to the fields declared in the FHidingSub2 class and not to the inherited fields from the FHidingSuper class. This is verified by running the FHidingTest2 class as listed in Listing 16-33. The output shows that the print() method of the FHidingSub2 class prints the num and name fields values from the FHidingSub2 class and not from the FHidingSuper class.

Listing 16-32: A FHidingSub2 class that inherits from FHidingSuper and declares two variables with the same name as declared in its superclass

```java
// FHidingSub2.java
package com.jdojo.chapter16;

public class FHidingSub2 extends FHidingSuper{
    // Hides num field in FHidingSuper class
    private int num = 200;

    // Hides name field in FHidingSuper class
    private String name = "Wally Inman";

    public void print() {
        System.out.println("num: " + num);
        System.out.println("name: " + name);
    }
}
```

Listing 16-33: A test class to demonstrate field hiding

```java
// FHidingTest2.java
package com.jdojo.chapter16;

public class FHidingTest2 {
    public static void main(String[] args) {
        FHidingSub2 fhSub2 = new FHidingSub2();
        fhSub2.print();
    }
}
```

```
Output:

num: 200
name: Wally Inman
```

The `FHidingSub2` class has four fields – two inherited (`num` and `name`) and two declared (`num` and `name`). The simple names of the fields refer to the field declared inside the class and not the inherited ones with the same name. If you want to refer to the inherited fields from the superclass, you need to qualify the field names with the `super` keyword. For example, `super.num` and `super.name` inside `FHidingSub2` refers to the `num` and `name` fields in `FHidingSuper` class.

The `print()` method of the `FHidingSub3` class in Listing 16-34 uses the `super` keyword to access hidden fields of the superclass and uses the simple names of the fields to access fields from its own class. You can see the output by running the `FHidingTest3class` as listed in Listing 16-35.

Listing 16-34: A FHidingSub3 class that demonstrates how to access hidden fields of superclass using the super keyword

```java
//FHidingSub3.java
package com.jdojo.chapter16;

public class FHidingSub3 extends FHidingSuper{
    // Hides num field in FHidingSuper class
```

```
        private int num = 200;

        // Hides name field in FHidingSuper class
        private String name = "Wally Inman";

        public void print() {
            //FHidingSub3.num
            System.out.println("num: " + num);

            //FHidingSuper.num
            System.out.println("super.num: " + super.num);

            //FHidingSub3.name
            System.out.println("name: " + name);

            //FHidingSuper.name
            System.out.println("super.name: " + super.name);
        }
    }
```

Listing 16-35: A test class that accesses hidden fields

```
// FHidingTest3.java
package com.jdojo.chapter16;

public class FHidingTest3 {
    public static void main(String[] args) {
        FHidingSub3 fhSub3 = new FHidingSub3();
        fhSub3.print();
    }
}
```

```
Output:

num: 200
super.num: 100
name: Wally Inman
super.name: John Jacobs
```

Figure 16-4: Memory layout for objects of FHidingSuper and FHidingSub2 classes.

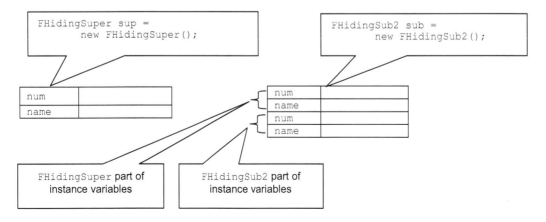

Recall that when an object is created, Java runtime allocates memory for all instance variables in the class of the object and all of its ancestors. When you create an object of the `FHidingSub2` or `FHidingSub3`.class, memory will be allocated for the four instance variables as shown in Figure 16-4.

Let us summarize the field hiding rules.

- Field hiding occurs when a class declares a variable with the same name as an inherited variable from its superclass.
- Field hiding occurs only based on the name of the field. Access level, data type and the type of field (`static` or non-static) are not considered when field hiding occurs. For example, a `static` field can hide an instance field. A field of `int` type can hide a field of `String` type, etc. A `private` field in a class can hide a `protected` field in its superclass. A `public` field in a class can hide a `protected` field in its superclass.
- A class should use the `super` keyword to access the hidden field of the superclass, whereas it can use a simple name or a name qualified with the keyword `this` to access the redefined fields in its body.

Early binding is used to bind a field of a class. Please refer to the *Early Binding* section in this chapter for more detailed examples of early binding for fields

Disabling Class Inheritance and Method Overriding

You can disable subclassing for a class by declaring it as `final`. We have seen the use of the `final` keyword before in declaring constants. The same `final` keyword may also be used in a class declaration. A `final` class cannot be subclassed. In other words, if you declare a class as `final`, no other class can inherit from that class. The following snippet of code declares a `final` class named `Security`.

```
public final class Security {
    // Code for Security goes here
}
```

You cannot inherit another class from a `final` class. The following declaration of class `CrackedSecurity` will not compile.

```
// Won't compile. Cannot inherit from Security
public final class CrackedSecurity extends Security {
    // Code for MyFinalClass goes here
}
```

You can also declare a method as `final`. A `final` method cannot be overridden or hidden by a subclass. Since a `final` method cannot be overridden or hidden, a call to a `final` method may be inlined by a code optimizer for better performance.

```
public class A {
    public final void m1() {
        // Code goes here
    }

    public void m2() {
```

```
        // Code goes here
    }
}

public class B extends A {
    // Cannot override A.m1() here because it is final in class A

    // OK to override m2() method because it is non-final in superclass
    public void m2() {
        // Code goes here
    }
}
```

You will find many classes and methods in the Java class library that are declared as `final`. Most notably, the `java.lang.String` class in Java class library is a `final` class. Why would you declare a class or a method as `final`? In other words, why would you want to prevent subclassing of a class or overriding/hiding of a method? The main reasons for declaring a class/method `final` are – security, correctness, and performance. If your class is important for security reasons, you do not want someone to inherit from your class and mess with security that your class is supposed to implement. Sometimes, you declare a `final` class or a `final` method to preserve the correctness of the program. A `final` method may result in better performance at runtime, because a code optimizer is free to inline the `final` method calls.

Abstract Classes and Abstract Methods

Sometimes, you may create a class just to represent a concept rather than to represent objects. Suppose you want to develop classes to represent different shapes. A shape is just an idea or a concept. It does not exist in reality. Suppose someone asks you to draw a shape. Your immediate response would be, "What shape do you want me to draw?" If someone asks you to draw a circle or a rectangle, it makes sense to you. Java lets you create a class whose objects cannot be created. Its purpose is just to represent an idea, which is common to objects of other classes. Such a class is called an *abstract class*. The term "concrete class" is used to denote a class, which is not abstract and whose objects can be created. So far, all our classes have been concrete whose objects may be created.

You need to use the `abstract` keyword in the class declaration to declare an abstract class. For example, the following code declares a `Shape` class as `abstract`.

```
public abstract class Shape {
    // No code for now
}
```

Since the `Shape` class has been declared `abstract`, you cannot create its object even though it has a `public` constructor (the default one added by the compiler). You can declare a variable of an `abstract` class type as you do for a concrete class. The following code snippet shows some valid and invalid uses of `Shape` class.

```
Shape s;                  // OK
new Shape();              // Error - Cannot create a Shape object using
                          // new Shape()
Shape s2 = new Shape();   // Error - Cannot create Shape object using
                          // new Shape()
```

If you look at the definition of the `Shape` class, it looks the same as any other concrete classes except the use of the keyword `abstract` in its declaration. If you remove the `abstract` keyword from it, it is considered a concrete class, and you can create its objects. A class has instance variables and instance methods to define the state and behavior of its objects. By declaring a class `abstract`, you indicate that the class has some incomplete method definitions (behaviors) for its objects and it must be considered incomplete for object creation purposes. What is an incomplete method in a class? A method which has a declaration, but its body is missing, is an incomplete method. Missing body of a method does not mean an empty body. It means no body. The braces that follow the method's declaration indicate the body of the method. In the case of an incomplete method, the braces are replaced with a semi-colon. If a method is incomplete, you must indicate it by using the `abstract` keyword in method's declaration. Our `Shape` class does not know how to draw a shape until you mention a specific shape. However, one thing is sure that we should be able to draw a shape no matter what kind of shape it is. In this case, we know the behavior name (draw), but we do not know how to implement it. Therefore, draw is a good candidate to be declared an `abstract` method (or incomplete method) in the `Shape` class. The `Shape` class looks as follows with an `abstract draw()` method.

```
public abstract class Shape {
    public Shape() {
    }

    public abstract void draw();
}
```

When you declare a class `abstract`, it does not necessarily mean that it has at least one abstract method. An `abstract` class may have all concrete methods. It may have all `abstract` methods. It may have some concrete and some abstract methods. If you have an `abstract` class, it means that an object of that class cannot exist. However, if a class has an `abstract` method (either declared or inherited), it must be declared `abstract`. Declaring a class as `abstract` is like placing an "under construction" sign in front of a building. If an "under construction" sign is placed in front of a building, it is not supposed to be used (not supposed to be created in case of a class). It does not matter if the building is complete or not. Just the "under construction" sign is enough to tell that it cannot be used. However, if some parts of the building is incomplete (like a class having abstract methods), you must place a "under construction" sign in front of it (must declare the class as `abstract`) to avoid any mishap, in case someone attempts to use it.

TIP
You cannot create an object of an `abstract` class. If a class has an `abstract` method, declared or inherited, it must be declared `abstract`. If a class does not have any `abstract` methods, you can still declare the class as `abstract`. An `abstract` method is declared the same way as any other method except that its body is indicated by a semi-colon.

Listing 16-36 has the complete code for our `Shape` class. Each shape will have a name. The `name` instance variable stores the name of a shape. The `getName()` and `setName()` methods let you read and change the name of the shape respectively. Two constructors let you set the name of the shape or leave the name to the default name "Unknown shape". A shape does not know how to draw and therefore, it has declared its `draw()` method as `abstract`. A shape also does not know how to compute its area and perimeter. Therefore, it has declared `getArea()` and `getPerimeter()` methods as `abstract`.

```java
// Shape.java
package com.jdojo.chapter16;

public abstract class Shape {
    private String name;

    public Shape() {
        this.name = "Unknown shape";
    }

    public Shape(String name) {
        this.name = name;
    }

    public String getName() {
        return this.name;
    }

    public void setName(String name) {
        this.name = name;
    }

    // Abstract methods
    public abstract void draw();
    public abstract double getArea();
    public abstract double getPerimeter();
}
```

An `abstract` class guarantees the use of inheritance (at least theoretically). Otherwise, an `abstract` class by itself is useless. For example, until someone supplies the implementations for the `abstract` methods of the `Shape` class, its other parts – instance variables, concrete methods, and constructors are of no use. We create subclasses of an `abstract` class, which override the `abstract` methods and provide implementations for them.

Listing 16-37 has code for a `Rectangle` class, which inherits from the `Shape` class. Note that we have not declared the `Rectangle` class as `abstract`, which means that it is a concrete class and its objects can be created. An `abstract` method is also inherited by a subclass like any other methods. Since the `Rectangle` class is not declared `abstract`, it must override all three `abstract` methods of its superclass and provide implementation for them. If the `Rectangle` class does not override all `abstract` methods of its superclass and provides implementation for them, it is considered incomplete and must be declared `abstract`. Our `Rectangle` class overrides the `draw()`, `getArea()` and `getPerimeter()` methods of the `Shape` class and provide implementation (body within braces) for them. The instance variables – `width` and `height`, are used to keep track of width and height of the rectangle. Its constructor accepts its `width` and `height`. Inside the constructor, we call the constructor of the `Shape` class using super keyword – `super("Rectangle")`, to set its name. Listing 16-38 has code for a `Circle` class, which inherits from the `Shape` class. It also overrides three `abstract` methods of the `Shape` class and provides implantation for them.

Listing 16-37: A Rectangle class, which inherits from the Shape class and provides implementations for the inherited abstract methods

```java
// Rectangle.java
```

```java
package com.jdojo.chapter16;

public class Rectangle extends Shape {
    private double width;
    private double height;

    public Rectangle(double width, double height) {
        // Set the shape name as "Rectangle"
        super("Rectangle");
        this.width = width;
        this.height = height;
    }

    // Provide implementation for inherited abstract draw() method
    // from Shape superclass
    public void draw() {
        System.out.println("Drawing a rectangle...");
    }

    // Provide implementation for inherited abstract getArea() method
    // from Shape superclass
    public double getArea() {
        return width * height;
    }

    // Provide implementation for inherited abstract getPerimeter()
    // method from Shape superclass
    public double getPerimeter() {
        return 2.0 * (width + height);
    }
}
```

Listing 16-38: A Circle class, which inherits from Shape class and provides implementations for inherited abstract methods

```java
// Circle.java
package com.jdojo.chapter16;

public class Circle extends Shape {
    private double radius;

    public Circle(double radius) {
        super("Circle");
        this.radius = radius;
    }

    // Provide implementation for inherited abstract draw() method
    // from Shape superclass
    public void draw() {
        System.out.println("Drawing a circle...");
    }

    // Provide implementation for inherited abstract getArea() method
    // from Shape superclass
    public double getArea() {
        return Math.PI * radius * radius;
    }
}
```

```
        // Provide implementation for inherited abstract getPerimeter()
        // method from Shape superclass
        public double getPerimeter() {
            return 2.0 * Math.PI * radius;
        }
}
```

It is time to use our `abstract` `Shape` class along with its concrete subclasses, `Rectangle` and `Circle`. Note that the only restriction that is applied to an `abstract` class, when it is used in code, is that you cannot create its objects. Apart from this restriction, you can use it the same way you can use a concrete class. For example, you can declare a variable of an `abstract` class type; you can call methods of the `abstract` class using that variable, etc. How do we call a method on a `Shape` variable, if we cannot create an object of the `Shape` class? This is a good point. Let us consider the following snippet of code.

```
Shape s = new Rectangle(2.0, 5.0); // Upcasting at work
double area = s.getArea();  // Late binding at work. Will call
                            // getArea() method of Rectangle class
```

If you look at the above code, it makes sense. The first statement creates an object of `Rectangle` class and assigns its reference to a variable of the `Shape` class, which is a simple case of upcasting. A superclass variable can refer to an object of any of its subclasses (to be specific any descendants). Since `Rectangle` is a subclass of `Shape`, a variable of `Shape` type (`s`) can refer to an object of the `Rectangle` class. In the second statement, we are calling the `getArea()` method using the `s` variable. The compiler only verifies the existence of the `getArea()` method in the `Shape` class, which is the declared type of the `s` variables. The compiler does not care if the `getArea()` method in the `Shape` class is incomplete (`abstract`) or not. It does not care if the `getArea()` method is `abstract` in the `Shape` class, because it is an instance method and it knows that late binding at runtime will decide which code for the `getArea()` method will be executed. All it cares about is the existence of a method declaration of the `getArea()` method. At runtime, the late binding process finds that the variable `s` is referring to a `Rectangle` object and it calls the `getArea()` method of the `Rectangle` class. Is it not like having one's cake and eating it too – Have an `abstract` class (incomplete class) and use it too? If you look at the above two lines of code, you would find that these magical two statements involve so many concepts of object-oriented programming – abstract class, abstract method, upcasting, method overriding, late binding, and runtime polymorphism. All of these features are involved in the above two statements to give you the ability to write generic and polymorphic code.

Listing 16-39 has code for a `ShapeUtil` class, which has two `static` methods – `drawShapes()` and `printShapeDetails()`. Both methods accept an array of `Shape` as a parameter. The `drawShapes()` method draws all the shapes by calling the `draw()` method of each element in the array passed to it.. The `printShapeDetails()` method prints details – `name`, `area` and `perimeter` of the shapes passed to it. The beauty about the code in the `ShapeUtil` class is that it never refers to any subclasses of the `Shape` class. It has no knowledge about the `Rectangle` or `Circle` class at all. It does not even care if a `Rectangle` class or a `Circle` class exists, although the code will work with a `Rectangle` object, a `Circle` object, or an object of any descendant of the `Shape` class. You may argue that we could have written the same code even if we did not declare the `Shape` class as `abstract`. So, what is the big deal about declaring the `Shape` class as `abstract`? We are getting two advantages by declaring the `Shape` class as `abstract`.

- If we did not declare the `Shape` class `abstract`, we were forced to provide implementation for the three `abstract` methods in the `Shape` class. Since the `Shape` class does not know what shape object it will take the form of, it is not appropriate for it to provide implementation for the draw(), getArea() and getPerimeter() methods. For now, let us assume that we can handle this issue by providing an empty body for the draw() method and returning zero (or maybe a negative number) from the getArea() and getPerimeter() methods in the Shape class. Let us move to the next advantage, which is more compelling.

- We are forced to declare the Shape class as abstract, because we had declared three abstract methods in it. The greatest advantage of declaring an abstract method in a class is to force its subclasses to override and provide implementation for it. The abstract methods in the Shape class forced the Rectangle and Circle subclasses to override them and provide implementation for them. Was it not what we wanted? In our example, the advantage of the abstract class is to force the subclasses of the Shape class to override and provide implementation of its draw(), getArea() and getPerimeter() methods. If we did not declare these methods as abstract in the Shape class, there was no way to force its subclasses to override these methods.

Listing 16-40 has code that tests the ShapeUtil class along with the Shape, Rectangle, and Circle classes. It creates an array of Shape of length 2. It populates one element of the array with a Rectangle object and another with a Circle object. It passes the array to drawShapes() and printShapeDetails() methods of the ShapeUtil class, which draws the shapes and prints their details according to the type of object placed in the array.

Listing 16-39: A ShapeUtil class that has utility methods to draw any shapes and print details about them

```java
// ShapeUtil.java
package com.jdojo.chapter16;

public class ShapeUtil {
    public static void drawShapes(Shape[] list) {
        for(int i = 0;  i < list.length; i++ ) {
            // Draw a shape, no matter what it is
            list[i].draw();     // Late binding
        }
    }

    public static void printShapeDetails(Shape[] list) {
        for(int i = 0;  i < list.length; i++) {
            // Gather details about the shape
            String name = list[i].getName(); // Late Binding
            double area = list[i].getArea(); // Late binding
            double perimeter = list[i].getPerimeter(); // Late binding

            // Print details
            System.out.println("Name: " + name);
            System.out.println("Area: " + area);
            System.out.println("Perimeter: " + perimeter);
        }
    }
}
```

Listing 16-40: A test class to test Shape, Rectangle, Circle, and the ShapeUtil class

```java
// ShapeUtilTest
package com.jdojo.chapter16;

public class ShapeUtilTest {
```

```
public static void main(String[] args) {
    // Create some shapes, draw, and print their details
    Shape[] shapeList = new Shape[2];
    shapeList[0] = new Rectangle(2.0, 4.0); // Upcasting
    shapeList[1] = new Circle(5.0);         // Upcasting

    // Draw all shapes
    ShapeUtil.drawShapes(shapeList);

    // Print details of all shapes
    ShapeUtil.printShapeDetails(shapeList);
}
}
```

```
Output:

Drawing a rectangle...
Drawing a circle...
Name: Rectangle
Area: 8.0
Perimeter: 12.0
Name: Circle
Area: 78.53981633974483
Perimeter: 31.41592653589793
```

We have finished discussing the main rules of declaring an `abstract` method and an `abstract` class. However, there are many other rules that govern the use of `abstract` methods and `abstract` classes in a Java program. Most of those rules (if not all) are listed below. All rules about an `abstract` method and an `abstract` class point to only one rule – "Abstract class should be subclassed to be useful and the subclass should override and provide implementation for its `abstract` methods".

- A class may be declared `abstract` even if it does not have an `abstract` method.
- A class must be declared `abstract` if it declares or inherits an `abstract` method. If a class overrides and provides implementations for all inherited `abstract` methods and does not declare any `abstract` methods, it does not have to be declared `abstract`..Although, it could be declared `abstract`.
- You cannot create an object of an `abstract` class. However, you can declare a variable of `abstract` class type and call methods using it.
- An `abstract` class cannot be declared `final`. Recall that a `final` class cannot be subclassed, which conflicts with the requirement of an `abstract` class that it must be subclassed to be useful in a true sense.
- An `abstract` class should not declare all constructors as `private`. Otherwise, the `abstract` class cannot be subclassed. Note that constructors of all ancestor classes (including an `abstract` class) are always invoked when an object of a class is created. When you create an object of a `Rectangle` class, constructors for the `Object` class and the `Shape` class are also invoked. If you declare all constructors of an `abstract` class as `private`, you cannot create a subclass for your `abstract` class, which makes it the same as declaring an `abstract final` class.
- An `abstract` method cannot be declared `static`. Note that an `abstract` method must be overridden and implemented by a subclass. A `static` method cannot be overridden. However, it can be hidden.

- An `abstract` method cannot be declared `private`. Recall that a `private` method is not inherited and hence it cannot be overridden. The requirement for an `abstract` method is that a subclass must be able to override and provide implementation for it.
- An `abstract` method cannot be declared `native`, `strictfp` or `synchronized`. These keywords refer to implementation details of a method. The `native` keyword denotes that a method is implemented in native code as opposed to Java code. The `strictfp` keyword denotes that the code inside a method uses FP-strict rules for floating-point computations. The `synchronized` keyword denotes that the object on which the method is invoked must be locked by a thread before it can execute method's code. Since an `abstract` method does not have an implementation, the keywords that imply an implementation cannot be used for an `abstract` method.
- An `abstract` method in a class can override an `abstract` method in its superclass without providing implementation. The subclass `abstract` method may refine the return type or exception list of the overridden `abstract` method. Let us consider the following code. Class B overrides the `m1()` `abstract` method of class A and it does not provide its implementation. It only removes one exception from the throws clause. Class C overrides the `m1()` method of class B and provides implementation for it. Note that the change in return type or exception list as shown in `m1()` method for class B and class C must follow the rules of method overriding.

```java
public abstract class A {
    public abstract void m1() throws CE1, CE2;
}

public abstract class B extends A {
    public abstract void m1() throws CE1;
}

public class C extends B {
    public void m1(){
        // Code goes here
    }
}
```

- A concrete instance method may be overridden by an `abstract` instance method. This can be done to force the subclasses to provide implementation for that method. All classes in Java inherits `equals()`, `hashCode()` and `toString()` method of `Object` class. Suppose you have a class CA and you want all its subclasses to override and provide implementation for the `equals()`, `hashCode()` and `toString()` methods of `Object` class. You need to override these three methods in class CA and declare them `abstract` as shown below. In this case, concrete methods of the `Object` class have been overridden by `abstract` methods in CA class. All concrete subclasses of class CA are forced to override and provide implementation for `equals()`, `hashCode()`, and `toString()` methods.

```java
public abstract class CA {
    public abstract int hashCode();
    public abstract boolean equals(Object obj);
    public abstract String toString();
    // Other code goes here
}
```

Behind the Scenes

Method Overriding and Generic Method Signature

Java 5 has introduced generics (refer to the chapter on *Generics* for more details on generics). If you are using a version of Java prior to Java 5, this section does not apply. Java 5 lets you declare generic methods. When Java code with generics types is compiled, the generic types are transformed into raw types. The process that is used to transform the generic type parameters information is known as type erasure. Let us consider the GenericSuper class in Listing 16-41. It has a generic type parameter T. It has two methods: m1() and m2(). Its m1() method uses the generic type T as its parameter type. Its m2() method defines a new generic type to use it as its parameter type.

Listing 16-41: A sample class that uses generic type parameter

```
// GenericSuper.java
package com.jdojo.chapter16;

public class GenericSuper<T> {
    public void m1(T a) {
        // Code goes here
    }

    public <P extends Employee> void m2(P a) {
        // Code goes here
    }
}
```

When the GenericSuper class is compiled, the erasure transforms the code during compilation and the resulting code looks as shown in Listing 16-42.

Listing 16-42: The GenericSuper class transformed code during compilation after erasure is used

```
// GenericSuper.java
package com.jdojo.chapter16;

public class GenericSuper {
    public void m1(Object a) {
        // Code goes here
    }

    public void m2(Employee a) {
        // Code goes here
    }
}
```

The GenericSub class in Listing 16-43 inherits the GenericSuper class. Its m1() and m2() methods override the corresponding methods in the GenericSuper class. If you compare the methods m1() and m2() between Listing 16-41 and Listing 16-43 for overriding rules, you would think that they do not have the same signature, because the code in Listing 16-41 uses generics. The rules for checking for override equivalent method signature is that if a method uses generic parameters, you need to compare its erasure and not the generic version of its declaration. When you compare erasure of m1() and m2() method's declaration in the GenericSuper class (in

Listing 16-42) with `m1()` and `m2()` methods declarations in Listing 16-43, you would find that `m1()` and `m2()` methods are overridden in the `GenericSub` class.

Listing 16-43: A GenericSub class that inherits the GenericSuper class and override m1() and m2() methods

```java
// GenericSub.java
package com.jdojo.chapter16;

public class GenericSub extends GenericSuper{
    public void m1(Object a) {
        // Code goes here
    }

    public void m2(Employee a) {
        // Code goes here
    }
}
```

Beware of Typo Danger in Method Overriding

Sometimes it is easy to get it wrong when you try to override a method in a class. It may seem that you have overridden a method when it is not overridden. Let us consider following two classes `C1` and `C2`.

```java
// C1.java
package com.jdojo.chapter16;

public class C1 {
    public void m1(double num) {
        System.out.println("Inside C1.m1(): " + num);
    }
}

// C2.java
package com.jdojo.chapter16;

public class C2 extends C1 {
    public void m1(int num) {
        System.out.println("Inside C2.m1(): " + num);
    }
}
```

The intent was that the `m1()` method in class `C2` overrides the `m1()` method of class `C1`. However, the `m1()` method in `C2` does not override the `m1()` method in `C1`. It is a case of method overloading and not method overriding. The `m1()` method in `C2` is overloaded – `m1(double num)` is inherited from class `C1` and `m1(int num)` is declared in `C2`.. Things becomes more difficult when you start running your program and you do not get the desired result. Consider the following code snippet.

```java
C1 c = new C2();
c.m1(10);  // which method is called - C1.m() or C2.m2()?
```

What should be printed when you execute the above code? It prints the following.

```
Inside C1.m1(): 10.0
```

Are you surprised to see the output of the above snippet of code? Let us discuss in detail what happens when the above snippet of code is compiled and executed. When the compiler comes across the second statement, `c.m1(10)`, it does the following things.

- It finds out the compile-time type of the reference variable `c`, which is `C1`.
- It looks for a method named `m1` in `C1`. The argument value, 10, passed to the method `m1()` is of `int` data type. The compiler looks for a method named `m1` (inherited or declared) in the class `C1`, which accepts an `int` type parameter. It finds that class `C1` has a method `m1(double num)`, which accepts a `double` parameter and not an `int` parameter. It tries type-widening conversion and finds that `m1(double num)` method in class `C1` can be used for `c.m1(10)` method call. At this time, the compiler binds the method signature for the call. Note that the compiler binds the method signature and not the method code. The method code is bound at runtime, because `m1()` is an instance method. The compiler does not decide which `m1()` method's code will be executed, when `c.m1(10)` will be executed. It decides only the method signature - a method named `m1` will be executed, which accepts a parameter of type `double`. Keep in mind that the compiler's decision is solely based on its knowledge about class `C1`. When `c.m1(10)` is compiled, the compiler does not know (or care) about the existence of any class, e.g., class `C2`. You can see what code is generated for `c.m1(10)` method call by the Java compiler. You need to use the `javap` command line utility with –c option to disassemble the compiled code as follows. You need to pass the fully qualified name of the class to the `javap` command.

```
javap -c your-fully-qualified-class-name
```

For the above code snippet that contains `c.m1(10)` call the `javap` will print instructions that are generated by the compiler. We have shown only one instruction below

```
12:   invokevirtual   #14; //Method com/jdojo/chapter16/C1.m1:(D)V
```

The `invokevirtual` instruction is used to denote a call to an instance method that will use late binding. The `#14` (it may be different for you) indicates the method table entry number, which is the entry for `C1.m1(D)V` method. The syntax is a little cryptic for us. The character `D` denotes `double`, which is the parameter type and `V` denotes `void`, which is the return type of the method `m1()`.

- At runtime when the JVM attempts to run `c.m1(10)`.It uses the late binding mechanism to find the method code that it will execute. Note that the JVM will search for `m(D)V` method signature, which is the compiler syntax for `void m1(double)`. It starts the search by looking at the runtime type of `c`, which is class `C2`. Class `C2` does not have a method named `m1`, which accepts a parameter of type `double`. The search moves up in the class hierarchy and it goes to class `C1`. The JVM finds the method in class `C1` and it executed it. This is the reason why you got the output that indicates that `m1(double num)` in the class `C1` is called for `c.m1(10)`.

Such mistakes are very difficult to hunt down. Java 5 lets you avoid such mistakes by using `@Override` annotation (see the chapter on *Annotations* for more details on annotations) with the overriding method. It has compiler support. The compiler will make sure a method that is annotated with `@Override` annotation really overrides a method in its superclass. Otherwise, it will generate a compile-time error. Using the `@Override` annotation is easy. Just add it to the method declaration anywhere before the method's return type. The following code for class `C2` uses `@Override` annotation for the `m1()` method.

```
public class C2 extends C1 {
    @Override
    public void m1(int num) {
        System.out.println("Inside C2.m1(): " + num);
    }
}
```

When you compile the above code for class C2, the compiler will generate an error stating that the method m1() in class C2 does not override any method in its superclass. By using the @Override annotation with a method that is supposed to override a superclass method saves you lots of debugging time. Note that the @Override annotation does not change the way method overriding works. It is used as an indicator to the compiler that it needs to make sure the method really overrides the method of its superclass. If the method does not override a superclass method, the compiler needs to generate an error.

Is-a, has-a and part-of Relationships

A software application, which is designed based on an object-oriented paradigm, consists of interacting objects. Objects of one class may be related to objects of another class in some ways. Is-a, has-a and part-of are the three most commonly used relationships that exist between objects of two classes. We have already discussed that is-a relationship is modeled using inheritance between two classes. For example, the relationship – "A part-time manager *is-a* manager", is modeled by inheriting PartTimeManager class from Manager class.

Sometimes, an object of a class contains an object of another class, which indicates a whole-part relationship. This relationship is called *aggregation*. It is also known as *has-a* relationship. The example of has-a relationship is – "A person has an address." As a whole-part relationship, the person represents the whole and the address represents the part. Java does not have any special feature that lets you indicate has-a relationship in your code. In Java code, aggregation is implemented by using an instance variable in whole, which is of type part. In our example, the Person class will have an instance variable of type Address as shown below. Note that an object of the Address class is created outside of a Person class and passed in to the Person class constructor.

```
public class Address {
    // Code goes here
}

public class Person {
    // Person has-a Address
    private Address addr;

    public Person(Address addr) {
        this.addr = addr;
    }

    // Other code goes here
}
```

Composition is a special case of aggregation in which the whole controls the life cycle of the part. It is also known as part-of relationship. Sometimes, *has-a* and *part-of* relationships are used interchangeably. The main difference between aggregation and composition is that in composition the whole controls the creation/destruction of the part. In composition, the part cannot exist by itself. Rather, the part is created and destroyed as a part of the whole. Consider the relationship – "A CPU is part-of a computer." You can also rephrase the relationship as "A computer has a CPU". Does the existence of a CPU outside a computer make sense? The answer is no. It is true that a computer and a CPU represent a whole-part relationship. However, there are some more constraints to this whole-part relationship and that is – "The existence of a CPU makes sense only inside a computer". You can implement composition in Java code by declaring an instance variable of a type part and creating the part object as part of creation of the whole as shown below. An object of `CPU` is created when an object of `Computer` is created. The `CPU` object is destroyed when the computer object is destroyed.

```java
public class CPU {
    // Code goes here
}

public class Computer {
    // Person part-of Address
    private CPU cpu = new CPU();

    // Other code goes here
}
```

Java has a special class type called inner class, which can also be used to represent composition. An object of an inner class can exist only within an object of its enclosing class. The enclosing class would be the whole and the inner class would be the part. We can represent the part-of relationship between CPU and computer using an inner class as follows. Compare this implementation of composition between a computer and a CPU with the previous one. When you use an inner class, an object of the `CPU` class cannot exist without an object of the `Computer` class. This restriction may be problematic when the object of the same class, say `CPU`, is part of another object in a composition relationship.

```java
public class Computer {
    private CPU cpu = new CPU();

    // CPU is inner class of Computer class
    private class CPU {
        // Code goes here
    }

    // Other code goes here for Computer class
}
```

Composition also denotes owner-owned relationship. A computer is an owner and a CPU is owned by a computer. The owned object cannot exist without an owner object. Typically, but not necessarily, the owned object is destroyed when the owner object is destroyed. Sometimes, when the owner object is being destroyed, it passes the reference of the owned object to another owner. In such cases, the owned object survives the death of its current owner. The point to note is that the owned object always has an owner.

Sometimes, programmers get confused between the choice of using inheritance and composition and they use inheritance instead of composition. You can find this kind of mistake in the Java class library where `java.util.Stack` class is inherited from `java.util.Vector` class. A `Vector` is a list of objects. A `Stack` is also a list of objects, but is not simply a list of object as `Vector` is. A `Stack` is supposed to allow you to add an object to its top and remove an object from its top. However, a `Vector` allows you to add/remove an object at any position. Since the `Stack` class inherits from the `Vector` class, it also inherits methods that will let you add/remove an object at any position, which are simply wrong operations for a stack. The `Stack` class should have used composition to use a `Vector` object as its internal representation rather than inheriting from it. The following code snippet shows the correct use of a "has-a" relationship between the `Stack` and `Vector` classes.

```
public class Stack {
    // Stack has-a Vector
    private Vector items = new Vector();

    // Other code goes here
}
```

TIP

Whenever you are in doubt in choosing between composition and inheritance, give preference to composition. Both let you share the codes. However, inheritance forces your class to be in a specific class hierarchy. Inheritance also creates a subtype, whereas composition is used to create a new type.

No Multiple Inheritance of Classes

Java does not support multiple inheritance. It supports single inheritance. A class in Java cannot have more than one superclass. Inheritance lets a class inherit implementation and/or interface from its superclass. In the case of implementation inheritance, the superclass provides implementation for functionality that its subclass inherits and reuses. For example, the `Employee` class has implemented the `getName()` and `setName()` methods, which are inherited by the `Manager` class. In this case, the `Manager` class inherits implementations of `getName()` and `setName()` methods from its superclass `Employee`. In the case of interface inheritance, the superclass provides specification for functionality that its subclass inherits and implements. Note that declaring `abstract` methods in Java defines a specification whereas declaring a concrete (non-abstract) method defines an implementation. For example, the `Shape` class has specification for a `draw()` method, which is inherited by its subclasses (e.g. `Rectangle` and `Circle`). It does not provide any implementation for the `draw()` method. All concrete subclasses of the `Shape` class must provide implementation for its `draw()` method.

Multiple inheritance is defined as having a class inherit from more than one superclass. It poses some problems when a class inherits an implementation from multiple superclasses. Suppose there are two classes - `Singer` and `Employee`, and both provide implementation for processing salary (say `pay()` method). Further, suppose we inherit a class `SingerEmployee`, which inherits from the `Singer` and `Employee` classes. The new class, `SingerEmployee` inherits the `pay()` method from two different superclasses, which have different implementations. When the `pay()` method is invoked on a `SingerEmployee` object, which `pay()` method should be used – from the `Employee` class or from the `Singer` class? Multiple inheritance makes programmer's job as well as language designer's job complex. Java supports multiple inheritance of interfaces, not implementations. It has a construct, called `interface`, which is different from a `class`. An interface can have only `abstract` methods and constants declarations. An interface can inherit from multiple interfaces. A class can implement multiple interfaces. Java's approach to support multiple inheritance avoids problems for programmers as well as its designers. Multiple interfaces inheritance is easier to understand and design than the multiple implementations inheritance.

Appendix A. ASCII Character Set

ASCII Characters

ASCII is an acronym for *American Standard Code for Information Interchange.* Table A-1 *has the list of ASCII character set.*

Table A-1: ASCII character set

Decimal	Hexadecimal	Binary	Character	Official Name
0	0	0	NUL	NULL
1	1	1	SOH	Start of heading
2	2	10	STX	Start of text
3	3	11	ETX	End of text
4	4	100	EOT	End of transmission
5	5	101	ENQ	Enquiry
6	6	110	ACK	Acknowledge
7	7	111	BEL	Bell
8	8	1000	BS	Backspace
9	9	1001	HT	Horizontal tabulation
10	0A	1010	LF	Line feed
11	0B	1011	VT	Vertical tabulation
12	0C	1100	FF	Form feed
13	0D	1101	CR	Carriage return
14	0E	1110	SO	Shift out
15	0F	1111	SI	Shift in
16	10	10000	DLE	Data link escape
17	11	10001	DC1	Device control one
18	12	10010	DC2	Device control two
19	13	10011	DC3	Device control three
20	14	10100	DC4	Device control four
21	15	10101	NAK	Negative acknowledge
22	16	10110	SYN	Synchronous idle
23	17	10111	ETB	End of transmission block
24	18	11000	CAN	Cancel
25	19	11001	EM	End of medium
26	1A	11010	SUB	Substitute
27	1B	11011	ESC	Escape

28	1C	11100	FS	File separator
29	1D	11101	GS	Group separator
30	1E	11110	RS	Record separator
31	1F	11111	US	Unit separator
32	20	100000	SP	Space
33	21	100001	!	Exclamation mark
34	22	100010	"	Quotation mark
35	23	100011	#	Number sign
36	24	100100	$	Dollar sign
37	25	100101	%	Percent sign
38	26	100110	&	Ampersand
39	27	100111	'	Apostrophe
40	28	101000	(	Left parenthesis
41	29	101001	)	Right parenthesis
42	2A	101010	*	Asterisk
43	2B	101011	+	Plus sign
44	2C	101100	,	Comma
45	2D	101101	–	Hyphen-minus
46	2E	101110	.	Full stop = period
47	2F	101111	/	Solidus = slash
48	30	110000	0	Digit zero
49	31	110001	1	Digit one
50	32	110010	2	Digit two
51	33	110011	3	Digit three
52	34	110100	4	Digit four
53	35	110101	5	Digit five
54	36	110110	6	Digit six
55	37	110111	7	Digit seven
56	38	111000	8	Digit eight
57	39	111001	9	Digit nine
58	3A	111010	:	Colon
59	3B	111011	;	Semicolon
60	3C	111100	<	Less-than sign
61	3D	111101	=	Equals sign
62	3E	111110	>	Greater-than sign
63	3F	111111	?	Question mark
64	40	1000000	@	Commercial at
65	41	1000001	A	Latin capital letter A
66	42	1000010	B	Latin capital letter B
67	43	1000011	C	Latin capital letter C

68	44	1000100	D	Latin capital letter D
69	45	1000101	E	Latin capital letter E
70	46	1000110	F	Latin capital letter F
71	47	1000111	G	Latin capital letter G
72	48	1001000	H	Latin capital letter H
73	49	1001001	I	Latin capital letter I
74	4A	1001010	J	Latin capital letter J
75	4B	1001011	K	Latin capital letter K
76	4C	1001100	L	Latin capital letter L
77	4D	1001101	M	Latin capital letter M
78	4E	1001110	N	Latin capital letter N
79	4F	1001111	O	Latin capital letter O
80	50	1010000	P	Latin capital letter P
81	51	1010001	Q	Latin capital letter Q
82	52	1010010	R	Latin capital letter R
83	53	1010011	S	Latin capital letter S
84	54	1010100	T	Latin capital letter T
85	55	1010101	U	Latin capital letter U
86	56	1010110	V	Latin capital letter V
87	57	1010111	W	Latin capital letter W
88	58	1011000	X	Latin capital letter X
89	59	1011001	Y	Latin capital letter Y
90	5A	1011010	Z	Latin capital letter Z
91	5B	1011011	[	Left square bracket = Opening square bracket
92	5C	1011100	\	Reverse solidus = Backslash
93	5D	1011101	]	Right square bracket = Closing square bracket
94	5E	1011110	^	Circumflex accent
95	5F	1011111	_	Low line = Spacing underscore
96	60	1100000	`	Grave accent
97	61	1100001	a	Latin small letter A
98	62	1100010	b	Latin small letter B
99	63	1100011	c	Latin small letter C
100	64	1100100	d	Latin small letter D
101	65	1100101	e	Latin small letter E
102	66	1100110	f	Latin small letter F
103	67	1100111	g	Latin small letter G
104	68	1101000	h	Latin small letter H
105	69	1101001	i	Latin small letter I
106	6A	1101010	j	Latin small letter J

107	6B	1101011	k	Latin small letter K
108	6C	1101100	l	Latin small letter L
109	6D	1101101	m	Latin small letter M
110	6E	1101110	n	Latin small letter N
111	6F	1101111	o	Latin small letter O
112	70	1110000	p	Latin small letter P
113	71	1110001	q	Latin small letter Q
114	72	1110010	r	Latin small letter R
115	73	1110011	s	Latin small letter S
116	74	1110100	t	Latin small letter T
117	75	1110101	u	Latin small letter U
118	76	1110110	v	Latin small letter V
119	77	1110111	w	Latin small letter W
120	78	1111000	x	Latin small letter X
121	79	1111001	y	Latin small letter Y
122	7A	1111010	z	Latin small letter Z
123	7B	1111011	{	Left curly bracket = Opening curly bracket
124	7C	1111100	|	Vertical line = Vertical bar
125	7D	1111101	}	Right curly bracket = Closing curly bracket
126	7E	1111110	~	Tilde
127	7F	1111111	DEL	DELETE

References

Bloch, Joshua. *Effective Java: Programming Language Guide.* Addison-Wesley, 2001.

Cormen , Thomas H., Charles E. Leiserson, Ronald L. Rivest, and Clifford Stein. *Introduction to Algorithms.* 2nd Edition. The MIT Press, 2001.

Cornell, Gary, and Cay Horstmann. *Core Java 1.2.* Vol. 1. Prentice Hall Computer Books, 1998.

—. *Core Java 1.2.* Vol. 2. Prentice Hall Computer Books, 1998.

Downing, Troy Bryan. *Java RMI: Remote Method Invocation.* Wiley Publishing, 1998.

Eckel, Bruce. *Thinking in Java.* 1st Edition. Prentice Hall, 1998.

Freeman, Elisabeth, Eric Freeman, Bert Bates, and Kathy Sierra. *Head First Design Patterns.* O'Reilly Media, 2004.

Gamma, Erich, Richard Helm, Ralph Johnson, and John Vlissides. *Design Patterns: Elements of Reusable Object-Oriented Software.* Addison-Wesley Professional, 1994.

Goetz, Brian, Tim Peierls, Joshua Bloch, Joseph Bowbeer, David Holmes, and Doug Lea. *Java Concurrency in Practice.* Addison-Wesley Professional, 2006.

Gosling, James, Bill Joy, Guy Steele, and Gilad Bracha. *The Java Language Specification.* 3rd Edition. Addison-Wesley, 2005.

Grosso, William. *Java RMI.* 1st Edition. O'Reilly Media, 2001.

Hall, Marty. *Core Servlets and Javaserver Pages.* Prentice Hall, 2000.

Harold, Elliotte Rusty. *Java I/O.* 1st Edition. O'Reilly Media, 1999.

—. *Java Network Programming.* 2nd Edition. O'Reilly Media, 2000.

Horton, Ivor. *Beginning Java.* Wrox Press, 1997.

Hyde, Paul. *Java Thread Programming.* Sams, 1999.

"Java SE 7 Documentation." *Oracle Corporation Web site.* http://download.oracle.com/javase/7/docs/ (accessed 2011).

Lakshman, Bulusu. *Oracle and Java Development.* Sams, 2001.

Lea, Doug. *Concurrent Programming in Java: Design Principles and Patterns.* 2nd Edition. Addison-Wesley, 1999.

Liskov, Barbara, and John Guttag. *Program Development in Java: Abstraction, Specification, and Object-Oriented Design.* Addison-Wesley Professional, 2000.

Mano, M. Morris. *Computer Engineering: Hardware Design.* Prentice Hall, 198.

Oaks, Scott. *Java Security.* 2nd Edition. O'Reilly Media, 2001.

Oaks, Scott, and Henry Wong. *Java Threads.* 2nd Edition. O'Reilly Media, 1999.

Patterson, David A., and John L. Hennessy. *Computer Organization and Design: The Hardware/Software Interface.* 2nd Edition. Morgan Kaufmann, 1997.

Pawlan, Monica. "Reference Objects and Garbage Collection." *Pawlan Communications.* 8 1998. http://www.pawlan.com/monica/articles/refobjs/ (accessed 7 2011).

Preiss, Bruno R. *Data Structures and Algorithms with Object-Oriented Design Patterns in Java.* Wiley, 1999.

Shirazi, Jack. *Java Performance Tuning.* 1st Edition. O'Reilly Media, 2000.

Topley, Kim. *Core Java Foundation Classes.* Prentice Hall PTR, 1998.

Travis, Greg. "IBM DeveloperWorks." *Getting started with new I/O (NIO).* July 09, 2003. https://www.ibm.com/developerworks/java/tutorials/j-nio/ (accessed September 01, 2008).

Venners, Bill. *Inside the Java 2 Virtual Machine.* 2nd Edition. McGraw-Hill Companies, 2000.

Walsh, Aaron E, Justin Couch, and Daniel H. Steinberg. *Java 2 Bible.* Wiley Publishing, 2000.

Index

Made in the USA
Lexington, KY
18 August 2012